## ON EXODUS

Samuel David Luzzatto's
Interpretation of
the Book of *Shemot*

translated and edited by
Daniel A. Klein

KODESH PRESS

© Daniel A. Klein 2015
ISBN: 978-0-9978205-7-7

All rights reserved. Except for brief quotations in printed reviews, no part of this publication may be reproduced, stored in a retrieval system, or transmitted in any form or by any means (printed, written, photocopied, visual electronic, audio, or otherwise) without the prior permissions of the publisher.

Published & Distributed by
Kodesh Press L.L.C.
New York, NY
kodeshpress@gmail.com

To
Bia Thorman Hirsch Klein
בינה בת יעקב
עמו״ש
*mia carissima moglie*
שמעו בנים מוסר אב והקשיבו לדעת בינה

# CONTENTS

Preface . . . . . . . . . . . . . . . . . . . . . . 9
Introduction . . . . . . . . . . . . . . . . . . . 13

*Shemot* . . . . . . . . . . . . . . . . . . . . . . 34
*Va'era* . . . . . . . . . . . . . . . . . . . . . . 91
*Bo* . . . . . . . . . . . . . . . . . . . . . . . 128
*Beshallaḥ* . . . . . . . . . . . . . . . . . . . 171
*Yitro* . . . . . . . . . . . . . . . . . . . . . . 253
*Mishpatim* . . . . . . . . . . . . . . . . . . . 315
*Terumah* . . . . . . . . . . . . . . . . . . . . 387
*Tetsavveh* . . . . . . . . . . . . . . . . . . . 406
*Ki Tissa* . . . . . . . . . . . . . . . . . . . . 423
*Vayak'hel* . . . . . . . . . . . . . . . . . . . 455
*Pekudei* . . . . . . . . . . . . . . . . . . . . 465

Sources . . . . . . . . . . . . . . . . . . . . . 473
Primary Source Index . . . . . . . . . . . . . . 494
Subject & Author Index . . . . . . . . . . . . . 508

# PREFACE

In 1872, seven years after the author's death, the Paduan printer Francesco Sacchetto issued Volume 2 of *Il Pentateuco volgarizzato e commentato da Samuel Davide Luzzatto*. The work contained two elements: an 1858 Italian translation by S.D. Luzzatto ("Shadal") of the Book of Exodus (*Shemot*), plus his commentary on Exodus in Hebrew, a much fuller version than one that had been printed in 1846. It is only now—for the first time in 143 years—that the work has been republished in its entirety, in this new all-English edition.

Since 1998, when my English translation of Luzzatto's Genesis appeared,[1] there has been something of a flowering of Shadal scholarship. A conference held in Israel at Bar-Ilan University and Hebrew University in May 2000, commemorating the bicentennial of Shadal's birth, featured lectures by Israeli, "Anglo-Saxon," French, and Italian scholars, and led to the publication of a multilingual volume of essays in 2004.[2] An English translation of Shadal's 1836 book of Hebrew grammar appeared in 2005,[3] and Shmuel Vargon's incisive writings on various aspects of Shadal's exegetical work culminated in a full-length Hebrew volume in 2013.[4] The

---

1. *The Book of Genesis: A Commentary by Shadal (S. D. Luzzatto)*, Northvale, NJ, and Jerusalem, Jason Aronson Inc., 1998.
2. Robert Bonfil, Isaac Gottlieb, and Hannah Kasher, eds., *Samuel David Luzzatto: The Bi-Centennial of His Birth*, Jerusalem, Hebrew University Magnes Press, 2004.
3. *Prolegomena to a Grammar of the Hebrew Language*, trans. Aaron D. Rubin, Piscataway, NJ, Gorgias Press, 2005.
4. Shmuel Vargon, *S.D. Luzzatto: Moderate Criticism in Biblical Exegesis*, Ramat Gan, Bar-Ilan University Press, 2013.

following year, a three-part study comparing Shadal's approach to those of his contemporaries Zvi Hirsch Chajes and Samson Raphael Hirsch appeared.[5] And in 2015 came the welcome news that a new edition of Shadal's Hebrew commentary on the Torah, based on a manuscript by two of his students, was being published in Israel.[6]

Supplementing this flow of books was the publication of several new Shadal-related articles.[7] Also noteworthy is the research in the field of "Shadalia" conducted by Shimon Steinmetz, who has posted the interesting results on his blog, "On the Main Line." Josh Waxman, too, has made a significant contribution by posting on his "Parshablog" a serial translation and discussion of Shadal's controversial *Vikkuaḥ al Ḥokhmat ha-Kabbalah*.

There has even been an English translation of Shadal's commentary on all Five Books of Moses.[8] This is not a complete version, however, because it is based on the 1965 Israeli Hebrew edition,[9] which omits Luzzatto's text translation, leaves many of his cryptic references unexplained, and expurgates many of the names and cited passages of non-Jewish authorities.

When I first began to teach myself Italian at the age of twelve, in response to a challenge from my father, I never suspected how this unusual hobby would change my life. My grandmother, believing that I would be interested in seeing the Bible in Italian, showed and ultimately gave me her father's original edition of Shadal's *Pentateuco*. At first I was amused, but then came to be deeply impressed with what became my favorite commentary. I was

---

5. Ephraim Chamiel, *The Middle Way: The Emergence of Modern-Religious Trends in Nineteenth-Century Judaism Responses to Modernity in the Philosophy of Z.H. Chajes, S.R. Hirsch and S.D. Luzzatto,* Brighton, MA, Academic Studies Press, 2014, based on Chamiel's 2006 doctoral dissertation (Hebrew University).
6. Yonatan Bassi, ed., *Perush Shadal la-Torah,* Jerusalem, Carmel Publishing House, 2015.
7. Martin Lockshin, "Some Approaches to the Tension between Peshat and Midrash Halakhah" (Hebrew), *Studies in Bible and Exegesis,* vol. 8, pp. 33-45 (2008); Daniel A. Klein, "Who Counted Righteousness to Whom? Two Clashing Views by Shadal on Genesis 15:6," *Jewish Bible Quarterly,* vol. XXXVI, No. 1 (141), pp. 28-32 (2008); Daniel A. Klein, "A Letter to Almeda: Shadal's Guide for the Perplexed," *Ḥakirah*, vol. 10, pp. 225-241 (2010). Mention should also be made of Harlan J. Wechsler's essay, "Beyond Particularity and Universality: Reflections on Shadal's Commentary to Genesis 18-19," in Diana Lipton, ed., *Universalism and Particularism at Sodom and Gomorrah,* Atlanta: Society of Biblical Literature, 2012.
8. *Torah Commentary by Samuel David Luzzatto* (4 vols.), trans. Eliyahu Munk, Brooklyn, Lambda Publishers, 2012.
9. Pinhas Schlesinger, ed., *Perush Shadal al Ḥamishah Ḥumshei Torah,* Tel Aviv, Dvir, 1965.

# Shadal on Exodus

on a summer break from law school when I took on the ambitious project of translating both the Italian and the Hebrew components into English. This demanding and exhilarating work has been part of my life, on and off, for almost forty years.

The publication of my Genesis volume led me to form special friendships with a coterie of fellow Shadal enthusiasts, including Mitchell First, Shimon Steinmetz, Meylekh Viswanath, and Ari Kinsberg. I thank them for their help, support, and encouragement. My thanks also go to a close friend whose opinion and feedback I value, Rabbi Chaim Hisiger.

Since 1998, Judaica research has been revolutionized by the availability online of many formerly obscure and hard-to-find primary sources. The thrill of searching out and touching the pages of these aging materials in the sanctum of a library has largely been replaced with the pleasure and convenience of summoning them up anywhere and instantly on a computer screen. Still, I did have occasion in the course of my preparation of this Exodus volume to dig into the printed collections of Yeshiva University, the New York Public Library, and the Jewish National and University Library at Hebrew University's Givat Ram campus in Jerusalem. For helping me access those few materials that I found it hard to get my hands on, I thank Shimon Steinmetz, Dr. Martin Lockshin of York University in Toronto, Joseph Holub of the University of Pennsylvania, Dr. Bruce Nielsen of Penn's Katz Center for Advanced Judaic Studies, and Dr. Shalom Rackovsky of Cornell University, who is almost as much a brother as a friend.

In preparing for a 2014 lecture in New York on Shadal and his Bible interpretation, Rabbi Adam Mintz tracked me down and asked for my help, which I gladly provided. He returned the favor by mentioning me and my work in the lecture, for which I express my *hakkarat ha-tov*.

How I wish my father, Sidney B. Klein, of blessed memory, were still here to share in the joy of this new Shadal volume. He took pride in referring to me as his "Italian son," and he delighted in taking on various research assignments to help me complete the Genesis translation. In our very last conversation in 2000, when he asked me and my brother about our current activities, I made sure to remind him that I was at work on the next volume. I am moved whenever I look at his copy of my first book, in which his favorite parts are copiously marked with yellow highlighting. At this time I also miss my grandmother, Elizabeth Isaacs Gilbert, to whom I dedicated the first book with a wish that she live to 120, *centovent'anni*. In the event, she fell short of this goal by only sixteen years and did live to see my daughter's first child—that is, her oldest grandson's oldest grandson.

# Shadal on Exodus

It was Mitch First who performed the valuable service of a *shadkhan* in suggesting that I submit my Exodus volume to Alec Goldstein of Kodesh Press. I am most grateful to Rabbi Goldstein for the enthusiasm and expertise with which he has embraced this project. He has declared his interest in publishing the remaining books of the Shadal Humash; I have made some progress on Leviticus, and I pray that the *Santo Benedetto Signore* will grant me the time and the mental acuity to see this work through. I also realize that I will have to start moving faster.

When my first Shadal book appeared, I was the father of four growing children: Coby, Liora, Aviva, and Yehudit. Now they are grown and making their mark on the world, and I have a fine group of children-in-law and an expanding crop of adorable grandchildren, *ken yirbu*. I am thankful for their love and support, and that of my mother, Nancy Klein, and my parents-in-law, Yale and Davida Hirsch. To all my friends and all my family members (official and otherwise), I say *rov todot*.

For 35 years and counting, my guiding compass in life has been my wife Bia. To paraphrase a line from one of her favorite singing groups, the Ribbono Shel Olam only knows *where* I'd be without her, and it is to her, on this her birthday, that this book is gratefully and lovingly dedicated.

Daniel Abraham Klein  
Rochester, New York  
April 17, 2015

# INTRODUCTION

Samuel David Luzzatto (1800-1865), known by his Hebrew acronym Shadal (שד"ל), was the preeminent Italian Jewish scholar of the nineteenth century. A superb linguist, writer, educator, and religious thinker, Shadal devoted his talents above all to *parshanut ha-mikra*, the interpretation of the Jewish Scriptures. Although he was a devout believer in the divinity, unity, and antiquity of the Torah, Shadal approached the text in a remarkably open spirit of inquiry, drawing upon a wide variety of sources, ancient and contemporary, Jewish and non-Jewish, and focusing on the "plain" meaning (*peshat*) as he saw it.

A great-grandnephew of Moses Hayyim Luzzatto (1707-1747), the author of *Mesillat Yesharim*, and related to later distinguished figures including New York's mayor Fiorello LaGuardia, Shadal was born in the seaport of Trieste.[1] His formal schooling was cut short by illness at the age of thirteen, but he continued to study Talmud with his father and with the city's chief rabbi, Abraham Eliezer ha-Levi. Shadal's mastery of the science of grammar, Western philosophy, and several ancient and modern languages was the product of an ambitious self-education. For more than 35 years he served as a professor of Bible, Hebrew, and Jewish history and religion at the Collegio Rabbinico of Padua, where he mentored many of the future leaders of Italian Jewry.

Although he insisted that he was neither a rabbi nor a decisor of Jewish law,[2] recent scholarship has revealed that Luzzatto did indeed hold a form of

---

1. For biographical details concerning Shadal, the best single source remains Morris B. Margolies, *Samuel David Luzzatto: Traditionalist Scholar* (New York: Ktav, 1979). Shadal's *Autobiografia* (Padua, 1878), focusing on his earlier years, was translated into Hebrew by Moses A. Shulvass and published as *Pirkei Hayyim* (New York: Talpiot, 1951).
2. Letter to Hirsch B. Fassel (Sept. 18, 1838), *Iggerot Shadal* (Przemysl and Cracow, 1882-94), p. 544.

*semikhah*. In a parchment "diploma" written on April 26, 1838, and replete with praise for Shadal's scholarship and personal qualities ("An all-containing cluster, a reasoning thinker and intellectual… in Bible as well as in Mishnah and Gemara"), Rabbi Abraham Reggio, Chief Rabbi of Gorizia, made the following declaration: "I place my two hands upon him and invest him with a glorious crown, and I authorize him to be called to the Torah with the title of 'the most excellent, learned, intelligent, and wise Signor Samuel David Luzzatto (*Magnalad Achacham*)'"—the Italian Jewish pronunciation of *ma'alat ha-ḥakham*, "the exalted scholar," i.e., Rabbi. Apparently this honor was conferred upon him at the behest of the Collegio to enhance the dignity of its ceremonial occasions. The honoree, though grateful, seldom if ever made personal use of the title, and the entire incident came to be forgotten.[3]

Shadal's prodigious literary output included *Ohev Ger* (1830), a study of Targum Onkelos; *Yesodei ha-Torah* (1840, published in 1880), an interpretation of the fundamentals of Judaism in light of human ethics and psychology; *Diwan Le-Rabbi Judah ha-Levi* (1864), a groundbreaking collection and study of medieval Jewish poetry; and several texts on Hebrew grammar. But what unified his body of work into a "mosaic of rare beauty"[4] was his *parshanut*, which included translations of and commentaries on the Five Books of Moses, Isaiah, and Job, as well as commentaries on Jeremiah, Ezekiel, and Proverbs. As we shall see, his treatment of the Book of Exodus in many ways epitomizes not only the brilliance of his scholarship, but his sharpness of expression and his frank and forthright style.

## The Passionate Scholar— With an Occasional Touch of Humor

> "…you are of a torrid temperament in keeping with the temperament of your native land."[5]

As professional and meticulous a scholar as Luzzatto was, he did not always maintain one of the usual attributes of his trade: scholarly detachment. A man

---

3. The relevant documents, published by Shadal's son Isaia in August 1877 in the Italian Jewish periodical *Corriere Israelitico*, were rediscovered on microfilm in 2012 by Shadal researcher Shimon Steinmetz; see http://onthemainline.blogspot.com/2012/11/shadal-series-14-on-shadals-unusual.html.

4. Israel Abrahams, "Samuel David Luzzatto as Exegete," *Jewish Quarterly Review* 57 (1966), p. 88.

5. Letter to Shadal from S.J. Rapoport, May 19, 1833, *Iggerot Shir*, p. 17, cited by Margolies, p. 149.

of deeply held convictions, he did not hesitate to express them forcefully, and at times his "torrid" Italian temperament led him to use intemperate language. Here are some choice examples from his Exodus commentary, aimed at particular figures whose views aroused his ire:

- Samuel Cahen: "What business would this man have translating and interpreting such a book [Exodus]? Would that he had never reached out his hand to touch it!" (3:21).
- Johann Gottfried Eichhorn: "See to what extent the effrontery of this heretic has reached" (7:27).
- Isaac Marcus Jost: "Let lying lips be dumb!" (12:29).
- Baruch Spinoza: "This is Judaism; its exact opposite is Spinozism" (15:3).

When it came to Maimonides, Shadal's criticism was at times more muted: "Blessed be the Omnipresent, Who has freed us from that philosophy that prevailed in Maimonides' days, toward which he tended more than he should have, even if his intention was for the good" (20:1). But elsewhere (21:10), without actually naming him, Shadal inveighed against "sophisticates [*mithakkemim*] for whom a wife is like a maidservant and a medication for the preservation of their health"—making it clear to whom he was referring by citing the *Mishneh Torah*—and concluded, "However, one whose Torah is the Torah of Moses, the Mishnah, and the Talmud will love his wife as much as his own self and will honor her more than himself."

Against R. Abraham Ibn Ezra, a fellow commentator whom he accused of having a cryptic style and irreverent attitude, Shadal reserved his sharpest barb, over a dispute as to the meaning of the word *mish'arotam* (Exod. 12:34). Shadal translated this word as "their dough," theorizing that the Israelites came out of Egypt with dough wrapped in their clothing in an effort to keep it warm and ready to ferment. Ibn Ezra, however, understood the word to refer to wooden vessels that the people carried because their donkeys were already fully laden with clothes. "Some admirer of his," Shadal remarked drily, "may choose to believe him—that our ancestors were such asses that they loaded wooden vessels on their backs and loaded their garments on the donkeys."

On the other hand, Luzzatto lavished praise where he felt it was due: "Blessed be He Who chose Rashi and bestowed upon His worshippers a seeing eye and a hearing ear" (22:1). And with admirable fairness, his comment on the Tenth Commandment (20:14) concludes, "See the words of Ibn Ezra, for they are pleasing."

# Shadal on Exodus

At times Shadal engaged in a kind of linguistic humor so subtle that it might easily be missed. An example is found in his comment on Exod. 7:27 ("If you, then, refuse to let them go…"), where the Hebrew word for "refuse" is *ma'en*. Shadal expresses the view that this word is a variant and equivalent of *mema'en*. He goes on to note that Rashi rejects this view—and the word that Shadal uses for "rejects," apparently with tongue in cheek, is *mema'en*.[6]

## Shadal's Place in the Jewish World

Where did Luzzatto stand within the spectrum of Jewish religious ideology? Somewhat paradoxically, he may be best described as an "Orthodox *maskil*." On the one hand, that is, he firmly believed in *Torah min ha-shamayim* (the Divine origin of the Torah) as well as the Torah's unity and accurate transmittal by Moses,[7] and it has been noted that the "observance of the commandments in all of their particulars was a matter which Luzzatto regarded as absolutely essential to the Jew, ethically and ethnically."[8] On the other hand, as an Italian Jew, an openness to the best of secular culture and a readiness to employ secular learning and categories of thought in the service of *parshanut* came naturally to Shadal. Accepting truth wherever he found it, Shadal frequently cited not only the classic medieval Jewish commentators, but also newer sources farther afield, including Dutch Calvinist and French Huguenot scholars, and in particular two leading German "Orientalists" of his day, Gesenius and Rosenmueller.[9] His spirit of rational inquisitiveness led him to espouse modern (for his time) linguistic methods and sometimes unconventional views, though rejecting the source criticism and emendations of the Torah text that contemporary Bible critics had begun to advocate. Shadal himself was well aware that people would find him difficult to pigeonhole.

"*Moi aussi je me crois orthodoxe*," he once remarked in a letter to Abraham Geiger (the Reform leader who was at once his colleague in scholarship and his opponent in ideology)—"I, too, believe myself to be Orthodox, but not sufficiently so according to the ideas of the majority of the 'kosher' Jews, and not at all according to Maimonides and all of his *adorateurs*."[10]

---

6. Another instance of such quiet humor is found in Shadal's comment on Gen. 45:26, where he connects the word *va-yafog* to the Rabbinic Hebrew *pikpuk*, meaning "hesitation" or "doubt." Noting that other authorities had interpreted *va-yafog* differently, he says, "I doubt this [*ani mefakpek ba-zeh*]."
7. *Ha-Ensiklopediyah ha-Ivrit*, s.v. "Luzzatto, Shemuel David."
8. Margolies, *Samuel David Luzzatto*, p. 78.
9. For particulars about the authorities cited by Shadal in his Exodus commentary, some of whom were his own students, see the "Sources" section of this volume.
10. Letter to Geiger (March 2, 1851), *Index raisonné des livres de correspondance de feu Samuel David Luzzatto* (Padua, 1878), pp. 100-101.

# Shadal on Exodus

# Innovative Interpretations

With his linguistic acumen and his love of free inquiry, Shadal arrived at interpretations that may often strike even the modern reader as fresh and novel. Among his most interesting comments on the Book of Exodus are the following:

- Even when performing miracles, God prefers to adhere to the ways of nature in part. Thus, the plagues of Egypt resembled in some respect phenomena that were natural in Egypt, some occurring in one year and some occurring in another, except that in the year in question, all of them came clustered together, and each one contained a novel aspect that was not found in nature (see at Exod. 7:20). Similarly, the splitting of the Red Sea was a miraculous event mixed with natural elements, not entirely unlike a phenomenon that saved the Dutch fleet during a seventeenth-century war with England (see at Exod. 14:21). In so holding, Shadal rejected on the one hand the extreme attempts by some moderns to naturalize the Exodus miracles, and on the other hand any fanciful embellishments by more traditional scholars that "unnecessarily overloaded the Torah's account with signs and wonders."
- The Israelites resided in Egypt for literally 430 years, not an abbreviated 210 years as in the traditional rabbinic view (see at Exod. 6:20, 12:40). Only such a lengthy time span would account for the large population totals given later in the Torah. To accommodate this view, Shadal accepted the suggestion of some non-Jewish scholars that the listed names such as Levi, Kohath, and Amram were not of consecutive generations, but that there were other generations between them.
- As indicated above, Shadal expressed the view that the Israelites took their dough with them as they hastened out of Egypt hoping that it would ferment, because they had not yet been commanded to make a festival of *matsot*, nor was *hamets* yet forbidden to them (see at Exod. 12:14, 21, 29, 34). They had even added leaven to their dough, but due to the conditions of their flight, the dough failed to rise and they had to bake it in the form of *matsah*. If they had already been commanded that night to eat their bread unleavened (as per the talmudic view), they would have baked the dough immediately after kneading it rather than carrying it with them unbaked. It was only after they came out of Egypt that Moses told them that in order to commemorate the occasion in the future, there would be

an annual prohibition of *ḥamets* and commandment to eat *matsot*, for only then would they have understood that this would be a reminder of the miracle of their sudden expulsion from Egypt.

- In the phrase *tehomot yekhasyumu* ("the depths covered them") in the Song of the Sea, the grammatically strange and unique word *yekhasyumu* is best explained as a use of onomatopoeia—that is, the employment of an imitative and naturally suggestive word for rhetorical effect—because the double "u" sound arouses an impression of darkness and depth and thus portrays to the listener's ear the enemy's sinking into the deep waters (see at Exod. 15:5). In fact, Shadal's treatment of the entire Song is the pearl of his Exodus commentary. In the course of his analysis of chapter 15, he includes, among other things, (1) a discussion of why ancient Hebrew poetry contains traces of Aramaic, (2) a thorough explanation of the poetic device of parallelism, (3) an essay on the derivation and semantics of the word *kodesh* ("holiness"), and for good measure, (4) a stinging diatribe against the philosophy of Spinoza.
- One of the purposes behind the collection of the silver half-shekel for the Tabernacle was to diminish the people's fear of the "evil eye" (see at Exod. 30:12). They were being counted, and the people believed that a census might arouse the evil eye unless they paid a "ransom" to help build the sanctuary. God did not wish to abolish the folk belief in the evil eye altogether, since it had the beneficial effect of keeping the people from putting too much trust in their own might or wealth. In fact, said Shadal, what the common people attributed to the evil eye—and modern scholars just as misguidedly dismissed as coincidence—was a Divinely decreed phenomenon of nature, that "pride goeth before the fall."

Also worthy of special mention are Shadal's theory as to the social utility of the Second and Fourth Commandments—that is, avoidance of the human jealousy, hatred, and rivalry that inevitably resulted from a belief in multiple gods (see at Exod. 20:3), and the fostering of love and solidarity among the Jewish people that would flow from observing a single, weekly common day of rest (see at Exod. 20:11)—as well as his explication and justification of the concept of God's demanding account from the children for the sins of their fathers (see at Exod. 20:5). As for Luzzatto's commentary on the book's legal portions, most notably in the *parashah* of *Mishpatim* (chapters 21 to 23), his approach to this material is so distinctive, and so potentially subject to misunderstanding and controversy, that it calls for an extended discussion, as follows below.

# Shadal on Exodus

# Shadal and the Oral Torah

"This is a proper law [*din emet*] even though it does not reflect the plain meaning of the verse" (Shadal on Exod. 21:28).

"This is a correct rule of law, only it is not the plain meaning of the verse, but merely an *asmakhta*" (Shadal on Exod. 22:2).

When dealing with the legal sections of the Book of Exodus, a commentator who is as devoted to the *peshat* as Shadal is faced with a dilemma. In many cases, the Rabbis of the talmudic era set down authoritative interpretations of these passages that diverge from what would appear to be the "plain" meaning of the text. Some of these rules of law are purportedly based on constructions of the Torah's language (*derashot*) that may strike the modern reader as arbitrary, fanciful, or far-fetched. What is the role of a post-rabbinic Torah commentator who endeavors to explain these legal passages?

As Martin Lockshin has pointed out,[11] two of the available options are opposite extremes: (1) to reject the rabbinic interpretations out of hand; or (2) to deny that there is any tension between *peshat* and *derash*—that is, to disregard the *peshat* entirely, or to insist that the rabbinic interpretation *is* in fact the "plain" meaning. Neither one of these two extremes is acceptable to those commentators who hold fast to halakhic observance and yet find value in identifying a *peshat* that is independent from the *derash*. This subset of scholars, which includes Shadal, must adopt some other option.

One model is furnished by R. Samuel ben Meir (Rashbam, 1080-1158), a unique figure who was not only a leading talmudic scholar of the Tosafist school but also a biblical commentator who—to an even greater degree than his grandfather Rashi—preferred adhering to the *peshat*. That is, he was not averse to offering interpretations of the Torah's legal provisions that differed from or even opposed the normative halakhic view, but at the same time he acknowledged that the latter was controlling in practice. How did he justify the Rabbis' non-*peshat* constructions of the law? In many cases, Rashbam would explain that rabbinic interpretation was based on subtle cues provided by *yitturim*,[12] apparent textual superfluities that according to *peshat* should be ignored or treated as literary flourishes.

---

11. Martin (Meir) Lockshin, "Some Approaches to the Tension between Peshat and Midrash Halakhah" (Hebrew), *Studies in Bible and Exegesis (Iyyunei Miqra u-Farshanut)*, vol. 8, (2008), p. 33-35.
12. Lockshin, p. 36.

## Shadal on Exodus

But then, why did he consider it so important to examine the *peshat* of the legal provisions along with the *derash*? Elazar Touitou has suggested two reasons: Rashbam was participating in an intellectual movement of his time in Northern France among Jewish and Christian scholars alike who favored *peshat* interpretations of the Jewish Scriptures, and he also found the *peshat* approach useful as a means of refuting Christian polemicists.[13] Perhaps there was another, more basic motive: sheer intellectual honesty. Quite possibly he took the view that the "plain" meaning was undeniably there, whether or not it had any practical significance, and so it deserved to be discussed for its own sake. Perhaps, too, Rashbam believed—as did the Vilna Gaon, some 600 years later—that the *derash* could not be fully understood without first examining the *peshat*. As the Gaon strikingly put it, "the Oral Law, which was handed down as law to Moses on Sinai... registers as a reverse impression [of the Written Law], like a stamp leaves a reversed impression on clay.... And therefore one must know the *peshat* of the Torah, in order to recognize the stamp."[14]

A contemporary of Rashbam, R. Abraham Ibn Ezra (1089-1164), was another classic Torah commentator who generally valued the *peshat* and yet accepted the *derash* as binding in practice. Lockshin identifies him as the originator of a different method of dealing with rabbinic legal constructions that veer from the text's plain meaning.[15] According to Ibn Ezra, such constructions were not to be seen as fanciful or faulty *parshanut* (exegesis), because they were not *parshanut* at all. Instead, they were to be understood as *asmakhta*, a term that he borrowed and adapted from the Talmud, meaning the use of a scriptural text as a support or "peg" on which to hang a rule of law as a kind of aide-memoire, even though that rule was not truly derived from that text but originated elsewhere. Ibn Ezra's innovation lay in his extension of the *asmakhta* concept to cover many rabbinic constructions that were not so characterized in the Talmud, and in his use of the term to refer specifically to those constructions that were in tension with the *peshat*. What, then, was the true source of these rules of law if not from the text itself? In Ibn Ezra's view, such rules originated from traditions (*mesorot*) that the Rabbis received from their forebears.[16]

---

13. Elazar Touitou, *Ha-Peshatot ha-Mithaddeshim be-Khol Yom: Iyyunim be-Feirusho shel Rashbam la-Torah*, Ramat Gan: Bar-Ilan University Press, 2003, p. 179.
14. *Aderet Eliyahu* (R. Elijah of Vilna's commentary on the Torah), comment on Exod. 21:6.
15. Lockshin, pp. 37-39.
16. Lockshin, p. 39.

# Shadal on Exodus

As we have seen, Samuel David Luzzatto did not generally count himself among Ibn Ezra's admirers. It may therefore seem ironic that Shadal not only accepted the *asmakhta* approach but expanded it boldly:

> Our ancient Sages did not learn the laws by distorting the Scriptures or by means of interpretations that were far from the plain meaning of the texts. Rather, the laws were those that they received from their predecessors from mouth to mouth, or *takkanot* [regulations, ordinances, reforms] that they enacted with deep and wondrous wisdom, according to the need of the times, and in keeping with that which the Torah commanded us, to heed the judge who would exist in our days. The interpretations that depart from the plain meaning are merely *asmakhta*.[17]

Here Shadal was introducing a new principle: many of the rules of law that were presented as derived from *derash* were not handed down from time immemorial, but were newly crafted in response to changing times. Besides expanding the concept of *asmakhta*, Shadal was broadening the term *takkanah* to include laws that had traditionally been regarded not as rabbinic enactments, but as originating from the Torah itself.[18] In the following excerpt from his 1847 work *Beit ha-Otsar*, Luzzatto gave his thesis a fuller explanation:

> The *Soferim* ["Scribes," from the time of Ezra on onward] promulgated *takkanot* for the good of the nation according to the needs of the generations, and anything that was not explicated or defined in the Torah of Moses they explicated and defined according to their wisdom, under the authority granted to them from Sinai, and in accordance with the principles of the Torah and its secret teachings that had been handed down to them from Sinai. Thus did

---

17. S.D. Luzzatto, letter to Osias Schorr, 1838, published in *Meḥkerei ha-Yahadut* I, part 2, p. 242.

18. It should be noted that Shadal did not necessarily mean to demote any such laws from the status or force of *mi-de-oraita* (lit., "from the Torah") to *mi-de-rabbanan* (lit., "from the Rabbis"). These classifications are halakhic terms of art and are not always tied to the actual origin of a particular law. Thus, for example, there are laws of rabbinic origin that are called "*de-oraita*" because they have an *asmakhta* from the Torah, e.g., the prohibition of *melakhah* on intermediate festival days (Tosafot, *Avodah Zarah* 22a; see *Encyclopedia Talmudit*, s.v. *asmakhta*). "It may even happen that the traditional interpretation got by the application of the… hermeneutical rules conflicts with the natural sense of the text, and yet, from the standpoint of Jewish law, the resulting legal rule is *deorajtha*, that is, Pentateuchal" (Isaac Herzog, *The Main Institutions of Jewish Law*, p. 3).

all the sages and scribes in every generation; in their hands the Torah was not like a book of the dead or a thing without the spirit of life, but rather the words of the Living God, a thing that was always alive and thriving, beneficial and useful at all times, according to the needs of every generation. For this reason they did not want to reduce their words to writing, so as not to lock the door to those who would come after them, but rather to enable them as well to promulgate *takkanot* for the needs of their times.

The *Soferim*... did not bother to force the words of the Torah so as to bring them into agreement with their *takkanot*, for there were none among the people who would have raised any objection against them; rather, all the people would obey the judges of their times, as prescribed in the Torah of Moses. Only for the need of a particular time, when the Sadducees raised claims against them, did the Sages adduce proofs from the Torah.... However, toward the end of the Second Temple period, when the Hasmonean dynasty ceased, when Herod ruled and society became corrupted and men of violence prevailed, and when honor and governing authority were taken from the Sages, who were no longer the nation's judges and administrators but rather its wise men and teachers, then they began to support the laws and statutes that had been handed down to them by citing verses from the Torah. It was then that they devised some hermeneutical rules for interpreting the Torah, and they began to teach their students Midrash, i.e., homiletic explanations of the verses (Mekhilta, Sifra, and Sifrei). However, they would privately inform the greatest of their students (in keeping with the secret teachings of the Torah) that these explanations were merely *asmakhta*, and that Scripture never loses its plain meaning.

From then on, homiletical interpretations began to appear in the Mishnah and the *baraitot*, followed by the casuistic reasonings in the Talmud, especially among the Babylonian sages, who were the more sharp-witted ones.... Then the Talmud was completed and reduced to writing, but the secret Torah teachings were never written down; perhaps they had already been forgotten because they had only ever been confided to the elite few, and perhaps they had intentionally been left unwritten because it was not appropriate to hand them down to everyone. It was then that the *asmakhtot*, which had been of subordinate importance, assumed primary importance.[19]

---

19. S.D. Luzzatto, *Beit ha-Otsar* ("The Treasurehouse"), Chamber 1, pp. 13-14.

# Shadal on Exodus

Notice that Shadal does not assert that the Sages were legislating with carte blanche. Rather, he says that they were operating "in accordance with the principles of the Torah and its secret teachings that had been handed down to them from Sinai." In other words, the "Oral Torah" (*Torah she-be-al peh*) did indeed have a Sinaitic core, even if much of what developed from that core was manmade. To be sure, there is no way to verify a theory of secret Torah teachings, and perhaps this is a reason why Shadal did not refer to it in his later writings, as Ephraim Chamiel has noted.[20] But Shadal was convinced that the Rabbis' *takkanot* were indeed in accordance with the Torah's principles and, in many cases, could even be said to reflect the "deepest intention" of the Torah, even when departing from the *peshat*.[21] In any case, Shadal based the binding authority of the *takkanot* on a written Torah passage of crucial importance: "According to the teaching [*torah*] that they [the legal authorities of your time] will give you, and according to the decision that they will pronounce, you will do; you must not stray to the right or to the left from the decision that they communicate to you" (Deut. 17:11).[22]

To best understand the thinking of Luzzatto and his contemporaries as to these matters, it is helpful to consider the state of the European Jewish community in the first half of the nineteenth century. As a result of powerful political, social, and economic changes, the values of "modernity" had begun to take hold in the Jewish mind; among these values were innovation

---

20. Ephraim Chamiel, *Life in Two Worlds—The "Middle-Way" Religious Responses to Modernity in the Philosophy of Z.H. Chajes, S.R. Hirsch and S.D. Luzzatto* (Hebrew). Ph.D. dissertation, Hebrew University, 2006, p. 185. In any case, Shadal was not the first to suggest such a theory of secret teachings. He may have adopted the concept from Judah ha-Levi (*Kuzari* 3:73).
21. Shmuel Vargon, "Samuel David Luzzatto's Critique of Rabbinic Exegesis Which Contradicts the Plain Meaning of Scripture" (Hebrew). *Jewish Studies, an Internet Journal*, vol. 2, 2003, p. 120. At the same time, it should be noted that Shadal reserved the right as a commentator to take issue with particular rabbinic opinions, at least in theory: "If we had lived then, they would not have rebuked us for disagreeing with them, so just because I have come later, have I lost out?" (Letter to S.J. Rapoport, 1819, in *Iggerot Shadal*, Przemysl and Cracow, 1882-94, p. 32). In a later letter to Rapoport (1833), he even seemed to indicate that as a matter of personal practice, he followed the peshat as opposed to the *halakhah* with respect to shaving (*Iggerot Shadal*, p. 246). As Vargon observes (pp. 99-100, nn. 7, 11), this is a surprising and anomalous statement on Shadal's part, and his wording is susceptible to more than one interpretation.
22. This might be regarded as the Torah's "elastic clause," analogous to that of the United States Constitution: "The Congress shall have the power… To make all laws which shall be necessary and proper for carrying into execution the foregoing powers…" (Art. I, sec. 8, cl. 18).

for its own sake, individual autonomy, critical thinking, and historical consciousness.[23] These values, plus an impulse toward assimilation with the surrounding culture, led many Jews to question the continuing worth of certain traditional religious practices. In particular, even though many early leaders of the Reform movement "felt bound by the law of the Torah because of their belief in its divine authorship," they "did not feel similarly obliged by the Rabbinic interpretations of the Torah, especially when many of those interpretations *seemed to violate the simple, plain meaning of the text.*"[24] Consequently, those who felt called upon to respond to the challenge of modernity were compelled to address the *peshat/derash* issue in one way or another.

Some, including Rabbis Samson Raphael Hirsch, Jacob Tsevi Meklenburg, and Meir Loeb Malbim, wrote Bible commentaries in which they sought to demonstrate the unity of the Written Torah and the Oral Torah by showing that *derash* was compatible with *peshat*. Others, such as Rabbi Zechariah Frankel and Heinrich Graetz, among the founders of the "Positive-Historical" school that is regarded as the forerunner of Conservative Judaism, distinguished *derash* from *peshat* and promoted the idea that the Rabbis issued new halakhah-changing legislation according to the needs of their time—a view similar to Shadal's. However, they at least intimated that Deut. 17:11 empowered and perhaps even obligated post-rabbinic authorities of every generation to effect further changes.[25] This, it seems, would have been a step too far for Shadal, at least in practice. Consider the following pair of statements:

1. …in every instance in which the Rabbis turned away from the plain meaning of the Scriptures, where the statement is not an individual's opinion but is agreed to without dissent, it is not a mistake that they made, but rather a *takkanah* that they instituted, according to the needs of the generations—and who is a *Reformator* like they were? But their *takkanot* were made with deep wisdom, fear of God, and love of humankind, not for their own benefit or honor, and not in order to find favor in the eyes of flesh and blood.[26]
2. This, too, I believe with a perfect faith, that all the men who are seeking to institute reforms [*takkanot*] and innovations in Israel are

---

23. Chamiel, p. 14.
24. Michael S. Berger, *Rabbinic Authority*. New York: Oxford University Press, 1998, p. 148 (emphasis mine).
25. Chamiel, p. 185. The modern Conservative movement has certainly espoused this position.
26. Shadal, comment on Lev. 7:18 (1847).

all like babes and sucklings in relation to our ancient Rabbis, of blessed memory, who in their Jewish wisdom received from Sinai succeeded in fortifying Israel like a column of iron and a wall of bronze against all the [evil] times that befell us.[27]

On the one hand, Shadal is acclaiming the talmudic Sages as "reformers" *par excellence*. But on the other, he is casting serious doubt on the qualifications and motives of their nineteenth-century would-be successors.[28] According to Chamiel, these two statements indicate that "in Luzzatto's view, reforms are only a theoretical possibility. The authority that would be able to formulate decisions in matters of reform would have to be a Rabbinical body with fear of Heaven and expertise in halakhah. It would have to love humankind, be humble and free of human biases, and understand the spirit of the people and its needs with deep wisdom and broad vision, like our Sages. Such a body does not exist and, practically speaking, cannot come into existence, and therefore from a practical standpoint, it is impossible to promulgate reforms in halakhah."[29]

Shadal's approach to the history and development of Jewish law is seen in his comment on what is traditionally regarded as the very first *mitsvah*, "Proliferate and multiply" (Gen. 1:28). Although not saying in so many words that the *halakhah* differs from the *peshat*, he points out that this directive was given to humankind as a whole when the human race was small in number, and that there was no need to issue such a command to the Israelites when the Torah was given because the earth was already settled, "yet the Rabbis did well in including 'Proliferate and multiply' among the *mitsvot*.... Especially after the destruction [of the Jewish commonwealth], when the people decreased, were they obligated to reinforce this *mitsvah*. Blessed be He Who chose them and their learning, for were it not for their remonstrances and enactments, the nation would have disappeared from the earth, just as many great and mighty nations have disappeared and been forgotten." That is to say, the Rabbis' treatment of this phrase as a specifically Jewish legal

---

27. Shadal, letter to Osias Schorr, 1838, in *Meḥkerei ha-Yahadut* I, part 2, p. 248.
28. In fact, Shadal regarded the Reform movement of his time as misnamed: "Some Israelites, eager to exonerate themselves from the religious practices connected with Judaism, and wishing to do so with a sort of legality, so as not to have to be regarded as impious transgressors of the Law of God, mask their project of totally abolishing the Mosaic law under the specious name of Reform" (letter to A. J. Fürst, Sept. 1, 1843, in *Epistolario italiano francese latino* [Padua, 1890], pp. 424-425).
29. Chamiel, p. 180, n. 240.

obligation departed from the plain meaning of the verse, was influenced by historical and sociological changes, and was a wise decision.

Luzzatto's Exodus commentary contains several applications of this approach. For example:

- In Exod. 12:6, the people are commanded to bring the Passover sacrifice *bein ha-arbayim*, literally, "between the evenings." "This undoubtedly means 'at twilight,' as per the Karaites and Ibn Ezra," says Shadal. "However, the [halakhic] opinion of the Rabbis, that the time for the paschal sacrifice begins after the noon hour [Mishnah *Pesaḥim* 5:3], is also correct, for on Passover as observed by the generations [in the land of Israel], they all had to slaughter their lambs in the Temple courtyard and sprinkle the blood on the altar, and it would have been impossible to complete this ceremony during the twilight hour alone, so they began after noon."
- In Exod. 12:43, it says that no "stranger" (*ben nekhar*) shall eat of the Passover sacrifice. "This," says Shadal, "is undoubtedly to be understood literally: 'no foreigner [*nokhri*].' However, the Rabbis interpreted it to mean 'one who has made himself a stranger to his Father in Heaven,' i.e., an apostate [*meshummad*]. This was an interpretation that originated much later [than the giving of the Torah], when the Greeks arose and forced apostasy upon Israel. In accordance with the needs of that time, the Rabbis said that *ben nekhar* includes not only a foreigner, but also a Jew who acts in a foreign manner."
- In Exod. 21:8, if a master does not wish to marry his maidservant, her father is admonished not to sell her *le-am nokhri*, understood by Shadal as "to a foreign people" or "to a man of another Israelite tribe." However, he notes that "with the passage of generations, the sense of kinship between members of a given tribe was forgotten, and even such members were strangers and foreigners to each other, and no man would redeem anyone but his close relative. For this reason the Rabbis were constrained to interpret the phrase *le-am nokhri* as *li-gevar oḥoran* ("to another [Israelite] man") [as per Onkelos], for they knew that any Israelite, even one from the same tribe, would be a 'stranger' to the girl and would not redeem her to set her free; rather, if he acquired her, he would keep her in bondage as a maidservant."

Social change was not the only motivating factor suggested by Shadal for rabbinic modifications of *halakhah*. To those accustomed to viewing the

Rabbis' legislation as building ever-expanding restrictive "fences" around the law, it may come as a surprise that Shadal often saw a rabbinic tendency toward leniency. For example:

- In Exod. 21:12, the Torah states, "One who strikes a man, and the latter dies of it, will be put to death." Shadal comments, "According to the plain meaning, even if the striker did not intend to cause death when he knowingly and intentionally struck, he is put to death if the victim dies of the beating and not of some additional cause that happens to occur." But he goes on to say that the Rabbis "tended to be lenient rather than strict in this matter; see *Sanhedrin* ch. 9"—where the Mishnah states that the striker is not subject to the death penalty unless he intended to cause death and used lethal force.
- In Exod. 22:11, the rule is given that when one delivers to his neighbor an animal to guard, and the animal is stolen from the neighbor, the latter must compensate the owner. Shadal explains that according to the *peshat*, such compensation is required even if the neighbor is only an unpaid guardian (*shomer ḥinnam*, "gratuitous bailee"), since he nevertheless took it upon himself to guard the animal and was negligent. However, Shadal observes, the Rabbis were lenient and applied this rule only to a paid bailee (*shomer sakhar*).

In one instance, Luzzatto discerned a combined motive of leniency and response to social change, resulting in what might be viewed as one of the Rabbis' most daring legal innovations: "With all the *mitsvot* of the Torah, the text speaks in masculine gender, but women, too, are included. However, the Sages exempted women from the positive *mitsvot* that are time-bound [*she-ha-zeman gerama*]; apparently, in their times the status of women had changed, and men had been laying a heavier yoke upon them" (comment on Exod. 20:10). In other words, as Shadal seems to imply, the only way that the Rabbis felt able to alleviate the social condition of women in their time was not to enact "equal rights" legislation, but to reinterpret the Torah so as to release women from many of their former halakhic obligations.

At times, however, Shadal offers no particular theory as to why the Rabbis chose to depart from the *peshat*. For example, with respect to the phrase in Exod. 23:2, *ve-lo ta'aneh al riv lintot aharei rabbim lehattot*, he gives the *peshat* translation, "nor shall you give testimony in a cause, inclining after the many, in order to bend [twist] (justice)," an admonition addressed to potential witnesses. In his comment on this verse, he says that the Rabbis' homiletical interpretation of the phrase *aḥarei rabbim lehattot* (literally, "after the many to bend")—that judges are to decide the law according to majority vote— is merely an *asmakhta*, for "undoubtedly there is no way to decide the law other than by majority." Apparently, Shadal felt that the Rabbis made use of this phrase as a Scriptural anchor for their rule simply because the wording happened to lend itself to such a *derash*.

In light of the above discussion, it becomes possible to understand correctly a statement of Shadal that on first sight may appear quite shocking: "Far be it from me to twist the scriptural texts in order to make them agree with the *halakhah*."[30] Elsewhere, he makes a similar statement, but with a crucial addition: "It is not our duty to distort the Scriptural texts in order to make them agree with the halakhah, *but it is our duty to act according to halakhah,* as it says, 'According to the teaching [*torah*] that they will give you....'"[31]

Even taking into account that crucial addition, Shadal's approach to the "Oral Torah" may be taken by some with misgivings. A leading twentieth-century Modern Orthodox rabbi, Walter Wurzburger, once wrote a critique of a Conservative scholar's work, using language that almost could have been aimed at Shadal himself.[32] Below are some of Rabbi Wurzburger's challenges, followed by defenses that may be offered on Shadal's behalf.

1. "If [as this scholar claims] the talmudic sages were entitled to change the Written Law to keep abreast with the requirements of their age, why should our generation feel constrained to uphold the immutability of the principles formulated by Talmudic Judaism?"[33]

As we have seen, Shadal believed that the talmudic Sages enacted their *takkanot* with "deep wisdom, fear of God, and love of humankind," in sad contrast with the wrongly motivated "babes and sucklings" who were proposing reforms in his generation. Presumably, his opinion of would-be halakhic innovators of "our generation" would have been no higher.

---

30. Luzzatto, introduction to *Ha-Mishtadel*, first page.
31. *Meḥkerei ha-Yahadut* I, part 2, p. 21 (emphasis mine). It should be noted that in one important instance, Shadal vigorously defends the Rabbis' halakhic reading of a verse as the actual *peshat*: he maintains that Exod. 13:9, "And you will have it for an insignia on your arm, and for a memorial between your eyes," is not merely a metaphoric expression, as per the Karaites and even Rashbam, but rather refers to the *mitsvah* of wearing *tefillin*.
32. Walter Wurzburger, "The Oral Law and the Conservative Dilemma," *Tradition*, vol. 3 no. 1, pp. 83-88 (Fall 1960), a review of *Law and Tradition in Judaism* by Boaz Cohen (New York: Jewish Theological Seminary, 1959).
33. Wurzburger, p. 83.

2. "[This scholar] implies that the Rabbis were cognizant of the fact that their ingenious methods of interpretation constituted an actual modification of the original law. Accordingly, they devised the hermeneutical rules and developed the Midrashic exegesis as a subterfuge, because they wanted to conceal under the guise of interpretation what, in point of fact, amounted to a deliberate modification of religious law."[34]

Shadal might have countered that there was nothing ethically wrong with the Rabbis' fostering the impression among the common people that their *derashot* reflected the actual meaning of the Torah texts, because (1) their enactments were in fact wise and beneficial applications of the Torah's underlying principles and intentions; (2) they were legislating under the authority granted to them by Deut. 17:11; (3) the unsettled political conditions of the late Second Temple period compelled them to start supporting their rules of law by citing Torah verses; and (4) they never let the scholarly elite forget that such supports did not reflect the actual *peshat*.

3. "The real issue is this: were the changes and developments that occurred during the Talmudic period the result of the creation of an Oral Law that was superimposed upon biblical Judaism, or did the Rabbis, employing principles that ultimately derived from divine revelation on Mt. Sinai, interpret both the Written and the Oral Torah in the light of the historic conditions of their time?"[35]

Shadal might have chosen to thread between these two supposedly opposite alternatives. If by "Oral Law" or *Torah she-be-al peh* we mean the body of law that is not to be found in the textual *peshat*, he might have said, then yes, this was largely a new creation of the talmudic legislators. But at the same time it must again be emphasized that those legislators were not driving without a roadmap; even if their legislation was not actually derived from the texts that they used for formal support, their enactments in response to new historic conditions were ultimately based on their expert understanding of the fundamental "principles of the Torah"—perhaps even its "secret teachings"—"that had been handed down to them from Sinai." This specialized knowledge, Shadal might have said, was the God-given core of the "Oral Torah."

---

34. Wurzburger, p. 84.
35. Wurzburger, p. 85.

# Shadal on Exodus

Such an approach, though perhaps outside the traditional mainstream, is not without support from tradition-minded scholarship. Ephraim Urbach, the eminent twentieth-century Orthodox authority on the history of *halakhah*, expressed the view that the Rabbis' recognition of the *derashah* as a legitimate basis for *halakhah* was a slow process that began as a result of the weakening of internal government, undermining of the social order, and the stripping of the Sanhedrin of its authority, and that eventually the whole Oral Law—even including the *halakhot* that derived from ordinances, enactments, and legal precedents and decisions—was deduced from the biblical text by exegetical processes.[36]

On the other hand, Shadal's "modern" approach has come under challenge from what might be called a "postmodern" approach, which takes the Rabbis and their *derashot* at their word. "Our sense and the rabbis' sense of what constitutes simple, literal meaning do not always agree," David Weiss Halivni has said. "Their sense of the simple, literal meaning was more inclusive."[37] He elaborates:

> The modern state of mind demands a greater faithfulness to the simple, literal meaning (to the peshat), and a greater obligation to preserve it. Only in the face of virtually insurmountable problems is this approach abandoned. The presence of an extra word, letter, or even an entire phrase can easily be seen as a stylistic peculiarity. Peshat, from this point of view, is synonymous with exegetical truth, and one does not abandon truth lightly. But to the rabbis of the Talmud, deviation from peshat was not repugnant. Their interpretive state of mind saw no fault with an occasional reading in. It was not against their exegetical conscience, even though it may be against ours.[38]

The difficulty with this postmodern approach is that it reopens the halakhic system to a line of attack from the left: does it not simply mean that the Rabbis

---

36. Ephraim Urbach, "The Derasha as a Basis of the Halakha and the Problem of the Soferim" (Hebrew), *Tarbiz* 27/2, pp. 166-182 (1958); see English abstract. Urbach differs with Shadal's theory in that he suggests that the "Soferim" were not the early governing authorities and legislators, but rather a separate class of scholars, i.e., the early exegetes who were the ones who developed the hermeneutical rules of Biblical interpretation, and that their methods were eventually adopted by the Rabbis: "the sages became Soferim."
37. David Weiss Halivni, *Peshat and Derash: Plain and Applied Meaning in Rabbinic Exegesis*, New York: Oxford University Press, 1991, p. 12.
38. Halivni, p. 9.

were able to "delude themselves into thinking that their forced interpretations were not distortions but elucidations of the real intent of the biblical text"? If so, and if "the operations of the rabbinic mind reflect sheer naiveté in matters historical or philological, it is difficult to see why sophisticated scholars should feel constrained to uphold the authority of religious leaders whose rulings were predicated upon gross ignorance of pertinent and relevant data. In [such a] case, we would have ample grounds for disqualifying the teachers of old from serving as mentors for our age."[39] This difficulty is obviated, of course, if we assume as Shadal did that the Rabbis were quite aware that their *derashot* did not reflect the true plain meaning of the Torah text, and that the actual basis for their enactments was (to use Oliver Wendell Holmes' phrase) the "felt necessities of the time," coupled with their "deep wisdom, fear of God, and love of humankind."

Still, Luzzatto himself acknowledged that he was facing battle on two fronts—with the traditionalists on the right and the "heretics" on the left—and yet he expressed confidence in the ultimate outcome:

> And if some sincere and upright men, who are devoted to the Talmud and *posekim*, will say to me… "Even if your intention is good, your actions are not, for in your intention to raise up the Written Torah, you are lowering the Oral Torah; while meaning to give honor to our Sages, you are saying that their words come from wisdom and not from tradition…"—I would say to them, "My words are not meant for you, but for those who love free inquiry".… Therefore you, my sincere and upright brothers, who sigh and moan over all the abominations that are being perpetrated among us, do not declare war against me, for I am with you, not with your enemies, Heaven forbid! But my heart is confident and sure that only the moderate faith that I uphold is God's desire, and that it will forever be established…."[40]

## About This Translation

In preparing to present Shadal's Hebrew commentary to the English-speaking public, I decided early on that it was equally important to include an English version of his Italian translation of the Torah text itself. Thus, both of these elements are featured together in the present edition: the English version of

---

39. Wurzburger, pp. 84, 85.
40. Letter to Osias Schorr, 1838, in *Meḥkerei ha-Yahadut* I, part 2, pp. 247-249.

the text translation appears verse by verse in boldface, interspersed with the translated comments on each verse.

While translating Shadal's Italian rendering of the Torah text into English, I generally kept as close as I could to his wording and style, though at the same time keeping an eye on the Hebrew original. The standard American English system of quotation marks has been introduced. However, I have made no editorial insertions. Thus, within the text translation, any brackets or parentheses are those that appeared in the 1872 printing.

In translating the Hebrew commentary, my work was facilitated by Shadal's wonderfully lean, down-to-earth writing style, but a few modifications were in order. To accommodate the modern reader's eye, I have freely inserted new sentence and paragraph breaks. I also felt it necessary to add occasional insertions and notes to clarify or finish implied thoughts that might not be obvious to the reader, to identify obscure references, and to supply materials that Shadal alluded to with a bare citation. In addition—although I did not generally consider it part of my role as editor to pass judgment on Shadal's comments—I took the liberty of adding notes in some instances where modern scholarship has something pertinent to say about a point that Shadal raised. Within the translated commentary, any supplementary words or phrases in square brackets are my own editorial insertions, unless otherwise noted, while parenthesized statements are generally those that were so marked in the original. There were no footnotes in the original; all footnotes in the present work are my own.

In transliterating Hebrew words, I have generally followed a slightly modified version of the *Encyclopaedia Judaica*'s system, reflecting the popular Israeli "Sephardic" pronunciation.

With regard to the translation of biblical verses that appear in cross-references, (1) any verses cited from within the book of Exodus are, of course, translated as they appear in the present work; (2) verses from the other four books of the Torah are translated according to my English rendering of Shadal's Italian version of those verses; and (3) verses from the rest of the Bible (*Nevi'im* and *Ketuvim*) are translated, in general, as they appear either in the 1917 Jewish Publication Society version (as used in the Soncino Books of the Bible) or the 2004 Keter Crown Bible Chorev, with some exceptions, mainly the substitution of "you" for the archaic "thou" and "thee."

# Shadal on Exodus

# In Conclusion

An ideal new edition of Shadal's Torah interpretation would be a large and multifaceted work in three languages. In order to present a faithful portrait of the man and his scholarship while reaching the broadest likely audience, this edition would have to include: (1) Shadal's text translation in Italian, (2) a complete and annotated version of his commentary in Hebrew, and (3) an English rendering of both. Although such a deluxe publication may never see the light of day, modern Shadal studies have progressed to a point where some of these features are available in pieces. The original Italian and Hebrew printing from the 1870's, long a rarity, can easily be viewed online, while the 2015 edition of the Hebrew commentary, though lacking notes, breaks new ground by presenting the full *perush* as it changed and developed over the course of Shadal's career. And now, those who are more comfortable with English than with Italian or Hebrew have access to a new cross section of the Shadal oeuvre with the publication of this comprehensive and annotated Exodus volume. It is my hope that the translating efforts that I have made—and, *se Dio vuole*, will continue to make—will help to advance the English-reading public's appreciation for a man who, 150 years after his passing, remains one of the most interesting Jewish thinkers of his or any other age.

# *Shemot*

*The righteous Egyptian midwives • A good child saved from the water • Dealing crookedly with the wicked • "I am not a speaker" • "A bloodstained bridegroom you are to me" • "Why do you distract this people from its labors?"*

**1:1. These are the names of the children of Israel, gone to Egypt—who had gone there with Jacob, each one with his own family:**

***These are the names.*** Because the Torah is about to state that "the children of Israel proliferated, propagated themselves…" it first mentioned that when they came to Egypt, they numbered only seventy (Rashbam, Mendelssohn).

**1:2. Reuben, Simeon, Levi, and Judah.**

***Reuben, Simeon.*** The sons of Jacob are arranged here according to the order in which he took his wives, for first he took Leah, whose sons were Reuben, Simeon, Levi, Judah, Issachar, and Zebulun. Then he took Rachel, and she bore Joseph and Benjamin; Benjamin is mentioned first and Joseph is mentioned at the end, for Joseph did not come with his brothers, but was already there when they came. Then he took Bilhah, whose sons were Dan and Naphtali, and finally Zilpah, whose sons were Gad and Asher (per my late father).

# *Shemot*

**1:3.** Issachar, Zebulun, and Benjamin.
**1:4.** Dan and Naphtali, Gad and Asher.
**1:5.** The persons originating from Jacob's thigh were in all seventy-two souls. Joseph was then (already) in Egypt [and thus he is not mentioned here with the other brothers, who had gone there with their father].

***thigh*** *(yerekh).* See at Gen. 46:26 [where it is explained that the term *yerekh*, in this context, is a euphemism for the organ of reproduction].

**1:6.** Joseph died, as well as all of his brothers, and all of that generation.
**1:7.** And the children of Israel proliferated, propagated themselves, and became exceedingly numerous and strong, and the country [of Goshen] became full of them.

***propagated themselves*** *(va-yishretsu).* See at Gen. 1:20 [where it is explained that the verb *sharats* literally means "to swarm"].

***and the country became full of them.*** The country of Goshen [not Egypt proper].

**1:8.** There arose then a new king over Egypt, who had not known Joseph.

***There arose then a new king.*** In the opinion of the scholar Jost *(Allgemeine Geschichte des Israelitischen Volkes* [1832], vol. 1, p. 94), the Pharaoh at the time of the Exodus was (according to modern authorities who have succeeded in understanding the writing of the ancient Egyptians) the fifth one of the Rameses family, and the kings of that family had wiped out, about 200 years previously, the shepherd kings who had come from Arabia, conquered the Egyptians, and ruled over them for 100 years. Jost says that the shepherd kings had preferred the children of Israel because those kings were Semites and Asiatics and spoke a language related to Hebrew; perhaps they, too, were called "Hebrews" *(Ivrim),* having descended from Joktan son of Eber.

The Pharaoh of Joseph's time, who preferred the Hebrews, settled the sons of Jacob in the best part of the country, in the land of Rameses. It is likely that this land was the property of one Egyptian family, called the family of Rameses, and that the Israelites took all or part of their inherited land and settled in it; after 200 years, the members of the Rameses family rebelled against the foreign shepherd king, wiped out his family, and ruled in their stead. Because the Rameses family hated the Israelites, who had taken away their inheritance and had been preferred by the shepherds, [the new] Pharaoh decreed what he did regarding Israel.[1]

**1:9. He said to his people, "Here the people of the Israelites is [making itself] more numerous and strong than we.**
**1:10. "Now then, let us study some stratagem against him, so that he does not increase so much that, some war occurring, he would be able to join himself to our enemies, make war against us, and then depart from the country."**

*let us study some stratagem against him* (nitḥakkemah lo). "Let us make ourselves wise [ḥakhamim] on his account and deal cleverly with him." Ḥokhmah ("wisdom") denotes prudent conduct toward an intended goal. There is general *ḥokhmah* and specific *ḥokhmah*: general *ḥokhmah* is conduct toward a general goal, which is a person's success in all his affairs throughout his life. To arrive at such general success, a person's conduct must always be wise, and he must master his will and act at all times with skill, righteousness, and fear of God; this is what is referred to simply as *ḥokhmah* in Scripture. Specific *ḥokhmah*, on the other hand, is conduct toward a specific goal, whatever it may be, good or evil; e.g., "And Jonadab [Amnon's friend] was a very subtle [ḥakham] man" (2 Sam. 13:3); he was a man who always knew how to act prudently in order to achieve his objective, whatever it might be.

So here, *nitḥakkemah lo* means, "Let us make ourselves wise with respect to this people in order to achieve our objective: that the people not increase

---

1. According to one modern system of chronology, the period of the Hyksos, or so-called "shepherd kings" of Asiatic origin, lasted from the 17th or 16th century B.C.E. to about 1570 B.C.E., when they were expelled by the first ruler of the 18th Dynasty, Ahmes (Ahmosis) I. The first of the "Ramesides" to rule was the second king of the 19th Dynasty, Rameses I (ruled 1320-1318 B.C.E.). The Pharaoh of the Exodus has often been identified as either Rameses II (1304-1237 B.C.E.) or Merneptah (1236-1223 B.C.E.), the fourth and fifth kings of the 19th Dynasty respectively.

A different proposed chronology asserts that it was a pre-Hyksos Pharaoh who befriended Joseph, and that the Hyksos rulers were "insecure about their staying power as usurpers" and "suspicious of the Israelites' loyalty," and thus oppressed and enslaved the Israelites (see Judah Landa, "The Exodus: Convergence of Science, History and Jewish Tradition," *Ḥakirah*, vol. 14, pp. 187-235 [2012]).

It has been pointed out that the translation "shepherd kings" for "Hyksos" (attributed by Josephus [*Against Apion* 1:14] to the Egyptian priest-historian Manetho) is mistaken, and that Hyksos is actually derived from two Egyptian words meaning "rulers of foreign lands" (see, e.g., Rosalie David, *Handbook to Life in Ancient Egypt* (New York: Oxford University Press, 1999, p. 32).

so as to be able to make war against us." In contrast, the expression *al tithakkam yoter*, "neither make yourself overwise" (Eccl. 7:16), refers to general *hokhmah*, i.e., "Do not make yourself too wise with regard to love of righteousness," as it says [in the same verse], "Be not righteous overmuch."

Wessely (in his book *Gan Na'ul*) did not distinguish between general and specific *hokhmah*, and therefore he was forced into error as to some verses, including the present one. He thought that the verb [*hakham*, "to be wise"] appears in the *hitpa'el* (reflexive) conjugation to indicate that it was *hokhmah* only in the imagination of Pharaoh and his advisers. It is not true, however, that the *hitpa'el* generally indicates an action that is imagined and not real. In the verse, "There is one who pretends himself rich [*mit'asher*], yet has nothing; there is one who pretends himself poor [*mitroshesh*], yet has great wealth" (Prov. 13:7), the words "yet has nothing" and "yet has great wealth" themselves indicate that the action of *hit'asherut* and *hitrosheshut* (lit., "becoming rich," "becoming poor") is not real but false—not that this is within the function of the *hitpa'el*, as the author of *Anaf Ets Avot* has pointed out (p. 29).

**some war occurring** *(ki tikrenah milhamah)*. The ending *–nah* [in the verb *tikrenah*, seemingly indicating the plural] is superfluous; cf. "her hand she put *(tishlahnah)* to the tent-pin" (Judg. 5:26); "The crown of pride… shall be trodden *(teramasnah)* underfoot" (Isa. 28:4).

**make war against us, and then depart from the country.** Rashbam and Mendelssohn interpret, "And it would not be to our benefit to lose our slaves." The Korem objected that the Israelites were not yet slaves; he interprets the phrase "and then depart from the country" as meaning, "He will take with him all the wealth and property that he will have acquired in our country." But this, too, is incorrect, for their wealth and property would be theirs, and the Egyptians would have no right to it. Besides, if this explanation were correct, the main point [of Pharaoh's statement] would be missing.

My late son, Ohev Ger [Filosseno] upheld Rashbam and Mendelssohn's interpretation, saying that even before the Egyptians enslaved the Israelites, from the beginning, the Israelites helped Egypt by virtue of their shepherding, since the Egyptians were not shepherds but needed shepherds; thus, if the Israelites were to leave Egypt, this would cause damage to the kingdom.

I myself would say that the correct view is that the new king who arose over Egypt was fearful that the Egyptians would rebel, but he was certain that if they started to rebel, he would defeat them and kill their leaders, and the people would hear and be afraid. However, he was more fearful of the

Israelites; since they were foreigners and sojourners in that country, and unlike the Egyptians, they were not emotionally attached to the land, it was likely that they would rise against him as soon as they had the opportunity, and even if the king were to prevail against them and his enemies, he would not be able to take revenge upon the Israelites, for they would go out of the country to the land of the enemies with whom they would have joined.

According to the scholar Jost, it is found in the books of the ancients that the shepherd people conquered Egypt as far as Memphis, and there they installed a king. Afterwards they built Avaris, which he identifies with Heroöpolis and which is the same as Pi-ha-Hirot [below, 14:9] (for *pi* is the equivalent in Egyptian of the definite article *ha*).[2] Later, when the king of Thebais [the southern Egyptian region where the city of Thebes was located] rose against them and defeated them, they fled there [to Avaris], and the Egyptians, unable to bring them under their rule, expelled them from there as well. Accordingly, Jost interprets "make war against us, and then depart from the county" to mean that Pharaoh was afraid that Israel might join with Egypt's enemies, the shepherd people, who were at Pi-ha-Hirot near Goshen, and that they would make war against Egypt by leaving the country, joining the remnants of the people from Arabia, and attacking the Egyptians together. However, it seems to me that according to this theory, it should first have said "and depart from the country" and *then* "join himself to our enemies."

**1:11. So they set up over that (people) commissioners of levy [charged with selecting the strongest individuals], in order to oppress him with their burdens. He built cities for Pharaoh for use as storehouses, Pithom and Ra'amses.**

*So they set up.* After Pharaoh said, "Let us study some stratagem against him," he apparently added, "Let us set up commissioners of levy over him," except that the Torah abbreviated the account.

*commissioners of levy (sarei missim).* Officials appointed to exact the *mas*, a term which sometimes means giving something [as tribute] and sometimes means performing some service needed by the king. It seems to me that *mas* (although seemingly derived from the root *masas*, "to melt," "to dissolve") is

---

2. Modern scholarship does not identify Avaris with Pi-ha-Hirot, although both were in the eastern Nile Delta region. Avaris has instead been identified with Tso'an (Zoan or Tanis); see *Encyclopaedia Judaica*, s.v., "Hyksos," "Pi-ha-Hirot," and "Zoan."

actually derived from the root *nasa*, "to raise," and is related to the expression *va-yissa massa'ot*, "he offered them [offerings]" (Gen. 43:34). *Mas* is similar to *terumah* ("tribute") [lit., "raising"]; persons chosen for the king's service are themselves called *mas*, since they are "raised" from among the public; cf. "And king Solomon raised a levy [*va-ya'al… mas*] out of all Israel; and the levy was thirty thousand men. And he sent them to Lebanon" (1 Kings 5:27-28). My late son Ohev Ger said that similarly in Italian, the term *leva* ("levy") is derived from the concept of "raising" and "lifting" [*levare*, "to raise"] and refers to the military vanguard that the king conscripts from among the people.

***in order to oppress him with their burdens.*** So that through their enslavement with hard labor, their strength would be diminished and they would not multiply so greatly, and those who would be born would not be so healthy or strong.

***with their burdens*** *(be-sivlotam)*. The Heb. does not refer precisely to the bearing of loads on one's shoulders (as Kimhi and Mendelssohn interpreted it), but the term was transferred to denote any labor that one imposes on another (as in the Italian *peso* ["burden," lit., "weight"] and *carico* ["burden," lit., "load"]). Cf. "And the man Jeroboam was a mighty man of valor; and Solomon saw the young man that he was industrious, and he gave him charge of all the labor of [*sevel*] the house of Joseph" (2 Kings 11:28).

***He built*** *(va-yiven)*. It is possible that these cities had already been in existence, for the root *banah* ("to build") is also used to denote the renovation or reinforcement of that which has already been built (Rashi, Clericus, and Rosenmueller).

***cities… for use as storehouses*** *(arei miskenot)*. In which to store grain; [*miskenot* is] the equivalent of *mikhnasot*, from the root *kanas* ("to gather"). Cf. "Storehouses also [*u-miskenot*] for the increase of corn, wine, and oil" (2 Chron. 32:28). *Arei miskenot* are mentioned in 2 Chron. 8:4, 8:6, and 17:12.

***Pithom.*** Herodotus [2:158] mentions a city named Patumos and says that it is near the Red Sea (Rosenmueller and Gesenius).

***Ra'amses*** (רַעְמְסֵס). Vocalized with a *patah* at the *ayin* [as opposed to "the land of Rameses (רַעַמְסֵס)" (Gen. 47:11)]. According to Jablonski, this is

Heliopolis, the "city of the sun," for *re* in the Egyptian language means "sun" and *messe* means "field."[3]

The traveler of ancient routes, Forskal, told Niebuhr that on his way from Cairo to Alexandria he came upon a village that they called "Ramsis," and near that village there were ruins of an old city (Rosenmueller). The opinion of the scholar Jost is that Pharaoh decreed that the Israelites build and reinforce the city of Rameses, which had earlier belonged to his kinsmen. Perhaps Pharaoh stationed soldiers there to supervise the Israelites and prevent them from rebelling.

**1:12. But the more they oppressed him, the more he increased, and the more extraordinarily he increased, so that they were vexed on account of the children of Israel.**

***the more extraordinarily he increased*** *(ve-khen yifrots)*. The root *parats* [in its most basis sense] is a transitive verb denoting "breaking," as in, "He breaks me [*yifretseni*] with breach upon breach [*ferets al penei farets*]" (Job 16:14), and in particular the breaking down of fences and walls, as in, "Why have You broken down [*paratsta*] her fences?" (Ps. 80:13). Later it was used as if it were an intransitive verb; thus it was said, "And you will extend [*u-faratsta*] westward, eastward…" (Gen. 28:14), meaning, "You will break down every boundary, overcome every obstacle, and spread out westward and eastward."

---

3. Shadal's comment on Gen. 47:11 notes that Jablonski derived "Ramses" from the Egyptian *rem* ("man") and *sos* ("shepherd"). Modern scholarship, however, derives it from *R'-ms-sw* ("Re is he that has borne him") and apparently draws no distinction between Ra'amses and Rameses (see *Encyclopaedia Judaica*, s.v. "Ramses"). With respect to Luzzatto's treatment of ancient Egyptian words and writing in general, he seems to have relied mainly on pre-Rosetta Stone scholarship, even though he was acquainted with at least some of the work of Jean-François Champollion (1790-1832), whose decipherment of the Stone, first announced in 1822, opened the way to the correct understanding of the Egyptian hieroglyphics. (See, for example, Shadal's reference in his *Grammatica* § 258 to Champollion's *Grammaire égyptienne*, 1836.) Why Shadal continued to make use of apparently outdated Egyptology is not entirely clear, but it should be noted that Champollion's work had not yet been definitively accepted during Shadal's lifetime. It was not until 1866, when the Decree of Canopus was successfully deciphered using Champollion's method, that his reputation was cemented as the true decipherer of the hieroglyphs (see Lesley Adkins and Roy Adkins, *The Keys of Egypt: The Obsession to Decipher Egyptian Hieroglyphs*, New York: HarperCollins, 2000, p. 294).

*Shemot*

The term was transferred to denote anything that increases to a greater extent than normal, as if it were breaking through the bounds that nature set for it, as in, "While the little that you had before me [i.e., flocks] has greatly multiplied [*va-yifrots la-rov*]" (Gen. 30:30); "And his possessions [lit., "cattle"] are increased [*parats*] in the land" (Job 1:10). It would also be said of a person that he was *porets*, meaning that his possessions were increasing, as in, "And he became exceedingly rich [*va-yifrots... me'od me'od*], and he possessed numerous flocks" (Gen. 30:43). Perhaps the term *peritsah* was also used in the sense of an increase in strength or power; this was the opinion of the Aramaic translator [i.e., Onkelos, on the present verse], who rendered the phrase *ken yirbeh ve-khen yifrots* as *ken sagan ve-khen takfin* ("the more he increased and the more they became powerful").

In my opinion, [the expression *ve-khen yifrots* in the verse] does not depart from the meaning of "increase in number," as if it said, "The more they oppressed him, the more he multiplied," and Israel's increase was greater than natural.

**1:13. Then the Egyptians made the Israelites serve with rigor.**

**with rigor** *(be-farekh)*. The Hebrew appears also in Lev. 25:43, 46, and 53, and in Ezek. 34:4, and it is an Aramaic term for "breaking" or "crushing" (Rashbam, Kimhi). In [normal] Hebrew, "oppression" is called *ritsuts* [lit., "crushing"], as in:

- "Whom have I oppressed [*ratsoti*]?" (1 Sam. 12:3);
- "Vexed and oppressed [*ve-ratsuts*]" (Deut. 28:33);
- "And to let the oppressed [*retsutsim*] go free" (Isa. 58:6);
- "And they oppressed and crushed [*va-yerotsetsu*] the children of Israel" (Judg. 10:8);
- "That crush [*ha-rotsetsot*] the needy" (Amos 4:1).

**1:14. And they embittered their life with toilsome labors, with mortar and with bricks, and with every labor of the fields; every labor to which they subjected them (they subjected them to it) with rigor.**

**with mortar and with bricks.** The manufacture of mortar and bricks, which is hard labor because one needs to stand near the furnace.

**with mortar** *(be-ḥomer)*. Cf. Gen. 11:3 [where the term occurs in connection with the Tower of Babel].

***every labor to which they subjected them*** *(et kol avodatam)*. Some interpret this phrase to mean "besides all their labor"; this interpretation is correct according to the accents.[4] The preferable explanation, however, is Ibn Ezra's: that [the verse is to be understood] as if the words *avedu vahem* ("they subjected them") were written twice [as in the translation].

The term *avad be-* is equivalent to *he'evid*, "subjected" [using the root in a *hif'il*, i.e., causative sense], except when the *be-* means "for," as in, "And Israel served for a wife [*va-ya'avod Yisra'el be-ishah*]" (Hos. 12:13) (Ibn Ezra).

**1:15. Then the king of Egypt said to the midwives of the Hebrews, of whom one was named Shiphrah, and the other Puah.**

***to the midwives of the Hebrews*** *(la-meyalledot ha-ivriyyot)*. In the opinion of the Sages, Onkelos, Rashbam, Mendelssohn, and Rosenmueller, these midwives were of Israelite stock, but according to the Alexandrian translator, Jerome, Josephus Flavius [*Antiquities* 2:9], and Abravanel, the "midwives of the Hebrews" were Egyptian, and this seems likely, for how could Pharaoh have commanded Israelite women to kill all the sons of their people, without suspecting that they would reveal the matter?

Clericus argued that if they were not Hebrews, it would have said *la-ivriyyot* [i.e., "midwives *to* the Hebrews" not *ha-ivriyyot*, "the Hebrews"]. Rosenmueller, emending the text, said that it should have read *et ha-ivriyyot* [the word *et* is a direct object marker, making the phrase mean, "those who assisted the Hebrews in giving birth"]. This is not a convincing argument, however, for although the text could have read *la-meyalledot et ha-ivriyyot*, it could just as well have conveyed the same meaning by saying *la-meyalledot ha-ivriyyot*, without the *et* [to indicate that *ha-ivriyyot* was the direct object]; cf. *kol ha-adam ha-okhel ha-boser*, "every man who eats the sour grapes" (Jer. 31:29) [where there is no *et* to introduce the object, *ha-boser*].

Insofar as their claim was based on the statement that "the midwives feared God" (below, v. 17), this is no claim at all, for it is not written [that they feared] "the Lord" (YHVH), but rather "God" (*Elohim*), and anyone who has a God (whether it be a true God or a false god) would surely fear to slay sinless infants, regardless of their nationality.[5] This is illustrated by what

---

4. The word *et* is marked with a disjunctive accent (*yetiv*), which may indicate that it means "with" or "besides," rather than merely serving to introduce a direct object.

5. All too many atrocities perpetrated by various professed monotheists in the 20th and 21st centuries have unfortunately cast doubt on this seemingly reasonable assumption.

is said of Amalek: "Without fearing God [*Elohim*], he slew you all the weak ones remaining behind, while you were weary and tired" (Deut. 25:18). My late beloved student, the scholar R. Jacob Hai Pardo, added that if the midwives were of another people, it would [indeed] be fitting to say that they acted out of "fear of God" rather than love, while if they had been Hebrews, there would have been no need to mention the fear of God, for everyone loves his own people.

As for the claim that the names "Shiphrah" and "Puah" are not Egyptian but are derived from Hebrew roots, this is no claim either, for in my opinion, these midwives were not technically Egyptian, but were from the land of Goshen, which was near the land of Canaan (see at Gen. 46:34), and it is likely that they spoke the language of Canaan and that their names were Canaanite or Hebrew.

Now it obvious that a great and multitudinous people would not likely have only two midwives, and therefore Ibn Ezra (followed by Rosenmueller) said that these two were the chiefs of all the midwives. According to R. Ovadiah Sforno, Pharaoh spoke first with the midwives who were in his city, and after they failed to carry out his word, he no longer trusted the ones in other places. This, however, seems unlikely to me, for the Israelites were in Goshen, not in Egypt [proper]; the phrase "and the country became full of them" (above, v. 7) does not mean that they spread throughout Egypt, for below, too, we find that it was only in Goshen, where the Israelites were, that there was no hail (Exod. 9:26).

I say that Pharaoh did not wish to speak with all the midwives at once, for if all of them were to kill Israelite boys at the same time, the matter would become widely known. This would not happen if only two of them, and not the others, were to kill; they would be able to say that it was an accident. It was, in fact, his intention to give the command to all the midwives, one after another at random, so that the matter should not become known.

**1:16. He said, that is, "When you assist the Hebrew women in childbirth, you shall observe over the chair [or, over the vessel for washing the newborn]: if it is a son, you shall cause it to die; and if it is a daughter, let it live."**

***When you assist... in childbirth*** *(be-yalledkhen).* With regard to the distinction between the *pi'el* and *hif'il* conjugations, see *Bikkurei ha-Ittim* 5588 (1827), p. 130.[6]

---

[6]. This article, apparently written by Shadal, notes that the *meyalledet* ("midwife,"

***over the chair*** *(al ha-ovnayim).* Some interpret the Hebrew to mean the chair of the woman giving birth, while others interpret it as "the womb." According to some, the word is derived from *even* ("stone"), while others derive it from *banah* ("to build") or *ben* ("son"). Gesenius says that the *ovnayim* consisted of two stones, one concave and the other on top as a covering, and that in the concave stone they used to wash the newborn infant. Thévenot moreover noted that the kings of Persia used to command that their relatives' sons be put to death while being washed. According to this opinion, the *ovnayim* referred to here resembles the *ovnayim* mentioned in Jer. 18:3; see there.[7]

***you shall cause… to die*** *(va-hamitten* וַהֲמִתֶּן*).* From *hemit* ("to cause to die") [whose root is *mut*] were derived the form *hematta* and *hamitota* ("you caused to die"), analogous to *hekamta* and *hakimota* ("you raised") [from *hekim*, whose root is *kum*]. In the vocabulary of Scripture, however, [a form like *va-hamitten*] is nowhere else found in connection with roots whose middle letter becomes silent [like the *vav* in *mut* and *kum*]; it is proper to say [in the second person plural, masculine] *hekamtem* (with the first syllable vocalized with a short *hataf segol*, not a long *tseireh* as written in *Netivot ha-Shalom*, for with the multiple vowels resulting in the displacement of the accent [toward the end of the word], one of the vowels should be shortened to a *sheva* if there is nothing to prevent it; see *Toledot Rambeman,* Vienna edition, last page), or *hakimotem*. Here, too, the proper form would have been *ve-hematten* (וְהֵמַתֶּן) (and not והמתתן, for one would not say *shavat'ta* or *natan'nu,* but rather *shavatta* or *natannu* [with a single *tav* or *nun* marked with a *dagesh*]), or *va-hamatten* or *va-hamitoten*.

[The actual form] *va-hamitten* is vocalized with a *hirek* on the model of *tsad* [which yields] *tsiddo* and *pat* [which yields] *pittekha*. In the case of these

---

from the *pi'el* conjugation of the root *yalad,* "to give birth to") is one who assists at a birth, while the *molid* ("begetter," from the *hif'il* of the same root) is the one who proximately causes the birth.

7. The *ovnayim* in Jeremiah is generally understood to be a "potter's block." Shadal, in his comment on Jer. 18:3, cites R. Jonah ibn Janah, who reported having seen a potter from "the lands of the east" who used a wooden implement consisting of two millstone-like components, a large lower one and a small upper one; R. Jonah said that this implement was called *ovnayim,* meaning, "two stones," because of its resemblance to millstones. However, Shadal questions this interpretation due to the vocalization of the word. As for a connection between the midwives' *ovnayim* and the potter's *ovnayim,* Cassuto (*Commentary on the Book of Exodus,* p. 14), notes that the Egyptian god to whom the creation of human beings was attributed was commonly depicted as sitting beside a potter's wheel, fashioning human figures out of clay.

nouns, which are derived from geminate verbs (*tsad*, "side," from *tsadad*; *pat* "bread," from *patat*), the *hirek* properly appears, for if they were to be written out in full form, they would be צדדו* (*tsid'do*, with a double *dalet*) and פתתך* (*pit'tekha*, with two *tavs*), on the model of *bigdi* and *bigdekha* [from the noun *beged*, "clothing"]. Because the word *ve-hematten* seemed as if it were derived from a geminate root [the hypothetical *matat*], in which case a double *tav* would have been proper (והמתתן, *ve-hemat'ten*), they pronounced it with a *hirek* on the model of the geminates.

This peculiarity is not to be ascribed [merely] to the [Masoretic] vocalizers, as if they had made it up themselves, for we do find the form וַהֲמִיתִּיו, *ve-hamittiv*, "and I slew him," (1 Sam. 17:35), with a *yod* [between the *mem* and the *tav*], which proves that such was the pronunciation of the ancients. Similar to this peculiarity is a [plural] form derived from *morag*, "threshing board": *moriggim* (1 Chron. 21:23); this word, too, is found with a *yod* [between the *resh* and the *gimel*].[8]

*... let it live (va-ḥayah).* Through frequent use of the root *ḥayah* ("to live"), sometimes they said *ḥai* instead of *ḥayah*, e.g., "Arpachshad lived [*ḥai*]" (Gen. 11:12). Here too *va-ḥayah* appears instead of [the proper feminine form] *ve-ḥayatah*. The *yod* is "weak" [i.e., has no *dagesh*], for the word is actually not derived from a geminate root [חיי]. According to Gussetius, the word is derived from a root חוי, but the phrase *Arpakhshad ḥai* stands against this theory, for if the word had been derived from חוי, the *ḥet* would have been vocalized with a *kamats* [חָי instead of חַי].[9]

**1:17. However, the midwives feared God, and they did not carry out that which the king of Egypt had commanded them, but they let the boys live.**

***but they let the boys live** (va-teḥayyena).* They left them alive; cf. *lo teḥayyeh kol neshamah*, "Do not leave any soul alive" (Deut. 20:16).

**1:18. Then the king of Egypt called the midwives, and he said to them, "How is it that you did such a thing, that you have, that is, let the boys live?"**

---

8. However, the standard reading here and in 2 Sam. 24:22 is מוֹרַגִּים, without a *yod* between the *resh* and *gimel*.

9. Thus וְאַרְפַּכְשַׁד חַי proves the root is חיי not חוי.

## Shadal on Exodus

***How is it (maddua) that you did...*** Not [as it might have been translated], "*Why* did you do such a thing?" Rather, "How was it that you dared to annul my command?" (See *Otsar ha-Shorashim*.)[10]

***that you have... let... live (va-teḥayyena).*** [This is the same word as the one in the previous verse that means "but *they* let live," but] it is well known that the verb form *tifkodna* is identical for the second person and third person feminine plurals.

**1:19. The midwives said to Pharaoh, "Because the Hebrew women are not like the Egyptians, but they are vigorous: before the midwife has come to them, they have already given birth."**

***Vigorous (ḥayot).*** An adjective [*ḥayeh* in the masc. sing.] derived from the root *ḥayah*, "to live," on the model of *daveh*, "sick, sad" [from the verb *davah*], *raveh*, "well-watered," [from the verb *ravah*]. The noun *ḥayyah*, "beast," however, is derived from a geminate verb root [חיי], and this [i.e., the fact that the *yod* in *ḥayyah* is strengthened with a *dagesh*] serves to distinguish between [the adjective *ḥayah*, which has] the meaning of "healthiness" and "strength," and [the noun *ḥayyah*, which has] the meaning of "animal," even though the *ḥayyah* was originally so called only because of its strength and power.

**1:20. God benefitted the midwives, and the people became numerous and exceedingly strong.**

***God benefitted the midwives.*** He benefitted them in that He caused Pharaoh to have mercy upon them and not put them to death in his anger. If Pharaoh had killed them and appointed others in their place, the new ones would have carried out his decree in order to avoid being put to death, and so as a result of the good with which God benefitted the midwives, it also occurred that "the people became numerous and exceedingly strong" (Judah Aryeh Osimo).

**1:21. Now, since the midwives feared God, He made them houses [that is, families, in other words, He gave them numerous progeny].**

***He made them houses.*** Rashi, citing the Sages, explained that God made the midwives houses of priesthood, *Leviyyah*, and kingship.[11] Likewise, Ibn Ezra

---

10. By Judah Leib Ben Ze'ev (Vienna, 1807-1808). Under the root *mada* (p. 350, 1839 ed.), it is explained that *maddua* is used when the questioner wishes to know the cause for an act or a failure to act.
11. Rashi, adopting the traditional identification of Shiphrah with Jochebed and

said that this was a reward from God to the midwives, and similarly, the opinion of Clericus and Rosenmueller was that as a reward for letting the Israelite children live, He increased their families and descendants (cf. "Then they shall be built up in the midst of My people" [Jer. 12:16]; "God makes the solitary to dwell in a house" [Ps. 68:7]).

Gesenius (*Thesaurus*, p. 193) interpreted "houses" (*batim*) in the sense of wealth and riches, as in, "Through wisdom is a house builded" (Prov. 24:3). Similarly, Gussetius said that the idea of "success" is included with multitude of descendants, as in, "They that work wickedness are built up" (Mal. 3:15). However, Rashbam, R. Isaac Arama, and the Korem maintained that Pharaoh built houses for the midwives in order to keep them from going to the Hebrew women in childbirth. This is far from the meaning of the expression, however, and [if this explanation were to be adopted,] the main idea would be missing [from the text], as Nachmanides noted.

R. Moses Hefez (*Melekhet Maḥashevet*) expressed the view that after the midwives' righteousness became known, they had an increase in the number of houses that called them, as we say [in Italian] of midwives, *ha molte case* ("she has many houses"). Mendelssohn understood this verse as connected with the next one: "Now, since the midwives feared God, and since God made them [the Israelites] houses and many families, Pharaoh then commanded all of his people, 'Every son that is born....'" Still, however, the expression "He made them houses" remains difficult, as it is an unusual way of denoting an increase of offspring; what does this expression add, since we already know that Israel had many families?

My late father maintained that the Israelites wished to reward the midwives, and since they were trained in the use of mortar and bricks, they built them houses. Even according to this explanation, however, there is a difficulty, for the text should have read *va-yiven* ("he built"), while the term [that actually appears,] *va-ya'as* ("he made") is on the model of, "The Lord will make you a house [i.e., a dynasty]" (2 Sam. 7:11), and appears to lend support to the view of the Sages.

It seems to me that it was the custom that only the women who had no children and no household responsibilities became midwives, but God blessed these midwives and gave them children, and they proliferated, multiplied, and established "houses."

---

Puah with Miriam, meant to say that "Shiphrah," through Aaron and Moses, became the ancestress of the priests and the Levites, while "Puah," through her descendants by Caleb of the tribe of Judah, became the ancestress of the house of David.

## Shadal on Exodus

***them*** *(lahem).* The Hebrew [properly a masculine indirect object pronoun] appears instead of *lahen* [the feminine form]; cf. below, 2:17, *tsonam* ("their sheep") [instead of *tsonan*].

**1:22. Pharaoh then commanded all his people, saying, "Every son that is born [to the Israelites] you shall cast into the Nile, and every daughter you shall let live."**

***all his people.*** Once he saw that his plan to do the thing secretly had not succeeded, and his command to the midwives had perhaps already been revealed, he made the matter public and commanded all of the Egyptians that when they happened to see or hear a Hebrew infant, they should cast him into the Nile.

***Every son that is born.*** The meaning undoubtedly is "born to the Hebrews," as Onkelos and the Jerusalem Targum translated.

***Every son that is born*** *(ha-yillod).* [The Heb. is equivalent to] *ha-nolad*; compare:

- "The child that is born [*ha-yillod*] to you" (2 Sam. 12:14);
- "The people that were born [*ha-yillodim*] in the wilderness" (Josh. 5:5);
- "Those that were born [*ha-yillodim*] to him in Jerusalem" (2 Sam. 5:14);
- "[The sons and the daughters] that are born [*ha-yillodim*] in this place" (Jer. 16:3).

It is an adjective that takes the place of a passive participle; it serves to indicate past or future, as is the case with participles. Clericus said that the word should likely be read *ha-yillud*, but it does not seem so to me, since we find the form הַיְלָדִים, without a *vav*.

**2:1. A man of the family of Levi had gone and taken a daughter of Levi.**

***had gone*** *(va-yelekh).* This is the expression used for one who bestirs himself to do something. Compare:

- "Reuben went [*va-yelekh*] and lay with Bilhah" (Gen. 25:22);
- "So he [Hosea] went [*va-yelekh*] and took Gomer" (Hos. 1:3) (Nachmanides); [other examples are:]
- "Who passes over [*va-yelekh*], that is, to render worship to other gods" (Deut. 17:3);

- "And he [Ahab] went [*va-yelekh*] and served Baal" (1 Kings 16:31);
- "But she also went [*va-telekh*] and played the harlot" (Jer. 3:8).

Now this "taking" had happened previously, for Miriam and Aaron had already been born. [However,] the Sages said that Amram had dismissed his wife on account of Pharaoh's decree, but afterwards brought her back on the advice of Miriam; see also below, Exod. 6:20.

**2:2. The woman, having become pregnant, bore a son; and seeing that he was good, she kept him hidden for three months.**

*that he was good (tov).* Ibn Ezra, Sforno, Mendelssohn, Rosenmueller, and Gesenius interpreted this to mean "that he was good-looking," for they did not understand how it could be said of a newborn boy that he was "good." Rashbam gave the explanation that the boy was born at the end of six months, and that his mother observed him and saw that he was fully formed and viable, not a stillborn.[12]

It seems clear to me, however (from my late father), that the proper interpretation of *tov* is the literal one, and that a baby is called "good" when he does not cry or shout. If he had shouted, it would have been impossible to hide him, for his voice would have been heard from afar. However, because he was "good," she was able to hide him.

**2:3. But not being able to keep him hidden, she took him a box of papyrus, daubed it with bitumen and pitch, placed the child in it, and placed it in the reeds, on the bank of the Nile.**

*to keep him hidden* (הַצְּפִינוֹ, *hatsefino*). The *dagesh* marking the letter *tsadi* is for the purpose of embellishing the reading; they did this in order to make the *sheva* vowel "mobile" and lengthen the word [which would otherwise have been pronounced *hatspino*], and the purpose of this was to allow the *segol* [*segulta*] accenting the word to be sung well, for there is no word before it with an auxiliary accent that would aid its cantillation. A similar treatment is found in the phrase *mikkedash* (מִקְּדָשׁ) *YHVH konenu yadekha* ("to the sanctuary, O Lord, that Your hands will render firm") [below, Exod. 15:17].[13]

---

12. Rashbam based the figure of six months on the fact that the child was hidden for three months afterward, the assumption being that it was feasible to hide him until his expected birth date, but no later.

13. In both cases, there would normally have been a *dagesh kal* in the succeeding letter; it "should" have been *hatspino* with a *dagesh kal* in the *pe*, and *mikdash*

# Shadal on Exodus

[The word *hatsefino*] is the *pa'il* (active) form [of the root *tsafan*, "to hide"]. One who is *tsofen* [in the *kal*] hides another person, but the other is able to come out of his hiding place if he does not wish to remain hidden. Not so the *matspin* [in the causative *hif'il*], for he forces the other to stay hidden. Jochebed, even after the first three months, could have continued to hide her son, but she would not have been able to force him to remain hidden, for he would have cried aloud and Egypt would have heard him. Cf. "O that You would hide me [*tatspineni*] in the netherworld" (Job 14:13), meaning, "Would that You would slay me, so that You would force me to be hidden out of Your sight, and I would not walk before You in the land of the living, and the Divine justice would not be able to touch me."

**papyrus** *(gome)*. [A plant] that grows by the Nile, so called [in Hebrew] after the expression, "Please let me try [or "sip"] [*hagmi'ini*] a little water" (Gen. 24:17), as if it needs to drink. Thus Lucan calls it *bibula papyrus* ("thirsty papyrus"). They made clothes, shoes, baskets, and even boats out of it; in the words of Lucan (*Pharsalia* 4.136), "The boats of Memphis are framed of thirsty papyrus" (Rosenmueller and Gesenius).

My student Isaac Judah Klineberger says that first they called this plant *gome,* and [only] later it happened that they drank water with a stalk of papyrus—as where a person who needed to take a drink from a stream took a papyrus that was growing by the stream, make it into a straw, and drank of the stream's water sip by sip—and this type of drinking became known as *gemi'ah* after the *gome.*

**daubed it** *(va-taḥmerah)*. A verb derived from *ḥemar* ("bitumen"). The [final letter] *he* would properly have been marked with a *mappik* [a dot to strengthen the sound and indicate the object "it"].

**in the reeds** *(ba-suf)*. Cf. "The reeds and flags [*va-suf*] shall wither" (Isa. 19:6). This is a type of plant that grows by the Nile, called *Sari* in Egyptian. Pliny *(Natural History* 13.13) states as follows: "The sari, too, that grows on the banks of the Nile, is one of the shrub genus. It is generally about two cubits in height, and of the thickness of one's thumb."[14]

---

with a *dagesh kal* in the *dalet*. However in both cases, the *dagesh* was moved to the preceding letter (*tsadi* and *qof*), and it became a *dagesh chazak*.

14. Based on the translation by Bostock and Riley (London, 1855). There, however, the citation is to Book 13, ch. 45, and the name of the plant is given as "saripha."

*Shemot*

The mother's intention in placing her child in a box at the Nile's edge was (per Sforno) that perhaps some Egyptian might see him and take him home with him like any foundling. I would add that the mother said to herself, "It would be better for him to live in an Egyptian's house than to die," and yet she did not despair of him, but sent her daughter in order to know what would become of him; she passed her thoughts on to her, so that the girl said to Pharaoh's daughter, "Do you want me to go call you a nursing woman, from among the Hebrews?" [below, v. 7]. In this way the mother was able to let the child know that he was a Jew and to teach him the language and faith of his ancestors.

**2:4. And his sister placed herself far off, in order to know what would become of him.**

*placed herself* (*va-tetatsav* וַתֵּתַצַּב). A strange word, for the proper form would have been *va-tityatsev* [in the reflexive]. Perhaps it could be said that the vocalization ought to be *va-tattsev*, i.e., *va-tatsev* ("and she stationed [his sister]"), referring back to the child's mother, for she was the one who had his sister stand far off so as to know what would happen with her son. She did not place him there so that he should die, for a mother would not likely kill her own child for fear that he might be killed, unless she were to choose for him an easier form of death. In this case, even the Egyptians would not have done any worse than casting him into the Nile, while she [if it were her intention to kill him] by placing him in the box, would have caused him to die of starvation, which is a much harsher form of death than drowning.

As we know, the root *yatsav* ("to stand") is conjugated in the manner of verbs that are *ḥaser nun* [derived from a root whose initial letter *nun* disappears in some forms], as in the Aramaic *tinda* ("you will know") from the root *yada* ("to know"), and that sometimes in Aramaic, a *tav* is added to *naḥ* verbs [those containing a letter that disappears or is not pronounced in some conjugations] so that the syllable before the main vowel can have a "mobile" *sheva*, as occurs in regular verbs: for example, in the *itpe'el* conjugation, *ittekam* [from *kum*] and *yittezin* [from *zun*], where the *tav* is strengthened with a *dagesh*, and in Syriac, אֶתְּתְקַם and אֶתְּתְרִים. As a result, in Aramaic there are roots beginning with a letter *tav* that does not occur in Hebrew; for example [the root *tenaḥ*, which yields] *atnaḥ*, "to give rest," equivalent to the Hebrew *heniaḥ* (and the source of *etnaḥta* [an accent mark indicating "pause"]). Cf. "They would leave [*matneḥei*] signs" (*Eruvin* 53a). So here, the root *yatsav* yielded *va-tattsev* ("and she stationed her").

***in order to know*** *(le-de'ah)*. [The Hebrew is irregular and appears] instead of *la-da'at*; cf. *le-ledah* ["to give birth," instead of the regular form *la-ledet*] (1 Kings 19:3).

**2:5. Pharaoh's daughter had come down to bathe by the Nile, and her maids went walking on the bank of the Nile; she saw the box amid the reeds, and she sent her servant girl, who took it.**

***to bathe by*** *(al,* lit., "on") ***the Nile.*** Rashi, Mendelssohn, and Rosenmueller interpreted this to mean that she went down to *(el)* [אל] the Nile to bathe in it. However, this was not the opinion of the accentuator [who, by placing a disjunctive *pashta* at the words *bat Par'oh* ("Pharaoh's daughter"), separated the preceding verb *va-tered* ("had come down") from the subsequent phrase *lirḥots al ha-ye'or* ("to bathe by the Nile")]—and he was correct, for it would not make sense to say *va-tered al* [to mean "she went down to"]. The correct explanation is that she went down to bathe alongside the Nile.

***her servant girl*** *(amatah)*. Her maid; the word is not to be interpreted as "her arm" (and is not to be read as *ammatah*), for *ammah* is a term that specifically refers to an arm's measure [i.e., a cubit], not to the arm itself. This term is found only once to refer to the arm, in the verse, "[Og's bedstead] is nine cubits [*ammot*] in length and four in width, [measured] with the arm of [*be-ammat*] a [common] man" (Deut. 3:11), but even there it means an arm's measure and not the arm itself.[15]

**2:6. She opened it, and she saw him, the baby, and finding that he was a crying child, she had pity on him, and she said, "This is one of the babies of the Hebrews."**

***She opened it*** *(va-tiftaḥ,* with no object in the Hebrew). The box *(tevah)*; apparently there was a cover on it, as there was on the ark *(tevah)* of Noah.

***and she saw him, the baby*** *(va-tir'ehu et ha-yeled)*. The words *et ha-yeled* are superfluous, for we already knew what was in the box. Therefore it is written *va-tir'ehu* with a pronominal suffix, while the words *et ha-yeled* are added to suggest the great astonishment that she had when she saw a baby in

---

15. Cf. Rashi's comment, which although favoring *amatah* as "her servant" on grammatical grounds, explains that the Rabbis asserted that Pharaoh's daughter's arm miraculously extended several cubits to reach the child (quoting *Sotah* 12b).

a papyrus box that had been cast into the reeds. Once she saw him and saw that he was a crying child, she took pity on him.

***This is one of the babies of the Hebrews.*** She surmised that one of the Hebrews had likely placed his son there, so that an Egyptian might take him in and he would not be put to death.

**2:7. His sister said to Pharaoh's daughter, "Do you want me to go to call you a nursing woman, from the Hebrews, who would nurse the baby for you?"**

***from the Hebrews.*** For many Hebrew women were lactating, since many of them had children that had been put to death ([explained] my late father). An alternative explanation is that [such a nursing woman] would love and care for the baby more [than another would], since both he and she were Hebrews (Rosenmueller).

**2:8. Pharaoh's daughter said to her, "Go." And the maiden went, and she called the mother of the baby.**
**2:9. Pharaoh's daughter said to her, "Take this baby with you, and nurse him for me, and I will give (you) your pay." The woman took the baby and nursed him.**

***Take (heilikhi).*** The Hebrew is the equivalent of *holikhi* [in the *hif'il* conjugation of *halakh*, "to go"], on the model of *heitivi* or *heiniki* (Ibn Ezra, Gersonides, Mendelssohn, Rosenmeller, and Gesenius).[16] Some have interpreted it as *he likhi* ("here [it is] for you"), but we do not find the [Aramaic] form *likhi* in Scripture. Besides, the word *et* [which introduces the next words *ha-yeled ha-zeh,* "this baby," as a direct object] would not go well with *he likhi.* Perhaps it is written *heilikhi* in place of *holikhi* to make the word conform with *ve-heinikihu* ("and nurse him") (as per Dubno).

**2:10. The baby having grown, she brought him to Pharaoh's daughter, who kept him as a child, and she named him Moses, adding, "For from the water I saved him."**

---

16. When a root begins with a *yod,* like *yada* ("to know"), or *yarad* ("to go down"), in the *hif'il,* the *yod* changes to a *vav.* Thus *yada* becomes *modi'a* ("to inform") and *yarad* becomes *morid* ("to bring down"). The famous exception is *meitiv,* "to make good," rather than \**motiv.* The root *halakh* is treated as if it began with a *yod,* thus *molikh* (e.g., Isa. 63:12), so the formulation *heilikhi* (rather than *holikhi*) is unexpected.

***and she named him Moses…*** Abravanel interprets "and she named him" to mean that it was his mother who named him, not Pharaoh's daughter, and he interprets *meshitihu* (מְשִׁיתִהוּ) [here translated as "I saved him"] as the equivalent of *mashit oto*, "you (f.) saved him," similar to *yolidtini*, "you have borne me" (Jer. 15:10), or *libbavtini*, "you have ravished my heart" (Songs 4:9). As proof he cites the lack of a *yod* after the *tav* [in *meshitihu*, which seems to argue against the first-person "I saved him"].

However, since the boy had become the son of Pharaoh's daughter, who did not know that the nurse was his [real] mother, the correct explanation is that Pharaoh's daughter named him. In any case, his name was *Mosheh* (and not some other name such as Monios, as was Ibn Ezra's opinion),[17] for *mo* in Egyptian means "water," and *ushe* means "saved," and thus *Mosheh* means "saved from water." It is for this reason that the Alexandrian translator always writes *Mosheh* as "Moyses," since the original form was *Mo-ishe*. Similarly, Josephus Flavius [*Antiquities* 2:9] wrote that the word was compounded from *Mo-yses*, meaning "saved from water" (Jablonski, Rosenmueller, and Gesenius). Also, Clement of Alexandria (*Stromata*, Book I) wrote that the Egyptians gave the name "Moisheh" to anyone who came out of the water alive.[18]

It seems to me that the Hebrew verb *mashah* ("to pull out") was derived from the name *Mosheh*, and this root is found only in the sense of saving from water: "He drew me out [*yamsheni*] of many waters" (2 Sam. 22:17, Ps. 18:17); "So that He caused to remember the ancient times, the times of the one who drew His people out of the water [*mosheh ammo*]" (Isa. 63:11), after which it is specified [in the next phrase], "Where is he [Moses] now who brought them up out of the sea?"[19] Not that the verb was derived from the name of Moses our teacher [himself]; rather, I say that anyone who fell into the water and was rescued was called *Mosheh* by the Egyptians, and the Israelites, having learned of this while they were in Egypt, constructed a verb *mashah* to refer to rescue from the water.

My student, Rabbi Mordecai Mortara, maintains that they said *mashah* because they already had the verb *mashakh* ("to draw"), which is similar in meaning to the verb *mashah*; this is correct. Thus it resulted that the Hebrew *mashah* does not exclusively mean rescue from water, but "pulling out" in general, and therefore Scripture specifies, "For from *the water* I saved him [*meshitihu*]," and, "He drew me out [*yamsheni*] of many waters."

---

17. According to Ibn Ezra, citing various authorities, Monios was his original Egyptian name, which was translated into Hebrew as *Mosheh*.
18. Modern scholarship derives *Mosheh* from an Egyptian word for "son"; cf. the royal name Thutmose, "son of Thoth."
19. Based on Shadal's Italian translation of and comment on this verse.

The Korem adopts Abravanel's position [that it was Moses' mother who named him], and he adds that Moses grew up not with Pharaoh's daughter, but with his mother; he interprets the phrase *va-y'hi lah le-ven* ("who kept him as a child") to refer back to "his mother," who did not receive wages as a nurse, but instead asked Pharaoh's daughter to return the baby to her. This is quite illogical, for in that case it should have said not *va-y'hi lah le-ven*, but *va-teshivehu el immo* ("and she returned him to his mother") or something similar. Furthermore, the subsequent statement, "He went out to his brothers" (next v.) indicates that he had not been with his brothers.

***For from the water I saved him.*** She said this in Egyptian, but Scripture records it in Hebrew, using the verb *mashah* in a play on words.

**2:11. Now in that time, Moses having grown, he went out to his brothers, and he observed their burdens; he saw an Egyptian man who was striking a Hebrew man, from among his brothers.**

***he went out to his brothers.*** For he had been told about his kindred, and he wished to see his brothers (Mendelssohn). Perhaps this was because his mother, who had nursed him, used to come occasionally to see about the boy's welfare, as nurses customarily do; when he had grown a little, perhaps she told him that he was an Israelite and she was his mother.

***and he observed their burdens*** *(va-yar be-sivlotam)*. The preposition *be-* indicates that he "looked upon" their sufferings with a compassionate eye; cf. "Yes, the Lord has seen my misery [*ra'ah... be-onyi*]" (Gen. 29:32). Similarly, the Midrash [*Exodus Rabbah* 1:32] and Rashi say that he set his eyes and his heart to feel distressed over them.

**2:12. Having turned here and there, and having seen that there was no one, he struck the Egyptian, and he hid him in the sand.**
**2:13. Having gone out another day, he saw two Hebrew men who were coming to blows; and he said to the one who was in the wrong, "Why are you beating your neighbor?"**

***were coming to blows*** *(nitsim)*. The Hebrew is the *nif'al* form of the root *nutsah*, with the *nun* of the root missing [i.e., the form would properly have been *nintsim*].[20]

---

20. This is evidenced by the *dagesh* in the *tsadi* of *nitsim* (נִצִּים).

*to the one who was in the wrong (la-rasha*, lit., "to the wicked one"). To the one who seemed to him not to be the innocent party.

**2:14. But that man said, "Who has appointed you lord and judge over us? Do you think to kill me, as you killed the Egyptian?" Moses was afraid, and he said (to himself), "Then the thing is known."**

*Who has appointed you.* Because they saw that he had hidden the slain man in the sand, they realized that he had no authority from the king. Therefore that Hebrew man dared to say to him, "Who has appointed you lord?" (Klineberger).

**2:15. Pharaoh, having heard this thing, sought to kill Moses; but Moses fled from Pharaoh, and he went to dwell in the country of Midian, and [at first] he stopped nearby a well.**

*and he went to dwell in the country of Midian.* Ibn Ezra wrote that the Midianites were subordinate to Pharaoh, and that therefore Moses was forced to become a shepherd, so as not to stay in a settled area. This is nonsense, for it is unlikely that the priest of Midian would always have been outside the city; rather, he was undoubtedly a well known man in the city, and his sons-in-law would have been known as well. According to Ibn Ezra's thinking, Moses should have married one of the poor and nameless among the people, not the priest's daughter.

**2:16. The priest of Midian had seven daughters. They came, drew water, and filled the watercourses, to give to drink their father's flocks.**

*the watercourses (ha-rehatim).* See Gen. 30:38 [where the same term is used].[21]

**2:17. The shepherds having come, they chased them away; but Moses arose and defended them, and he gave their flocks to drink.**
**2:18. They having arrived near to Reuel their father [grandfather], he said, "How is it that you have come quickly today?"**

---

21. In his comment there, Luzzatto says that the term denotes "running" in Aramaic, i.e., a place of running water.

*Reuel their father.* He was their grandfather, Jethro's father.[22] J.D. Michaelis said that Reuel was mentioned here because he was still alive and the head of the household; afterwards he died, and Jethro was then mentioned because he succeeded him as head of the household.

**2:19. And they said, "An Egyptian man freed us from the shepherds, and he also drew for us and gave the flocks to drink."**

*and he also drew for us.* Even though they had already drawn and filled the watercourses, the water they had drawn did not suffice, so Moses drew again (Ibn Ezra).

**2:20. And he said to his daughters, "And where is he? Why have you abandoned that man? Invite him, so that he may come to dinner."**

*Invite him (kir'en)* Properly *kerenah*, but the [final] *nun* was left without a vowel; cf. *shema'an koli* ("listen to me") [Gen. 4:23] instead of *shema'nah*. This is in the manner of the Aramaic, for in [the related] Syriac, the imperative feminine plural form is *ketulein*.

**2:21. Moses consented to stay with that man, and he gave to Moses Zipporah his daughter.**
**2:22. She gave birth to a son, to whom (Moses) gave the name Gershom, for he said, "I have become a stranger in a foreign land."**
**2:23. Now after a long time, the king of Egypt died, and the Israelites sighed and cried out because of the slavery, and their outcry on account of the slavery arose to God.**

*the king of Egypt died.* This is by way of introduction to the subsequent statement, "For all those who sought your person are dead" (below, 4:19) (Rashbam).

*and the Israelites sighed.* Even during the king's life they had sighed, but it had not been possible for them to gather and call an assembly and a fast, for

---

22. In biblical times, the word *av* (lit., "father") was almost certainly used by grandchildren to refer to their grandfather, since there was no more specific term (*Leksikon Mikra'i*, s.v. *mishpaḥah*). For a more extensive discussion of the identity of Reuel and the names of Moses' father-in-law, see Shadal's comment on 18:1, below.

they had no day of rest. Now, at the king's death, when the Egyptians were mourning and eulogizing him, the Israelites also gathered and cried out to God (A. H. Mainster).

**2:24. God heard their groan, and He was mindful of the promise made to Abraham, Isaac, and Jacob.**
**2:25. God saw (the condition of) the Israelites, and God knew [He decided what He had to do].**

*and God knew.* He decided what He would do for them. Compare:

- "And I will decide [lit., "know"] how to treat you" (Exod. 33:5).
- "Now advise you [lit., "know"] and consider what answer I shall return to Him that sent me" (2 Sam. 24:13).
- "Tomorrow the Lord will decide [*ve-yoda*, lit., "will make known"] who should belong to Him" (Num. 17:5); see my comment there.[23]

**3:1. Moses pastured the flocks of Jethro his father-in-law, priest of Midian; and (one time) guiding the flocks along the open country, he arrived at the mountain of God, at Horeb.**

*and guiding the flocks, etc. (va-yinhag,* lit., "and he guided"). And once it happened that while he was guiding the flocks along the open country, he went far from his place until he came to Mount Horeb.

*along the open country (ahar ha-midbar).* The term *midbar* [usually translated as "desert"] is not used exclusively to mean a desolate place, but includes any area that is not a sown, cultivated field, even if it has pasturage; see Ps. 65:13 ["The pastures of the *midbar* do drop (with fatness)"]; Jer. 9:9 ["And for the pastures of the *midbar* a lamentation"] and 23:10 ["The pastures of the *midbar* are dried up"] (Rosenmueller). *Ahar ha-midbar* means that little by little, he went far from his place as he was accompanying his flocks along the way of the *midbar,* through its length and breadth, which stretched to Mount Sinai.

According to Kimhi, a place of pasture is called *midbar* from the root *devar,* meaning "to lead" in Aramaic. According to Ludovico de Dieu, *midbar*

---

23. In that comment, Shadal suggests that the word *ve-yoda* might be vocalized as *ve-yeda* or *ve-yada,* lit., "and He will know," meaning "He will decide"; in support of this suggestion, Shadal cites the present verse and the one in 2 Samuel.

is derived from a similar root meaning "mountain" in the Ethiopian language, but the first opinion is correct. Perhaps because the term *midbar* was used for places of pasturage with no houses or trees but only wide, open space, the term was retained for dry desert places which are likewise wide and open without houses or trees (A.H. Mainster).

***the mountain of God.*** So called with reference to the future [Revelation at that site] (Onkelos and Rashi), or else this is what Moses wrote after the giving of the Torah (my student, Elisha Zammatto). Some say it was so called because of its height—cf. *harerei El* ("mighty mountains," lit., "mountains of God") [Ps. 36:9]—but the first interpretation is the correct one.

***at Horeb.*** Horeb and Sinai were two different mountains, or two peaks of the same mountain. These are the words of Pietro della Valle: "There are two mountains in one place, that is, Horeb and Sinai, both of which arise, as I say, from one foot and are divided afterwards continuously the higher they ascend."[24]

**3:2. An angel of the Lord appeared to him from the midst of a bush, in a flame of fire. He saw (that is) that the bush was burning in the fire, and the bush was not consumed.**

***An angel of the Lord appeared.*** What he saw is subsequently specified; God sends His messages through every means.

***in a flame of fire*** *(be-labbat esh)*. *Labbah* takes the place of *lehavah*; this is the derivation of the Mishnaic expression, "If another person comes and fans the flame [*ve-libbah*], the one who fans [*ha-malbeh*] is culpable" (*Bava Kamma* 6:4) (Saadiah Gaon, Dubno, and Rosenmueller).

***from the midst of a bush*** *(ha-seneh)*. A type of bramble that was found in that mountain, on account of which the mountain was called "Sinai" (Ibn Ezra). Now the bush was "burning in the fire," but it was not actually burning; rather, it was surrounded by flames like an object on fire, for the fire was flaming between the thorns but was not catching in them. At first Moses saw the fire within the bush and [thought he saw] the bush was on fire, but

---

24. By "Horeb" and "Sinai," della Valle was referring to Jebel Musa and Jebel Katherin (see Wilfred Blunt, *Pietro's Pilgrimage* [London: James Barrie, 1953], p. 63).

afterwards he saw that the bush was not burnt. Then he said, "Let me draw near and see... how it could be that the bush is not consumed" [next. v.].

The root *ba'ar* ("to burn"), in the *kal* conjugation [as in this v.] is an intransitive verb (see Kimhi and *Netivot ha-Shalom, contra* Ibn Ezra) and denotes the flaming of a fire and also the burning of the object that is on fire, for in the usual course of nature a flame does not separate from the burning object. Here, however, the bush was flaming but was not burnt.

***consumed*** *(ukkal).* The Hebrew is a participle in the *pu'al* conjugation; see my *Grammar* §§422, 374.[25]

**3:3. Moses said, "Let me draw near and see this great phenomenon, how it could be that the bush is not consumed."**
**3:4. The Lord having seen that he was drawing near to see, God called him from the midst of the bush, and He said, "Moses! Moses!" And he said, "Here I am."**
**3:5. And (God) said, "Do not come near here. Remove the shoes from your feet, for the place on which you stand is holy soil."**

***Remove*** *(shal).* The Hebrew is from the root *nashal* ("to draw off," "drive out"); cf. "And you will have chased from your presence [*ve-nashal*] many nations" [Deut. 7:1].

**3:6. Then He added, "I am the God of your father, the God of Abraham, the God of Isaac, and the God of Jacob." Moses hid his face, for he was afraid to look toward God.**
**3:7. The Lord added, "I have seen the misery of My people that is in Egypt, and I have hear the cries that it sends forth because of its oppressors. Yes, I know its pains.**
**3:8. "I have therefore descended to free it from the Egyptians, and to make it pass out of that country to a good and spacious country, to a land that flows with milk and honey, to the land (that is) of the Canaanites, of the Hittites, of the Amorites, of the Perizzites, of the Hivites, and of the Jebusites.**

***that flows with milk and honey.*** See below at 13:5.

---

25. In § 422, Shadal notes that the form *ukkal* here is a participle without the usual initial *mem*, i.e., an irregular form of *me'ukkal*. This same point is made in § 374, where Shadal observes generally that the participle of the *pu'al* sometimes lacks the initial *mem*.

**3:9.** "Now then, behold, the cries of the children of Israel have reached Me, and I have also seen the oppression that the Egyptians make them suffer.
**3:10.** "Now then, come so that I may send you to Pharaoh; and you shall take My people, the children of Israel, out of Egypt."

*and you shall take…out (ve-hotsei,* lit., "and take out"). The Heb. is an imperative that takes the place of a verb in the future tense because it is preceded by another imperative, *lekhah* ("come"); cf. "Keep my commandments, and you will live (*ve-ḥ'yeh,* lit., "and live") [Prov. 4:4]. Similarly, in my manuscript *ḥumash* (written in the year 5171 [1411] or earlier), the word appears in the Targum as *ve-tappek* ("and you will take out").[26]

**3:11.** Moses said to God, "Who am I, that I may go to Pharaoh, and take the children of Israel out of Egypt?"
**3:12.** And (God) said, "(Yes,) for I will be with you, and this (phenomenon that you see here) serves you as a sign that it is I Who send you. When you take the people, then, out of Egypt, you shall render worship to God upon this mountain."

*for I will be with you.* "With regard to what you say, 'Who am I that I may go,' etc., know that it is not from you, but rather I will be with you; and this phenomenon that you see in the bush is a sign for you that I, God, am the One Who sends you" (Rashi, Rashbam, Ibn Ezra, and Mendelssohn).

*When you take… out, etc.* This is a separate matter, a command that he should make a memorial to that first sign that God made him, and that he should do this by sanctifying that mountain and worshipping God there, as Moses in fact did: "He built an altar beneath the mountain… And he sent the youths of the children of Israel, who immolated burnt offerings," etc. (below, 24:4, 5). Here there was no need to tell him that at this mountain God would reveal Himself to the entire people and cause them to hear His words; rather, it seems to me that He merely told him what was fitting in order to encourage him to believe that through him the Israelites would come out of Egypt.

*When you take… out (be-hotsi'akha,* lit., "in your taking out"). "During the time of your taking out," for when they were at Mount Sinai and had not yet

---

26. Most editions have *ve-appek,* in the imperative.

reached settled land, the exodus from Egypt was not yet complete. The verb stem with the prefix *be-* denotes "during the time of the action," while the stem with the prefix *ke-* denotes "after the action"; [for illustrations of this rule,] see *Bikkurei ha-Ittim* 5589 (1828), p. 93. I have since found a similar explanation by R. Solomon Pappenheim (*Yeri'ot Shelomoh*, part 1, p. 4, columns 3, 4) and by Gussetius (letter *bet*). However, Mendelssohn's comment here is completely null and void, though followed by Rosenmueller and others.[27]

**3:13. Moses said to God, "Here I go to the children of Israel, and I say to them, 'The God of your fathers sent me to you.' If they say to me, 'What is His name,' what should I tell them?"**

*If they say to me, 'What is His name.'* Maimonides aptly raised the issue (*Guide for the Perplexed* 1:63) as to how this question could have been so pertinent that Moses sought to know how to respond to it—for Israel must either have known that name or never heard it at all, and if it were known to them, Moses would have no claim [on their credence] by telling it to them, for his knowledge would be just like theirs, while if it were unheard of among them, what proof would Moses have that this was God's name, if knowledge of His name was proof [of Moses' authority]?

According to Maimonides, Moses said, "Perhaps they will ask me to prove to them the existence of God," to which God responded by saying, "*Ehyeh asher ehyeh*" [next v.], meaning, "The One Who exists is the One Who exists," in other words, "He Who must necessarily exist."

According to Mendelssohn, the many years of Israel's exile and enslavement nearly caused them to forget God's holy names, and Israel—except for the tribe of Levi—became like the other nations who believe in the hosts of heaven, as if there were no God besides these. Mendelssohn translated *Ehyeh asher ehyeh* as "the Entity that exists forever"; a similar explanation of this name is given by Saadiah Gaon.

In my opinion, the fact that the people believed that God had remembered them when Moses appeared to them and performed wonders before them proves that they were not ignorant of God's existence and were not unfamiliar

---

27. Mendelssohn wrote, "The use of the prefix *be-* with the verb stem indicates the past, while the use of the prefix *ke-* indicates the future. Accordingly, the proper form would have been *ke-hotsi'akha*, but an expert in the true meaning of tenses knows that here there is no future per se, but rather a combination of future and past [i.e., future perfect, "when you will have taken out"], for the people would not worship God on the mountain until after they left Egypt."

with the Lord of their fathers—for it is unlikely that they would acquire such knowledge in an instant upon seeing the wonders, but rather the wonders merely helped validate for them the [Divine] agency of Moses. In my view, Moses knew that Israel knew the Lord, the God of their fathers, but he thought that they would ask which descriptive name He had used to characterize Himself when He sent Moses, for He is named after His actions (since the Biblical Hebrew expression "by the name of [*be-shem*] so-and-so" means "fitting such and such a description," as in, "Afterwards you shall be called the City of Righteousness" [Isa. 1:26], meaning, "Then you shall *be* the city of righteousness." There are many more such expressions).

The purpose of this question would be to find out what God's intention was in sending Moses to them: perhaps the matter was not to be entirely for their benefit, but rather to punish the Egyptians and not to save the Israelites afterward, or perhaps He would have some other intention. By asking, "What is His name," they would be asking by which description He revealed Himself to Moses, and by which name He called Himself so that His intent could be discerned. It was as if a person were to ask, "How did so-and-so's face appear and how did his voice sound? What were his motions as he spoke these words to you?" So as to reveal thereby his thought and intent.

The answer that God gave was "*Ehyeh* is My name," and then He added "*asher ehyeh*" ("for I will be"), that is, "The description with which I reveal Myself to you and to them is *Ehyeh*, for indeed 'I will be'" (*asher ehyeh* is an explanation of the name *Ehyeh*). The meaning is, "I will be with you; I will be accessible to you; you will always see that there is a God among you" (cf. the Rabbis' interpretation, "I will be with you in this enslavement"), "for I will not leave you without doing what I promised you. With this description and purpose I send Moses, for I have determined to redeem you at all costs, and there will never be a moment in which I will not be with you even if there is no one to stand before Me. You will always see that there is a God among you, and you will never ask, 'Where is God?' For I will always be."

Now this name [*Ehyeh*] served a temporary need, but it was not a sufficient general answer to the question "what is His name" taken absolutely. Therefore He went on to say, "So shall you say to the children of Israel: 'The Lord [*YHVH*], God of your fathers... sent me to you.' This is My name forever, and this is My title for all ages" [next v.]. That is, "The Lord [the Tetragrammaton] is My name forever and My title for all ages, but the name *Ehyeh* refers only to this particular mission to take the people out of Egypt."

My student, Rabbi Abraham Hai Mainster, maintains that the question, "what is His name," is equivalent to the question, "Who is the Lord, that I should have to obey Him?" [below, 5:2]—that is, "Who is this God Who sends you to us, and what is His reason for sending us a messenger? After abandoning us and hiding His face from us throughout this long time and in all the great trouble that we are in, what name and what right does He have over us, to send us a messenger to command us to do anything?" This is what Moses thought that Israel might say when they saw him come in God's name, that they might think that he was coming only to impose commandments upon them. When in Midian, Moses did not know if they still believed and trusted in their fathers' God, and he suspected that with the greatness of their oppression and the length of their trouble, they had already despaired of mercy.

Then [according to Mainster] God answered Moses, "*Ehyeh asher ehyeh*," that is, "It is true that until now I have done nothing for them, and I have no name or right over them; it is as if I were nothing to them, as if I did not exist. However, from this day forward I will be for them what I will be, I will do for them what I will do, I will acquire the name and right over them that I will acquire. Therefore say to the children of Israel, '*Ehyeh* sent me to you': He Who until now was as if He were nothing to you, but Who says, 'That which I have not been, I will be; that which I have not done, I will do'—He is the One Who sends me to you."

Now this answer [according to Mainster] was to be given only if Israel said to Moses, "What is His name?" In fact, they said so such evil thing to him, for their hearts still clung to the God of their fathers, and they believed the tradition that they had, according to which God would show Himself mindful of them. God, Who examines hearts, knew they would not say such a thing, and therefore He went on to tell Moses, "So shall you say to the children of Israel: the Lord, God of your fathers, God of Abraham, God of Isaac, and God of Jacob, sent me to you." Then he added to Moses (not to be repeated to Israel), "This is My name forever, and there is no need for another name, for that which I did to Abraham, Isaac, and Jacob is sufficient to make known in every generation My greatness and My attributes."

**3:14. And God said to Moses, "*Ehyeh asher ehyeh* [I will be what I will be; that is, I will do for you that which I have never done until now]." Then He said, "So shall you say to the children of Israel: '*Ehyeh* [I will be] sent me to you.'"**

*And God said, etc.* Now after thirty years, I have changed my explanation of this verse somewhat, and it appears before you in my printed Italian translation, meaning, "I will be what I will be; I will do what I have never done." This is the correct explanation.

3:15. God added to Moses, "So shall you say to the children of Israel: 'The Lord, God of your fathers, God of Abraham, God of Isaac, and God of Jacob, sent me to you. This is My name forever, and this is My title for all ages."
3:16. "Go, assemble the elders of Israel, and say to them, 'The Lord, God of your fathers, appeared to me – the God (that is) of Abraham, Isaac, and Jacob – saying, "I have thought of you, and that which is being done to you in Egypt.

*the elders of* (ziknei) *Israel.* Rashi interpreted this well [by saying that the term refers to the people's leaders, not literally to all its old men], unlike Mendelssohn's translation [*"die Aeltesten"*].²⁸

3:17. ""And I have decided to take you out of the misery of Egypt, and to bring you to the country of the Canaanites, the Hittites, the Amorites, the Perizzites, the Hivites, and the Jebusites, to a country (that is) that flows with milk and honey."'
3:18. "They will listen to you; then you and the elders of Israel will go to the king of Egypt, and you will say to him, 'The Lord, God of the Hebrews, has manifested Himself to us. Now then, please permit us to go into the desert, to a distance of three days' journey, and let us make sacrifices to the Lord, our God.'

*has manifested Himself to us* (nikrah aleinu). When a person wishes to find something and then the thing suddenly presents itself before him, it is said of the thing that it was "called" (*nikra*) before him, i.e., it happened to be there as if someone had called it; cf. "And Absalom chanced to meet [*va-yikkarei*] the servants of David" (2 Sam. 18:9)—he happened before them as if they had called to him, "Come and let us kill you." Similarly, "Please cause me to make a [fortunate] encounter [*hakreih na le-fanai*] today" (Gen. 24:12); see *Bikkurei ha-Ittim* 5589 (1828), p. 88.²⁹

The term *nikrah* (נקרה) was derived from *nikra* (נקרא), but sometimes they made a distinction in writing and wrote the word with a *he* when the meaning was "a chance happening," but with an *alef* when the meaning was literally "calling." Here, the expression *nikrah aleinu* means, "He has

---

28. Although the German *die Aeltesten* literally means "the oldest ones," it does also carry the meaning of "the elders" in the sense of "leaders."
29. There, in a discussion of the word *nikra,* Shadal says that *hakreih nah le-fanai* means, "Please make it so that the thing that I seek should be called [*nikra*] and summoned before me."

happened before us, His servants, who wish to worship Him." Rosenmueller says that the expression is to be understood as if it were written with an *alef*, as in, "Because Your name is called [*nikra*] upon Your city and Your people" (Dan. 9:19) and similar expressions, and that it is not to be understood in the sense of Divine revelation, for God did not reveal Himself to the elders of Israel, but only to Moses. I say, however, that this is not a convincing claim, for God revealed Himself to Israel by means of his revelation to Moses; besides, that expression [*nikra*] would not likely have been used without the word *shem* ("name"), and would properly have appeared as, "The name of the Lord [was called upon us]."

**Now then, please permit us to go,** *etc.* Undoubtedly this request would be deceitful, for they would have no intention to return. Inasmuch as Pharaoh had detained and enslaved them unlawfully, it should not be surprising that God commanded Moses to deal crookedly with the wicked. Moreover, there is no doubt that if Moses was so reluctant to go on God's mission, he would have been even more reluctant if God had commanded him to tell Pharaoh to release Israel permanently; then Moses would not have accepted the mission at all, for he would not have dared to say to the king, "You have done evil to this people; now send them out free."

It is also possible that if Moses had so spoken to Pharaoh, then Pharaoh would have put him to death and would have dealt more and more cruelly with Israel, which may be inferred *a fortiori* from the way that he made their yoke heavier by saying, "Idle you are, idle; let the labor be worsened on the people, and let the straw not be given to them" [cf. below, Exod. 5:17, 9, and 10]. God does not change a person's nature, especially the nature of thoroughly wicked persons who deserve punishment and not reward.

The author of the *Akedah* [R. Isaac Arama] wrote, "This was a divinely profound plan designed to reveal to all Pharaoh's stubbornness and hardness of heart. By commanding [Moses] to request only that Pharaoh let them alone for about ten days to go three days' distance into the wilderness to make sacrifices to their God—it being apparently understood from their words that they would return afterwards—which request Pharaoh would nevertheless not heed, [God meant to demonstrate that] all the more so, if they were to tell him to release them completely [Pharaoh would refuse]." This is incorrect, however, for the main reason for Pharaoh's refusal was his fear that they would not return, as he said, "Who are those who are to go?" (Exod. 10:8); "Go you [only] the men" (10:11); "But let your flocks and herds remain here" (10:24)—that is, as a pledge. If he was [merely] afraid that they would not return, he should not have been punished for this.

My student, R. Isaac Pardo, responds that if Pharaoh had asked for a pledge immediately, he would have been in the right, but he did not say, "Go you only the men" until after [most of] the plagues. To the contrary, at the beginning he did not only fail to say, "Give me a pledge for your return," but he became crueler and more oppressive to them, and in this he demonstrated his wickedness.[30]

**3:19. "And I know that the king of Egypt will not let you go, if not (constrained) by force.**

***if not (constrained) by force*** *(ve-lo be-yad ḥazakah*, lit., "and not by a strong hand"). Only by a strong hand, i.e., only against his will (Rashi, Gersonides, Clericus, the Alexandrian translator, Jerome, and Pagninus). Similar instances of this usage of the word *ve-lo* are found in, "If not [*ve-lo*], I pray you, let my brother Amnon go with us" (2 Sam. 13:26); "If not [*ve-lo*], yet I pray you, let there be given to your servant two mules' burden of earth" (2 Kings 5:17), where the meaning is "if not so," "at least."

Nachmanides, Mendelssohn, and Rosenmueller interpret this as "not even by a strong hand," but if so, what is the meaning of the statement, "But I will stretch out My arm... and then he will let you go" (next v.)? God's wonders are themselves the "strong hand," and the verse states that after the wonders, Pharaoh would not refuse to let them go; elsewhere it is specifically stated, "For [constrained] by force [*ve-yad ḥazakah*] he will let you go; rather, by main force [*u-ve-yad ḥazakah*] he will drive you out of his country" (Exod. 6:1). After this event, Scripture attests in many places that with a "strong hand," God took us out of Egypt.

---

30. Nehama Leibowitz (*Studies in Exodus*, p. 94) criticizes Shadal's view as "quite out of character with his usually delicate moral scruples," and she finds "more plausible" the view propounded by Arama. In point of fact, Shadal's opinion here is entirely in keeping with his moral system, which tolerates deception under certain specific circumstances for the sake of a greater good. See, for example, his comment on v. 21 below, where he forcefully advances the opinion that the people were to be commanded by Moses, speaking in God's name, to trick their Egyptian neighbors into lending them furnishings and garments: "God wished, rightly and justly, that Israel should not leave Egypt empty-handed, and He commanded them to deal crookedly with a wicked nation." In a similar vein is Shadal's interpretation of the law of the bride accused of unchastity (Deut. 22:13-21). Supporting R. Eliezer ben Jacob's opinion in *Ketubot* 46a, Shadal's comment on v. 17 maintains that for the sake of marital harmony and to save the bride from a death penalty, the couple's stained bedsheet could serve as conclusive evidence of her virginity—despite the fact that such evidence might well have been fabricated.

Rashbam and Ibn Ezra interpret this as "and not because of his strong hand," that is, "not because his power is strong before Me." This conforms with Targum Onkelos, as the text appears in most books, *ve-la min kodam de-ḥeileh takkif* (see *Ohev Ger,* p. 48),[31] but if so, it should have said *ve-lo mi-yad ḥazakah* or *ve-lo me-ḥozek yado.*

In a manuscript *ḥumash* on parchment in my possession, written before the year 5171 (1411), the Targum reads *ve-la ellahein min kodam de-ḥeila takkif.* Here the scribe mixed together two versions, and the one who added the vowel points vocalized the word *ve-la* but left the word *ellahein* unvocalized, while vocalizing the word *de-ḥeila* (דחילא) with a *tseireh.* It seems to me, however, that to the contrary, the version with *ellahein* (which is also the version of Antwerp that I cited in *Ohev Ger*) is to be preferred, and the *ḥet* in דחילא should be vocalized with a *ḥirek (de-ḥila),* to mean "fear."

**3:20. "But I will stretch out My arm, and I will strike Egypt with the many wonders that I will work in its midst; and then he will let you go.**
**3:21. "And I will put this people in favor in the eyes of the Egyptians, so that when you go, you will not go empty-handed.**

*you will not go empty-handed (reikam).* This does not mean, "without your own money, flocks, and herds," but, "without money in addition to yours"; cf., "Do not send him [the Hebrew servant] empty-handed. But you shall make him a present: you shall give him of your sheep" (Deut. 15:13-14). This is inferable from the context, for first it says, "And I will put this people in favor in the eyes of the Egyptians," and then it says, "A woman will ask of her neighbor," etc. [next v.]. However, the term *reikam* is used for both of these meanings, as in, "I went out full, and the Lord has brought me back *reikam*" (Ruth 1:21), meaning, "empty of my money," and, "Go not *reikam* to your mother-in-law" (Ruth 3:17), meaning "empty of presents."

**3:22. "A woman will ask of her neighbor, and of the lodger of her house, furnishings of silver and of gold, and garments, which you will place upon your sons and on your daughters, thus making spoil (of the things) of the Egyptians."**

---

31. There, Luzzatto notes that this version was cited by Rashi but was not in accordance with Rashi's own interpretation, "Pharaoh will not let you go if I do not show him My strong hand." Luzzatto asserts that Rashi's preferred reading of Onkelos began with the word *ella,* "but only," and that copyists had changed this word to conform with the Hebrew. He further notes the reading *ellahein* in the Antwerp edition and the hybrid reading in the 1411 manuscript discussed below.

***A woman will ask*** *(ve-sha'alah), etc.* There is no doubt that this was to be an act of trickery, for they would not tell them that they would never come back, but rather that they would be going on a three-day journey and would return. Also, the word *sha'alah* ("will ask") is known to mean "on condition of returning": "When one borrows [*yish'al*] from his neighbor [some animal], and [the latter] becomes crippled or dies, if the owner was not with him, he will pay for it" (Exod. 22:13).

Rashbam interpreted *ve-sha'alah* to mean an outright gift, as in, "Ask [*she'al*] of Me, and I will give the nations for your inheritance" (Ps. 2:8), but Mendelssohn aptly wrote (on Exod. 11:2) that there is no need to take the verse out of its plain meaning, and that the Rabbis long ago gave the proper response that the Israelites rightfully took from the Egyptians that which they had lent to them. The truth is that this was a trick ordained by God; cf. "Set you an ambush for the city behind it" (Josh. 8:2); "[The Lord said to Samuel,] 'Take a heifer with you and say, "I have come to sacrifice to the Lord"'" (2 Sam. 16:2). God wished, rightly and justly, that Israel should not leave Egypt empty-handed, and He commanded them to deal crookedly with a wicked nation, for besides the fact that all of their oppressive slave labor for Egypt was paid for with onions and garlic, they were leaving with the Egyptians all the movable property that they could not take with them, and also the fields and dwellings; a similar explanation was given by the Gentile scholar Justi.

S. Cahen, the author of the French translation, wrote on this verse:

> Those who have attacked the Israelites with respect to this matter are wrong. It is understandable that slaves who are reaching out to break their chains will have no scruples about tricking their former oppressors; such an action may be excused. It is in keeping with what we know about the ancient Asiatic peoples, in the customs of those regions. In order to judge impartially the morality of a people, one must know its particular notions concerning the just and the unjust, and not judge antiquity according to our current notions.

But this man who not only makes no connection between this incident and a Divine command, just as he does not at all acknowledge the divinity of the Torah or the other prophecies—does not even connect this incident to a command of Moses, but rather to the impetuosity of the people sunken in slavery. If so, then the Torah of Moses is nothing but a storybook of vanities and falsehoods, for in his opinion, Moses was a wise and righteous man who would not have commanded such a thing; yet here it is written that he commanded it at the word of God. If this is the case, what business would this man have translating and interpreting such a book? Would that he had never reached out his hand to touch it! "The unclean and the fool shall not pass over it; it shall be called the way of holiness."[32]

In any case, there are those who would respond, "It is true that the Israelites were justified in taking the articles lent to them by the Egyptians who had enslaved them, and in whose hands the Israelites left their movable property and lands upon their departure. But how could God command an act of trickery? Would this command not have made a harsh and evil impression on the hearts of the Israelites, who would have learned from this to use deceitful language and deal corruptly? Could God not have enriched His people without commanding them to commit fraud?

I say that Israel—having suffered what they did at the hands of the Egyptians and being well aware of the Egyptians' evil dealings with them—upon receiving this command and fulfilling it by borrowing from the Egyptians as Moses told them, would by no means have gained the impression that it was permissible to engage in acts of fraud and deceit. To the contrary, it was impressed upon their souls that God repays a person for his actions and punishes cruel evildoers for their evil, for indeed the Israelites did not do this of their own accord, and perhaps in their great desire to remove themselves from their oppressors and the land that devoured their children, they never would have taken the effort to do such a thing. Nevertheless, they did it because they were commanded to do so by their leader who spoke to them in the name of God. What was impressed upon them was that God despises evildoers but saves and favors those who are crushed in spirit; in turn, it was impressed upon them that if they themselves, in successful times, were to oppress others, God would avenge them and transfer their wealth to those others. Thus, Moses later warned them several times to remember that they had been slaves and that God had redeemed them.

The proof of all this is that both here and below (Exod. 11:3, 12:36), the Torah makes it clear that it was God's will to put the people in favor in the eyes of the Egyptians so that they would lend articles to them; that is, the Israelites realized that the Egyptians, who hated them, would not have lent them their precious objects if it were not for God's will by way of a miracle. In a similar vein, it is explicitly stated below, "The children of Israel did according to the orders of Moses" (Exod. 12:35), which indicates that it was not on their own initiative that they did so, but in order to do the command of their leader and deliverer. It is also clear that this episode did not damage their

---

32. A paraphrase of Isa. 35:8.

hearts and souls, but to the contrary, it strengthened their hearts with reverence for God and love of justice.

This is the reason that God wanted Israel to put to death the seven nations [of Canaan]—to teach Israel how God punishes evildoers, as Moses said to them, "For those who inhabited this land before you practiced all these abomination… and the country vomited out its inhabitants… Remain obedient to Me, so as not to practice any of the abominable statutes that were practiced before you" (Lev. 18:27, 25, 30). It was for the same reason that the Torah recorded God's statement to Abraham, "In the fourth generation they [i.e., the Israelites] will return here, for the iniquity of the Amorites is not yet full" (Gen. 15:16), to let it be known that those peoples would be extirpated solely because of their wickedness, and that before their measure was full, Israel would not be able to take their land from them. Furthermore, from Moses' statement to Israel, "Do not say in your heart, when the Lord your God drives them away from your presence, 'Because of my probity the Lord has brought me to conquer this country,' while (on the other hand) it is because of the wickedness of these nations" (Deut. 9:4), it is clearly seen that they tended toward the opinion that the fate of each nation was determined by its actions and by God's decree and providence.

If so, it is clear that this episode as well, in which the Egyptians lent them their silver and gold, was viewed by Israel as caused by God to punish one people and reward another, and that it was impossible for them to have learned anything from this that would have corrupted their ways or actions.

**4:1. Moses, responding, said, "And if they will not believe me, and will pay me no heed, but will say, 'The Lord did not appear to you'?"**

*And if (ve-hen).* As in the Aramaic, "Now then, if [*hen*] it seems good to the king… whether it be so [*hen*] that a decree was made of Cyrus the king" (Ezra 5:17). Similarly, in Biblical Hebrew, "And see if [*hen*] there has been such a thing" (Jer. 2:10); "If [*hen*] I shut up heaven that there be no rain, or if [*ve-hen*] I command the locust to devour the land, or if [*ve-im*] I send pestilence among My people" (2 Chron. 7:13). The word *hen* may also appear in place of the [prefix] *he* of interrogation: "Could we slaughter [*hen nizbah*] before the eyes of the Egyptians that which is sacred for them, without their stoning us?" (Exod. 8:22). From the word *hen* was derived the *he* of interrogation and astonishment.

**4:2. And the Lord said to him, "What do you have in your hand?" He said, "A staff."**

***What do you have in your hand.*** As one person would say to another, "Do you acknowledge that this object before you is stone?" When the other says, "Yes," the first person says, "I will turn it into wood" (Rashi).

**4:3. And He said, "Throw it on the ground." He threw it on the ground, and it became a serpent, and Moses fled from its presence.**
**4:4. The Lord said to Moses, "Stretch forth your arm and take hold of its tail." He stretched forth his arm and seized it, and it became a staff in his hand.**
**4:5. [The Lord added], "So they will believe that there appeared to you the Lord, God of their fathers, God of Abraham, God of Isaac, and God of Jacob."**

***So they will believe.*** This is an abbreviated verse, meaning, "And the Lord said, 'Perform this miracle before them, so that they will believe...'" It was abbreviated because it is self-evident that God showed Moses wonders so that he should perform them before the people in order that they believe him (Nachmanides, Mendelssohn).

**4:6. The Lord said to him once more, "Put your hand in your bosom." He put his hand in his bosom, then he took it out, and he found it leprous, of the color of snow.**

***leprous, of the color of snow*** *(metsora'at ka-shaleg,* lit., "leprous like snow"). White as snow; the whitest form of leprosy, called *Leuce,* is exceedingly difficult to heal, as the ancient physician Celsus attested (Clericus and Rosenmueller, preceded by Sforno).

**4:7. Then He said, "Put your hand back in your bosom." He put his hand back in his bosom, then he took it out of his bosom, and he found it returned to the color of his flesh.**
**4:8. [The Lord added], "Now, if they do not believe you, and do not pay attention to the first miracle, they will believe the second.**

***and do not pay attention to*** *(ve-lo yishme'u le-kol,* lit., "and do not listen to the voice of") ***the first miracle.*** *Shemi'ah le-kol* ("listening to the voice") is an idiom for paying attention, as in, "Which hearkens not to the voice of charmers" (Ps. 58:6); "And hearken to the voice of them that contend with me" (Jer. 18:19).

The meaning of this verse is, "If they do not believe you after the first miracle—which would happen only because they would not observe it carefully to investigate it properly, for in their anxiety and hard labor their minds would not be clear enough to examine what they saw, and thus they would fail to recognize the greatness and truth of the wonder—then they will believe you after the second miracle." It was not that the two miracles would prove the prophet's agency better than one, for the first had no fault or flaw and was as trustworthy as a hundred witnesses. Rather, those who might not carefully observe the first on account of their distress would observe the second, and as a result they would believe. The phrase "if they do not believe you…" means that *those who* do not believe the first will believe the second.

**they will believe** (*ve-he'eminu le-kol*, lit., "they will believe the voice of"). The seemingly superfluous [word] *le-kol* was added after "they will believe" in order to make the phrase parallel to the one preceding, *ve-lo yishme'u le-kol*.

**the second** (*ha-aharon*, lit., "the last"). The miracle after, not literally "the last" [see next v.]; a similar use of the term *aharon* is, "Leah and her children behind [*aharonim*] [and Rachel and Joseph last (*aharonim*)]" (Gen. 33:2).

**4:9. "If, then, they do not believe even these two miracles, and they do not listen to you, you will take of the water of the Nile, and you will pour it on the dry ground; and that water which you will have taken from the Nile will become blood on the dry ground."**
**4:10. And Moses said to the Lord, "Please, Lord! I am not a speaker, neither (was I one) in the past, nor (did I become one) after You spoke to Your servant; but I am slow of mouth and slow of tongue."**

***I am not a speaker, etc.*** (*lo ish devarim anokhi*, lit., "I am not a man of words"). Rashbam long ago revolted against the theory that Moses was a stammerer, and said, "This idea is not contained in the words of the Tannaim and Amoraim, and one need not mind the irreligious books." He maintained that Moses was not fluent in the Egyptian language, but this, too, is truly unlikely, since Moses had been raised in Egypt and in the king's house.

Ibn Ezra upheld the view that Moses was a stammerer, and he interpreted the phrase "and I will teach you that which you must speak" [below, v. 12] to mean that God would put in his mouth words that did not contain the letters that were difficult for him. If so, let Ibn Ezra show us which letters are not found in the passages that Moses spoke to the entire people—apart from the fact that it is blasphemous to say that God would choose as His messenger, who would give the Torah to His people, a man who would have to choose the words that he could pronounce.[33]

The truth is that Moses was not a "man of words"—i.e., a powerful orator who could speak at length before any audience and not cringe before anyone—in conformance with what is written of him, "While Moses himself is the meekest man there is on the face of the earth" (Num. 12:3) [and thus did not defend himself against the complaints of Miriam and Aaron]. This is somewhat similar to Jeremiah's statement, "Behold, I cannot speak" (Jer. 1:6), except that Jeremiah was able to add, "For I am a child," but Moses was old. It was even more difficult for him, after having spent so many years as a shepherd, to go before a great king and argue with him.

God answered him, "Who is it who made a mouth for man, or who is it who makes one mute," etc. [next v.]—that is, is it not in My power to remove your slowness of tongue?—"Now then, go; and I will be with you, and I will put words in your mouth until you are a man of words to the proper extent and you do not lack the power of speech." This change, however, was not to come upon Moses suddenly in that instant, but little by little, for it was not to be a physical change but a spiritual one in the powers of mind and strength of heart. For this reason, Moses did not feel any change in himself at that time, and so he said once more, "Charge anyone [else] whom You want to charge" (v. 13). We have further proof of his lack of self-confidence at that time from God's statement to him, "Go, return to Egypt, for all those who sought [to take possession of] your person are dead" (v. 19).

If Moses had been a stammerer, inevitably God would either have cured him or not cured him; if He had cured him, Moses would have felt the change in himself immediately and would not have refused again, while if He had not cured him, the statement, "Who is it who made a mouth for man" would

---

33. Such an expedient was in fact resorted to by Lionel Logue, speech therapist to King George VI. To circumvent the King's stuttering problem, Logue would study the text of a royal address, "spotting any words that might trip the King up, such as those that began with a hard 'k' or 'g' sound or perhaps with repeated consonants, and wherever possible, replace them with something else." (Mark Logue and Peter Conradi, *The King's Speech: How One Man Saved the British Monarchy*, [New York: Sterling, 2010], p. 7.) However, Shadal is no doubt correct in suggesting that a search of all of Moses' recorded public statements would fail to reveal the consistent omission of any particular phonemes.

have been sheer mockery, Heaven forbid. Some interpret the statement to mean, "I know that You are a stammerer, for I purposely made you a stammerer, but nevertheless I am commanding you to go." But who could not see that this is not an answer that would have persuaded Moses to go, for Moses would have said to himself, "If He wants me to go on His mission, let Him first cure my defect."

In addition, the subsequent statement, "There is indeed Aaron your brother, the Levite" (Exod. 4:14), clearly appears to mean, "I know that he would not refuse like you, but would take it upon himself to speak." If the meaning had been, "Is not Aaron a stammerer like you, and yet he will speak," the statement would have concluded with the words *hu yedabber* ("he will speak") without the word *yada'ti* ("I know").

**4:11. And the Lord said to him, "Who is it who made a mouth for man, or who is it who makes one mute, or deaf, or seeing, or blind? Is it not I, the Lord?**

*Who is it who made a mouth for man.* "Who is it who gave man his powers and his wholeness, and who makes a man disabled from the start of his formation and lacking one of his powers? Who is it that gave man a mouth, and who makes some of them mute from birth, or deaf from birth or *in utero* so as to remain mute, as a result of not hearing others speak? Similarly, who made one seeing or blind, that is, who gave man the power of sight, and who made this power diminished? Is it not I, the Lord?"

The mute and the deaf are both mentioned here in connection with the question, "Who is it who made a mouth for man," for they both lack the power of speech. Afterwards the sighted and the blind are mentioned, that is, the power of sight and the lack of that power. Let the lying lips be dumb which say that the phrase ought to read "or lame [*pisse'ah*] [instead of *pikke'ah*, "seeing"] or blind," for the intent of the verse is not merely to attribute disabilities to God, but rather to say that it is God Who grants powers and wholeness, and from Whom also proceed disabilities and lack of powers, for at the beginning of the statement He says, "Who is it who made a mouth for man?"

**4:12. "Now then, go; and I will be with you, and I will teach you that which you must speak."**
**4:13. And he said, "Please, Lord, charge anyone (else) whom You want to charge."**

*charge anyone (else) whom You want to charge (shelaḥ na be-yad tishlaḥ).* "Anyone You want except for me" (Rashbam, Mendelssohn). It is the way of the Hebrew language to repeat the verb where the meaning is "whoever" or "whatever" [or the like], as in:

- *ve-shama ishah be-yom shom'o,* "And her husband comes to know of it whenever it may be" (Num. 30:8);
- *u-ve-yom pokdi u-fakadti,* "Then, whenever it may be, I will make them pay" (Exod. 30:34);
- *ve-shama ha-shome'a,* "And whoever hears it" (2 Sam. 17:9).

**4:14. And the Lord became kindled with wrath against Moses, and He said, "There is indeed Aaron your brother, the Levite; I know that he will not refuse to speak. Indeed, he is about to come to meet you, and upon seeing you he will rejoice of heart.**

*the Levite.* Apparently the Levites were more learned than the other tribes and were eloquent speakers, and therefore they were better qualified for the priesthood than the rest of the nation. God was thus saying to Moses, "Aaron, although he is your brother, is a [true] Levite by character, for it is as if you are not a Levite, since you refuse so vehemently to go on My mission."

*Indeed, he is about to come, etc.* "For I will speak to him," as it is written below (v. 27). According to the plain meaning of the verse, God's anger, as mentioned here, does not seem to have left any trace,[34] but the Torah [in describing God as angry] was speaking in human terms, for God was speaking like a man who says to his fellow, "I will not plead with you any further. If you do not want to fulfill my mission, which would have brought you honor, I will bestow the honor on another man who I know will not refuse."

**4:15. "You will speak to him, and you will put the words in his mouth; and I will be with you and him when you speak, and I will teach you that which you must do.**
**4:16. "He will speak for you to the people. He will serve you as an interpreter, and you will be to him as a divinity.**

---

34. As Rashi explains, R. Joshua ben Korhah expressed the view, in *Zevaḥim* 102a, that God's "anger" usually leaves a "trace," i.e., some punishment usually ensues, but no such consequence is mentioned here; however, R. Yosi maintained that there was a consequence, in that Aaron "the Levite" was given the priesthood that had formerly been destined for Moses and his descendants.

## Shemot

***He will speak for you (lekha) to the people.*** At the end of Rashi's comment [explaining that *lekha*, lit., "to you," here means "on your account"], it is written [in many editions] *leshon aleihem*, but this should read *leshon al hem* ("they are the equivalent of *al*"), that is, words such as *li*, *lo*, and *lahem* ("to me," "to him," "to them"), when appearing next to the verb "to speak," indicate *al* ("about") or *bishvil* ("for," "on account of").[35]

**4:17.** "Take with you, then, this staff, with which you will do the miracles."
**4:18.** Moses went, and he returned to Jether his father-in-law, and he said to him, "Let me go and return to my brothers [relatives], who are in Egypt, and see if they are still alive." And Jethro said to Moses, "Go in peace."
**4:19.** The Lord said to Moses in Midian, "Go, return to Egypt, for all those who sought (to take possession of) your person are dead."

***Go, return, etc.*** "And do not hold back for fear of the king and his ministers who were seeking your life on account of the killing of the Egyptian, for they are already dead." He added this to encourage him, for He knew that he was afraid.

**4:20.** Moses took his wife and his sons, he had them mount upon an ass, and he returned toward the country of Egypt; and Moses took with him the divine staff.

***the divine staff.*** So called because with it he would perform the miracles that were within the divine power.

**4:21.** The Lord said to Moses, "As you go to return to Egypt, take care that all the miracles, with which I charge you, you execute before Pharaoh; but I will render his heart strong [obstinate], and he will not let the people go.

***take care*** *(re'eh*, lit., "see") ***that all the miracles.*** "See that all the miracles, with which I charge you, you perform before Pharaoh, but that he will not listen to you, for I will make his heart strong...." He let him know this so that he should not be discouraged upon seeing that Pharaoh would not listen to him. In the same vein is [the warning by God to Isaiah] in Isaiah 6; see my comment there.[36]

---

35. Modern editions generally have the correct reading *leshon al hem*.
36. On Isa. 6:10, where God tells the prophet, "Make the heart of this people fat,

**4:22.** "And [finally] you shall say to Pharaoh, 'Thus says the Lord: "Israel is My firstborn son.**

***Israel is My firstborn son.*** "Even though I will, in the end of days, 'turn to the peoples a pure language, that they may all call upon the name of the Lord, to serve Him with one consent' (Zeph. 3:9), nevertheless Israel is more honorable to Me than any of them, since they were the first to serve Me, when all the other peoples strayed away from Me" (Sforno). See also Rashi on Jer. 3:18.[37]

**4:23. ""'I say to you, let My son come to serve Me—and you refuse to let him come. Behold, I will kill your firstborn son.'"**

***Behold, I will kill your firstborn son.*** One might ask, this was to be the last of the plagues, and Moses did not mention it to Pharaoh until the end, so why should it be mentioned now? The way I see it is this: since Moses said to Jethro, "Let me... see if they are still alive" (Exod. 4:18), this proves that Moses did not tell him anything about God's mission, but said only that he longed to see his relatives. If so, when he took with him his wife and sons, who knew nothing about the mission, there is no doubt that his wife and older son—upon seeing that he was to go before the king of Egypt to tell him to set Israel free—would seek to deter him from performing his mission, out of fear that Pharaoh would kill him. God knew this and disapproved of his taking his wife and sons with him, especially since Moses had already been unduly swayed by his wife in that he delayed the circumcision of his [younger] son after the passage of eight days, for if [his departure] had been within eight days of his son's birth, his wife would not likely have accompanied him on the journey. Thus, it seems that he heeded her advice to perform the circumcision at the age of thirteen, in conformance with the practice of the Ishmaelites and Midianites (as noted by Deyling and before him Gussetius).

It was for this reason that God made this statement to him, so that he should understand that if he were to fail to fulfill his mission so as to impede Israel's exodus from Egypt, he himself would be subject to such a punishment—God would kill Moses' firstborn. Thus it occurred that when they were at a lodging place, and it displeased God that Moses was journeying with his wife and sons, "the Lord assailed him, and He threatened to make

---

and make their ears heavy," Shadal comments that this "command" was intended to let Isaiah know that the people would not heed his words.

37. Apparently this should be Jer. 3:19, where Rashi interprets the phrase, "How would I put you [Judah] among the sons" as referring to God's "other" sons, i.e., the idolatrous nations.

him die" (next v.). I say this means, "to make his firstborn son die," the term "firstborn son" having been mentioned twice [immediately] above [in v. 22 and the present verse]. Then Moses told Zipporah that this had happened to them because they had delayed the circumcision of their younger son, whereupon Zipporah hastened without hesitation to circumcise her son—not the sick son alluded to by the words *hamito* ("to make him die") and *va-yifgeshehu* ("assailed him"), for he was the older son who was already circumcised, but the younger son, who was not yet thirteen but had remained uncircumcised. She made the blood reach Moses' feet, and she said, referring to Moses, "A bloodstained bridegroom you are to me—it is your fault and not mine that our older son is sick, and you are the cause of his death." Perhaps she thought that the exertion of the journey was the cause of his sickness. Then, when she saw that her son was immediately cured, she said, "A bloodstained bridegroom for the circumcision."

Since they were still close to Midian, Zipporah returned with her sons to her father's house and Moses went on alone; this was God's will, so that Moses should have no impediment in performing his mission. This is what is meant by the phrase "after he had sent her back" (Exod. 18:2), for at this time he sent her back to her father's house.

**4:24. Now, during the journey, in the lodging place, the Lord assailed him [He struck one of Moses' sons with a grave illness], and He threatened to make him die.**

***in the lodging place*** *(ba-malon).* A place where they hid away for the night, not a *malon* ("inn") such as we have nowadays, but perhaps a cleft of a rock or the like.

***assailed him*** *(va-yifgeshehu).* In my opinion, the pronominal suffix *–hu* ("him") refers back to Moses' firstborn son, Gershom, for God had said, "Israel is My firstborn son" [above, v. 22] and "Behold, I will kill your firstborn son" [above, v. 23]. Here, too, "the Lord assailed him" means Moses' firstborn, as I explained in the previous verse.

Other commentators say that this refers to Moses. Rabbenu Hananel (cited by Rabbenu Bahya) made it refer to the younger son, for in his opinion, Moses was not at the lodging place, having sent his family ahead on the donkey, but this is unlikely. My student Rabbi Moses Cohen Porto, like Rabbenu Hananel, interprets "assailed him" as referring to the younger son; in his opinion, the illness affected the son's genital organs, and this led

Zipporah to think that it was a consequence of their failure to circumcise him, so she then hastened to do so.

Rashbam and Parhon, even though maintaining that it was Moses [who was "assailed"], nevertheless explained the reason for the illness as Moses' tarrying on his journey and bringing along his wife and sons.

**4:25. Zipporah took a flint and cut the foreskin of her son, and she made (the blood) reach his [Moses'] feet, and she said, "A bloodstained bridegroom you are to me [some sin of yours is the cause of the son's death]."**

*a flint (tsor).* A sharp stone; so to this day it is the custom of some Ethiopians to circumcise with such a stone (Ludolf, *Historia Aethiopica* 5.1.21). Similarly, it seems that this was also the custom in Israel in the time of Joshua, who took *ḥarvot tsurim* ("knives of flint") [for this purpose] (Josh. 5:2). Accordingly, Onkelos renders [*tsor*] as *tinnara* ("rock," "flint").

In the same vein, Herodotus wrote that the Egyptians, when dissecting their dead to remove the internal organs and mummify them, would cut them with an "Ethiopian stone." So also Pliny (*Natural History* 55.12) wrote that the priests of Cybele [a nature goddess of Asia Minor] used to castrate themselves with a stone (Clericus, Rosenmueller).

*and cut the foreskin of her son.* It does not say "his foreskin," for the sick son was Gershom, while the one that she circumcised was Eliezer [the younger son], as I explained above.

*and she made [the blood] reach his [Moses'] feet (va-tagga le-raglav).* Cf., "then you shall sprinkle [*ve-higga'tem*] the lintel... from the blood collected in the basin" (Exod. 12:22); i.e., she sprinkled the blood of the circumcision at Moses' feet.

**4:26. (The Lord) having then left him [that is, the son having been cured], she said, "Bloodstained bridegroom for the circumcision [that is, the threatened death was for the delay of the circumcision]."**

*having then left him (va-yiref mimmennu).* Then God let the boy alone (*rafah min ha-na'ar*), that is, His hand was "weakened" (*rafetah yado*) from upon the boy, and he was cured. Then she said, "You are not absolutely a bloodstained bridegroom to me, but only *la-mulot*," i.e., with respect to the circumcision only. According to both Gussetius and Deyling, she said *la-mulot*, in the plural, to refer to two circumcision [customs], the Hebrew circumcision of eight days and the Ishmaelite circumcision of thirteen years; the reason that Moses appeared to her as a "bloodstained" man was that he wanted to circumcise his sons at eight days, when they were [allegedly] too tender. It is also possible that she [actually] said *la-mulat* [an archaic singular, which reading is obtained with a change of vowels but not of written consonants], on the model of *ezrat* [instead of *ezrah*] *mi-tsar* ("help against the adversary") (Ps. 60:13, 108:13).

**4:27. The Lord then said to Aaron, "Go toward Moses in the desert." And having gone, he met him in the mountain of God, and he kissed him.**
**4:28. And Moses explained to Aaron all the speeches with which the Lord had charged him, and all the miracles that He had commanded him [to do].**

***all the speeches** (divrei)* ***with which the Lord had charged him.*** All the addresses that God had sent him to deliver to the people and to Pharaoh, as is later specified: "Aaron explained all the things [*ha-devarim*] that the Lord had said to Moses, and he did the miracles in the presence of the people" (below, v. 30).

**4:29. Moses and Aaron went and assembled all the elders of the children of Israel.**
**4:30. Aaron explained all the things that the Lord had said to Moses, and he did the miracles in the presence of the people.**
**4:31. The people believed, and hearing that the Lord had thought of the children of Israel, and that He had seen [taken into account] their misery, they bowed and prostrated themselves.**

**5:1. Then Moses and Aaron went, and they said to Pharaoh, "Thus says the Lord, God of Israel: 'Let My people go to celebrate a festival to Me in the desert.'"**
**5:2. Pharaoh said, "Who is the Lord, that I should obey Him to let Israel go? I do not know the Lord, nor do I wish to let Israel go."**

***I do not know the Lord.*** Even if he had heard His name, he said, "I do not know Him," that is, "I ascribe no divinity to Him; I have not tested the extent of His power." Cf., "other gods, unknown to you [that is, that have not given you proof of their divinity]" (Deut. 11:28).

**5:3. And they said, "The God of the Hebrews has manifested Himself to us. Permit us, please, to go into the desert a distance of three days' journey, and let us make sacrifices to the Lord our God, so that He does not assail us with pestilence, or with the sword."**

***The God of the Hebrews has manifested Himself (nikra) to us.*** The meaning of *nikra* here, even though it is spelled with a [final] *alef*, is as it is above (Exod. 3:18), where it is spelled *nikrah*, with a *he*, that is, "revealed to us." That which I wrote in *Bikkurei ha-Ittim*, 5589 (1828), p. 88, was a mistake on my part, for the expression, "His name was called [*nikra*] upon us" would never appear without the word *shem* ("name"), as I wrote above (on 3:18) *contra* Rosenmueller.

It seems to me, however, that when they heard Pharaoh say, "I do not know the Lord," they explained that this God Who had manifested Himself to them was the God of the Hebrews, which [appellation] was better known, besides the fact that God had commanded them to say, "The Lord, God of the Hebrews" (Exod. 3:18), not the "God of Israel" (as the Korem also points out). Because they understood his statement, "I do not know the Lord," to mean that Pharaoh did not know the extent of His power, they added, "so that He does not assail us with pestilence," etc., that is to say, "We know that He is capable of punishing with pestilence or the sword."

Joseph Jarè adds that they mentioned "pestilence" and "the sword" in order to induce Pharaoh to fear that the pestilence would afflict Egypt as well, and similarly, that the "sword," which signifies war, would not be upon Israel alone but upon all the people of the land.

**5:4. The king of Egypt said to them, "Why, Moses and Aaron, do you want to distract this people from its labors? Go to (carry out) your tasks."**

***to distract (tafri'u).*** The alternative explanation cited by Kimhi in *Shorashim* appears correct, i.e., that the Hebrew signifies distancing or diversion away; this is the derivation of the term *le-mafre'a* ("backwards, "out of order," "irregularly").

***to distract this people from its labors.*** It seems to me that on this occasion, Moses was accompanied by the elders of Israel, as had been commanded previously (Exod. 3:18). Pharaoh understood that Moses and Aaron had already told the people all that God had said, and so Pharaoh said, "Why do you distract this people from its labors—for when you tell them that their

God wants them to go to celebrate in His honor, they will begin to prepare themselves for the festival, and all of their attention will be upon this, not upon performing the king's labor." Then he said to the elders of the people, "Go to your tasks," i.e., you and the rest of the people.

**5:5. Pharaoh added, "This people, moreover, is numerous, and you would like to make them cease from the labors laid upon them."**

*This people, moreover, is numerous, etc.* "And it would cause a great loss if they ceased from their labors, since they are so numerous" (Rashi, Ibn Ezra). According to Igel, Pharaoh meant to say, "They are numerous and they could rebel, so why do you make them cease from their labors, so that their minds will be free to rebel against me?"

**5:6. Pharaoh commanded on that day the [Egyptian] taskmasters appointed over the people, and the [Israelite] superintendants, saying—**

*the taskmasters (ha-nogesim).* Egyptian appointees who forced them to work; the "superintendants" (*shoterim*) were Israelites (Rashi).

**5:7. "Do not continue to give the people straw for making the bricks, as previously; let them go themselves and cut the straw for themselves.**

*straw (teven).* The long [stalks] that are harvested with the sheaves (Italian, *paglia*), while the term *kash* (Italian, *stoppia*, "stubble") refers to the short pieces that are placed in the field as fodder for the animals (as per the Ri [R. Isaac ben Samuel] in Tosafot on *Shabbat* 36b).

At first, Pharaoh used to give the Israelites straw of his own for brickmaking, but now he forced them to wander in the fields to collect stubble, and thus Israel was in great distress; perhaps it was even Pharaoh's intention that the Egyptians should quarrel with them and kill them.

The word *koshesh* (to "cut" or "gather" straw) is similar to *katsats* ("to cut," "to chop") (cf., *mekoshesh etsim*, one who "gathered wood," Num. 15:33). *Kash*, stubble, is what is left over after the chopping and harvesting.

*and cut the straw for themselves.* That which would take the place of straw for them, as is specified below, "to cut stubble [to make use of it] for straw" (v. 12).

## Shadal on Exodus

**5:8. "Impose, then, upon them the same quantity of bricks that they made previously, without any diminution; for they are idle, therefore they shout, saying, 'Let us go to make sacrifices to our God.'"**

***quantity*** *(matkonet).* The root *takhan* (תכן) indicates knowledge of something in precision, whether in measure, weight, number, or any other manner. The expression "*matkonet* of bricks"—cf., "the [customary] number [*tokhen*] of bricks" (v. 18)—refers to number; "and you shall not make of it [the sacred oil] anything similar with those same measurements [*u-ve-matkunto*]" (Exod. 30:32) refers to number and weight; "the money which had been counted [*ha-metukkan*]" (2 Kings 12:12) refers to number; "and metes out [*tikken*] the waters by measure" (Job 28:25) refers to measure; while precise knowledge is referred to in:

- "But the Lord weighs [*ve-tokhen*] the hearts" (Prov. 21:2);
- "But the Lord weighs [*ve-tokhen*] the spirits" (Prov. 16:2);
- "And by Him actions are weighed [*nitkenu*]" (1 Sam. 2:3).

Similarly, the phrase, "The way of the Lord is not equal [*lo yittakhen*]" (Ezek. 18:25) means that it is impossible to know it, that is, the mind cannot fathom it.

On the other hand, the root *takan* (תקן), with a *kof*, found only once [in the Bible] in Eccl. 12:9 ("and set in order [*tikken*] many proverbs"), has a different meaning (pertaining to setting up or establishing) and is an Aramaic term that entered Ecclesiastes and the language of the Sages. This is the source of the phrase *tikkanta Shabbat,* which is spelled with a *kof* [rather than the usual *kaf*] in many manuscript *siddurim*, and this is the correct reading.[38] See my comment on Isa. 40:12.[39]

**5:9. "Let the labor be increased upon these people, so that they be occupied with it, and let them not be diverted by lies."**

***and let them not be diverted by lies*** *(ve-al yish'u be-divrei sheker).* Rashi, properly making a fine distinction, said that if the word *yish'u* were related to the expression *va-yisha YHVH el Hevel* ("and the Lord showed approval to

---

[38]. This phrase, which appears in the Musaf *Amidah,* has generally been translated as, "You have instituted (or "established") the Sabbath."

[39]. There, on the phrase *ve-shamayim ba-zeret tikken* ("and meted out heaven with the span"), Luzzatto cross-references to the present verse and makes many of the same observations that are made here.

Abel") (Gen. 4:4), the phrase here should have read *el divrei sheker* or *al divrei sheker* [instead of *be-divrei sheker*]. He interpreted *yish'u* in terms of "speech," and he gave a similar interpretation to the phrase v*e-esh'ah ve-ḥukkekha tamid* (i.e., "and I will speak of Your statutes continually," Ps. 119:117). It seems to me, however, that the word *yish'u* does not depart from its [usual] meaning of "turning," only that when this verb is followed [as here] by the preposition *be-*, it means turning by way of distraction (as in the Italian, *divertirsi* ["to divert oneself"], which is similarly derived from *vertere*, meaning "to turn"). Thus *ve-esh'ah ve-ḥukkekha* [is to be understood as "and I will be diverted by Your statutes"]. From the root *sha'ah* was derived *sha'ashua* ("amusement," "entertainment").

**5:10. The taskmasters of the people and their superintendants went out and said to the people, "Thus says Pharaoh: I do not give you straw.**
**5:11. "You go and take straw where you find it, for your labor is not decreased at all."**
**5:12. The people scattered throughout all the country of Egypt to cut stubble (to make use of it) for straw.**

*scattered (va-yafets).* The Heb. is an intransitive verb in the *kal* form, and is a *naḥ ayin yod* verb [i.e., the root is *pits* (פי"ץ), and the middle letter *yod* disappears in some conjugations, as here; the normal form would have been *yafits*] on the model of *az yashir* (Exod. 15:1). Similar forms are, "And the people were scattered [*va-yafets*] from him" (2 Sam. 13:8), and "The east wind scattered [*yafets*] upon the earth" (Job 38:24). However, in the phrase, "The Lord dispersed [*va-yafets*] them thence" (Gen. 11:8), the verb is in the *hif'il* (causative) conjugation, although it would be possible to read it *va-yafots*, thus making it into a *kal* form of a *naḥ ayin vav* verb [i.e., the root would be *puts* (פו"ץ), with the middle letter *vav* disappearing], as in, "And let Your enemies be dispersed [*ve-yafutsu*]" (Num. 10:35).[40]

*to cut stubble (to make use of it) for straw.* To pluck the stubble left over in the field to make use of it instead of [proper] straw; see above, v. 7.

**5:13. The taskmasters then insisted, saying, "Finish your labors, the daily task, as when there was straw."**

*insisted (atsim).* The Heb. is from the root *its* (אי"ץ).

---

40. Hebrew verbs that have a middle vowel letter that often does not occur are known as "weak" or "hollow" verbs.

***as when there was straw.*** Formerly it seemed to me that this phrase referred back to the beginning of the verse, i.e., the taskmasters would insist as when there was straw (although this interpretation is against the accents [because the phrase is not set off with a major disjunctive]). It seemed unlikely to me that the taskmasters themselves would say, "Finish your labors now that you have no straw, just as you did when you had straw," for this seemed to be an illogical statement. It is to be noted that in the subsequent verse it says, "How is it that you have not completed, either yesterday or today, the established quantity of bricks to make, as you did previously?"—without adding, "as when there was straw." I maintained that the only job of the taskmasters was to spur the workers on, to collect from the superintendants the daily amount of bricks, and to beat them if they came up short, but that they had nothing to do with the straw, whether or not it was to be given to the workers. Thus they would pretend not to know that it was not given to them, and they would say, "Finish your labors, your daily task. How is it that you have not completed, either yesterday or today, the established quantity of bricks to make?" In other words, "What innovation is this that you do not complete your established quantity?" This is the meaning of [the initial word of the question in v. 14] *maddua*—"How did this innovation come to be?" (Exod. 1:18); thus it seemed explicitly stated that they pretended not to know the reason.

But now (Adar 5614 [1854]), I see that all of the above is unlikely, for previously (vv. 6, 10) it is specified that it was the taskmasters themselves who received the command from Pharaoh and transmitted it to the people, saying, "Thus says Pharaoh: I do not give you straw." If so, how could they have pretended not to know that they had no straw? Besides (as my student R. David Hazak alerted me), the beaten superintendants should have answered the taskmasters' question, "How is it that you have not completed the established quantity?" by saying that the reason was that they had no straw, but the superintendants did not so respond, for the taskmasters had anticipated them by saying, "Finish your labors, your daily task, *as when there was straw.*" When the superintendants saw that the taskmasters were compelled by Pharaoh's command to shut their ears against their complaint, they went and complained to Pharaoh himself.

The word *maddua*, too, can be successfully reconciled. The meaning of the question [in v. 14] is, "How is it that you dared to violate the king's command"—cf., above, 1:18—"For you are idlers and slackers, and the lack of straw is not a sufficient excuse, since you have plenty of free time to gather stubble and make the bricks, but you are lazy and waste your time with idle matters."

**5:14. The superintendants of the children of Israel, appointed over them by Pharaoh's taskmasters, were beaten, saying, "How is it that you have not completed, either yesterday or today, the established quantity of bricks to make, as you did previously?**

***How is it that you have not completed,*** *etc.* "How is it that you have not completed, either yesterday or today [*gam temol gam ha-yom*] (as you did previously [*ki-temol shilshom*]) the established quantity of bricks to make?" (Rashi). It is surprising that Onkelos [seemingly] divided *ki-temol shilshom* in two [translating it as *ke-me-itmallei u-mi-de-komohi*, lit., "as yesterday and the day before"], though they refer to only one day (Dubno).

One of my students said that *itmallei*, with an initial *alef*, means, "the day before yesterday," while *temallei*, without an *alef*, means, "yesterday," and therefore Onkelos was precise in translating [the first word of the phrase *ki-temol shilshom*] as *ke-me-itmallei* and [the second two words in the phrase *gam temol gam ha-yom*] as *af temallei*. I then reviewed every instance of *temol* and *etmol* in the Bible, and I found that all of them were translated [in the Targum] as *itmallei,* except for [*yom temol*] here and in three other instances that are translated *temallei*:

- *gam temol gam ha-yom* (1 Sam. 20:27), where the meaning is precisely "yesterday";
- *gam temol gam shilshom* (2 Sam. 3:17) ("in times past"); and
- *temol bo'ekha* (2 Sam. 15:20) ("you came but yesterday"), even though the last two instances do not mean precisely "yesterday."

The correct explanation is given by Igel: *me-itmallei u-mi-de-komohi* is an Aramaic idiom referring to time past, not precisely to "yesterday," and the matter does not depend on the presence or lack of an initial *alef*, for *temallei* and *itmallei* are the same, just like the Hebrew *temol* and *etmol*; however, the Hebrew *temol shilshom*, like the Aramaic *me-itmallei u-me-de-komohi,* is an idiom referring to a long period of time in the past.

**5:15. The superintendants of the children of Israel went and complained to Pharaoh, saying, "Why do you treat your servants so?**
**5:16. "Straw is not distributed to your servants, and still we are told, 'Make bricks.' Then your servants are beaten, and your people is rendered culpable."**

*and your people is rendered culpable (ve-ḥatat ammekha).* The word *ve-ḥatat,* as it is vocalized, is the equivalent of *ve-ḥat'ah* [the feminine third person singular of the verb *ḥatah,* "to transgress"] – cf., *ve-karat etkhem ha-ra'ah* ("and evils will happen to you," Deut. 31:29) [where *ve-karat* takes the place of *ve-kar'ah*]—and its meaning is as per the Targum, "and your people are sinners against us in that they are beating us, and against our brethren in that they are demanding of them something that they are powerless to do." The word *am* ("people") [normally a masculine noun] would be feminine here, as in, "Why is this people [*ha-am ha-zeh*] slidden back [*shovevah* (f.)]" (Jer. 8:5). This statement should properly have read, "And you [Pharaoh] are culpable," but out of respect, the superintendants employed a euphemism and said, "Your people are culpable" (Ibn Ezra).

Mendelssohn interpreted this phrase to mean, "They are treating us—we who are your people—as is customarily done with transgressors, beating us although we are innocent," but this (as per Korem) is far-fetched. [Alternatively] it would be possible to read the phrase as *ve-ḥattat immakh* ("and the transgression is with you").

**5:17. And he said, "Idle you are, idle; it is for this reason that you say, 'Let us go to make sacrifices to the Lord.'**
**5:18. "Now then, go, labor, without your being given the straw; and the (usual) number of bricks you must supply."**
**5:19. The superintendants of the children of Israel saw themselves in a bad way, hearing it said, "You shall not decrease (anything) of your bricks, (that is) of the daily task."**

*saw themselves (otam,* lit., "them"). The superintendants saw the children of Israel (Rashi); however, according to Ibn Ezra, Nachmanides, and Rosenmueller, the superintendants saw themselves.

*hearing it said (lemor,* lit., "saying"). When Pharaoh said this to them.

*You shall not decrease (anything) of your bricks, etc.* From the bricks that are imposed upon you, that is, from that which is the daily task.

**5:20. Having then, on their coming forth from Pharaoh, encountered Moses and Aaron, for whom they were watching—**

*for whom they were watching (nitsavim likratam,* lit., "standing to meet them"). Waiting to hear the king's answer.

**5:21.** They said to them, "Let the Lord see, and let Him lay blame on you and judge, for you rendered us odious to Pharaoh and his servants, (as if) putting the sword in their hand, so that they might kill us."

*you rendered us odious (hiv'ashtem et reiḥenu,* lit., "you caused our odor to stink") *to Pharaoh.* You made us appear to him as if our odor were stinking; you rendered us odious and hateful in his eyes.

**5:22.** Moses returned to the Lord, and he said, "Lord! Why have You done [more and more] evil to this people? Why have You sent me?

***Moses returned to the Lord.*** To the place where he had been speaking with Him (Rashbam, Mendelssohn). Perhaps this was outside the city, in accordance with [Moses' subsequent statement], "When I will have left the city, I will stretch out my palms toward the Lord" (Exod. 9:29).

**5:23.** "While ever since I came to Pharaoh to speak in Your name, he has done [more and more] evil to this people, nor have You brought any salvation to Your people."

**6:1.** The Lord said to Moses, "Now you will see what I will do to Pharaoh; for (compelled) by force he will let them go, or rather by main force he will drive them out of his country.

***for (compelled) by force*** *(ki ve-yad ḥazakah,* lit., "for with a strong hand") ***he will let them go.*** Because of strong hands that will overpower him, he will let them go.

***or rather by main force*** *(u-ve-yad ḥazakah,* lit., "and with a strong hand") ***he will drive them out.*** Against Israel's will, he will drive them out, and they will not have enough time to make provisions for themselves; similarly, it says, "And the Egyptians pressed the people strongly, so that they should go quickly away from the country" (Exod. 12:33) (Rashi). This is one of the poetic usages in Hebrew, to employ one word or expression in two different senses. For example:

- "If you will return [*tashuv,* i.e., repent], O Israel, says the Lord, then you will be established [*tashuv*] to Me" (Jer. 4:1).[41]

---

41. This translation is in accordance with Luzzatto's comment on Jer. 4:1, in

- "Among the smooth stones of [*be-ḥallekei*] the valley is your portion [*ḥelkekh*]" (Isa. 57:6).
- "Gad, attacked [*yegudennu*] by enemy hordes, will cut [*yagud*] their heel" (Gen. 49:19).
- "Does one turn away [*yashuv*, i.e., turn from God] and not return [*yashuv*]?" (Jer. 8:4).
- "He will trample [*yeshufekha*] on your head, and you will wrap [*teshufennu*] around his heel" (Gen. 3:15).

Otherwise, it is possible to translate the verse according to its plain meaning: "By My strong hand he will let them go, and by My strong hand he will not only let them go, but will drive them out of his country."

---

which he expresses the view that the second *tashuv* is actually a form of the root *yashav*, "to sit," "to stay," "to be established," and the proper form would have been *teshev*, but that for the sake of a play on words, the form *tashuv* was employed.

# *Va'era*

*Hardening Pharaoh's heart • The sorcerers' arcane arts • Miracles: natural and supernatural aspects • From blood to hail • "It is the finger of God" • "I and my people are at fault"*

**6:2. Then God spoke to Moses, and He said to him, "I am the Lord."**

*I am the Lord (YHVH).* The Worker of Good and Evil, and I want Israel to know that evil as well as good comes from My hand.

**6:3. "I showed Myself to Abraham, Isaac, and Jacob as God Omnipotent; but as that which My name 'the Lord' signifies, I did not make Myself known to them.**

*I showed Myself... as God Omnipotent (be-El Shaddai); but... My name 'the Lord' (u-shemi YHVH), etc.* "To the patriarchs I showed My power to save them and to do them good, but I was not known to them in the aspect of 'Worker of Good and Evil,' which My name YHVH signifies,[1] for I did not do evil to them. Now, however, that you have said, 'Why have you done evil to this people,' know that this is My way, and indeed it is My will that Israel

---

1. See Luzzatto's comment on Exod. 15:3, below, and on Gen. 2:4, where he interprets the name YHVH as a compound of a cry of joy (*yah*) and a cry of woe (*wah*), i.e., Worker of Good and Evil.

should recognize that I am the Worker of Good and Evil, so that they will fear Me always."

Many commentators [among them Rashi] have interpreted the name YHVH as "Keeper of My promises."

It cannot be said that the patriarchs did not know the name YHVH, since we find, "Abraham called that place YHVH Yir'eh" (Gen. 22:14), and similarly, "And He said, I am YHVH, Who brought you out of Ur Casdim" (Gen. 15:7). Rashi aptly said, "*Lo hoda'ti* ("I did not make [My name] known to them") is not written here, but rather *lo noda'ti* ("I was not known to them")."

The words *u-shemi YHVH*, according to Ibn Ezra (preceded by Judah ha-Levi, *Ma'amar* 2 [of the *Kuzari* 2:2]), are the equivalent of *u-ve-shemi* ("but by My name"), for the prefix *bet* in *be-El Shaddai* carries another one with it. From Ibn Ezra's statement that according to Saadiah Gaon, the word *levaddo* ("only") is missing from this phrase, as if He said, "But by My name YHVH alone I was not known to them; rather, at times [I was known as] El Shaddai and other times as YHVH," it seems that Saadiah Gaon, too, understood *u-shemi* as *u-ve-shemi*.

According to Igel, *u-shemi* signifies "but I in all My aspects."

**6:4.** "And I also made to them a solemn promise to give them the land of Canaan, the country of their wandering, where they lived as strangers.
**6:5.** "And I Myself have also given heed to the groans of the children of Israel, whom the Egyptians hold in slavery, and I recalled to memory My promise.
**6:6.** "Therefore, say to the children of Israel, 'I am the Lord; and I will draw you out from under the burdens of the Egyptians, and I will save you from their slavery, and I will liberate you with outstretched arm [with force], and with great punishments.
**6:7.** "'And I will take you for My people, and I will be your (guardian) God; and you will know that I, the Lord your God, am the One Who draws you out from under the burdens of Egypt.
**6:8.** "'And I will bring you to the country that I swore to give to Abraham, Isaac, and Jacob; and I will give it to you as an inheritance [in perpetual ownership]. I am the Lord [Who promises this].'"
**6:9.** Moses spoke thus to the children of Israel; but they did not pay heed to Moses, because of the anxiety they were in, and because of the hard slavery.

***because of the anxiety*** *(mi-kotser ruaḥ,* lit., "because of shortness of breath," Italian, *l'ambascia).* "Anyone who is in anguish is short of breath and cannot draw long breaths" (Rashi). Similarly in Italian, the words *ambascia* and *affanno* denote "shortness of breath" and are transferred to indicate sorrow and affliction.

**6:10. The Lord spoke to Moses, saying:**
**6:11. "Go, speak to Pharaoh, king of Egypt, so that he may let the children of Israel go from his country."**
**6:12. And Moses spoke before the Lord, saying, "Behold, the children of Israel did not listen to me, and how will Pharaoh listen to me? Whereas I have impeded [not fluent] lips."**

***impeded lips*** *(aral sefatayim,* lit., "uncircumcised lips"). Sealed (Rashi). The term *orlah* (lit., "foreskin") is used for anything that covers over another thing and prevents it from performing its function. Here, the expression is a figurative one like "slow of mouth and slow of tongue" (Exod. 4:10), for Moses fit neither of these descriptions [literally]; rather, he was not a "man of words," and he thought that he would be unable to sway the king's heart his way without speaking a multitude of words.

**6:13. Then the Lord spoke to Moses and to Aaron, and He charged them concerning the children of Israel, and concerning Pharaoh king of Egypt, (with the mission) of bringing the children of Israel out of the country of Egypt.**

***Then the Lord spoke,*** *etc.* Because Moses had said, "I have impeded lips," God joined Aaron to him (Rashi).

**6:14. These are the heads of their lineages. The sons of Reuben firstborn of Israel (were): Hanoch and Pallu, Hezron and Carmi; these are the families of Reuben.**

***These are the heads of their lineages.*** It is known that the people of the East are quite particular about genealogies; therefore, now that it is mentioned that Moses and Aaron were appointed and raised to greatness, their genealogy is given. It begins with Reuben in order to state that the tribe of Levi, too, is among the oldest of the sons of Jacob.

# Shadal on Exodus

As for those who say that this genealogy was added on and was not written by Moses, their words are most improbable, for below (vv. 29-30), it says once more, "The Lord spoke to Moses" and "Moses spoke before the Lord"; this is repeated because [the narrative that was begun in v. 13 above] was interrupted by the genealogy. If the Torah were [composed merely of unconnected] extracts, such a thing would be out of place. In fact, we know that the style of the ancients in arranging the words of their books was quite different from ours today (Rosenmueller).

***these are the families of Reuben.*** From these four sons came four families. It may be that Reuben had other sons, and their descendants did not branch out into families but were called by the names of their [ancestors'] brothers; this may have been the case with the rest of the tribes. Perhaps it was only from those who went down to Egypt that families were formed.

**6:15. The sons of Simeon: Jemuel, Jamin, Ohad, Jachin, Zohar, and Shaul son of the Canaanite woman; these are the families of Simeon.**
**6:16. These, then, are the names of the sons of Levi, (subdivided afterwards) in their progeny: Gershon, and Kohath, and Merari. The years of Levi's life were one hundred thirty-seven.**
**6:17. The sons of Gershon (were): Libni and Shimi, heads of the respective families.**
**6:18. And the sons of Kohath: Amram, and Izhar, and Hebron, and Uzziel. The years of Kohath's life (were) one hundred thirty-three.**
**6:19. And the sons of Merari: Mahali and Mushi. These are the families of Levi, (subdivided afterwards) in their progeny.**
**6:20. Amram took to wife Jochebed his aunt, who bore him Aaron and Moses. The years of Amram's life (were) one hundred thirty-seven.**

***Amram took, etc.*** We are constrained to say that Scripture omitted some of the generations between Kohath and Amram, for in Numbers (3:28), the number of males of the age of one month and up registered to Kohath was 8,600, and he had had only four sons who had established families; thus each one of the four sons of Kohath would have had 2,150 sons. Moreover, Amram fathered only Aaron, Moses, and Miriam, and Moses fathered only two sons and Aaron four; how is it possible that Amram—and [his brothers] Izhar, Hebron, and Uzziel—would have had 2,150 souls in the second year after their exodus from Egypt?

## Va'era

Therefore we must agree with J.B. Koppe in his work, *Israelitas non 215, sed 430 annos in Aegypto commemoratos esse* ("The Israelites stayed in Egypt not 215 but 430 years"), Göttingen, 1777, who said (and with whom Rosenmueller concurred) that Levi, Kohath, and Amram were not of consecutive generations, but that there were other generations between them. Accordingly, the number of 430 years that the children of Israel dwelled in Egypt [Exod. 12:40] can be reconciled literally, and the great numerosity of the children of Israel in Egypt, which the Torah does not describe as actually miraculous, can be understood as well.

The scholar Jost (Part I, p. 2) says that these names mentioned here are the names of families, for it may be said that during the time that a father was alive, his descendants usually formed one group in a single clan (even though the children sometimes separated during their father's life, as for instance Isaac and Ishmael during Abraham's life, and Jacob and Esau during Isaac's life), and upon the father's death, the family would divide, and at times it would not divide until some time after the father's death. The meaning of this section, in his opinion, is that the family of Levi remained as one family and was called by the name of Levi throughout 137 years after the death of Jacob, and then after the time of Levi's death, it was divided into three families that were named for Gershon, Kohath, and Merari. Similarly, the family of Kohath remained in one group for 133 years and afterwards was divided into four families. At the time of the exodus from Egypt, 137 years had passed in which the family of Amram remained one family, from which came Moses and Aaron. If you add these three figures of 137, 133, and 137, and add to them the 17 years that the Israelites passed in Egypt before the death of Jacob, you will have 424 years, in other words, close to 430 years. Therefore (he says), every time it says "son of Izhar," "son of Kohath," or the like, the meaning is "from the seed of Izhar," "from the seed of Kohath."

**6:21. And the sons of Izhar: Korah, and Nepheg, and Zichri.**
**6:22. And the sons of Uzziel: Mishael, and Elzaphan, and Zithri.**

*And the sons of Uzziel.* The sons of Hebron [brother of Amram, Izhar, and Uzziel] are not mentioned, because there was no need to mention their names subsequently in the Torah, as there was a need to mention the children of these three [brothers]: the children of Amram—Moses, Aaron, and Miriam—are mentioned frequently in the Torah; the sons of Izhar [are listed here] because of the episode of Korah [Numbers 16]; the sons of Uzziel [are listed here] because of Mishael and Elzaphan (Leviticus 14). The sons of Korah [are listed] because of the subsequent statement, "But the sons of Korah did not die" (Num. 26:11). Similarly, the sons of Aaron and Phinehas son of Eleazar are mentioned [here and later] in the Torah, but the sons of Itamar are not listed [here] because there was no need to mention them subsequently in the Torah (Rashbam, Ibn Ezra, Mendelssohn, and Rosenmueller).

**6:23. Aaron took to wife Elisheba daughter of Amminadab, sister of Nahshon, who bore him Nadab, and Abihu, Eleazar, and Ithamar.**

*sister of Nahshon.* This is mentioned here to honor Aaron and his sons, for Nahshon was the prince of the children of Judah. The woman's name is mentioned because it is the way of Scripture to trace the ancestry of important individuals on the mother's side as well, as with the kings [of Judah], "And his mother's name was…" (Mendelssohn and Rosenmueller).

**6:24. And the sons of Korah: Assir, and Elkanah, and Abiasaph. These are the families of the Korahites.**
**6:25. And Eleazar son of Aaron took to wife one of the daughters of Putiel, who bore him Phinehas. These are the heads of the lineage of the Levites, (subdivided) in their respective families.**

*Putiel.* The name appears to be compounded from an Egyptian word, *puti* (see Gen. 37:36) [i.e., "devoted to"],[2] and the Hebrew name El, and its meaning is "devoted to the glory of God" (my late eldest son). Gesenius interpreted the name as "afflicted by God."

**6:26. These are (that) Aaron and (that) Moses to whom the Lord said, "Bring the children of Israel out of the country of Egypt, (placing yourselves) at the head of their ranks.**

*These are (that) Aaron and (that) Moses.* These are they, and this is their genealogy. Here, Aaron is mentioned first in accordance with their birth order; subsequently [next v.] it reverts and says, "These are (that) Moses and (that) Aaron" in accordance with their rank (Rashbam, Ibn Ezra, and Mendelssohn).

*at the head of their ranks (al tsive'otam).* See below at Exod. 12:51.

---

2. There, Shadal cites the view that the name Potifar means "devoted to the sun."

## Va'era

**6:27. These are they who spoke to Pharaoh king of Egypt, in order to bring the children of Israel out of Egypt. These are (that) Moses and (that) Aaron.**
**6:28. Now, when the Lord spoke to Moses in the country of Egypt —**

*Now, when the Lord spoke* (va-y'hi be-yom dibber YHVH). This phrase is connected to the one below (Rashi) [even though they are separated by a space in the written version]. The word *be-yom* (lit., "on the day of") means "at the time," "when He spoke."

**6:29. The Lord spoke to Moses, saying, "I am the Lord. Speak to Pharaoh king of Egypt all that I speak to you."**

*The Lord spoke, etc.* This is the same statement that was made above (vv. 10-12), but because the subject was interrupted by the genealogical account, the statement was once again repeated (Rashi). However, the verses are not duplicated word for word, but are somewhat different in terminology, and this is a sign that the verses were not repeated at random, but that the author repeated them intentionally.

**7:1. And the Lord said to Moses, "See, I appoint you (as) divinity toward Pharaoh, and Aaron your brother will be your prophet.**

*divinity (elohim) toward Pharaoh.* The Hebrew denotes an actual "god," and similarly "your prophet" (*nevi'ekha*) denotes an actual prophet (as per Mendelssohn), but here both terms are metaphors: not that Moses was an actual god or Aaron was an actual prophet, but because Moses was to speak his words to Pharaoh through Aaron, the situation resembled God's speaking through a prophet.

**7:2. "You will speak as much as I command you, and Aaron your brother will speak to Pharaoh, and he will let the children of Israel go out of his land.**
**7:3. "(First, however) I will harden Pharaoh's heart, and I will multiply My miracles and portents in the country of Egypt.**

*I will harden Pharaoh's heart.* This phrase may be interpreted as per the early commentators (Maimonides, Nachmanides, and others) in its plain sense, for in consideration of the magnitude of Pharaoh's sins, it would have been only just to block him from the paths of repentance (see Maimonides, *Teshuvah* 6:5). Rashi anticipated and recorded this opinion, but in his concise manner of expression, he added a fine and worthy concept: that withholding the paths of repentance from Pharaoh was not due to the magnitude of his sins alone, but there was another reason, which was that it was known to God that even if Pharaoh were to repent, his repentance would not have been complete; see Rashi's brief comment, for it is pleasing.[3]

It would also be possible to follow the interpretation of Mendelssohn, Clericus, and Rosenmueller, that here there was no Divine punishment or actual miracle; rather, Pharaoh himself hardened his heart, for all actions are attributable to God in some sense, as He is the First Cause. I would add that the actions which are attributed to God in the Scriptures are the strange actions whose reasons are incomprehensible to us. So here, Pharaoh's stubbornness despite his having seen several signs and wonders is a strange and astonishing thing, and therefore it is attributed to God. Cf., "And yet the Lord did not give you until this day a mind to understand, and eyes to see, and ears to hear" (Deut. 29:3);[4] "Because the Lord has said to him, 'Curse David'" (2 Sam. 16:10).[5]

R. Saadiah Gaon (*Emunot ve-De'ot* 4:4) expressed the view that God "strengthened" Pharaoh's heart, that is, his spirit and vitality, in that he would not succumb and die in the earlier plagues until God completed the later plagues, as it is said, "Indeed at this time I would have stretched forth My hand and struck you and your people with pestilence, and you would have disappeared from the earth. But it is for that reason that I let you exist, in order (that is) to make you see My power" (Exod. 9:15-16). However, it is far from the plain meaning of the expression, "I will harden [*aksheh*] his heart" or "I will strengthen [*aḥazzek*] his heart" to say that it means only, "I will keep him alive."

The author of the *Ikkarim* [R. Joseph Albo] (4:25) wrote that a wicked person, when struck by an affliction, [normally] relents and returns to God

---

3. Rashi goes on to say, "[God said,] 'It would be better for his heart to be hardened, so that My signs might be multiplied against him and that you [Israel] might recognize My power.' This is the way of the Holy One, blessed is He: He inflicts punishment on the nations so that Israel will hear and see, as it is said, 'I have cut off nations, their corners are desolate… I said, "Surely you will fear Me, you will receive correction"'" (Zeph. 3:6-7)."
4. Meaning, the children of Israel had behaved as if they had not seen the miracles of the Exodus, until they spent forty years in the desert (as per Shadal's comment on that verse).
5. Shimi ben Gera, who dared to curse David in the presence of the king's soldiers, was acting irrationally.

## Va'era

out of fear of the punishment that is imposed on him, as Pharaoh said, "I have sinned; [I see it] finally. The Lord is the one Who is right" (Exod. 9:27). Because such conduct is compelled and is not voluntary, God is said to "strengthen" such a person's heart by giving him some rationale to which he can attribute the affliction, so that he can say it came by chance rather than by Divine Providence. Thus he can remove from his heart the timidity that was induced by the affliction and remain in his natural state, with his free will uncoerced.

**7:4. "Pharaoh will not listen to you, and I will place My hand upon Egypt, and I will take My hosts, My people, (that is) the children of Israel, out of the country of Egypt, by means of great punishments.**
**7:5. "And the Egyptians will know that I am the Lord, when I stretch forth My arm over Egypt and take out the children of Israel from among them."**
**7:6. Moses and Aaron obeyed; as the Lord commanded them, so they did.**
**7:7. Moses was eighty years old, and Aaron eighty-three, when they spoke to Pharaoh.**
**7:8. The Lord said to Moses and to Aaron as follows:**
**7:9. "When Pharaoh says to you, 'Give a proof of your assertions,' you will say to Aaron, 'Take your staff, and cast it before Pharaoh; let it become a serpent!'"**

*Give a proof of your assertions* (*tenu lakhem mofet*, lit., "give a sign for yourselves"): as proof of your words. *Mofet* (מופת) means "proof," as in, "This is the sign [*mofet*] which the Lord has spoken" (1 Kings 13:3). The word is derived from the root יפע and is the equivalent of מופעת, i.e., that which is apparent (*mofi'a*) and obvious to all and cannot be doubted.

*let it (yehi) become a serpent.* This phrase, it seems to me, is a continuation of Moses' statement, for Moses [not only] had to tell Aaron to cast his staff before Pharaoh, but he also had to say before Pharaoh, "Let this staff become a serpent!" Thus it was properly written *yehi*, in the *tsivvui*,[6] not *yihyeh* in the future tense.

---

6. Although *tsivvui* is usually translated as "imperative," the same term is sometimes applied to a verb form that modern linguists call the "jussive" or "mild imperative." The word *yehi* is best understood as a jussive form.

It cannot be proven from the accents that the accentuator's opinion was otherwise. Although, in accordance with my opinion, it would have been proper to accent the word "Aaron" with a *zakef* [rather than the weaker *revia*], which is a stronger disjunctive than the *tipha* under the word "Pharaoh," it is in fact a norm of accentuation that when there is a quotation consisting of two clauses, the verb *amar* ("said") that introduces the quotation is marked with a lesser disjunctive than the one marking the word at the end of the first clause; cf. "They said [*tipha*], 'Let us call the maiden [*etnahta*, a stronger disjunctive], and let us ask her wish" (Gen. 24:57).[7]

**7:10. Moses and Aaron, having come to Pharaoh, did so, as the Lord had commanded. Aaron cast his staff before Pharaoh, and before his servants, and it became a serpent.**
**7:11. Pharaoh, too, called the sages and the wizards; and they, too, the sorcerers of Egypt, did the same with their arcane arts.**

***with their arcane arts*** *(be-lahateihem)*. Elsewhere [below, v. 22, and in Exod. 8:3 and 8:14] it is written *be-lateihem*, but these terms are the same, for the roots *lut* and *lahat* are equivalent, just like the roots *bush* and *behat* [the Hebrew and Aramaic words, respectively, for "to be ashamed"], *ruts* and *rehat* [Hebrew and Aramaic for "to run"], and *mul* and *mahal* [two Hebrew words for "to circumcise"]. The root *lut* denotes covering and concealment, and *lutim* or *lehatim* were the sorcerers' arts (*artes arcanae*) that were "hidden" from the understanding of the common people (Rosenmueller). Perhaps it was for this reason that sorcerers were called *harashim*, or in Aramaic *harashaya*, from the term *heresh*, meaning "in secret" (*hashai*) (Josh. 2:1).[8] In turn, the word *hashai* come from the root *hashah*, which is synonymous with *harash* and *heherish*, "to be silent."

In the Jerusalem Targum, mistakenly called Targum Jonathan, the sorcerers of Egypt are called Jannes and Jambres; in Num. 22:22 this Targum refers to them [by these names] as the two servants of Balaam; in *Menahot* (85a) they are called Yohana and Mamra; in Midrash Tanḥuma (*Ki Tissa* [19]) they are called Yunus and Yumbrus; in the Book of Zohar they are called the sons of Balaam; Paul, too, in one of his epistles (2 Timothy 3:8), mentions

---

7. In other words, the fact that the introductory phrase *ve-amarta el Aharon* ("you will say to Aaron") is set off with a relatively light disjunctive *revia*, while the subsequent phrase ending in "Pharaoh" is set off with a stronger *tipha*, does not prevent the next and final phrase *yehi le-tannin* ("let it become a serpent") from being construed as the second clause of a two-clause quotation.
8. "And Joshua... sent out of Shittim two spies secretly [*heresh*]."

them and says that they disputed with Moses (all this is from Buxtorf, *Lexicon Chaldaicum Talmudicum* [1640], p. 945).

Their memory is preserved also in various non-Jewish works, such as Pliny [*Natural History*] Book 30, ch. 1: "There is yet another branch of magic, derived from Moses, Jannes, Iotapes, and the Jews." So also Apuleius (*Apologia* [90]): "I am ready to be any magician you please—the great Carmendas himself or Damigeron or Moses, or Jannes or Apollobex or Dardanus himself, or any sorcerer of note from the time of Zoroaster and Ostanes till now." Eusebius, too, cited Numenius Pithagoricus, who mentions Jannes and Jambres as sorcerers of Egypt who disputed with Moses (to whom he refers as Museus) (all this is from Clericus and Rosenmueller).

With respect to the actions of the sorcerers, R. Hiyya bar Abba (*Sanhedrin* 67b) said that *be-lateihem* refers to the work of demons (*shedim*), while *be-lahateihem* refers to the work of wizardry (*keshafim*). Similarly, some of the commentators agreed that the sorcerers actually performed supernatural feats through wizardry, but Ibn Ezra wrote that it was nothing but an illusion. In the same vein, J.D. Michaelis wrote that the sorcerers took sleeping, motionless snakes that resembled staves, and by casting them on the ground, they woke them and made them appear as serpents; there are still men in Egypt who are experts in this work, especially with a kind of viper called *haje*, as Cahen attests.

According to Eichhorn (*De Aegypti anno mirabili*), Moses' actions themselves were illusions as well. Rosenmueller retorted, "Indeed, how scarcely credible it is that Moses would have persuaded himself that with this sort of craft, common enough in that land, he could deceive the king's own servants, nor is it likely that he, who had been brought up in the royal court and had been instructed in all the learning of Egypt, would have been unaware that this trick was known to the sorcerers."

**7:12. Each one cast his own staff, and they became serpents. Then Aaron's staff swallowed their staves.**
**7:13. But Pharaoh's heart was strengthened, and he did not heed them, as the Lord had predicted.**
**7:14. Then the Lord said to Moses, "Pharaoh's heart is heavy [weighty, hard to move, obstinate]; he (Pharaoh) has refused to let the people go.**
**7:15. "Go to Pharaoh in the morning; he must go out (to go) to the water. Wait for him on the bank of the Nile, and take with you the staff that was changed into a serpent.**

*he must go out… to the water.* Perhaps to see how many degrees the Nile had ascended (as per Ibn Ezra and Mendelssohn), or to go for a walk and take the air (as per Rashbam and R. Jacob Baal ha-Turim), or to bathe as Pharaoh's daughter had done (my student, R. Samuel Solomon Olper). God commanded Moses to speak to Pharaoh by the Nile rather than in his house, because Moses would have to strike the waters of the Nile before the eyes of Pharaoh and his servants.

**7:16. "And say to him, 'The Lord, God of the Hebrews, sent me to you, to say, "Let My people go to render worship to Me in the desert" – and behold, you have not given heed until now.**
**7:17. "'Thus says the Lord: "By this you will know that I am the Lord." Behold, I strike with the staff that I have in my hand upon the water that is in the Nile, and it will turn into blood.**

*that I am the Lord.* That I am the Lord Who is speaking to you through Moses and Aaron, and that they are not operating on their own.

*and it will turn into blood.* I think it fitting to cite here the opinion of R. Naphtali Herz Wessely regarding the plagues of Egypt: All the plagues that God brought upon the Egyptians can be divided into four classes of three plagues each, as follows. The first class consists of the serpents, blood, and frogs; the second—lice, mixture [of beasts or insects], and fatality [*dever*, i.e., pestilence]; the third—boils, hail, and locusts; and the fourth—darkness, striking of the firstborn, and splitting of the Red Sea. These four classes correspond to the "four sore judgments," mentioned in Ezekiel 14, by which God judges the world, namely, pestilence (*dever*), the sword, famine, and evil beasts. Each of these classes begins with a wonder that constitutes a minor plague and serves as a warning that if the Egyptians do not repent, He will strike them afterwards with greater plagues. These chastisements are the serpents, lice, boils, and darkness, and these are the ones referred to as "miracles and portents," for through their miraculous nature, they serve as signs of the plagues to follow. Each of the plagues is preceded by a warning, but not these four, since they are not plagues *per se* but rather chastisements and warnings of what is to come. This is Wessely's opinion; see the scholar Reggio's comment at v. 3 above.[9]

---

9. Reggio essentially follows Wessely's system and adds that the four classes of judgments are paralleled in *Behukkotai* (Leviticus 26) and *Ha'azinu* (Deuteronomy 32), as well as in *Avot* 5:8.

## Va'era

Rashbam (at v. 26 below) wrote that Moses would give warning for two plagues but not for a third. This occurred with each of [three] classes: he gave warning for the blood and frogs, but not for the lice; he gave warning for the mixture and fatality, but not for the boils; he gave warning for the hail and locusts, but not for the darkness.

R. Jacob Baal ha-Turim wrote that no warning was given for every third plague, in keeping with the statement of the Rabbis that "one who has been flogged twice [for the same transgression punishable by *karet* and then transgresses a third time] is put into a prison cell [and given a fatal diet]" (Mishnah *Sanhedrin* 9:5). Nachmanides wrote that warnings were given only for those plagues that involved human death.

**7:18. "'And the fish that are in the Nile will die, and the Nile will stink, and the Egyptians will seek in vain to drink water from the Nile.'"**

*and the Egyptians will seek in vain (ve-nil'u).* See my comment on Isa 1·14 [10]

**7:19. Then the Lord said to Moses, "Say to Aaron, 'Take your staff, and stretch out your arm over the waters of Egypt, over their rivers, over their canals, over their pools, and over their every receptacle of water, and they will turn into blood.' And there will be blood throughout all the country of Egypt, and (even) in the vessels of wood and of stone."**
**7:20. Moses and Aaron did so, as the Lord commanded: Aaron raised (his arm) with the staff, and he struck the Nile, in the presence of Pharaoh and his servants; and all the water of the Nile turned into blood.**

*and all the water of the Nile turned into blood.* Eichhorn's opinion, followed by others, was that the "blood" and all the rest of the plagues were natural phenomena that commonly occurred in Egypt every year, but that Moses' intention was to make Pharaoh understand that it was the Lord, the God of the Hebrews, Who activated these phenomena, and that He was the Ruler of all the earth. It is known that the waters of the Nile, after rising and flooding the land of Egypt in [the summer month of] Tammuz, appear red and thick (whether because of the ruddiness of the land of Cush from which they come, or whether from the multitude of swarming creatures that make the water ruddy in other countries as well and cause the common people to believe

---

10. There, on the phrase *nil'eti neso* ("I cannot bear"), Shadal comments that the verb *nile'ah* always means "cannot" or "try unsuccessfully," and he cross-refers to the present verse.

that blood falls from the skies—see [Diderot's] *Encyclopédie*, s.v. *Pluie prodigieuse*)[11]— and are ill-smelling and bad for drinking.

Eichhorn added that Moses and Aaron did not turn all the waters of the Nile red at the moment that the staff was stretched forth; rather, through sleight of hand they turned red the contents of a vessel that they had filled with Nile water. Their intention was to convey the message that the God Who had taught them how to cause the water in the vessel to turn red was the God Who caused the ruddiness of the Nile waters and Who was telling Pharaoh to let His people go.

To this, Rosenmueller appropriately responded that the taking of the Nile water and pouring it on the dry ground was to be done only in the sight of the Israelites (Exod. 4:9), but what was done now in Pharaoh's sight was different, for they did not take [a sample] of the Nile's water, but rather Aaron stretched forth his hand over the Nile and immediately all of its water turned to blood. Besides, it is unlikely that Moses would have thought he could convince the king by means of natural phenomena that occurred every year, without performing before him some supernatural wonder.

Now it is well known that even in performing miracles, God prefers to adhere to the ways of nature in part. Thus, with respect to the plagues of Egypt it is likely, in my opinion, that they resembled in some respect phenomena that were natural in Egypt, some occurring in one year and some occurring in another, except that in that year, all of them came clustered together; in addition, each one contained a novel aspect that was not found in nature.

So, too, with respect to the plague of blood, we see that the redness of the water was novel in its ill effects, to the extent that all the fish within it died, something that we never find mentioned in the writings of the travelers of ancient routes. This is proof that the water's foul odor and quality were much more intense than in other years and departed from the course of nature, as if the water had actually turned to blood.

**7:21. And the fish that was in the Nile died, and the Nile stank, and the Egyptians could not drink water from the Nile, and the blood was all over the country of Egypt.**

**7:22. The sorcerers of Egypt did likewise with their arcane arts, and Pharaoh's heart became strong, and he did not heed them, as the Lord had predicted.**

---

11. The article in question (vol. 12, p. 796) states that small aquatic insects may multiply during the summer "in muddy ditches and channels in such quantities that they render the surface of the water completely red," causing ignorant people to believe that it rained blood, and to derive from this phenomenon "all kinds of sinister omens."

***The sorcerers of Egypt did likewise.*** It seems to me that the event described in v. 21, "and the blood was all over the country of Egypt," did not occur immediately; rather, the verse concludes the account of the water turning into blood. However, at the moment when Aaron struck the Nile in the presence of Pharaoh, the Nile's water immediately turned to blood, and immediately the sorcerers took vessels with water that was not from the Nile and that had not yet turned to blood, and through their trickery they turned that water into blood. Afterward, the plague took hold in all the water in the houses of Egypt and in all their receptacles of water.

**7:23. Pharaoh turned away and went to his house, and he did not take heed even to this.**
**7:24. The Egyptians then all dug around the Nile (some wells, in order to have) water to drink, not being able to drink the water of the Nile.**

***The Egyptians then all dug... water*** *(va-yaḥperu... mayim).* They dug *and brought forth* water (a "pregnant" construction); cf., "and dig [for] it more than [for] hidden treasures" (Job 3:21). According to this explanation, it would have been proper to place the [disjunctive] *tipḥa* at the word *mayim* (ויחפרו כל-מצרים סביבת היאר מָיִם לשתות), but the accentuator [in placing the *tipḥa* at *ha-y'or* ("the Nile") and connecting the words *mayim lishtot*, "water to drink"] interpreted the phrase as "the Egyptians dug in order to drink water" [similar to the translation given here].

**7:25. Then, seven days having passed since the Lord had struck the Nile —**

***Then, seven days having passed.*** In *Exodus Rabbah* (9:12, 10:7) it was said that similarly, each plague lasted seven days, but this is not necessarily so. Rashbam wrote [in his comment on this verse], "Such was the plague of the Nile," that is, this one alone lasted seven days. According to Ibn Ezra and Nachmanides, the rest of the plagues did not last as long.

In Ibn Ezra's opinion, the Israelites were also struck by this plague, and by the frogs and lice as well, and God did not distinguish between Egypt and Israel except where it says so specifically in the Torah. R. Jacob Baal ha-Turim commented on this, "His departure from the words of the Sages and his hasty pursuit of the *peshat* (the "plain" meaning) led to this opinion—far be it from God to strike Israel, for there is nothing to impede God from saving whom He wishes or from striking whom He wishes."

## Shadal on Exodus

It seems to me that the land of Goshen, as per the modern scholars, was not in Egypt proper, but on its border, near Arabia, and therefore that land did not drink from the Nile's water. Thus Goshen was not struck by the plagues of blood and frogs, and there was no need for Scripture to mention this point, for it was known to the Israelites, who were familiar with the nature of the land where they had lived. However, if a few Israelites were outside Goshen, we cannot deny that they, too, were struck by these plagues, and that they, too, were forced to drink from wells that they dug.

**7:26. The Lord said to Moses, "Go to Pharaoh, and say to him, 'Thus says the Lord: "Let My people go the render Me worship.
7:27. "If you, then, refuse to let them go, I will scourge all of your territory with frogs.**

***all of your territory*** (*kol gevulekha*, lit., "all of your border") — But not the land of Goshen, which was not within the border of Egypt proper; see also below, Exod. 10:4 (R. Moses Ehrenreich).

***with frogs.*** It is well known that after the Nile recedes, having watered the land of Egypt, many species of creeping things are spawned in the remaining mud. Bochart wrote that [the plague of frogs] was miraculous in that (1) one particular species—the frogs—multiplied so greatly; (2) they appeared the moment that Moses spoke; (3) they left the water, their normal habitat, and came upon the dry land and into houses; and (4) they were wiped out at Moses' word, at the time that Pharaoh set for him.

Eichhorn bemoaned and bewailed the fact that none of the travelers of ancient routes who wrote of Egyptian matters ever made an observation of frogs or reported the phenomenon of their multiplying every year and coming upon dry land. See to what extent the effrontery of this heretic has reached: he says that the multiplicity of the frogs and their intrusion into houses is a natural occurrence in Egypt that happens every year, even though there is no one who has attested or recorded such a thing.

***refuse*** (*ma'en*). The Hebrew is the equivalent of *mema'en* [the intensive (*pi'el*) form of the root *ma'an*] (see my *Grammar* § 374).[12] Rashi, however, rejects this (*mema'en ba-zeh*), and in his opinion the word is not a present tense *pi'el* form, but rather an adjective [i.e., "if you are reluctant to let them

---

12. There, Luzzatto says that the participle of the *pi'el* conjugation sometimes lacks the usual prefix *mem*, and as an example he cites *ma'en*.

go"].[13] The copyists misunderstood his meaning and corrupted his comment by deleting the [negative introductory] word *ve-ein*, but there is no doubt that he himself wrote it this way: *ve-ein ma'en kemo mema'en* ("*ma'en* is *not* the equivalent of *mema'en*").

My student Shalom Simeon Modena adds that it was for this reason that Rashi, in his initial comment [on the phrase *ve-im ma'en attah*], said, "If you are a refusing one [*sarvan*]," employing an adjectival form, and then went on to say, "*Ma'en* is not the equivalent of *mema'en*, 'refuse' [*mesarev*]," employing a present tense verb rather than repeating the form *sarvan*.[14]

**7:28. ""The Nile will swarm with frogs, which will go up (on the land) and enter into your house, into your bedroom, and upon your bed, and into the house of your servants, and upon your people, and into your ovens, and into your kneading troughs.**

**and into your kneading troughs** (*u-ve-mish'arotekha*). The Hebrew is also found to refer to the dough itself (e.g., "their dough [*mish'arotam*] wrapped in their clothes" [Exod. 12:34]). The word is derived from *se'or* ("leaven"), even though the latter word is spelled with a *sin* [rather than a *shin*] (Abravanel). Kimhi wrote that perhaps the word was derived from *she'er*, meaning "food." Joseph Jarè suggests that *se'or* is derived from *she'ar* ("remainder"), for the *se'or* is the portion of the dough that remains from the previous day and has fermented.

There is no doubt that Moses and Aaron went and said all this to Pharaoh [although it is not so specifically stated], but the Samaritans added to the text, "And Moses and Aaron came to Pharaoh and spoke to him, 'So says the Lord, "Let My people go to render Me worship, and if you refuse,"'" etc.

**7:29. ""The frogs, in sum, will go up upon you, your people, and all of your servants.""**

***upon you, your people,*** *etc.* They will even go up upon individuals, that is, on their clothes and their bodies.

---

13. Modern grammarians would classify the word *ma'en* as a "stative verb," that is, a verb that describes a state of being rather than an action.
14. The supercommentary *Sefer ha-Zikkaron* likewise favored the negative reading *ve-ein*, though Rosenbaum and Silbermann (p. 34) claim that such a reading is based on a "misunderstanding" of Rashi. Chavel's edition (pp. 194-195) does not have the word *ve-ein*, but does cite a supercommentary (*Be'er Rehovot* by Isaac Auerbach, 1730) which lends support to the idea that Rashi viewed *ma'en* as an adjectival form.

**8:1.** Then the Lord said to Moses, "Say to Aaron, 'Stretch forth your arm with your staff, over the rivers, over the canals, and over the pools, and cause the frogs to go up upon the land of Egypt.'"

**8:2.** Aaron stretched forth his arm over the waters of Egypt, and a quantity of frogs went up and covered the land of Egypt.

**8:3.** The sorcerers of Egypt did likewise with their arcane arts, and they made the frogs go up upon the land of Egypt.

***The sorcerers of Egypt did likewise.*** They took a vessel full of water that contained frog eggs, and with their arcane arts (that is, their knowledge of nature), they hastened the hatching of the frogs from the eggs.

**8:4.** Pharaoh called Moses and Aaron, and he said, "Pray to the Lord, that He may remove the frogs from me and from my people; and I will let the people go to make sacrifices to the Lord."

***Pharaoh called Moses and Aaron.*** With respect to the blood, it was said, "And Pharaoh's heart became strong" (Exod. 7:22), for that plague did not touch his own body or flesh, since the people had dug around the Nile and found water. In this case, however, the frogs had entered the king's own house. But Ibn Ezra's comment—that Pharaoh saw that the sorcerers had only added onto the plague but could not diminish it—is nonsense, for Pharaoh had not summoned them to remove the plagues, but to recreate them with their arcane arts.

**8:5.** And Moses said to Pharaoh, "I want you to be able to boast over me. For when do you want me to pray in favor of you, of your servants, and of your people, so that the frogs may cease from you and from your houses, and remain only in the Nile?"

***I want you to be able to boast over me*** *(hitpa'er alai).* "Exalt yourself over me, and make yourself master over me, in that you may set me a time for which I should pray for you." After Pharaoh set him a time, Moses said to him, "So that you may know that there is none like the Lord, our God" [next v.], that is, "I have not said this for your honor, but for the honor of my God."

***For when do you want me to pray in favor of you*** *(le-matai a'tir lekha).* "For what time should I pray now that they should be removed?" See Rashi.[15]

---

15. Rashi here observes that if the first word of this phrase had been *matai*, "when," the phrase would have meant, "When should I pray?" but that *le-matai*

**8:6. And he said, "For tomorrow." And Moses added, "(Let it be) as your word, so that you may know that there is none like the Lord, our God.**

*For tomorrow.* Pharaoh thought that Moses knew that the time had come when the frogs would cease immediately, so in order to test him, he put off the time and said, "For tomorrow" (R. Samuel ben Hofni, cited by Ibn Ezra). Nachmanides thought to the contrary, that Pharaoh thought Moses was seeking a distant time, so he gave him a short time. This is incorrect, for if so, Pharaoh should have told him that the frogs should cease immediately, not "tomorrow."

**8:7. "The frogs will cease from you and from your houses, from your servants and from your people; and they will remain only in the Nile."**

*will cease (ve-saru).* Cf., "from which the change [i.e., plague of leprosy] will be ceased [*ve-sar*]" (Lev. 13:58). The meaning is not that the frogs would go away alive; therefore Moses did not say that they would merely return to the Nile, but that they would die wherever they were. The Korem erred in his understanding of the word *ve-saru* [which could be translated as "will turn aside"] and thought that Moses was promising that the frogs would return to the Nile alive, but that God was not willing [to comply].

**8:8. Then, Moses and Aaron having come forth from Pharaoh, Moses exclaimed to the Lord, on account of the frogs, with which He had aggravated Pharaoh.**

*Moses exclaimed (va-yits'ak).* This was because the plague of blood had lasted seven days and had ceased without a prayer, but here—the first time Moses prayed for a plague to cease—the term *tse'akah* is used, which indicates a more forceful prayer than the term *ha'atarah* ("solicitation"), which is used in connection with the rest of the plagues (my student Moses Cohen Porto). Another reason (as per Ibn Ezra) is that Moses had already promised Pharaoh, without God's authorization, that the frogs would cease at the time that Pharaoh would set for him.

**8:9. And the Lord did as the word of Moses, and the frogs died from the houses, from the courtyards, and from the fields.**

---

indicates, "I will pray for you today that the frogs will cease at the time that you set for me."

*as the word of Moses.* As Moses had spoken to Pharaoh, that the frogs would cease "tomorrow."

**8:10. They piled them in heaps and heaps, and the country stank of it.**
**8:11. Pharaoh, seeing comfort restored, rendered his heart obstinate, and he paid no heed to them, just as the Lord had predicted.**

*comfort (harvaḥah,* lit., "spacing"). Cf., "Out of my straits I called upon the Lord; He answered me with great enlargement [*be-merḥavyah*]" (Ps. 118:5). Trouble is described in terms of a person who is sitting in a narrow place in which he cannot move about or act at will (so also the expression *tsarah ve-tsukah*, "trouble and anguish" [lit., "narrowness and pressure," see, e.g., Isa. 30:6]). The opposite is to sit in a place that is "enlarged" (*raḥav*) or "spacious" (*meruvvaḥ*).

*rendered... obstinate (ve-hakhbed).* The form *hakhbed* is an infinitive, which is to be understood as taking on the tense of the preceding verb, whether past or future.[16]

**8:12. Then the Lord said to Moses, "Say to Aaron, 'Stretch out your staff, and strike the dust of the land, and it will become lice in all the country of Egypt.'"**

*and it will become lice (ve-hayah le-khinnim).* In the Alexandrian translation, *scniphos* ("gnat"). Philo of Egypt, in his *Life of Moses* [Book 1, 23:130], wrote that this was a tiny flying insect with a very painful sting; it would also enter the ears and nostrils, and one had to take great care to protect one's eyes. Perhaps this is the *culex pulicaris* [a variety of mosquito] of Linnaeus, or the *culex molestus* [another mosquito mentioned by Forskal, which is found in Egypt and is very bothersome to sleepers at night.[17] Eichhorn says that in the word *kinnim,* the element *–im* is not a plural suffix, but rather *knim* or *knif* is the name of the insect (*scniph*) in the Egyptian language (Rosenmueller).

---

16. Here, the infinitive *hakhbed* assumes the past tense of the verb *va-yar*, lit., "and he saw."
17. Forskal's description of this mosquito includes the following statement: "Rosetta, Cairo and Alexandria tremendously abundant, bothers sleepers at night and difficult to avoid them unless with well-closed curtains" (*Descriptiones animalium, avium, amphibiorum, piscium, insectorum, vermium, quae in itinere orientali observavit Petrus Forskål* [Copenhagen, 1775], p. 85). Ironically, Forskal is said to have died of malaria (see Sources).

## Va'era

In my opinion, after the Israelites left Egypt and entered their own land, where this insect was not found, they used the word *kinnim* to denote a different species of insect that stings the flesh, and thus Onkelos translates it as *kalmeta* ("vermin"), and similarly in the Syriac translation, *kalma*. This is mentioned in the Talmud: "Gossip comes from peddlers and vermin (*kalmei*, i.e., "lice") from rags" (*Berakhot* 51b). In the Tosafot (*Shabbat* 12a), there is a dispute between R. Joseph of Orleans and Rabbenu Tam as to whether the *kinnah* is the white one (i.e., the louse) and the *par'osh* is the black one (i.e., the flea), or vice versa.

In the Midrash (Yalkut [*Va'era* 182]) it says, "He brought twelve [or fourteen] varieties of *kinnim* upon them; the smallest of them was the size of a hen's egg, and the largest the size of a goose egg." However, in the Talmud (*Sanhedrin* 67b) it says, "'And the sorcerers said, "It is the finger of God"': R. Eliezer said, 'From here we deduce that the demon [*shed*] cannot create a creature smaller than a barleycorn.'"

**8:13. They complied; and as soon as Aaron stretched out his arm with his staff, and struck the dust of the land, a multitude of lice was on the people and on the animals; all the dust of the land was lice in all the country of Egypt.**

*a multitude of lice (ha-kinnam)*. The Hebrew is the name of the species [lit., "the louse"], like *ha-tsefardea* [lit., "the frog," above, v. 2]. From here there is proof that the *mem* in *kinnim* is not a plural suffix but is part of the root, as per Eichhorn. There is no proof to the contrary from the forms *reikam* ("empty-handed") and *ḥinnam* ("gratuitously") cited by Mendelssohn, for in those words the *mem* is added to indicate an adverbial form, but here the word [*kinnam*] is the name of a species, and we never find such names with a *mem* suffix.

*all the dust of the land was lice.* So it appeared to the people because of the extreme multitude of the lice; this is [merely] by way of hyperbole.

**8:14. The sorcerers endeavored likewise, with their arcane arts, to produce the lice, but they could not. And the lice were on the people and on the animals [but not elsewhere, as the sorcerers would have wanted to produce them].**

*but they could not.* According to Nachmanides and Mendelssohn, they had been able to do so with the blood and the frogs, since those plagues had not involved any act of creation, but the plague of lice was a new creation, for it is not in the nature of dust to turn into lice.

Formerly I interpreted the phrase *le-hotsi et ha-kinnim* ("to produce [lit., "to take out"] the lice") to mean "to remove" the lice from upon them. Under this interpretation, the subsequent phrase, "And the lice were on the people and on the animals," would have fit in well, for the sorcerers could not remove them or take them off. The sorcerers' later statement, "It is the finger of God" [next v.], would also have fit in well. However, this does not appear to be the true meaning of *le-hotsi*. Also, according to that interpretation, it should not have said that the sorcerers "did likewise" [the literal meaning of the phrase that is translated here as "endeavored likewise"].

The correct explanation is that God was abusing (*hit'allel*) the Egyptians (as is seen in Exod. 10:2, below), and that one of the ways in which He abused them was that he began with miracles and portents of such a nature that the sorcerers were able to duplicate them to some extent. The object was to harden Pharaoh's heart so that he and his people should receive the punishment that they deserved. However, He did not wish to continue in this way till the end, so that the Israelites would be led astray and find fault with Moses' miracles. Therefore, after the first two miracles, He no longer allowed the sorcerers to duplicate His portents and wonders.

***And the lice were on the people and on the animals.*** This means, in my view, that the lice were on the people and animals *only*, for the sorcerers could not produce the lice in other places where they had not been present through the actions of Moses and Aaron. If the sorcerers had been able to accomplish this, they would have said that the incident was [merely] a human trick, but now they were forced to say that it was "the finger of God."

**8:15. And the sorcerers said to Pharaoh, "It is the finger of God." But Pharaoh's heart became strong and he paid no heed to them, just as the Lord had predicted.**

***It is the finger of God.*** Ibn Ezra interpreted this as "a Divine plague," in the sense of "the hand of the Lord" (Exod. 9:3), and so Onkelos, *maḥa min kodam YHVH* ("a plague from the presence of the Lord"). According to this interpretation, they were not admitting that it was Moses' God Who had done this, but only that it was a plague from "the gods."

It seems to me, however, that "finger" is not the equivalent of "hand," for one strikes with a hand, not a finger; but rather, "finger" is said in reference to a command, as in, "The putting forth of the finger" (Isa. 58:9). Thus, "the finger of God" signifies a Divine command, the will of God. The sorcerers did admit that Moses and Aaron's action was at the command and word of God, and therefore they made no more efforts with their arcane arts.

It should not be said that the sorcerers made no such admission, and that it was for this reason that Pharaoh's heart was strengthened, for below it is said, "Pharaoh sent, and he found that not one of the animals of the Israelites had perished; and [still] Pharaoh's heart was obstinate, and he did not let the people go" (Exod. 9:7). This can only mean that despite seeing the miracle, he made his heart obstinate. Here, too, even though the sorcerers admitted, he did not, or he acted contrary to what he would have had to admit in his heart, as is the manner of heretics.

**8:16. Then the Lord said to Moses, "Having risen tomorrow morning, present yourself to Pharaoh – he must surely go out (to betake himself) to the water – and say to him, 'Thus says the Lord: "Let My people go to render Me worship.**
**8:17. "'"For if you do not let My people go, behold, I will send against you, your servants, your people, and your houses the mixture (of beasts or insects); and the houses of the Egyptians, and also the land on which they stand, will be filled with the mixture.**

*the mixture (he-arov).* According to the [major] commentators and Josephus Flavius, [*Antiquities* 2:14] this was a mixture of noxious beasts. Support for this is found in Ps. 78:45, "He sent among them *arov*, which devoured them." Rashbam interpreted this as wolves of the evening (*erev*), whose nature it is to prey at night, while the Greek translation, followed by Philo [*Life of Moses* 1:130], was "dog flies," apparently of a type of insect called *Tafani* ("gadflies," "horseflies"). Aquila, followed by Jerome, translated *arov* as a mixture of all kinds of flies, flies of various species (Rosenmueller). This last opinion seems likely to me, for it is not readily understood how wild beasts could have entered the houses without the doors being closed against them. Under this interpretation, the word *va-yokhelem* ("which devoured them") in the Psalms is a hyperbolic expression, as is the subsequent phrase, "And frogs, which destroyed them" (Ps. 78:45). Similarly, it is commonly said that lice and fleas "devour" a person, and so other such expressions.

**8:18. "'And I will then distinguish the country of Goshen, upon which My people stand, so that there will be no mixture there, in order that you**

may know that I, the Lord, am amidst (the things) of the earth [I watch over and govern them].

*that I, the Lord, am amidst (the things) of the earth.* "That I am the God Who watches over the lower realm and Who works good and evil"; cf. "Behold, because my God is not in my midst [does not protect me], I was seized by these evils" (Deut. 31:17); "Is the Lord among us, or is He not?" (Exod. 17:7), referring to Divine Providence. Distinguishing between one nation and another is a sign of such Providence.

**8:19. "'I will thus make a distinction between your people and Mine. Tomorrow this miracle will happen.'"**

*a distinction (pedut,* lit., "redemption"). A separation; similarly, the terms *yeshu'ah, hatsalah, ḥilluts,* and *purkan* [all lit., "rescue" or "salvation"] are all expressions of distinction or separation (Rashbam). According to Nachmanides and Mendelssohn, this "distinction" was that even in Egypt [proper], if the beasts were to encounter an Israelite, they would not harm him. In my opinion, however, this verse is only a general statement following particulars [and thus does not come to add a new detail].

**8:20. The Lord did so, and there came a grave mixture into the house of Pharaoh, into the house of his servants, and into all the land of Egypt. The country suffered damage, on account of the mixture.**

*into the house of Pharaoh… and into all the land of Egypt (u-ve-khol erets Mitsrayim).* The *etnaḥ* [major disjunctive] should properly have been placed here [at the word *Mitsrayim,* "Egypt," rather than previously at *avadav,* "his servants"]. Otherwise, it should have said "in all the land of Egypt" without the [conjunctive] *u-* ("and").[18]

**8:21. Pharaoh called Moses and Aaron, and he said, "Go, make sacrifices to your God within the country."**

*make sacrifices… within the country (ba-arets).* "But do not go into the desert" (Rashi). This statement reveals Pharaoh's malicious nature, for until

---

18. Some translations, including Shadal's own, follow the approach taken in Shadal's comment and attach the phrase *u-ve-khol erets Mitsrayim* to the first half of the verse. Others (e.g., the 1917 JPS version) attach the phrase to the second half and render it, "and in all the land of Egypt the land was ruined."

now he had not even allowed the people this much, and had not given them any rest from their labor.

**8:22. And Moses said, "It is not suitable to do so, for we must sacrifice to our God that which is sacred for the Egyptians. Could we slaughter before the eyes of the Egyptians that which is sacred for them, without their stoning us?**

***for we must sacrifice... that which is sacred for the Egyptians*** *(to'avat Mitsrayim*, lit., "the abomination of Egypt"). According to R. Yeshuah (cited by Ibn Ezra), Moses recorded [his statement] this way in order to deprecate idolatry, but to Pharaoh he [actually] said "the gods of Egypt." This seems to be Rashi's opinion as expressed in his first explanation, but Rashi's second explanation, followed by Rosenmueller, is "that which its slaughter would be an abomination to the Egyptians." It seems to me, however, that the Hebrew *to'evah* is the equivalent of "sacred" or "taboo," like the Latin *sacer* ("sacred," "devoted to a deity for destruction," "accursed"), i.e., something set apart that is forbidden to be used.

Years after [writing the above opinion], I found that in the Egyptian [Coptic] language, *uab* and *ethuab* denote "purity" and "holiness," and similarly, *suab* and *tubo* mean "to purify." It seems to me that the Hebrew root *ta'av* is derived from the Egyptian and [properly] denotes purity and holiness, but that the Hebrews used it in the opposite sense. The Arameans, too, used the term *se'ev* to refer to impurity, in contrast to the use of *suab* in Egyptian to indicate purity. See my *Grammar* § 258.[19]

***Could we slaughter*** *(hen nizbaḥ)*. The Hebrew is equivalent to *ha-nizbaḥ*; see above at 4:1.

---

19. There, Shadal (citing sources including Champollion) refers to these same Coptic and Aramaic words, and says, "It is probable that because of religious antipathy, the Semites would have used in a completely contrary sense those words that, among the Egyptians, signified purity and sanctity."

This opinion is virtually echoed by the twentieth-century scholar A.S. Yahuda, who in connecting the Hebrew *to'evah* to the Egyptian *w'b* and *św'b* ("pure," "to purify"), comments as follows: "That in Hebrew this word should present a meaning contrary to that of its Egyptian original should cause no surprise since that which was for the Egyptians pure and holy, was for the Hebrews impure and abhorrent, as *vice versa* the sacrifices of the Hebrews appeared to the Egyptians as an abomination (Ex. 8, 22)." (*The Language of the Pentateuch in its Relation to the Egyptian*, vol. I [London: Oxford University Press, 1933], p. 95.)

***without their stoning us.*** As late as the time of Juvenal, the Egyptians were still contending with each other on their festival days because the gods of one city were not those of another city, and thus they would wage war and stone each other (Satire 15):

> Between the neighboring towns of Ombi and Tentyra there burns an ancient and long-cherished feud and undying hatred, whose wounds are not to be healed… because each hates its neighbors' Gods…. So when one of these peoples held a feast, the chiefs and leaders of their enemy thought good to seize the occasion… they now search the ground for stones… and hurl them with bended arms against the foe…[20]

Plutarch, too, wrote that a clever king decreed that each city's gods should be different from one another, so that the people of Egypt should be unable to unite in a powerful conspiracy and rebel against him. Plutarch also recorded [in *Isis and Osiris*] that in his time, it occurred that the people of one city [Cynopolis] ate a fish that was worshipped in another city [Oxyrhyncus], and the people of the other city ate the dogs that were worshipped in the first city, with the result that a war broke out between them until the Romans came and made peace between them (Clericus).

**8:23. "We must enter into the desert a journey of three days; then we will make sacrifices to the Lord our God, according to what He will say to us."**
**8:24. And Pharaoh said, "I will let you go to make sacrifices to the Lord your God in the desert, but do not go far. (Meanwhile) pray for me."**
**8:25. And Moses said, "Here I go out from before you, and (soon) I will pray to the Lord, and the mixture will cease from Pharaoh, from his servants, and from his people, tomorrow. But let Pharaoh not make mockery, by not letting the people go to make sacrifices to the Lord."**

***and the mixture will cease*** *(ve-sar).* See above at v. 7.

***make mockery*** *(hatel).* See Gen. 31:7 and Isa. 30:10.[21]

---

20. Translated by G. G. Ramsay, Loeb Classical Edition (1918).
21. Shadal's comment on the phrase *hetel bi* ("mocked me") in Gen. 31:7 derives the verb from the root *talal*. His comment on the word *mahatallot* ("delusions") in Isa. 30:10 similarly derives the word in question from *talal*, and Shadal goes on to explain that the roots *talal*, *tul*, and *hatal* are all related and ultimately derive from a two-letter root *tal*.

## Va'era

**8:26.** Moses, having gone out from before Pharaoh, prayed to the Lord.
**8:27.** And the Lord carried out the word of Moses, and the mixture ceased from Pharaoh, from his servants, and from his people; there did not remain of those (animals) even one.
**8:28.** But Pharaoh made his heart obstinate this time as well, and he did not let the people go.

**9:1.** Then the Lord said to Moses, "Go to Pharaoh, and say to him, 'So says the Lord, God of the Hebrews: "Let My people go to render Me worship.
**9:2.** """For if you refuse to let them go, and you continue to hold onto them—
**9:3.** """Behold, the hand of the Lord will be on your animals [that is, He will strike your animals] that are in the field, on the horses, on the asses, on the camels, on the oxen, and on the flocks; [that is, there will be] an exceedingly grave fatality.

*the hand of the Lord will be on.* With respect to the plagues of fatality [pestilence] and the striking of the firstborn [Exod. 11:4ff.], both of which involved loss of life, Moses and Aaron performed no action as a signal, neither the raising of the staff nor anything else. Rather, they attributed the act to God Himself: "The hand of the Lord will be on..." (this v.); "Near midnight I [the Lord] will go forth in the midst of Egypt" (Exod. 11:4).

*will be (hoyah).* The Hebrew is a participle of the root *hayah* ("to be"). We find [the alternate form] *hoveh*, but [its feminine] *hovah* was not used, so as not to be confused with a noun, as in, "Calamity [*hovah*] shall come upon calamity [*hovah*]" (Ezek. 7:26).

*an exceedingly grave fatality.* Eichhorn says that the large number of vermin (the lice and the mixture of animals) caused the fatality, for the insect eggs scattered in the air and settled with the dew on the vegetation of the field, and the [domestic] animals, after eating the vegetation, fell ill and died. He adds that the Israelites' cattle did not die, since the Israelites had been shepherds for a long time and were experts in the ways of healing animals.

I do not deny that there was a natural aspect to this, except that along with it there was a miraculous aspect that went beyond the natural order of the world. The large number of lice and mixed animals, and the fact that the mixture did not spread into the land of Goshen, was in the way of a miracle, and this itself was perhaps the reason that the Israelites' cattle did not die.

**9:4.** "''And the Lord will make a distinction between the cattle of the Israelites and that of the Egyptians, and nothing will perish of that which belongs to the children of Israel.'''"

**9:5.** The Lord fixed a time, saying, "Tomorrow the Lord will carry out this thing in the country."

**9:6.** And the Lord carried out this thing on the following day, and all the animals of the Egyptians died, and of those of the Israelites there died none.

**9:7.** Pharaoh sent, and he found that not one of the animals of the Israelites had perished; and (still) Pharaoh's heart was obstinate, and he did not let the people go.

**9:8.** Then the Lord said to Moses and to Aaron, "Take your fists full of furnace soot, and let Moses scatter it through the air in the presence of Pharaoh."

*furnace soot (piaḥ kivshan).* Rashbam interpreted this to mean fine ash that is blown in the air. However, since the word *piaḥ* is attached by *semikhut* to the word *kivshan* ("furnace"), it is more likely that *piaḥ* is that which blows and rises in the smoke and adheres to the furnace, and this is what has been commonly translated as *fuliggine* ("soot").

*and let Moses scatter it through the air.* Not that this would be the [actual] cause of the [ensuing plague of] boils, but he had to perform some action before the wonders came into being, so as to make it known that it was through the will of God, Who had sent the prophet who was performing this action, that the miracle came to be. This was analogous to raising the staff, speaking to the rock (Num. 20:8), and the like. Perhaps He chose this signal in particular, as Abravanel explained, to symbolize that all of the air of Egypt would be damaged, and that it would be hot and burning and productive of boils.

*and let Moses scatter it.* From the plague of boils onward, it was Moses and not Aaron who performed these signs (stretching forth the staff, etc.), perhaps because of the severity of these plagues, which involved people's sickness and death or the cutting off of their sustenance.

**9:9.** "And it will become a powder (that will fall) on all the country of Egypt, which will produce on the people and on the animals, in all the country of Egypt, ulcers, boils breaking forth.

## Va'era

***And it will become a powder.*** A metaphoric and hyperbolic expression, as if the soot would turn into a powder and scatter throughout the land of Egypt, and upon falling over the people and animals, would turn into boils, etc. (Clericus and Rosenmueller).

**ulcers** *(shehin).* An affliction mentioned in Job (2:7), "With sore boils [*shehin*] from the sole of his foot even unto his crown." According to Rashi, the word is derived from a term for "warmth," as in the Mishnaic expression *shanah shehunah*, "a hot year" (*Yoma* 55b). Perhaps the affliction (*ulcera*) was so called in the sense of "warmth," but *shehin* does not mean "inflammation," as was the opinion of Clericus, Mendelssohn, Rosenmueller, and Reggio; they thought that the verse meant that the *shehin*, i.e., the warmth, caused the boils (*ava'bu'ot*) to break forth. This is not so; rather (as the accentuator wisely accented the phrase [by connecting the words *shehin* and *pore'ah*, and separating *pore'ah* and *ava'bu'ot*]), the word *pore'ah* ("breaking forth") modifies *shehin*, as specified afterwards (below, v. 10), "ulcers, boils, broke forth [*shehin ava'bu'ot pore'ah*] in the people and in the animals."

The expression *shehin pore'ah* is analogous to *tsara'at pore'ah*, "leprosy, sprouting forth" (Lev. 13:42, 57), meaning that it springs up without an external cause, or that it springs up repeatedly, and is difficult to heal.

**boils** *(ava'bu'ot).* This term explains what the *shehin* was; its root is *bu'a* or *nava* ("to bubble"), for the *ava'bu'ot* resembled a spring (*mabbua*) from which a fluid exuded. Eichhorn said that these were the ulcers of pestilence (*vomicae pestilentiales*), and that they were a natural phenomenon that was common in Egypt. Rosenmueller fittingly responded that the *shehin* recorded here was not a fatal affliction, for if it had been, Moses would not have refrained from saying so. Further proof is afforded by Moses' statement to Pharaoh, "Now at this time I would have extended My hand and struck you… with pestilence…" (v. 15), which indicates that God had [in fact] not sent them a [fatal] pestilence.

**9:10. And they took the furnace soot and, having presented themselves to Pharaoh, Moses scattered it through the air; and (at once) ulcers, boils, broke forth in the people and in the animals.**
**9:11. The sorcerers could not remain before Moses, by reason of the ulcers, for the ulcers were in the sorcerers and in all the Egyptians.**

*The sorcerers could not remain before Moses.* Apparently the sorcerers, even if they were not performing any act with their arcane arts—as in the case of the fatality and the mixture—always stood before Moses when he was speaking with Pharaoh, in order to scrutinize his words and actions and to cast doubt on them. Now, however, in the case of the ulcers, they could not remain standing before him, since the plague afflicted their own bodies (Abravanel).

**9:12. But the Lord rendered Pharaoh's heart strong [obstinate], and he did not pay heed to them, as the Lord had predicted to Moses.**
**9:13. Then the Lord said to Moses, "Having risen tomorrow morning, present yourself to Pharaoh, and say to him, 'So says the Lord, God of the Hebrews: "Let My people go to render Me worship.**
**9:14. ""For this time I am about to send all My scourges to your heart, and in your servants and in your people, so that you know that there is no equal to Me in all the land.**

*all My scourges.* This refers to the hail (below, v. 18); since it destroyed the grain and caused famine, it was more severe than all the [previous] plagues, and they were all included in it. This is what Rashi meant [in his comment on this verse], in saying that the plague of *batsoret* ("famine") was equal to all the plagues. This is the reading [of Rashi's comment] in the Lisbon edition and in many manuscripts, and this is also the correct reading according to the author of *Sefer ha-Zikkaron*, rather than "the plague of *bekhorot* [firstborns]" which has no relevance here. See also Mizrahi.[22]

*to your heart.* He did not say "in you," as he said, "in your servants and in your people," for a plague of famine would not affect the king, who would lack no food; but it would touch his heart, for he would be troubled by his people's misfortune (my student, Rabbi Moses Ehrenreich).

**9:15. ""Now at this time I would have extended My hand and struck you and your people with pestilence, and you would have disappeared from the earth.**

*Now at this time I would have extended* (ki attah shalaḥti). "It would have been fitting for Me to do so," on the model of:

---

22. As Chavel notes (*Perushei Rashi al ha-Torah*, p. 197), Mizrahi favored the reading *bakkurot* ("first fruits"), since the hail struck only the spring crops. Both Chavel and Rosenbaum and Silbermann (*Pentateuch With Rashi's Commetary*, p. 235) also mention the alternate reading *batsoret*.

- "They should have spoken [*dabber yedabberu*] at first, saying, 'Would they ask [for peace] in Avel?'" (2 Sam. 20:18);
- "You should have eaten [*akhol tokhelu*] it in a holy place" (Lev. 10:18).

See also my comments on Isa. 2:9 and Ezek. 20:25.[23]

**9:16. ""But it is for this that I let you exist, for the purpose (that is) of making you see My power, and so that My name may be celebrated through all the earth.**
**9:17. ""Are you, then, still showing yourself haughty against My people, not wanting (to give in) to let them go?**

***showing yourself haughty against My people*** *(mistolel be-ammi)*. Exalting yourself and acting proudly; the Hebrew is related to, "Extol [*sollu*] Him that rides upon the skies" (Ps. 68:5); "Extol her [*salseleha*], and she will exalt you" (Prov. 4:8); and also the word *mesillah* ("roadway") (Kimhi, [*Shorashim*] at the root *salal*), so called because roads are "raised up" in order to straighten them (not because stones and obstacles are "lifted off" them, as per Kimhi). However, the expression is still difficult, for it would have been proper to say *mistolel al ammi* and not *be-ammi*. Therefore I say that this word includes another concept that derives from haughtiness, that is, arrogance, evildoing, and harshness toward inferiors (*tyrannus*), as Onkelos translated, *at kevish leih le-ammi* ("you are oppressing My people").

This verse is in the conditional: "If you are still showing yourself haughty... [then I will make the hail fall]." Otherwise, it is the equivalent of, "If so, are you still holding fast to your position?"

**9:18. ""Behold, tomorrow at this time I will cause to rain down an exceedingly grave hail, like to which there has not been in Egypt, from the day that it was founded until now.**

***it was founded*** *(hivvasedah)*. This expression is used for the beginning of the settlement of the land of Egypt, for the Nile floods it every year, and the land was not fit for habitation until it was "founded" [i.e., embanked] by means of works specially adapted to the purpose. Similarly, with respect to the land

---

23. On the phrase *ve-al tissa lahem* in Isa. 2:9, Shadal comments that it means, "You should not have forgiven them." Similarly, he interprets the phrase *ve-gam ani natatti lahem ḥukkim lo tovim* (Ezek. 20:25) to mean, "I should have given them illogical and unhelpful laws"; his comment there cross-refers to the present verse.

of the Chaldeans, which was inundated by the waters of the Euphrates, it was said, "When Assyria founded it [*yesadah*] for shipmen" (Isa. 23:13, and see my comment thereon [which cross-refers to this verse and echoes the observations made here]). So also the city of Venice was founded upon the waters, and to this day, the streets that are situated at the water's edge in that city are called *fondamenta*, meaning "foundations."

***hivvasedah.*** If this word were an infinitive (in which case the final letter *he* would properly have been marked with a *mappik* [to indicate that the *he* was a suffix, and that the word meant "its founding"]), the preceding words would properly have been *le-min yom* ("from the day of") rather than *le-min ha-yom* ("from the day that"). Thus the word must be in the past tense. If it were in the *nif'al* conjugation, the proper form would have been *nosedah*, and if it were in the *hitpa'el*, the proper form would have been *hityassedah*, with the letter *samekh* marked with a *dagesh*; if it were in the *af'el*, it would have been *husdah*. Thus the word must be in the *hinfa'el* conjugation, which is the "father" of the *nif'al* and the "son" of the *hitpe'il*, an example of the latter being *hitpakedu* (Judg. 20:15).

The Masoretes undoubtedly erred in including this word in a list of eighteen words that lack a *mappik he*, that is, words that should have been marked with a *mappik* but were not. Nevertheless, this is proof of their clean hands, for they did not reach out to emend these words as a matter of logic and add the *mappik* that they thought should have been present.

**9:19. ""Now then, send and have sheltered your cattle and as much as you have in the field. All of the people and animals that will be found in the field and will not be withdrawn to the house will be struck by the hail, and they will die.""**

***have sheltered*** *(ha'ez)*. The imperative of the root *oz* in the *hif'il* conjugation, indicating a gathering into a guarded place. Cf., "The inhabitants of Gibeon flee to cover [*he'izu*]" (Isa. 10:31); "Put yourselves under cover [*ha'izu*], you children of Benjamin" (Jer. 6:1).

It is strange that God should have given advice to Pharaoh as to how to be saved from the plague, for if all the Egyptians had feared the word of God, they would all have been saved. Nachmanides answered this difficulty by saying that the main purpose of the plague was to destroy the produce of the soil, not to kill the people or the animals, and so He showed the sinners how to save themselves from the hail. My student Joseph Jarè responds that this warning could not have spread throughout Egypt, since the hail was to come the next day, and in fact it seems that the warning was made known only to Pharaoh's servants who were at his side and heard Moses' words, for it says, "One who, among Pharaoh's servants, feared the word of the Lord caused his own servants and animals to flee into the houses" (next v.); however, the rest of the Egyptians knew nothing of this. If so, Nachmanides' answer is insufficient, and likewise the words of Wessely (in *Hokhmat Shelomoh*, p. 106), cited in Reggio's commentary, are not sufficient,[24] since the warning was not made known to most of the Egyptians.

Abravanel wrote that this verse was not part of God's words, but that Moses, in order to ingratiate himself with the wicked, gave Pharaoh this advice as if he were his friend. I say, however, that here there is neither a warning nor advice. Rather, when Moses said, "Behold, tomorrow at this time I will cause to rain down an exceedingly grave hail, like to which there has not been," Pharaoh's servants undoubtedly heard his words; if they believed that there was substance to his words, they would have hastened to have their cattle and servants flee indoors without any warning from Moses. God, Who knew that some of Pharaoh's servants believed in Moses (these are the ones who later said, "Do you not yet understand that Egypt is destroyed?" (Exod. 10:7)), anticipated this and said to Pharaoh, "The choice is yours to be saved in part from this plague, for this is why I tell you that the plague will occur tomorrow and not today." Indeed, God so decreed in order that there would be a distinction between those who feared Him and those who did not, so that this distinction would be impressed upon the hearts of the Israelites, and that even the Egyptians, when retelling the events of that year, would record that if a man feared the word of God, his cattle and his men were saved from the hail.

**9:20. One who, among Pharaoh's servants, feared the word of the Lord caused his own servants and animals to flee [that is, withdrew them promptly] into the houses.**
**9:21. One, however, who did not set his mind to the word of the Lord abandoned his own servants and animals in the field.**
**9:22. And the Lord said to Moses, "Stretch forth your arm toward the heaven, and let there be hail in all the country of Egypt, on the people, on the animals, and on all the vegetation of the field, in the land of Egypt."**

***Stretch forth your arm.*** With your staff (Ibn Ezra).

---

24. Reggio said that God told the Egyptians that their salvation from the hail depended on their free choice, so as to teach them that God loves those who do right and punishes those who do wrong.

# Shadal on Exodus

**9:23. And Moses stretched forth his staff toward the heaven, and the Lord sent thunders and hail, and fire ran down toward the earth; the Lord, that is, made hail rain upon the country of Egypt.**

***and fire ran down*** *(va-tihalakh).* Lightning and "arrows of God" (thunderbolts). The vocalization *tihalakh* is unusual; cf., "And their tongue walks [*tihalakh*] through the earth" (Ps. 73:9). The proper form would have been *tehelakh* or *tahalakh*, or *tehallekh* or *telekh*.

**9:24. There was hail, and a fire catching in itself [that is, not fed by anything] was in the midst of the hail, which was exceedingly grave, like to which there was not in all the land of Egypt, ever since it had become an inhabited country.**

***and a fire catching in itself*** *(mitlakkaḥat).* Cf. Ezek. 1:4, "A great cloud, with a fire flashing up [*mitlakkaḥat*]." Wessely interpreted this in the sense of *aḥizah* ("catching," "taking hold"), i.e., that the fire caught in itself and did not need to catch in something else as our [normal] fire does; this is correct. He read the phrase against the accents [i.e., disregarding the disjunctive *zakef gadol* separating the words *esh*, "fire," and *mitlakkaḥat*], i.e., "in the midst of the hail there was fire catching in itself." However, it is also possible to interpret the phrase in conformance with the accents: "and fire was catching in itself in the midst of the hail." See also Pliny [*Natural History*], Book II, ch. 49, and Seneca, *Naturales Quaestiones,* Book 5, ch. 13 (Clericus).[25]

***ever since it had become an inhabited country*** *(me-az hayetah le-goi).* See *Bikkurei ha-Ittim* 5587 (1826), p. 174.[26]

---

25. In the Loeb edition of Pliny's *Natural History*, lightning is discussed in Book II, chapters XLIX to LVI. In ch. L, Pliny says that if a blast of wind "flared up as soon as it burst the cloud, and had fire in it, [but] did not catch fire afterwards, it is a thunderbolt [*fulmen*]." In ch. LI, Pliny claims that Egypt's excessive heat made that country "immune" from thunderbolts. In ch. LIII, he records that nine gods, including Jupiter, were said to hurl thunderbolts.

Seneca devotes an entire book (numbered Book II in the Loeb edition) within *Naturales Quaestiones* to a discussion of lightning and thunder. Chapters 12 ff. deal with "celestial fire" and the origin of lightning. In ch. 14, Seneca theorizes that lightning descends because something in the lower atmosphere "which has the capacity to attract fire is kindled by the heat of the atmosphere above it." In ch. 16, he defines a "lightning bolt" (*fulmen*) as "fire that has been compressed and hurled violently."

26. There, Shadal cites the present verse in support of the view that the word *goi*

**9:25.** The hail killed in all the country of Egypt whatever there was in the field, men and animals; it struck also all the grass of the fields, and all the trees of the fields it broke.

**9:26.** Only in the country of Goshen, where the children of Israel were, there was no hail.

**9:27.** Pharaoh, having sent to call Moses and Aaron, said to them, "I have sinned, (I see it) finally. The Lord is the One Who is right, and I and my people are at fault.

**I have sinned… finally** *(ha-pa'am*, lit., "the time"). He did not sin this time any more than he had at other times; rather, *ha-pa'am* is to be understood as in, "This one finally [*ha-pa'am*] is bone of my bones and flesh of my flesh" (Gen. 2:23). It means, "Finally, I see that I have sinned."

***and I and my people are at fault.*** The people, too, had sinned, for Pharaoh had consulted with them from the beginning and said, "Here the people of the Israelites is [making itself] more numerous and stronger than we" (Exod. 1:9). If they had not been at fault, they would have tried to divert his anger from its destructive goal, but they said nothing to him. Instead, they agreed with him at once, and "they" (not Pharaoh) "set up over that (people) commissioners of levy" (Exod. 1:11). Now we see that the midwives, for all their weakness, did not do what Pharaoh had commanded them, nor did he punish them. How much more so could the entire people have annulled his decrees or softened them.

**9:28.** "Pray to the Lord, and let the thunders of God and the hail cease; and I will let you go, nor will you be detained any further."

***and let… cease*** *(ve-rav)*. A past-tense verb converted [by the conjunctive prefix *ve-*] into the future tense, meaning "and it will be enough," i.e., "it will cease."

**9:29.** And Moses said to him, "When I will have gone out of the city, I will stretch forth my palms toward the Lord, (and at once) the thunders will cease, and the hail will be no more, so that you may know that the earth is the Lord's.

---

originally referred to land rather than people and was derived from *gai* ("valley"). He refers to the same article in his comment on the phrase *le-mishpehotam be-goyeihem* in Gen. 10:5, where he says that *be-goyeihem* could be translated as "in the lands of their habitation."

# Shadal on Exodus

***When I will have gone out of the city.*** Perhaps the hail was not in the city but in the fields, and thus Pharaoh's messengers had been able to go and summon Moses and Aaron. Therefore, Moses said, "When I will have gone out of the city" (R. Isaac Pardo), for such was their custom, to look upon the thing that they were praying about; cf., "Isaac made supplication to the Lord regarding (*le-nokhah*, lit., "opposite") his wife" [Gen. 25:21].[27]

**9:30. "But you and your servants, I know that you will not yet fear the Lord God."**

***you will not yet fear*** *(terem tir'un)* — i.e., "you will still not fear" (see Rashi) [who comments that *terem* should be understood as *adayin lo* ("not yet") rather than "before"]. Ibn Ezra wrote that Rashi interpreted *terem* as the equivalent of *lo* ("not"), but perhaps this is a scribal error, for in fact Ibn Ezra, in expressing an alternate view (in his short commentary to Exodus) attributed this interpretation not to Rashi, but to R. Judah the Spanish grammarian.

**9:31. Meanwhile, the flax and the barley had been struck, for the barley was almost ripe, and the flax was on the stalk.**

***on the stalk*** *(giv'ol).* The Hebrew is derived from *gavia* ("chalice," "cup") and is the equivalent of the floral term *calix* [or "calyx," i.e., a flower's cup-like sepals]. This was the opinion of Gesenius, who cited proof from R. Ovadiah Bertinoro, who commented on the phrase *giv'olim she-lo gamelu* (*Parah* 11:7), "when the flower is within its cup before it blossoms." Expressing the same opinion were R. Parhon ("*giv'ol* – a flower that has not yet put forth its bud"), and R. Jonah [ibn Janah] and R. Judah ben Kuraish in their Arabic books in manuscript.

**9:32. The wheat and the spelt had not been struck, for they are later.**
**9:33. Moses came forth from Pharaoh outside the city, and he stretched forth his palms toward the Lord; and (at once) the thunders and the hail ceased, and the rain did not drop to the earth.**

***did not drop*** *(lo nittakh).* The Hebrew indicates a pouring or falling of a liquid (like the word *nasakh*), as in, "Until water was poured [*nittakh*] upon them from heaven" (2 Sam. 21:10). The meaning is that not even a little rain

---

27. There, Shadal comments that *le-nokhah* is to be understood literally, and he cross-refers to the present verse.

fell, for along with the hail there had indeed been rain, as it subsequently says [next v.], "the rain… had ceased."

**9:34. And Pharaoh, having seen that the rain and the hail and the thunders had ceased, continued to sin, and he rendered his own heart obstinate, he as well as his servants.**
**9:35. Pharaoh's heart having been made strong, he did not let the children of Israel go, as the Lord had predicted through Moses.**

# *Bo*

*The final plagues • The paschal sacrifice • "Their dough, not yet leavened" • The fertility of the Hebrews • "A night awaited by the Lord" • "An insignia on your arm"*

**10:1. Then the Lord said to Moses, "Go to Pharaoh, for I have rendered his heart and that of his servants obstinate, in order to perform these wonders of Mine in their midst.**

**Go to Pharaoh.** For I wish to strike Egypt with more plagues, as it was for this reason that I rendered his heart obstinate.

**10:2. "And in order that you should tell your children and grandchildren how I trifled with the Egyptians, and the wonders that I carried out in them; and you will know that I am the Lord."**

***I trifled with** (hit'allalti be-) **the Egyptians.** Compare:

- "Because you are mocking me [*hit'allat bi*]" (Num. 22:29).
- "And they abused her [*va-yit'allelu vah*] all the night" (Judg. 19:25).
- "When He had made a mock of them [*hit'allel ba-hem*] [the Egyptians]" (1 Sam. 6:6).
- "[Lest they come] and make a mock of me [*ve-hit'allelu vi*]" (1 Sam. 31:4).

# *Bo*

- "Lest they deliver me into their hand, and they mock me [*ve-hit'allelu vi*]" (Jer. 38:19).

All these examples, followed as here with the preposition *be-*, indicate injury connected with shame. The verb *hit'olel* is, however, found without a *be-* following, and it indicates action, as in, "To be occupied [*le-hit'olel*] in deeds of wickedness" (Ps. 141:4).

It seems to me that *le-hit'allel be-* has the basic meaning of "having one's way with" someone, that is, to that person's misfortune (as the preposition *be-* often denotes), and the *hitpa'el* verb form indicates this, just as *hit'hallekh* [the *hitpa'el* form of *halakh*, "to go"] means "to go here and there at one's will," without going in any single, fixed direction. *Hit'allel be-* may be translated [in Italian] as *malmenare* ("to abuse").[1]

**10:3. Moses and Aaron, having come to Pharaoh, said to him, "Thus says the Lord, God of the Hebrews: 'Until when will you refuse to yield before Me? Let My people go to render Me worship.**

***to yield*** *(le-anot).* The Hebrew is the equivalent of *le-he'anot*, in the *nif'al*, and means, "to yield"; it is related to *oni* ("affliction") and *anavah* ("humility"). Cf., "He was oppressed, though he humbled himself [*ve-hu na'aneh*]" (Isa. 53:7); see my comment there.[2] Perhaps the proper reading would have been *la-anot*, in the *kal*, as in, "I am greatly afflicted [*aniti*]" (Ps. 116:10); "Nor will he abase himself [*ya'aneh*] for the noise of them" (Isa. 31:4).

**10:4. "'For if you refuse to let My people go, behold, tomorrow I will bring the locusts into your territory.**

***the locusts.*** This plague is found in Egypt only occasionally. Eichhorn said that because locusts travel in formation like troops, with the vanguard in front and the rearguard behind, Moses saw the vanguard and understood that the locusts would arrive the next day. Rosenmueller fittingly responded that it would have been unlikely for Moses to have been the only one in all of Egypt who saw this, and if others in Egypt had seen it, they would have realized that nothing miraculous was occurring.

---

1. Here, however, Shadal's Italian translation of *hit'allalti be-* employs a different term, *mi trastullai con* ("I 'trifled' or 'amused myself' with").
2. Shadal interprets *ve-hu na'aneh* as "and he did not resist, but he bore it with humility [*anavah*]." His comment cross-refers to the present verse.

*into your territory (bi-gevulekha*, lit., "in your border"). See above, 7:27.

**10:5.** "'They will cover the sight of the earth, so that the earth will not be able to be seen, and they will eat the scarce residue that remained to you after the hail, and they will despoil all the trees that are sprouting to you from the field.

***the scarce residue*** *(yeter ha-peleitah)*. The entire residue was but little.

**10:6.** "'Your houses, the houses of all your servants, and the houses of all the Egyptians will be full of them, a thing that neither your fathers nor your grandfathers saw, since they existed on the land until this day.'" Then, having turned away, he went forth from Pharaoh.
**10:7.** But the servants of Pharaoh said to him, "Until when must that man be a stumbling block for us [to cause us harm]? Let that people go to render worship to the Lord their God. Do you not yet understand that (otherwise) Egypt is lost?"
**10:8.** Then Moses and Aaron were made to return to Pharaoh, who said to them, "Go to render worship to the Lord your God. (But) who are those who are to go?"

***were made to return*** *(va-yushav et)*. See *Bikkurei ha-Ittim* 5587 (1826), p. 178.[3]

**10:9.** And Moses said, "We will go with our young and our old, with our sons, with our daughters, with our flocks and cattle we will go, for we must celebrate a feast to the Lord."
**10:10.** But he said to them, "So may the Lord help you, as I will let you go together with your children! Consider that some evil threatens you.

***that some evil threatens you*** *(ki ra'ah neged peneikhem*, lit., "that evil is before your faces"). On the model of, *ki tov neged ḥasidekha*, "for good awaits Your pious ones" (Ps. 52:11); that is, "See that evil will come to you, for if you persist in seeking to have your entire people go, the result will be not only that I will not let you go, but that I will punish you in anger, since I

---

3. There (actually p. 179), Shadal explains that *va-yushav* (which appears to mean "he was returned") is actually a transitive and impersonal verb ("one caused to return"), with "Moses and Aaron" as the direct objects, as indicated by the particle *et*.

will then know for sure that your intention was to flee and to mock me" (this also seems to be Ibn Ezra's interpretation).

**10:11.** **"Not so, but let (only) the men [the adult males] go, and render worship to the Lord, for that is the thing that you are seeking." And he expelled them from the presence of Pharaoh.**
**10:12. Then the Lord said to Moses, "Stretch forth your arm over the country of Egypt, for the locusts (so that they may come), and let them attack the country of Egypt and eat all the vegetation of the land, all that the hail has left to put forth."**
**10:13. And Moses stretched forth his staff over the country of Egypt, and the Lord caused an east wind to come in the country all that day and all the night; and when it was (the next) morning the east wind had borne the locusts.**

*an east wind* (*ruaḥ kadim*). If it was indeed an east wind, the locusts came from Arabia, but locusts are more common in the land of Cush, and accordingly the wind should have been a south wind. According to Bochart, following the Alexandrian translation, this *ruaḥ kadim* was a south wind. Rosenmueller said that perhaps it was a southeasterly wind, and he cited support from Psalm 78:26, "He caused the east wind [*kadim*] to set forth in heaven, and by His power He brought on the south wind"—for the wind that brought the quails [in the Sinai desert] was called both "east" and "south," i.e., southeasterly.

It should not be said that *kadim* is [merely] a term for a strong wind from any direction, for below (v. 19) it is expressly stated that a "west wind" was the opposite of this wind. Therefore one should not insist that the locusts came from the land of Cush, for it was not beyond God's power to bring them from Arabia.

**10:14. The locusts attacked all the country of Egypt, and they alighted on all the territory of Egypt. They were exceedingly numerous; before them there had not been such a quantity of locusts, nor will there be the like afterward.**

*Before… afterward.* This was said by way of poetic expression and hyperbole; cf., Joel 2:2 ["There has not been ever the like, neither shall be any more after them," referring to a locust plague] (Clericus and Rosenmueller). It might be said that the expression means [only] "there had not been such a quantity *in Egypt*" (Jacob Hai Pardo), but even so, it is unlikely that Scripture would have bothered to speak [literally] about the future here and to declare that there would never be anything like it again.

**10:15. They covered the sight of all the country, so that the country was darkened, and they devoured all the vegetation of the land and all the fruits of the trees that the hail had left to put forth; and there remained nothing green in the trees, nor in the vegetables of the field, in all the land of Egypt.**

*so that the country was darkened.* A similar event was seen by Forskal in Egypt in 1761: "While they flew on high in marching formation, from far away the air suggested the appearance of smoke."

**10:16. Pharaoh hastened to call Moses and Aaron, and he said, "I have sinned against the Lord your God, and against you.**
**10:17. "Now then, please pardon my sin this one time, and pray to the Lord your God, that He may remove from me this only death [this only plague]."**
**10:18. Moses, having exited from Pharaoh, prayed to the Lord.**
**10:19. And the Lord raised a contrary western wind, exceedingly strong, which carried away the locusts and sank them in the Red Sea. Not one locust remained in all the territory of Egypt.**
**10:20. But the Lord rendered Pharaoh's heart strong, and he did not let the children of Israel go.**
**10:21. Then the Lord said to Moses, "Stretch forth your arm toward the heaven, and let there be darkness in the country of Egypt, and let one go groping in the darkness."**

*and let one go groping in the darkness* (ve-yamesh ḥoshekh). There are those [e.g., Rashi] who explained this as the equivalent of *ve-ya'amesh,* from *emesh,* meaning "night" or "dark," but it would make no sense to say, "And let the darkness be dark." Others derived *ve-yamesh* from *mashash* ("to feel," "to grope"), and this is correct, but they said that the air became so thick that it could be felt.

The proper explanation is that this is a poetic expression, like "They grope in the dark [*yemasheshu ḥoshekh*] without light" (Job 12:25), where the Hebrew is the equivalent of *yemasheshu ba-ḥoshekh* [i.e., the word "in" is understood]. Similarly, the Jerusalem Targum has *vi-y'hon memashmeshin ba-ḥashokha* ("and let them grope in the darkness") (as I have since found in Clericus).

## Bo

Eichhorn attributed this plague to a strong, hot, and destructive wind which in Arabic is called *samum* [*simoom*] and in Turkish *samiel*, and which blows in Egypt from Passover to Shavuot, during those fifty days which are still called *ḥamsin* ("fifty") by them; during that time, people are forced to sit in their houses and not go outside. However, none of this does Eichhorn any good, for it is not in this wind's nature to produce a darkness so complete that people cannot see one another in their house (see v. 23 below). We do find that a great darkness sometimes occurred in Egypt, but this was always the result of a great windstorm and tempest, and here nothing if this kind is mentioned.

**10:22. Moses stretched forth his arm toward the heaven, and there was somber darkness in all the country of Egypt for three days.**
**10:23. They did not see one another, and they did not move from where they were [that is, they did not leave the house] for three days; but the children of Israel all had light in their residences [in the land of Goshen].**

*and they did not move from where they were (ve-lo kamu ish mi-taḥtav).* They did not leave their houses; cf., "Remain where you are [*shevu ish taḥtav*], let no one go forth from his place on the seventh day" (Exod.16:29) (Rashbam, Ibn Ezra, Mendelssohn, and Rosenmueller).[4]

*but the children of Israel all had light in their residences.* In the land of their residence.

**10:24. Then Pharaoh called Moses, and he said, "Go render worship to the Lord, but let your flocks and cattle remain here; let your offspring also go with you."**

*Then Pharaoh called (va-yikra,* lit., "and [he] called"). At the end of the three days of darkness.

**10:25. And Moses said, "You yourself, rather, will place animals at our disposition, to make of them sacrifices and burnt offerings to the Lord our God.**
**10:26. "And our cattle, too, will come with us, not a hoof will remain of them, for we will have to make use of them to render worship to the Lord our God; and we do not know what worship we must render to the**

---

4. *Contra* Rashi, who comments that the Egyptians literally could not move from their standing or sitting positions.

Lord [what quality and quantity of sacrifices we must make], until we arrive there."

***what worship we must render to the Lord.*** What sort of worship He may command of us; we do not know what kind [of animals] and how many of each kind He will command us to sacrifice (Ibn Ezra). Rashi's statement, "Perhaps He will demand more than we have," means that "we will not be able to bring only some of our cattle and leave some behind, lest He demand more than we will have taken with us."

**10:27. But the Lord rendered Pharaoh's heart strong, and he did not consent to let them go.**
**10:28. Pharaoh said to him, "Go away from me; guard yourself from coming before me any more, for on the day that you come before me, you will die."**
**10:29. And Moses said, "You have spoken well; I will come before you no more."**

**11:1. But the Lord had said to Moses, "Yet one more scourge will I bring upon Pharaoh and upon Egypt, then he will let you go from here; rather, having given you permission to go, he will completely expel you from here.**

***But the Lord had said to Moses*** *(va-yomer YHVH el Mosheh*, lit., "And the Lord said to Moses"). These three verses (vv. 1-3) are a kind of parenthetical statement, while the statement beginning "Near midnight" (v. 4) is the continuation of Moses' response, "I will come before you no more." Here, *va-yomer YHVH* means, "the Lord had said," i.e., before Moses went to Pharaoh at this time, God had informed him about the plague of the firstborn. Thus it was that Moses said to Pharaoh, "I will come before you no more," for he knew that Pharaoh would come to him (Exod. 12:31).

***having given you permission to go.*** "After he permits you to go, this will not suffice him, but he will drive you out and press you to hurry away."

***completely*** *(kalah)*. "All of you, men, women, children, and cattle" (Rashbam). The meaning is that Pharaoh would drive them away permanently, for it was always his intention that they would come back after worshipping their God, as he said to them, "And go render worship to the Lord as you said" (Exod. 12:31). See also my comment on Gen. 3:23.[5]

---

5. There, on the word *va-yshallehehu* ("and He sent him out"), Shadal explains

*Bo*

**11:2. "Speak to the people, so that they ask each man of his own friend, and each woman of her own friend, furnishings of silver and gold."**

*Speak to the people.* When God said to Moses, "Yet one more scourge will I bring upon Pharaoh" (v. 1), He also said this (even though He had already told this to him in Midian [Exod. 3:22]) in order to remind him and to spur him on at the time that the deed was to take place, and additionally (as per Abravanel) in order that they would ask of the Egyptians prior to the plague of the firstborn, which was to be a time of panic.

**11:3. The Lord then put the people in favor among the Egyptians; and Moses, too, in particular was in great consideration in the country of Egypt, among Pharaoh's servants and among the people.**

*The Lord then put, etc.* After relating this command, the Torah adds that God helped His people in this matter, as He had previously said, "And I will put this people in favor in the eyes of the Egyptians" (Exod. 3:21). When the Egyptians saw the great plagues and wonders that had come upon them at Moses' word with regard to Israel, they began to recognize Israel's merit in that this people had a powerful, redeeming God, and they began to understand the injustice that they had done to them, and that the Israelites were human beings like themselves. It is in fact the way of people flushed with success to view the oppressed poor as if they were not fellow human beings, and to see no wrong in adding to their suffering. However, when such miserable people begin to rise out of the depths to some degree, then the successful people begin to ascribe importance to them and to show them mercy and love; cf., "Now after these things, the wife of his master turned her eyes toward Joseph" (Gen. 39:7).

**11:4. Then Moses added, "So says the Lord: 'Near midnight I will go forth in the midst of Egypt.**

*Near midnight (ka-ḥatsot ha-lailah). Hatsot* is a noun, as in Ps. 119:62 ["In a moment they die, even at midnight *(va-ḥatsot lailah)*]." The prefix *ba-* that would properly have followed the prefix *ka-* is missing [but understood], and thus the proper form would have been *ke-va-hatsot ha-lailah*, that is, "near midnight." Compare:

---

that the verb *shillaḥ*, in the *pi'el*, means to cause a person to wander wherever he wishes. A form of the same verb, *ke-shalleḥo* ("having given you permission to go") is used in the present verse.

- "You have broken [the oppressor's rod] as in the day of [*ke-yom*] Midian" (Isa. 9:3), where *ke-yom* is the equivalent of *ki-ve-yom*.
- "And I will purge away your dross as with lye [*ka-bor*]" (Isa. 1:25), instead of *ke-va-bor*.
- "Awake, as in the days [*ki-y'mei*] of old" (Isa. 51:9), instead of *ke-vi-y'mei*.
- "And I will build it as in the days [*ki-y'mei*] of old" (Amos 9:11) (same).
- "As in the days [*ki-y'mei*] of Gibeah" (Hosea 9:9) (same).
- "As in the days *(ki-y'mei)* of the appointed season (Hosea 12:10) (same).
- "As through a wide breach [*ke-ferets*] they come" (Job 30:14), instead of *ki-ve-ferets*.
- "And she returns to her father's house, as in her childhood [*ki-ne'ureha*]" (Lev. 22:13), instead of *ke-vi-ne'ureha*.

**11:5.** "'**And every firstborn in the country of Egypt will die, from Pharaoh's firstborn, destined to sit on his throne, to the maidservant's firstborn, who is behind the millstones [to turn the wheel of the mill], as well as every firstborn of the animals.**

**destined to sit** *(ha-yoshev,* lit., "who sits") — who was to have sat in the future.

**behind the millstones** — who pushes the beam that makes the millstones turn.[6]

**11.6.** "'**And there will be in Egypt great cries, like which there have never been, nor will there ever be again.**

**like which** *(asher kamohu).* The Hebrew refers back to *lailah* ("night"), not to *tse'akah* ("cries"), i.e., "such that, as on that night, there has never been a cry" (Sforno).[7]

---

6. Modern archeology shows that the mills of this period operated by passing the upper millstone back and forth over the lower stone. It was only at the end of the Persian period that the turning upper millstone—which revolved on an axis over the stationary lower millstone—came into use. See *Encyclopaedia Judaica*, s.v. "Millstone."

7. This comment seems to be based on the fact that *kamohu* has a masculine suffix, which should refer to a masculine noun such as *lailah*, rather than a feminine noun such as *tse'akah*. In any case, this comment obviously takes a different approach from that of the translation. It also differs somewhat from Sforno's comment, which interprets the phase as "there has never been such a cry on a night like that," i.e., a peaceful night as opposed to a wartime night.

## *Bo*

**11:7. "'But among all the children of Israel not even a dog will whet its tongue; neither man nor beast (will die), so that you may know that the Lord makes a distinction between the Egyptians and the Israelites.'**

*not even a dog will whet its tongue.* There will be no outcry among Israel, and everything that belongs to Israel will remain quiet; even the dogs will not bark, though when they hear shouting they [normally] bark.

*whet (yeḥerats).* The Hebrew denotes "sharpening"; see Rashi and Gesenius.[8]

*neither man nor beast.* Neither man nor beast will die, and thus there will be no outcry in Israel; the Hebrew is an elliptical phrase. Clericus understood it to mean that neither man nor beast would cry out, but in my view, a man would [normally] cry out over the death of his kin, but a beast would not.

*neither man (le-me-ish)* [For a similar grammatical form] compare "both great *(le-mi-gadol)* and small" (Esth. 1:5).

**11:8. "And all these servants of yours will come to me, and they will bow to me, saying, 'Go you forth, and all the people that follow you,' and then I will go forth." And (having so said) he went forth from Pharaoh, kindled with anger.**

**11:9. And the Lord said to Moses, "Pharaoh will not pay heed to you, so that My wonders may be increased (even more) in the country of Egypt."**

*And the Lord said.* Mendelssohn and Rosenmueller understood this to mean "the Lord had said," but this is unnecessary. Rather, after Moses informed Pharaoh about the plague of the firstborn, God told Moses that even this warning would not avail, for only when the plague came would Pharaoh listen to them (my student, R. [Joseph] Shabbetai Basevi).

**11:10. So Moses and Aaron did all these wonders in Pharaoh's presence; but the Lord rendered Pharaoh's heart strong, and he did not allow the children of Israel to go out of his land.**

---

8. Rashi cites other biblical verses in support of this interpretation. In the Gesenius *Lexicon*, the root *ḥarats* is translated as "to sharpen" or "to cut to a point," and the phrase here is interpreted to mean "not a dog shall sharpen (point) his tongue," i.e., "no one shall even slightly offend or provoke them."

## Shadal on Exodus

***So Moses and Aaron did,*** *etc.* Because the account of Moses and Aaron's mission to Pharaoh ends here—for they did not come before him again—this is said by way of conclusion.

**12:2. "This month is for you the head of the months; it must be for you the first among the months of the year.**

***the head of the months; it must be for you the first,*** *etc.* So that Iyyar would be called the second month, and so the rest [of the months would be numbered thereafter], even though they already considered the beginning of the year to be in Tishrei, and so it remained afterwards, as it says, "And the festival of gathering [Sukkot] at the going out of the year" (Exod. 23:16). Similarly, the jubilee year began on the tenth day of the "seventh" month [Tishrei]. This [numbering of the months] was in commemoration of the redemption from Egypt. God did not command Moses and Aaron to tell Israel about this; rather, He was letting them know that the people would be redeemed during that month [Nisan]. God told them that after the people left the house of bondage, they would commemorate the month of their redemption by calling it "the first month."

**12:3. "Speak to all the Community of Israel, saying that on the tenth of this month they should provide themselves, each one (for himself), a lamb [or kid] for each family, [or, if the family occupies more than one house] a lamb for every house.**

***Speak to all the Community of Israel, saying*** *(lemor).* My student, Joseph Jarè, raised the difficulty that the word *lemor* is superfluous, because [this word generally introduces a direct address, but] the phrase "they should provide themselves" is not in the second person. However, it seems to me that *lemor* is written so that it should not be thought that Moses and Aaron were to deliver this command on the tenth of the month ("Speak to all the community of Israel on the tenth of the month").

The accentuators, however, seeing that the word *lemor* did not go well with the word *ve-yikḥu* ("that they should provide"), placed the *etnaḥ* (major disjunctive) at the word *ha-zeh* [i.e., at the end of the phrase "on the tenth of this month"], so that the verse should be understood to mean, "Speak to all the Community of Israel and say these words to them on the tenth of the month." Then the verse leaves off without specifying the exact words that they were to say; rather, God told them the gist of the matter, that the people were to provide themselves with lambs, etc. This entire section is mixed [grammatically], partly in second person and partly in third person (26 Tammuz 5623 [1863]).

***they should provide for themselves, each one** (ish), etc.* That is, "they should provide for themselves a lamb for each family," but they were not to do this collectively, but rather *ish*, i.e., each one for himself.

**12:4. "If the house is too small to allow for (the consumption of) a lamb, he [the head of the family] will take it together with his neighbor, who is close to his house, having made a count of the persons. You shall take into account, for (the provision of) the lamb, each individual, according to that which he is accustomed to eat.**

***having made a count of** (be-mikhsat).* The Hebrew is derived from the root *kasah* and is similar to *mekhes* ("tribute," Num. 31:28), from the root *kasas*, which in turn yields *takhossu* ("you shall take into account," in this verse); also similar is *memer* ("bitterness," Prov. 17:25), from the root *marar*. In my opinion, from this [root *kasah*] is derived the term *yom ha-kese* ("the full moon") (Prov. 7:20). (See *Ohev Ger*, p. 116.)[9]

**12:5. "You shall provide yourself with a small animal, immaculate, male, and born within the year; either from among the lambs or from among the kids you may take it.**

***either from among the lambs**, etc.* For *seh* ("small animal") is a term denoting an individual member of the class of *tson* ("small cattle," "flocks"), which encompasses sheep and goats. Thus we find *seh kevasim ve-seh izzim* ("the lamb and the kid," Deut. 14:4).

**12:6. "You shall keep it until the fourteenth day of the month, and (on that day) all of the assembly of the Community of Israel will slaughter it, toward evening.**

***toward evening** (bein ha-arbayim,* lit., "between the evenings"). This undoubtedly means "at twilight," as per the Karaites and Ibn Ezra, for below it says, "At night [*bein ha-arbayim*] you will eat meat" (Exod. 16:12), and [in

---

9. There (pp. 113-114 in the 1895 edition), Shadal discusses the root *kasas*, which in Syriac means "rebuke" or "chastise."

the following verse] it says, "Now, at night [*ba-erev*] the quails rose up" [and the people caught them for food]. Onkelos, too, translates [*bein ha-arbayim*] as *bein shimshaya* ("at twilight").

However, the [halakhic] opinion of the Rabbis, that the time for the paschal sacrifice begins after the noon hour (Mishnah *Pesaḥim* 5:3), is also correct, for on Passover as observed by the generations [in the land of Israel], they all had to slaughter their lambs in the Temple courtyard and sprinkle the blood on the altar, and it would have been impossible to complete this ceremony during the twilight hour alone, so they began after noon. In contrast, on [the first] Passover in Egypt, each individual slaughtered the lamb in his own home, all the Israelites at the same time.[10]

**12:7. "And they will take of that blood, and they will place it on the two doorposts and on the lintel of the rooms in which they will eat it.**

***the lintel*** *(ha-mashkof)*. The root *shakaf* seems to have the basic meaning, as [does its cognate] in Arabic, of stretching something out on top of something else (Gesenius).

***the… doorposts*** *(ha-mezuzot)*. Rashi's comment that the *mezuzot* are the "upright posts" (*ha-zekufot*) (which does not appear in the Mekhilta [the halakhic Midrash which is the source of many of Rashi's comments in this chapter]) seems to have been based on a foreign [i.e., European] language, for in the Venetian dialect, doorposts are called *erte,* which means "uprights."[11]

**12:9. "Do not eat of it half raw, or boiled, (that is) cooked in water, but roasted with fire, (roasted whole) with the head, the legs, and the entrails.**

***half raw*** *(na)*. [The equivalent] in Arabic means "raw," insufficiently cooked (Rashi, Ibn Ezra, Rosenmueller, and Gesenius).

***or boiled, cooked in water*** *(u-vashel mevushal ba-mayim)*. It seems to me [that this phrase is to be interpreted] against the accents [which connect the words *u-vashel mevushal,* seemingly yielding an expression meaning

---

10. In effect, Shadal is saying that although *bein ha-arbayim* literally means "at twilight," the Rabbis were justified in construing the term for halakhic purposes (as does Rashi on this verse) as "from noon to evening."

11. The Italian expression *all'erta* ("look out," "beware," lit., "to the watchtower") is the source of the English word "alert" (Random House Dictionary).

"boiled at all"], for *bashel* is an adjective[12] ("boiled") and *mevushal ba-mayim* is its explanation ("that is, cooked in water"). This was Mendelssohn's interpretation.

**12:10. "Do not leave remains of it until the morning; and that which you let remain of it until the morning, you shall burn.**
**12:11. "And thus shall you eat it: with your loins girded, with your shoes on your feet, and with your staff in your hand; you will eat it in haste; it is the sacrifice of Passover (in homage) to the Lord.**
**12:12. "I will scour through the country of Egypt on that night, and I will strike every firstborn in the country of Egypt, of the men and of the beasts, and upon all the gods of Egypt as well I will exert punishments. I am the Lord.**

*I will scour through.* Inasmuch as this plague was to be different from all the others, in that only the firstborn were to die and, furthermore, not one of the Israelite firstborn would die, it was attributed [directly] to God, as if He were passing from house to house and distinguishing between firstborn and non-firstborn and between Egyptian and Israelite. And yet the Torah does not describe God as if He Himself were doing the striking; rather, God was passing through accompanied by the destroying angel; God would say to the destroyer, "Strike this one," and he would do so. This may be understood from that which is written below, "And He will not allow the destroyer to enter into your houses to strike" (v. 23).

The statement of the Sages [in the Passover Haggadah], "I and not an angel [will strike the firstborn]," means that the task was not delegated to any angel who could strike without a specific command from God, for He alone knows hidden things and distinguishes between firstborn and non-firstborn.

**12:13. "And the blood on the houses in which you live will serve as a countersign for you; that is, I will see the blood, and I will pass over you, and the scourge will not make a slaughter of you when I strike in the country of Egypt.**

*and the scourge will not make a slaughter of you (ve-lo yihyeh vakhem negef le-mashḥit).* "The scourge [*negef*] will not be a destroyer [*mashḥit*] among you." The prefix *le-* in *le-mashḥit* indicates the predicate; *mashḥit* does not modify *negef*, but is its predicate. Compare:

---

12. Or, in modern terminology, a stative verb.

- "And the blood… will serve as a countersign [*le-ot*]" (present verse).
- "And let them [My words] be to you for frontals [*le-totafot*]" (Deut. 11:10).
- "This will be your trimming [*le-tsitsit*]" (Num. 15:39).

**12:14. "That day will come to be commemorated by you, and you will solemnize it as a festival to the Lord. For all the ages to come, as a perpetual law, you will celebrate it.**

*That day will come to be commemorated by you* — in future generations. However, in the year they left Egypt, they were not commanded to make a festival of *matsot*, nor was *ḥamets* forbidden to them, and they did not celebrate on the first day or the seventh day [of the future holiday of Passover]; see below at v. 21.

**12:15. "For seven days you will eat unleavened bread; you will even cause it to be that on the first day there will be no leaven in your houses; for whoever, between the first and the seventh day, eats leaven, that person will be cut off from the midst of Israel [that is, that person will leave no descendants].**

*you will even cause it to be that on the first day, etc.* So that when the first day begins, the leaven will have already been removed from the houses (Ibn Ezra and Mendelssohn), the *be'ur* ("removal" or "burning" of the leaven) having taken place beforehand. However, there is no basis for interpreting "on the first day" *(ba-yom ha-rishon)* to mean "the day before" (as per the school of R. Ishmael [in the Mekhilta and *Pesaḥim* 5a] and Rashi [in his comment on the present verse]). The phrase [cited by Rashi], *rishon adam* (Job 15:7) means "the first one of the human race" [and not one born "before Adam," as Rashi maintained]; see my translation.[13] And if it is written, "Do not shed over [that is, having in the house] leavened bread the blood of My sacrifice" (Exod. 34:25), this is a separate commandment which is not included in the present verse [although R. Ishmael, followed by Rashi, regards Exod. 34:25 as proof that leaven must be removed on the day before the "first day"].

---

13. *"Nascevi forse tu il primo del genere umano? Eri tu partorito innanzi alle colline?"* ("Were you perhaps born the first of the human race? Were you delivered before the hills?" (*Il libro di Giobbe*, Trieste: 1853.)

*will be cut off (ve-nikhretah).* See at Gen. 17:14 [where Shadal comments that the punishment of *karet* consists of untimely death and childlessness, rather than banishment, as Clericus had maintained].

**12:16. "On the first day there will be a holy convocation [religious assembly], and on the seventh day there will be a holy convocation among you; no work shall be done on them; only that which is wont to be eaten by every person, that alone may be made [prepared] by you.**

*a holy convocation (mikra kodesh).* According to Rashi and others, "you shall call that day holy," i.e., on the first day, you shall perform the action of calling that day holy; in other words, that day will be holy to you. Onkelos translated *mikra* in the sense of "happening" (*mikrah*) or "event." But since we see in Isaiah the phrase "new moon and Sabbath, the calling of *mikra*" (Isa. 1:13), without the word *kodesh* ("holy"), it seems that *mikra* means a gathering of the people to celebrate a holiday, while *mikra kodesh* means a gathering and celebration of holiness, that is, for the honor of God.

The word *kara* ("to call") sometimes denotes gathering, as in, "Though a multitude of shepherds be called forth [*yikkarei*] against him" (Isa. 31:4), for people are gathered by means of calling. Similarly, the roots *tsa'ak* and *za'ak* ("to shout") are used in connection with the gathering of people, as in:

- "And Barak gathered [*va-yaz'ek*] Zebulun and Naphtali" (Judg. 4:10).
- "And Sisera gathered together [*va-yaz'ek*] all his chariots" (Judg. 4:13).
- "And the people were gathered together [*va-yitsa'aku*] after Saul" (1 Kings 13:4).

**12:17. "You shall observe (the law of) the unleavened breads, for on the same (above-mentioned) day I will cause your ranks to come out of the country of Egypt; you shall therefore observe that day in all the ages to come as a perpetual law.**
**12:18. "In the first (month), on the fourteenth of the month, you shall eat unleavened breads, until the twenty-first of the month, at night.**
**12:19: "For seven days leaven must not be found in your houses; for whoever eats a leavened thing, that person shall be cut off from the midst of the Community of Israel, whether he be a foreigner [who has embraced Judaism] or a native.**
**12:20. "Any leavened thing you shall not eat; in all your residences [in any part of your country] you shall eat unleavened breads."**

## Shadal on Exodus

**12:21. Moses called all the elders of Israel, and he said to them, "Go, take for yourselves of the flocks in proportion to your families, and slaughter the paschal sacrifice.**

*Go (mishkhu,* lit., "draw"). Cf. "All the men draw [*yimshokh*] after him" (Job 21:33); "Go and draw [*u-mashakhta*] toward mount Tabor" (Judg. 4:6) (Coccejus and Clericus).

In this section, Moses does not at all mention to Israel the matter of the eating of *matsot* and the prohibition of *hamets*, even though he had already been commanded concerning this in the previous section. The correct explanation is that God had mentioned to Moses the matter of the eating of *matsot* and the prohibition of *hamets* because He knew that they would be chased out without time for their dough to ferment, but Moses did not say any of this to them, because they would not have been able to understand why they should eat *matsot*. It was only after they came out that he specified to them (Exodus 13) the prohibition of *hamets* and the commandment of *matsot*, for then they understood that this was a reminder of the miracle that they had been expelled from Egypt without being able to linger.

However, even though Moses did not tell them [here] about the prohibition of *hamets*, it nevertheless seems that he did tell them (even if it was not so recorded) to eat the paschal sacrifice with *matsot* and bitter herbs, even if he did not tell them to eat *matsot* for seven days. Eating the paschal sacrifice with *matsot* also seems to be derived from the haste in which they were commanded to eat it. Similarly, I have since found it written by the *Baal ha-Turim* below (at v. 29), "Or perhaps it should be understood in the plain sense, that their expulsion from Egypt was the reason that they baked [their dough] as *matsot*, and if they had remained, they would have made it *hamets*, for on the [first] Passover in Egypt they were commanded to eat *matsah* on the first night only."

So also, the Ran [Rabbenu Nissim] commented[14] on the chapter *Arvei Pesahim*, "[We eat] this *matsah* to commemorate their redemption, as it says, 'From the dough... they baked... and they could not linger' (Exod. 12:39), i.e., if they had been able, they would have leavened it, for the Passover in Egypt was observed for one night and day, like *Pesah Sheni* (Num. 9:6-13), and the next day they would have been allowed to eat *hamets* and do work. Thus, if they had been able to linger, they would have leavened their dough for the needs of the day after, for they had not been warned against having

---

14. More specifically, the Ran's comment is on R. Isaac Alfasi's *Halakhot* (Alfasi, *Pesahim* 25b, s.v. *matsah*). Here Alfasi is summarizing material found in chapter 10 (*Arvei Pesahim*) of the tractate *Pesahim*, 116b.

leaven in their sight. However, because of their lack of time, they baked it as *matsah*, and to commemorate that redemption they were [subsequently] commanded to eat *matsah*."

A strong proof that they were not commanded in Egypt concerning the removal of *hamets* is found in the statement, "The people carried away on their backs their dough, not yet leavened" (below, v. 34), which happened apparently only because of their haste, in that they could not bake it because they were waiting for it to rise. If they had already been commanded concerning the *matsah*, they would have baked their dough immediately after kneading it and would not have waited for it to rise. As for the phrase, "For they were expelled from Egypt, and they could not linger, and they did not even prepare any provisions" (below, v. 39), this means that their dough had no time to rise and therefore they did not bake it [until after they left Egypt], and they had no provision to eat except for the dough.[15]

**12:22. "And having taken a bunch of hyssop, you shall infuse it in the blood that is (collected) in a basin; then you shall sprinkle the lintel and the two doorposts with the blood that is in the basin. And none of you shall go out from the door of his own house until the morning.**

***in the basin** (ba-saf)*. A vessel, cf. *sippot kesef* ("cups of silver," 2 Kings 12:14), and similarly Onkelos translates it as *be-mana* ("in a vessel of a maneh's weight"). However, Gussetius understands the term in the sense of *saf ha-sha'ar* ([Latin] *limen*, "threshold"), and so the Alexandrian translation and that of Jerome, but it seems to me that if this were so, it would have said *al ha-saf* ("on the *saf*"), not *ba-saf* ("in the *saf*").

***hyssop** (ezov)*. The Swedish scholar Hasselquist saw a type of moss called *Bryam trunclulatum* growing in the walls of Jerusalem, and he said that

---

15. The Talmud (*Pesahim* 96b) takes the view that the Israelites were forbidden to eat *hamets* on the first night and day of the original Passover. Accordingly, some commentators, including Nachmanides (on v. 39, below), explain that the Israelites intended from the start to bake their dough as *matsah*, but that they had no time to do so until after they left Egypt. However, the Ran says that the ban on eating *hamets* did not then extend to having *hamets* in one's possession, so the Israelites could have made their dough *hamets* for the next day's consumption, only they had no time to prepare it properly. Apparently the Ran takes the view that they added no leaven, but planned to let the dough ferment naturally (i.e., through the action of ambient yeast) to the extent possible. Shadal goes one step further: the people prepared their dough *with* leavening (see below at v. 39) in the vain hope that it would ferment overnight in transit.

perhaps this was the ancient *ezov* that was said to grow in a wall (Cahen). However, Gesenius identified *ezov*, as had Saadiah Gaon, R. Jonah [ibn Janah], Maimonides (comm. to *Negaim* 14:6), Kimhi, and R. Tanhum, as *origanum* ("origan," "wild marjoram") [a relative of oregano], whose aroma is pleasant.

**12:23. "And the Lord will pass to strike the Egyptians, and having seen the blood on the lintel and on the two doorposts, the Lord will pass over that door, and He will not allow the destroyer to enter into your houses to strike.**

*and He will not allow (ve-lo yitten*, lit., "and He will not give"). He will not permit. See above at 12:12.

**12:24. "You shall observe this thing as a law for you and for your children in perpetuity.**
**12:25. "Now when you have entered into the country that the Lord will give you, as He has promised, you shall observe this rite.**
**12:26. "And when your children will say to you, 'What is this rite that you have?' —**
**12:27. "You shall say, 'The sacrifice of the Passover, (in homage) to the Lord, Who passed over the houses of the children of Israel in Egypt, when He struck the Egyptians, and our houses He saved.'" The people [having heard this] bowed and prostrated themselves.**
**12:28. The children of Israel went and did so: according to that which the Lord had commanded Moses and Aaron, so they did.**
**12:29. Now at midnight, the Lord struck every firstborn in the country of Egypt, from the firstborn of Pharaoh, destined to sit on his throne, to the firstborn of the prisoners, who was in the underground house, as well as every firstborn of the animals.**

*the Lord struck every firstborn.* According to Eichhorn, they died of the disease *variolae pestiferae* ("pestilential pox") which occasionally visits Egypt and kills young men. Rosenmueller fittingly responded that it would not kill firstborns in particular. Jost expressed the opinion, by way of hint (in a book printed in Berlin 15 years ago),[16] that Moses killed the firstborns with his men by moonlight, and that the firstborns of each house had been separated from the rest of the household, for they were consecrated to their gods, and they also had with them animals that had been set aside for sacrifice.

---

16. *Allgemeine Geschichte des Israelitischen Volkes* (Berlin, 1832), p. 87.

## Bo

Let lying lips be dumb! Besides the fact that he must bring proof that the firstborns used to sit in special houses or rooms, it is impossible to understand how Moses would have dared to announce to Pharaoh in advance that every firstborn would die. Would it not have been inevitable that some of them would have kept vigil that night to see how the matter would turn out?

Furthermore, with how many men would Moses have accomplished this? He had, after all, commanded the whole [Israelite] people not to leave their houses until morning. Perhaps it might be said that the Levites were with him, but some of them would inevitably have been neighbors of members of other tribes, and since they would join each other to eat the Passover sacrifice, some Israelite could not have failed to notice that some Levite was not at home.

Also, who could imagine that among the Israelites were men who were so brave as to enter the houses of their masters, the Egyptians, and even Pharaoh's house, to kill their firstborn? We see how fainthearted they were, for they did not stand up to the Egyptians when their sons were cast into the Nile, or when they were told that they would no longer be given straw, or [even subsequently] when they saw the Egyptians while encamped by the sea.

Moreover, who would believe that Pharaoh's house was not shut and guarded, so that someone could kill his firstborn son without anyone knowing, especially after he had been warned that his son would die? And how could it be that men who entered the houses in haste to kill the firstborn sons would turn and kill the firstborn animals, and of what use would this have been for them? How would they have put themselves in danger of being discovered, in order to kill the animals? And as for the firstborn of the prisoners in the underground chambers, what reason would Moses have had to kill them, there being no use to him to do this? And how would his men have entered the underground chambers?

Even if it could be believed that all this happened, could it be believed that the thing would not have been discovered, and that no Egyptian would see any of Moses' agents enter or leave his house, so that the thing would have become known to the people and the king? For surely if Pharaoh had had any suspicion that it was the Israelites who were striking the firstborn, he would not have sent them away in peace, but would have taken revenge against them in anger and rage.

See how many vain arguments the heretics load upon themselves so as not to accept that it is God Who does wonders in the midst of the earth to keep His people alive, so that the knowledge of His Oneness and His qualities may be preserved within it for the benefit of all the world's inhabitants.

**12:30. Pharaoh arose at night, he, all his servants, and all the Egyptians; and there were great cries in Egypt, for there was not a house where there was not someone dead.**

**12:31. He called Moses and Aaron at night, and he said, "Rise up, go forth from the midst of my people, both you and the children of Israel, and go to render worship to the Lord as you said.**

**12:32. "Take also your flocks and herds, as you said, and get you gone; then bless me also [when rendering worship to your God, pray also for me]."**

***then bless me also.*** [He asked them] to pray for him as well (Onkelos, Rashi, Rashbam, Ibn Ezra, and Mendelssohn), for when they worshipped God with their sacrifices, they would pray that He would accept their worship and bless them; Pharaoh requested that when praying to God to bless them, they should pray that He bless him as well.

**12:33. And the Egyptians pressed the people strongly, that they should go quickly out of the country; for they said, "(If they do not go) we will all die."**

**12:34. The people carried away on their backs the dough, not yet leavened; (they carried, that is) their dough wrapped in their clothes.**

***their dough*** *(mish'arotam).* Even though the original meaning of this term was the vessel [trough] in which they kneaded the dough and added the leaven (*se'or*)—for the word *mish'eret* is derived from *se'or* (as per Abravanel), notwithstanding that the former word has a *shin* and the latter a *sin* [see above at 7:28]—nevertheless it seems that here the term refers to the dough to which the *se'or* had been added. It is unlikely that they would have bundled their kneading troughs in their clothes, while on the contrary, it is readily understood why they would have put the dough in their clothes: so that it should warm up and ferment.

Onkelos translated *mish'arotam* as *motar atsvatehon*, i.e., that which remained in their troughs—the dough that was left over (*nish'ar*) after they baked the *matsot* that they had eaten with the meat of the Passover sacrifice; so also Rashi (based on the Mekhilta), "the remains of the *matsah* and bitter herbs."

Ibn Ezra understood the term to mean "a wooden vessel," [which they carried] because their donkeys were [already fully] loaded with garments. Some admirer of his may choose to believe him—that our ancestors were such asses that they loaded wooden vessels on their backs and loaded their garments on the donkeys.

**12:35. The children of Israel did according to Moses' orders, and they requested of the Egyptians furnishings of silver and of gold, and garments.**
**12:36. The Lord had then put the people in favor among the Egyptians, and the latter loaned to them. Thus they made spoil of the Egyptians' things.**
**12:37. The children departed from Rameses toward Sukkot, (numbering) about six hundred thousand foot-passengers, (that is) the adult men, besides the little ones [below the age of twenty].**

*about six hundred thousand, etc.*, — besides those less than 20 years old. Now the population of the Israelites was two million at least, and it is very strange and far removed from the way of the world that from seventy souls there should be born such a nation in 400 years. Johann David Michaelis sought to reconcile this with nature in several ways. First, he said that the men of the East marry at the age of 13 or 15, but this is nonsense, for taking a wife at a young age weakens the body and decreases fertility. Second, he said that the Israelites took more than one wife, but this too is nonsense, for if one man were to take many wives or even only two, other men would be left without a wife, since the number of women born is close to the number of males and does not exceed it by much. In addition, he said that the Israelites lived a hundred years or more, but this is nonsense as well, for Moses said, "The days of our years are seventy years" (Ps. 90:10), and Caleb told Joshua that he was 85 years old but still strong enough for war (Josh. 14:10), implying that most of the men of his generation were not so.

The Sages said that the Israelite women bore six at a time (*Exodus Rabbah* 1:7), and ancient writers attest that the Nile waters increased fertility and that the Egyptian women usually bore twins or even more than two at a time. Aristotle wrote, "Frequently and in many lands [women] bear twins, as for instance in Egypt especially" (*History of Animals*, Book VII, part 4). Pliny wrote, "That women may bring forth three at one birth appears evident... But to go above that number is reputed and commonly spoken to be monstrous, and to portend some mishap, except in Egypt, where women are more than ordinarily fruitful, by drinking of Nile water, which is supposed to help generation" (*Natural History* 7.3). Shortly thereafter he wrote, "Trogus is my author [who attests] that in Egypt it is an ordinary thing for a woman to have seven at a burden." Similarly, Seneca wrote, "No explanation can be given as to how Nile water increases fertility" (*Natural Questions* 5.23). (Besides these sources, Clericus cited also the words of Paulus Jurisconsultus, who wrote, "It was reported by not unreliable sources… that many Egyptians gave birth seven at a time.")

Perhaps circumcision was also a cause for increased procreation, as Philo wrote in his book on circumcision,[17] and similarly the Jewish physician S.B. Wolfsheimer, *De Causis Fecunditatis Hebraeorum Nonnullis Codicis Sacri Praeceptis Innitentibus* ("On the Causes of the Fertility of the Hebrews, Supported by Some of the Teachings of the Sacred Codes"), Halle, 1742.

It might further be asked, how could the land of Goshen have supported them all? To this J. D. Michaelis responded that it seems clear that not all of the Israelites remained in Goshen, but that they spread throughout Egypt; see Rashi on v. 13 above, s.v. *u-fasahti*.[18] The land of Egypt was quite well known among the ancients for its goodliness and its numerous inhabitants. It also seems likely that the Israelites spread out to pasture their herds outside Goshen, in the wilderness between Goshen and the land of Israel, as it is written, "The men of Gath that were born in the land [of Canaan] slew them [the sons of Ephraim] because they came down to take away their cattle" (1 Chron. 7:21).

Such was Michaelis' explanation. But all of this is insufficient to account for the magnitude of the increase mentioned above. Without a doubt, God's Providence was with Israel to preserve their health and strength, as can be inferred from the words of the midwives, who said, "Because the Hebrew women are not like the Egyptians, but they are vigorous" (Exod. 1:19). God's Providence and blessing defended and saved the Israelites from fatal childhood maladies, in order to fulfill the promise that He had made to Abraham, so that at the end of four hundred years they should become a nation capable of arising and establishing itself in the land of its inheritance that God had sworn to give them (Av 5623 [1863]).

**12:38. And also many alien people came along with them, and flocks and herds, exceedingly numerous cattle.**

*And also many alien people* (erev rav). It has been said that these were Egyptians who mixed with the Israelites in order to become proselytes,

---

17. This treatise is included in his book *Special Laws* I:1-11; the reference to fecundity is found at I:7.
18. There, Rashi comments that during the plague of the firstborn, God passed over the Israelite houses and struck the Egyptian houses, for the houses of the Israelites were intermingled with those of the Egyptians.

upon seeing the prodigious wonders that God had done for them, and that these people were the *asafsuf* ("alien multitude") mentioned elsewhere (Num. 11:4). It seems to me, however, that even if some people were stirred to become proselytes, there would have been no reason for them to leave with the Israelites, for the Israelites had never said they were going away permanently, but were supposed to return immediately. It would thus have been unlikely that alien people would mingle with them on the festival that they were celebrating to their God if, up to that day, the aliens had never feared God, adhered to the Israelites, or become circumcised; thus, "No uncircumcised one must eat of it [the Passover sacrifice]" (below, v. 48).

However, we find in Nehemiah (13:3), "They separated from Israel all the alien mixture [*erev*]," meaning mixture by way of intermarriage. Therefore it seems to me that this *erev rav* had previously mixed with the Israelites, and that they were Egyptian men who had married Israelite women and Egyptian women who had married Israelite men—and these were the *asafsuf*.

In the Targum [Onkelos], *ha-asafsuf* is translated *aravravin*. Here, too, the Samaritan text has, "And also *aravrav* came along with them," [changing *erev rav* into] a single word, which would be a doubled form like *yerakrak*, "greenish," *adamdam*, "reddish" (Lev. 13:49), and *petaltol*, "perverse" (Deut. 32:5). This would be an exact parallel to *asafsuf*. However, there is no need for this, since we find in Nehemiah the phrase, "They separated from Israel all the *erev*"; this indicates that in Hebrew the term *erev* was used to signify *asafsuf*.

**and flocks and herds.** Belonging to the Israelites; first the adult men, the little ones, and the alien people are mentioned, and afterward the livestock. However, according to Sforno, these were the flocks and herds of the alien people, while according to my student Judah Luzzatto, they belonged to either group.

**12:39. From the dough that they carried with them from Egypt, they baked unleavened cakes, for it had not become leavened; for they were expelled from Egypt, and they could not linger, and they did not even prepare any provisions.**

*for it had not become leavened (ki lo ḥamets).* This indicates [only] that the dough did not ferment, not that they had failed to add leavening. It seems to me that on the night of the fifteenth [of Nisan], perhaps after having eaten the Passover sacrifice, they kneaded the dough for the next day, put the leaven in it, and let it rest there, as it was customary to leave dough overnight so that it should rise. After midnight, however, they were expelled from Egypt and they could not bake their dough, so they took it with them on their backs. The dough grew cold after having been brought out of a place where it had been concealed and brought into the outside air, especially since the night air is cold, and as a result, the dough did not rise, even though they had placed it in their clothes to keep it warm.

**and they did not even prepare any provisions.** They did not know that they would be leaving Egypt that night (especially—as my student Hezekiah Matsliah Ashkenazi pointed out to me—since Moses had told them not to leave their houses until morning), and they prepared no provisions, but only kneaded the dough as they usually did for the next day.

Nachmanides and R. Isaac Caro interpreted this to mean that they baked the dough on their way, and outside Egypt, for they had been expelled from Egypt, and they indeed baked it into unleavened cakes, for so they had been commanded.

**cakes** *(ugot)*. See at Gen. 18:6.[19]

**12:40. The residence that the children of Israel made in Egypt was of four hundred and thirty years.**

***The residence that the children of Israel made.*** See above at 6:20. The opinion of the Sages was that they dwelled in Egypt only 210 years, and that the 400 years were from the time of Isaac's birth (Isaac was 60 when he fathered Jacob, and Jacob was 130 when he stood before Pharaoh; this yields 190 years, leaving 210 to complete the 400). The figure of 430 recorded here would have been from the time of the "covenant between the pieces" (Genesis 15), which they said occurred 30 years before Isaac's birth.

Some (cited by Abravanel) said that Scripture did not bother to record [in God's statement] to Abraham the 30 additional years, for the greater figure [of 400] absorbs the lesser. According to Nachmanides and Abravanel, the 30 years were added on because of the Israelites' sins in Egypt.

It should be noted that in the Samaritan version it is written, "The residence that the children of Israel *and their forefathers* made in *the land of Canaan and* the land of Egypt was four hundred and thirty years," and so it appears in the Alexandrian translation; this is one of the [Alexandrian]

---

19. Here, Shadal's comment describes *ugot* as thin cakes of the kind that Arabs still baked, and he says that the term was derived from a word meaning "circle."

emendations mentioned in the Talmud (*Megillah* 9a). The leading modern scholars, such as Richard Simon, Vater, Jahn, J.D. Michaelis, Koppe, Ravius, Rosenmueller, and Gesenius, have agreed that this is merely an emendation based on conjecture. The Jerusalem Targum has, "Thirty *shemittah* cycles of years, totaling two hundred and ten years."

**12:41. Now at the end of four hundred thirty years, on the same (abovementioned) day, all the ranks of the Lord went forth from the country of Egypt.**
**12:42. It was a night awaited by the Lord, to take them out of the country of Egypt; and this same night is (holy) to the Lord, to be observed by all the children of Israel, for all the ages to come.**

***It was a night awaited by the Lord*** *(leil shimmurim hu la-YHVH)*. As Rashi explained [i.e., that God was awaiting that night so that He could fulfill His promise to take them out], for the word *la-hotsi'am* ("to take them out") cannot be interpreted properly any other way. The word *shimmurim* ("anticipation") comes from an expression [such as] "His father remained in waiting [*shamar*] for the matter" (Gen. 37:11). Similarly, [it was a night of] *shimmurim* for all the children of Israel, as in, "Observe [*shemor*] the month of the first ripening" (Deut. 16:1), i.e., they were to set their minds [to anticipate] when it would come, and to fulfill all its laws.

**12:43. The Lord said to Moses and to Aaron, "This is the statute of the paschal sacrifice. No stranger shall eat of it.**

***No stranger*** *(ben nekhar)* ***shall eat of it.*** This is undoubtedly to be understood literally: "no foreigner [*nokhri*]." However, the Rabbis interpreted it to mean, "one who has made himself a stranger to his Father in Heaven," i.e., an apostate (*meshummad*). This was an interpretation that originated much later [than the giving of the Torah], when the Greeks arose and forced apostasy upon Israel. In accordance with the needs of that time, the Rabbis said that *ben nekhar* includes not only a foreigner, but also a Jew who acts in a foreign manner.

The word *meshummad* is apparently derived from *shemad* (denoting "destruction," "persecution") and [originally] described one who converted against his will during a time of persecution and, after the evil decree was annulled, did not repent. The word *mumar*, in contrast, described one who willingly converted.

[In his comment on this verse,] Nachmanides sought to explain the word *meshummad* as derived, with the dropping of the letter *ayin*, from *shemoda* or *ishtemoda*, [i.e., a variant of] *meshumda*, one who acts like a stranger toward his God. The Korem properly objected that [the phrase in the Targum to Gen. 42:8] *ve-ishtemoda Yosef le-aḥohi ve-innan la ishtemode'eh* conveys the meaning of *hakkarah* ("recognition") [i.e., "Joseph recognized his brothers, but they did not recognize him"], not *hitnakkerut* ("acting like a stranger"). However, the Korem himself fell into error and wrote, "It is true that the word *ve-ishtemoda* contains two meanings in one, for Onkelos translated the word *va-yitnakker* ("pretended to be a stranger") in Gen. 42:7 as *ve-ishtemode'innun*." This is wrong, because *ve-ishtemode'innun* is the translation of the Hebrew *va-yakkirem* ("and he recognized them"), while the subsequent phrase *va-yitnakker aleihem* is translated as *ve-ḥasheiv mah di yemalleil immehon*. Thus, the Korem's objection to Nachmanides' opinion remains strong and valid, for *ishtemoda* does not imply *hitnakkerut* ("acting like a stranger") but *hekker* ("recognition"), and the correct explanation is as I wrote above, with respect to the derivation of *meshummad* and its distinction from *mumar*.

It should be noted that in a manuscript book of grammar in my possession (lacking a title and author's name, but among the older works), I found that according to the grammarian R. Jonah [ibn Janah], *meshummad* is a variant of *meshu'amad*, and that the root *amad* in Syriac and Arabic means immersion for the purpose of accepting the Christian faith [i.e., baptism]. This opinion was shared by R. Judah ha-Levi in the *Kuzari* 3:65, which reads as follows in manuscript:

> As regards the Sadduceans and the Boethosians, they are nothing but apostates and sectarians who deny the World to Come; they are the sectarians who are anathemized in our prayer. But the well-known one [Jesus] and his followers are the *meshummadim* who adopted the doctrine of baptism [*torah ha-ma'amudit*], being baptized in the Jordan.[20]

But this opinion, too, seems quite unlikely to me, and the correct explanation is the one I have given.

**12:44. "Every slave bought with money, when you have circumcised him, will be able to eat of it.**

---

20. This translation is based on that of Hirschfeld, p. 188, as modified to reflect the version quoted by Shadal.

## Bo

***Every slave.*** The circumcision of [male] slaves has been the master's obligation ever since Abraham (Gen. 17:12), and we have also been commanded to allow slaves to rest on the Sabbath and holidays; all this raises the status of a slave, who is only slightly inferior to his master. Thus, as soon as the slave is circumcised, he eats like his master on Passover.

However, toward the end of the Second Temple period, the people's moral standards were corrupted by the kings of the Herodian dynasty, and Israel learned the ways of the gentiles. In particular, the kings, the nobles, and the wealthy aspired to imitate the Romans, who we know were cruel to their slaves. There were then Jewish masters who were unwilling to circumcise their slaves, so that they should not think of themselves as Israelites or as human beings. It was then that the Sages of Israel arose and decreed that whoever did not circumcise his slaves would not be allowed to eat the Passover sacrifice. Their intention, in my opinion, was that anyone who did not consider slaves to be human was not worthy of being included among the celebrators of the Festival of Freedom.

This was the approach of the majority of the Rabbis, and it is reported without attribution (*setam*) in the Mekhilta [on this v.] (although in Rashi's version, cited in his comment on this verse, it is attributed to R. Joshua, while in the version cited by Tosafot on *Yevamot* 70b, it is attributed to R. Akiva). However, R. Eliezer [ben Hyrcanus] said that a master's refusal to circumcise his slaves did not prevent him from eating the Passover sacrifice, for R. Eliezer adhered to the ways of Shammai, as I explained in *Kerem Ḥemed* vol. 3, p. 220, and opposed any innovation that was not in the Torah or tradition, and he would say nothing that he had not heard from his teachers. The other Sages of Israel, however, would issue new regulations according to the needs of the times, and they were compelled to excommunicate R. Eliezer [as related in *Bava Metsi'a* 59b], who resisted anything that deviated from what he had received from his teachers (29 Sivan 5614 [1854]).

**12:45. "The resident foreigner and the hireling [non-Israelites, living in Palestine without embracing Judaism] will not eat of it.**

***The resident foreigner*** *(toshav)* — a foreigner who settles among the Israelites but does not observe their Torah. According to the Rabbis, this was one who accepted the seven Noahide commandments; see below at v. 18.

***and the hireling*** *(ve-sakhir).* A foreigner who works for an Israelite and is hired for a number of days; even though he [generally] eats with Israelites, he does not eat the Passover sacrifice. All of this [was enacted] to further impress the Exodus from Egypt on the mind of the Israelite.

Ibn Ezra understood this to refer to an Israelite resident or hireling who was not counted within a *ḥavurah* [a company of eaters; see at v. 47 below], but there is no reference at all here to the matter of *ḥavurot*. Besides, the hireling is in his master's house, and consequently (if he has no wife or children) he is included among the household.

**12:46. "In one single house it shall be eaten; do not take of (its) meat out of the house, and do not break any bone of it.**

*and do not break any bone of it.* In keeping with [the command of] eating it in haste (Rashbam), or in order to show respect for the sacrifice, so that it should not be treated in a gluttonous manner (Gersonides), or else in order to eat it in a style of freedom and not like food for slaves.

**12:47. "All of the Community of Israel will do it.**

*All of the Community of Israel, etc.* [In his comment on this v.] Rashi abridged the words of the Mekhilta, and his words remain unclear. What the Mekhilta meant to say was that on Passover as celebrated by subsequent generations, they would be able to form a *ḥavurah* of ten people from ten different families ("all the Community of Israel," whoever they may be), but for purposes of Passover in Egypt it is said, "He will take it together with his neighbor" (v. 4)—he and all the members of his household, and his neighbor and all the members of his neighbor's household (for they were not allowed to leave their houses).

According to the plain meaning, the commandment of the Passover sacrifice was explained previously (at the beginning of this chapter), but here there is an additional explanation as to the law of the slave, the resident foreigner, the hireling, and the *ger* ("foreigner"). Before discussing the *ger*, Scripture first makes it known that the slave, the resident foreigner, and the hireling may eat the Passover sacrifice, but they may not do the sacrifice themselves; only "all the Community of Israel will do it." Subsequently it is specified that even the *ger*, once he is circumcised, may do the sacrifice for himself with the members of his household, without having to participate in a *ḥavurah* of [native born] Israelites (21 Av 5623 [1863]).

**12:48. "When a foreigner dwells among you, and he wishes to make the paschal sacrifice to the Lord, every male who pertains to him must be**

circumcised, and then he will be admitted to do it, and he will be equal to the native; but no uncircumcised one must eat of it.

*When a foreigner (ger) dwells among you.* According to the Rabbis, this refers to a *ger tsedek* ("righteous proselyte"), who accepts the entire Torah. However, from this verse it is clear that he is called a *ger* even before he is circumcised, and thus the *ger* [according to the plain meaning] has not accepted all the *mitsvot*, has not been circumcised, and does not belong to the people of Israel.

According to the literal meaning [of these verses], it seems that a *ger* is of lesser status than a *toshav* ("resident foreigner"), for the *toshav* has settled in the country, while the *ger* has come to dwell [temporarily] and then return after some time to his country. How, then, could it be said categorically of a *toshav* that "he will not eat of it," while it is said of a *ger* that if he becomes circumcised, then he may eat of it?

Johann David Michaelis wrote that a *ger* has no land and a *toshav* has no house, but I say that a *toshav* is one who comes alone, without a wife or children, and settles in the house of an Israelite (this is the meaning of *toshav kohen*, "the resident foreigner who has settled with a priest" [Lev. 22:10]) and becomes like his slave or servant ("He will be with you as a hireling or as a resident foreigner [*ke-toshav*]; and he will serve with you until the year of the Jubilee" [Lev. 25:40]).

A *ger*, on the other hand, comes with his entire household, his wife and his children, and lives apart with his family, not with an Israelite like the *toshav*. Therefore it says, "Every male who pertains to him must be circumcised," that is, from among the members of his household. There is no doubt that a *toshav*, too, could eat of the Passover sacrifice if he wanted to become circumcised, but this is mentioned in connection with the *ger*, because of the novel rule enabling him to observe Passover on his own, as I have explained at the previous verse.

As for the phrase, "And also of the children of the resident foreigners [*toshavim*] dwelling with you, you may purchase" (Lev. 25:45), it is specified [later] in the same verse, "begotten in your country"—that is, [this case concerns] a resident foreign man who married a resident foreign woman or a Canaanite bondwoman, not a foreigner who came to the country already married.

Accordingly, there is no doubt that the *toshav* was not an idolater, for he was part of an Israelite household, and we find that the Torah made him eligible to eat of the sabbatical year's grain like an Israelite or a slave

## Shadal on Exodus

(Lev. 25:6), and he was punished [like an Israelite] for homicide, and the cities of refuge took him in as well (Num. 35:15).

With respect to the *ger*, it appears from the present verse itself ("When a foreigner dwells among you… every male who pertains to him must be circumcised") that he did not accept upon himself all of the commandments, and we do not find a rule that "there shall be one law for you and for the *ger*" in connection with all the commandments in general. Specifically, however, in connection with the Passover sacrifice (here and in Num. 9:14), it is provided that if the *ger* wishes to do it, he must do so according to the commandment and must not eat of it uncircumcised.

So also with respect to the offering of [other] sacrifices, if he wishes to bring a burnt offering (*isheh*), "he must do the same as you do" (Num. 15:14-16). The *ger* contracted impurity like any Israelite, and if he wished to purify himself, he needed the ashes of the red heifer like any Israelite (Num. 19:10). Indeed, we find:

- "And all the congregation of the children of Israel will be pardoned, and the foreigners [*ve-la-ger*] dwelling in your midst" (Num. 15:26);
- "Whether it is a native among the children of Israel or a foreigner [*ve-la-ger*] dwelling among them, you will have one same law for one who does [sins] in error" (Num. 15:29);
- "But one who does [transgresses] with a raised hand, whether a native or a foreigner [*ha-ger*], [will become extinct]" (Num. 15:30).

All of this apparently concerns a *ger* who has voluntarily become circumcised and has joined the people of Israel; such a person is called a *ger tsedek* ("a righteous *ger*"). However, not every *ger* is a *ger tsedek*, as I have proved from the present verse ("when a foreigner dwells among you"), and thus our obligation to love the *ger* and not to oppress him applies to any *ger* in general, even if he is not a *ger tsedek*.

**and he wishes to make** *(ve-asah,* lit., "and he makes") **the paschal sacrifice.** He wishes to make the sacrifice for himself, with the members of his household.

**and then he will be admitted to do it.** He will be deemed fit to make the Passover sacrifice for himself.

**12:49.** "The same law will be for the native and for the foreigner who dwells among you."

# *Bo*

**12:50. All the children of Israel did so; they did (that is) as the Lord had commanded to Moses and to Aaron.**

*All the children of Israel did so.* It has already been stated above (v. 28) that "the children of Israel went and did so," etc., but that was in reference to the slaughtering of the Passover sacrifice and the placing of its blood on the lintel and the doorposts. Here, it is repeated that they "did so" with respect to the eating of the sacrifices: they did not let any stranger eat of it, they ate it in one house, and they did not break any bone of it.

Ibn Ezra wrote that perhaps this statement refers to the Passover sacrifice that they made in the wilderness of Sinai (in the second year) (see Numbers 9), for it was then that they circumcised the *gerim*, and the events of the Torah are not all recorded in chronological order. However, there is no need for such an explanation here.

**12:51. Now, on that same (above-mentioned) day, the Lord brought the children of Israel out of the country of Egypt, at the head of their ranks [that is, guiding them with the pillars of cloud and fire].**

*Now, on that same day, etc.* This, too, was already stated above (v. 41), but it is duplicated in order to conclude [this section] with a remembrance of the exodus from Egypt, which is the basis for the subsequent section, "Declare sacred to Me every firstborn... Remember this day, on which you came forth from Egypt" (Exod. 13:2-3).

According to Rashbam, Ibn Ezra, and Gersonides, this verse is attached to the next section: on that same day that the Lord brought the children of Israel out of Egypt at the head of their ranks, He gave Moses the commandment, "Declare sacred to me every firstborn." It seems to me, however, that if this were so, it should have said, "Now on that same day on which [*asher*] the Lord brought..."

Nachmanides says that this verse means that not all of the people left at night, but that on the next day they came out of Egypt completely.

*at the head of their ranks (al tsive'otam*, lit., "on their ranks"). Rashi (above at 6:26) understood this as the equivalent of *be-tsive'otam* ("with their ranks"), on the model of *ve-al ḥarbekha tiḥyeh* [Gen. 27:40, understood as *be-ḥarbekha,* "with your sword"], and *amadtem al ḥarhekhem* (Ezek. 33:26) [similarly understood as *be-ḥarbekhem*]. However, the meaning of the word *al* in the verses that he cited is quite distinct from its meaning here, according to the nature of the phrase.

Rosenmueller translated *al* here as *secundum* ("by," "alongside"), and cited as analogous usage "each one by [*al*] his camp, and by [*al*] his army corps" (Num. 1:52). But this, too, has no relevance here, for there the meaning is "each one attached to his camp and corps," but how could it be said that all the children of Israel [collectively] were "attached" to their ranks?

Coccejus said that the expression is equivalent to *le-tsive 'otam* ("according to their ranks"), which fits the context of the verse, but I have not found any similar usage; he cited as analogous, "These stones will bear [*tihyena al*] the names of the children of Israel" (Exod. 28:21), but this has no relevance here, for the "stones" and the "names" are two different things, while "Israel" and "their ranks" are the same thing. I have found no example of the usage of the word *al* to refer to a thing that is inseparable from another thing.

Nachmanides interpreted the expression to mean "with all their ranks," i.e., the ranks of the women and the alien people accompanying them, but this, too, is unlikely, for the women were not in separate ranks, while the alien people would not likely be referred to as part of the Israelites' ranks.

Therefore it seems to me that this should be taken to mean that the Lord was at the head of their ranks; cf., "These are [that] Aaron and [that] Moses to whom the Lord said, 'Bring the children of Israel out of the country of Egypt, [placing yourselves] at the head of their ranks [*al tsive'otam*]'" (Exod. 6:26). That is, God, Moses, and Aaron were *al tsive'otam*, i.e., their leaders; cf., "at the head of his army [*ve-al tseva'o*] Nahshon son of Amminadab" (Num. 1:7). Here, the meaning is that God went before them with a pillar of cloud or fire.

**13:1. The Lord spoke to Moses, saying:**
**13.2. "Declare sacred to Me every firstborn, everyone born first of the children of Israel, both of the men and of the animals; they are Mine."**

**Declare sacred to Me** *(kaddesh li,* lit., "sanctify to Me"). By oral statement (that is, "Tell the Israelites that the firstborn are sacred to Me"); cf., the expressions *ve-tiharo ha-kohen* ("the priest will declare him pure") and *ve-timme'o ha-kohen* ("the priest will declare him impure" [Leviticus 13] (Yefet [ben Ali] the Karaite, cited by Ibn Ezra).

**everyone born first** *(peter kol reḥem,* lit. "opening of every womb"). *Peter* means "opening" (according to all the commentators) and "release" and "bringing forth"; cf., "when one lets out [*poter*] water" (Prov. 17:14); "they shoot out [*yaftiru*] the lip" (Ps. 22:8); and also, "but he slipped away [*va-

*yiftor*] out of Saul's presence" (1 Sam. 19:10). So also [we find] *niftar* ("to die," lit., "to be freed") in Rabbinic Hebrew, and *itpetar* ("to escape") in the language of the Targum and in Syriac.

Bochart objected that in 34:19-20 below, it is written *peter shor va-seh* ("the firstborn of the oxen and of the lambs") and *peter ḥamor* ("firstborn of a donkey"), without the word *reḥem* ("womb"). In his opinion, the word *peter* is from the Arabic, for *alfatar* in Arabic means "beginning" or "first." This proves nothing, however, for the root *pataḥ* ("to open") is also used (especially in Rabbinic Hebrew) to refer to any beginning. The Arabs likely did the same and used [the equivalent of] the root *patar* for any beginning. In Hebrew, people left off the word *reḥem* and used *peter* for every firstborn, though not for every beginning.

In Rabbinic Hebrew, the root *patar* was used in the sense of "completion" (as in *maftir*), but even this sense is not far removed from "coming forth." Similarly in Latin, *exitus* means "going out" and also "end" or "conclusion."

Note that the word *reḥem* was omitted [after *peter*] only where it had already been written previously. In v. 12 below, it says, "You shall offer every *peter reḥem* to the Lord," and then in v. 13 it says, "Every *peter* of a donkey you shall redeem with a lamb."

**they are Mine.** This is a separate statement, which supplies a reason for the command, "Declare sacred to Me every firstborn," as Rashi wrote: "I have acquired them for Myself by having stricken the firstborn of Egypt" (and the firstborn of Israel I saved).

**13:3. Then Moses said to the people, "Remember this day, on which you came forth from Egypt, where you were slaves; for (that is) with a strong arm the Lord brought you out of here, and let no leaven be eaten.**

***Then Moses said to the people,*** *etc.* Before telling Israel about the command of the firstborn, he mentioned the command of the feast of *matsot*, which had been told to him before they left Egypt but had not been told to the people until afterwards (see above at 12:14, 21).

***Remember this day.*** Every year.

**13:4. "It is today that you are leaving, in the month (that is) of the first ripening [of the barley].**

***the first ripening*** *(ha-aviv).* The beginning of the ripening of the grains; cf., "for the barley was almost ripe [*aviv*]" (Exod. 9:31); "of nearly ripe grain [*aviv*] toasted in fire" (Lev. 2:14). Apparently, barley is called *aviv* at its first ripening, and wheat is called *karmel.* The word has no relation at all to the word *av* ("father"), as Ibn Ezra thought; he wrote, "*Aviv* is to be interpreted as *bikkur* ["first fruit"], for it is derived from *av*, as if it were the first [product] of its begetter." Kimhi went astray after him and (at the root *aviv*) interpreted the term *be-ibbei ha-naḥal* ("at the green plants of the valley") (Songs 6:11) as equivalent to *be-atsei ha-naḥal* ("at the trees of the valley"), and wrote, "The ear [of grain] with its stalk is called *aviv*, after the stalk itself, which is called the 'tree,' for a tree is like a father that begets branches."

All of this is error, for we never find *aviv* referring to a tree or a stalk, or to an ear [in general], but only specifically to an ear at the start of its ripening; see R. Elijah [Levita]'s *Nimmukim* [on Kimhi's *Shorashim*]. We find [forms of] the noun *av* in the phrases *be-ibbei ha-naḥal* (Songs 6:11) and *odennu ve-ibbo*, "while it is yet in its greenness" (Job 8:12), denoting a sprouting plant that is not yet ripe. Apparently the doubled *bet* in *aviv* serves to distinguish between that word and *av*, and to indicate a plant in a later stage of growth that has arrived at [the point of] ripeness. A similar pattern is seen in the phrase *sabbuni gam sevavuni*, "they surrounded me, yea, they encompassed me" (Ps. 118:11), [where the second verb, derived from the geminate root *savav*] is stronger than the first [which is derived from the simpler root *sov*].

In Aramaic we find the root *avav* referring to a fruit-bearing tree; the phrase "as the first-ripe in the fig tree at her first season" (Hosea 9:10) is translated by Targum Jonathan as *ke-vikkurah ve-teinata di va-aval me'abbeva.* However, it seems to me that this is derived not from *aviv*, but rather from *inba*, which is Aramaic for "fruit." Thus we see that Jonathan was not content to say *me'abbeva*, but preceded it with *va-aval*, meaning "at the beginning." This indicates that *me'abbeva* means only "producing fruit" [and does not itself imply newly ripening fruit].

Similarly, we find "in the month of Bul" (1 Kings 6:38) translated by Jonathan as *be-yeraḥ meisaf ibbevaya*, which further indicates that *avav* in Aramaic refers only to "fruit" (for the month of Bul is the [autumn] month of Marheshvan, in which there are neither first fruits nor *aviv*). The word *ibbevaya* has the same significance as *ibba* and *inba* (which are interchangeable and related forms, just as we find *kintsei* in place of *kitsei*, Job 18:20).

In a manuscript Rashi in my possession, [the comment on this verse begins], "Would they not have known [in which month they went out]?" (not "Would we not have known") [as found in most editions], and this is correct.[21]

---

21. The reading favored by Shadal also appears in Chavel's edition.

## *Bo*

**13:5. "Now, when the Lord will have brought you to the country of the Canaanites, the Hittites, the Amorites, the Hivites, and the Jebusites, which He swore to your fathers to give you, a land that flows with milk and honey—you will practice this rite in this month.**

*a land that flows with milk and honey.* We find a similar expression among the poets of the ancient peoples, such as Ovid (*Metamorphoses* I, 111):

> From veins of valleys, milk and nectar broke,
> And honey sweating through the pores of oak.

He was preceded by Theocritus (Idyll 5):

> Let the Imera run milk for water, and the Crati
> Of reddening banks...
> Let the Sibarite, too, run honey, and tomorrow
> Let the damsel draw honeycombs for water.

Similarly, Euripides (in his play *The Bacchantes*) wrote, "With milk and wine and streams of luscious honey flows the earth." So also in the Prophets: "The mountains shall drop down sweet wine, and the hills shall flow with milk" (Joel 4:18). This is a poetic expression by way of hyperbole.

**13:6. "Seven days shall you eat unleavened bread, and on the seventh day [besides the first, already mentioned above, will be] a feast to the Lord.**

*Seven days shall you eat unleavened bread.* The Samaritans emended this (and so it is translated in the Greek version ascribed to the seventy elders) to read, "Six days shall you eat unleavened bread," to conform with Deut. 16:8. They failed to see that prior to this statement in Deuteronomy, "Six days shall you eat unleavened bread," it had been said, "Do not eat with it [i.e., the Passover sacrifice] leavened bread; for seven days following it you shall eat unleavened bread" (Deut. 16:3). Then, after stating, "And on the next day you may turn and go to your tents" (Deut. 16:7), it says, "Six days shall you eat unleavened bread," that is, aside from the first day. After that, it is added that the last of these days, the seventh, is to be an "assembly" (v. 8). Here, however, where there is no detailed discussion about the first day, it says, "Seven days shall you eat unleavened bread," and subsequently it is added that the last of those seven days is to be a feast.

**13:8. "And you shall then explain the thing to your son, saying, '[This is done] for the sake of all that the Lord did for me, when I came out of Egypt.'**

***And you shall then explain*** *(ve-higgadta,* lit., "you shall tell") ***the thing to your son.*** You shall explain to him the reason for what you are doing; cf., "to them that declared [*le-maggidei*] the riddle" (Judg. 14:19), meaning those who explained it.

***for the sake of all that the Lord did for me*** *(ba-avur zeh asah YHVH li).* "I am observing this holiday and eating this *matsah* because of what the Lord did for me" (Rashbam, Nachmanides). The words *zeh* and *zu* mean "that" or "which," as in:

- *am zu yatsarti li,* "the people that I formed for Myself" (Isa. 43:21).
- *am zu ga'alta,* "the people that You liberated" (Exod. 15:13), *am zu kanita,* "that people that You made" (Exod. 15:16).
- *be-oraḥ zu ahallekh,* "in the way that I walk" (Ps. 142:4).
- *har Tsiyyon zeh shakhanta bo,* "mount Zion, in which You have dwelt" (Ps. 74:2).
- *el mekom zeh yasadta lahem,* "to the place that You have founded for them" (Ps. 104:8).
- *ve-zeh ahavti nehpekhu vi,* "and they whom I loved are turned against me" (Job 19:19).

The word *zu* is derived from *di,* which is Aramaic for "that," just as *zeh* is derived from [the Aramaic] *da* and *den* ("this"). Similarly in German, the word *so* is [sometimes] used to mean "that."[22]

Mendelssohn wrote that the accents in this verse [which set off *zeh* with a disjunctive *revia*] agree more with the interpretation of Rashi and Ibn Ezra ("in order that I should observe His commandments, God did for me") [i.e., they understood *zeh* to mean "this" and *ba-avur zeh* as "for the sake of this observance"]. This is not so, however, for the word *zu* in the phrases *am zu ga'alta, am zu kanita, am zu yatsarti li,* and *be-oraḥ zu ahallekh* is also marked with a disjunctive and is thus connected with the word preceding it, just like the word *zeh* in the expression *ba-avur zeh asah YHVH li.*

---

22. The German *so* is pronounced like the Hebrew *zo.* Perhaps Shadal meant to imply that these words were etymologically linked.

## Bo

**13:9. "And you will have it for an insignia on your arm, and for a memorial between your eyes—so that the law of the Lord may be in your mouth [may always be present to you]—for with a strong arm the Lord brought you out of Egypt.**

*And you will have it for an insignia (ve-hayah lekha le-ot), etc.* This is to be understood as if it said, "And you will have it for an insignia on your arm, and for a memorial between your eyes, for with a strong arm the Lord brought you out of Egypt, and this is so that the law of the Lord may be in your mouth" (Nachmanides). This is the proper understanding of the plain meaning of the verse, and v. 16 below is proof for this interpretation. However, the Karaites say that this is [merely] a metaphor [and not a literal command to wear *tefillin*], but Ibn Ezra refuted them well.[23]

Rashbam, too, inclined toward the Karaite view and wrote, "Let it be for you as a constant reminder, as if it were written on your arm, similar to the phrase, 'Set me as a seal [*ka-hotam*] upon your heart' (Songs 8:6). 'Between your eyes' as a kind of ornament or gold chain that is customarily placed on the forehead for beauty."[24] In our day, the Korem has also upheld the opinion of the Karaites. However, there is no doubt that if this were a [mere] allegory, it should have said "as an insignia [*ke-ot*] on your arm, and as a memorial [*u-khe-zikkaron*] between your eyes," not *le-ot* and *u-le-zikkaron*, since the *mitsvot* are not allegory and poetry (as are the prophecies of Isaiah, who said, "Behold, I have graven you upon the palms of My hands" [Isa. 49:15]), but rather straightforward expressions.

---

23. Ibn Ezra, noting that the Karaite interpretation is based on an analogy to various metaphorical expressions (e.g., "For they shall be a chaplet of grace on your head, and chains about your neck") in the book of Proverbs, says that the introductory words of that book, *Mishlei Shelomoh*, indicate that the book deals with *meshalim* (metaphors), but that in contrast, the words of the Torah are to be taken literally unless common sense dictates otherwise.

24. It has been pointed out that although Rashbam felt free to offer a metaphorical interpretation of this verse, he clearly did not mean to adopt the Karaite view in practice and negate the *mitsvah* of *tefillin* (see footnote 26 in S. Vargon, "Samuel David Luzzatto's Critique of Rabbinic Exegesis Which Contradicts the Plain Meaning of Scripture" (Hebrew), *Jewish Studies, an Internet Journal*, vol. 2 (2003), http://www.biu.ac.il./JS/JSIJ). In particular, it has been noted that (1) Rashbam maintained that the "legal" portion of the Torah begins when the people assemble at Sinai; (2) the present verse, which precedes that event, would thus not be intended to establish a rule of law; and (3) although Rashbam does not comment on Deut. 6:8 ("And you will bind them for an insignia on your arm…"), he would apparently have understood that verse as referring to the commandment of *tefillin*. (See Elazar Touitou, *Ha-Peshatot ha-Mithaddeshim be-Khol Yom: Iyyunim be-Feirusho shel Rashbam la-Torah* [Ramat Gan: Bar-Ilan, 2003], p. 187.)

# Shadal on Exodus

The Korem, in a clever attempt to remove the difficulty of these *lameds* (*le-ot, u-le-zikkaron*), explained that the father [continuing the statement in v. 8] is saying to his son, "This holiday, through the sacrifice of the paschal offering and the baking of *matsot*, will be for an insignia on your arm, for these things are done by hand, and for a memorial between your eyes, for you will see the *matsah* and bitter herbs placed before you." This, however, is a distortion of the verse, for it is not the son but the father who is doing these actions, so how could the father say "on *your* arm"? Similarly, it says below (v. 15), "Therefore *I* sacrifice to the Lord all the firstborn males," [and then in v. 16,] "And let it be for an insignia on *your* arm."

Furthermore, how could the father be telling the son that God "brought *you* out" of Egypt, instead of "brought *me* out" or "brought *us* out," especially since he had just said, "For the sake of all that the Lord did for *me*"? Besides, this insignia was to be a permanent symbol, not a seasonal act, so how could it follow from those [Passover-related] actions, which were performed once a year, that the law of the Lord would be "in our mouths," that is, constantly spoken of (cf., "This song, which will not pass into oblivion, but will be preserved in the mouth of his progeny" [Deut. 31:21])?

Another thing: what would [the allegorizers] say about the phrase, "And you shall bind them for an insignia on your arm" (Deut. 6:8)? The Karaites (cited by Ibn Ezra) said this was an expression similar to:

- "Bind them continually upon your heart" (Prov. 6:21);
- "Bind then about your neck, write them upon the tablet of your heart" (Prov. 3:3);
- "Bind them upon your fingers, write them upon the tablet of your heart" (Prov. 7:3).

They did not understand, however, that all these are [indeed] poetic figures of speech—the proof being "write them on the tablet of your heart," which cannot be taken literally—and if the Torah had used such an expression, we would have said it was a metaphor, like, "Circumcise the foreskin of your heart" (Deut. 10:16), but the Torah tell us to bind on the arm and between the eyes, and to write upon the doorposts of our houses (Deut. 6:8-9), and who can tell us that this is all a mere metaphor? Indeed, who can tell us which of the *mitsvot* are to be taken literally and which of them figuratively?

If the matter needed reinforcement, I would add that we know that this was in fact the custom of ancient peoples—and that even today in Eastern countries, people wear cultic symbols on their bodies—for it is written,

*Bo*

"Nor shall you make in yourselves incised writing" (Lev. 19:28). So, too, modern-day Arabs write verses from their scripture on their doorposts and their city gates. Some say that it was the custom of ancient peoples to write on their skin, and on pieces of paper or tablets that they would wear on their foreheads, magical inscriptions and amulets. God wanted to distance Israel from such customs, and so He commanded us to wear on our skin some of the words of His Torah, so that the law of the Lord might always be in our mouths and never depart from the mouths of our children.

According to the simple meaning (*peshat*) of the verse, the essential inscription [of the *tefillin*] would be these words: "With a strong arm the Lord brought us out of Egypt." This is the epitome of the entire Torah, encompassing two main principles of our faith, which are (1) reward and punishment, that is, that God watches over everyone's actions in order to render to each person according to his deeds; and (2) the eternal covenant, that is, that God chose Jacob for His own. Rabbi Judah Aryeh Osimo adds that just as the High Priest wore a sacred diadem on which it was written "Holy to the Lord" (Exod. 28:36), so it was—as the entire congregation was to be holy and a kingdom of priests—that God commanded them to have a sign on their bodies, and just as the phrase "Holy to the Lord" symbolized the High Priest's greatness and importance over all of Israel, so the phrase "With a strong arm the Lord brought us out of Egypt" would indicate Israel's glory over all the nations.

Isaac Pardo responds, however, that the High Priest's diadem served to make his holiness known to all who saw him, while the purpose of *tefillin* was not to gain us human glory, but rather to keep the Torah in our mouths. He says that the *tefillin* on the arm serves as a sign to its wearer, who sees it and remembers that the Lord brought us out of Egypt, while the *tefillin* on the head is a sign for the wearer's brother Jew who sees it, for every Jew who sees another Jew wearing *tefillin* on his forehead will remember that with a strong arm, the Lord brought us out of Egypt.

**13:10. "You shall observe this statute in its established time, from year to year.**

*You shall observe this statute, etc.* This refers back to the beginning of Moses' statement to Israel, "Remember this day, on which you came forth from Egypt" (Exod. 13:3).

## Shadal on Exodus

*from year to year (mi-yamim yamimah,* lit., "from days to days"). Cf., "Throughout a year [*yamim*] it may be recovered" (Lev. 25:29), after which it is specified, "But if it is not recovered before an entire year [*shanah*] has passed" (v. 30), and before which it says, "Its right of recovery will last until the end of the year of [*shenat*] its sale" (v. 29). The phrase "until the end of the year of its sale" might have been taken to mean "until the new year," even if twelve months had not passed from the day of sale. For this reason, the phrase "throughout a year [*yamim*] it may be recovered" was added, and then it says, "But if it is not recovered before an entire year [*shanah*] has passed."

The terms *yamim* and "entire year" are synonymous; an entire year was called *yamim* because it includes every kind of day, long and short. The year was called *shanah* because the days and the seasons (planting and harvest, cold and heat, summer and winter) [see Gen. 8:22]) return again [*pa'am sheniyyah*] annually. All of this refers to the natural [solar] year of 365 days, beginning from any date, for a person who sells a house [as in Lev. 25:29] may sell it on any day that he wants, and at the end of 365 days [after the sale], an entire year is completed, otherwise called *yamim.* The concept of the "leap year" is not mentioned in the Torah.

Wessely, commenting on Leviticus 25 (followed by Reggio on the present verse) sought to distinguish between *shanah* and *yamim,* and said that *shanah* is a 365-day year proper, while *yamim* means a year as set according to the calendrical cycle, which year is sometimes 354 days long [and sometimes 384]. This is nonsense, for in the case of one who sells a house, as well as in the case of Jephthah's daughter (Judg. 11:40), both of the terms *yamim* and *shanah* are mentioned, and it is unlikely that there should be any difference between them. How would it be possible to interpret [the verse in Lev. 25] as follows: "Its right of recovery will last until the end of the year of its sale [365 days]"; "throughout a year [354 or 384 days] it may be recovered"; "but if it is not recovered before an entire year [365 days] has passed"? Rather, the correct explanation is according to Rashi (on Lev. 25:29-30): the days of a full year are called *yamim.*

**13:11. "Now, when the Lord will have brought you to the land of the Canaanites and will have given it to you, as He swore to you and to your fathers —**
**13:12. "You shall offer every firstborn to the Lord. That is, of all the firstborn of the animals that you will have, you shall sacrifice the males to the Lord.**

***You shall offer*** *(ve-ha'avarta*, lit., "you shall pass"). A term denoting "setting aside" (Rashi).

***of all the firstborn*** *(peter reḥem)*. Here [Moses] specifies what is first stated in a general way: "You shall offer every firstborn to the Lord, *that is* [these words are added in translation], of all the firstborn of the animals... you shall sacrifice the males.... Every firstborn of an ass you shall redeem with a lamb.... And every firstborn of the human species... you shall redeem."

***That is, of all the firstborn*** *(peter sheger)*. *Shigger* in Aramaic signifies "sending," [and thus *sheger* means] that which an animal "sends forth" from its womb. This term includes all of its young without distinction, as in the phrase *shegar alafekha* ("the offspring of your cattle") [e.g., Deut. 28:4], while *peter* refers to the firstborn, which opens the womb *(reḥem)*.

**13:13. "Every firstborn of an ass you shall redeem with a lamb [or a kid]; and if you do not want to redeem it, you shall kill it. And every firstborn of the human species, (that is) of your sons, you shall redeem.**

***you shall kill it*** *(va-arafto)*. [The Hebrew is] derived from *oref* ("neck") and denotes the cutting of the neck. This [unusual] term was used so that the owner should not slaughter it in the manner of a sacrifice, for no sacrifices were to be brought from impure animals [such as an ass]. The redemption procedure was [seemingly] the same for any other impure animal (Num. 18:15), but [here] the Torah was speaking of the most common case, for the ass was widespread among them. However, in the Mekhilta they said that no impure animal other than an ass was to be redeemed.[25]

**13:14. "Now, when in the future your son will ask you, saying, 'What is this?' – you will say to him, 'With a strong arm the Lord brought us out of Egypt, where we were slaves.**
**13:15. "'And when Pharaoh made difficulties in letting us go, the Lord killed in the country of Egypt every firstborn, both those of the men and those of the animals; for this reason I sacrifice to the Lord all the firstborn males, and I redeem every firstborn of my sons.'**

---

25. Both the Mekhilta and the Talmud (*Bekhorot* 5b) acknowledge that the general nature of the wording of Num. 18:15 might suggest that even the firstborn of a horse or camel should be redeemed with a lamb, but regard the specific references to "the firstborn of an ass" in Exod. 13:13 and 34:20 as excluding the redemption of any other impure animal.

***made difficulties in letting us go*** *(hikshah... le-shallehenu).* He let us go with difficulty; cf., *va-tekash be-lidtah* ("and she had a difficult birth") [Gen. 35:16]; *behemah ha-makshah leiled* ("an animal that gives birth with difficulty") (Mishnah *Hullin* 4:1). *Hikshah* [from *kashah*, "to be difficult"] is a verb that serves in place of an adverb, analogous to *heitavta lir'ot*, "you have seen well" (Jer. 1:12). The meaning here is that first Pharaoh said he would let them go when a plague would cease, then he went back on his word, then he said that they should leave their offspring, then he told them to leave their flocks and herds, and only after the plague of the firstborn did he let them all go. Similarly, with regard to the animal *ha-makshah leiled*, every pang that the animal undergoes helps it to give birth, and when the last pang comes, the animal gives birth.

**13:16. "And let it be to you for an insignia on your arm, and for a frontal between your eyes, that with a strong arm the Lord brought us out of Egypt."**

***And let it be to you,*** *etc.* These are not the father's words; rather, the Torah is concluding the matter and once again referring to the *mitsvah* of *tefillin*, whether to add urgency on account of its great importance, or whether to specify how we should write the *tefillin*, for above (v. 9), it said "brought *you* out," but here it says "brought *us* out," which is exactly what we were to write [in the *tefillin*, according to the *peshat*]: "With a strong arm the Lord brought us out of Egypt."

***and for a frontal*** *(u-le-totafot).* The Hebrew is from the root *tuf*, and the proper form of the word is *taftafot*, just as "Babel" is properly *Balbel*. The root *tuf* in Arabic signifies "going around," and the term *totefet* is used for an ornament that encircles the head or the arm; the phrase "and the bracelet that was on his arm" (2 Sam. 11:10) is translated by Targum Jonathan as *ve-totafta de-al dar'eih* (Fullerus, Rosenmueller, and Gesenius).

# *Beshallaḥ*

*"The Lord will do combat for you"* • *"And the waters were divided"* • *"I sing to the Lord"* • *Parallelism and onomatopoeia* • *Judaism and its opposite* • *The meaning of holiness* • *"The Lord will reign forever"* • *"What will we drink?"* • *Bread from heaven* • *Erase the memory of Amalek*

**13:17. Now, when Pharaoh let the people go, God did not guide them in the direction of the country of the Philistines, for it was (too) near; for God said, "The people, upon seeing war, could change its mind and go back to Egypt."**

***when Pharaoh let... go** (be-shallaḥ)*. The Hebrew is not *ke-shallaḥ* (which would have meant "after he let go"), but *be-shallaḥ* (which means "at the time that he let go"), for God did not have this thought [only] after they departed.

***God did not guide them**, etc.* God does not suddenly change people's hearts; rather, He deals with each individual slowly according to the individual's nature and characteristics. When Israel left the house of bondage, it was not possible for them to be strong and courageous (see Ibn Ezra on Exod. 14:13)[1]

---

1. There, Ibn Ezra comments that it should not be surprising that 600,000 Israelite men were afraid to attack their Egyptian pursuers, for they had been conditioned to act as submissive slaves.

and do battle immediately against the seven nations [of Canaan] and take possession of the land. Even if God had delivered their enemies into their hands amid signs and wonders, they would not have been in a proper condition to become an independent nation governing itself with wisdom and understanding. Slaves who are suddenly released from the heavy yoke of oppression will either remain fainthearted, or else will turn to the other extreme and sink into anarchy, unable to exercise the functions of government for lack of the power and wisdom that are necessary for the establishment of a free society.

For this reason, God did not wish to bring them immediately into the land and into warfare, for upon seeing war in their timid condition, they would have chosen slavery and gone back to Egypt. Instead, He guided them toward the desert so that they would remain there for some time and gradually gain training, acquiring the character traits they would need in order to govern themselves in their land. There was another reason for this as well: in the great desert, it would be possible for them to receive the Torah and the commandments as one people together, to become educated in the fear of God and the knowledge of His ways, and to learn to trust in God under His leadership and that of Moses His servant. If they had come immediately to take possession of the land, they would have dispersed, each one to his allotted territory, and it would have been impossible for them to be educated together as one.

Even if they had not been delayed in the desert for forty years on account of the spies, they would have stayed there for a few months until they received the Torah and the commandments while encamped around Mount Sinai, with manna to eat and without the burden of working the soil.

*for it was (too) near.* That "direction" (*derekh*, lit. "way").

**13:18. But God caused the people to turn toward the desert, along the Red Sea. Yet the children of Israel departed armed from the country of Egypt.**

**armed** *(va-ḥamushim).* With weapons; just as the term *ḥalutsim* ("pioneers," "vanguard") is derived from *ḥalatsayim* ("hips," "loins"), *ḥamushim* is derived from *ḥomesh* ("hip," "groin") (see, e.g., 2 Sam. 20:7), the part of the body where the sword is girded. This statement indicates that it was not for lack of arms that God said, "The people could change its mind," but because of their faintheartedness.

## Beshallaḥ

**13:19.** Moses then took with him the bones of Joseph, for he had adjured the children of Israel, saying, "God will show Himself mindful of you, and (then) you will transport my bones from here with you."
**13:20.** They departed from Sukkot, and they encamped in Etam, at the edge of the desert.
**13:21.** And the Lord went before them by day by means of a pillar of cloud to show them the way, and by night with a pillar of fire to make light for them, so that they might journey both by day and by night.

***And the Lord went before them,*** *etc.* John Toland, in his book *Tetradymus* (London, 1720), and many others among the modern deniers [of miracles], said that Aaron or some other person would conduct the fire before the people, just as the Persians used to do, as Curtius wrote [in his *Life of Alexander*] (Book 5, ch. 7) [Book 3, ch. 3 in standard editions]: "Now the order of the procession was such: a fire signal, which itself they called sacred and eternal, was carried in front on a silver altar." It has been said that the fire was seen from a distance by day on account of the smoke that rose from it, while by night the fire was visibly bright. Thus, Curtius himself relates that Alexander would light bonfires when his camp traveled: "A fire was observed by night, and smoke by day" [Book 5, ch. 2]. They also cite the statement of the Englishman [Joseph] Pitts that the Arabs who travel through the desert in caravans light their way at night with a fire that they place in an iron brazier, which is raised on a tall pole.

The correct explanation is given by J.E. Faber, in his book *Archäologie der Hebräer*: God made the sign and wonder in conformance with what was customary among the peoples of those times and places. Perhaps one might say that the verse in question does not absolutely require [us to believe] that this pillar was of a miraculous nature, for we find a similar-sounding statement, "and the Ark of the pact of the Lord went before them… to provide them with rest" (Num. 10:33), and we know that the ark did not travel miraculously, but that the Levites carried it. Also, we often find that a messenger of God (even if human) is called by the name of his Sender. Thus it might be possible to interpret the phrase "the Lord went before them" as referring to a select and holy man who went before them by command of God.

However, I say that what we find below—

- "Then the angel of God departed, he who was going before the camp of Israel… and the pillar of cloud departed from before them" (Exod. 14:19);

- "And he was (for the former) cloud and darkness, and (for the latter) he brightened the night" (Exod. 14:20);
- "The Lord looked [turned] toward the camp of the Egyptians with a pillar of fire and of cloud, and He threw the camp of the Egyptians into confusion" (Exod. 14:24).

—demonstrates that this phenomenon was miraculous. In addition, Moses' statement, "[The Canaanites,] who have heard that You, O Lord, are in the midst of this people, for it was manifestly seen that You, O Lord, that is, Your cloud, stood over them, and with a pillar of cloud You went before them during the day, and with a pillar of fire during the night" (Num. 14:14), indicates that this was an overt miracle that was seen by all the nations, for even the gentiles recognized that it was supernatural.

Similarly, the Psalmist mentions among the wonders [of the Exodus], "He spread a cloud for a screen, and fire to give light in the night" (Ps. 105:39). So also Nehemiah, after saying that God had divided the sea before them, went on to say, "In a pillar of cloud You led them by day…" (Neh. 9:12).

**13:22. The pillar of cloud did not (ever) cease by day, nor the pillar of fire by night, before the people.**

***did not cease** (yamish)*. The Hebrew is an intransitive verb in the *kal* conjugation, from the root *mish*, as in, "[Joshua] did not move [*yamish*] from the tent" (Exod. 33:11); "Neither shall it cease [*yamish*] from yielding fruit" (Jer. 17:8).

***before the people** (lifnei ha-am)*. The Hebrew properly should have been *mi-lifnei ha-am* ("from before the people"), but the [prefix] *mem* was omitted; cf., "Guard yourselves from going up [*alot*, instead of *me-alot*] on the mountain" (Exod. 19:12).

Some say that the verse should be construed as, "The pillar of cloud and the pillar of fire that were before the people did not cease." So it is rendered in the Jerusalem Targum: *le-madbera kodam ama*, that is, "that went before the people."

In Rashi's comment [on this verse], the word *mashlim* means "hand over" ["The pillar of cloud would hand over [*mashlim*] to the pillar of fire," etc.] (as in Ezra 7:19 [*hashlem kodam Elah Yerushelem*, "deliver [the vessels] before the God of Jerusalem"]). My student, Rabbi Moses Cohen Porto, says that soldiers on guard duty wait at their post until their replacement arrives, and then they (verbally) "hand over" what they must guard. Rashi's comment [on the phrase "pillar of cloud"] in *Shabbat* 23b says that [the pillar of cloud would] "hand over [*mashlim*] its light" [to the pillar of fire], but this is an inexact rendering. Below, at 14:19 [on the phrase "and the pillar of cloud departed from before them"], Rashi himself wrote, "The pillar of cloud handed *the camp* over to the pillar of fire," and this conforms exactly to Moses Cohen Porto's explanation that the guard hands over to his fellow *what he must guard*.

**14:1. And the Lord spoke to Moses, saying:**
**14:2. "Speak to the children of Israel, that they should turn back and camp before Pi-ha-Hirot, between Migdol and the sea, before (that is) Baal-zephon. Facing this you will camp, by the sea.**

***before Pi-ha-Hirot.*** According to Jost (*Allgemeine Geschichte* I.90), this is the city of Heroöpolis (near Suez), for *pi* in the Egyptian language is the equivalent of the definite article *ha-* [in Hebrew], and the word *polis* in Greek means "city." For Jablonski's opinion, see Gesenius' *Thesaurus*, p. 1102.[2]

***Migdol.*** A city at the northern border of Egypt, mentioned also in Jer. 44:1 and 46:14, and Ezek. 29:10 and 30:6.

***Baal Tsefon.*** Apparently *Tsefon* is the equivalent of Typhon, the name of an Egyptian evil angel (*cacodaemon*); it seems that this name was given to places in the uncultivated area between the Nile and the Red Sea (J.R. Forster, Rosenmueller, and Gesenius).

This [command of God] was in order to mislead the Egyptians, who would say that their god was hard to overcome (as per Rashi), for when the Israelites came near to that evil deity, [it would appear that] they had lost their way and were confused. Perhaps, too, when the Egyptians saw that the Israelites were encamped in that place, they would realize that the Israelites did not intend to celebrate a holiday [to God], for this would not be an appropriate location, since it was sacred to the evil deity.

**14:3. "And Pharaoh will think that the children of Israel are encumbered in the country, that the desert closed passage to them.**

---

2. Jablonski derived the name from the Coptic *pi-achi-roth*, "the place of meadows."

***the desert closed passage to them*** *(sagar aleihem ha-midbar*, lit., "the desert closed on them"). The desert closed their way to them (Mendelssohn).

**14:4.** **"I will then render Pharaoh's heart strong, and he will pursue them; then I will make Myself honor [I will demonstrate My power] in Pharaoh and in all of his army, and the Egyptians will know that I am the Lord." And they did so.**
**14:5. It was told to the king of Egypt that the people had fled [that is, that they did not intend to celebrate a holiday and then return], and the mind of Pharaoh and his servants was turned to the people; and they said, "What have we done, letting Israel go from serving us?"**

***that the people had fled*** — that they did not intend to celebrate a holiday and return, for they were encamped before Baal-zephon.

***and the mind of Pharaoh and his servants was turned to*** *(va-yehafekh... el)* ***the people.*** This does not mean that they "changed their mind"; rather, the expression is similar to *nehpakh el ha-rodef* ("turned back upon the pursuers," Josh. 8:20). Once the Egyptians realized that the Israelites had fled, they turned their mind to them, just as a person turns his mind toward anything that he once had but lost, for when Israel was under their control, they did not realize how valuable their labor was to them. Now that the Israelites had fled, the Egyptians began to consider to matter and said, "What have we done?"

**14:6. And (Pharaoh) tied up his carriages, and he took his people with him.**

***And (Pharaoh) tied up his carriages*** *(rikhbo).* The noun *rekhev* can refer to the animal that one rides (*rokhev*) upon, as in:

- "And David slew of the Arameans seven hundred *rekhev*" (2 Sam. 10:18);
- "And David houghed all the *rekhev*" (2 Sam. 8:4);
- "And you shall be filled at My table with horses and *rekhev*" (Ezek. 39:20).

Here, too, it seems to me that *rekhev* refers to the horses that the horsemen (*parashim*) rode.[3] I do not deny that there were also carriages there, for it is

---

3. Shadal's text translation of *rikhbo* (It. *i suoi cocchi*) obviously does not conform to his comment.

written, "And He detached the wheels of their carriages [*markevotav*]" (below, v. 25), but the term "tying up" (*asirah*) pertains to animals, as in:

- "Harness [*isru*] the horses" (Jer. 46:4);
- "And tie [*va-asartem*] the cows to the cart" (1 Sam. 6:7);
- "But the horses [were] tied [*asur*], and the asses tied [*asur*]" (2 Kings 7:10).

One cannot argue from the phrase, "Joseph, his carriage [*merkavo*] having been harnessed [*va-ye'sor*]" (Gen. 46:29), for indeed *merkavah* can also refer to horses, and in particular to [a team of] four horses, as it is written, "And a *merkavah* came up and went out of Egypt for six hundred shekels of silver, and a horse for a hundred and fifty" (1 Kings 10:29). Later, the vehicle with a seat that was drawn by horses came to be called *rekhev* and *merkavah*, as in the term *rekhev barzel* ("iron chariot"), even though "sitting" is not the same as "riding," and the term *rekhivah* properly refers not to sitting in a vehicle, but to riding on an animal. It is only by way of transferred meaning that a vehicle in which one sits came to be called *merkavah* or *rekhev*.

***and... his people*** — those who went on foot.

## 14:7. He took six hundred chosen carriages, besides all the other carriages of Egypt; and all of them carried strong warriors.

***six hundred chosen carriages*** *(rekhev baḥur)*. Having mentioned that he had taken "all the [other] *rekhev* of Egypt," it would seem unnecessary for the text to say that he took six hundred chosen *rekhev*. However, the meaning is that he had more than this number of chosen *rekhavim*, but he did not take them all with him, so that the rest might be spared. The rest of the *rekhev* of Egypt, which were not as distinguished, were all taken.

***and... strong warriors*** *(ve-shalishim)* — men of valor. According to Ibn Ezra, the second in rank after the king was called the *mishneh* (which is true), and the third in rank was called the *shalish* [from *shalosh*, "three"]. Abravanel said that each *shalish* was an officer in charge of thirty (*sheloshim*) men.

In the Greek translation ascribed to the seventy elders [the Septuagint], the word is rendered *tristatai* ("soldiers fighting from chariots"). Origen explained that they were so called because in each chariot there were three men, i.e., one driver and two warriors; this was also the view of Gesenius.

According to Jacob Lydius, they were called *triarii* in Latin, since they went into battle only after two other battle lines fell. He added that perhaps *shalish* merely denotes "very strong," for the number three indicates a superlative degree; cf. *kadosh kadosh kadosh*, "holy, holy, holy" (Isa. 6:3), *trismegistus* ("thrice greatest") [an epithet of Hermes].

**14:8. The Lord rendered strong the heart of Pharaoh king of Egypt, and he ran after the children of Israel, while the children of Israel went forth [journeyed] with a high hand [that is, without fear or haste].**

***with a high hand*** *(be-yad ramah)*. They were not at all anxious until they saw Pharaoh and his people pursuing them; then they were "exceedingly afraid" (below, v. 10) (Rashbam). Cf., "But one who acts [transgresses] with a raised hand [*be-yad ramah*]" (Num. 15:30). Onkelos, however, rendered this expression as "with a bare head," for bare-headedness was considered an indication of fearlessness, while a covered head was a sign of submission.

**14:9. The Egyptians having pursued them, they overtook them (while they were) encamped by the sea; (there pursued them, that is) all the horses of Pharaoh's carriages, his horsemen, and his army, (and they overtook them) by Pi-ha-Hirot, before Baal-zephon.**

***all the horses of Pharaoh's carriages*** *(kol sus rekhev Par'oh)* — all of his riding horses, i.e., those ridden by horsemen.[4] It might seem that since the horsemen are mentioned, it would not have been necessary to mention the horses, but the horses are separately mentioned in order to describe for us the causes for Israel's fright. Besides being frightened by the sight of the horsemen and the army, they were terrified by the sight of the horses themselves. The horses are mentioned first because they were the first to be seen and heard; only afterwards did the people see the horsemen, and then they saw the soldiers.

**14:10. And as soon as Pharaoh was near, the children of Israel, having raised their eyes and seen the Egyptians marching behind them, were exceedingly afraid, and they cried out to the Lord.**

***was near*** *(hikriv)*. The Hebrew is an intransitive verb, "became near" [even though it is in the *hif'il* or "causative" conjugation].

---

[4]. Here again, as in v. 6 above, the translation and the commentary differ as to the meaning of the word *rekhev*.

**14:11. And they said to Moses, "Is it perhaps because graves were lacking in Egypt that you have led us to die in the desert? What is this that you have done to us, to bring us out of Egypt?**

***Is it perhaps because… were lacking*** *(ha-mi-beli ein).* The Hebrew [lit., "without not"] is a double negative, where one would have sufficed; cf. *ha-rak akh be-Mosheh*, "[Has the Lord spoken] only [lit., "only, only"] with Moses?" (Num. 12:2).

***What is this that you have done to us.*** But had they not seen with their own eyes all the plagues that God had inflicted upon Egypt, and understood that it was not Moses who had done all this? Abravanel said that perhaps they thought that it had been God's will [merely] to lighten the burden of Egypt from upon them and to release them from their labor, but not that they should leave the country. This is unlikely, for Moses had indeed mentioned to them the matter of leaving the country; when speaking of the Passover, he had said to them, "Now, when the Lord will have brought you to the country of the Canaanites…" (Exod. 13.5).

In my opinion, the correct explanation is that according to the popular belief of the times, God's priests and confidants could perform supernatural deeds by means of divine power, even without a command from God Himself, for they believed that God formed an alliance with His priests, who knew the methods of worshipping Him, and that God could be enticed by them and would do their will (see my comment on Isa. 1:11).[5] Thus, it was possible for the Israelites of that time to believe that the plagues of Egypt were supernatural signs and wonders, but that nevertheless, their exodus from Egypt was not by Divine will, but by the will of Moses.

**14:12. "Did we not already say to you in Egypt, 'Let us be, that we may serve the Egyptians'? For it would be better for us to serve the Egyptians than to die in the desert."**

---

5. There, commenting on God's admonition ("To what purpose is the multitude of your sacrifices to Me?") Shadal said that the Israelites of Moses' time "believed that the signs and wonders they had seen were indeed miraculous and accomplished through Divine power, but they thought that God formed an alliance with His priests and wise men… and that God could be enticed by them and would do their will. Thus it seemed likely to them that their exodus from Egypt was by virtue of Divine power, with genuine and Divine wonders, and yet was not according to God's will or command, but rather through the will of Moses and Aaron, His priests, who had enticed Him with their worship and could sway Him to do whatever they wished."

## Shadal on Exodus

***Did we not already say,*** *etc.* We do not find that they actually said this to him. However, the Samaritans added a verse after Exod. 6:9 ("But they did not pay heed to Moses, because of the anxiety they were in, and because of the hard slavery"): "And they said to Moses, 'Let us be, and let us serve the Egyptians, for it would be better for us to serve the Egyptians than to die in the desert.'" But how could it be that amid the pain of hard slavery, the danger of the desert would enter their minds? And if in fact they were concerned about dying in the desert, then their failure to heed Moses was not because of their anxiety and hard slavery, but was due to wisdom, prudence, and presence of mind.

The correct explanation is in accordance with the statement in the Mekhilta, "Where did they say such a thing? 'Let the Lord see, and let Him lay blame on you and judge' (Exod. 5:21)." It was then that they complained that Pharaoh had made their yoke heavier, and they said to Moses, "If you had not come, we would have been serving the Egyptians in peace." But the latter part of the statement here, "For it for it would be better for us to serve the Egyptians than to die in the desert," seems (as per Abravanel) to be an amplification that they were adding now.

The reason that they said "…than to die in the desert" and not "…than to die by Egypt's sword" is that it never occurred to them to do battle with their masters the Egyptians, but rather they immediately thought of fleeing. There was nothing ahead of them but the sea and the desert, and it seemed to them that in any event they would be facing death. Moses understood this and told them not to be afraid, for God would do combat for them against Egypt.

**14:13. But Moses said to the people, "Do not be afraid. Stand to see the salvation that the Lord will work for you today. For after having seen the Egyptians today, you will never see them again.**

***For after having seen the Egyptians,*** *etc.* That is, "After the sight that you have seen of them today, you will never see them again." The Rabbis made this into a negative commandment, which is supported by the statement, "The Lord has said to you, 'Do not ever return on this way'" (Deut. 17:16). According to the plain meaning of the verse here, it is undoubtedly a reassurance that contains within it a command; that is, "God promises you that you will never see them again, and furthermore, it is not proper for you ever to go back among them willingly."

My student R. David Hazak explains this verse by reversing the words [*asher re'item et Mitsrayim*], as if it said *et Mitsrayim asher re'item*, "These Egyptians that you see today, you will never see them again"; this was the translation given by Diodati and also Jerome.

## Beshallaḥ

**14:14. "The Lord will do combat for you, and you will stay quiet."**

*will stay quiet (taharishun).* The Hebrew means "to be quiet as a deaf-mute" (*heresh*); cf. "O God of my praise, keep not silent [*al teherash*]" (Ps. 109:1). A similar verb root is *hashah*, as in, "Be not deaf [*al teherash*] to me, lest You be silent [*tehesheh*] to me" (Ps. 28:1); "And we are still [*maḥshim*]" (1 Kings 22:3). See also Gen. 34:5.[6]

**14:15. And the Lord said to Moses, "Why are you crying out to me? Speak to the children of Israel, and let them be on their way.**

*Why are you crying out to me?* God did not inform Moses in advance about the splitting of the Red Sea; all He had said was, "I will make Myself honor in Pharaoh..." (above, v. 4). Thus, when Moses saw the Egyptians moving after them, he did not know how or by what means God would save the Israelites, so he told them to "stand to see the salvation that the Lord will work for you today," so as to encourage them, but then he prayed to God (Nachmanides, Mendelssohn).

**14:16. "And you, raise your staff, and stretch forth your arm toward the sea, and divide it; and the children of Israel will enter in the midst of the sea in the dry land.**
**14:17. "I will then render strong the hearts of the Egyptians, and they will enter after them; and I will make Myself honor in Pharaoh and in all his army, in his carriages and in his horsemen.**
**14:18. "And the Egyptians will know that I am the Lord, My power being demonstrated in Pharaoh, in his carriages, and in his horsemen."**
**14:19. Then the angel of God departed, he who was going before the camp of Israel, and he went behind them; and the pillar of cloud departed from before them, and its stood behind them.**
**14:20. He (the angel) came between the camp of the Egyptians and that of Israel, and he was (for the former) cloud and darkness, and (for the latter) he brightened the night; and throughout that night the one camp did not come close to the other.**

*He came between the camp.* Today, 21 Iyyar 5619 (1859), it seems to me that this is to be taken in the literal sense, with a distinction between "the angel"

---

[6]. There, on the phrase "but Jacob remained silent [*ve-heḥerish*]," Shadal cross-refers to the present verse and similarly discusses the roots *harash* and *hashah*.

and "the cloud." This is why the text repeated itself and said [first] of the angel that "he went behind them," and [then] said of the cloud that "it stood behind them." The phrase "came between the camp" refers not to the cloud [*contra* Rashi], but to the angel: it was the angel who was cloud and darkness for the one group and who brightened the night for the other group.

***and he was cloud and darkness.*** For the Egyptians, for the pillar of cloud went behind the Israelites.

***and he brightened the night.*** The aforementioned angel of God brightened the night for the Israelites; that is, when night came, he served as a pillar of fire for them, as they were accustomed to have every night.

***the one camp did not come close to the other.*** The Egyptians did not come close to the Israelites, on account of the cloud and darkness that was in front of the Egyptians.

**14:21. Moses then stretched forth his arm toward the sea, and the Lord made the sea flow by means of a powerful east wind throughout the night, and He reduced the sea to dry land, and the waters were divided.**

***And the Lord made the sea flow,*** *etc.* The splitting of the Red Sea, as recounted in the Torah, was a miraculous event mixed with natural elements, for if God had not wished to make any use at all of the forces of nature, what was the "powerful east wind" for? The text itself explicitly states that God made the sea flow with a strong wind; thus Rashbam wrote, "As in the normal way of the world, the Holy One, blessed is He, caused the wind to dry and congeal the streams."

Therefore, in order to explain how this came about, Clericus (followed by many) said that the Israelites crossed the Red Sea [i.e., the Gulf of Suez] at its northern end, toward Suez and Pi-ha-Hirot (as is the tradition among the Arabs), and they passed through it as its waters were turning back and receding, but when Moses stretched forth his arm over the sea, God sent a powerful wind that blew from north to south and prevented the waters from returning quickly, so that the low tide lasted many more hours than normal. They said this because if it had been the power of the wind alone that had dried the sea, it could not be understood how people could have passed through it without being swept away by the wind.

# Beshallaḥ

A similar occurrence was cited by Clericus as having taken place in 1672, during a war between the English and the Dutch, when a strong wind blew and prolonged the absence of sea water up to twelve hours; the English [ships] could not enter the dry land, and the result was a great salvation for the people of Holland.[7]

Clericus and his followers maintained that this wind was not literally an "east wind," but rather a north wind, but because the east wind was strong and harsh in those regions, they would call any strong wind an "east wind," as in:

- "With the east wind You break the ships of Tarshish" (Ps. 48:8);
- "The east wind has broken you in the heart of the seas" (Ezek. 27:26);
- "I will scatter them as with an east wind before the enemy" (Jer. 18:17);
- "He has removed her with His rough blast in the day of the east wind" (Isa. 27:8);
- "The east wind carries him away, and he departs" (Job 27:21).

On the other hand, the scholar Jost (*Allgemeine Geschichte* I.92.92) says that the splitting of the Red Sea was not at all due to the return of the [tidal] sea waters in the course of nature, but rather was caused entirely by a great and powerful storm wind. In answer to the question of how the Israelites could have crossed the sea during such a storm, he says that the storm took place on the previous day and night, turning the sea into dry land, and that Moses had the Israelites cross the sea after the fury of the storm had passed but before the waters returned to their place. He understood the phrase "and the Lord made the sea flow" (*va-yolekh YHVH et ha-yam*) to mean "the Lord *had* made."

In any event, there is no doubt that this phenomenon consisted of miracles mixed with natural occurrences. The scholar Niebuhr, who was there in 1762 (*Description de l'Arabie*), proved that it could not have been a completely natural event, for although he himself crossed the Red Sea at Suez by camel, accompanied by Arabs who walked through water that reached only up to their knees, it is unlikely that so numerous a people as Israel could have done

---

7. Historical accounts of the Third Anglo-Dutch War (1672-1678) indicate that Clericus was most probably referring to the first Battle of Schooneveld, which took place in May 1673 when English and French ships attacked a Dutch fleet in the coastal waters at the mouth of the Schelde River. Although these accounts do not corroborate Clericus (as cited by Luzzatto) in full, they attest that the battle was delayed by stormy weather, that the delay allowed the Dutch to prepare a surprising and successful counterattack, and that the shallow waters and shoals hampered the invading ships.

so. The caravans traveling between Cairo and Mount Sinai never crossed the Red Sea, despite the fact that if this had been possible, it would have been of great advantage to them. Besides, it is known that 3,000 years ago, the sea was deeper and wider than it is now, and that through the ages, the floor of the sea became much higher, on account of the buildup of sand, than it had been in ancient times.

As for the slight difficulty raised by some as to how the Israelites could have crossed the Red Sea floor, covered as it [allegedly] was with coral, this too was answered by Niebuhr, who said that this does not exist at all at the end of the sea toward Suez, for there the sea floor is entirely sand and is easy to walk on. This scholar also attested that the algae (*suf*) that grows plentifully in the Red Sea (*Yam Suf*) does not grow at all at the end in question.

It should be noted that the matter of the drying of the Red Sea's waters remains in the tradition of [some] peoples of the earth. Thus, Diodorus Siculus (*Bibliotheca Historica* 3:39) recorded that a people that lived on fish (*Ichthiophagi*) and dwelled near the Red Sea had a tradition received from their ancestors that this entire area had once been turned into dry land.

Wessely, on the basis of what he found in the book of wisdom falsely attributed to King Solomon [i.e., the pseudepigraphic Wisdom of Solomon], unnecessarily overloaded the Torah's account with signs and wonders, and said that the sea floor rose up, while the sea waters split and were piled up on either side of the newly formed pathway, standing like a heap until the Israelites passed through, and that when the Egyptians came, the sea floor suddenly fell and the waters collapsed over them.[8] See the commentary of my friend, the scholar Reggio,[9] and see also, in Ibn Ezra's commentary (below on v. 27), the opinion of Hiwi [al-Balkhi], who claimed that it was all a natural occurrence, and Ibn Ezra's rejoinders to his fantasies.[10]

***and the Lord made the sea flow*** (*va-yolekh et*, lit., "made go"). Compare:

---

8. Perhaps Wessely was elaborating on these passages from the Wisdom of Solomon: "...dry land emerging where water had stood before, an unhindered way out of the Red Sea, and a grassy plain out of the raging waves, where those protected by thy hand passed through as one nation, after gazing on marvelous wonders" (19:7-8, Revised Standard Version).
9. Reggio's conception of the splitting of the Red Sea is essentially similar to that of Wessely.
10. Hiwi al-Balkhi (9th century C.E.), whose heretical views were condemned by Rabbanites and Karaites alike, maintained that Moses relied on his knowledge of the Red Sea tides and had the people cross over the sea at low tide, while Pharaoh's ignorance of the tides led to his drowning.

- "And we traveled through [*va-nelekh et*] all that desert" (Deut. 1:19);
- "And He knew your going through [*lekhtekh et*] this great desert" (Deut. 2:7);
- "And by His light I walked through [*elekh*] darkness" (Job 29:3);
- "Though he walks [*halakh*] in darkness" (Isa. 50:10).

The phrase here is the equivalent of "the Lord caused an east wind to go through the sea"; it was the wind that went, not the sea. God caused the wind to go as described above: "And the Lord caused an east wind to come in the country" (Exod. 10:13) (21 Iyyar 5619 [1859]).

**14:22. And the children of Israel walked in the middle of the sea in the dry land, having the waters as walls on the right and on the left.**

*having the waters as walls, etc.* According to Ibn Ezra, the waters froze and then, after the Israelites passed through, they melted, as it is written below, "The waters piled up; they stood upright like a heap" (Exod. 15:8). However, the correct view is that of Gersonides and Abravanel: the waters were not [literally] high [walls] to the right and left; rather, the wind moved them there and restrained them from flowing, as is seen with sea waves that gather at the shore during a storm. Then was formed the path on which they crossed like a bridge from one side to the other, and on either side [of the path] the waters piled up and could not pass over and flood the pathway.

The expression "as walls" means that the waters were about them on the right and left, not literally like a wall or a heap, even though it says, by way of poetic simile, "They stood upright like a heap." Clericus brings proof for this from the expression in Nahum, "Are you better than No-Amon, that was situate among the rivers, that had the waters round about her; whose rampart was the sea, and of the sea her wall?" (Nah. 3:8).

**14:23. And the Egyptians, pursuing them, entered behind them, (that is) all Pharaoh's horses, his carriages, and his horsemen, into the sea.**
**14:24. Now, in the morning watch [in the last hours of the night], the Lord looked [turned] toward the camp of the Egyptians with a pillar of fire and of cloud [sending thunder and lightning], and He threw the camp of the Egyptians into disorder.**

*in the morning watch.* At the end of the night, for the night is divided into watches, the last of which is called the "morning watch" (*Berakhot* 3b).

***the Lord looked toward the camp of the Egyptians.*** He turned toward them with an evil intent, by means of a pillar of fire and cloud that He sent before them. Apparently what is meant is thunder, lightning, and "arrows of God" [see above on 9:23], as the Psalmist said:

> You have, with Your arm, redeemed Your people…
> The waters saw You, O God…
> The clouds flooded forth waters;
> The skies sent out a sound;
> Your arrows also went abroad.
> The voice of Your thunder was in the whirlwind;
> The lightnings lighted up the world;
> The earth trembled and shook (Ps. 77:16-19).

In addition, we find the term *hamam* ("to throw into disorder," "to discomfit") [which appears here in the phrase *va-yahom et mahaneh Mitsrayim*, "and He threw the camp of the Egyptians into disorder"] used in connection with lightning and thunder:

- "But the Lord thundered with a great thunder on that day against the Philistines, and discomfited them [*va-yhummem*]" (1 Sam. 7:10);
- "And He shot forth lightnings, and discomfited them [*va-yhummem*]" (Ps. 18:15);
- "Cast forth lightning, and scatter them; send out Your arrows, and discomfit them [*u-t'hummem*]" (Ps. 144:6).

Josephus Flavius, too, gave a similar account.[11]

***and He threw the camp of the Egyptians into disorder*** (*va-yahom et mahaneh Mitsrayim*). The root *hamam* sometimes denotes destruction, as in:

- "Making them perish [*le-hummam*] from amidst the camp" (Deut. 2:15);
- "[Nebuchadnezzar] has devoured me, he has crushed me [*hamamani*]" (Jer. 51:34);
- "To discomfit them [*le-hummam*], and to destroy them" (Esth. 9:24).

---

11. Josephus' retelling of the aftermath of the splitting of the Red Sea (*Antiquities* 2:16) contains the following passages: "Showers of rain also came down from the sky, and dreadful thunders and lightning, with flashes of fire. Thunderbolts were also darted upon them [the Egyptians]…" (trans. Whiston).

## *Beshallaḥ*

Otherwise it denotes scattering, that is, a scattering after defeat or destruction, as in:

- "And I will put in disorder [*ve-hammoti*] every people where you will enter, and I will compel all your enemies to turn their necks to you" (Exod. 23:27);
- "And He sent out His arrows, and scattered them; and He shot forth lightnings, and discomfited them [*va-yehummem*]" (Ps. 18:15).

Here, too, the pillar of fire and cloud—that is, the thunder, lightning, and "arrows"—destroyed and scattered the camp of the Egyptians. This fits in best with Jost's view that there was a great storm which had abated when the Israelites crossed over, but then returned to wreak destruction on the Egyptians; this occurred so that the Egyptians should know before their death that it was God Who was doing combat against them for Israel (as He said above, v. 18), which would not have been known if the Egyptians had suddenly drowned in the sea.

**14:25. And He detached the wheels of their carriages, thus making them go with great difficulty. Then the Egyptians said, "Let us flee from the Israelites, for the Lord is doing combat for them against the Egyptians."**

*And He detached.* [The subject, missing in the Hebrew, is] God, acting by means of his "arrows."

*thus making them go* (*va-y'nahagehu*). God drove (*nahag*) the Egyptians, i.e., He caused them to go with difficulty.

**14:26. But the Lord said to Moses, "Stretch forth your arm toward the sea, and let the waters come back over the Egyptians, on their carriages, and on their horsemen."**
**14:27. Moses stretched forth his arm toward the sea, and the sea at the break of morning returned to its natural state, and the Egyptians, fleeing, went toward it. Thus the Lord hurled down the Egyptians in the midst of the sea.**

*to its natural state* (*le-eitano*) — to its previous condition. Schultens (followed by Rosenmueller and Gesenius) said that *eitan* is derived from the root *yatan*, which means "was continuous" in Arabic; they understood the expression *naharot eitan* (Ps. 74:15) as rivers that flow constantly, without interruption. Even they, however, were compelled to acknowledge that in the expression *va-teshev be-eitan kashto*, "but his bow vigorously resisted" (Gen. 49:24), *be-eitan* means "with strength."

It seems to me that the basic meaning of this root refers to something permanent and unchanging, but it was later transferred to mean anything strong or hard that is also permanent and unchanging. The word *le-eitano* means "to what its nature always was," not as Gesenius wrote in his *Lexicon*, "perennial, ever-flowing."

**hurled down** *(va-yna'er)*. He caused them to fall into the sea; cf., "That it [the dawn] might take hold of the ends of the earth, and the wicked be shaken [*ve-yinna'aru*] out of it" (Job 38:13).

**14:28. The waters returned (to their place), and they covered the carriages and the horsemen, all the army of Pharaoh that came after them [the Israelites] into the sea. Not one individual remained of them.**

**all the army of Pharaoh** *(le-khol ḥeil Par'oh)*. The prefix *le-* [in *le-khol*, lit., "to all"] signifies "that is"; cf., "[Who smote many nations, and slew many kings:] Sihon [*le-Siḥon*] king of the Amorites..." (Ps. 135:11). Sometimes this prefix means "in sum," as in, "[And you will make its pots... and it shovels, and its basins, and its forks, and its paddles;] all [*le-khol*] of its furnishings you will make with copper" (Exod. 27:3); "All [*le-khol*] the furnishings of the tabernacle" (Exod. 27:19).

**14:29. And the children of Israel had walked on the dryness in the midst of the sea, having the water as a wall on the right and on the left.**
**14:30. Thus the Lord saved the Israelites on that day from the hands of the Egyptians, and the Israelites saw (some of) the Egyptians (lying) dead on the shore of the sea.**

**dead on the shore of the sea.** The Israelites had hastened on their way and did not see the downfall of the Egyptians, but saw only some of them dead on the shore, for most of them had been swallowed into the depths of the sea—as it says, "the earth swallowed them" (Exod. 15:12)—and only a few of them were thrown up by the storm waters onto the shore.

# Beshallaḥ

**14:31. The Israelites saw [recognized] the great power that the Lord had exercised against the Egyptians, and the people were pervaded with fear of the Lord, and with faith in the Lord and in Moses His servant.**

**15:1. Then Moses and the children of Israel sang to the Lord the following hymn, saying, "I sing to the Lord, for He has shown Himself supreme; horse and rider has He thrown into the sea.**

***Then Moses… sang.*** Some of the critics of our time (Nachtigal, De Wette, and others) date this song much later than Moses. First, they say that it is improbable that he would have composed it instantaneously at that time. This assertion (even if we say that Moses uttered this song from the heart, in order to thank God for the great salvation that He had granted His people) should pose no difficulty at all for us, given that this song—like all other songs in the Bible—is not bound by the cords of meter and rhyme, but is composed entirely of free speech, such that wherever the spirit and yearning of the poet may lead him, he will go. So we find that Jacob and Moses delivered their blessings at the time of their deaths, and similarly, David composed several psalms while his spirit was troubled, when he was fleeing from Saul or Absalom.

These critics raise another difficulty from the song's allusion to the Temple ("And You will lead them, and You will establish them in the mountainous region [lit., "mountain"] of Your patrimony" [below, v. 17]). But they do not see that Moses' intention in leading the people out of Egypt was undoubtedly that they should fear God and make Him a sanctuary.

They further object that it would have been impossible for all of Israel to learn this song so as to be able to sing it. This is a valid point, but long ago the Rabbis were divided as to how the song was sung at the sea (*Sotah* 30b).[12] I say that Moses declared, "I sing to the Lord, for He has shown Himself supreme; horse and rider has He thrown into the sea," and Israel responded, "Horse and rider has He thrown into the sea"; Moses said, "My strength and my song, He is Yah; He was my salvation," and Israel responded, "Horse and rider has He thrown into the sea." Similarly, Moses said each line (or sometimes half a line), and Israel responded with nothing but these words, "Horse and rider has He thrown into the sea." It would have been easy for the people to learn these four words [Hebrew *sus ve-rokhevo ramah va-yam*] by heart.

---

12. There, R. Akiva expressed the view that after each phrase that Moses sang, the people responded, "I sing to the Lord"; R. Eliezer son of R. Yosi ha-Gelili said that the people repeated the entire song phrase by phrase; and R. Nehemiah said that Moses and the people sang the entire song together.

# Shadal on Exodus

On the same model, we find in Psalm 136, "O give thanks to the Lord, for He is good, for His mercy endures forever," that the words "for His mercy endures forever" are repeated at the end of every verse. Similarly, in the case of the Song of Deborah (Judges 5), it seems to me that after each verse, the people responded, "Bless the Lord" [*Barekhu YHVH*, the concluding phrase of v. 2]. So also with respect to David's song (Psalm 18), the revised version [of the song found in 2 Samuel 22] that was apparently adapted for singing in the Temple, I say that the people responded after each verse, "I love You, O Lord, my strength" (Ps. 18:2).

Hence it can be deduced why all three of these songs [i.e., Moses' Song of the Sea, the Song of Deborah, and Psalm 18] are written [in the Masoretic text] in a distinctive style, "half bricks set over whole bricks": as a reminder that originally, below each verse were written the words that the people would respond; for example [in the Song of Deborah, Judg. 5:2]:

*Bi-fero'a pera'ot be-Yisra'el    be-hitnaddev am*
            *Barekhu YHVH*
*Shime'u melakhim    ha'azinu rozenim*
            *Barekhu YHVH*

You might ask, "If so, then why is Psalm 136 not written 'half bricks over whole bricks' like the three other songs?" The answer is that this would not have been possible, for the response appears after each line [and not after every two phrases].

As for my statement above that biblical songs are not bound by the cords of meter and rhyme, but consist entirely of free speech, this is not the place to prove the truth of this assertion, but it will be explained, God willing, in another place. Some of my writings [on this subject] have been printed in *Der Orient*, 1840, *Literaturblatt* pp. 6, 7, 20, 21, 42, 43, and 44.

The interpretations of this verse by R. Azariah [de' Rossi] (in his book *Me'or Einayim*) and Nachmanides are completely without foundation.[13]

---

13. Although *Me'or Einayim* apparently contains no interpretation of this verse in particular, ch. 60 discusses the nature of biblical poetry. Citing several verses from the Song of the Sea as examples, R. Azariah says that biblical poems, though not based on syllabic meter, can be seen as made up of clauses with two or three "measures" or "feet" based on the number of "ideas" in the clause (see Joanna Weinberg's translation, p. 713). Shadal scrutinizes this theory in his 1840 article in *Der Orient*, "On the Art of Hebrew Poetry," and speaks of its "insufficiency" and "inconsistency," noting that R. Azariah himself conceded that "perhaps the [verses that are] exceptions outnumber those that are applicable." As for

## Beshallaḥ

***for He has shown Himself supreme*** *(ki ga'oh ga'ah)*. The verb *ga'ah* implies height and exaltedness; terms denoting height and superiority are often transferred to refer to one person's overpowering of another. Thus, the verb *gavar* ("to prevail," "to overcome") is derived from *gavah* ("to be high"). Similar expressions in Italian are *superare* ("to surpass," "to surmount") and the adjective *superiore*. Here, the phrase *ga'oh ga'ah* means that God is exalted and prevails over others, that is, those who rise up against Him.

In Hebrew, [conjugated] verbs sometimes serve a descriptive function without denoting any action, as in, "How fair [*yafit*, from the verb *yafah*] and how pleasant [*na'amt*, from the verb *na'am*] are you" (Songs 7:7), and expressions such as *ḥakhemu* ("were wise"), *tsadeku* ("were righteous"), and many others. Here, too, it would have been possible to interpret *ga'oh ga'ah* to mean [simply], "He is high and exalted." However, elsewhere the verb *ga'ah* never denotes [merely] the quality of exaltedness, but rather means "to rise up," as in, "Can the reed shoot up [*ha-yig'eh*]" (Job 8:11); "For the waters were risen [*ga'u*]" (Ezek. 47:5). Moreover, it seems that a verb which serves merely a descriptive function does not occur in a doubled form with the infinitive absolute; thus, one would not say *yafoh yafit*, *ḥakhom ḥakhemu*, or *tsadok tsadeku*. Here too, then, *ga'oh ga'ah* must denote an action and not a description.

However, since it would be impossible to interpret *ga'oh ga'ah* to mean that God became high and exalted after not having been so, there is no alternative but to understand the phrase to mean that "He has shown Himself high and exalted," i.e., that He performed an act through which His exaltedness and supremacy were demonstrated; see v. 7 below.

***horse and rider has He thrown into the sea.*** This [half of the verse] comes to explain the phrase *ki ga'oh ga'ah*.

***horse and rider*** *(sus ve-rokhevo)*. In poetic language, the singular is preferred over the plural, for a much stronger impression is made when the listener's attention is concentrated on a single subject, rather than wandering among many subjects. Consider, for example, the phrase "Judge the orphan, plead for the widow" (Isa. 1:17). If it had said, "Judge the orphans, plead for the widows," the expression would have lost much of its force, for the reader's thought would have wandered among many orphans and widows, but as the phrase

---

Nachmanides, Shadal's disagreement with him is apparently directed at his assertion that the reason for the use of the "future" tense in the phrase *az yashir Mosheh* (lit., "then Moses will sing") is that the narrator is inserting himself at the beginning of the action, as if announcing what is about to happen.

stands, one's attention is concentrated entirely on one orphan and one widow. So also below, it says "the God of my father" (next v.) not "of my fathers."

***has He thrown (ramah) into the sea.*** *Ramah* is an Aramaic word, the Targum equivalent of [the Hebrew] *hishlikh*. It is found [in Hebrew] only in poetic expressions, e.g., *moshekhei romei keshet*, "archers handling the bow" (Ps. 78:9). Similarly, many Aramaisms are unique to Hebrew poetry, such as:

- *enosh* instead of *adam* ("man");
- *atah* instead of *ba* ("come");
- *millah* instead of *davar* ("word");
- *kedem* instead of *olam* ("ancient days").

This is because poetic expression prefers to use words that are not customary among the masses, as well as archaic and foreign words (as in Italian, in which poets choose words from Latin or archaic Italian), for their unusual nature adds to their pleasantness and charm (as has been noted by the author of *Melitsat Yeshurun* [Solomon Lewisohn] on the last page of his book.

Hebrew and Aramaic were originally a single language, but little by little they divided and grew distant from one another.[14] Words that are now Aramaic were once shared by Hebrew and Aramaic, but Hebrew abandoned them and left them to Aramaic. Since these words were archaic and unusual in Hebrew, poets chose them in order to add charm to their expressions. Some of the latter-day critics, however, did not understand this, and everywhere in Scripture that they found Aramaic words or Aramaic-style expressions, they hastened to judge that the book or section in question was written in the Babylonian exile, "at a time when the Hebrew language had lost its glory and had ceased from the lips of its speakers, for their language had been confused in the land of Babel, where they spoke Aramaic."

They did not understand that Aramaisms are proof of a late date of composition [only] when they appear in simple language and not in prophecy or song, as in the books of Daniel, Ezra, Nehemiah, Chronicles, and Esther. There it is clear that the writer chose Aramaic words and expressions not in order to embellish his style, but because he was following his usual speech pattern, being more fluent in Aramaic than in Hebrew. However, in the case

---

14. Modern linguists generally agree that Hebrew and Aramaic are both members of the Northwest Semitic subgroup of Semitic languages and that they separated from a common ancestor; see, e.g., John Huehnergard, "What Is Aramaic?", *Aram* vol. 7 (1995), pp. 261-282.

of the prophetic and poetic books, whose language is refined with the utmost precision and with wondrous wisdom, who would ever say that these words unwittingly slipped through the hands of the sublime poets and rhetoricians, as if they were not experts in the language in which they uttered their soaring expressions and delightful poetry?

Who would believe [for example] that the author of the Hallel, through a careless slip of the tongue, would have said *kol tagmulohi* ("all His bountiful dealings," Ps. 116:12) in the Aramaic style, instead of [the regular Hebrew] *tagmulav*? Or that the author of the Song of Songs unintentionally said *mittato she-li-Shlomoh* ("Solomon's palanquin," lit., "his palanquin, of Solomon," 3:7), an Aramaism, or *shallamah ehyeh ke-otiyah* ("for why should I be as one who veils herself," 1:7), where *shallamah* is derived from the Aramaic *dilma* or *di-lemah* (Ezra 7:23)? Or that the author of Psalm 139 did not know Hebrew because he said *ki ein millah bi-lshoni* ("for there is not a word in my tongue," v. 4) using [the Aramaism] *millah* instead of *davar*?

Who would believe that the author of the Book of Job "spoke half in the speech of Ashdod [and could not speak in the Jews' language," Neh. 13:24], because he said *kattar li ze'eir va'ahavvekka* ("suffer me a little, and I will tell you," Job 36:2), which is an entirely Aramaic utterance? Or that the author of the Song of the Sea was standing in Babylonia, because he said *ramah* instead of *hishlikh*? See below, on the phrase *tevi'emo ve-titta'emo* (v. 17).[15]

**15:2. "My strength and (the subject of) my song is Yah; He was my salvation. This is my God, and I will celebrate Him; He is the God of my father, and I will exalt Him.**

*My strength (ozzi)*. God is my strength and might, for with His help I will overcome all my enemies; compare:

- "O Lord, my strength [*uzzi*] and my stronghold" (Jer. 16:19);
- "The Lord is a strength [*oz*] to them, and He is a stronghold of salvation to His anointed" (Ps. 28:7);
- "God is our refuge and strength [*va-oz*]" (Ps. 46:2).

There is no need to remove the word from its literal meaning and interpret it in the sense of "praise" or "greatness" (as did Rosenmueller and Gesenius).

---

15. Although Shadal's comment on this phrase does not in fact make any reference to Aramaisms, his comment on the word *yokheleimo* (below, v. 7) notes that the suffix *–o* is a poetic embellishment of Aramaic derivation.

# Shadal on Exodus

In the expressions "Give to the Lord glory and *oz*" (Ps. 29:1) and "Give *oz* to God" (Ps. 68:35), the word *oz* does not mean "praise"; rather, these expressions mean, "Ascribe strength and might to God," that is, "Know and understand in your hearts, and acknowledge with your mouths, that strength and might are His." See below on the word *ve-anvehu* ("and I will celebrate Him").

On the subject of the *kamats* (עָזִּי) with which the word *ozzi* is vocalized, it should be noted that the "closed" vowels *i* and *u* precede a letter strengthened with a *dagesh* (when that letter is not preceded by an accent, as in סָבִּי [*sobbi*, where the *munah* accent alters the pronunciation from the regular *subbi*]), while the "broad" vowels *e* and *o* precede a letter marked with a quiescent *sheva*, as the following pairs of words illustrate:

| Words with dagesh | Words with quiescent *sheva* |
|---|---|
| *hukki* ("my law") | *hok'kha* ("your law") |
| *hukkah* ("stricken") | *hofkad* ("appointed") |
| *ittekhem* ("with you") | *etkhem* ("you," accusative plural) |

However, there are exceptions, such as *kollu, kossu, me'oddam* [all words with a *dagesh*], and *muktar* and *yushlakhu* [both words with a quiescent *sheva*].

Rashi correctly pointed out [in his comment on this verse] that every two-letter word that is vocalized with an *o* sound, such as *rok* and *hok*, is instead vocalized with an *u* sound when the word is expanded to three letters, as in *rukki* and *hukki* (except when the second letter has a quiescent *sheva*, as in *hok'kha*), but that in all three instances in which the phrase *ozzi ve-zimrat Yah* appear in Scripture, the letter *ayin* in *ozzi* is marked with a *kamats hatuf* [*kattan*], and that this is a great oddity [since we would have expected to find the word vocalized as *uzzi*]. This oddity constrained Rashi to say that *ozzi* does not mean "my strength," but that the *-i* suffix is superfluous (on the model of *shokheni seneh* [Deut. 33:16]), and that the meaning of the phrase is "the strength and the song of God." [Nevertheless] it is remarkable that Rashi was able to be precise to a hair's breadth in the matter of vowel shifts, even though this was not his special area of expertise and he never saw the books of the fathers of Hebrew grammar, who wrote in Arabic.

Ibn Ezra attacked Rashi and said that there is no [significant] difference between *ozzi* and *uzzi*, just as [there is no such difference where] in once place it is written *hukki* and in another place *hok'kha*, but this last point was already noticed by Rashi, which is why he added [the caveat] "except when the

## Beshallaḥ

second letter has a *sheva*." Ibn Ezra brought further proof from the word *be-ozzekha* [below, v. 13, where the word seemingly should have been vocalized as *be-uzzekha* under Rashi's system]. However, it seems that even this did not escape Rashi's attention, and for this reason he wrote "except when the second letter has a *sheva* or a *hataf*" (as it appears in a manuscript Rashi in my possession).[16] Apparently Rashi used the word *sheva* to mean a quiescent *sheva*, and he used the word *hataf* to mean a mobile *sheva*, in order to account for both *ḥok'kha* [with a quiescent *sheva*] and *ozzekha* [with a mobile *sheva*]

In any case, one truly cannot avoid acknowledging that there is no [significant] difference between *ozzi* and *uzzi*, just as there is no [such] difference between *kollu* and *va-yekhullu*, or *yeḥonnenu* and *yeḥunnekha*, or other such instances.

**and my song** *(ve-zimrat)*. The Hebrew is not in the construct *(semikhut)* state [i.e., it does not mean "the song of"], and therefore it is vocalized with a *kamats* (וְזִמְרָת); cf., *ezrat mi-tsar*, "help against the adversary" (Ps. 60:13); *af naḥalat shaferah alai*, "yea, I have a goodly heritage" (Ps. 16:6). This form is unique to poetic speech and is apparently shortened from *zimratah* and *ezratah* [variants of *zimrah* and *ezrah*], with an intrusive *tav*, on the model of the Aramaic *ḥokhmeta* [the equivalent of the Hebrew *ḥokhmah*] and the like. The Aramaic *sheva* [e.g., the second vowel in *hokhmeta*] switches to a *kamats* in Hebrew, as in:

| Aramaic | Hebrew |
| --- | --- |
| *pekad* | *pakad* |
| *besar* | *basar* |

As for the meaning of the word, there is no doubt that the pronominal suffix *–i* was dropped, and that *zimrat* is the equivalent of *zimrati* ("my song"), as per R. Moses Cohen (cited by Ibn Ezra), i.e., "the One in Whose honor I sing is Yah." The commentators who understood *ve-zimrat* as in the construct state [i.e., "the song of"] resorted to forced interpretations. Thus, Rashi interpreted the phrase as "the strength and the song of God," and Ibn Ezra as "my strength and the song of my strength is God."

---

16. In most editions, the phrase appears as *bi-sheva be-ḥataf*, while in Shadal's copy it appears as *bi-sheva ve-ḥataf*. In an attempt to explain the usual reading *bi-sheva be-ḥataf*, Rosenbaum and Silbermann suggest that the word *bi-sheva* is merely a gloss, since Rashi always referred to a mobile *sheva* by the term *ḥataf* (p. 75a).

# Shadal on Exodus

Ibn Ezra found support for his claim from *menat ha-melekh*, "the king's portion" (2 Chron. 31:3), where *menat* has a *kamats* [instead of the expected *patah*] and yet is in the construct state. This is no proof, however, for the word does indeed preserve a *kamats*, but that *kamats* is Aramaic (as in the Syriac *menata*, which should appear [instead of *manata*] in our Targum on 2 Sam. 6:19), not a Hebrew *kamats* that takes the place of an Aramaic *sheva* or *patah*. Because it is an archaic *kamats*, it does not change [to a *patah*]; compare:

- *she'ar* (שְׁאָר) *ammo*, "the remnant of his people" (Isa. 11:11);
- *yekar* (יְקָר) *tif'eret*, "the honor of his excellent [majesty]," (Esth. 1:4);
- *pitgam* (פִּתְגָם) *ha-melekh*, "the king's decree" (Esth. 1:20);
- *ketav* (כְּתָב) *ha-dat*, "the writing of the decree" (Esth. 4:8);
- *galuti* (גָלוּתִי), "My exiles" (Isa. 45:13);
- *ma'badeihem* (מַעְבָּדֵיהֶם), "their works" (Job 34:25)

—and others (among which should be *ketavei* [not *kitvei*] *ha-kodesh*, "the holy Scriptures," and *shetarei* [not *shitrei*] *hovoteinu*, "the records of our guilt"), where the *kamats* does not change to a *sheva* or a *patah*, since it is an archaic *kamats* of the type that is also found in Aramaic, rather than a Hebrew modification on the [above-mentioned] model of *pakad* and *basar*. There is much to say on this topic, which I have previously explicated in my book *Prolegomeni*.

According to Rashi, the phrase *va-y'hi li li-y'shu'ah* (lit., "and He was my salvation") is not an independent statement, but the meaning of the verse is, "The strength and vengeance of God was my salvation." For this reason, he was compelled to cite examples in which the initial *vav* of *va-y'hi* is superfluous. Ibn Ezra retorted that this was not the usage of either Hebrew or Arabic. I say, however, that it is not appropriate to bring proof from Arabic, because that language does not contain the *vav ha-hippukh* [the "conversive" *vav* that changes a verb from past to future or vice versa], while in Hebrew there are many instances of such a *vav* that does not serve as a conjunction ("and"). This is especially true of the word *va-y'hi*, as in all instances where this word introduces a book or a narrative. Some of the verses that Rashi cites here do, in fact, demonstrate that it is not contrary to Hebrew usage to say *va-y'hi li li-y'shu'ah* and to mean "He was my salvation."

The *Me'ammer*, in a well-intentioned effort to save Rashi from Ibn Ezra's grasp, imagined that there was another Rabbi Solomon, and said that Ibn Ezra was not referring to Rashi [R. Solomon Yitshaki]. He also said that the verses cited by Rashi were intended to show not that *va-y'hi* could be the equivalent of *hayah* ("was"), but rather that the *vav ha-hippukh* could appear in the middle of a verse (!!!).

What is this like? It is like the statement that the commentator to *Netivot ha-Shalom* [Aaron Jaroslav], Num. 9:13, made in order to save Ibn Ezra from a serious error that had escaped his pen—in that Ibn Ezra had interpreted the phrase *u-v'-derekh* (ובדרך) *lo hayah* ("and was not on a journey") to mean *o ve-derekh* (או בדרך) *lo hayah* ("*or* was not on a journey"), [taking the normally conjunctive *vav* to mean "or"] as in the phrase *u-makkeh aviv ve-immo* ("one who strikes his father *or* his mother," Exod. 21:15). The commentator said that Ibn Ezra meant only to instruct us that the initial *vav* in *u-v'-derekh* should be read as if it were preceded with an *alef* (אובדרך) [instead of *ve-ve-derekh*]. The *Me'ammer* understood that these words of the commentator were nonsense and expressed his astonishment over them, and he took Ibn Ezra's interpretation at face value. However, he did not discuss the error that resulted from this interpretation,[17] nor did he understand the reason why the commentator had felt compelled to take the position that he did.

**Yah.** The good and beneficent God; see on the next verse.

**and I will celebrate Him** *(ve-anvehu)*. The Hebrew is from *naveh*, meaning "pleasant" and "beautiful," and the sense is, "I will beautify and glorify Him with my praises." Similarly, *va-aromemenhu* [in this same v.] means, "I will exalt Him with my words." In other words, "I will give Him beauty and exaltedness," that is, "I will ascribe these qualities to Him," as in, "Give strength to God" (Ps. 68:35); see above at the start of the comment to this verse.

**He is the God of my father.** That is, "of my fathers"; [for the reason why the singular is used,] see above at the comment on the phrase "horse and rider" [v. 1].

***This is my God, and I will celebrate Him; He is the God of my father, and I will exalt Him.*** This is an idea expressed twice in different words, a device quite commonly found in biblical poetry, where statements are divided into

---

17. Num. 9:13 states that if a person fails to offer the Passover sacrifice at the proper time, he incurs the penalty of *karet* if he was *tahor* (in a proper state of purity) *and* he was not on a journey. Ibn Ezra's reading would seemingly impose *karet* for such a failure even if the person was not *tahor*, or even if he was on a journey, despite the fact that in either case he would have had a legitimate excuse.

two corresponding parts; this is what is called "parallelism." Sometimes the two parts compare one thing to another, as in:

- "As a lily among thorns / So is my love among the daughters" (Songs 2:2).

Sometimes the two parts contrast one thing to another, as in:

- "A wise son makes a glad father / But a foolish son is the grief of his mother" (Prov. 10:1);
- "Children I have reared and brought up / And they have rebelled against Me" (Isa. 1:2).

Sometimes the second part explains the first, as in:

- "I sing to the Lord, for He has shown Himself supreme / Horse and rider has He thrown into the sea" (above, v. 1).

Sometimes the second part is a continuation of the first, but repeats a word or two, as in:

- "With me from Lebanon, O bride / With me from Lebanon come" (Songs 4:8).

Sometimes the second part is a continuation of the first, repeating an idea but not repeating words, as in:

- "Listen, heavens, and I will speak / And let the earth hear the sayings of my mouth" (Deut. 32:1).

Sometimes the second part merely repeats the first in different words, as in:
- "My speech will drip like the rain / My word will trickle like dew" (Deut. 32:2),

and as in the present verse.

This device seems to have been intended to divide a statement into small components, in order to make a greater impression on the listener and also to render the statement easier to sing. Perhaps the origin of the device was, as has been said, that the wise men of old composed many proverbs (*meshalim*, lit., "similes") in which one thing was compared to another, for example:

## *Beshallaḥ*

- "As a ring of gold in a swine's snout / So is a fair woman who lacks discretion" (Prov. 11:22);
- "Where no wood is, the fire goes out / And where there is no whisperer, contention ceases" (Prov. 26:20).

These sayings were given the name *mashal* because they comprised one element that was compared (*nimshal*) to another. These *meshalim* attained great popularity, for people find the *mashal* pleasing because of the innovation that it contains, in that it points out the similarity between two very different things, such as "a ring of gold" and "a fair woman," or "a swine's snout" and "a woman who lacks discretion," or "wood" and "whisperer," or "fire" and "contention."

This very innovation, however, which is the reason for the pleasing quality of the *mashal*, is also the reason for its rarity, for it is quite difficult to find such similarities between different things. As a result, when some of the poets could not come up with true *meshalim* comparing one thing to another, they invented the artificial *mashal*, which—although not containing any such comparison—resembled the *mashal* in form, in that it contained two parallel parts expressing the same idea in different words. This artificial *mashal* was itself called a *mashal*, with the result that any poem was called a *mashal*, for Hebrew poetry contains many such doubled sayings. When a *mashal* was made to be sung to a melody in a pleasant voice, it was called a *shir* or *shirah*, but when it was not made to be sung, it was [simply] called a *mashal*, as in the *meshalim* of Balaam (Numbers 23-24) and Solomon (*Mishlei Shelomoh*, the Book of Proverbs).

**15:3. "The Lord is (a) warlike (God); the Lord is the name that is ascribed to Him.**

***The Lord is (a) warlike (God)*** *(YHVH ish milḥamah,* lit., "The Lord is a man of war"). He is the One Who truly deserves, more than anyone else, to be called an *ish milḥamah*, for there is no one who can stand up against Him.

***the Lord is the name that is ascribed to Him*** *(YHVH shemo,* lit., "the Lord is His name"). This is the appropriate name for Him, for He does good or ill as He desires, with none to restrain Him.

In my opinion, the Tetragrammaton is a compound of two sounds: *Yah*, a sound of joy, by which name God is known in His aspect as the Worker of Good; and *Wah*, a sound of weeping and sorrow. The sacred name composed of these two sounds denotes the God Who is the source of all good things and all evil things (see my comment on Isa. 38:11, in my commentary printed at the beginning of the late scholar Rosenmueller's exegetical work on Isaiah, 1835).[18] This is not the place to discuss this matter at length. I will add only that the idea of referring to the Tetragrammaton as the *shem ha-havayah* ("the name of Being") is only a later innovation. This name was never taken to denote eternity (as moderns have customarily translated it, *der Ewige*, "the Eternal"), for even the gods of other nations were thought to be eternal by their worshippers, but not one of them (even according to pagan belief) was the source of all good and all evil. This could be ascribed only to a single God. The name *Ehyeh asher ehyeh* (Exod. 3:14) has nothing to do with the name YHVH and does not at all refer to "eternity"; I have already explained this above [at 3:13 and 3:14].

One of Spinoza's disciples [Immanuel Wolf] thought to glorify our people by saying that the Tetragrammaton signified the oneness of Being, i.e., the unity of all existence (see *Zeitschrift für die Wissenschaft des Judentums*, Berlin 1822, p. 3). But this is the exact opposite of that which all the holy books teach about Him, for they all clearly state that the Creator is one thing and the creation is another: one is active and the other passive, one is Master and the other servant. According to Spinoza, everything that exists in the world is of necessity, and not at all a matter of will; but according to the Jews (from Abraham until today), nothing exists of necessity, and everything is a product of God's will. The faith of Spinoza and the faith of the Hebrews are as distant from each other as east and west, and the opposition of one to the other is total.

The [true] glory of Judaism is this: it is Judaism that taught humankind of the Oneness of God and the unity of creation. That is, all people are the children of One Father, and the nations did not come forth from the womb of their native soil (*autochthones*), nor are some the children of one god and some the children of another god. Rather, they are all brothers, children of one man and creatures of One God. So, too, all creation: heaven and earth, sea and dry land, sun and moon and stars, domestic and wild animals, birds and reptiles and fish are all the work of One God. But the Creator and the creation are infinitely separate from one another, and the whole world is in the hand of the Creator, like clay in the hand of the potter. It is not beyond His power to change His creatures as He desires, and all changes that take place

---

18. In his comment on the phrase, "I shall not see Yah… in the land of the living" (Isa. 38:11), Shadal gives the paraphrase, "I will no longer enjoy the goodness and mercies of God."

in the world are according to God's will. It is He Who confers good or punishes, all according to His will, and nothing at all exists of necessity. This is Judaism; its exact opposite is Spinozism.

And these are their fruits: the one implants in our hearts love and compassion for others; it comforts us in our troubles and strengthens our hearts with hope. The other hardens our hearts toward our fellows and causes us to despair in our time of evil, presenting us with a primeval and eternal necessity of nature, not subject to any commander or susceptible to any change whatsoever.

**15:4. "The carriages of Pharaoh, and his army, did He thrust into the sea; and the best of his strong ones were drowned in the Red Sea.**

***did He thrust*** *(yarah)*. The basic meaning of the Heb. is "to thrust in to the ground," as in, "Or who laid [*yarah*] the cornerstone [of the earth]?" (Job 38:6); "And here is this monument stone, that I establish [*yariti*] between me and you" (Gen. 31:51). Here, too, the meaning is "sank with force," in accordance with the earlier verse, "Thus the Lord hurled down the Egyptians in the midst of the sea" (Exod. 14:27).

***and the best of his strong ones*** *(u-mivḥar shalishav*, lit., "the choice of his strong ones") — his strong ones who were the best chosen. [For similar construction,] compare:

- "And accepted of the multitude of his brethren [*le-rov eḥav*]" (Esth. 10:3), i.e., "his many brethren";
- "Every green plant [*yerek esev*, lit., 'greenness of a plant']" (Gen. 1:30);
- "The flashing sword [*lahat ha-ḥerev*, lit., 'the flash of the sword']" (Gen. 3:24);
- "And any chosen thing [*mivḥar nidreikhem*, lit., 'the choice of your vow'] of which you will have made a vow to the Lord" (Deut. 12:11).

***were drowned*** *(tubbe'u)* ***in the Red Sea.*** The verb *tava* is found in Scripture to refer to sinking not into water, but into mud (Jer. 38:6, 22; Ps. 69:3, 15), or the earth (Lam. 2:9), or the forehead [of Goliath] (1 Sam. 17:49). From this sense were derived the nouns *matbe'a* ("die") and *tabba'at* ("signet ring"), because they are used for engraving. Here, the term is used in order to convey that [the carriages and army] were driven into the water with force, as if they were sunk into the floor of the sea. To confirm this meaning, the word was vocalized *tubbe'u* [in the *pu'al*, or passive intensive conjugation] rather than *tibbe'u* [in the active *pi'el* conjugation], to indicate that they did not fall into the water on their own or by accident, but were thrust in by force.

**15:5. "The depths covered them; they sank in the abysses like stone.**

***The depths*** *(tehomot)*. Deep waters.

***covered them*** *(yekhasyumu)*. [In the syllable *yu*,] the final *he* of the root *kasah* ("to cover") becomes a *yod*, as in *natayu* [from *natah*] and *yirbeyun* [from *ravah*]. Because of this added *yod*, the *dagesh* that normally would have appeared in the [preceding letter] *samekh* was dropped, as in the word *shalmonim* (Isa. 11:23; see my comment thereon).[19] The normal form of the word would have been *yekhassum*, or with the added *yod*, *yekhasyum*, but the final *-u* was added by way of poetic usage, as in the words *tevi'emo* and *titta'emo* (below, v. 17), although [according to that model] it should have been vocalized with a *holam* [i.e., *yekhasyumo*].

Hebrew grammarians (including R. Elijah [Levita] in his *Sefer ha-Harkavah* [Rome, 1518], as well as Rashbam, say that the [letter *mem* in *yekhasyumu*] is vocalized with a *shuruk* in order to match the pronunciation of the preceding *yod*, which is also vocalized with a *shuruk*. This explanation seems worthless to me, for we find examples of such vowel-matching only with respect to two words, as in:

- *horo ve-hogo* (Isa. 59:13);
- *tse'enah u-re'enah* (Songs 3:11);
- *et motsa'akha ve-et mova'akha* (2 Sam. 3:25);
- *u-motsa'av u-mova'av* (Ezek. 43:11).

However, we find no such thing with respect to the vowels in a single word; to the contrary, we find that the Hebrew language prefers variation in such cases. Thus, we say *yahpots* and not *yahpats*, *ye'ehav* and not *ya'ahav*, *ekal/tekal* and not *akal/takal*, *yokhal* and not *ya'akhal*, *ye'ehaz* and not *ya'ahaz*.

In vain do these grammarians cite support from words such as *vi-y'rishtem*, *she'iltiv*, and *she'eltem*, as Ibn Ezra comment on *vi-y'rishtem* (Deut. 4:11): "Since the *yod* was deprived of a vowel following the *hirek* of

---

19. Shadal's comment observes that *shalmonim* is a variant of *shillumim*, and that the introduction of the letter *nun* took away the *dagesh* that would otherwise have appeared in the *lamed*.

## Beshallaḥ

the initial *vav*, the second letter of the root [the *resh*] was also given a *ḥirek*" [i.e., the word normally would have been vocalized *ve-yarashtem*, but the change of the initial syllable to *vi-* carried with it the shift to *–ri*]. This means nothing, for we also find *u-fishtem* [instead of the expected form *u-fashtem*] (Mal. 3:20) without any other *ḥirek*, and just as we find *ve-hitgaddilti ve-hitkaddishti* [instead of *hitgaddalti ve-hitkaddashti*] (Ezek. 38:23), where one *ḥirek* does follow another, so we also find *ve-hitkaddishtem* (Lev. 11:44) where [an unexpected *ḥirek* appears] without any other *ḥirek*. It is well know that the *pataḥ* vowel sometimes shifts to a *ḥirek*, as in *tsad/tsiddo* or *pat/pittekha*, but not once [other than in the word *yekhasyumu* here] does the suffix *–mo* shift to a *shuruk* [*-mu*].

Therefore, I say that the reason for the *shuruk* [in *yekhasyumu*] is to portray to the listener's ear the sinking into the depths and the submerging under the water, for the function of the *u* sound seems to be to arouse in us an impression of darkness and depth. Anyone who is familiar with the value of the poetic device known as onomatopoeia [the use of imitative and naturally suggestive words for rhetorical effect] will not scoff at this. And if one assumes that the *shuruk* at the end of the word *yekhasyumu* is for the purpose that I have stated, this justifies to some extent the opinion of the grammarians that this *shuruk* serves to match the pronunciation of the preceding *yod*. Indeed, if there had been no other *shuruk* (if, for example, it had been written *yekhassemu*), a single *shuruk* standing alone at the end of the word would not have had the power to arouse an impression of sinking and darkness. Only with another *shuruk* preceding it does the final *shuruk* have the power to arouse such an impression.[20]

*Yekhasyumu* (lit., "will cover them") is a future-tense verb that takes the place of a past-tense verb; cf. the phrase *tir'ats oyev*, "shatters [lit., 'will shatter'] the enemy" (next v.). There are many such examples in prophetic and poetic language; not that the future form actually functions as the past, but the poet uses it to describe what is, so to speak, before his eyes, and the future functions as a present tense, which does not exist in [Biblical] Hebrew.[21]

---

20. For examples of similar onomatopoeia in English employing repeated *u* sounds, consider the expression "doom and gloom," and the name of the title character of Edgar Alan Poe's lugubrious poem, "Ulalume."

21. The forms that Shadal refers to as "future" and "past" are known by modern grammarians as "imperfect" and "perfect" in the context of Biblical Hebrew. According to William Chomsky (*Hebrew: The Eternal Language,* pp. 162-163), (1) the imperfect was used to describe an "uncompleted" action, not necessarily a future action; (2) no special form for the present tense existed in Biblical Hebrew, which used an "adjectival" form instead; and (3) true past, present, and future tenses came into use only in post-Biblical or Mishnaic Hebrew.

Thus, in the phrase *tehomot yekhasyumu*, the poet imagines that now, before his eyes, the depths are covering the Egyptians.

***in the abysses*** *(bi-m'tsolot)*. The word *metsolah*, too, means "deep water." Even though this noun is derived from the root *tsul*, it looks as if it were derived from *tsalal* ("to sink"), as in the phrase *tsalalu ka-oferet*, "sank like lead" (below, v. 10). The [equivalent of the] verb *tsalal* in Arabic means "was lost," "disappeared from view," and sometimes "was buried." Apparently, deep water was called *metsolah* because anyone who fell into it would be lost and would disappear. Some proof for this is furnished by the phrase, "[You placed me in the lowest of pits,] in dark places, in the deeps [*bi-m'tsolot*]" (Ps. 88:7). Thus, *metsolah* resembles the Latin *vorago* ("abyss," "depth") [seemingly related to *vorare*, "to swallow" or "devour"].

**15:6. "Your right hand, O Lord, You Who are girt with might, Your right hand (I say), O Lord, shatters the enemy.**

***girt with might*** *(ne'dari ba-koah)*. This phrase refers back to God (as per the Rabbis in the Mekhilta). The verse is elliptical [and is to be understood as translated, with the words, "You Who are" added]. If the phrase referred back to "Your right hand [*yeminkha*]" (as per Rashi and Gesenius), the word "girt" would properly have appeared [not as *ne'dari*, but in the feminine form] *ne'deret*.

***girt*** *(ne'dari)*. It seems to me that the root *adar* is a "brother" to the root *azar* ("to gird") in Hebrew and the root *hadar* ("to surround") in Syriac, and that *ne'dari ba-koah* is the equivalent of *ne'zar bi-g'vurah*, "Who are girded about with might" (Ps. 65:7). A derivative of this root [*adar*] is *adderet* ("mantle"), a garment that surrounds the entire body, and also *addir* ("mighty"), whose most basic meaning is "girt," but which was transferred to denote strength; cf. "I have girded you [*a'azerkha*], though you have not known Me" (Isa. 45:5), meaning, "I have strengthened you."

***shatters*** *(tir'ats)*. The root *ra'ats* is related to [the Hebrew] *ratsats* and the Aramaic *ra'a*. The structure of this verse resembles that of the following:

- "For lo, Your enemies, O Lord / For lo, Your enemies shall perish" (Ps. 92:10);
- "God, to Whom vengeance belongs, O Lord / God to whom vengeance belongs, shine forth" (Ps. 94:1);

## Beshallaḥ

- "How long shall the wicked, O Lord / How long shall the wicked exult?" (Ps. 94:3);
- "With me from Lebanon, O bride / With me from Lebanon come" (Songs 4:8);
- "It is not for kings, O Lemuel / It is not for kings to drink wine" (Prov. 31:4);
- "Awake, awake, Deborah / Awake, awake, utter a song" (Judg. 5:12).

According to Ibn Ezra, the meaning of the verse is that "time after time—innumerable times—You do this, that is, Your right hand shatters the enemy." This is erroneous; the truth is that this mode of expression [merely] adds force to the statement, for the listener is in suspense and waits to hear what the conclusion will be, and when he hears it, it is more pleasing to him, as is any valuable thing that is sought for but not found immediately.

**15:7. "And with Your great, irresistible force, You bring down those who rise against You; You send forth Your burning wrath, it devours them like straw.**

*Your... irresistible force* (ge'onekha). *Ga'on* sometimes means a mighty force that cannot be withstood, as in:

- "And here shall your proud waves [*bi-g'on gallekha*] be stayed" (Job 38:11);
- "Yet how will you do in the high waves of [*ge'on*] the Jordan?" (Jer. 12:5);

and in a different noun form:

- "You rule the proud swelling of [*be-ge'ut*] the sea" (Ps. 89:10);

and with reference to God:

- "In the strength of the Lord, in the majesty of [*bi-g'on*] the name of the Lord his God" (Micah 5:3).

*Ga'on* is close in meaning to *oz* ("vehemence," "impetus"); compare also, "From before the terror of the Lord, and from the glory of His majesty [*ge'ono*] when He arises to shake the earth mightily" (Isa. 2:19). (See also above at the phrase *ki ga'oh ga'ah* [v. 1].)

*You bring down* (taharos). You throw down with force; cf. "And from your station shall you be pulled down [*yehersekha*]" (Isa. 22:19); "Break [*haros*] their teeth in their mouth" (Ps. 58:7). This expression is directed against "those who rise against You," i.e., "bring them down to the ground." Later the term *harisah* was used in the sense of "tearing down" the wall of a house or a city, and still later in the sense of bursting through a boundary (as in 19:24 below ["Let neither the priests nor the people step forward [*yehersu*] to go up toward the Lord"]), as if to throw down a border fence.

***Your burning wrath*** *(haronekha).* The noun *haron* is derived from the verb *harah* (a "brother" to *harar*), indicating "heat" or "burning." Thus it is fitting to say that "it devours them like straw," that is, it consumes them quickly, just as fire consumes straw.

***it devours them*** *(yokhelemo).* The *vav* suffix (*-o*) is a poetic embellishment of Aramaic derivation. In Aramaic, the equivalent of [the Hebrew] *otam* ("them") is *himmo*, as in *u-t'karev himmo*, "and you shall offer them" (Ezra 7:17). At first this was simplified to *u-t'karevemo*, and then the *vav* was dropped and they said *u-t'karevem*. However, the poets chose to use archaic forms, and they restored the *vav* to its place.

**15:8. "With a breath from Your face, the waters piled up; they stood upright like a heap, the flowing waves; the depths congealed in the heart of the sea.**

***With a breath from Your face*** *(appekha). Appayim,* in the dual form, does not [literally] mean "nose" or "nostrils," but rather "face" (like *anpin* in Aramaic); compare:

- "With the sweat of your face [*appekha*] will you eat bread" (Gen. 3:19);
- "And bowed down with his face [*appayim*] to the earth" (Gen. 19:1);
- "And she fell before [*le-appei*] David" (1 Sam. 25:23), where *le-appei* is the equivalent of *lifnei* ("before," lit., "in the face of") (so in Rabbinic Hebrew, *kelappei*, "towards" or "against," was formed from *ki-le-appei*).

Here, [the poet] imagines that the powerful east wind, which was a miraculous occurrence, was God's own breath, as if He had blown on the water with His face and the water stood as a single heap.

***piled up*** *(ne'ermu).* Became like a stack of (*aremat*) wheat.

## *Beshallaḥ*

***like a heap*** *(ned)*. *Ned* is close in meaning to *aremah* ("stack"), as in, "A heap [*ned*] of boughs" (Isa. 17:11). However, in the Mekhilta on this verse, it says, "Just as a *nod* ("goatskin bottle") is tied up and lets nothing in or out [so was the spirit of the Egyptians]," and thus it seems that they read the word [as if it were vocalized] as *nod*. Similarly, in the Jerusalem Targum attributed to Jonathan ben Uzziel, the phrase is translated as *kamu lehein tseririn he khezikin*, and *zika* is [Aramaic for] *nod*; so also in Ps. 33:7, "He gathers the waters of the sea together as a heap [*ka-ned*]," the Targum reads *de-makhnis heikh zika moi de-yama*.

Perhaps Onkelos, too, read the word as *nod* [in this v.], but since a *nod* is a small, insignificant article, he used a grander image to appeal to the listener's ear, and translated the word as *ke-shur*, "like a wall." Also, perhaps because *ne'ermu* ("piled up") and *nitsevu kemo ned* (or *nod*) ("they stood upright as a heap") are one idea expressed twice in different words, Onkelos chose to introduce a variation, and interpreted *ne'ermu* in the sense of *ormah*, "cleverness" [*hakhimu maya*, "the waters became wise"]. There is a similar instance below (v. 16) with regard to the phrase, "until Your people passes, O Lord / Until that people passes that You have made," where Onkelos removed the duplication and interpreted the first half of the phrase to refer to the crossing of the Arnon, and the second to refer to the crossing of the Jordan.

***congealed*** *(kafe'u)*. As in, "And curdled me [*takpi'eni*] like cheese" (Job 10:10). By way of poetic hyperbole, the waters are described as standing as if congealed.

**15:9. "The enemy said, 'I will pursue, I will overtake, I will divide spoil, my desire will be satiated in them; I will unsheathe my sword, my hand will exterminate them.'**

***The enemy said.*** By way of poetic expression, the poet imagines the words of another; cf., "And you said in your heart, 'I will ascend into heaven'" (Isa. 14:13).

***I will pursue, I will overtake*** *(erdof assig)*. The lack of a conjunctive *vav* between these verbs (*asyndeton*) indicates the quick succession of these actions, as if the pursuing, overtaking, and dividing of spoil would follow each other immediately. A similar usage in Scripture is, "At her feet he sank, he fell, he lay" (Judg. 5:27), and a similar usage in world literature is the statement of Julius Caesar, *"Veni, vidi, vici"* ("I came, I saw, I conquered"). So also below, "You blew with Your breath, the sea covered them" (v. 10).

***will be satiated in them*** *(timla'emo)* — lit., "will fill them," as in, "And the houses of the Egyptians... will be filled with [*u-male'u*, lit., 'will fill'] the mixture" (Exod. 8:17). A similar usage is found with the root *sava* ("to satisfy"), the meaning of which is close to the root *malei* ("to fill"): *tisbe'u lahem*, "you will be satiated with bread," lit., "you will satiate bread" (Exod. 16:12); *u-sva'tem oto*, "and you shall be satisfied with it," lit., "and you shall satisfy it" (Joel 2:19). So here, *timla'emo nafshi* means "my soul and desire will be full of them and satisfied by them."

***my desire*** *(nafshi,* lit., "my soul"). Cf., "You will be able, at your will [*ke-nafshekha*], to eat of the grapes to satiety" (Deut. 23:25). According to Ibn Ezra, the phrase *timla'emo nafshi* is connected to [the preceding phrase] *ahallek shalal* ("I will divide spoil"), but this was not the view of the accentuator [who separated the phrases with a major disjunctive *etnahta*], which was more precise, for if Ibn Ezra were correct, it should have said *timla'ehu nafshi*, "my desire will be satiated in *it* [i.e., the spoil]." Since it says *timla'emo* [in the plural], this indicates that the meaning is "my desire for revenge," i.e., "my desire to take vengeance of them and to destroy them will be satiated in them, for I will unsheathe my sword, and my hand will exterminate them." After some time, I found that my friend, the scholar Moses Landau, translated *nafshi* as *meine Rachgier* ("my desire for revenge").

***I will unsheathe my sword*** *(arik harbi,* lit., "I will empty my sword"). "I will draw my sword from its sheath"; cf. "Abram... led forth [*va-yarek*] the servants whom he had trained" (Gen. 14:14); "And [Moab] has not been emptied [*hurak*] from vessel to vessel" (Jer. 48:11). The expression is transferred, for at first the verb *herik* ("to empty") referred to the vessel that remained empty, but later the word was extended to refer to that which was taken out of the vessel (as per Rashi). There is an analogous usage in Latin (*evacuare gladios*, "to unsheathe [lit. "empty"] a sword"). See my comment on Gen. 32:26.[22]

***my hand will exterminate them*** *(torishemo).* The Hebrew denotes destruction, as in, "I will strike it with the plagues and destroy it [*ve-orishennu*]" (Num. 14:12). The basic meaning of the verb *horish* was "to cause one's possessions

---

22. There, Shadal explains the phrase *va-teka kaf* ("[Jacob's] thigh bone was dislocated") as literally referring to the socket of the bone, "[e]ven though it was the thigh bone and not the socket that was dislocated." He then cross-refers to the phrase *arik harbi* in the present verse.

to become an inheritance [*yerushah*]," i.e., by killing the owner. In order to indicate the ease of the victory that the enemy was imagining, [the poet] first mentioned the beginning of the battle, which was the drawing of the sword, and then the end of the victory, which [to be] the destruction of the foe. The connection of these two actions without a conjunctive *vav* indicates the rapid succession of one to the other.

**15:10. "You blew with Your breath, (and at once) the sea covered them; they sank, like lead, in terrible waters.**

***You blew*** *(nashafta)*. The Hebrew is synonymous with *neshivah* ("blowing"). With metathesis, this [root *nashaf*] yields *nefesh* ("breath," "soul"), as in, "His breath [*nafsho*] kindles coals" (Job 41:13). Similarly, *ruaḥ* and *neshamah* (synonyms for "soul") originally referred to the air that living creatures inhale and exhale. It is well known that in all languages, words that refer to intangible things were originally used for physical things.[23]

***You blew with Your breath*** *(be-ruḥakha)*. A figure of speech like the one above, "With a breath [*u-v'-ruaḥ*] from Your face" (v. 8). In the [narrative] account [preceding the Song], there is no [express] mention of wind in connection with the drowning of the Egyptians; this supports my comment above (on 14:24) that the statement that "the Lord looked toward the camp of the Egyptians with a pillar of fire and of cloud" implies that there were thunder, lightning, and "arrows of God" as well as a stormy wind.

***they sank*** *(tsalalu)*. See above on the word *bi-metsolot* (in v. 5).

---

23. This linguistic theory, a key component of Shadal's commentary (see also, for example, his etymology of the word *kodesh*, next v.) is supported by modern scholarship. According to the Israeli linguist Guy Deutscher, in *The Unfolding of Language* (New York: Henry Holt and Co., 2006), "The only way we have of expanding our expressive range to encompass abstract concepts is to draw on concrete terms" (p. 128). "The truth of the matter is that we simply have no choice but to use concrete-to-abstract metaphors. And when one stops to think about it, this is not even so surprising, since after all, if not from the physical world, where else could terms for abstract concepts come from? ... The mind cannot just manufacture words for abstract concepts out of thin air—all it can do is adapt what is already available. And what's at hand are simple physical concepts" (p. 127). "[C]onsider the verb 'decide,' which in English derives from a Latin verb meaning 'cut off.' At first this image may seem unusual, but in fact, the physical activities of cutting or separating seem to be the source of the concept of 'deciding' in many languages... [including] biblical Hebrew *Bazar*, and Chinese *jue*" (p. 126).

***like lead.*** Which, because of its weight [i.e. density], is quick to sink and disappear from view.

***terrible*** *(addirim).* Mighty; see above (v. 6) on the phrase *ne'dari ba-koaḥ.*

**15:11. "Who is equal to You among the gods, O Lord? Who is equal to You, (Who are) girt with holiness, worthy of awesome praises, worker of wonders?"**

***Who is equal to You among the gods, O Lord?*** This verse is similar in structure to "Your right hand, O Lord, You Who are girt with might / Your right hand, O Lord, shatters the enemy" (above, v. 6). That is, the first part of the verse is repeated, but the idea is not completed until the end of the verse. So here, "Who is equal to You among the gods, O Lord" is not a complete statement; rather, the meaning is, "Who among the gods is girt with holiness, awesome, and a worker of wonders equal to You, O Lord?" (as per Mendelssohn's comment).

However, this verse differs from v. 6 and similar verses in that the second part is missing the word *ba-elim* ("among the gods") (for [in order to fit the model,] the verse should have read, "Who is equal to You among the gods, O Lord / Who is equal to you *among the gods*, girt with holiness"). In the same vein is the verse, "Wherewith Your enemies have taunted, O Lord / Wherewith they have taunted the footsteps of Your anointed" (Ps. 89:52), where the word *oyevekha* ("Your enemies") is missing from the second part.

A somewhat similar example is, "Is it kindled against the rivers, O Lord / Is Your anger against the rivers?" (Hab. 3:8), which means, "Is Your anger kindled against the rivers?" The first part of this verse is missing the word *appekha* ("Your anger"), while the second part is missing the word *ḥarah* ("kindled"). The verse should not be interpreted according to the view of the accentuator [who joined the words *ḥarah YHVH* in the first part with a conjunctive *munaḥ*], for [in that case] the phrase should have read *ḥarah af YHVH* ("the Lord's anger is kindled"), since the phrase *ḥarah YHVH* is not found anywhere.

***among the gods*** *(ba-elim).* The Hebrew is the equivalent of *ba-elohim*, that is, the gods of the nations, as in, "And [the king] shall speak strange things against the God of gods [*elim*]" (Dan. 11:36). So also, "Who among the *benei elim* can be liked unto the Lord" (Ps. 89:7), meaning *benei Elohim* ("sons of God"), i.e., the angels; similarly, "Ascribe unto the Lord, *benei elim* / Ascribe unto the Lord glory and strength" (Ps. 29:1). Other than in these verses, we do not find *elim* as the equivalent of *elohim*, but rather denoting "strength" or "might," as below, "the magnates of [*eilei*] Moab" (v. 15); so also, "When he raises himself up, the mighty [*elim*] are afraid" (Job 41:17).

The reason for this is that the primary meaning of *el* is "strong" or "powerful," and from this was derived *eloah* and *elohim*, but these words are altered in form, so that anyone who hears the term *elohim* knows that it refers to an object of worship, whether [truly] possessing strength and might (as does the true God) or whether lacking any strength or might (as do the gods of the nations). On the other hand, the word *elim* is not altered in form, and one who hears it must necessarily understand it to refer to strong or powerful beings. Therefore, the Israelites chose not to use this term to refer to the gods of the nations, and the prophets used it only where the context shows that these *elim* are not in fact strong or powerful—as in the present verse, which says that there are none among the *elim* that are girt with might, worthy of awesome praises, or workers of wonders; and in the verse from Daniel, where the phrase "the God of gods [*elim*]" indicates that the *elim* are under the power of the true God.

**girt with holiness** *(ne'dar ba-kodesh)*. See above on *ne'dari ba-koah*, v. 6. The meaning is "girt [*ne'ezar*] and surrounded by Divine might, Godly attributes," etc. In other words He is the true God, and not in name only. See what I wrote in *Bikkurei ha-Ittim ha-Hadashim* 5606 (1845/46), p. 35.[24]

**with holiness** *(ba-kodesh)*. It seems to me that *kodesh* was derived from *kad esh*, that is, *yekod esh*, "a burning of fire" (as per the homiletical interpretation in the Talmud, *Kiddushin* 56b, of the phrase "otherwise the produce of the planting would become sacred [prohibited] [*tikdash*]" [Deut. 22:9]—"otherwise it would be set afire [*tukkad esh*]"), and that the term originally applied to sacrifices that were burned in order to honor God. Later the term was transferred to anything that was set aside for God's honor and removed from profane use, even if no burning was involved, e.g., the *kedushah* ("holiness") of Sabbath, the "holy convocations" (*mikra'ei kodesh*), the "holy mountain" (*har ha-kodesh*), and the "holy Temple" (*beit ha-mikdash*).

Similarly, a person would be called *kadosh* ("holy") by reason of being devoted to God and set apart for His service. The terms "holy garments" (*bigdei kodesh*) and "holy oil" (*shemen ha-kodesh*) referred to the garments

---

24. The reference is to an article on pp. 35-37 on the root *kadash*, apparently reproduced in its entirety in the next comment.

and the oil that were special to the priests and removed from the rest of the people, and which served to symbolize the setting aside of the priests for God's service.

The word *kadosh* came to denote anything divine or pertaining to God, and likewise *kodesh* came to mean "godliness," "Divine power," "Divine attribute," and the like. The expression *ne'dar ba-kodesh* means "girt with Divine power, Divine attributes," etc., that is He is truly Divine, and not in name only. This sense of the term was extended so that God [Himself] was said to be *kadosh*, that is, He is Divine and exalted above all human imperfection.

The term *kedushah* was also transferred to describe anything from which no benefit is to be derived, and from which people keep apart as if it is set aside for Heaven, even if this is not the case and the article in question possesses no "holiness," but is merely forbidden. This is the meaning of the phrase "otherwise the produce of the planting would become sacred [prohibited] [*tikdash*]" (Deut. 22:9).

Because sacrifices were to be eaten in a state of purity, people would purify themselves before eating them, and thus it was said, "For the Lord has prepared a sacrifice, He has consecrated [*hikdish*] His guests" (Zeph. 1:7). They would also purify themselves before coming to the Temple, and in this sense it was said, "Sanctify [*kaddeshu*] a fast, call a solemn assembly, gather the elders... to the house of the Lord your God" (Joel 1:14). Similarly, before the giving of the Torah, when the people came into the presence of God, it was said, "Have them sanctify themselves [*ve-kiddashtam*] today and tomorrow" (Exod. 19:10). Joshua, too, told the people, "Sanctify yourselves [*hitkaddashu*], for tomorrow the Lord will do wonders among you" (Josh. 3:5); that is, he told them to purify themselves as if they were coming into God's presence, so that they should be impressed with the greatness of the miracle that God was to perform for them in causing them to cross the Jordan on dry land.

Other examples are, "Sanctfiy yourselves [*hitkaddeshu*] for tomorrow, and you will eat meat" (Num.11:18), i.e., "prepare yourselves for the miracle [of the quails]"; and also, "Up, sanctify [*kaddesh*] the people, and say, 'Sanctify yourselves [*hitkaddeshu*] against tomorrow'" (Josh. 7:13)—that is, Joshua wanted the people to purify themselves before he cast the lot to determine who had misappropriated the devoted things, as if they were coming into God's presence to hear their judgment, and this was in order to impress upon them that the lot that he would cast among them would result in a Divine judgment.

## *Beshallaḥ*

The term *mitkaddeshet* was later transferred to a woman who was cleansing herself of her menstrual impurity (2 Sam. 11:14), even if her ritual immersion was not done for the purpose of partaking of *kodashim* (sacred offerings), but rather to become pure for her husband, or perhaps because she would be obligated, after giving birth, to go to the Temple and bring a sacrifice. Also, because soldiers would bring sacrifices before going to war so as to pray that God would be with them—and because, even when at war, they were admonished to keep themselves in a state of *kedushah* and purity, as it is written, "For the Lord, your God, walks in the midst of your camp… therefore your camp must be holy [*kadosh*]" (Deut. 23:15)—they would use the expression *kaddesh milḥamah* ("sanctify war") [in the sense of "prepare for war"], as in Jer. 6:4, Joel 4:9, and Mic. 3:5, and those who were prepared for war were called *mekuddashim* (Isa. 13:3).

As for the verse, "And they set apart [*va-yakdishu*] Kedesh in Galilee [as a city of refuge]" (Josh. 20:7), it is true that it would have been proper to use the verb *va-yavdilu*, as in, "Then Moses separated [*yavdil*] three cities" (Deut. 4:41), but it seems that out of a preference for plays on words, it was written *va-yakdishu et Kedesh*. In any case, the term *kedushah* is well employed with respect to cities of refuge, for the refuge given to manslayers was originally a distinction unique to sanctuaries and altars, as it is written, "From My very altar shall you tear him [the intentional murderer] away" (Exod. 21:14); "And [Joab] caught hold on the horns of the altar" (1 Kings 2:28). Because the Torah banned the *bamot* ("high places," or local altars) and commanded the entire nation to have only one sanctuary and altar—and thus not all manslayers could flee to the Temple, which was too distant for some—the six cities of refuge were ordained, as if there were six sanctuaries and altars in the land of Israel to give refuge to those who killed unintentionally. Hence, it was fittingly written *va-yakdishu et Kedesh*, as the word *va-yakdishu* does not depart from the essential meaning of *kedushah*.

In the verse, "But prophesy not again any more at Bethel, for it is the king's sanctuary [*mikdash melekh*], and it is a royal house" (Amos 7:13), the term *mikdash melekh* does not mean "the king's house," but literally a "sanctuary," the site where [Jeroboam's] golden calf was worshipped. It was called *mikdash melekh* because it was there that the king would bring his sacrifices, not at the other worship site in Dan, which was at the far border [of the northern kingdom of Israel] and distant from the royal city [of Samaria].

Moreover, the terms *kadesh* and *kedeshah* [the masculine and feminine words, respectively, for "sacred prostitute"] do not depart from the essential meaning of *kedushah*, for there were pagan gods (such as Ashtoret, alias Astarte and Venus) whose worship consisted of acts of harlotry, and the *kedeshim* and *kedeshot* consecrated themselves and their hire to those gods. During the reigns of some of the sinful kings of Judah, these abominations were performed even in honor of the true God, and in His house, and the *kedeshim* had houses within the Temple (2 Kings 23:7), even though the Torah had already forbidden all of this by declaring, "There shall not be a prostitute [*kedeshah*]... You must not let into the House of the Lord... the hire of a harlot..." (Deut. 23:18-19).

It is clear that most or all of the commentators (led by Onkelos and Jonathan) were mistaken in thinking that the term *kedushah* applies to any "preparation." Rashi (on Num.11:18) sought to bring proof from Jeremiah (2:3), "And prepare them [*ve-hakdishem*] for the day of slaughter," but not even that verse lends decisive support, for the more likely explanation, as per my student, David Hai Ashkenazi, is that the prophet is comparing the slain to sacred sheep (*tson kodashim*) that are slaughtered on a day of sacrifice; cf. "For the Lord has prepared a sacrifice" [Zeph. 1:7, referring to the slaughter of sinners].

Now every enlightened person knows that words indicating spiritual, intellectual concepts that are not perceptible to the senses are all transferred terms that originally indicated tangible things.[25] For example, the three words *nefesh*, *ruaḥ*, and *neshamah* (all meaning "soul") originally referred to "breath" and the intake of air, and because inhalation is an action that is necessary for life, these nouns were later transferred to refer to the vital essence of all living things, the cause of human life and thought. Similarly in other languages, [words such as the Latin] *anima* ("soul") originally meant "wind," "air," or "breath." The concept of *kedushah*, too, is exalted and far removed from the senses, and it is unlikely that its root originally conveyed such an exalted meaning. [It is true that] if we search through the languages cognate to Hebrew, we find in all of them this root in the sense of "holiness," and not in any other tangible sense that might be thought to have been transferred to denote "holiness." However, according to my view, the original sense of the word *kodesh* reflected a tangible thing, the burning of sacrifices, and the word was later transferred to anything specially dedicated to the honor of God even if it was not burned.

There is a similar instance in Latin, according to Servius, the ancient commentator to the poems of Virgil: "*Sancire* ("to sanction") properly refers to something holy, that is, 'to consecrate by pouring the blood [*sanguine*] of an enemy'; and to say *sanctum* is as if [to say] 'consecrated with blood.'"[26]

---

25. See note 22 above.
26. From Servius' comment on Virgil's *Aeneid* 12:200, "Let Jupiter hear, who sanctions [*sancit*] covenants by his thunder."

## Beshallaḥ

I hereby revoke what I wrote in *Bikkurei ha-Ittim* 5587 (1826), p. 204, and in *Kerem Ḥemed* vol. 3, p. 210, on the verse "Six hundred thousand on foot" (Num. 11:21).[27] I now say that when God said, "Sanctify yourselves [*hitkaddeshu*] for tomorrow, and you will eat meat" (Num. 11:18), this was already an intimation that the matter would be way of a miracle. It seems to me that if God had promised the people a new type of food (as in the case of the manna), Moses would not have expressed astonishment. However, God said that He would give them meat, and Moses saw that there was no settled land around them where there would be herds and flocks, and no sea with fish, and even birds were not to be seen in that great and terrible desert; therefore he was astonished.

In his *Thesaurus*, Gesenius made of the expression *mitkaddeshet mitum'atah*, "she was purified from her uncleanness" (2 Sam. 11:4) the basic source for the entire concept of *kedushah*; he thought that the original sense of the word indicated purity and cleanliness. This is not so, for *kedushah* always denotes a higher state than [mere] purity. *Kedushah* means that a thing is set aside for the honor of God, and this concept is not at all included in the meaning of the word *tohorah* ("purity"). It should be obvious that in the case of the phrase, "Therefore the Lord blessed the Sabbath day and declared it holy [*va-y'kaddeshehu*]" (Exod. 20:11), it could certainly not have been said *va-yetaharehu* ("and declared it pure"). Similarly, in the vast majority of other places, the term *kedushah* could not be replaced by the term *tohorah*, for the principal meaning of *kedushah* refers to a thing's relation to God, unlike the principal meaning of *tohorah*.

As for the derivation of the word, Gesenius found no root similar to *kadash* except for *ḥadash* ("to be new"), which also (according to him and others) mainly denotes that which is clean and bright, but all of this is unlikely. The root *kadash* contains the letter *shin* even in Aramaic, while the Aramaic equivalent of *ḥadash* is *ḥadat*. According to others cited by Gesenius, the original meaning of the root *kadash* had to do with "setting aside," and the root is derived from *kadad*, which in Arabic and Syriac denotes "cutting" or "splitting." But how many other roots do we have in Hebrew that indicated "cutting"—can it be that out of all of them, only this one was chosen, which appears in Hebrew only in another sense (that of "bowing to the ground")?

---

27. There, Shadal expressed the view that when God commanded Moses to assemble seventy elders (Num. 11:16), Moses thought that he and these elders would have to slaughter enough meat or gather enough fish to feed the people for a month, i.e., that the people's request for meat would be granted through natural means rather than by way of a miracle.

And if we had to derive *kadash* from *kadad*, it would make more sense to say that it came from *kodkod*, "the top of the head," and that *kedushah* originally meant "height" or "exaltedness."

I concede that the compounding of one word from two words (*kodesh* from *kod esh*) is an unusual phenomenon in Hebrew and its cognate languages, and that I have retracted what I wrote twenty years ago, that *riggel* ("to spy") was derived from *ra gillah* ("to expose evil"), and that *yatur* ("will explore") was derived from *atah ra'ah* ("came and saw"). Nevertheless, it cannot be completely denied that compound roots do exist, such as:

- *mahar* ("tomorrow") from *yom ahar* ("day after");
- *belimah* ("nothingness") from *beli mah* ("without anything");
- *lulei* ("unless") from *lu lo* ("if not");
- *me'umah* ("anything") from *mah o mah* ("what or what"); and also, in my opinion:
- *immadi* ("with me") from *im yadi* ("with my hand");
- *etsel* ("next to") from *el tsela* ("at the side of");
- *zulati* ("except for") from *zu lo* ("this not") (on the model of *bilti, beli,* and *bal,* which I derive from *belo* [all meaning "without"]).[28]

If anyone still denies the existence of compound Hebrew words, such a person would be free to say that *kedushah* is derived from *yekod* ("burning"), but that the final *shin* was added to distinguish the idea of *kedushah* from the idea of "burning."

**worthy of awesome praises** *(nora tehillot,* lit., "awesome of praises"). Worthy of great and mighty praises; cf., *nora alilah,* "terrible in His doing" (Ps. 66:5), i.e., "master of awesome deeds."

**15:12. "As soon as you made a sign with Your right hand, the earth swallowed them.**

***As soon as you made a sign with Your right hand.*** Just as a person commands his servants with a sign of his hand and they hasten to do his will, so the earth hastened to do God's will and swallow them.

---

28. Perhaps Shadal would not have been surprised to know that compound words have been coined in Modern Hebrew: e.g., *karnaf* ("rhinoceros," from *keren af,* "nose-horn") and *ramzor* ("traffic light," from *remez or,* "sign of light").

***the earth swallowed them.*** First it says that "the sea covered them" and "they sank like lead" (above, v. 10), and now it says that they remained swallowed up in the floor of the sea. Nachmanides explained that after they drowned, the sea cast them out as is the custom of the waters, and their bodies decomposed and returned to the dust on the earth [on the shore] as they were—but this is forced.

**15:13. "You guide with Your benevolence the people that You liberated; You escort him with Your power to Your holy abode.**

***You guide,*** *etc.* Now that the depiction of the Egyptians' downfall has been completed, the poet turns his thought to Israel, and he describes God's mercy upon them in doing all of this for them; just as He took them out of Egypt without harm, so He will bring them in peace to the land that He promised them.

***You guide*** *(naḥita,* lit., "You guided")... ***You liberated*** *(ga'alta).* The Hebrew past tense forms appear instead of the present tense; the poet is depicting the future as if it were before his eyes. See above, v. 5, on the word *yekhasyumu* ("covered them," lit., "will cover them").

***with Your benevolence*** *(be-ḥasdekha).* With love and compassion for Your people.

***with Your power.*** With great might against any who would rise up against Your people.

***to Your holy abode*** *(el neveh kodshekha,* lit., "to the abode of Your holiness"). *Neveh kodesh* (lit., "abode of holiness") is the equivalent of *naveh kadosh* ("holy abode"), just as *anshei kodesh* ("people of holiness") means *anashim kedoshim* ("holy people"), and *anshei emet* ("people of truth") means *anashim ne'emanim* ("faithful people").

The "abode" is the land of Canaan (Rashbam). It is called "God's abode" because it was to be the place of His worship. God is said to "dwell" in any place where He is worshipped.

**15:14. "The peoples, hearing this, tremble; pangs assail the inhabitants of Philistia.**

***The peoples, hearing this, tremble*** *(shame'u ammim yirgazun,* lit., "the people heard, they will tremble"). "When You guide Your people with benevolence, then the peoples who have heard of this miracle will tremble, and they will remain immobile as stone when Israel passes by them (v. 16)." Both past and future tenses are used here to indicate the present, for the poet describes the event as if it is now before his eyes. First he refers to "the peoples" in general, and then he specifies Philistia, Edom, Moab, and Canaan.

***tremble*** *(yirgazun).* The basic meaning [of the root *ragaz*] is "shaking" or "trembling," as in, "The curtains do tremble [*yirgezun*]" (Hab. 3:7); "The foundations of the mountains did tremble [*yirgazu*]" (Ps. 18:8). The term was transferred to denote any emotional tumult or agitation for whatever reason, as in:

- "[The nations] shall fear and tremble [*ve-ragezu*]" (Jer. 33:9); "They will be agitated [*ve-ragezu*] and will tremble for fear of you" (Deut. 2:25); "A trembling heart [*lev raggaz*]" (Deut. 28:65)—all of these denoting the excitation of fear.
- "And the king was much moved [*va-yirgaz*]" (2 Sam. 19:1); "From your travail and from your trouble [*u-mi-rogzekha*]" (Isa. 14:3)—both of these denoting the excitation of sorrow.
- "And they that provoke [*u-le-margizei*] God" (Job 12:6); "In wrath [*be-rogez*] remember compassion" (Hab. 3:2)—both of these denoting anger.

In Aramaic, the word is used exclusively in the sense of anger. So also in Rabbinic Hebrew, *ragzan* means "an angry man." Here, however, the term is used in the sense of fear.[29]

***pangs*** *(ḥil).* This term, too, denotes "trembling," as in, "And the land quakes and is in pain [*va-taḥol*]" (Jer. 51:29); "The waters saw You, they were in pain [*yaḥilu*]; the depths also trembled" (Ps. 77:17). However, it seems to refer in particular to trembling with pain and suffering, as in, "Before she travailed [*taḥil*], she brought forth" (Isa. 66:7), although it is sometimes transferred to refer to inanimate things that feel no pain.

The peoples that are mentioned [here] first are those which were close to the pathways that Israel had to traverse in order to go to the land of Canaan. Afterwards the inhabitants of Canaan are mentioned, those whose land Israel

---

29. Much of this comment also appears at Gen. 45:24, on the phrase, "Do not become angry [*tirgezu*] on the way."

was coming to conquer. First it was necessary for the Philistines, Edom, and Moab to be afraid, so that they would not hinder the Israelites as they passed by them, and afterwards it was necessary for the Canaanites to be afraid, so that Israel could defeat them. Thus, with respect to Philistia, Edom, and Moab it says that "they remain immobile as stone, until Your people passes" (below, v. 16), while with respect to the inhabitants of Canaan it says [that they will remain immobile while] "You will conduct them [the Israelites] and You will establish them" (below, v. 17).

**15:15. "At once the tribes of Edom take fright, the magnates of Moab are assailed with trembling; all the inhabitants of Canaan turn to liquid [they lose all strength and courage].**

*At once (az*, lit., "then") — as soon as they hear of the splitting of the Red Sea and the drowning of the Egyptians.

*the tribes of (allufei) Edom. Allufim* are the heads of families, and a family headed by a chief is called an *elef*, as in:

- "Behold, my family [*alpi*] is the poorest in Manasseh" (Judg. 6:15);
- "By your tribes and by your families [*u-le-alfeikhem*]" (1 Sam. 10:19);
- "I will search him out among all the families of [*alfei*] Judah" (1 Sam. 23:23).

The *alluf* is the chief of the *elef* and prince of the clan, and the *allufei Edom* are the clans into which the nation of Edom is divided; each clan had an *alluf* and prince. These are the *allufim* mentioned in Gen. 36:40-43.[30]

There was also a king in Edom (Gen. 36:31, Num. 20:14); it seems to me that the *allufim* of Edom were not subject to the king of Edom, but had revolted against him or had never accepted a king over themselves, and that part of the nation was under the king's rule and part was under the rule of the *allufim*. This second part of the nation of Edom was known in particular as "the children of Esau" (see Rashbam on Deut. 2:4). The king of Edom did not take fright of the Israelites, but confronted them with a large force. In contrast, "the children of Esau" were afraid of them (Deut. 2:4).

---

30. In his comment on Gen. 36:43, Shadal said that he had once understood *alluf* as meaning "prince" or "ruler," but that he now preferred to translate the word as "clan" or "tribe." The comment here seems to waver between these two opinions.

***the magnates of*** *(eilei)* **Moab** — their mighty ones. The term is not derived from *ayil* ("ram") (which was Ibn Ezra's opinion), but is related to *el* and *elim* ("god," "gods"), and is sometimes [as here] written with a *yod*, for we do find the words *eyal* and *eyalut*; all of these denoted "strength" and "power."

*Eilim* was apparently the title of some of the officials: "And the king's wives, and his officers, and the chief men of [*eilei*] the land, he carried into captivity from Jerusalem to Babylon" (2 Kings 24:15); "And the mighty of [*eilei*] the land he took" (Ezek. 17:13). Of Moab it is [subsequently] said, "And that the Moabites were exceedingly afraid of that people, for it was numerous, and that the Moabites were in anguish, for fear of the children of Israel" (Num. 22:3).

***turn to liquid*** *(namogu)*. They dissolve, like a substance that liquefies in water. This is a figure of speech, as if to say that their heart's strength was lost and turned to water; cf., "And the hearts of the people melted [*va-yimmas*] and became as water (Josh. 7:5). In a similar vein, Ovid wrote, "My heart melts from unending sorrows as fresh wax is wont to do when fire is brought near" (*Ex Ponto* I.2.57).

It seems that these two roots, *mug* and *masas*, are distinguished from each other in that something which is *namog* is dissolved by water, as in the verses, "You make her soft [*temogegennah*]... with the showers" (Ps. 65:11); "And the mountains shall drop sweet wine, and all the hills shall melt [*titmogagnah*]" (Amos 9:13)—that is, they will turn to water. Similarly, "The gates of the rivers are opened, and the palace is dissolved [*namog*]" (Nahum 2:7)—that is, after the gates of the rivers are opened, the water floods the palace and it dissolves in water. And perhaps a similar example (if interpreted against the accents and the vocalization) is the phrase *namogu, ba-yam de'agah* ["they are melted away; there is trouble in the sea," which might be read as *namogu be-yam de'agah*], "they are melted away in a sea of trouble" (Jer. 49:23).

On the other hand, something that is *namas* is melted by fire or heat, as in:

- "Then as soon as the sun became hot, it [the manna] melted [*ve-namas*]" (Exod. 16:21);
- "My heart is become like wax; it is melted [*names*] in my inmost parts" (Ps. 22:15);
- "As wax melts [*ke-himmes*] before the fire" (Ps. 68:3);
- "The mountains melted [*namassu*] like wax" (Ps. 97:5);

- "And the mountains shall be molten [*ve-namassu*] under Him… as wax before the fire" (Mic. 1:4).

A similar root is *masah*, as in, "He sends forth His word, as melts them [*va-yamsem*]" (Ps. 147:18)—that is, by the heat of the sun. Two verses seem to be anomalous:

- "I melt away [*amseh*] my couch with my tears" (Ps. 6:7), and
- "The mountains shall be melted [*ve-namassu*] with their blood" (Isa. 34:3).

However, even in these verses the reference is to heat, for both fresh blood and tears are warm. [In the former verse, the poet] is saying that his tears are so plentiful that he would be justified in saying, "Every night I make my bed to swim" [Ps. 6:7, first half of the verse], and they are so boiling hot that they melt his couch, which might have been wholly or partly made of silver or gold. With regard to fear, however, the terms *namog* and *namas* are used without distinction, since such a figure of speech is merely transferred. One would say that one's heart or blood turned to water, without our knowing whether this resulted from excessive heat or excessive wetness.

**15:16. "Terror and fear fall upon them; by reason of Your great arm [that is, at the sight of the miracles] they remain immobile as stone, until Your people passes, O Lord, until that people passes that You made.**

*fall upon them* — upon Edom and Moab (Ibn Ezra).

*by reason of Your great arm (bi-g'dol zero'akha*, lit., "in the greatness of Your arm"). *Gedol* is the equivalent of *godel*; cf., "According to the greatness of Your power [*ke-godel zero'akha*] set free those that are appointed to death" (Ps. 79:11). The noun form *po'el* interchanges with the noun form *pe'ol*, as in, "May we be satisfied with… the holy place of *kedosh*] Your temple" (Ps. 65:5), where *kedosh* is the equivalent of *kodesh* or *kedushat*. So also, "Or on the height of [*gevo'ah*] his stature" (1 Sam. 16:7), where *gevo'ah* is the equivalent of *govah*. Similarly, *te'omim* ("twins") is the plural of *te'om,* while *to'omei* ("twins of") [an alternate form found in Songs 7:4] is the plural of *to'am* or *to'em*.

Likewise, the noun form *pe'el* interchanges with the forms *p'al, p'eil,* and *p'el,* as in the following pairs of words: *heder/hadar, hevel/haveil, shekhem/sh'khem,* etc. This is because all of these forms, which end with a *segol* vowel followed by an unvocalized letter, originally were vocalized with a *sheva* and a *patah*, or a *sheva* and *holam*, as in Aramaic; e.g., Hebrew *koshet*, Aramaic *keshot*; Hebrew *gever*, Aramaic *gevar*. There is much to say about this, but I have explained it at length in my book *Prolegomeni*.

The meaning of the phrase *bi-gedol zero'akha* is, "When they will see Your arm stretched forth over all who would harm Your people, they will remain immobile like a silent stone, and they will not prevent Israel from passing by them."

**they remain immobile** *(yiddemu)*. The Hebrew is in the *kal* conjugation of the root *damam*, on the model of *yittemu* (Deut. 34:8) from *tamam*.

**until Your people passes, O Lord,** *etc.* This phrase does not follow the pattern of "Your right hand, O Lord..." (above, v. 6), "Who is equal to You among the gods, O Lord..." (above, v. 11), or the like, for in those examples, the first clause is not a complete statement, but in this case it is. Perhaps this is because this phrase differs from those other doubled phrases in another way: they appear at the beginning of a verse, but this is at the end. When the meaning of such a phrase is doubtful and held in suspense, it is fitting and pleasing for the phrase to appear at the beginning, but not at the end.

Nevertheless, the second half of the phrase here does add somewhat to the first half; while the first half says, "Until that people passes, O Lord," the second half says, "Until that people passes that You made"—i.e., the people that You made to be Yours. They were Your people not only because they retained the custom of their forebears (worshipping You because their forebears did), but because now, having brought them out of the house of bondage, You have acquired them as servants, as it says, "They are My servants, whom I brought forth from the land of Egypt" (Lev. 25:42).

**15:17. "And You will conduct him, and You will establish him in the mountainous region of Your patrimony [favored by You]; (You will conduct him, I say) to the place that You, O Lord, destined for Your seat; to the sanctuary, O Lord, that Your hands will render firm.**

***And You will conduct him, and You will establish him*** *(tevi'emo ve-titta'emo)*. The opinion of the accentuator in this verse is quite correct, but the commentators did not understand it at all. This is how the verse is to be taken: "You will conduct him (after having established him in the mountainous region of Your patrimony) to the place that You destined for Your seat, which is the sanctuary that Your hands will render firm."

## *Beshallaḥ*

The word *tevi'emo* ("and You will conduct him") is attached to *makhon le-shivtekha* ("the place for Your seat"), which is the Temple, even though these two elements are not connected with a formative letter [i.e., the word *makhon* has no *le-* prefix, and the word "to" is supplied in translation only], as occurs in the phrases, "Enter into [*bo'u*] His gates with thanksgiving" (Ps. 100:4); "For she has seen that the heathen are entered into [*ba'u*] her sanctuary (Lam. 1:10), and many other such examples. However, the word *ve-titta'emo* ("and You will establish him") is perforce connected by the formative letter *bet* [to the subsequent phrase *be-har naḥalatekha*, "in the mountainous region of Your patrimony"]. Thus, the phrase *ve-titta'emo be-har naḥalatekha* is parenthetical, and for this reason the preceding word *tevi'emo* is set off with a [disjunctive] *revia*, separating it from *ve-titta'emo*.

**in the mountainous region of** *(be-har*, lit., "in the mountain of") **Your patrimony.** Any mountainous area is called *har*, e.g. *har Yehudah* and *har Efrayim*, and also:

- "That happy mountainous region [*ha-har*]" (Deut. 3:25);
- "And in this mountain [*ba-har ha-zeh*] will the Lord Tseva'ot make unto all peoples a feast" (Isa. 25:6);
- "And He will destroy this mountain [*ba-har ha-zeh*]" (Isa. 25:7);
- "For in this mountain [*ba-har ha-zeh*] will the hand of the Lord rest" (Isa. 25:10).

[In all of these examples] the reference is to the entire land of Israel.

**Your patrimony** *(naḥalatekha).* The land of Israel is called God's patrimony, as if it were His own property and inherited portion; such property is held dear by all people (and in particular by the ancients, as is seen from the incident of Naboth in 1 Kings 21:3). Cf., "The heathen are come into Your inheritance [*be-naḥalatekha*]" (Ps. 79:1); "You defiled My land, and made My heritage [*ve-naḥalati*] an abomination" (Jer. 2:7). Similarly, the people of Israel is called God's portion and patrimony, in order to indicate how dear it is to Him.

**the place** *(makhon)* **that You, O Lord, destined for Your seat.** The heavens are called God's "dwelling place" (*mekhon shivtekha*, 1 Kings 8:39, 43, 49; *mi-mekhon shivto*, Ps. 33:4), and the Temple is also so called: "A place for You to dwell in [*mekhon le-shivtekha*] forever" (1 Kings 8:13). *Makhon* means "place" (similar to the Arabic *makan*), as in, "I will hold Me still, and

I will look on in My dwelling place [*vi-mekhoni*]" (Isa. 18:4). Most of the uses of this word in this sense occur in poetry and in elevated speech, while in plain speech the forms *mekhonah* and *mekhonot* are used in the sense of "foundation" or "base." In poetry, we find the word used in this sense in the plural form: "Who did establish the earth upon its foundations [*mekhoneha*]" (Ps. 104:5).

**destined** *(pa'alta)*. "You set aside and ordained in Your thought"; compare:

- "Woe to them that devise iniquity, and work [*u-fo'alei*] evil upon their beds" (Mic. 2:1);
- "Yea, in heart you work [*tif'alun*] wickedness" (Ps. 58:3);
- "Who has wrought [*pa'al*] and done it?" (Isa. 41:4).

**the sanctuary** *(mikkedash)*. [Although the normal reading of the word is *mikdash*,] the *kof* is strengthened with a *dagesh* in order to embellish the reading. It seems to me that this was done for the purpose of making the *sheva* vowel [marking the *kof*] a mobile one, so as to increase the word's syllables [from two to three], thus enabling the *zakef gadol* [accenting the word] to be sounded better. A similar instance occurs with the word *hatsefino* (Exod. 2:3): since the word is accented with a *segulta* [*segol*], but is not preceded by a word with an auxiliary accent, [the Masoretes] wanted to increase the word's syllables so that the melody of the *segulta* could better be heard, even though this accent does not go well with any other *dagesh* added for embellishment.

Another similar instance is the replacement of a quiescent *sheva* with a *hataf patah* in the word *ha-timalokh* ("shall your reign," Jer. 22:15) in order to increase the word's syllables for the sake of the cantillation of the *zakef*, which is not preceded by an auxiliary.[31]

**Your hands will render firm** *(konanu)*. The Hebrew is not synonymous with *pa'alta* (as in Ibn Ezra's opinion), but denotes "setting up" and "establishing," as in, "And I will establish [*ve-khonanti*] the throne of his kingdom" (2 Sam. 7:13); "God establish it [*yekhoneneha*] forever" (Ps. 48:9). The meaning is that God will preserve His sanctuary from destruction, a statement analogous to the one that follows, "The Lord will reign forever."

**15:18. "The Lord will reign forever."**

---

31. The normal reading, *ha-timlokh*, is in fact found in standard printed versions.

## Beshallaḥ

***The Lord will reign*** *(YHVH yimlokh)* ***forever.*** This is not said by way of prayer, for if it were, it should have said *yimlokh YHVH*, "Let the Lord reign" (e.g., Ps. 146:10). Nor is this said by way of prophecy; rather, this is a poetic expression: "When God brings His people to His sanctuary, then God will be king forever," i.e., His people must serve Him forever.

***will reign.*** He will be king over Israel, so that they will serve Him and follow His Torah, and He will be at their head in place of a [human] king, for their appointment of a king over themselves would not be in keeping with the Torah's primary intention. Here there is also an allusion to a future event, that God will become King over all the earth, and God will be One and His name One.

***forever*** *(le-olam va-ed).* The basic meaning of the word *olam* refers to a time that is unknown (*ne'lam*) and indefinite, whether past or future. Thus, for example, "Remember the remote times [*yemot olam*]" (Deut. 32:7) refers to the ancient past that is distant and unknown to us, while the expressions *eved olam*, "a slave forever," *ahuzzat olam*, "an eternal possession," and *simḥat olam*, "eternal joy," refer to the future. The expression *me-olam ve-ad olam*, "from everlasting and to everlasting," refers to both past and future.

The word *ad*, "until," is transferred to mean (like *olam*) any distant time, whether past or future (and similarly, in Latin, poets sometimes say *usque* [lit., "up to," "until"] to refer to eternity). Thus, for example, "Do you not know this of old time [*ad*]" (Job 20:4) refers to the past, while "Trust in the Lord forever [*adei ad*]" (Isa. 26:4) refers to the future.

*La-ad* is the equivalent of *le-olam* ("forever"), and by way of hyperbole the expression is doubled to *la-ad le-olam* (Ps. 148:6) or *le-olam va-ed* (which expression is not defective, as in the opinion of Ibn Ezra, who thought that it was properly *le-olam ve-ad olam*). The word *va-ed* (וָעֶד) would properly have been vocalized *ve-ad*, or at the end of a phrase (for it is found in no other location) *va-ad*. The *segol* vowel under the *ayin* [in *va-ed*] is very strange. Ibn Ezra sought to resolve it but could not, for he ascribed it to its position at the end of the verse, analogous to *va-okhel* (Gen. 3:12), a variant of *va-okhal*. This, however, proves nothing: first, because the vowel in *va-ed* (וָעֶד) is a *segol*, while the vowel in *va-okhel* (וָאֹכֶל) is a *tseireh*; and second, even in positions other than the end of a verse, *naḥ peh alef* verbs [those whose first root letter *alef* disappears in some conjugations] in the future tense [such as *va-okhel/va-okhal*] are vocalized sometimes with a *tseireh* and sometimes with a *pataḥ*, e.g., *va-oḥez be-filagshi* (Judg. 20:6)—and except for *naḥ peh alef* verbs in the future tense, we never find a *pataḥ* changing to a *tseireh* at the end of a verse.

Rashi wrote that the *vav* in *va-ed* is part of the root (*yesod*) of the word and that "it" is *petuḥah* [i.e., vocalized with a *pataḥ*]. The author of [the supercommentary] *Siftei Ḥakhamim* [Shabbetai Bass] correctly explains that Rashi meant to refer to [the vocalization of] the *ayin* [and not the *vav*], for in [the contrasting phrase cited by Rashi], *ki anokhi ha-yode'a va-ed* (וָעֵד) (Jer. 29:23), where the word means "and witness," the *ayin* is *kemutsah*, that is, marked with a "*kamats katan*," which is [an archaic name for] *tseireh*, while in the case of וָעֶד, meaning "forever," the *ayin* is marked with a "*pataḥ katan*," which is [an archaic name for] *segol*.

On the other hand, Ibn Ezra was referring to the vocalization of the *vav* when he said, "It is the way of the Hebrew language that when the *tenu'ah* (this word [meaning "vowel"] seems to be a scribal error, and should be *neginah*, "musical accent") is on the letter following a *vav*, it is marked with a *pataḥ*, as in *shor ve-khesev va-ez* (Lev. 7:23), and for this reason there is a *pataḥ* in *va-ed*." He used the terminology of *petiḥah* to refer to the *kamats* [in *va-ed*], not that the *kamats* is actually called [*pataḥ*], but because it is a *petuḥah* [i.e., an "open" vowel] relative to the *sheva*, which is not a vowel at all. In Ibn Ezra's short commentary [to Exodus], he further expressed the idea: "Because the accent [*ta'am*] is on the first letter, as in *leḥem va-yayin* (Gen. 14:18), the *vav* is marked with a *pataḥ*."[32]

However, Rashi's statement that the *vav* in *va-ed* is "*yesod*" [usually understood as meaning "part of the root"] cannot be taken literally. Rashi was aware that the expressions *la-ad, minmi ad,* and *olmei ad* appear without a *vav*, so how could he have said here that the *vav* was *yesod*? Furthermore, his comment elsewhere (at Num. 21:14) [on the words *et vahev*, usually understood as referring to a place named Waheb], "*Et vahev* is the equivalent of *et yahev*, just as the root *ya'ad* yields וְעֵד," does not at all prove that he derives *va-ed* from the root *ya'ad*, for there he was [merely] referring to the appearance of a *vav* in place of a [root letter] *yod* in words such as *no'ad* and *mo'ed*, as well as *va'ad* (וַעַד, "council") in Rabbinic Hebrew, but he was not referring (as the *Me'ammer* thought) to the word *va-ed*, which as everyone knows is not derived from the root *ya'ad*, but from the word *ad*, as in *la-ad* and *le-olmei ad*.

---

32. For an opposing view, see Rosenbaum and Silbermann, p. 242: "There appears to be but little doubt that Rashi and Ibn Ezra had the reading וָעֶד or perhaps even וָעַד in place of our וָעֶד, and that the nomenclature of the vowels which Rashi employs here is the same as ours." In other words, Rashi did in fact mean to say that the *vav* (not the *ayin*) is marked with what we call a *pataḥ*.

## Beshallaḥ

It seems clear to me that this is what Rashi intended to say: in the word וָעֵד ("and witness"), with a *tseireh* marking the *ayin*, [the presence of the initial *vav* does not determine the vocalization of the *ayin*, for] the word עֵד appears without a *vav*; but the word וָעֶד, with a *segol* marking the *ayin*, cannot exist without the *vav*, for without it the word would be *ad* with a *pataḥ*, not *ed* with a *segol*. Thus, the *vav* is an inseparable element of the word וָעֶד, as if it were a root letter (*yesod*).

Similarly, in a comment below (v. 23) on the word *maratah*, Rashi wrote, "The *tav* appears in place of the root letter *he* of the word *marah*," and so also, on the word *va-ḥamato* [in the same comment], he wrote, "The *he* of the root changes to a *tav*." Thus, he characterizes as a "root letter" any letter that is inseparable from a word, and whose removal would alter the word's meaning, even if it is not truly part of the root—for the root of *marah* is *marar* [with a *resh*, not a *he*], and the root of *ḥemah* is [not *ḥamah*, with a *he*, but] *yaḥam*.

**15:19. For Pharaoh's horses, with his carriages and with his horsemen, entered into the sea, and the Lord caused the waters of the sea to turn back over them, and the children of Israel walked in the dryness in the midst of the sea.**

*For Pharaoh's horses, etc.* This verse is not part of the Song (as per Ibn Ezra), for the language of this verse is not like the Song's language, but is in the style of simple narration. However, it does have a connection to what is above: "Then Moses and the children of Israel sang.... For Pharaoh's horses... entered into the sea" (Nachmanides, Mendelssohn).

**15:20. And Miriam the prophetess, sister of Aaron, took the tambourine in hand, and all the women went out after her with tambourines and with sistra.**

*the prophetess (ha-nevi'ah).* One who utters praise or rebuke for the people is called a *navi*, "prophet" (Rashbam), and so Rashi (above, on 7:1) [where he says that a *navi* rebukes the people]. Here, the term seems to denote one who is expert in the art of song and music; compare:

- "The sons of Asaph, and of Heman, and of Jeduthun, who should prophesy [*ha-nibbe'im*] with harps, with psalteries, and with cymbals" (1 Chron. 25:1);

- "Who prophesied [*ha-nibba*] according to the direction of the king" (1 Chron. 25:2);
- "Who prophesied [*ha-nibba*] in giving thanks and praising the Lord" (1 Chron. 25:3).

**sister of Aaron.** Daughters were called after the eldest son (Rashbam), e.g., "[Mahalath, daughter of Ishmael,] sister of Nebaioth" (Gen. 28:9).

**the tambourine** *(ha-tof)*. A ring of metal or wood on which a skin is stretched, and from which hang small pieces of metal. The instrument is raised with the left hand and struck with the fingers of the right hand. It is quite common to this day in the lands of the East, where it is called *dof* [in Arabic]. The term is also found in the Mishnah: "Its skin [that of a lamb] is used in making a *tof*" (Mishnah *Kinnim* 3:5).

**and all the women went after her.** To this day, it is the custom among eastern peoples that the women sing among themselves, not with the men, and that the most prominent and respected young woman takes the lead in singing and dancing, with the rest following after her, dancing as she does and responding to her song.

**and with sistra** *(u-vi-m'holot)*. Many of the Gentile scholars, among them Rosenmueller and Gesenius—and also Mendelssohn—have understood this word as "dance," but the texts prove that *mahol* is the name of an instrument, like *tof*. Thus we find:

- "With *tuppim* and *meholot*" (here and Judg. 11:34);
- "Let them praise His name with *mahol*, with *tof* and harp" (Ps. 149:3);
- "Praise Him with *tof* and *mahol*; praise Him with stringed instruments and psaltery" (Ps. 150:4).

So also, the [Aramaic] word *hingin*, used here in Onkelos' translation, is the equivalent of the Hebrew *kinnor* ("harp"); the phrase "with *tof* and *kinnor*" (Gen. 31:27) appears in the Targum [in some editions] as *be-tufin u-ve-hingin*. [Even more] likely is Kimhi's view that the word *mahol* is derived from the root *halal* ("to be hollow") and is related to *halil* ("pipe," "flute"), and so we find "*tof* and *halil*" (Isa. 5:12).

The Gentile scholars, however, derived the word from *hul*, which in Arabic denotes going in a circle. Perhaps this is the correct interpretation in some instances, as in:

- "To dance [*la-ḥul*] in the dances [*ba-meḥolot*]" (Judg. 21:21);
- "Of them that danced [*ha-meḥolelot*]" (Judg. 21:23);
- "Did they not sing one to another of him in dances [*va-meḥolot*]" (1 Sam. 21:12);
- "And he saw the calf and the dances [*u-m'ḥolot*]" (Exod. 32:19);
- "Then shall the virgin rejoice in the dance [*be-maḥol*]" (Jer. 31:12).

If so, there are two types of *maḥol*, the dance and the instrument. Perhaps the second term was derived from the first, and the name *maḥol* was given to an instrument that was used during a dance.

I have translated the word [in Italian] as *sistri* [Lat. and Eng. "sistra," pl. of "sistrum"], in accordance with the author of *Shiltei ha-Gibborim* [Abraham Portaleone], who wrote that it was a round metal instrument resembling a large ring and open on all sides, and around the edge were set small bells that sounded when the instrument was shaken. It should be added that this instrument was often used in Egypt on their holidays, and thus it is likely that it was known to the Israelites as well.

**15:21. And Miriam sang to them (the above hymn, beginning thus): "Sing to the Lord, for He has shown Himself supreme; horse and rider has He thrown into the sea."**

*And... sang (va-ta'an*, lit., "and responded"). The Hebrew denotes "song," as in, "Did they not sing [*ya'anu*] one to another of him in dances" (1 Sam. 21:12). The term was derived from the practice of one [leader] singing and the rest of the people responding after him, as I have explained above (at v. 1).

*to them (lahem).* To "the women," even though the word is written with a *mem* [normally the masculine ending; the expected word would have been *lahen*]. Perhaps it is written this way because of the initial *mem* in the following word ("*lahem Miriam*"). Mendelssohn translated the phrase as, "And Miriam sang facing them," that is, facing Moses and the Israelites; but it seems to me that if this were so, it should have said *va-ta'an aḥareihem* ("and she sang after them"). Mendelssohn further said that if Miriam sang to the women, she should have begun her song with the word *shornah* [the feminine imperative], not *shiru* [the masculine imperative]. However, this is no proof, for *shiru* is a poetic imperative that does not refer back to any specific men or women, but to the whole world; there are many such examples in prophetic and poetic passages (see Kimhi on Isa. 35:3).[33]

---

33. In his comment on the imperative *ḥazzeku* in that verse, Kimhi says that such

Miriam said *shiru* and not *ashirah* ("I sing"), because she was not the author of this song, for Moses had already composed it. Apparently Miriam sang the entire song (as per the Mekhilta and Rashi), while the women responded after her, "Horse and rider has He thrown into the sea," just as the Israelite men responded after Moses.

**15:22. Then Moses caused Israel to depart from the Red Sea, and they entered into the desert of Shur. They walked for three days in the desert, without finding water.**

*the desert of Shur.* This is the desert between Egypt and the land of Israel, also called the desert of Eitam; perhaps one particular part of the desert of Shur was known as the desert of Eitam. Shur was the name of a city at the edge of Egypt (Gen. 16:7, 20:1, 25:18; 1 Sam. 15:7, 27:8). The name of the desert of Shur is now Jofar.

The statement cited by Mendelssohn in Ibn Ezra's name—that the people had the pillar of fire and the pillar of cloud only until they crossed the sea—is erroneous, as is made clear by Neh. 9:19 [where, in a review of Israelite history, it is said that even when the people had made a golden calf, "You... forsook them not in the wilderness; the pillar of cloud departed not from over them by day, neither the pillar of fire by night..."] (*Orient* vol. 32, 1846, p. 222).

**15:23. They arrived at Marah, but they could not drink of the water of Marah, for it was bitter; therefore (that place) had the name of Marah.**

*They arrived at Marah.* The Arabs have given the name Ayyun Musa ("Moses' springs") to some springs of bitter water that are located seven hours' distance from Suez and half an hour from the Red Sea. It is unlikely, however, that these are the waters of Marah referred to here, for the Israelites walked three days in the desert before their arrival at Marah. However, there are other bitter waters to the south of those springs. According to Burckhardt and Gesenius, Marah is at the site now called Bir Howara.

**15:24. And the people murmured against Moses, saying, "What will we drink?"**
**15:25. And he cried to the Lord, and the Lord showed him a wood, which he threw into the water, and the water became sweet. There (God) gave it [the people] a law and a rule, and there He tested it.**

---

imperatives are addressed not to any particular individuals, but to an indefinite audience.

***and the Lord showed him a wood.*** On the Coromandel coast [of India] there is a type of wood that they call Nellimoran ("nelli wood"), which sweetens bitter water, and they throw it into their springs. However, in the desert of Shur there is no such thing, and the inhabitants of those regions know of no wood with such powers, as Niebuhr attests. Nachmanides wrote, "From the plain meaning of the verse, it seems that this wood naturally sweetened water, and that this was its special property, and that God taught this to Moses…. It says 'the Lord showed him,' because this wood was not [generally] found in that place, but the Holy One, blessed is He, showed him where it was, or else produced it for him by way of a miracle."

***There (God) gave it [the people] a law and a rule.*** As is specified afterward, "If you obey the Lord…" (next v.). This is the general law and rule that He gave them when they first came under His leadership, before He gave them His particular commandments.

***and there He tested it.*** He supplied their need, as if to examine them to see whether their complaints were caused only by a genuine need, and whether they would be faithful to Him once that need was satisfied (as Exod. 16:4). Therefore He admonished them and said, "If you obey…."

**15:26. And He said, "If you obey the Lord your God, and you do that which is right in His eyes, and you give heed to His commandments, and you observe all His statutes, none of the infirmities [calamities] that I sent upon the Egyptians will I send upon you; but rather I, the Lord, will be your healer."**

***none of the infirmities,*** *etc.* For the sweetening of the bitter waters corresponded to the first plague that God had inflicted upon Egypt, when He turned their water to blood so that they could not drink it (Rashbam, Ibn Ezra).

***infirmities*** *(mahalah).* The Heb. is synonymous with *mahlah*, "plague," and *tahalu'im*, "diseases," (cf. Deut. 29:21), and includes all kinds of calamities.

***but rather (ki) I, the Lord, will be your healer.*** The word *ki*, when preceded by a negative [as here, in the phrase *lo asim alekha*, lit., "I will not send upon you"], means "but," [and thus this phrase means] "but to the contrary, I, the Lord, will be your healer, and I will remove from you any infirmities that may come upon you in the course of nature."

**15:27. Then they arrived at Eilim, and there were twelve springs of water and seventy palms; and they camped there by the waters.**

*at Eilim (Eilimah).* Said to be in the valley called Girondel, Gorondel, or Garendel, eight miles from the city of Tor, for there Shaw found nine springs and 2,000 date palms. Gesenius reports hearing Ehrenberg say that near this place, he had found a valley called עאלים.

**16:1. They departed from Eilim, and all the assembly of the children of Israel reached the desert of Sin, situated between Eilim and Sinai; (and this was) on the fifteenth day of the second month from their going out of the country of Egypt.**
**16:2. And all the assembly of the children of Israel murmured against Moses and against Aaron, (finding itself) in the desert.**

*murmured.* See my comment above on Exod. 14:11.

**16:3. That is, the children of Israel said to them, "Oh, if only we had died by the hand of the Lord [of a natural death] in the country of Egypt, sitting by the pot of meat, eating bread to the fill! While you have brought us out to this desert, to cause all this multitude to die of hunger."**

*we had died by the hand of the Lord.* A natural death, as any person dies (Rashbam, Mendelssohn).

*sitting by the pot of meat.* Elsewhere they said, "We remember the fish that we ate in Egypt, without expense" (Num. 11:5), but made no mention of meat. Perhaps (as per A. H. Mainster), the fish and the leeks, etc., were what they ate for free, that is, what the Egyptians gave them, while one who had much sheep and cattle at home would be brought meat by his wife, and they would cook it at their place of labor.

**16:4. The Lord then said to Moses, "Behold, I am about to make bread rain for you from the heaven; and the people will go out, and they will collect of it what is needed from day to day. I want to test them, whether they are ready to follow My law, or not.**

*I want to test them.* It was as if God was saying, "Now they are complaining, and they have a right to do so, for they have no bread to eat. But now I want

## Beshallaḥ

to supply their need, and then I will see whether they will follow My Torah and cease complaining—whether they will observe My commandments once they see that I am doing good for them—or whether, despite all this, their hearts will not be firm with Me." This is all in keeping with the principle that "the Torah speaks the language of man."

This verse and the ones that follows are a shortened version of God's statement to Moses, who was not commanded to tell all of this to Israel immediately; instead, he said, "At night you will know that it is the Lord..." (below, vv. 6-8). See below at v. 22.

**16:5. "On the sixth day, then, they will prepare that which they will have brought (home), and it will be double of that which they will collect daily."**

*they will prepare.* For the needs of the Sabbath.

*and it will be double, etc.* "And I rain down for them a double amount, so that they can prepare for the Sabbath."

**16:6. Moses and Aaron said to all of the children of Israel, "At night you will know that it is the Lord Who brought you out of the country of Egypt.**

*At night you will know, etc.* As it is specified below, "When the Lord gives you at night meat to eat" (v. 8), then when you see that He is satisfying your desires, you will recognize that it is He Who brought you out of Egypt, that is, He wanted us take you out of there and bring you into the desert, not as you said [to us], "You have brought us out" (Rashi, Rashbam).

**16:7. "And tomorrow morning you will see the majesty of the Lord when He shows that He has heard your murmurings against the Lord. We, then, what are we, that you murmur against us?"**

*And tomorrow morning, etc.* This does not at all refer (as Ibn Ezra maintained) to God's glory as seen in the cloud, but refers (as per Rashi, Rashbam, Nachmanides, and Mendelssohn) to the falling of the manna, which was a phenomenon that revealed the glory of God. This expression was not used in connection with the quails [i.e., the meat (below, v. 13)], for the quails were produced through God's Providence but were not completely miraculous.

***when He shows that He has heard*** *(be-shom'o,* lit., "when He hears"). By means of the manna, He showed that He had heard their murmurings.

**16:8. And Moses added, "(Yes,) when the Lord gives you at night meat to eat, and in the morning bread to satisfy you, the Lord thus showing that He has heard the murmurings that you make against Him. We, then, what are we? Your murmurings are not against us, but against the Lord."**

***when the Lord gives you.*** "That which I said [that the Lord will show that He has heard you] will occur by virtue of His giving you [meat and bread]."

**16:9. Moses said to Aaron, "Say to all the assembly of the children of Israel, 'Draw near before the Lord, for He has heard your murmurings.'"**

***Draw near before the Lord.*** Apparently the pillar of cloud [see the next v.] did not [then] appear while they were camping, but only while they were traveling; it was only after the Tabernacle was built that the cloud was present above it even during their encampment, as it is written, "All the time that the cloud remained above the tabernacle, they were encamped" (Num. 9:18). Here, when Aaron spoke to the people, they did not have the pillar of cloud, yet suddenly God's majesty appeared to them in the cloud—that is, the cloud appeared to them.

When Aaron said to them, "Draw near before the Lord," this did not mean that they should [literally] go anywhere or move in any direction; rather, the meaning was, "Come to us and we will cause you to hear the word of God," whereupon God was at once revealed in the cloud, so as to validate Moses' words. This is why Moses said to Aaron, "Say to all of the assembly of the children of Israel," so that Aaron would summon them and Moses would speak to them.

At first, apparently, when Moses and Aaron told the people, "At night you will know that it is the Lord..." (above, v. 6), they did not listen to them or cease their murmurings; but now, as a result of seeing the cloud, they paid heed to their words, and then Moses said to them [echoing God's statement in v. 12, below], "Thus says the Lord: 'I have heard the murmurings.... At night you will eat meat....'" Even though it is nowhere mentioned in the Torah that Moses [actually] said this to them, the fact that God told him [in v. 12] to "speak to them, saying..." indicates without a doubt that he did say this to them.

## Beshallaḥ

**16:10. And as soon as Aaron had spoken to all the assembly of the children of Israel, they—having turned to the desert—saw the majesty of the Lord, which appeared in the cloud.**

**16:11. And the Lord spoke to Moses, saying:**

**16:12. "I have heard the murmurings of the children of Israel. Speak to them, saying, 'At night you will eat meat, and in the morning you will have your fill of bread; and you will know that I, the Lord, am your God.'"**

*that I, the Lord, am your God* — i.e., "that I watch over you."

**16:13. Now at night the quails arose [came in flight], and they covered the camp; and in the morning there was the expanse of dew around the camp.**

*the quails (ha-selav) arose.* Selav is the Arabic name for the bird called *coturnix* in Latin and *quaglia* in Italian. These birds fly from land to land and are found in numberless quantities in Arabia, arriving there from the Red Sea. They fly close to the ground and can be caught by hand. [The miracle consisted in the fact that] God caused them to appear on the very day that the people complained of hunger. Abravanel was likely correct in saying that the quails came to them on that day only, not every day like the manna (as per Nachmanides and some of the Sages; see *Arakhin* 15b), until they returned in Kibroth-hattaavah (Num. 11:31).

*the expanse of (shikhvat,* lit., "layer of") *dew.* The dew lay spread over the ground.

**16:14. Then, the expanse of dew having risen [evaporated], there was seen on the face of the desert something minute, in the form of grains, minute (that is) like the frost on the earth.**

*the expanse of the dew having risen.* When the dew rose into the air, that is, when the sun shone and the dew evaporated into the air as usual, then there appeared the manna that was underneath it (Rashi and Clericus). It seems to me that the [untranslated] word *ve-hinneh* (lit., "and behold") [preceding "on the face of the desert"] confirms this interpretation, for *ve-hinneh* in all instances means only "then he saw," "then they saw," "then the thing was revealed."

***something minute*** *(dak*, with the word "something" supplied in translation). On the face of the desert they saw something minute, made in the form of small grains.

***in the form of grains*** *(meḥuspas)*. The Hebrew appears nowhere else and has no cognate in other languages, and thus we do not know its meaning. In *Yoma* 75b, the Rabbis interpreted it as something that is "softened in the palm of the hand," (*namo'aḥ al pisat ha-yad*) [from which phrase the word *meḥuspas* is supposedly abbreviated], or "absorbed by the 248 parts of the body" (after the numerical value of the letters of *meḥuspas*). Rashi's comment on this verse, "Some say that *meḥuspas* has the same meaning as *ḥafisa* ("valise" [in the language of the Mishnah])," is not from the Talmud [in *Yoma*], for the statement there that there was "dew above and dew below, as if [the manna] were placed in a box," is not an interpretation of *meḥuspas*, but is merely a homiletical statement based on the phrase [in this v.] "the expanse of dew having risen," taken together with Num. 11:9, "And when the dew, during the night, descended upon the camp, the manna descended upon it," from which they deduced that there was a layer of dew above and a layer below.

Onkelos, according to the standard version appearing in most books, translated *meḥuspas* as *mekallaf* ("peeled"), similar to his translation of *maḥsof ha-lavan*, "exposing the white" (Gen. 30:37). However, given that we find in the Targum to this verse the word *ke-gir* ("like plaster"), which does not correspond to any word in the Hebrew text (as Rashi noted), and given that we find that the reading of this word in Nachmanides and in ancient versions (see *Ohev Ger*) is *degir*, meaning "piled in heaps," I suspect that *degir* is the translation of *meḥuspas*, and that the intended version was as follows: "On the face of the desert was something minute, *degir*, minute like the frost of the earth." The word *mekallaf* is thus an interpolation added by later copyists who did not understand the word *degir* and thought that no translation had been supplied for *meḥuspas*, so they translated it as if it were derived from *maḥsof*, which is translated in the Targum to Gen. 30:37 as *killuf*. From this they made the form *mekallaf*, which does not fit here at all.

Gesenius interpreted *meḥuspas* as "peeled off, skinned (*decorticatum*), that is, like scales," but I do not understand how *decorticatum* can mean "like scales." Ibn Ezra and Kimḥi interpreted *meḥuspas* as "round" (in his short commentary, Ibn Ezra presented this as an alternative view), while Rashi interpreted it as "uncovered," perhaps deriving it from the root *ḥasaf* ("to bare"), even though he said that the word has no other like it, that is, in its four-letter form [as if derived from a four-letter root *ḥaspas*] and spelled with a *samekh* and not a *sin*.

## Beshallaḥ

Gussetius gave the meaning as "hard as clay," *ḥaspa* being the Aramaic word for "earthenware." J.D. Michaelis (followed by Rosenmueller) derived it from the Arabic, meaning "like snow." The Jerusalem Targum translates it as *mesargal*; *sirgul* means "marking lines." Perhaps this translator was of the opinion that the manna was spotted and speckled with many colors.

According to the context, the best opinion seems to be the alternative view cited by Ibn Ezra—not that *meḥuspas* means "round" (*agul*), for if so, why would the text not have said *agul*?—but because *meḥuspas* may describe something composed of small, round granules. Because *meḥuspas* was a strange word, the Torah amplified it with the phrase *dak ke-kefor*, "minute like the frost" (A.H. Mainster).

**like the frost.** Dew that freezes in the cold, composed of many granules. The "manna" known to medicine [as a laxative] is a type of resin that exudes from certain trees at given times; in the Sinai desert much of it is found exuding from tamarisk trees in the month of Sivan. Some of the greatest and most respected ancient scholars (such as Avicenna) believed that this manna fell from the air onto the trees. The type of manna found in Persia, called in their language *terenjabin*, is white as snow and resembles coriander seeds [see v. 31 below]; it too is found only in certain months of the year and on tree branches.

In the account of the travels (*Sibbuv*) of R. Petahiah [of Regensburg], regarding the mountains of Ararat, it is written:

> The mountains are full of thorns and other herbs; when the dew falls upon them, manna falls upon them, but when the sun shines warm it melts. They therefore carry off the manna together with the thorns and herbs, which they are obliged to cut off, since they are very hard. It is white like snow. The herbs and nettles are very bitter. However, when boiled together with the manna they become sweeter than honey and every other sweet stuff. Were it boiled without the nettles the limbs of the partaker thereof would become disjointed for excessive sweetness. They look like small grains. They gave him [Petahiah] a few to taste; they melted in his mouth; they were sweet, penetrating into all his limbs, so that he could not bear the sweetness.[34]

Now despite all the efforts of the researchers and nonbelievers to reconcile the matter of the manna with nature, they are still constrained to admit that

---

34. Tranlation by Abraham Benisch (1856), p. 49.

the "manna" known to us is not a nutritious food, and this consideration is aside from the other miraculous aspects of the manna, which did not fall on the Sabbath, fell in double amounts on Friday, and bred worms on all days except the Sabbath. See Ibn Ezra [on v. 13 above] and Abravanel.[35]

**16:15. The children of Israel, having seen this, said to one another, *"Man hu?"* [what is it?], for they did not know what it was. And Moses said to them, "It is the bread that the Lord gives you to feed upon.**

***Man hu*** — i.e., *mah hu* ("what is it?"). The word *man* (מָן), with a *kamats*, means "what" in Syriac, while מַן, with a *patah*, means "who"; see *Ohev Ger* p. 112.[36]

**16:16. "This is what the Lord has commanded. Gather of it each one according to his own consumption; take of it an omer per head, according to the number of your people, each one for as many as he has in his tent."**

***each one according to his own consumption.*** According to what was needed for the members of his household, according to their number.

**16:17. The children of Israel did so, and they gathered of it some more and some less.**

***The children of Israel did so,*** *etc.* If they obeyed Moses, they did not gather either too much or too little [only to find the next day that everyone miraculously possessed their correct amount] (as Rashi and others maintained), but rather [they each gathered their correct amount] according to measure, one omer per head; why should we take what was commanded and turn it into a miracle? The correct explanation is that of Ibn Ezra, that they gathered of it some more and some less, each according to the number

---

35. Ibn Ezra's comment criticizes Hiwi al-Balkhi, the ninth-century anti-Bible polemicist, for maintaining that the biblical manna was the Persian *terenjabin*. Ibn Ezra's ten arguments include those of Luzzatto. Abravanel's comment on v. 14 adopts and supplements Ibn Ezra's arguments and adds two of his own: if the manna was merely a natural substance, the well known "medical" manna, then (1) why would the Israelites have been commanded to preserve a sample of manna for posterity (below, v. 33), and (2) why would Moses have described the manna as something "unknown to you and to your fathers" (Deut. 8:3)?

36. There (p. 115 in the Krakow edition), s.v. *man*, Shadal notes the difference between מַן and מָן, and he attributes to Ludovico de Dieu the interpretation of *man hu* as *mah hu* ("what is it?").

of persons in his tent. However, Ibn Ezra says that the phrase "they measured with the omer" (next. v.) means that each one found the amount that he had estimated; apparently, it was his view that they did not gather according to measure but by estimation, and afterwards they measured and found that they had gathered exactly one omer per head; this was Gersonides' opinion. But this, too, is an unnecessary miracle.

In my opinion, they [simply] obeyed Moses and gathered a measured amount of one omer per head. The phrase "and they gathered of it some more and some less" (*ha-marbeh ve-ha-mam'it*) means that one would gather much and another little, according to the number of persons in his tent, e.g., ten omarim or five omarim according to his head count. Afterwards it specifies that "they measured with the omer," i.e., that they had gathered according to measure and not by estimation, and "one who took much did not take more and one who took little did not take less," that is, one who gathered ten omarim did not exceed his quota and gather more than an omer per head, while one who gathered five omarim did not fall short of his quota and gather less than an omer per head. Rather, "each one gathered according to his own consumption," one omer per head.

**16:18. They measured, that is, with the omer: one who took much did not take more (than one measure per head), and one who took little did not take less (than one measure per head); each one gathered according to his own consumption.**
**16:19. And Moses said to them, "No one must leave over of it until the morning."**
**16:20. Some did not obey Moses, and they left over of it until the morning; but it produced worms and stank. Moses became angry with them.**

**but it produced** (*va-yarum*). The Hebrew is related to *rimmah ve-tole'a* ("worms and maggots," Isa. 14:11; Job 21:26) and thus it is vocalized with a *kibbuts* (וַיָּרֻם) to distinguish it from [another verb whose root is likewise *ramam* but indicates] "exaltation" (*romemut*). However, even though it is derived from the root *ramam*, its proper form would have been *va-yarom*, on the model of *va-yasov* [from the root *suvuv*].

**Moses became angry with them.** For they did not trust in God, as if they would have nothing to eat the next day; therefore the manna produced worms, so that they would have to rely on a miracle [i.e., the next day's manna]. It was not [otherwise] in the nature of manna to produce worms, just as it did not produce worms on the Sabbath.

**16:21. They gathered it from morning to morning, each one according to his own consumption. As soon as the sun became hot [that is, made itself felt], it [the manna] melted.**

*As soon as the sun became hot (ve-ḥam ha-shemesh).* Not when the sun rose, but when it grew hot—that is, as its heat grew strong over the land—the manna would gradually melt.

Rashi's citation from *Sanhedrin* 67[b] comes to explain the meaning of the word *pashar* ("melted") which appears in the Targum [as a translation of *ve-namas* in this verse].[37] In manuscript, the word *ve-namas* does not follow the word *mafshir* [in Rashi's comment], but comes after the phrase *shivḥan shel Yisrael* [as it does in standard printed versions], as follows: "*ve-names*, translated in the Targum as *pashar* [as in *posherim*, 'tepid water']," etc. It seems to me, however, that they [i.e., the uses of the word *pashar* in the sense of 'melting' and 'tepid'] refer to two distinct things, and thus the author of the *Arukh* [R. Nathan of Rome] made them into two separate entries."[38]

**16:22. Now on the sixth day they gathered double bread, two omer for each one; and all the princes of the community went and told (this) to Moses.**

*they gathered double bread.* Ibn Ezra fittingly observed that the verse says "they gathered" rather than "they found," which indicates that they gathered the double bread intentionally, which in turn indicates that Moses had told them to do so in accordance with what God had said to him (v. 3), except that he had not specifically mentioned to them the matter of the Sabbath.[39] Thus it was that the princes came and told Moses that the people had done his bidding, and they asked him what they should do with it [the extra manna], since Moses had previously told them, "No one must leave over of it until the morning" (above, v. 19). This was Abravanel's view as well.

---

37. In the *Sanhedrin* passage cited by Rashi, the term *pashar* is actually used in a transferred sense to denote the "vanishing" of a magical creature when a spell was broken.
38. In the *Arukh*, a talmudic lexicon, the first entry for *pashar* cites passages referring to tepid water, while the second cites the *Sanhedrin* passage as well as the Targum to the present verse.
39. *Contra* Rashi, who maintained that it was only after the people brought the sixth day's manna into their tents and measured it that they discovered that they had gathered a double amount, and that Moses had never yet told them that they should do this.

## Beshallaḥ

**16:23. And he said to them, "It is just what the Lord has predicted [that on the sixth day it would descend in a double amount]. Day of rest, holy Sabbath, in honor of the Lord, it is tomorrow. That which you wish to bake, bake; and that which you wish to boil, boil; and all the remainder you shall hold in reserve until the morning."**

*That which you wish to bake, bake.* Given that he did not say, "That which you wish to bake tomorrow, bake today," it seems (as per Ibn Ezra) that this does not mean, "That which you intended to bake tomorrow, bake today," but rather this is what he told them: "Bake and boil of this manna as much as you need for today's eating, and all the remainder you shall hold in reserve until tomorrow, and tomorrow I will tell you what you should do."

It would have been possible to say that just as the people had done work (*melakhah*) on several Sabbaths before the descent of the manna, so they did work on that first Sabbath, except that they did not gather manna because it did not fall. The statement above, "They will prepare that which they will have brought" (v. 5), might have been understood to refer to all other Sabbaths except for that first one, while the statement below, "The people then rested on the seventh day" (v. 30), might have been understood to refer to the other Sabbaths, or to the act of going out to gather manna, or to any categories of work other than food preparation. However, from Moses' instruction to the people, "Eat of it today" (below, v. 25), not "boil it today" or "bake it today." It seems more likely that on that Sabbath they ate the manna raw, without cooking, for it could also be eaten as it was.

*bake (efu).* The initial *alef* of the Hebrew is vocalized with a *tseireh* instead of a *ḥataf [segol]* [i.e., אֵפוּ instead of the regular form אֱפוּ] in order to lengthen the sound of the *alef*, as occurs in Syriac (see *Ohev Ger*, p. 95, and my *Grammar* §183); cf., וַאֲסֵרֶם [instead of וְאֶסְרֵם] (Zech. 7:14); אֵתָיוּ [instead of אֱתָיוּ, Isa. 21:12].[40]

**16:24. They left it until the morning, as Moses commanded; but it did not stink, nor did it produce worms.**
**16:25. And Moses said, "Eat it today, for today is Sabbath, in honor of the Lord; today you will not find it in the field.**

---

40. In *Ohev Ger*, p. 95 (p. 100 in the Krakow edition), Shadal says that a vowel shift from *ḥataf pataḥ* to *tseireh* (e.g., *amar* to *emar*, *akhal* to *ekhal*) occurs in Syriac with words whose first root letter is *alef*. In the *Grammar (Grammatica della lingua ebraica)* §183, Shadal says that in Hebrew, an initial *alef* sometimes changes a "composite *sheva*" (e.g., a *ḥataf pataḥ* or *ḥataf segol*) into a vowel such as a *tseireh*, and he gives the example אֵפוּ for אֱפוּ.

**16:26. "Six days shall you gather it; the seventh day, however, is Sabbath; on it there will be none."**

***the seventh day, however** (u-va-yom ha-shevi'i)**, is Sabbath.*** "On the seventh day it will be Sabbath for you, and on it there will be no manna" (Rashi). Ibn Ezra said that the word *bo* ("on it") is an extra clarification [duplicating the *va-* in *u-va-yom ha-shevi'i*], but this is not so, as Mendelssohn has pointed out.[41] However, it is true that the *bet* in *u-va-yom* (וביום) is not needed, for it would have been sufficient to have said *ve-yom* (ויום) *ha-shevi'i* ("but the seventh day") (as it is written in the Ten Commandments [below, 20:10]). Similar instances occur below:

- "And the seventh day [*u-va-yom ha-shevi'i*] is a day of great rest" (Exod. 31:15);
- "And the seventh day [*u-va-yom ha-shevi'i*] will be holy for you" (Exod. 35:2); and similarly:
- "On the first day [*ba-yom ha-rishon*] there will be a holy convocation, and on the seventh day [*u-va-yom ha-shevi'i*] there will be a holy convocation" (Exod. 12:16).

Even though these *bet* prefixes are not needed, they are not superfluous [i.e., devoid of any meaning], for for the phrase *ba-yom ha-shevi'i shabbat* means [not merely "the seventh day is Sabbath," but] "*on* the seventh day you shall rest," and the phrase *ba-yom ha-shevi'i yihyeh lakhem kodesh shabbat shabbaton* means [not merely "the seventh day will be holy to you, a great rest," but] "*on* the seventh day you shall call a holy convocation and you shall rest."

**16:27. Now on the seventh day some of the people went out to gather, but they did not find.**
**16:28. And the Lord said to Moses, "Until when will you refuse to observe My commandments and My laws?**

***And the Lord said to Moses.*** He told him to say to the people, "Until when will you refuse [*me'antem*, in the plural]" (Ibn Ezra).

---

41. Mendelssohn's *Biur* explains that the part of this verse starting with *u-va-yom* consists of two separate clauses, with "Sabbath" as the predicate of the first clause, and that the second clause would have made no sense without the word *bo* to refer back to "Sabbath."

## Beshallah

**16:29. "Mind you that the Lord has imposed the Sabbath upon you: therefore He gives you, on the sixth day, bread for two days. Remain where you are; let no one go forth from his place on the seventh day."**

*Mind you (re'u,* lit., "see"). Understand that God has given you the Sabbath, that it is God Who commanded you concerning the Sabbath.

*Remain where you are (shevu ish takhtav).* Each in his tent (Ibn Ezra); cf., "And they did not move from where they were [*ve-lo kamu ish mi-tahtav*]" (Exod. 10:23).

*let no one go forth from his place on the seventh day* — to gather the manna. The main point of this verse concerns the gathering of manna, while the prohibition of the Sabbath limits [not to go 2000 cubits beyond the last house of a city] is a rabbinic enactment (Rashi).[42] Just as future generations were to cease from going out to the fields to work the land or tend the herds, so they [the Israelites in the desert], who had no other kind of work for finding their sustenance but to go out and gather the manna, were forbidden to go forth from their places to gather it, since this was their main occupation.

**16:30. The people then rested on the seventh day.**

*The people then rested.* On that day, and henceforward on every Sabbath.

**16:31. The Israelites called it manna, and it resembles the coriander seed; it is white, and it has the taste of a cake flavored with honey.**

*and it resembles the coriander seed (ke-zera gad).* In shape, but white in appearance (Rashbam) [who notes that coriander seeds are not white]. The ancients translated *gad* as "coriander," and Dioscorides wrote that the people of Africa (Carthage) called coriander *goid*.

*a cake flavored with honey (ke-tsappihit bi-d'vash)* — dough kneaded with honey. *Tsappihit* is from the root *tsafah*, [the equivalent of] which in Arabic signifies "stretching out," and it denotes dough that is stretched out and thin.

---

42. On the phrase "let no one go forth from his place," the Mekhilta comments, "These are the two thousand cubits," i.e., the Sabbath limit. Rashi cites this comment but adds that the Sabbath limit is not expressly mentioned in this verse because it is merely *mi-divrei Soferim*, i.e., a rabbinic enactment.

Closely related to *tsafah* is *tafah*, from which is derived *tefah* ("span") and *mitpahat* ("sheet"), each denoting something stretched or spread out (Gesenius).

In another place (Num. 11:8) it is written that the taste of the manna was like "soft oiled dough." Rashbam and Ibn Ezra correctly explained that when it was eaten as it was, raw, it tasted like a cake flavored with honey, but when it was ground up, it tasted like soft oiled dough.

**16:32. And Moses said, "Here is what the Lord has commanded. A full omer of it shall you keep in reserve for the ages to come, so that they may see the bread that I caused you to eat in the desert, when I brought you out of the country of Egypt."**

**16:33. Afterwards [after the erection of the tabernacle], Moses said to Aaron, "Take a receptacle, and place in it a full omer of manna, and deposit it before the Lord, in reserve for the ages to come."**

*a receptacle (tsintsenet).* The Hebrew has no other occurrence in Scripture and not even an equivalent in languages cognate to Hebrew. Gesenius compares it to *tene* ("basket") [which is *tsanna* in Aramaic and in the Talmud, and *zana* in Italian; this in my opinion, is the derivation of the phrase *ve-el metsinnim yikkahehu* (Job 5:5)][43] and he interprets *tsintsenet* as a kind of basket. This is unlikely, however, for the manna was comprised of small granules, and besides, a basket does not last for ages. Onkelos translated *tsintsenet* as *tseluhit* ("flask"), and Rashi interpreted it as an earthen vessel. In the Greek translation attributed to the seventy elders [Septuagint] it is translated as "golden pot."

*and deposit it before the Lord.* This was said by Moses to Aaron after the tabernacle was erected, and these three verses (33-35) were written by Moses in the fortieth year.

**16:34. As the Lord commanded Moses, Aaron deposited it in reserve before (the Ark of) the law.**

*before the law (ha-edut).* Before the ark of the law, which was so called because of the tablets that contained God's commandments and *edot* ("laws," lit., "testimonies").

---

43. This part of the text was bracketed in the original. The word *metsinnim*, understood by Shadal as "baskets," has otherwise been translated as "thorns."

## Beshallah

**16:35. The children of Israel ate the manna for forty years, until they arrived in inhabited land; they ate the manna (that is) until their arrival at the verge of the country of Canaan.**

***The children of Israel ate the manna for forty years,*** *etc.* There is no proof (as some claim) that Moses did not write this verse, for Moses could have written it at the end of his life, especially since he did not write "and the manna ceased," as it is written in Joshua (5:12); rather, he said only that they ate the manna until they arrived at the verge (*ketseh*) of the country of Canaan, where they were at the end of Moses' life.

How pleasant are the words of R. Saadiah Gaon (in the introduction to *Emunot ve-De'ot*): the manna was more wonderful than the other miracles, for a continual phenomenon is more wonderful than one that does not endure; one cannot imagine a trick that would sustain a nation numbering close to a million people for forty years, where such sustenance stemmed not from a [natural] substance, but from a new type of food that the Creator innovated for them out of the air. If there were any basis for a trick that would supply even a part of such sustenance, the ancient philosophers would have been the first to sustain their disciples with it. Neither can it be imagined that the Israelite masses would have agreed to fabricate this account and pass it on to their children if it were not truly so, or that their children would have accepted this account from them if in fact they had been sustained through a natural process.

To this it should be added that the Israelites would have been able to examine the matter of the manna every day in order to discern whether Moses was resorting to any trickery, for there was no thunder or lightning that would have prevented them from closely inspecting how the thing came to be. Thus it is unimaginable that any suspicion of fraud could be associated with this miracle, and therefore, in my opinion, it is a foundation for our belief in the Divine origin of the Torah *(Torah min ha-shamayim)*.

**16:36. Now the omer is a tenth of the efah.**

***a tenth of the efah.*** See Rashi [who elaborates on various ancient measurements]. The quantities of such measurements are known to us by tradition only. It seems that the *efah* was better known to them (Abravanel), while the term *omer* was not as commonly used; thus it is that in several places in the Torah itself, it is written "a tenth of an efah"—and the [use of the synonymous] term *issaron* ("one tenth") supports this theory—even though the measure's proper name was *omer*. Perhaps this was the amount of grain that was produced from one sheaf (*omer*) of ears. Similarly, the *ḥomer* (which was ten *efot*) was perhaps the amount of grain that was produced from a heap (*keri* or *ḥomer*, as in the expression *ḥomarim ḥomarim*, "heaps and heaps" [Exod. 8:10]) of one hundred *omarim*, and from the term *keri* came the synonymous term [for *ḥomer*,] *kor*.

**17:1. All the community of the children of Israel departed from the desert of Sin, in various movements [that is, stopping in various places], following the command of the Lord; then they encamped in Rephidim, and there was no water for the people to drink.**

*in various movements (le-mas'eihem*, lit., "according to their journeys"). In various stages, for they did not travel from the desert of Sin to Rephidim in one movement, but from Sin to Dophkah, then to Alush, and from Alush to Rephidim [see Num. 33:12-14] (Ibn Ezra and Mendelssohn); the rest of their travels were similar. The use of the word *le-mas'eihem* is analogous to *le-mino* and *le-minehu* ("of various species," lit., "according to its species") (Gen. 1:11).

*for the people to drink (lishtot ha-am*, lit. "to drink, the people") — so that the people should drink. Cf., "all of them wait for You, that You may give them their food [*latet okhlam*, lit., 'to give their food']" (Ps. 104:27); there are many such examples.

**17:2. The people contended with Moses, saying, "Give us water so that we may drink." And Moses said to them, "Why do you contend with me? Why put the Lord to the test?"**

*Why do you contend with me?* For I am only God's messenger.

*Why put the Lord to the test?* They did not yet need water, for they had water that they had brought with them from Alush, but as soon as they came to Rephidim and found no water [source], they began to contend, for they did not trust in God to watch over them and provide for their needs (Nachmanides and Abravanel). Their demand was by way of a test, to see if He would be able to give them what they asked as soon as it occurred to them.

**17:3. But the people, having become thirsty, murmured against Moses, and said, "Why have you brought as out of Egypt, to cause me, my children, and my cattle to die of thirst?"**

## Beshallaḥ

**17:4. Moses shouted to the Lord, saying, "What am I to do to this people? Yet a little, and they will stone me."**

*Yet a little, and they will stone me.* "In a little while, because of the urgent need that will come upon them, they will stone me" (Abravanel); "If this trouble lasts a little longer, they will stone me" (Wessely, *Ḥokhmat Shelomoh*, p. 50), *contra* Rashi and Mendelssohn [who interpret the phrase as, "If I wait a little longer, they will stone me"].

**17:5. And the Lord said to Moses, "Pass before the people, and take with you some of the elders of Israel; and your staff with which you struck the Nile [7:20], take in your hand, and go.**

*Pass before the people.* And have no fear that they will stone you.

*and take with you some of the elders.* As witnesses, for they will see that it will be through your action that water will come forth from the boulder, and they will not say that springs had been there since ancient times (Rashi).

**17:6. "I am about to go before you there over a boulder, in Horeb, and you will strike that boulder, and water will come forth from it, and the people will drink." Moses did so, in the presence of the elders of Israel.**

*I am about to go before you there.* "There you will see My glory, and in that way you will know which boulder it is that you should strike." Cf. [God's command to Abraham to offer up Isaac] "upon the one of the mountains that I will tell you" (Gen. 22:2) (A. H. Mainster).[44]

**17:7. That place was named Massah and Meribah, because of the contention that the children of Israel made, and their testing of the Lord, saying, "Is there the Lord among us, or is there not?"**
**17:8. Then came Amalek and attacked the Israelites in Rephidim.**

*Then came Amalek.* Son of Eliphaz, son of Esau; his land was in Arabia, between Egypt and Canaan.

---

44. In his comment on Gen. 22:4, Shadal adopts the Rabbis' view that God identified the mountain in question by "a cloud binding the top of the mountain, or some other miraculous sign."

**17:9. And Moses said to Joshua, "Make a selection of men for us, and go forth to battle against Amalek. Tomorrow I will place myself on the top of the hill, with the staff of God in my hand."**

***Joshua.*** The grandson of Elishama son of Ammihud, the prince of the tribe of Ephraim (1 Chron. 7:27) (Ibn Ezra). It seems that God wanted Israel to see that it was not by sword or spear that God would save them, and if Moses and Aaron [themselves] had gone into battle, it could have been claimed that they fought and won by means of trickery.

***Tomorrow.*** At the time of battle I will place myself (Rashi).

***I will place myself on the top of the hill,*** *etc.* "To bring upon you God's salvation by way of a miracle," for it was by taking hold of his staff that Moses would perform signs and wonders. Since this was their first war, and Israel was not yet trained for battle, it was necessary to strengthen their hearts to trust in God, and therefore it was necessary that they be saved by way of a miracle (my student, R. Moses Ehrenreich). Moses went up to the top of the hill so that he could see the battle, for whenever he raised his hand with his staff, he would face toward the thing that was the occasion of the miracle. Although it might have seemed that his intention was to pray [as Ibn Ezra thought], this was not so, for the spreading forth of hands [in prayer] is to be distinguished from the raising of the hand with the staff.

If Rashbam were correct in comparing Moses' action to the raising of a battle standard, then they ought to have placed Moses' staff on a tall pole and led it before the people. It seems to me that the reason that Moses did not go forth to lead the people was so that there should be no room for them to ascribe their salvation to a natural occurrence, on the order of Rashbam's explanation. Rather, it was to be deemed entirely miraculous, like the rest of the wonders that Moses performed.

**17:10. Joshua did as Moses told him, with respect to battling against Amalek; and Moses, Aaron, and Hur went up upon the top of the hill.**

***Joshua did.*** He made a selection of men.

***and Hur.*** The Rabbis identified him as Miriam's son; Josephus Flavius [*Antiquities* 3:2] said that he was her husband.

# Beshallaḥ

**17:11. Now when Moses held his hand high, the Israelites won; and when he laid his hand down, Amalek won.**

*Now when Moses held his hand high, etc.* It was as if everything depended on the raising of his hand with the staff, that is, that their salvation was from God and by way of a miracle, like the other signs and wonders that Moses performed. When they saw that victory in battle depended on Moses raising his hand, they supported his hands on either side. This was analogous to the offering of sacrifices and the performance of services in order to appease God and draw His Providence toward us. If God had nevertheless not wished to save Israel, it would not have been beyond His power to cause even Aaron and Hur to lose the strength to support his hands.

**17:12. Moses' arms were heavy (for him), and they took a stone, put it under him, and sat him upon it, and Aaron and Hur supported his hands, one on each side, and (so) his hands remained steady until the setting of the sun.**

*heavy (kevedim).* The Hebrew is masculine and thus irregular, as it refers to *yadayim,* "hands" (feminine); cf. Ezek. 2:9 [where the masculine *bo* ("in it") refers back to *yad* ("hand")].

*and they took a stone... and sat him upon it.* My student R. Joseph Shabbetai Basevi says that this was not because Moses' legs were tired from standing, but rather it was in order to support his hands well and without exertion, for if Moses had not been sitting, Aaron's and Hur's hands would have become heavy as well, while as long as Moses was sitting and they were standing, it would be easy for them to support his hands, and this was something that experience would have shown him. However, [my students] Foà, Cohen, and Hazak[45] object and say that if Moses was sitting and they were standing, it would be all the more difficult for them to support his hands. The correct explanation is, just as his hands were heavy, so was it hard for him to stand, and therefore they sat him down and also supported his hands.

*supported his hands, one on each side.* At first he was holding his staff in one hand, and after that hand grew tired, he held it in both hands. According to my

---

45. "Foà" is probably Hezekiah (Cesare), "Cohen" is probably Moses Cohen Porto, and "Hazak" is probably David Forti, all of whom were students of Shadal in the 1850's; see Sources.

student R. Isaac Pardo, the staff was always in one of his hands, but he would transfer it from the right to the left, and when it was in his right hand, Aaron would support it, and when in his left hand, Hur would support it.

*steady (emunah*, lit., "steadiness"). Ibn Ezra wrote that the Hebrew was a noun signifying a thing that was standing and permanent. Mendelssohn quoted this comment and added that the word *emunah* was the equivalent of *be-emunah* ("in steadiness"). However, these two interpretations contradict each other, for if *emunah* means a standing and permanent thing, there is no need to add the *bet* prefix of *be-emunah*.

The correct explanation is that *emunah* is an adverb and is [in fact] the equivalent of *be-emunah*. Cf., "I know, O Lord, that Your judgments are righteous, and that in faithfulness [*ve-emunah*, lit., 'and faithfulness'] You have afflicted me" (Ps. 119:75), meaning, "faithfully and justly have You afflicted me and chastised me." According to Ibn Ezra's approach, the meaning [here] would have been that Moses' hands turned into something standing and permanent, but this was not so; rather, as long as his hands were supported, they remained steady. After some time I found a similar explanation in the *Me'ammer*, in the name of R.Y. Wisse.

**17:13. Joshua put Amalek and his people to rout at the edge of the sword. 17:14. The Lord said to Moses, "Write this for a record in a book, and put it in the ears of Joshua [call it in particular to his attention]; for (that is) I will erase the memory of Amalek from beneath the heaven."**

***Write this for a record in a book*** *(ba-sefer*, lit., "in the book"). This does not mean, "the well known book" [i.e., the Torah or the *Book of the Wars of the Lord*, as per Ibn Ezra]; rather, [this is an expression] equivalent to "write this down on paper." Cf., "Oh, that they were inscribed in a book [*ba-sefer*]" (Job 19:23)

***and put it in the ears of Joshua.*** We find nowhere else [in Scripture] the expression "put in the ears of so-and-so." Rashi's comment—"For he [Joshua] would lead the Israelites into the land, so that he would command Israel to pay back [Amalek] what they deserved"—is quite far-fetched, for even though this matter [i.e., Moses' death and succession by Joshua before the entrance into the land of Israel] was foreknown to God, He would not likely have hinted of this to Moses immediately after the exodus from Egypt, as this would have disheartened him.

Rashbam and Ibn Ezra modified [Rashi's approach] somewhat and said that Joshua was destined to rule over Israel and make war against the people of Canaan, but this explanation is still unlikely, for Joshua did not fight Amalek [in the land of Israel], so what was the need to tell him about this in particular? Was it not foreknown to God that there would be no war against Amalek until several generations after Joshua? What use, then, would there have been to alert Joshua to forewarn the Israelites about this?

Nachmanides commented, "He said, 'Put it in the ears of Joshua,' to command him to remind Israel about all the travails that came upon them through him [Amalek], for he [Joshua] was the one who knew and witnessed." But what need was there for Joshua's testimony? All the Israelites were equally witnesses to what he would have told them.

It seems to me that the meaning is, "Speak in his ears and he will write it," for just as in the case of the war against Amalek, where Moses commanded and Joshua did the fighting, so in the case of recording the event, Moses was to tell Joshua to do the writing. This would have brought satisfaction, honor, and prestige to Joshua as recompense for his activity in the war.

***for I will erase***, *etc.* Because the war had weakened Amalek but had not destroyed it, God told Moses to record that event for eternal remembrance. Israel was to remember what Amalek had done to them, for it was indeed God's will to erase the memory of Amalek from beneath the heaven.

**17:15. Moses built an altar, and he named it "The Lord is my banner."**

**The Lord is my banner** *(YHVH nissi).* "That for which a banner serves for other nations—in that whenever the warriors see it, they prevail, but whenever it is brought down or falls into the enemy's hands, they flee or are beaten—all of this God was for me, for when my hand and the staff were held high, Israel prevailed, but when my hand was low, Amalek prevailed." In other words, "from God comes salvation" (A.H. Mainster). Many names [in Scripture] are an entire phrase; for example:

- Immanuel, "God is with us" (Isa. 7:14);
- *YHVH tsidkenu*, "The Lord is our Righteous One" (Jer. 23:6);
- Hephzibah, "My delight is in her [*heftsi vah*]" (2 Kings 21:1, Isa. 62:4);
- *YHVH shammah* "The Lord is there" (at the end of Ezekiel [48:35]).

See also Gen. 33:20 [*El Elohei Yisrael*, "Mighty is the God of Israel"] and Isa. 9:5 [*Pele yo'ets El gibbor avi ad sar shalom*, "God the mighty, the everlasting Father, the Lord of peace, decrees wonders"].[46]

**17:16. And he added, "Yes, Yah has His hand upon His throne [that is, He swears]. The Lord will be at war with Amalek, from generation to generation [perpetually, until the extinction of that people]."**

***Yes, Yah has His hand,*** *etc.* God swears by His throne that He will be at war with Amalek from generation to generation, forever.

***Yes, Yah has His hand upon His throne*** *(ki yad al kes Yah).* Similar to the expression, "Yes, I raise My hand toward the heaven" (Deut. 32:40) (Rashbam, Ibn Ezra). Clericus interpreted this phrase to mean that Amalek was putting forth his hand on God's throne, i.e., on Israel, in whose midst God dwells, and therefore the Lord will be at war with Amalek forever. Besides this interpretation, another one occurred to Clericus on the basis of an emendation of the word *kes* ("throne") to *nes* ("banner"): Moses named the altar "The Lord is my banner [*nissi*]" because Amalek had put forth his hand against God's banner, and therefore the Lord would be at war with Amalek. In his view, "God's banner" was the hosts of Israel, who were God's hosts, or else it was Moses' staff, which was known as God's staff. All of this, however, is most unlikely; besides, the reading of *kes*, with the letter *kaf*, is extremely ancient, for the Samaritans emended it [not to *nes* but] to *kissei* [the more regular form of the word for "throne"].

***from generation to generation*** *(mi-dor dor).* Cf., "None shall pass through it forever and ever [*mi-dor la-dor*]" (Isa. 34:10).

---

46. Such are the meanings of these names according to Shadal's translations and comments on the respective verses.

# *Yitro*

*"Select persons of merit"* • *A realm of priests and a holy nation* • *"Then God uttered all these words"* • *Idol worship and social evil* • *Demanding account of the sins of the fathers* • *Sabbath and social benefit* • *"In order to test you has God come"*

**18:1. Jethro, priest of Midian, father-in-law of Moses, heard all that God had done to Moses, and to Israel his people, (that is) that the Lord had brought Israel out of Egypt.**

***Jethro... father-in-law of (ḥoten) Moses, heard.*** Below, it is written, "Then Moses let his father-in-law depart, and he went away to his country" (v. 27), while in Num. 10:24, it is written that in the second year [in the desert], "Moses said to Hobab son of Reuel the Midianite, father-in-law of Moses, ['Come with us']," which would indicate that he was still in the Israelite camp. If someone were to say that Reuel and not Hobab was Moses' father-in-law, we find in Judg. 4:11, "From the children of Hobab the father-in-law of Moses."

[In the Talmud] there was a dispute between the sons of R. Hiyya and R. Joshua ben Levi, the former maintaining that [the episode of] Jethro occurred before the giving of the Torah, and the latter maintaining that it occurred after the giving of the Torah. They were preceded by the Sages of the Mishnah, who asked, "What report did Jethro hear?" R. Joshua said that he heard about the war with Amalek (and not the giving of the Torah, for he arrived before then), while R. Elazar ha-Moda'i said that he heard about the giving of the Torah (*Zevaḥim* 116a).

Some scholars chose to cut this knot that was difficult for them to untie, and they said that Hobab was not Jethro. The first to follow this path was the revered grammarian, R. Jonah ibn Janah, who said that Hobab was Jethro's son and Zipporah's brother; he maintained that a wife's brother [and not only her father] was called her husband's *ḥoten* (this opinion was cited by Kimhi [in his *Shorashim*] under the root *ḥatan*, but he rejected it). Later, Mendelssohn strongly endorsed this interpretation of *ḥoten*, although he said (in the *parashah* of *Beha'alotekha*) that Jethro and Hobab were both brothers of Zipporah, and that the three of them were the children of Reuel. Ibn Ezra, too, though conceding that Hobab was Jethro, said that he was Zipporah's brother, not her father.

This opinion with regard to the word *ḥoten* is most unlikely, for we never find anywhere [else] the word *ḥoten* or [its feminine counterpart] *ḥotenet* used in this sense. To the contrary, we find, "Cursed be he who lies with his mother-in-law [*ḥotanto*]" (Deut. 27:23). The wife's sister is permitted to the husband after the wife's death,[1] so how could there be a curse with two meanings expressing two different laws, the one [referring to an act that is] prohibited at some times but permitted at other times?

Most scholars indeed, modern and ancient, Jew and Gentile, have distanced themselves from the approach of R. Jonah and agreed with the Sages that Hobab was Jethro, and that Reuel was Jethro's father and Zipporah's grandfather.[2] Nachmanides said that Hobab was a new name that was given to Jethro when he adopted the religion of Israel, for this is customary with respect to anyone who converts, as "He calls His servants by another name" (Isa. 65:15). It is not unlikely that Hobab was a new name that the Israelites called Jethro, whether derived from *ḥavivut* ("affection") or from some other derivation unknown to us today. But as for the statement of Nachmanides and others that Jethro became a proselyte, this seems unlikely to me.

If Jethro converted, how could he have replied to Moses, "I do not want to come, but I want to go to my country and to my kin" (Num. 10:30)? There

---

1. Luzzatto himself married his deceased first wife's sister, Leah Segre.
2. A plausible alternative has also been suggested: "Re'uel is a leadership name, similar to Avimelech or Pharaoh, that was used by the Kohein Midian, whoever he was at the time. Moshe's father-in-law Re'uel (also known as Yisro, Chovav, etc.) bore this name because he held this position. So did his father before him, also known as Re'uel" (Yacov Balsam, "Who Was Re'uel? Finding a New Solution to an Age-Old Puzzle," *Ḥakirah*, vol. 8, pp. 157-179 [2009]).

is no doubt that these words denote a complete departure, not going for the purpose of converting his household and returning. Furthermore, after that generation we find that Heber the Kenite [a descendant of Hobab; see Judg. 4:11], although residing in the land of Israel, was at peace with Jabin, the enemy of Israel. I do not say that the house of Heber the Kenite favored Jabin, for the incident of [Heber's wife] Yael proves the opposite [see Judg. 4:17-22], but Jabin was at peace with the house of Heber, and [Jabin's captain] Sisera trusted Yael; this would have been illogical if the Kenites had been full proselytes and had mixed with the Israelites for some time beforehand.

Moreover, in the time of Saul the Kenites lived among Amalek; is it possible that full proselytes would have established their dwelling place among the abominated people whose memory God had commanded to be wiped out? Besides, Saul said to the Kenites, "You showed kindness to all the children of Israel, when they came up out of Egypt" (1 Sam. 15:6); he did not say, "You observe God's Torah, and your God is my God."

What led the commentators astray was the matter of the family of the Rekabites, who lived in the midst of the Israelites (Jeremiah 35); in 1 Chron. 2:55 it is written, "These are the Kenites that came of Hammath, the father of the house of Rekab." The Sages, in Sifrei (*Beha'alotekha*), *Sotah* 11a, and *Sanhedrin* 104a, in order to emphasize the exalted quality of proselytes—who must not be disparaged, who are equal to Israel in every respect, and who are worthy even to sit on the Sanhedrin—said that the Kenites referred to in Chronicles are the same as the children of the Kenite, Moses' father-in-law. This, however, is merely by way of a homiletical statement (*derash*) with a Scriptural text used for support (*asmakhta*); happy is the one who pays heed to the good moral lesson that comes from it. However, according to the plain meaning, it seems that the Kenites in Chronicles and the Rekabites in Jeremiah were descended from Judah and had no relation to the children of the Kenite, Moses' father-in-law.

Perhaps the Rekabites were called "Kenites" because they dwelled in tents and wandered from place to place like them [i.e., the real Kenites]. If one likes, it may be said that both groups were called Kenites after Cain (*Kayin*), who was "wandering and restless" throughout the land.

Now there is one verse that appears to support those who say that the children of the Kenite, Moses' father-in-law, became proselytes: the statement in Judges that "the children of the Kenite, Moses' father-in-law, went up out of the city of palm trees [Jericho] with the children of Judah into the wilderness of Judah, which is in the south of Arad; and they went and dwelt with the people" (Judg. 1:16). However, after everything we have seen [cited] above, it makes no sense for us to infer from this verse that they became full proselytes (*gerei tsedek*), rather than *gerim toshavim* [i.e., resident foreigners].

In fact, I very much doubt that this verse is to be understood in accordance with the commentators, that is, that the Kenites dwelled together with the children of Judah, for I have not found a sufficiently exact explanation for the wording of the verse. Perhaps the true meaning is the opposite of what the commentators thought: that the Kenites, who were nomadic tent-dwellers, just then happened to be staying near the city of palm trees, and when they saw that the children of Judah were going out to war against the Canaanites, the peace-loving Kenites (who were called *shalma'ah* in Aramaic) distanced themselves from the battle areas and went up to the wilderness of Judah, to the south of Arad, and went and "dwelt with the people," that is, the Amalekites and Canaanites who inhabited the land. Where it says that they "went up out of the city of [*me-ir*] palm trees with [*et*] the children of Judah," perhaps it should be understood as "*me-et* ['from among'] the children of Judah," with the prefix *mem* in the word *me-ir* carrying with it another prefix *mem*. It is otherwise plausible to interpret the phrase as meaning that they "went up out of the city of palm trees, *where they had been* with the children of Judah" beforehand.

I will now return to the matter at hand: those commentators who concede that Hobab was Jethro are in dispute as to how to resolve the contradiction between the present episode and the one in *Beha'alotekha* (Numbers 10). According to Nachmanides (whose approach was maintained by Rabbenu Bahya and also Rosenmueller), Jethro came to the Israelites twice, the first time before the giving of the Torah—which is the time mentioned here—after which he departed and then returned after the giving of the Torah; this return is not mentioned here, but only later in Numbers (10:29), where Moses says, "We are about to set out… Come with us," and he replies, "I do not want to come, but I want to go to my country" (v. 30). Moses then urges him, "Please do not abandon us" (v. 31), and he (according to Nachmanides) is persuaded and remains with the Israelites. Under this interpretation, the failure to mention Jethro's return [to the Israelites] after the account of his departure to his country (below, v. 27) is a great difficulty.

Rashbam, Ibn Ezra, and Kimhi (at the beginning of the Book of Judges) said that Jethro came only once, after the giving of the Torah, and that the account here is given out of chronological order, for various reasons (see Rashbam at v. 13 below and Ibn Ezra on the present verse),[3] which,

---

3. In these comments, Rashbam says that the account of Jethro's visit is given here, rather than after the episode of Mt. Sinai, so as not to interrupt the accounts

however, are not strong enough to remove from one's mind a great sense of astonishment that this account should appear here. Despite these reasons, other commentators agree that the coming of Jethro occurred before the giving of the Torah, and that his return home did not occur now [i.e., at the end of the episode narrated here], but rather in the year after. The last verse (v. 27, below), which tells of Jethro's return home—or even the three preceding verses, which tell of the appointment of the judges [as Jethro had suggested]—may be out of place; these verses appear here in order to conclude the episode. Here they are stated in general terms, while elsewhere (in *Beha'alotekha* and in Deuteronomy 1) the account is spelled out in detail; this is the opinion of Gersonides, Abravanel, R. Isaac Arama, Sforno, Nicolaus de Lira (here, but not in *Beha'alotekha*), Clericus, and my friend, the scholar Reggio (here, but not in *Beha'alotekha*).

R. Wolf Meir, author of the *Me'ammer*, added support for this interpretation and said, "We know that this is the way of the Torah, to conclude episodes in a general way in one place, and to relate the end of a matter early on; for example, 'Afterwards Moses said to Aaron, "Take a receptacle [and place in it a full omer of manna... for the ages to come]"' (Exod. 16:33)—this command was given in the second year, after the erection of the Tabernacle, but Scripture recorded it here [in the first account of the manna]. Similarly, 'The children of Israel ate the manna for forty years' (Exod. 16:35) [is a concluding statement recorded long before its actual occurrence]."

In fact, this does not provide a complete proof [for the view of Gersonides et al.], for the command to set aside a receptacle of manna and the statement as to the duration of the manna do not reappear at another place in the Torah, unlike the account of Jethro's return to his country, which is written here (below, v. 27) and again in Numbers (10:24-32); similarly, the account of the appointment of the judges (below, vv. 13-26) is repeated in Deuteronomy (1:9-18). However, this type of repetition is [an example of] the thirteenth of the [32] hermeneutical rules of R. Eliezer ben R. Yose ha-Gelili: when a general statement (*kelal*) is followed by a narrative, the latter is merely a more particular elaboration (*perat*) of the former. Thus, "God created man in His image" (Gen. 1:27) is a *kelal* that is followed by a narrative *perat*: "The Lord God formed man" (Gen. 2:7); "The Lord God caused a slumber to fall upon the man" (Gen. 2:21); "The Lord God constructed from the rib... a woman" (Gen. 2:22). The hearer may think that this is an unrelated narrative, but it is actually an elaboration of the general statement.

---

of the giving of *mitsvot*, while Ibn Ezra says that Jethro's visit is recounted here in order to provide a positive contrast to the preceding episode of the attack by Amalek.

## Shadal on Exodus

This explanation is, in my opinion, the correct way to resolve the inconsistency that [seemingly] exists between this episode and *Beha'alotekha*. Saadiah Gaon, too, said that Jethro came before the giving of the Torah, but we do not know if his opinion was like ours, or if he held that Jethro departed and came back, as per Nachmanides, for we know nothing of the Gaon's words beyond the few of them cited by Ibn Ezra.

Rashi, unwilling to decide a matter that had divided the Sages of the Mishnah and Talmud, said only (at v. 13 below) that even according to one who says that Jethro came before the giving of the Torah, his departure to his country did not occur until the second year.

**18:2. And Jethro, father-in-law of Moses, took Zipporah, Moses' wife, after he had sent her back,**

*after he had sent her back.* See above, 4:23 ff.

**18:3. and her two sons as well, of whom one was named Gershom, for (Moses) said, "I have become a wandering man in a strange land."
18:4. And the other was called Eliezer, for (he said), "The God of my father was my help, and He saved me from Pharaoh's sword."
18:5. Jethro, father-in-law of Moses, with the latter's wife and sons, came toward Moses, in the desert where he was encamped, to the mountain (that is) of God.**

*in the desert (el ha-midbar).* If the word *ha-midbar* were to be accented with a *zakef*, it would properly be with a *pashta-zakef* (אֶל־הַמִּדְבָּר)—and it is so accented in a manuscript *ḥumash* on parchment in my possession—but not with a *zakef gadol* (אֶל־הַמִּדְבָּר).[4] However, there is no doubt that this is only a scribal error, and it seems to me that the word should be accented with a *revia* [אֶל־הַמִּדְבָּר], which is less of a disjunctive than the *tipḥa* under the word *sham* [in the subsequent phrase *asher hu ḥoneh sham*, "where he was encamped"]. [Such an accentuation, rather than the stronger disjunctive *zakef*, would correctly bring out the meaning as] "in the desert where he was encamped, *that is*, to the mountain of God."

So it appears in a manuscript *Tanakh* on parchment, from the year 5249 (1489), that was in Mendelssohn's possession. In the margin it is written רביע כ"ה, i.e., *ken hu* ("so it should be") with a *revia* (see *Tikkun Soferim* by

---

4. Some modern editions, including Koren, have אֶל־הַמִּדְבָּר, while others have אֶל־הַמִּדְבָּר.

# *Yitro*

Dubno). It also appears this way in a magnificent manuscript *Tanakh* in the possession of R. Jacob Saphir in Jerusalem.[5]

*the mountain of God.* See above, 3:1.

**18:6. And he said [caused to be said] to Moses, "I, your father-in-law Jethro, come to you, and your wife as well, as with her your two sons."**

*And he said.* Through a messenger (Rashi).

**18:7. And Moses went out toward his father-in-law, he prostrated himself to him and kissed him, and they asked each other about their wellbeing; then they entered into the tent.**
**18:8. Moses told his father-in-law all that the Lord had done to (inflicted upon) Pharaoh and to the Egyptians for the sake of Israel, all the travails that had come upon them on the journey, and from which the Lord had saved them.**
**18:9. Jethro rejoiced at all the good that the Lord had done to Israel, freeing them from the hands of the Egyptians.**
**18:10. And Jethro said, "Blessed be the Lord, Who freed you from the hands of the Egyptians and from the hands of Pharaoh, Who rescued the people from the power of the Egyptians.**

*Who freed you.* Moses and Aaron (Rashbam, Abravanel, Sforno).

**18:11. "Now I know that the Lord is greater than all the gods. Yes, (I recognize it) in the way that they offended against you [and for which they were then punished in such an exemplary manner]."**

*Yes (ki), in the way, etc.* The word *ki* is used as an intensifier.

*in the way that they offended against you.* From the way in which the Egyptians lorded it over the Israelites, oppressing them without fear until they succeeded in embittering their lives with all kinds of torment, casting their sons into the Nile and even withholding the straw that they needed to make bricks, it was obvious that Israel could not have been saved from their hands in a natural manner, but only through God. If the Israelites had not been so extremely weak and degraded, the Egyptians would not have offended

---

5. This reading also appears in the *Keter Crown Bible* (Jerusalem: Chorev, 2006).

against them to the degree that they did, for they would have had to fear that the Israelites would rise up against them. Thus, the God of Israel, Who had the power to save a poor and weak people from the hand of a mighty nation like Egypt, while Egypt's gods did not come to its defense, was greater than all the other gods.

***in the way*** *(va-davar*, lit., "in the matter") — in the manner or measure; cf., "This is the reason [*ha-davar*] why Joshua circumcised them" (Josh. 5:4).

**18:12. Jethro, father-in-law of Moses, offered to God burnt offerings and sacrifices; and Aaron and all the elders of Israel came to eat with Moses' father-in-law before God.**

***and sacrifices*** *(u-z'vaḥim).* Sacrifices of contentment (*shelamim*).[6]

***before God.*** Such terminology is used in connection with the eating of sacrifices (*kodashim*, lit., "holy things").

**18:13. On the next day, Moses sat to judge the people, and all the people stood about Moses from the morning to the evening.**
**18:14. Moses' father-in-law, having seen how he conducted himself with the people, said, "What is this way that you keep with the people? How is it that you sit (to judge) by yourself, and all the people stand about you from the morning to the evening?"**

***How is it that you sit*** — in judgment.

***and all the people****, etc.* And consequently, all the people stand about you from morning till evening (Rashbam).

**18:15. And Moses said to his father-in-law, "Because the people come to me to consult God.**

***to consult God.*** This is a general statement followed by specifics: "When they have any suit…" (next v.), that is, any monetary disputes or other types of litigation, and any matters of public administration. "I must necessarily

---

6. In his comment to Lev. 3:1, Shadal says that the *shelamim* (lit., "peace offerings") were sacrifices of joy that were eaten in communal celebrations; he translates the term as "sacrifice of contentment [of rendering thanks, and payment of a vow]."

judge alone, for they come to me to consult [*li-drosh*, lit., 'to seek'] God, i.e., to hear from me God's response, and there is no one else besides me who can give them such a response."

**18:16. "When they have any suit, it is brought to me, and I judge between the one and the other; and I make known the statutes of God and His laws."**

*it is brought to me (ba elai).* [The subject of the verb is] "the suit"; cf., "Neither does the cause of the widow come to them [*yavo aleihem*]" (Isa. 1:23). In other words, "Whenever they have any dispute, that dispute is brought to me" (*contra* Rashi and Mendelssohn).[7]

*the statutes of God (ḥukkei Elohim), etc.* That which God told him as a temporary directive for the management of the people; this does not refer to the commandments for posterity, and it is not to be inferred from here that Jethro came after the giving of the Torah. Moses declared the commandments to the entire assembled people, not to each individual, and [for this purpose] he would not have had to sit before them all day. It is true that the word *ḥok* does not refer to the announcement of judgment in a private suit, but rather denotes a general law to last throughout the generations. However, the meaning [here] is that Moses would decide private suits according to the general laws that God made known to him.

**18:17. And Moses' father-in-law said to him, "The way that you have is not good.**
**18:18. "You will grow exhausted, both you and this people that stands about you, for the thing is too heavy for you; you cannot carry it out alone.**

*You will grow exhausted (navol tibbol).* See Rashi [who follows the Targum, "You will grow weary," and interprets the Hebrew to denote "withering," like a leaf that becomes "weary" and falls away].

**18:19. "Now then, listen to me, let me advise you, and may God help you. Stay, for the people, close to God; (that is) you will present the suits to God.**

---

7. Rashi interprets *ba elai* as "[the litigant] comes to me." Mendelssohn reads the phrase as follows: "When they have any suit that is brought to me, then I judge between the one and the other."

*and may God help you (vi-y'hi Elohim immakh,* lit., "and may God be with you"). "May He help you, in His affection for you." This is an expression similar to "may God have mercy on you," and other such phrases.

*for the people (la-am).* For the sake of the people.

*close to God (mul ha-Elohim,* lit., "facing God"). Nearby Him; compare:

- "Coming close to [*ve-karavta mul*] the territory of the Ammonites" (Deut. 2:19);
- "And even the cattle… let them not pasture toward [*mul*] that mountain" (Exod. 34:3);
- "And he turned away from him toward [*mul*] another" (1 Sam. 17:30).

The meaning is, "Reserve for yourself anything that requires a prophecy from God, and give over the rest to others."

**18:20. "You will advise them of the statutes and of the laws, and you will make known to them the way that they must keep, and the actions that they must do.**

*of the statutes and of the laws, etc.* Anything pertaining to the public or private conduct of the people you will tell them by way of a commandment for posterity, before any suit comes before you.

**18:21. "You will then select, among all the people, persons of merit, fearers of God, men of loyalty, despising connivance; and you will place them at their head (in the rank of) chiefs of thousands, chiefs of hundreds, chiefs of fifties, and chiefs of tens.**

*despising connivance (son'ei vatsa).* The root *batsa*, related to the root *baka*, originally denoted splitting something in two, in which sense it was commonly used in Aramaic. This is the origin of the rabbinic expression *betsi'at ha-pat* ("breaking bread"). It was later transferred to refer to two persons splitting between themselves that which they took from someone else dishonestly. It is in this sense that every occurrence of the verb *botse'a* in Scripture is used. Similarly, the noun *betsa* always means the profit that two or more persons split among themselves.

Here, too, *son'ei vatsa* are those who despise to share with a thief, that is, to share with a culpable party in order to declare the guilty innocent and the innocent guilty. Perhaps it was later that the word *betsa* was transferred to denote any kind of profit.

***chiefs of thousands*** *(sarei alafim), etc.* According to the Sages, every ten men in Israel had one chief, every five of those chiefs had a "chief of fifties" over them, and so on. Ibn Ezra expressed astonishment over this, for it this were the case, one eighth of the people would all have had to be "persons of merit, fearers of God, men of loyalty, despising connivance," which is quite unlikely in the way of the world. He himself gave an explanation with language that can be understood in two different ways. Gersonides and Abravanel criticized him,[8] but perhaps his intended meaning was not as they understood it, but rather conformed to one of the interpretations given by Abravanel on this verse: those who were called "chiefs of thousands" were the chiefs to whom the people or a king gave a thousand men to guard him and take orders from him, and the "chiefs of hundreds" and the rest are to be similarly understood.

Abravanel offered an alternate interpretation for this verse: the "chiefs of thousands" were a council and a large court of a thousand men, and so similarly there was a court of a hundred, and so on.[9] Gersonides maintained that the "chiefs of thousands" had many thousands under them, with only one such chief per tribe; the "chiefs of hundreds" had many hundreds under them; and similarly the "chiefs of fifties" and "chiefs of tens" had many fifties and tens under them. To this interpretation my opinion tends; I would add that these titles were indeed first applied to those who had under them ten, fifty, a hundred, or a thousand, as the Sages said. A proof of this is the phrase, "A

---

8. Ibn Ezra expressed the view that the "chiefs of thousands" were those who had under them a thousand men, "his slaves, servants, or hirelings." Abravanel found it improbable that any of the newly freed Israelites would have had such a large personal retinue.

9. Abravanel, who was not only a Jewish scholar but also an international statesman, referred in this comment to the governmental system then in place in his adopted home city of Venice. "Thus Abrabanel [sic] identifies the 'governors of thousands,' mentioned in the Bible, with the Maggior Consiglio, the 'rulers of hundreds' with the Senate, and the 'rulers of tens' with the Council of Ten. In order to draw this analogy, however, this Iberian philosopher was obliged to bend the biblical text, for while in the Mosaic constitution the 'governors of thousands' were at the apex of the pyramid, Abrabanel had to set the 'rulers of tens' at the top so they could be identified with the Council of Ten" (Riccardo Calimani, *The Ghetto of Venice* [trans. Katherine Silberblatt Wolfthal], New York: M. Evans and Company, Inc., 1987, p. 43). This Venetian regime remained in power until Napoleon conquered the city in 1797, three years before the birth of Shadal in nearby Trieste.

captain of fifty [*sar ḥamishim*] with his fifty" (2 Kings 1:9), which is followed by, "Let my life, and the life of these fifty your servants, be precious in your sight" (2 Kings 1:13). However, the title "chief of thousands" was also used for one who had many thousands under him, "chief of hundreds" for one who had under him many hundreds but fewer than a thousand, "chiefs of fifties" for one who had under him more than fifty but fewer than a hundred, and "chiefs of tens" one who had under him more than ten but fewer than fifty.

I disagree with Gersonides, however, in that he said that the chiefs of thousands were only one per tribe. It seems to me that the "chiefs of thousands" are to be distinguished from the princes of the tribes, and that the chiefs of thousands were the leaders of many thousands but not any entire tribe, nor did they lead some thousands from one tribe and some thousands from another tribe. A.H. Mainster adds that these chiefs were apparently not subordinate to one another, for it does not say that the chiefs of tens were to bring difficult matters to a chief of fifty; rather, all of them were to judge cases themselves or else bring them to Moses. It was only according to each one's wisdom and qualities that he was appointed to be over many people or few.

In his short commentary, Ibn Ezra adopted that which he rejected in his long commentary, and he maintained that one eighth of the camp of Israel were wise men.

**18:22. "These will judge the people at any moment, but every great question they will present to you, and they will judge by themselves every small question; thus will they lighten the burden, bearing it together with you.**

***thus will they lighten*** *(ve-hakel)*. "By this means they will alleviate your burden." *Hakel* (lit., "to lighten") is an infinitive, but it takes on the tense and person that are indicated by the preceding verb [*yishpetu*, "they will judge"], for out of a preference for brevity, [Hebrew speakers] would omit that which was already known. Compare:

- "And they proclaimed before him, "Avrekh!"; so that they placed [*ve-naton*, lit., 'and to place'] him at the head" (Gen. 41:43);
- "The kings of Assyria have laid waste all the countries… and have cast [*ve-naton*, lit., 'and to cast'] their gods" (Isa. 37:18-19);
- "And they blew the horns, and broke [*ve-nafots*, lit., "and to break"] the pitchers" (Judg. 7:20);
- "Yea, the hind also calved in the field and forsook [*ve-azov*, lit., 'and to forsake'] it" (Jer. 14:5);

## Yitro

- "I cause your iniquity to pass from you, and I clothe [*ve-halbesh*, lit., 'and to clothe'] you" (Zech. 3:4);
- "When you fasted and mourned [*ve-safod*, lit., 'and to mourn']" (Zech. 7:5);
- "Men shall buy fields for money, and sign [*ve-khatov*, lit., 'and to sign'] the deeds and seal [*ve-ḥatom*, lit., 'and to seal'] them, and call [*ve-ha'ed*, lit., 'and to call'] witnesses" (Jer. 32:44);
- "You shall donate it to the foreigner living in your cities, or you shall sell [*makhor*, lit., 'to sell'] it to some stranger" (Deut. 14:21).

**18:23. "If you do this thing, God will give you His orders, and you will be able to stand [have the strength and the time to carry them out]; and also this whole people will be able to go to the proper place [to the nearest judge] in peace [without having an overcrowding at one single court producing confusion and quarrels]."**

*and you will be able to stand.* To withstand that which God will command you henceforward, for if you [continue to] judge alone, you will not be able to carry out what He commands you, as a result of overburdening.

*will be able to go to the proper place in peace.* They will not all have to come to you; rather, each one will go to the nearest chief, that is, to the closest place. Thus their going to judgment will be in peace and not confusion, for many people will not go to a single chief.

**18:24. Moses gave heed to his father-in-law, and he carried out all that he had said.**

*Moses gave heed, etc.* There is no doubt that if Moses had begun his leadership in a high-handed way, and had not made himself visible to the people and heard their claims both small and large, the hearts of the people would not have inclined toward him, and they would not have accepted his Torah and commandments. Therefore God did not tell him to do this thing [i.e., appoint other judges], but rather let him do it after the people had already tested his heart and his ways, and had grown attached to him.

**18:25. Moses, that is, selected men of merit from among all Israel, and he constituted them as chiefs over the people, chiefs of thousands, chiefs of hundred, chiefs of fifties, and chiefs of tens.**

**18:26. These judged the people at any moment; the difficult questions they brought to Moses, and every small question they judged by themselves.**

***they judged*** *(yishputu)*. The Hebrew is vocalized with a *shuruk* instead of a *sheva* [i.e., *yishputu* instead of the regular form *yishpetu*]; cf., *lo ta'avuri* [instead of *ta'averi*] (Ruth 2:8). According to Ibn Ezra, the *shuruk* replaces a *ḥolam* [i.e., the expected form would have been *yishpotu*], as if the word were at the end of the verse, since it is followed by only one short word (*hem*, "by themselves"); an analogous instance would be *teḥatellu vo* (Job 13:9), where the word is marked with a *tseireh* [rather than a *sheva*] because it appears at the end of the verse [except for the short word *vo*]. However, this explanation will not suffice for the word *ta'avuri*, which is not followed by a short word [and does not appear at the end of a verse]. Moreover, the word *teḥatellu* is marked with a *tseireh* not because it is a "pausal" form, but because the word is derived from a geminate root [*talal*, "to mock"] (as in the expression *hokha ve-itlula*, "derision and jest").

Rashi correctly noted that the verbs *ve-shafetu, yavi'u,* and *yishpetu* in v. 22 are in the future tense proper ("will judge," "will present," "will judge"), and that these forms were used by way of imperative, to indicate what the judges were to do; but that the verbs *ve-shafetu, yevi'un,* and *yishputu* in this verse ("judged," "brought," "judged") indicate [not the future but] that which they were accustomed to do [i.e., the frequentative]. Ibn Ezra, in his rashness, did not understand, and thought that Rashi intended to distinguish [in meaning] between *yishpetu* and *yishputu*; he wrote, "Rabbenu Shelomoh wished to make a distinction between them, but he did not succeed." This, however, is a falsehood without foundation.

**18:27. Then Moses let his father-in-law depart, and he went away to his country.**
**19:1. In the third month after the Israelites' going forth from the land of Egypt, on this day [that is, on the first of the month, on the day of the new moon, for the Hebrew word for "month" properly signifies "renewal"] they arrived at the desert of Sinai.**

***on this day.*** On the day of the [third] new moon, or *rosh ḥodesh*, for this is the principal meaning of the word *ḥodesh* ("month," lit., "renewal") (as per R. Moses ha-Cohen, cited by Ibn Ezra), even though the word was later transferred to denote the entire length of the month, that is, the 29 or 30 days from the renewal of the moon until its subsequent renewal.

**19:2. Having departed, that is, from Rephidim, they arrived at the desert of Sinai, and they encamped in the desert. Israel encamped there, opposite the mountain.**

***Having departed, that is, from Rephidim*** *(va-yise'u me-Refidim*, lit., "and they journeyed from Rephidim"). First there was a general statement that the people arrived on the first of the month at the desert of Sinai; now it is specified how this came to be, in keeping with the narrative style of Scripture (Mendelssohn).

***Israel encamped there, opposite the mountain.*** After the general statement that the people encamped in the desert, it is specified that they encamped opposite the mountain that was located in that desert, namely, Mount Sinai, which gave its name to the desert of Sinai.

Ibn Ezra (followed by Mendelssohn) thought that the statement "and they encamped [*va-yahanu*] in the desert" referred to all of Israel, while the statement "Israel encamped [*va-yihan*]," in the singular, referred to only a few of them, i.e., the heads of the tribes and the elders, who encamped opposite the mountain because of their [superior] honor. This is nonsense, for the reference to the people in the singular does not mean to speak of a few of them, but on the contrary, the intention is to speak of the entire people taken as a single entity (see what I wrote in *Bikkurei ha-Ittim* 5589 [1828], pp. 90-91).[10]

When it says that the people encamped in the desert, it says *va-yahanu*, in the plural, for in the great and broad desert, they looked as if they were scattered here and there; but when it says that they encamped opposite the mountain, this mountain was at the center of them all, with everyone facing it, and they formed one group and a single body, for the eyes and hearts of all were toward that mountain, which they already knew was the "mountain of God," as is evident from the statement above, "in the desert where he was encamped, to the mountain (that is) of God" (Exod. 18:5). For this reason it is written in the singular, "Israel encamped [*va-yihan*] there"—the whole people, as one man—"opposite the mountain."

**19:3. Moses then went up to God. The Lord, that is, called him from the mountain and said to him, "So shall you say to the family of Jacob and announce to the children of Israel.**

---

10. There (actually pp. 91-92), Shadal says that Hebrew collective nouns are sometimes construed as plural, when the speaker means to refer to many individuals, and sometimes as singular, when the reference is to a single body comprising many parts.

# Shadal on Exodus

***Moses then went up to God*** — to the mountain, but not to its summit.

***The Lord, that is, called him*** *(va-yikra elav YHVH,* lit., "and the Lord called him"). [Moses went up] because God had previously called him (Ibn Ezra, *Me'ammer,* and Bekhor Shor).

***So shall you say,*** *etc.* This is a poetic statement in parallelistic form, so phrased in order that the statement—which is an introduction to the entire Torah—would enter more easily into the hearts of the people.

***and announce*** *(ve-taggeid).* The Hebrew is spelled with a *yod,* in the manner of the indicative form [*ve-taggid*], but is vocalized with a *tseireh,* in the manner of the imperative.

Rashi's statement [that Moses was to explain to the men the details of the commandments in words that were] *kashin ke-giddin* ("as harsh as *giddin*") is taken from *Shabbat* 87a; *giddin* is a bitter herb—the author of the *Arukh* points out that the *dalet* in the word [*giddin*] has a *dagesh*—and is the Aramaic equivalent of *la'anah* ("wormwood") [see the Targum to Lam. 3:15].

**19:4. "'You have seen how I have treated the Egyptians, and how I lifted you (as if) on the wings of the eagles, and brought you near to me.**

***and how I lifted you.*** As if I had lifted you on eagles' wings, that is, as if I had caused you to fly in the air, for otherwise you would not have been able to come out from under the hand of Egypt.

***and brought you near to me.*** "I brought you out of Egypt's domain and brought you into Mine, to a place where you have no masters but I." The meaning is not "to this mountain where My presence is" (as per Ibn Ezra), for the main purpose of the Exodus was not to go to the desert, and why would it have been a praiseworthy act for Him to bring them to Mount Sinai? Their entire hope and desire was to go and inherit the land of Israel, and although receiving the Torah would indeed be an even more glorious thing than inheriting the land, He had not yet told them that He would proclaim the Torah to them on that mountain.

**19:5. "'Now then, if you obey Me and observe My pact [My law], you will be My treasure among all the peoples. For to Me belongs the whole earth —**

***treasure*** *(segullah)* — like a person's dearest possession.

***For to Me belongs the whole earth.*** And all the peoples are Mine, and the entire human race is dear to Me, but nevertheless you will be for Me a realm of priests and a holy nation (Sforno).

**19:6. "'But you will be for Me a realm of priests, and a holy nation.' These are the words that you shall say to the children of Israel."**

***a realm of priests, and a holy nation.*** Because the nations believed that priests were especially close and dear to their gods, and that their gods would do for them anything that they wished, God said that the entire people would be close to Him, and that He would be close to them whenever they called to Him and would watch over all their affairs, as if the entire congregation were holy men and priests—but only if they would observe His commandments.

**19:7. Moses went and called the elders of the people, and he put before them all of these things that the Lord had commanded him (to declare to them).**

***and he put before them*** *(va-yasem lifneihem).* In the natural course of things, when a person wants to use a thing for his benefit, he sets it up in front of himself (because the eyes see forward and not backward, and eating and other activities are indulged in while facing forward). That which is in front of a person is within his domain and subject to his enjoyment and use at will, and one who seeks to prevent him from doing so will first take it away from before him. Thus, the word *lifnei* ("before," "in front of") was transferred to mean that a thing is in someone's domain to be enjoyed at will, as in:

- "My country is at your disposal [*lefanekha*]" (Gen. 20:15);
- "And the country will be at your disposal [*lifneikhem*]" (Gen. 34:10);
- "The land of Egypt is at your disposal [*lefanekha*]" (Gen. 47:6);
- "Joshua son of Nun, who is at your service [*lefanekha*]" (Deut. 1:38);
- "Let our God now command your servants, who are before you [*lefanekha*]" (1 Sam. 16:16), that is, "we are ready to do as you command";
- "As I have served in your father's presence [*lifnei avikha*], so will I be in your presence [*lefanekha*]" (2 Sam. 16:19);

and other such examples. This is also the origin of the Aramaic expression *kodam malka* ("before the king"), which was said by way of honor instead of "to the king" [as in Dan. 2:36, "And we will tell its interpretation before the king"] (see *Ohev Ger*, p.13); its principal meaning was to indicate submission, i.e., that the person speaking with the king makes himself always ready to do anything that he might command him.

The expression *sam lifnei* ("put before") is found in its original sense, as in:

- "There having been presented to him [*va-yusam lefanav*] food to eat" (Gen. 24:33);
- "And set it [meat] before [*va-yasem lifnei*] Saul" (1 Sam. 9:24);
- "And let me set before you [*ve-asimah lefanekha*] a morsel of bread, and eat" (1 Sam. 28:22).

For this no explanation is needed. However, we also find it in a transferred sense in three places: one is here ["and he put before them"]; the second is below (21:1), "These, then, are the laws that you will present to them [*tasim lifneihem*]; and the third is in Deuteronomy (4:44): "This, then, is the law that Moses presented to [*sam... lifnei*] the children of Israel." These three instances have one meaning, and that is that Moses declared the words of God to Israel, leaving it up to the people to accept them or not, for at first the Torah was given to Israel without command or compulsion. Rather, the people willingly entered into a covenant with their God, as it is written here [next. v.], "And all the people responded together, and said, 'All that which the Lord has spoken, we will carry out.'"

So, too, with respect to the laws (*mishpatim*), it is written, "Moses went and told the people all the words of the Lord, and all the laws; and the whole people responded with one voice, and they said, 'All that which the Lord spoke, we will carry out'" (Exod. 24:3). Subsequently it is written, "And he took the book of the pact, and he read it before the people; and they said, 'All that which the Lord spoke, we will carry out obediently'" (Exod. 24:7). Then Moses sprinkled [sacrificial] blood upon the people and entered them into the covenant.

Just as Moses had done with the fathers when they left Egypt, so he did with the sons in the fortieth year. This is the meaning of the verse, "This then is the law that Moses presented to the children of Israel"; this "law" (*torah*) is the covenant that God made with them in the plains of Moab (Deuteronomy chs. 5-28). The reason that the people did not once more respond, "All that which the Lord spoke, we will carry out" is that they had already been accustomed to accept God's word through Moses for forty years and more, and they did not need to say explicitly, "We will carry out obediently"; their silence was consent. Not so here, at the start of Moses' mission, when they had to speak their minds and say, "All that which the Lord spoke, we will carry out."

Now an intelligent person understands that God did not actually leave it up to Israel to accept His Torah or not, for previously He had said to them, "Until when will you refuse to observe My commandments and My laws?" (Exod. 16:28). However, the truth is that it was foreknown to Him that at this time, immediately after their exodus from slavery to freedom, if He had asked them whether they were willing to accept His Torah and enter into a covenant under which they would be His people and He would be their God, they certainly would not have refused or drawn back. Therefore He put the matter before them so that they could choose of their own free will. Similarly, in the fortieth year, after He had defeated before them the Amorite kings, Sihon and Og, and had given their land to the people, it was clear that they would willingly have entered into a covenant with Him.

Joshua, in his old age, took a similar action and said to Israel, "And if it seems evil to you to serve the Lord, choose this day whom you will serve" (Josh. 24:15), not that they were given permission to abandon God's Torah, but Joshua knew that because of their love for him and his God, and their happiness that He had brought them to the county of their rest and heritage, they would certainly have responded (as they did), "Far be it from us that we should forsake the Lord" (Josh. 24:16). As a result, even after some time they would observe His commandments more zealously, since they had accepted them upon themselves out of free will.

The expression *natan lifnei* [often translated, like *sam lifnei*, as "put before"] is also found in its original sense, as in:

- "And put it [food] before them [*va-yitten lifneihem*]" (Gen. 18:8);
- "How should I set this [food] before [*etten... lifnei*] a hundred men?" (2 Kings 4:43);
- "And I set before [*va-etten lifnei*] the sons of the house of the Rekabites goblets full of wine" (Jer. 35:5);
- "And before [*lifnei*] a blind person do not place [*titten*] a stumbling-block" (Lev. 19:14);

and this, too, needs no explanation. I see no distinction between *natan lifnei* and *sam lifnei* when these expressions are used in their original and not transferred senses, but we do find *natan lifnei* in a transferred sense, as in:

- "Like all this law that I present to you [*noten lifneikhem*] today" (Deut. 4:8);
- "Take care to carry out all the statutes and the laws that I place before you [*noten lifneikhem*] today" (Deut. 11:32);
- "Because they have forsaken My law which I set before them [*natatti lifneihem*]" (Jer. 9:12).

These, in my opinion, have a different meaning, for the phrase "Take care to carry out" is an absolute command, so how could [Moses] have said afterwards, "...that I place before you today" if the meaning was "that I leave up to you to [immediately] accept or not to accept"? Similarly, what is the meaning of [the question and answer in Jer. 9:11-12] "Why is the land perished... Because they have forsaken My law which I set before them"? The main point seems to be missing; it should have said, "...which I set before them *and they accepted.*" See also:

- 1 Kings 9:6 ["But if you turn away... and not keep My commandments and My statutes which I have set before you [*natati lifneikhem*]"];
- Jer. 26:4 ["If you will not hearken to Me, to walk in My law, which I have set before you [*natatti lifneikhem*]"];
- Jer. 44:10 ["Neither have they... walked in My law... that I set before you [*natati lifneikhem*]"].

Therefore I say that the expression *sam lifnei*, used in a transferred sense, means that a person is to immediately choose whether or not to accept something—as here, "And he put before them [*va-yasem lifneihem*] all of these thing that the Lord had commanded him"—which is followed directly by, "And all the people responded together, and said... 'we will carry out.'" However, *natan lifnei* is an action done with the intention that a person should choose [whether or not to accept] at any time he pleases; for example:

- "Behold, today I place before you [*noten lifneikhem*] blessing and curse" (Deut. 11:26);
- "Now when these things will have come upon you, the blessing and the curse, that I placed before you [*natatti lifneikhem*]" (Deut. 30:1);
- "Life and death have I placed before you [*natatti lifneikhem*], the blessing and the curse" (Deut. 30:19).

In all these instances, the meaning is not that they should [necessarily] choose immediately, but that either immediately or in subsequent generations, whenever they please, they should choose for themselves the blessing or the curse. Similarly, God placed the Torah before us so that we should adhere to it or distance ourselves from it any time we please.

It is true that in the passage in Jeremiah, "Behold, I set before you [*noten lifneikhem*] the way of life and the way of death. He who abides in this city shall die..." (Jer. 21:8-9), where the subject matter pertains not to future generations but to the current moment, the language is not precise, and it should have said *sam* or *mesim*, not *noten*. However, Jeremiah wanted to retain the language used in the Torah, "Life and death have I placed before you [*natatti lefanekha*]," even though the reference there (Deut. 30:19) is to future generations and here it is to the current moment. It is well known that this was Jeremiah's way, to take his expressions from those of the prophets who preceded him.

**19:8. And all the people responded together, and said, "All that which the Lord has spoken, we will carry out." And Moses reported [that is, he went to report] to the Lord the words of the people.**

*And Moses reported to the Lord.* He returned to God's presence at the mountain with the people's response. Indeed, all is known before Him, and he did not ask Moses, "What did the people respond to you?" However, as soon as Moses came before God, He said, "I am about to reveal Myself to you in a thick cloud..." (next v.), and then Moses told God the words of the people. He said to Him, "Master of the universe, Your children are believers and they accept on themselves all that You say" (Nachmanides). [Moses said,] "They have already shown that they are believers, for the words that I have spoken to them in Your name are Your words, and if they suspected that I had made them up myself, they would not have said, 'All that which the Lord has spoken, we will carry out.' Therefore, there is no need for them to hear Your voice so that they should have faith in me, for they believe in me already."

**19:9. And the Lord said to Moses, "I about to reveal Myself to you in a thick cloud, so that the people may hear Me speak to you, and may also have faith in you forever." Moses then related to the Lord the words of the people.**

*I about to reveal Myself.* "Until now, I have proclaimed My words to you without any visible manifestation, for you have no need to see remarkable sights in order to know My greatness. But this time I wish to come to you in a thick cloud and speak to you from the midst of the fire and cloud, so that all the people may see the great spectacle, hear My voice speaking to you, and gain everlasting faith in Me and in you."

Here, God was hinting to Moses about the Revelation at Mount Sinai, but He did not tell him about it clearly all at once, for He did not say "so that the people may hear Me speak to *them*," as would have been proper if the intended reference was (as per Ibn Ezra and Maimonides [*Guide* 2:33]) to the Ten Commandments. Rather, He said "speak to *you*," referring (as per Saadiah Gaon and others) to that which was to take place before the giving of the Torah: "Moses spoke, and God responded to him in a loud voice" (below, v. 19).

Then Moses told Him the people's response, as if to say, "There is no need for this"—for Moses did not yet know that God's intention was to proclaim the Torah to all the people. Subsequently, God said to him, "Go to the people, and have them sanctify themselves… for on the third day the Lord will descend in the view of all the people to Mount Sinai" (below, vv. 10-11). He thereby hinted to Moses that His appearance in a thick cloud would not be for the stated purpose alone—that is, so that they should have faith in Moses—but that He wanted to prepare Israel for another great and glorious purpose, for which it would be fitting for them to sanctify themselves for two days, namely, that they should hear the Torah from His own mouth.

**19:10. Then the Lord said to Moses, "Go to the people, and have them sanctify themselves today and tomorrow, and wash their garments.**

*Go to the people.* God did not listen to Moses, but commanded him to summon the people to receive the Torah.

*and have them sanctify themselves.* That is, they [the men] were not to approach the women, and they were to bathe themselves in water, all this being by way of respect toward Heaven, and so that the matter would make a greater impression upon their hearts.

**19:11. "And let them be ready for the third day, for on the third day the Lord will descend in the view of all the people to Mount Sinai.**

*the Lord will descend.* That is, a manifestation of His glory, in the form of fire.

**19:12. "Fix limits for the people all around, saying, 'Guard yourselves from going up the mountain, and from touching (even) its extremity. Whoever touches the mountain, let him be put to death.**

***Fix limits for the people,*** *etc.* For Mount Sinai was, at that time, like a Divine sanctuary, as God was to be revealed there, and part of the holiness of a sanctuary is that the people should not enter within a certain boundary (Rosenmueller).

**19:13. "Let no hand touch him, but let him be stoned, or shot with an arrow; whether beast or man, let him not live. When the horn sounds, they will go up to the mountain [see below, 24:1, 9].**

***Let no hand touch him.*** "Whoever touches the mountain, let him be put to death," but they were not to go after him to kill him; rather, they were to put him to death from afar by means of stoning with stones or shooting (*yeriyyah*) with arrows (Rashbam, Ibn Ezra).[11]

***When the horn sounds,*** *etc.* "The Gaon [Saadiah] said that when Moses sounded the shofar, He then gave them permission to go up, and this was after Moses came down on Yom Kippur and commanded that the Tabernacle be built... [but] R. Samuel bar Hofni said that the word *hemmah* ['they'] refers [only] to Aaron, his sons, and the seventy elders, about whom it is written, 'Go up to the Lord, you and Aaron, Nadab and Abihu, and seventy of the elders of Israel' (Exod. 24:1), but to the rest of Israel He never gave permission to go up to Mount Sinai—and his [R. Samuel's] words seem right to me" (Ibn Ezra).

In my opinion, there is no need to interpret *hemmah* as referring to those men only, but *hemmah* is to be taken literally as "the people" plain and simple, while at the time of the actual event, He specified who was to go up, and the "elect" among the people (Exod. 24:11) stood in place of the entire people. Some things are first expressed in a general way and then are spelled out in detail; [in such cases] the detailed statement prevails over the generalization, e.g., "And he will serve him forever" (Exod. 21:6) [see the comment thereon].

**19:14. Moses descended from the mountain to the people, and he had the people sanctify themselves and wash their garments.**
**19:15. And he said to the people, "Be prepared for the third day; do not approach a woman."**

***For the third day*** (*li-sheloshet yamim*, lit., "for three days"). The Hebrew is the equivalent of *la-yom ha-shelishi*, on the model of, "At the end of

---

11. *Contra* Rashi, who cites *Sanhedrin* 45a for the proposition that a stoning victim was first to be "cast down" (*yiyyareh*) from a height.

three days [*be-od sheloshet yamim*], Pharaoh will decapitate you" (Gen. 40:19), which is followed by, "Now on the third day [*ba-yom ha-shelishi*]" (Gen. 40:20). Similarly, "And he confined them in a place of custody for three days [*sheloshet yamim*]" (Gen. 42:17), which is followed by, "But on the third day [*ba-yom ha-shelishi*]" (Gen. 42:18). (Ibn Ezra). [Thus] Moses did not add a day on his own initiative; see *Shabbat* 86b.[12]

**19:16. Now, on the third day, when it was morning, there was thunder and lightning, and a thick cloud was on the mountain, and (there was heard) a sound (as) of a horn, exceedingly loud; and all the people who were in the camp were frightened.**

***there was thunder and lightning*** *(va-y'hi kolot u-verakim)*. The Hebrew words are accented with a *kadma ve-azla,* a lesser disjunctive than the *pashta* that marks the words *ve-anan kaved* ("and a thick cloud"). This indicates that the thunder and lightning were only on the mountain and not on the camp.

**19:17. Moses drew the people out of the camp, toward God; and they placed themselves at the foot of the mountain.**
**19:18. Mount Sinai was all in smoke, for the Lord descended upon it in the fire; its smoke rose up like the smoke of a furnace, and the whole mountain trembled exceedingly.**
**19:19. The sound (as) of a horn kept growing exceedingly loud; Moses spoke, and the Lord responded to him in a loud voice.**

***Moses spoke.*** The correct view is that of [Saadiah] Gaon (cited by Ibn Ezra), that this is to be taken in the plain sense: Moses spoke with God, and He answered (with Scripture not bothering to record the words). This explains the phrase "so that the people may hear Me speak to you" (above, v. 9). [*Contra* Rashi,] there is no reference at all here to the Ten Commandments (for we heard all of them from God's own mouth, according to the plain sense of the verses). This is also Nachmanides' opinion; he says that God answered Moses with the commands that appear below, "Go down, warn the people…" (v. 21).

---

12. The Talmud, in *Shabbat* 86b-87a, records a dispute as to the date of the giving of the Torah: the majority view was that it was the sixth of Sivan, but R. Yosi maintained that it was the seventh. According to R. Yosi's view, Moses "added a day on his own initiative," and the people were to prepare themselves for three days in order to be ready on the fourth (that is, on the seventh day of the month). As Rashi points out in his comment on the present verse, those who say that the date was the sixth of Sivan do not agree that Moses added a day.

**19:20. When the Lord had descended upon Mount Sinai, to the summit of the mountain, the Lord called Moses to the summit of the mountain, and Moses ascended.**

**19:21. The Lord said to Moses, "Go down, warn the people, so that they do not advance toward the Lord to see, with a great slaughter coming of it.**

*so that they do not advance.* Not that they were forbidden to look, but they were not to come within the boundary in order to see better.

*advance (yehersu).* It seems to me that the Hebrew is transferred from the original sense of "breaking down" a wall, for one who enters a forbidden place is breaching a fence, as it were. An analogous usage is, "Why do you push yourself ahead [*mah paratsta*, lit., 'why do you breach']?" (Gen. 38:29) [said to Perez, son of Judah, who was born before his twin brother, although the latter had put out his arm first].

**19:22. "And also the priests who come near to the Lord [that is, officiate at the sacrifices], let them contain themselves in holiness [respectfully, and within the confines], so that the Lord does not make a massacre of them.**

*And also the priests (ha-kohanim).* The firstborns.

*who come near to the Lord.* Who stand by the boundary, or who customarily approach God when offering the sacrifices.

*let them contain themselves in holiness (yitkaddashu).* Let them be ready and careful to stand in awe and fear, so as not to say, "We are priests and [have the right to be] near to God" (Rashi, R. Joseph Bekhor Shor).

**19:23. Moses said to the Lord, "The people cannot go up to Mount Sinai, for You have warned us, saying, 'Place limits (around) the mountain and declare it holy.'"**

**19:24. And the Lord answered him, "Go, descend; then you will go up, and Aaron with you. But (for now) let neither the priests nor the people advance to go up toward the Lord, so that no slaughter be made of them."**

*Go, descend; then you will go up.* It seems to me that Moses wanted to stay on the mountain, and so he sought to avoid going down and warning the people, but God did not consent, and He told him to descend but to come back up the mountain with Aaron after the giving of the Torah. Thus it says below, "To Moses He then said, 'Go up to the Lord, you and Aaron...'" (Exod. 24:1). However, it seems clear to me that at the time of the giving of the Torah, Moses was not on the mountain but with the people, for they said to him, "Speak you with us, and we will listen" (Exod. 20:16).

This was Abravanel's opinion, except that he took the phrase "let neither the priests nor the people advance" as referring to that [later] time when Moses, Aaron, and the elders went up. It does not seem so to me; rather, the command not to advance should be understood in its plains sense as referring to "now," the time of the giving of the Torah.

The other commentators [notably Rashi, based on the Mekhilta] explain "then you will go up," etc., as meaning that at the time of the giving of the Torah, Moses was to have an assigned station (*mehitsah*) by himself [with Aaron having a station of his own at a lower level, and the priests at a still lower station]. However, there is no hint in the text of any assignment of different "stations" at the time of the giving of the Torah; rather, all the people, great and small, were to listen as one.

We find that Moses, after the giving of the Torah, approached alone toward the thick cloud (Exod. 20:18), while here it says, "Then you will go up, and Aaron with you." It should be noted that when Moses approached the cloud, the giving of the Torah was not yet completed, for the people said to Moses, "Speak you with us, and we will listen; and the let God not speak with us, so that we do not die" (Exod. 20:16). Then Moses approached God in order to receive the remainder of the "Torah," i.e., the *parashah* of *Mishpatim* (Exodus 21-23) with the five preceding verses (Exod. 20:19-23). However, the statement here, "Then you will go up, and Aaron with you," does not refer to that ascent, for that ascent would not have occurred if the people had not taken fright and been unable to receive the entire Torah [directly] from the mouth of God.

Rather, the ascent mentioned here ("Then you will go up," etc.) did not occur until after the receipt of the Torah was completed, at which time the leaders of the people went to worship the Giver of the Torah and to give Him thanks for it. Here, where God saw that Moses was refusing to go down, He told him, "Do not be aggrieved if you are now to be as one of the common people, for there will yet come a time when you will approach God, and all of Israel will know that you and Aaron are closer to Me than all of them are."

**19:25. Moses descended to the people, and he told it to them.**

## Yitro

***and he told it to them*** *(va-yomer aleihem,* lit., "and he said to them") — that which God had told him to warn them about.

**20:1. Then God uttered all these words, saying:**

***Then God uttered all these words.*** The correct opinion is that of the Rabbis in Midrash Hazita [*Shir Ha-Shirim Rabbah*] (on the verse, "Let him kiss me with the kisses of his mouth" [Songs 1:2]), and of Ibn Ezra and Abravanel, that all of the Ten Commandments were said by God in the hearing of the entire congregation of Israel, that is, that God miraculously caused a voice to be heard in the air as if a human being were producing those words, from "I am" (below, v. 2) until "anything belonging to your neighbor" (below, v. 14). Similarly, God miraculously caused a sound resembling that of a shofar (as per Gersonides) [who said that] creating such a sound without an actual shofar was a perfect wonder.

The verses prove this point: first of all, the verse here, "Then God uttered all these words." Second, "You have seen that from the heaven I spoke with you" (below, v. 19). Third, "And the Lord spoke to them from the midst of the fire... He declared to them His pact, (that is) the ten commandments" (Deut. 4:12-13), "And His words you heard from the midst of the fire" (Deut. 4:36). And fourth:

- "These words the Lord spoke to all your assembly in the mountain..." (Deut. 5:19);
- "And you, having heard that voice from the midst of the darkness" (Deut. 5:20);
- "And we have heard His voice from the midst of the fire; this day we have seen that God can speak with man, and the latter stays alive" (Deut. 5:21).

There is no hint in Scripture to what was said in the Talmud (*Makkot* 24a), that "I am the Lord" and "Do not have other gods" were heard directly from the mouth of the Almighty—that is to say, the other commandments were not so heard. Without a doubt, the Rabbis did not receive this idea by way of tradition; rather, there were conflicting homiletical statements as to this matter. In the Mekhilta they said that God spoke the Ten Commandments in a single utterance, and then repeated each of them separately; but in the Midrash Hazita (on the verse cited above), R. Joshua ben Levi contends that the first two commandments were heard directly from God's mouth, while the [other] Sages say that Israel heard all of the commandments from His mouth.

# Shadal on Exodus

Maimonides' opinion apparently was that the revelation at Sinai was entirely by way of a prophetic vision. In the first part of the *Guide for the Perplexed*, ch. 47, he wrote, "For this reason it says, 'All the people perceived the thunders and the flames' (below, v. 15), this statement itself being a prophetic vision." However, in the second part of the *Guide*, ch. 36, he wrote that (1) at the Sinai revelation, that which reached Moses did not reach all of Israel; (2) rather, God's speech was directed to Moses alone, and this is why the Ten Commandments are framed entirely in the second person singular (i.e., "your God," "who brought you out," "do not utter," "remember," "honor," "do not commit murder," etc.); and (3) Moses then went up to the foot of the mountain and told the people what he had heard.

Responding at length to Maimonides' statements were the distinguished scholar [Hasdai] Crescas, Abravanel in his fourteenth question [in his comment on Exod. 19:1], and the author of *Ma'asei Adonai* [R. Eliezer Ashkenazi], p. 145. In addition, Ibn Ezra responded to the claim that was made based on the fact that the third, fourth, and fifth commandments refer to God in the third person ("for the Lord will not leave unpunished," "His name," "in six days the Lord made," etc.), and said that [these commandments were nevertheless spoken directly by God Himself, for] "now that you have accepted this Name as that of your God, He has said to you, 'Do not utter the name of the Lord your God (swearing) falsely,' and also, 'For in six days the Lord made the heaven and the earth' (i.e., that God Whom you have accepted as your God); besides, it was the custom of Hebrew speakers to express themselves this way."

I will make no conclusion as to what Maimonides' rationale was in this exalted matter, for it is exceedingly difficult to penetrate its mystery. (See the commentary of the scholar R. Shem Tov [ben Joseph Ibn Shem Tov] on ch. 36 of the first part of the *Guide*.) Blessed be the Omnipresent, Who has freed us from that philosophy that prevailed in Maimonides' days, toward which he tended more than he should have, even if his intention was for the good.

Recently, the scholar Jost, in his book *Allgemeine Geschichte des Israëlitischen Volkes*, wrote (in Part 1, p. 109) that it was Moses who spoke the Ten Commandments to Israel; he took the phrase "Moses spoke" (Exod. 19:19) as referring to the Commandments, and the phrase "and the Lord responded to him in a loud voice" (ibid.) as referring to "the thunders and the flames" (below, v. 15) that were as loud as a shofar. You can see how far removed this is from the meaning of the Torah's words, which attest that Israel heard the Ten Commandments from God (that is, a miraculously created voice), not from a human mouth; for the people said to Moses, "Speak you with us... and let God not speak with us" (below, v. 16), and see all the other verses that I have cited above.

You can see, too, that the Torah always makes a distinction between "the thunders and the flames" and "the sound of a horn"; the words do not at all mean that the "thunders" sounded like a shofar. Besides, it is illogical to compare the thunders to the sound of a shofar, for thunder is a thing that is known to the entire people, and everyone knows that the sound of a shofar can never be as loud as thunder, so how can thunder be compared to the sound of a shofar?

Perhaps it might be answered that the comparison might be based not on the volume of the sound, but on its continuity, in that the thunder did not stop in a moment as usual. However, you can see that (besides the fact the text mentions the sound of the shofar separately from the thunder) it should then not have said "the sound of a horn, exceedingly loud" (Exod. 19:16), but rather "exceedingly prolonged," or the like.

This author [Jost] also said that apparently Moses did not draw out the entire people toward God (see Exod. 19:7), but only the heads of the tribes and the elders. He found support from what was written in Deut. 5:20, "And you, having heard that voice in the midst of the darkness, and the mountain burning in the fire, drew yourselves close to me, (that is) all the heads of your tribes, and your elders." But you can see that this is a support that has no substance, for even if the entire multitude was present, it would not have been appropriate for them to approach Moses to speak to him in a disorderly manner, like rebels, but instead the heads and elders would have approached him and spoken on behalf of all, especially since the multitude had taken fright and was standing at a distance (see below, v. 15).

You can see also that if only the heads and elders were present, there would have been no need to specify that it was only they who approached Moses; rather, it should have said [in Deut. 5:20] that "you… drew yourselves close to me, all of you," that is, everyone. To the contrary, the verse begins in an unspecified way, "And you, having heard," etc., for the entire people heard.

As for the verse that says, "I then stood between you and the Lord, to declare to you the word of the Lord; for you were afraid of the fire, and you did not go up on the mountain" (Deut. 5:5), this means only (as per Ibn Ezra's comment) that "from that day on, I stood between God and you; that is, at that time I became an interpreter between God and you, telling you His commandments, for you were afraid of the fire, even though you did not go up on the mountain but stayed beneath it as God had commanded. You were afraid to hear God's voice, and so you asked me to stand between God and you"—as it is specified below, "And you said, 'Behold, the Lord our God has shown us His majesty…. Approach you, and listen to all that which the Lord our God will say'" (Deut. 5:21, 24).

## Shadal on Exodus

Ibn Ezra, in his short commentary—on the verse, "Moses descended to the people, and he told it to them" (Exod. 19:25)—cited the verse "I then stood..." as proof that Moses and Aaron were within the boundary [i.e., on the mountain] when the Torah was given. However, this contradicts his comment on that verse in Deuteronomy [5:5], and it seems to me that his latter words should be considered authoritative, not his former words.

There is no conflict between the account here and the account in Deuteronomy. He uttered a falsehood who wrote that there remained only a general memory of the account of the giving of the Torah and Commandments, not a literal one, and that two versions of the Commandments remained, here and in Deuteronomy (as if Moses did not write Deuteronomy, but that after several generations it was written as it had been handed down from mouth to mouth). He also uttered a falsehood who attributed this opinion to Ibn Ezra, for the latter said only that God spoke the Ten Commandments in the version written here, and that they were so written on the tablets, while Moses, in restating them to Israel in the fortieth year, varied the wording slightly but preserved the sense, as is the way with all the repeated materials in the Torah. If only I could know whether, in the cases of Eliezer's recounting [of his arrangements to find a wife for Isaac] (Genesis 24) and Pharaoh's dream (Genesis 41), there likewise remained two versions in the memory of the people, as evidenced by the variations found in those cases between the narrator's account and those of Eliezer and Pharaoh in their [first-person] retellings!

**20:2. "I am the Lord your God, Who brought you out of Egypt, from the house of slaves [from that country which was a prison for you].**

*I am the Lord your God.* This verse is (as per Abravanel) an introduction to the commandments and admonitions that follow, and it means (as per Mendelssohn), "I, Who speak and command, am the Lord your God, Who brought you out of the land of Egypt, and thus it is proper for you to serve Me and not another besides Me."

There is a hint of such an explanation in the Mekhilta, where it is asked, why were the Ten Commandments not announced at the beginning of the Torah? A parable is then given of a king who enters a country and says to the people, "I will rule over you," whereupon they say, "Have you done any good for us that you should rule over us?" What did he then do? He built a wall for them, brought in water for them, and fought a war for them. Then, when he said, "I will rule over you," they responded, "Yes, yes." Just so, the Holy One, blessed is He, took Israel out of Egypt, split the sea for them, brought manna down for them, brought the quails over them, produced a well for them, and fought them a war with Amalek. Then, when He said, "I will rule over you," they responded, "Yes, yes." That is, "I, Who speak to you, am the Lord your God, Who has done good things for you, and so it is fitting that you should accept Me as your King and heed My voice."

According to this explanation, the word *anokhi* ("I") is the subject of the phrase, and the words *YHVH Elohekha asher hotseitikha* ("the Lord your God, Who brought you out"), etc., are the predicate. This is also the view of the accentuators [who marked *anokhi* with a disjunctive accent]. It would have been possible to divide the words in a different way, and to connect *anokhi* to God's name and mark the latter with a disjunctive. In that case, *anokhi YHVH* ("I, the Lord") would have been the subject, and "your God, Who brought you out" would have been the predicate. The meaning would have been, "I, Who am called the Lord, am alone your God, and I watch over you with a special Providence, for I have already brought you out of the land of Egypt."

Following this approach, Wessely gave the following interpretation in his commentary to the Wisdom of Solomon (p. 92): "That is to say, 'Hear, O Israel, I am the Lord, and there is no god beside Me. I am your One God, your Leader and King and thus you must serve Me through the laws and commandments that I will give you; I have not so commanded any of the other nations." In *Shirei Tif'eret,* part 6, he wrote:

Though I have been called God of all the earth,
God of all the peoples and nations together,
Even so you shall call Me God of Israel,
For I, the Lord, am your God.

Ibn Ezra, too, attached the Name to the word *anokhi*, saying, "The meaning of this commandment is that [Israel] was to believe and have faith in his heart, without any doubt, that [the God of] this Name, which is written but not spoken, was alone his God." However, it seems to me that if this were so, the verse would properly have been worded as, "I, the Lord, am your God Who brought you out [*asher hotsi'akha*]" [in the third person] (instead of *hotsetikha*, in the first person), or, "...for I brought you out [*ki hotsetikha*], or, "... I [*ani*] brought you out [*hotsetikha*]." To the contrary, the first explanation [above], which is the way that the accentuators followed, is the correct one in my view.

Perhaps this verse constitutes one of the Ten Commandments (*dibrot*) and yet is not a "command" (*mitsvah*). The author of the *Halakhot Gedolot* did not include it among the *mitsvot*; however, Maimonides deemed it a *mitsvah* and held that it was a command to believe in the existence of God (*Sefer ha-Mitsvot*, Pos. 1). His approach was followed by those who compiled lists of *mitsvot*, even though their opinions differed as to the definition of the *mitsvah* that it implied. [For instance,] the author of *Sefer Mitsvot ha-Gadol* [R. Moses of Coucy] was of the opinion that it was a command to believe that He Who gave us the Torah was the Lord God Who brought us out of Egypt.

However, we do not find in the Torah any command as to belief. It has been taught by no lesser an authority than R. Hasdai [Crescas] (the teacher of R. Joseph Albo) that the exercise of free will has no effect upon beliefs and opinions (see his book *Or Adonai, ma'amar* 2, *kelal* 5, ch. 5). Besides (as Abravanel noted), the statement "I am the Lord your God, Who brought you out..." is in the form of a narrative of a past event, and is not couched in language that indicates a command.

Why does it say, "Who brought you out of the land of Egypt," and not "Who created the heaven and the earth"? The reason is that the exodus from Egypt served as evidence for Israel that their God was the Ruler of heaven and earth; if it were not for the introductory signs and wonders [in Egypt], how would it have been made clear to them that their God was the One Who created heaven and earth? All the nations worshipped other gods, and perhaps each of them believed that its god was the creator of all. Since it was not the way of our Torah to issue commands as to belief, it would not have been appropriate for God to say, "I am the Lord your God, Who created the heaven and the earth," without citing some proof for His words. The statement "Who brought you out..." is the proof of the truth of His Divinity (this is the answer given by R. Judah ha-Levi in the *Kuzari*, sections 15 to 25 in the first *ma'amar*).

It may still be asked, however, why it did not say, "I, Who brought you out of Egypt, am the One Who created the heaven and the earth." The answer to this is that the creation of the world was a boon to all humankind alike, and it would follow that all humankind ought to worship Him, not that the Israelites in particular ought to observe numerous commandments and laws that He did not impose on other peoples. On the other hand, the exodus from Egypt was an act of mercy that God performed for the Israelites alone, from which followed their obligation to worship Him and observe His commandments, as per the Mekhilta that I cited above (and the similar comments of Ibn Ezra and Mendelssohn).

As for my statement that this verse is perhaps one *dibbur* among the Ten Commandments (*dibrot*), the reason is that even though there are undoubtedly ten *dibrot*—for it is written, "And [the Lord] wrote on the tablets the words of the pact, [that is] the ten commandments [*aseret ha-devarim*]" (Exod. 34:28)—there are doubts as to the manner of their division. According to the way the sections are divided in the Torah, the statements *anokhi* ("I am...") and *lo yihyeh lekha* ("Do not have..."), through *u-le-shomerei mitsvotai* ("and with the observers of My precepts") (below, v. 6) form only one section, while [the tenth commandment, below, v. 14] "Do not desire" is divided into two sections, making it appear as if "Do not desire the house of your neighbor" is the ninth commandment and "Do not desire the wife of your neighbor," etc., is the tenth commandment, but this (as per Abravanel) is a very strange idea that cannot be accepted.

In the Jerusalem Targum, called Targum Jonathan, "Do not desire" comprises one single commandment, while "I am" is referred to as the *dibra kadma'ah* ("first commandment") and "Do not have..." is referred to as the *dibra tinyana* ("second commandment"). It was the custom among the German and French communities, in early times, to read the Ten Commandments on the holiday of Shavuot with the Targum. Between "I am..." and "Do not have...," they would interpolate Aramaic *piyyutim*, and then they would say [the Targum's introduction to the second commandment], *dibra tinyana kad hava nafik*, etc. [followed by the Aramaic translation of the commandment itself,] *la yehavei lakh elaha oharan*, etc. As for the two statements beginning "Do not desire," they made them into a single commandment.

So it appears in the Mahzor Vitry and in some other very old books in manuscript; see also R. Wolf Heidenheim's *humash*, *Moda la-Binah*, at the end of the Book of Exodus. The Sages of the Talmud, too, refer to "I am..." and "Do not have..." as two commandments (*mitsvot*), and their intention was apparently to count them as two *dibrot* as well. This is undoubtedly more correct than the other approach of dividing "Do not desire" into two.

**20:3. "Do not have other gods to My face.**

***Do not have other gods.*** Just as I am your exclusive God, that is, your leader Who watches over you [in particular], so you are to accept Me exclusively as your God and not accept other gods to worship.

***to My face*** *(al panai)*. The expressions: *al penei*, *al panai*, and *al panekha* (lit., "on the face of, " "on my face," "on your face")—when not used in a literal sense, as in "he fell on his face [*al panav*]"—all connote pain, harm, fear, or anger, as in:

- "Haran died during the life of [*al penei*] Terah his father" (Gen. 11:28);
- "In the presence of [*al penei*] all his brothers did he [Ishmael] settle" [i.e., they were powerless to stop him] (Gen. 25:18);
- "And thus I will command respect of [*ve-al penei*] all the people" (Lev. 10:3);
- "But Nadab and Abihu died... during the life of [*al penei*] Aaron their father" (Num. 3:4) (as per Nachmanides, and as clearly stated in 1 Chron. 24:2, but against the accentuation);[13]
- "I will begin to render you formidable and fearsome to [*al penei*] the peoples" (Deut. 2:25);
- "He may not treat as firstborn the son of the loved one, in the face of [*al penei*] the son of the hated one" (Deut. 21:16)
- "And he will curse You to Your face [*al panekha*]" (Job 1:11);
- "Let not man prevail [let the nations be judged] against You [*al panekha*]" (Ps. 9:20, against the accents [which would favor the translation, "Let not man prevail; let the nations be judged in Your sight"]);
- "For surely to your faces [*al peneikhem*] I will not lie" (Job 6:28), meaning, "To your anger you will see that I am not lying and that the truth is with me";
- "Who shall declare His way to His face [*al panav*]?" (Job 21:31).

Similarly, all instances of the expression *shillaḥ me-al panav* ("sent away from upon his face"), *hesir me-al panav* ("removed from upon his face"), and *hishlikh me-al panav* ("cast away from upon his face") indicated removal of something that is painful for us to look at. The most convincing example [of the idiom *al penei*] is, "Violence and spoil is heard in her, before Me [*al panai*] continually" (Jer. 6:7).

An exception to the rule is the expression *avar al penei* ("to pass upon the face of"), as in:

---

13. In Num. 3:4, the full verse reads, "But Nadab and Abihu died before the Lord, presenting before the Lord a strange fire in the desert of Sinai, without having children—and Eleazar and Ithamar remained priests—during the life of [*al penei*] Aaron their father" (this rendering is more literal than that of Shadal, who rearranges some of the clauses). Nachmanides connects the phrase "*al penei* Aaron their father" to the opening phrase "But Nadab and Abihu died," notwithstanding that the verse's accentuation would connect "*al penei* Aaron their father" with the immediately preceding phrase "and Eleazar and Ithamar remained priests." Support for Nachmanides' and Shadal's reading is found in 1 Chron. 24:2, which says, "But Nadab and Abihu died before [*lifnei*] their father, and had no children; therefore Eleazar and Ithamar executed the priest's office."

- "He passed the present in front of him [*al panav*]" (Gen. 32:22);
- "The Lord, that is, passing in front of him [*al panav*]" (Exod. 34:6);
- "Six hundred men... passed on before [*al penei*] the king" (2 Sam. 15:18).

This expression means only "to pass before someone." Likewise, the use of the verb *ḥalaf*, which is synonymous with *avar*—as in "Then a spirit passed before my face [*al panai yahalof*]" (Job 4:15)—yields the meaning of "pass before." However, when not preceded by the verbs *avar* or *ḥalaf*, and when not conveying the literal meaning of "upon the face of," *al penei* always indicates pain. So here, "Do not have other gods to My face [*al panai*]," that is, "to My anger," "to incur My wrath." The meaning is, "Know that this angers Me," as it says below (next v.), "For I, the Lord your God, am a jealous God."

But why was the Holy One, blessed is He, so insistent as to the belief in His Oneness? Why should He care if we were to worship others besides Him? Does idol worship cause harm to civil society?

Yes, it does. This world in which we live, if examined part by part, will be found to contain much evil, as everyone knows. However, if the world is examined as a whole, every wise person understands that it is only good, for there is nothing in it that is evil per se; rather, anything [apparently] evil in the world is, in its essential nature, for the good. One who believes in One God finds it possible to imagine Him as essentially good and possessing every kind of perfection. This image would lead the believer to conclude that God loves goodness and good people, and that He hates evil and evil people. This, in turn, would lead the believer to better his ways, in order to find favor with his God.

On the other hand, one who believes in many gods, that is, one who accepts as divine the forces of nature, each one apart from the other, or some created beings, whichever they may be, will inevitably have one or more gods that are evil by nature, or that have some imperfection or diminution. This will result in his inclination toward evil or imperfection, as he will think that in so doing, he will find favor with such-and-such a god whose ways are so. This is known from experience, as anyone knows who has read the annals of the ancient peoples and their customs.

Besides, only a single God is likely to be conceived as possessing the epitome of perfection. If many gods are imagined to exist, each one of them must necessarily be lacking and imperfect, for the power of one will limit that of the other. As a result, jealousy, hatred, and rivalry will be ascribed to the heavens above, as is known from the beliefs of ancient peoples; and as a further inevitable result, human relations will suffer. Polytheistic beliefs cause the hearts of the various peoples to be sundered, for the members of one nation, who worship a particular god, will despise the members of another nation who worship another god, and they will claim to lack any relationship with them, as if those others were not human beings like themselves.

Only those who believe in One God know that we all have one Father, that One God created us, and that all humankind is dear to Him. Indeed, it was only after the Torah of Moses was spread throughout the world that the peoples began to recognize that we are all brothers. For all of these reasons, God wanted the knowledge of His Unity to be maintained in Israel, and thus He threatened them with all these threats [see below, v. 5] and employed such hyperbolic language, so that they should not worship other gods. All of this was not only for the benefit of Israel in particular, but for the benefit of the whole human race, for out of Israel was the Torah to come forth, and knowledge of God's Unity was to spread from them gradually to all humankind, so that in the end of days the world was to be filled with the knowledge of God.

How pleasant are the words of R. Judah ha-Levi (*Kuzari* 4:23):

> God has a secret and wise design concerning us, which should be compared to the wisdom hidden in the seed which falls into the ground, where it undergoes an external transformation into earth, water and dirt, without leaving a trace for him who looks down upon it. It is, however, the seed itself which transforms earth and water into its own substance.... In the same manner the law of Moses transforms each one who honestly follows it, though it may externally repel him.[14]

One should understand that this secret design that God has concerning us could not have been spelled out in the Torah, for to publicize it would have undercut its purpose; Israel would not have separated itself from the idolatries of the ancient peoples or guarded itself against assimilating with them unless God had attracted them toward His service with all the means that He, in His wisdom, saw fit to employ. Even now, it is not appropriate to make this known clearly to the common masses.

But if the giving of the Torah was to benefit the whole human race, why did God choose to reveal Himself to the Israelites alone, rather than to all humankind?

---

14. Trans. Hirschfeld, pp. 226-227.

## *Yitro*

This is the question of those deniers who think they can destroy thereby the entire palace of God's Torah to its foundations. However, it is not difficult to refute this claim, by arguing as follows: God's revelation to [any other] person or people to proclaim His Unity would necessarily have been of no benefit, for anyone who is accustomed to believing in many gods, even if he were to experience a revelation of God and be told that there is no god but the One, would not feel obligated to turn his heart toward Him and accept from Him the dogma of Unity. There would always remain a doubt in his mind, and he would say, "Perhaps this god is saying this merely to glorify himself, so that I should not worship another besides him. Tomorrow, another god may come and tell me that there is no god but he, or that he is a god equal to the other one." Therefore, with all the other peoples accustomed to polytheistic beliefs, it would not have been feasible for God to reveal Himself to them, for such a revelation would have been in vain.

Thus, once Abraham arose and, through his own discernment, recognized that there was only One God, immediately the Holy One, blessed is He, revealed Himself to him and brought him toward His service, promising him that He would multiply his descendants and make him a great nation, so that the seed of the true faith should be preserved in his posterity and not be lost. Furthermore, He gave him the commandment of circumcision, so that he and his descendants should be kept separate from all the idolatrous nations of the world and not intermix with them. Then, when the children of Jacob proliferated and became a people, still holding fast to the commandment of circumcision and faith in One God, He took them out of the house of slaves and gave them the Torah, so that they should be a people that sojourns apart [see Num. 23:9] and does not mix with the other nations, but rather preserves itself with its faith and Torah, which is its very life. All this was to be for their benefit at all times, and for the benefit of the entire human race in the future.

**20:4. "Do not make for yourself any likeness, or any image (of anything) that is in the heaven above, or (of anything) that is in the earth below, or (of anything) that is in the waters under the earth.**

***Do not make for yourself any likeness*** (*pesel*). A form made of wood or stone, so called because it is *nifsal*, that is, hewn with a blade and a hammer. It is distinguished from a *massekhah* (a "cast image"), which is of metal and made by casting. In four places only do we find *pesel* used where the reference is apparently to a *massekhah*:

- "Your graven images [*pesilei*] overlaid with silver" (Isa. 30:22);
- "The image [*ha-pesel*] which the craftsman has melted [*nasakh*]" (Isa. 40:19);
- "Who has fashioned a god, or molten an image [*u-fesel massekhah*]" (Isa. 44:10);
- "Every goldsmith is put to shame by the graven image [*mi-pesel*] his molten image [*nisko*] is falsehood" (Jer. 10:14, 51:17).

Even in these cases, it seems to me, the term *pesel* does not depart from its literal meaning, indicating an image of wood or stone, not metal, but overlaid with gold or silver, so that such an image is referred to as both *pesel* and *nesekh*. Thus, Isa. 30:22 refers to a *pesel* overlaid with silver; in Isa. 40:19 ("The image which the craftsman has melted, and the goldsmith spread over with gold"), the goldsmith puts a layer of gold on a *pesel* which has previously been made of wood. Similarly, in Jer. 10:14, the *pesel* is also a *nesekh*, for its interior is wood and its exterior is metal. In Isa. 40:19, the "craftsman" (*ḥarash*) is not a woodworker; rather, the word is used in the sense of "smith," as in, "Behold, I have created the *ḥarash* who blows the fire of coals" (Isa. 54:16), and the *ḥarash* is himself the "goldsmith" (*tsoref*).

The word *nesekh* [lit., a "poured" image] may be understood in the sense of the "pouring out" or casting of gold. Otherwise, it may be interpreted in the sense of "covering" or "overlaying," as in, "And the covering that is spread [*ve-ha-massekhah ha-nesukhah*] over all nations" (Isa. 25:7), i.e., a *pesel* that has been overlaid by a smith; see Kimhi's first interpretation. So also [in Isa. 44:10], the phrase *u-fesel nasakh* may be understood in this sense [i.e., "who has overlaid a *pesel*"].

Here, *pesel* is mentioned and not *massekhah*, for the Torah was referring to current conditions, in which there were no wealthy people to make for themselves gods of silver and gold, unless the entire nation were to cooperate, as they did in the making of the Golden Calf. Here in the Ten Commandments, God was speaking to each individual, while below (v. 20), He added a reference to "gods of silver and gods of gold."

A *pesel* could take any form; thus, it is written, "Any likeness [*pesel*] of the figure of any idol, of male or female form, of the form of any animal..." (Deut. 4:16-18). Here, however, since the term is followed by the phrase "or any image (of anything) that is in the heaven," etc., it seems that *pesel* refers to a human likeness. This is what is specified below (Deut. 4:16) in the reference to "male or female."

***or any image*** *(temunah), etc.* A form made to resemble something in the heaven, earth, or waters. The word *temunah* is derived from the root *mun*, related to the Arabic *man*, meaning "to lie, deceive," and is a term for an image that resembles something else, as in:

- "Any likeness of the figure of [*temunat*] any idol" (Deut. 4:16);
- "Likenesses of any figure [*temunat kol*]" (Deut. 4:23, 25).

It might have seemed from the following verses –

- "And you did not perceive any figure [*u-t'munah*]" (Deut. 4:12);
- "For you did not see any figure [*temunah*] on the day that the Lord spoke to you" (Deut. 4:15);
- "And he [Moses] contemplates the Divine appearance [*u-t'munat YHVH*]" (Num. 12:8);
- "A form [*temunah*] was before my eyes" (Job 4:16);
- "I shall behold Your face in righteousness; I shall be satisfied, when I awake, with Your likeness [*temunatekha*]" (Ps. 17:15) –

that *temunah* refers to a naturally occurring form, its appearance and look, rather than an artificial form made in its image (and so I wrote in *Bikkurei ha-Ittim* 5588 [1827], p. 89). However, having considered the rarity of this term, which does not appear in conjunction with the word *tsurah* ("form") in Ezek. 43:11 [where the *tsurah* of the Temple and its parts is discussed] and did not remain in use in Rabbinic Hebrew, and having examined in depth each of the verses in which the term appears (there being no others besides those that I have cited), I now take the view that the word *temunah* does not depart from its primary meaning, but always signifies a form that resembles something else. This can be understood from the expression "he contemplates the Divine *temunah*," which refers not to God's actual "appearance," but rather to a created form (a depiction of God's glory) which arouses in the heart of the prophet some description of the Creator.

Similarly, the phrase "I shall be satisfied, when I awake, with Your likeness [*temunatekha*]" (Ps. 17:15) refers to a depiction of Divine glory that is seen in a vision or dream (and the one who sees it is "satisfied" and rejoices in it even after awakening); this does not mean a form of God Himself. So also, "It stood still, but I could not discern its appearance; a form [*temunah*] was before my eyes" (Job 4:16) refers to a form in a prophetic vision that arouses some description [of God] that is not physical; in Latin [this idea is expressed by the term] *phantasma* ("mental image, imaginary likeness").

Likewise, the phrases "And you did not perceive any *temunah*" and "For you did not see any *temunah*" do not mean that "you did not see the form or image of God," but rather, "You did not see any created form that would arouse in your minds a description of the God Who was speaking to you; since you did not see any *temunah* that would substitute for His very essence, so you must not make any form to remind you of your God."

All of the verses that contain the word *temunah* can now be clearly explained, and it is clear that the meaning of this word is the same in each place and also agrees with the meaning of its root that is preserved in Arabic. From the same root [*mun*] comes the word *min*, which in Biblical Hebrew denotes something that resembles another thing, but is not equal to it. For example, "Every raven *le-mino*" (Lev. 11:15) means "the raven with all the other birds that resemble it but are not equal to it"; similarly, "Fruit trees producing fruit *le-mino*" (Gen. 1:11) means (in conformance with the accents and *contra* all the commentators, as I explained *ad loc.*) "fruit trees divided into many classes, each one resembling the other in that it is a fruit tree, but not equal to the other, for it is a different species." From this usage, the word *min* was later transferred in Rabbinic Hebrew to denote a class of many persons who resemble each other; similarly, the Latin word *species* originally meant "appearance" or "likeness," but was later transferred to denote the same thing as *min* [i.e., "class" or "kind"].

**or (of anything) that is in the waters under the earth.** Cf. "To Him that spread forth the earth above the waters" (Ps. 136:6). The Torah was speaking the language of human beings, in accordance with their beliefs [about nature] in that era.

**20:5. "Do not prostrate yourself to them, and do not render them worship; for I, the Lord your God, am a jealous God, Who with My enemies demands account of the sins of the fathers from the children, from the grandchildren, and from the great-grandchildren.**

**Do not prostrate yourself to them.** To the other gods, or to any *pesel* or *temunah*.

**and do not render them worship** *(ve-lo to'ovdem)*. "Do not serve them in any other manner." The word *to'ovdem* (תָּעָבְדֵם) is strange, because it is vocalized with two *kematsim*, though it properly would have received two *patahim*: *ta'avdem* (תַּעַבְדֵם), on the model of *ya'avdeni, ya'avdennu*,

## Yitro

*ya'avdem.* This word appears with two *kematsim* again below (23:24) and in Deut. 5:9; a similar form, *ve-no'ovdem,* occurs in Deut. 13:3. According to Kimhi (*Mikhlol,* Constantinople ed. [1532], p. 45), "The *mefo'arim* [i.e., the prefix letters that signal the number and gender of a verb] appear with a *kamats ḥatuf* [*kamats katan*] in the phrases *ve-lo to'ovdem* and *asher lo yeda'atam ve-no'ovdem*; the added-on letter [*tav* or *nun*] is vocalized with a *kamats* because of the *kamats hatuf* that follows it." Another example of such unusual vocalization occurs in Isa. 44:13, in which the word [that is vocalized as] *yeta'arehu* [where it first appears in the verse is instead vocalized as] *yeto'orehu* [where it appears the second time].[15]

The Gentile scholars say that the word *to'ovdem* is in the *hof'al* conjugation, but this does not fit the context, for the *hof'al* indicates compulsion by an outside force, but here the reference is to a voluntary act. This is especially so in the verse, "Let us follow other gods—unknown to you—and let us render them worship [*ve-no'ovdem*]" (Deut. 3:13), where there can be no idea of compulsion, and thus the *hof'al* would be out of place.

**jealous** *(kanna).* The original function of the root *kana* was to denote the reddening of a face to a shade approaching black. This meaning was preserved in Syriac, and the root appears in the Syriac translations of the phrases "redness [*hakhlilut*] of eyes" (Prov. 23:29) and "our skin is hot [*nikhmaru*] like an oven" (Lam. 5:10). A word related to this root is *kina'ah,* which is Aramaic for "smith," one whose occupation is to cause metal to be reddened in fire. In Arabic, too, *kana* means "very red."

In Hebrew this root was transferred to denote the "heating" of the heart and a strong emotion that causes the face to redden and darken, that is, a feeling of extreme anger, such as the anger of a husband whose wife strays from him, or a person who sees others receive that which ought to be give to him. Sometimes, too, one will become angry on another's behalf and be "jealous" for him, as when one sees his friend's garment being worn by others, or sees others taking what is rightfully his friend's; cf. [Moses' question to Joshua,] "Are you jealous [*ha-mekannei*] for me?" (Num. 11:29). Otherwise,

---

15. The word *yeta'arehu/yeto'orehu* means "he marks it out," referring to a person who is fashioning an idol. In his comment on Isa. 44:13, Shadal expresses the view that the word is given two different vocalizations in that verse for the sake of elegant variation. However, it is perhaps not coincidental that the words *to'ovdem, no'ovdem,* and *yeto'orehu* are all connected with idolatry. Cassuto's comment on Exod. 20:5 asserts that the vocalization of *to'ovdem* is "intended to express contempt... as though to indicate that the worship of idols does not merit the honorable name of 'service' but a distorted form of it."

one [may experience this emotion] upon seeing others causing any sort of pain to a third party, as in, "I am jealous [*kinneti*] for Jerusalem and for Zion with a great jealousy [*kin'ah*], and I am very sore displeased with the nations that are at ease; for I was but a little displeased, and they helped for evil" (Zech. 1:14-15).

Thus, the most basic meaning of the word *kin'ah* is merely "extreme anger." Maimonides (in *Guide for the Perplexed* 1:36) wrote that in all of the Torah and Prophets, the terms *ḥaron af* and *ka'as* ("anger") and *kin'ah* are never found [with respect to God] except in connection with [His reaction to] idolatry. In response, Nachmanides cited the phrases "And the Lord became kindled with wrath [*va-yiḥar af*] against Moses" (Exod. 4:14); "The Lord showed Himself angry [*va-yiḥar af*] to them [i.e., Aaron and Miriam]" (Num. 12:9); and "My wrath is kindled [*ḥarah appi*] against you and your two friends [i.e., against Eliphaz, Bildad, and Zophar]" (Job 42:7), but he concluded, "However, this is correct with respect to the term *kin'ah*," i.e., it is true that this term never appears except in connection with idolatry.

I say, however, that even this is not true, for we find, "The Lord is a jealous [*kanno*] and avenging God" (Nah. 1:2), where the prophet is speaking against Assyria, which did evil to Israel; it was for this evil that there was jealousy and vengeance, not on account of the idolatry that Assyria had committed, for (as per Nachmanides himself) Scripture records "jealousy" on the part of God only in connection with Israel's idolatry, not with that of the other nations.

Even though the present verse [Exod. 20:5] speaks of idolatry, it nevertheless seems to me that the phrases "a jealous God" and "demands account of the sins of the fathers" refer not only to idolatry, but are used in a general way, so as to say that He is an avenging and wrathful God; that is, a person who commits grievous sins is punished by Him with grievous blows, as if He were a human being whose anger was aroused.

**demands account of the sins of the fathers.** There is no doubt that one cannot conceive of a God Who is One, the Lord of all, all-knowing and all-Provident, Who rewards and punishes, without also believing that He is a just and true Judge—as Abraham said, "Shall the Judge of all the earth not do justice?" (Gen. 18:25). Moses, too, said, "The Fortress—immaculate is His work, for all His ways are justice. He is a God of loyalty, there is no falsehood in Him; just and upright is He" (Deut. 32:4).

However, the punishment of children for the sins of their fathers does not conform to true justice. The Torah itself warns judges not to judge in

## *Yitro*

this manner ("Let the fathers not be made to die for the children, and let the children not be made to die for the fathers," Deut. 24:16). Nevertheless, we see that it was a widespread belief among the Israelites that children were punished for their fathers' sins, to the extent that it became a proverb, "The fathers have eaten sour grapes, and the children's teeth are set on edge" (Jer. 31:28, Ezek. 18:2). Similarly, the Psalmist said [of a wicked man], "Let the iniquity of his fathers be brought to remembrance unto the Lord, and let not the sin of his mother be blotted out" (Ps. 109:14), and the Mourner said, "Our fathers have sinned, and are not; and we have borne their iniquities" (Lam. 5:7). There are many other such statements in the Scriptures.

In contrast, however, we see the Ezekiel strives to put the above-mentioned proverb to rest, and says, "The soul that sins, it shall die; the son shall not bear the iniquity of the father with him" (Ezek. 18:20). Likewise, Jeremiah declares that in future days this proverb will no longer be said (Jer. 31:28, 29). The Sages offered the explanation that demanding account of the sins of the fathers from the children occurs [only] when the children adhere to their fathers' actions, while Ezekiel's statement obtains when they do not adhere to their fathers' actions (*Berakhot* 7a).

One may still ask, however, "When the children adhere to their fathers' actions, does God punish the children more severely than they deserve for their own wickedness, or not?" If their punishment is not more severe than they themselves deserve, then there is no demanding account of the fathers' sins, but if their punishment is greater than they themselves deserve, then this is a perversion of justice.

Maimonides (*Guide* 1:54) says that "demanding account of the fathers' sins" means only that one of God's commandments is that in the case of an *ir ha-niddaḥat* (a city condemned for idolatry), "You shall strike the inhabitants of that city at the edge of the sword" (Deut. 13:16), including the children who have not sinned. You can see, however, how forced and far-fetched this explanation is. Besides, there is no proof for the idea that this principle applies only with respect to idolatry. Even though it is mentioned in connection with idolatry here, we find it also among the Thirteen Divine Attributes (Exod. 34:7), and there it does not refer to idolatry, but is stated in a general way. Who would think that one of the Thirteen Attributes refers only to one particular commandment [i.e., *ir ha-niddaḥat*], and one that rarely— and perhaps never—was put into practice? Besides, if "demanding account of the fathers' sins" referred to one particular commandment, it would be only fitting for the principle of "exercising benevolence up to the thousandth descendants" (below, v. 6) to refer to a single commandment as well; but just as the one idea is unlikely, so is the other.

# Shadal on Exodus

As I see it, the meaning of this verse is certainly that even from righteous children, God demands account of the sins of the fathers. Such was the belief of our ancestors, as it was said, "A righteous one who suffers evil—this is the righteous son of a wicked man" (*Berakhot* 7a). One senses [empirically] that this is so, for in countless positive and negative ways, a parent bestows things on a child, and a parent's actions, ways, and deeds inevitably cause good or evil to the offspring.

This phenomenon is one of the secrets of the hidden Providence behind all the events that occur in the world. God arranged this so that people should fear Him, for every father loves his offspring, and the concern that his sins might bring evil even to his children will restrain him, to a small or great extent, from always following his heart's resolve. Even if it does not restrain him, those who see his children laid low on account of his sins will raise a bitter cry against him; he will become a proverb and a byword, and many will see and hear this and refrain from his ways.

However, this evil that befalls the children on account of their fathers' sins is not an absolute or constant evil, "for He makes sore, and binds up; He wounds, and His hands make whole" (Job 5:18). No absolute evil comes forth from the Divine hand that controls all the events of our lives, and it is not beyond His power to draw forth great good from the depths of evil and woe. There is much more to be said about this, but here is not the place for it.

In sum, demanding account of the fathers' sins from the children is not for the purpose of taking vengeance on the wicked, but rather to benefit humankind by causing them to refrain from sin. Thus, it does not in fact constitute a perversion of strict justice. If a wicked person's child were to weigh the evil and good that befalls him from the day of his birth to the day of his death, it would become clear to him that no injustice will have been done to him, Heaven forbid, but rather a few dismaying evils and woes designed to keep a person far from sin.

It is for this reason that flesh-and-blood man is admonished not to punish children on account of their fathers, for a human being lacks the power to bind up the wound that he inflicts. Yet that which would be unrighteousness in flesh and blood is true justice in the Lord of all, Who holds all in His hand.

What I have said is clearly supported by the case of the wicked child of a righteous parent. Here (next v.) it says, "And with My friends... I exercise benevolence up to the thousandth descendants," and similarly we find it said by David, "Forever will I keep him for My mercy... his seed also will I make to endure forever" (Ps. 89:29-30)—but do wicked children escape punishment for their sins because of this? "If his children forsake My law...

## Yitro

Then I will visit their transgression with the rod, and their iniquity with strokes" (Ps. 89:31, 33).

So it is with the nation as a whole: God made a covenant with Abraham and chose his descendants, and He will never despise or reject them. But has He never punished them for their sins because of this? Thus it is clear that God's love for the patriarchs does not pervert strict justice or the letter of the law. If this is true of His benevolence, how much more so is it true of His chastisements? (And these verses themselves indicate that His benevolence is greater by far, for the demanding account of the fathers' sins falls only upon the children, grandchildren, and great-grandchildren, while His benevolence extends to "the thousandth descendants," that is, to the thousandth generation.) Surely there is no doubt that when God demands account of the fathers' sins from the children, He does not thereby pervert anyone's justice, for the scales of justice are God's, and He has many agents at His disposal to accomplish this demanding of account in order to admonish humankind, without doing actual injustice to the children.

In the days of Jeremiah and Ezekiel, when the prophets told the people that God was casting them from His presence because of the sins of the king Manasseh, who caused Israel to sin, it became a proverb among the people that "the fathers have eaten sour grapes, and the children's teeth are set on edge." However, for some of the people this became a stumbling-block for sin, discouraging them from repentance. For this reason Ezekiel had to rise up against this proverb and remind the people that "the Fortress—immaculate is His work, for all His ways are justice," that a child will not bear an absolute or constant punishment for his father's sin, but "the soul that sins, it shall die," that one who does not adhere to his father's sins shall surely live, and thus it behooves them to return to God so that He will take mercy on them. As he concludes, "Return and turn yourselves... Cast away from you all your transgressions... for why should you dies, O house of Israel? For I have no pleasure in the death of him who dies... turn yourselves, and live" (Ezek. 18:30-32).

My statement above, that the demanding account of the fathers' sins is a phenomenon that can be sensed, is similar to Gersonides' comment that the fathers' punishment continues against their children as a matter of fate, as in, "Our fathers have sinned, and are not; and we have borne their iniquities." However, in the year 5594 (1834) I challenged his view and said that the expression "demands account of the sins of the fathers from the children" (*poked avon avot al banim*) does not convey the meaning that the punishment continues against the children by [mere] fate, but rather than God brings punishment against the children with deliberate intent; cf. "I will make them pay for [*u-fakadti aleihem*] their sin" (Exod. 32:34); "And I will punish him [*u-fakadti alav*] for his ways" (Hosea 4:9). The term *pekudah* itself signifies deliberate punishment and not a chance evil: "The days of visitation [*ha-pekudah*] are come, the days of recompense are come" (Hosea 9:7); "And what will you do in the day of visitation [*pekudah*]" (Isa. 10:3).

Now, however, in the year 5605 (1845), I see that it is in fact the Torah's way to describe for us good and evil as descending from Heaven by way of deliberate reward or punishment, even though they come naturally in the way of the world. In truth, nothing in the world happens by "fate," but all follows from His causation, and everything traces back to the Prime Cause (see *Kuzari* 5:9[-10]). However, in order to admonish humankind and direct them on the proper path, God framed the laws of nature in such a way that the sins of the father would cause evil to his descendants. Moreover, in order to admonish the children of Israel, the Torah described God as a jealous, vengeful, and angry God, and said that He demanded account of the fathers' sins from the children, as if He did this by way of vengeance and anger, even though such things would occur only through natural processes and not, Heaven forbid, for the sake of vengeance; rather, all would be for the [ultimate] benefit of humankind.

Even when the Torah was compelled to describe God as vengeful and angry, at once it turned to describe for us how much greater was His benevolence than His retribution, by adding, "I exercise benevolence up to the thousandth descendants." This, indeed, is the cardinal principle of the entire Torah, to let us know that God exercises benevolence, justice, and righteousness in the world, for in these qualities He delights—that is, it is His will that one should adhere to God's way by behaving toward one's fellow with justice (i.e., meting out to every person what is due him) and with righteousness (i.e., bestowing on him what he ought to receive beyond the letter of the law).

**with My enemies** *(le-son'ai).* "With My enemies I so practice, to demand account of their sins from their children." Similarly, "With My friends [*le-ohavai*]... I exercise benevolence up to the thousandth descendants" (below, v. 6); i.e., "With My friends I so practice, to exercise benevolence with their children to the thousandth generation." The words *le-son'ai* and *le-ohavai* refer back to "the fathers" (as per Gersonides), not to "the children" (as was the view of Ibn Ezra, Rashbam, and perhaps also Rashi).

## Yitro

The Sages of the Talmud, who said that [God demands account of the fathers' sins from the children] when the children adhere to the ways of their fathers (*Berakhot* 7a), did not thereby interpret *le-son'ai* [as referring to "the children"], but merely meant to explain the verse as saying that such demanding of account occurs only when the children adhere to such ways. Similarly, Onkelos translated *le-son'ai* as *le-san'ai* [the Aramaic equivalent of *le-son'ai*] and then added the phrase (by way of supplement, not to interpret *le-son'ai*) *kad meshallemin benayya lemiḥtei batar avahat'hon* ("when the children follow exactly after their fathers to sin"). This supplementary phrase is not intended (as Mendelssohn and perhaps even Rashi thought) to interpret *le-son'ai* as meaning "if the children are My enemies," for if this were so, Onkelos ought to have omitted the word *le-san'ai* altogether, since the *kad meshallemin* phrase itself would have served as the interpretation of the word *le-son'ai*.

I will not conceal the fact that in a manuscript Targum on parchment in my possession, the word *le-san'ai* is missing but added in the margin. This, however, is nothing but a scribal error, for I looked in the *parashah* of *Va-ethannan* [where the phrase ending *le-son'ai* appears again (Deut. 5:9) in the repetition of the Ten Commandments], and there the word *le-san'ai* is not missing from the Targum.

I hereby revoke what I wrote about "the sins of the fathers" in *Ohev Ger*, p. 19.[16] The phrase "And they will confess their sins, and those of their fathers" (Lev. 26:40) is to be taken literally, as referring to "their sins" on the one hand and "those of their fathers" on the other; i.e., they will confess the sins that they committed, as well as those that were not committed by them, but by their fathers. So we find explicitly stated in Neh. 9:2: "And the seed of Israel... confessed their sins, and the iniquities of their fathers," which is followed by a lengthy recording of the fathers' sins in vv. 16-35.

Thus, the phrase in Jer. 14:20, "We acknowledge, O Lord, our wickedness, the iniquity [*avon*] of our fathers," is to be understood as missing a conjunctive *vav*: "our wickedness, *and* the iniquity [*va-avon*] of

---

16. There, Shadal says, " 'The sins of the fathers' is an expression which means, in Hebrew, not the sins that the fathers committed, but the sins that the children commit as a legacy from their fathers," in emulation of their fathers' behavior. In support of this interpretation, Shadal cites Lev. 26:40, "And they will confess their sins, and those of their fathers," claiming that the latter phrase means "those sins that they learned from their fathers." He also cites the verse, "We acknowledge, O Lord, our wickedness, the iniquity of our fathers," (Jer. 14:20), claiming that the lack of a conjunctive means that the sons are confessing that they themselves have committed "the iniquity of our fathers."

our fathers." The meaning in all of these verses is that since it is God's way to demand account of the fathers' sins from the children, one who confesses should confess not only his own sins, but also his fathers' sins, for he is liable for punishment for these as well; with confession, prayer, and repentance, he will achieve atonement for both sets of sins.

My friend, the noted scholar R. Isaac Reggio, writing in *Bikkurei ha-Ittim* 5606 (1845), seized upon my interpretation in *Ohev Ger*, adopting what I have [since] renounced, and completely denied the concept of the punishment of children for their fathers' sins. With regard to David's statement, "Let the iniquity of his fathers be brought to remembrance to the Lord, and let not the sin of his mother be blotted out" (Ps. 109:14), and Isaiah's statement, "Prepare slaughter for his children for the iniquity of their fathers" (14:21), he claimed that these were merely poetic expressions. This, however, is no answer, for from the utterances of poets of every nation and language we learn what the beliefs of that nation were in the time of those poets. If, in David's time, the belief in the punishment of children for their fathers' sins had not been widespread, how would it have occurred to him to make such a strange statement as "Let the iniquity of his fathers be brought to remembrance"?

In a similar vein, the scholar Gesenius, in his commentary on Isaiah, wrote that even if the verse "Your dead shall live, my dead bodies shall arise" (26:19) is to be understood as a poetic expression (as it is in fact), nevertheless it serves as proof that the belief in the resurrection of the dead was common in Israel in the writer's time.

However, my friend the noted scholar [Reggio] chose to twist the verses that he cited for the well-intentioned purpose of removing a complaint against our God, and in order to bring the Torah into agreement with philosophy. However, on the one hand, none of this is sufficient to remove the complaint, for the fact that children suffer for their fathers' sins can be sensed [empirically], and even if this concept were not written in the Torah, the problem of the suffering of the righteous would still remain. And on the other hand, I have already anticipated and answered this complaint by saying, "This evil that befalls the children on account of their fathers' sins is not an absolute or constant evil..." [see above].

Reggio said that even if it occasionally happens, for some particular reason, that a righteous person suffers as a result of the evil deeds of others, it still would be impossible to attribute to the Eternal God, Whose ways are all just, this characteristic of always punishing children for their fathers' sins. However, I say that this distinction between the usual and the unusual is nothing but a vain consolation; if we assume that sometimes an injustice occurs in the world and a righteous person suffers, even if this happens once in a thousand years, we have denied the doctrine of Divine Providence, for if there is a judging God in the world, surely it would not be beyond His powers to do justice even in this instance.

The truth is that "He Who sits above the circle of the earth, and its inhabitants are as grasshoppers" (Isa. 40:22) knows that there is no injustice in the world, neither always nor sometimes. Those who make a study of history understand that everything that has happened has been only for good, and that even if it seemed to people who lived during times of persecution (such as those of the Emperor Nero, Attila, Robespierre, and their ilk) that they were undergoing cruel injustice, it became clear after some time that all was for the [ultimate] good of the human race. So too, the demanding of account for the fathers' sins from the children is for the good of the human race. Even if it seems unjust in our eyes, it is not so in truth, "for He makes sore, and binds up; He wounds, and His hands make whole" (Job 5:18), as I have written above.

The *Me'ammer* says (on Lev. 20:5) that the demanding of account of the fathers' sins from the children means that [a wicked person's] children and grandchildren, and if he lives to see them, his great-grandchildren, will all die within his sight. However, the sense of the verse is not that they will die, but that they will be punished. If it were as he says, the verse would have said, "They will die childless." Rather, demanding account of the fathers' sins undoubtedly refers to punishment of the children, not punishment of the fathers.

**20:6. "And with My friends and observers of My precepts, I exercise benevolence up to the thousandth descendants.**

*I exercise benevolence.* "With My enemies, I demand account of their sins from their children, grandchildren, and great-grandchildren, but with My friends I exercise benevolence *la-alafim*," that is, to the descendants after a thousand generations, as is specified elsewhere (Deut. 7:9), "Who adheres to the promise and maintains benevolence to those who love Him and observe His precepts, for a thousand generations [*le-elef dor*]."

*up to the thousandth descendants (la-alafim).* *Alafim* is an adjective, like *shilleshim* and *ribbe'im* (lit., "third-generation" and "fourth-generation" descendants) (above, v. 5). The noun *banim* ("children"), which appears in the previous verse, is omitted here. The meaning is "thousandth descendants," "members of the thousandth generation" (Rashbam, Mendelssohn). The concept of "exercising benevolence up to the thousandth descendants" is in accordance with what we find with Abraham, who was called *ohavi* ("My friend") (Isa. 41:8; cf. 2 Chron. 20:7), and in whose merit God chose his descendants and made an eternal covenant with him. So also with Phinehas, "This will be for him, and for his progeny after him, a promise of everlasting priesthood" (Num. 2:13), and with David (2 Sam. 7:16, Jer. 33:17). None of this involves any perversion of justice, for any sinners would bear their own punishment, as is specified in 2 Sam. 7:14, "If he commit an iniquity, I will chastise him with the rod of men," and in Ps. 89:31, 33, "If his children forsake My law... Then I will visit their transgression with the rod"—as I have written on the previous verse.

**20:7. "Do not utter the name of the Lord your God (swearing) for falsehood, for the Lord does not leave unpunished one who utters His name for falsehood.**

*Do not utter, etc. (lo tissa).* Lit., "do not bear" on your lips; compare:

- "Nor will I take [*essa*] their names [those of idols] upon my lips" (Ps. 16:4);
- "And that you have taken [*va-tissa*] My covenant in your mouth" (Ps. 50:16).

The verb *nasa* is also found without any [explicit] reference to the "mouth" or "lips," in elliptical phrases such as:

- "Do not utter [*tissa*] false reports" (Exod. 23:1);
- "Nor takes up [*nasa*] a reproach against his neighbor" (Ps. 15:3).

From this usage comes the expression *nasa mashal* ("take up a parable," "utter poesy"), and also the term *massa* ("prophetic utterance," lit., "burden"). In a similar vein is the Latin verb *profero*, indicating "expression," derived from *fero*, "I bear."[17] The idiom *nesi'at shem YHVH* ("uttering the name of the Lord"), however, refers to the mention of God's name by way of an oath, as can be inferred from the context.

*for falsehood (la-shav). Shav* is synonymous with *sheker* ("lie," "falsehood"), but it can also mean something less than a *sheker*, i.e., a statement that cannot

---

17. Elsewhere, however, Shadal rejects this derivation of *massa*. In his comment on Isa. 13:1, he attributes it (with the Latin parallel) to Coccejus, Rosenmueller, and Gesenius, but calls it *hevel* ("nonsense"), asserting that *massa* is used only in connection with prophecy, and usually with a negative message that "burdens" the prophet.

stand, that has no support; such a statement is essentially a *sheker*. Later the term was transferred to denote any untrue statement, even if it has some support.

It seems to me that the original meaning of the word *shav* was "breath," and that it was related to the roots *nashaf, nashav*, and *sha'af* [all meaning "to breathe"]. That which cannot stand or endure was called *shav*, i.e., "breath," just as it was called *ruah* or *hevel*, both of which refer to the "wind" that leaves the mouth, as in, "The wind [*ruah*] shall carry them all away, a breath [*hevel*] shall bear them off" (Isa. 57:13). The expression *hevel peh* ("breath of the mouth") is known in Rabbinic Hebrew and Syriac. Later the term *la-shav* was used in the same sense as *le-ruah* or *la-hevel* [i.e., "for nought," "in vain"], as when a person works toward a certain goal but does not achieve it; for example:

- "In vain [*la-shav*] have I smitten your children; they receive no correction" (Jer. 2:30);
- "In vain [*la-shav*] do you make yourself fair; your lovers despise you" (Jer. 4:30);
- "In vain [*la-shav*] do you use many medicines; there is no cure for you" (Jer. 46:11).

This meaning, however, has no relevance here; if it did, the verse would mean, "Do not swear when you know that you will not be believed, but if you will be believed, you may swear even for falsehood." However, the prohibition of "uttering the name of the Lord *la-shav*" undoubtedly means swearing in His name for falsehood.

Furthermore, the term *shevu'at shav* in the Mishnah (*Shevu'ot* 29a) means a false oath taken to establish an assertion that is known to be untrue. Only in the Jerusalem Talmud do we find that one who swears that "two is two" [i.e., a true but frivolous oath] receives corporal punishment for making a *shevu'at shav*; Maimonides (*Shevuot* 1:4) included this among his four classes of *shevu'at shav*.

It should be noted that in manuscript and early printed versions of Rashi, the only example of *shevu'at shav* given is an oath that "a column of stone is of gold," but the mention of an oath that "[a column] of wood is of wood" is an addition that was inserted by later [copyists].[18] In my opinion, such an oath—which is true but useless and vain—was prohibited only by way of a preventive measure (*seyag*), for even such an oath shows disrespect for God's

---

18. Neither Chavel nor Rosenbaum-Silbermann includes the second type of oath in their editions of Rashi.

honor, and one who is accustomed to swear gratuitously will find it easy to fall into swearing falsely as well. Later on they included within this prohibition even the [mere] mention of God's name for no reason, for this, too, shows disrespect for God's honor, and in particular, the plain meaning of the words *lo tissa et shem* ("do not utter the name") indicates mere mentioning.

Onkelos, in order to avoid repeating the same word, translated the first *la-shav* [in this verse] as *le-maggana* ("in vain"), and the second one as *le-shikra* ("for falsehood"). He [thus] made the prohibition more stringent and expanded it to cover swearing in vain, while alleviating the major penalty, reserving it for false oaths.

***for the Lord does not leave unpunished,*** *etc.* One who swears falsely does not fear human judgment, for people will believe his words, and only rarely will his lying be discovered. Therefore it says that even if he goes unpunished by the judgment of humankind, he will not be left unpunished by the judgment of Heaven.

**20:8. "Remember the Sabbath day, to sanctify it.**

**Remember** *(zakhor) the Sabbath day.* This "remembering" does not mean (as I wrote in *Bikkurei ha-Ittim* 5588 [1827], p. 90), "Remember what you were previously commanded in the desert of Sin, to sanctify the Sabbath day." The term "remembering" *(zekhirah)* does not refer exclusively to the past, but is found also with reference to future events, as in:

- "She was not mindful of [*zakherah*] her end" (Lam. 1:9);
- "Neither did you remember [*zakhart*] the end thereof" (Isa. 47:7);
- "Because he remembered not [*lo zakhar*] to do kindness" (Ps. 109:16);
- "In wrath remember [*tizkor*] compassion" (Hab. 3:2).

[Here, too,] *zakhor* refers to the future, as does *shamor* ("observe") [the verb that takes the place of *zakhor* in the restatement of this commandment in Deut. 5:12]. In other words, "Place the Sabbath day on your heart, so that you anticipate when it should come in order to sanctify it; let it not be removed from your heart so that you profane it out of forgetfulness."

The Kiddush that the Sages instituted [to be recited at the beginning of the first Sabbath meal] is analogous to all the blessings that are recited in connection with *mitsvot*, in that the Sages required it to be said just before the performance of the *mitsvah*, so that the *mitsvah* should not be done by rote; rather, one should place it upon his heart that God so commanded, and should perform the deed with the intention of doing the will of his Creator.

## Yitro

***to sanctify it*** *(lekaddesho).* To distinguish it from the other days, not to use it for your own benefit to do all your work, but to dedicate it to Heaven like a sacrifice or a tribute *(terumah).* That is, withdraw your hand from making use of it for your own needs and business, and let it be wholly set apart for the honor of God; rest on that day in honor of the God Who commanded you to so rest.

**20:9. "Six days shall you labor, and you shall do all your work.**

***Six days shall you labor...*** The end of the verse explains the beginning: "Six days shall you labor, that is, you shall do all your work, everything that is necessary for you to do."

**20:10. "But the seventh day is Sabbath, in honor of the Lord your God; (on it) you shall not do any labor, neither you, nor your son, nor your daughter, nor your manservant, nor your maidservant, nor your beast, nor the wanderer who is in your cities.**

***you shall not do any labor, neither you*** *(attah,* masc.). This commandment undoubtedly encompasses both husband and wife, for with respect to minors it mentions "your son" and "your daughter," and with respect to servants, "your manservant" and "your maidservant." Thus the woman is equal to the man, and a wife is a free agent like her husband; if the wife were subordinate to her husband like a maidservant, it would have been necessary to caution the man as to the woman's [entitlement to] rest, just as he was cautioned as to his children's and servants' rest, for they are not free agents. Similarly, with all the *mitsvot* of the Torah, the text speaks in masculine gender, but women, too, are included. However, the Sages exempted women from the positive *mitsvot* that are time-bound *(she-ha-zeman gerama);* apparently, in their times the status of women had changed, and men had been laying a heavier yoke upon them.

**20:11. "For in six days the Lord made the heaven and the earth, the sea and all that is in them, and He rested on the seventh day; therefore the Lord blessed the Sabbath day, and declared it holy.**

***For in six days...*** Not one of the Ten Commandments has a reason spelled out for it. However, some of them have a reward or punishment specified: "For I, the Lord your God, am a jealous God..."; "for the Lord does not leave unpunished..."; "so that your days may be prolonged," etc. Here, too, no reason at all is specified for the commandment of the Sabbath, for it does not say, "So that you may remember that the Lord made the heaven and the earth in six days."

In Deuteronomy it is written, "And you shall remember that you were a slave in the land of Egypt, and the Lord your God brought you out of there with a powerful hand and with an outstretched arm; therefore the Lord your God commanded you to make the day of Sabbath" (Deut. 5:15). But even this is not (as I thought in *Bikkurei ha-Ittim* 5588 [1827], p. 91) the actual reason for which He commanded us to observe the Sabbath, just as it is unlikely that the reason we were commanded not to pervert the judgment of a foreigner or an orphan was in order that we remember the exodus from Egypt, even though it is written, "Do not pervert the judgment of the foreigner (or of the) orphan, and do not hold in pledge the garment of the widow. And you shall remember that you were a slave in Egypt, and the Lord, your God, freed you from there; *therefore* I command you to do this thing" (Deut. 24:17-18). Likewise with the *mitsvah* associated with the feast of Shavuot, "And you shall rejoice before the Lord, your God, you and your son and your daughter, and your manservant and your maidservant, and the Levite… and the foreigner and the orphan and the widow…" (Deut. 16:11-12).

These [*mitsvot*, with their reminders that "you were slaves,"] shed light on this [*mitsvah* of the Sabbath] (as per my friend, the scholar Reggio, in his commentary to *Behinat ha-Dat*, p. 63): each time that Scripture issues a command involving compassion, mercy, and assistance for foreigners and slaves, it adds a reference to the exodus from Egypt, as if to say, "You, too, were a slave and a foreigner in Egypt, and therefore the obligation falls upon you, more than any other human being, to show compassion for foreigners and strangers, to refrain from perverting their judgment, to give them furnishings of your possessions, to leave over young grapes for them, to gladden their hearts on your festivals, and so on." If so [says Reggio] we can infer that in the latter Commandments [i.e., the version in Deuteronomy], the only reason that the exodus from Egypt had to be mentioned was to go with the statement, "So that your manservant and your maidservant may rest like you" (Deut. 5:14). Therefore it is proper to say that the exodus from Egypt is given as the reason only for the command to give rest to slaves [and not for any of the other aspects of Sabbath observance].

The way I see it, the expressions "therefore [*al ken*] the Lord your God commanded you" and "therefore [*al ken*] I command you," as used in all these *mitsvot*, does not mean "so that you should remember the exodus from

## Yitro

Egypt," for remembering the exodus is not at all the reason for these *mitsvot*, nor even for giving rest to the manservant and maidservant. Rather, the meaning is that God knows that you will remember that you were a foreigner and a slave, and therefore you will not find it difficult to deal mercifully with foreigners, slaves, and poor people, for your heart (after all that you suffered) tends toward compassion and kindness. Thus it is that God commanded you to do all these merciful acts, and He did not refrain from so commanding you lest you find their burden too heavy. Rather, He is sure that you will act with a whole heart and a willing soul.

It follows that even in Deuteronomy, there is no mention at all of any reason for the *mitsvah* of the Sabbath. Elsewhere it is written, "For it [the Sabbath] is a signal for all the ages to come [of the alliance] between Me and you, so that it may be known that I, the Lord, have declared you holy" (Exod. 31:13). This, however, is [merely a way of] emphasizing the greatness of God's *mitsvah*, but is not actually a reason for it, since any number of things could just as well have served as a "signal" between Him and us.

This is Maimonides' opinion as to the reason for the Sabbath: "The object of the Sabbath is obvious, and requires no explanation. The rest it affords to man is known: one-seventh of the life of every man, whether great or small, passes thus in comfort, and in rest from trouble and exertion. This the Sabbath effects in addition to the perpetuation and confirmation of the grand doctrine of the Creation" (*Guide* 3:43).

As to this opinion, one might ask, "What need was there to command free people to rest?" Would they not cease work whenever they wished? It would have been sufficient to command a cessation of work for slaves and animals (and this question would be even stronger according to the opinion of the scholar Jost, who said (*Allgemeine Geschichte des Israëlitischen Volkes*, part 1, p.112) that the main reason [for the Sabbath] was to give rest to slaves and animals).

Therefore it seems appropriate to me to distinguish between the work cessation of a [free] Israelite and that of his slave or animal, for the latter is intended for its own sake as a matter of compassion and kindness, while the work cessation of the Israelites themselves on the seventh day is likewise, without a doubt, meant for their own benefit, but not merely so that they should rest, given that they would be free to rest any time they so desired. Rather, the purpose is that they should all rest *on one particular day*, in order that they should be able to gather together to eat and drink and converse with one another, so that love might increase among them, and also that they should be able to assemble in houses of worship and hear Torah from the mouths of the Sages.[19]

It is for this reason that the verse here says *va-yannaḥ* ("and He rested") and not *va-yishbot* ("and He ceased work"), in order to remind Israel that they are not only to cease from their labor, but they are also to rest and call the Sabbath an *oneg*, "delight" (Isa. 58:13); this will induce them to gather in groups in order to take delight in the day of rest. To this benefit, God added another: that the Sabbath day should serve as a reminder of the Creation, so that the people should remember that One God alone created the heaven and the earth, and that there is no god beside Him. On account of His great affection for this *mitsvah*, because of the powerful social benefit that results from it, as well as its serving as a reminder of the great principle of the Unity of God—and also because it is a law pertaining exclusively to Israel, for there was nothing like it among any of the ancient idolatrous peoples—God said that it was a "signal" between Him and us.

**20:12. "Honor your father and your mother, so that your days may be prolonged on the land that the Lord your God is about to give you.**

***Honor your father and your mother.*** Behave toward them as one would behave toward an honored and important person.

***so that (le-ma'an) your days may be prolonged.*** This does not mean "with the intention that your days may be prolonged," but rather, "for by this means will your days be prolonged." Often the word *le-ma'an* is used to indicate not an intended purpose, but rather a result, as in, "And I have done that which is evil in Your sight, that [*le-ma'an*] You may be justified when You speak" (Ps. 51:6); "And so the word of the law is unto them precept by precept... line by line... that [*le-ma'an*] they may go and fall backward" (Isa. 28:13).

***may be prolonged (ya'arikhun).*** The Heb. is an intransitive verb, even though it is in the *hif'il* (causative) conjugation. A similar phenomenon is found in the phrases "they shall be as white [*yalbinu*] as snow" and "though they be red [*ya'adimu*] like crimson" (Isa. 1:18).

---

19. The value of establishing a single common day of rest has similarly been recognized by the United States Supreme Court: "Obviously, a State is empowered to determine that a [mere] rest-one-day-in-seven statute... would not provide for a general cessation of activity, a special atmosphere of tranquility, a day which all members of the family or friends and relatives might spend together." (*McGowan v. Maryland* (1961), 366 U.S. 420.) Ironically, this argument was directed against the claim that a Sunday closing law was harmful to Orthodox Jewish storeowners.

## *Yitro*

***so that your days may be prolonged on the land,*** *etc.* The intended reference is to the nation as a whole, that they should not be exiled from their land (Ibn Ezra). Fulfillment of this commandment would lead to perfection of the family unit, which would allow for the perfection of the political unit, and the perfection of the political unit would foster concord among the people and lead their youth to accept the moral teachings of their elders (Gersonides). This is the principal strength of a nation, aside from the Divine aid that accompanies those who do His will. This reward is conferred not on the individual, but on the public, even though the commandment is upon each individual.

**20:13. "Do not commit murder. Do not commit adultery. Do not steal. Do not give false testimony against your neighbor.**

***Do not commit murder*** *(lo tirtsaḥ)*. One who kills another person intentionally and of his own volition is called a *rotse'aḥ*. This excludes an agent of the court who kills another under the authorization and command of the judges, and not of his own volition

***Do not commit adultery*** *(lo tin'af)*. *Ni'uf* (adultery) necessarily involves a married woman, as it is said, "And when one commits adultery [*yin'af*] with a married woman—commits adultery with the wife of his neighbor!—the adulterer and the adulteress shall be put to death" (Lev. 20:10); "You, wife, who commit adultery [*ha-mena'efet*] who take strangers instead of your husband" (Ezek. 16:32) (Rashi).

Ibn Ezra erred in contradicting this idea, finding support from the phrase "and she committed adultery [*va-tin'af*] with stones and with stocks" (Jer. 3:9). He did not understand that this is merely an allegory referring to idol-worship, for the nation is spoken of as if it were a woman married to God Himself, as is made clear throughout this section (Jeremiah 3).[20]

***Do not steal*** *(lo tignov)*. The taking of others' money without their knowledge. The Sages made this an admonition against kidnapping, for which a penalty is stated (Exod. 21:16) without a specific admonition. According to the plain meaning (*peshat*), this is an admonition against all types of theft, with their penalties specified below, each type separately.

---

20. Ibn Ezra understood *ni'uf* as a general offense synonymous with *zenut* ("unchastity").

# Shadal on Exodus

***Do not give** (lo ta'aneh) **false testimony against your neighbor** (be-re'akha).* [The word *be-re'ahka* is equivalent to] *neged re'akha* [i.e., *anah be-* means "to testify against"]; cf. "Here I am, witness against me [*anu vi*]" (1 Sam. 12:3).

*false testimony (ed shaker,* lit., "false witness"). Kimhi, Rosenmueller, and Gesenius understood *ed* as the equivalent of *edut* ("testimony"). Ibn Ezra, after many years of examination, interpreted the verse as meaning, "You, false witness, shall not testify against your neighbor." This is nonsense, for if one does not testify, how can he be a false witness? In his short commentary, Ibn Ezra rendered the verse as if it said *Lo ta'aneh be-re'akha* ve-attah *ed shaker,* that is, "Do not testify against your neighbor *while you are* a false witness"; "Do not testify against your neighbor as a liar." Similarly, Mendelssohn interpreted the verse as, "Do not testify against your neighbor anything that will render you a false witness."

It seems to me that the correct interpretation is, "Do not testify against your neighbor *the testifying of* a false witness," for the verb [here, *ta'aneh*] sometimes carries with it a noun [unstated but understood, here *aniyyat*, "the testifying of"] that is derived from it, as in *pen ishan ha-mavet* (Ps. 13:4, lit., "lest I sleep death"), meaning "lest I sleep *the sleep of* death" (*pen ishan shenat ha-mavet*). As Ibn Ezra commented on that verse, "For nouns come on the strength of verbs [*ki ha-shemot be-ko'ah ha-po'alim*]."

A similar instance is found below: "If you take in pledge [*ḥavol taḥbol*] the garment of [*salmat*] your neighbor, before the sun sets you shall return it [*teshivennu*] to him" (Exod. 22:25). There, the masculine suffix in the word *teshivennu* refers back [not to the feminine noun *salmat*, but rather] to the [missing but understood masculine] noun *ḥavol* ("pledge"), which comes on the strength of the verb *ḥavol taḥbol*. So also, "He has given the blessing (*u-verekh*, lit., "and He has blessed"), and I cannot take it back" (Num. 23:20), which means, "He has blessed with a blessing [*u-verekh berakhah*], and I cannot take back that blessing." And similarly, "But in the multitude of counselors [*yo'atsim*] it is established" (Prov. 15:22), meaning, "In the multitude of those who give counsel [*yo'atsim etsah*], counsel is established."

**20:14. "Do not desire the house of your neighbor; do not desire the wife of your neighbor, his manservant, his maidservant, his ox, his ass, or anything belonging to your neighbor."**

## Yitro

***Do not desire*** *(lo taḥmod), etc. Ḥemdah* is a desire for something that is currently in the possession of others and is forbidden to us, that is, it is not for sale. Although all such desire arises of itself in a person's heart upon seeing the desired object, it is within the person's power and will to suppress the desire as soon as it is born and to put it far from his heart, in the knowledge that attaining the desired object is impossible for him. Otherwise, he may preserve the desire in his heart and stoke its flame until he puts it into practice, finding that doing so is possible for him.

After God commanded "Do not commit adultery" and "Do not steal," thus forbidding to us anything that belongs to others, He told us that any possession of our neighbor must be seen by us as an unattainable object. By virtue of the fact that God commanded us not to take anything that is not ours, we will not desire it. Anyone who indulges in *ḥemdah* despises the word of God; injustice is a light thing to him, within the realm of possibility. But to one who fears the word of God, injustice is ruled out, and he considers that which is not his as if it were up in heaven, an object that he cannot take and will not desire. The latter person is content with his lot and rejoices in his neighbors' wellbeing, loving them and beloved by them, while the former person spends all his days in a tempest of desires and worries, coveting what is not his and doing injustice to his neighbor. Such a person, jealous of others, despising them and despised by them, "shall die for lack of instruction" (Prov. 5:23); "and envy slayeth the silly one" (Job 5:2).

See the words of Ibn Ezra, for they are pleasing.[21]

**20:15. All the people perceived the thunders and the flames, the sound of the horn and the mountain in smoke, and the people, seeing this, trembled, and they remained afar.**

***trembled*** *(va-yanu'u).* The verb *no'a* denotes trembling (Rashi, from the Mekhilta), as in, "And his heart trembled [*va-yana*], and the heart of his people, as the trees of the forest tremble [*ke-no'a*] with the wind" (Isa. 7:2); "The earth reels to and fro [*no'a tanu'a*] like a drunken man" (Isa. 24:20). This does not mean that the people "shook themselves" backward; rather (as per my student, R. David Hazak), this verse does not describe what happened after the utterance of the Ten Commandments, but indicates that when the

---

21. Ibn Ezra's comment on this verse includes the striking parable of the peasant who sees a beautiful princess but, knowing that he can never have her, does not desire her, just as he does not desire wings to fly off to heaven. Note that even in the case of Ibn Ezra, Shadal is willing to give credit where credit is due.

people came toward God and heard the thunders and saw the flames, they trembled and stayed far back, not approaching the mountain even up to the location that was permitted to them, as it is subsequently specified, "The people remained afar, and Moses approached toward the thick cloud" (below, v. 18) (this seems also to be the opinion of Rabbenu Bahya).

**20:16. And they said to Moses, "Speak you with us, and we will listen; and let God not speak with us, so that we do not die."**
**20:17. And Moses said to the people, "Do not be afraid, for in order to test you has God come, and so that the fear of Him may be impressed on you, so that you do not sin."**

*in order to test you* (nassot etkhem). It seems to me that this expression of "testing" (*nissayon*) is to be understood in the literal sense,[22] for God wanted to make all of Israel into "a realm of priests and a holy nation" (Exod. 19:6), and it was the custom among the Egyptians that when they would admit a person into their mysteries to make him holy to their gods (*initiatus*), they would test him with various trials and threats; if he showed fear and was unable to withstand all the tests, they would not accept him. The Israelites were indeed very frightened, but they did not turn back to their [the Egyptians'] gods; rather, they stood there to listen to the word of God, thereby showing themselves worthy of being a realm of priests (17 Adar I, 5624 [1864]).

**20:18. The people remained far off, and Moses approached toward the thick cloud, where God was.**
**20:19. And the Lord said to Moses, "So shall you say to the children of Israel: 'You have seen that from the heaven I spoke with you.**

*You have seen that from the heaven...* Without your making any image, or even any sanctuary or house in order to draw the Divine presence into your midst; rather, from the heaven, without any preparation on your part, I spoke with you.

**20:20. "'Do not make (any god) beside Me: gods of silver and gods of gold do not make for yourselves.**

---

22. *Contra* Rashi, who, following the Mekhilta, interpreted *nassot etkhem* as "exalt you," from *nes*, a banner that is held high.

***Do not make (any god) beside Me*** *(lo ta'asun itti).* According to the vocalization [of the word אתי to read *itti*, lit., "with Me"], this means, "Do not make anything to combine with Me," but such a reading does not fit in at all with what comes before or after. It seems to me that it should be read *lo ta'asun oti* [lit., "Do not make Me"], i.e., "Do not make My image," "Do not portray Me in any form." He then goes on to specify, "Gods of silver and gods of gold do not make for yourselves," even as a memento of Heaven (as per Rashbam), with the intention of drawing the Divine influence downward; "You have no need for any of this, but instead, an altar of earth you shall make for Me" (next v.). It should be understood that *itti* is an emended reading (*tikkun*) introduced by the Rabbis, for the expression "Do not make Me" would have been a difficult one for the masses.

**20:21. "'An altar of earth you shall make for Me, on which you shall sacrifice your burnt offerings and your sacrifices of contentment, whether of the flocks or of the herds. In every place that I will assign for you to invoke My name, I will come to you, and I will bless you.**

***An altar of earth you shall make for Me.*** In order to keep away idols and images, God let the people know that they had no need (in order to come close to Him) even for a stone altar, as an earthen altar would suffice for Him.

***In every place that I will assign for you to invoke My name*** *(asher azkir et shemi,* lit., "that I will make My name mentioned"). "That I will establish for you to mention My name, where I will command you to build Me an altar and pray before Me and give thanks to My name." This is what is meant by "mentioning" (*hazkarah*) of the name of God, as in, "But by You only do we make mention of [*nazkir*] Your name" (Isa. 26:13); "But we will make mention of [*nazkir*] the name of the Lord our God" (Ps. 20:8).

**20:22. "'But if you make Me an altar of stone, do not build it of chiseled stones, for raising your sword [the chisel] over the stones, you profane them.**

***do not build it of chiseled stones.*** It seems to me that the reason (as per Rashbam) was to keep away any hint of idol or statue, for if they had been permitted to chisel the altar's stones, they might have also made them in the shape of the sun, the moon, or other forms, and little by little they might have made themselves statues, idols, and cast images.

*for raising your sword, etc.* God ascribed [the reason for] this matter to the characteristic of iron as serving the purpose of killing, and thus not fitting to be used for the stones of an altar. He did not wish to mention the true reason, which was that they should not come to make images; if He had spelled out that the prohibition was for this reason, they would not have troubled themselves about it, for they would have said, "We will chisel the stones, but we will make no images."

**20:23. "'Nor shall you go up by steps upon My altar, so that you do not uncover your shameful parts upon it.'"**

*Nor shall you go up by steps.* This too, it seems to me, was to prevent them from making images in the steps of the altar, and He did not wish to reveal this true reason, but rather gave another reason, i.e., that no shameful parts should be exposed by means of taking broad steps.

# *Mishpatim*

*Hebrew servants, Canaanite slaves • Capital and non-capital offenses • "Eye for eye, tooth for tooth" • The goring ox • Theft, burglary, negligence • Seduction and witchcraft • "Do not oppress the foreigner" • "In what else will he sleep?" • Seeing God's face*

**21:1. "These, then, are the laws that you shall present to them.**

***These, then, are the laws*** *(ha-mishpatim). Mishpat* is a noun formed from a verb [*shafat*, "to judge"], and it means the decision of law that a judge decrees. "Do not commit murder," "Do not commit adultery," and "Do not steal" (Exod. 20:13) are not *mishpatim*; rather, they are great root principles that people do not need to learn from a judge, for everyone acknowledges them. On the other hand, the laws that appear in this section are "branches" that are subject to dispute, concerning which people need a judge to decide the law, and thus they are called *mishpatim*.

Because it is the way of a judge to decide who is obligated to whom, who should give and who should receive, people came to use the word *mishpat* for something pertaining to a particular person or thing—whether for good, as in:

- *ke-mishpat ha banot*, "according to the right of girls" (below, v. 9);
- *mishpat ha-kohanim*, "the right of the priests" (Deut. 18:3);
- *mishpat ha-bekhorah*, "the right of primogeniture" (Deut. 21:17);

—or for ill, as in:

- *mishpat mavet la-ish ha-zeh*, "this man is worthy of death" (Jer. 26:11);

—and even to inanimate objects, as in:

- *ha-mishkan ke-mishpato*, "the tabernacle in the suitable manner" (Exod. 26:30);
- *ke-ḥukkat ha-pesaḥ u-khe-mishpato*, "according to the statute and the law of the paschal sacrifice" (Num. 9:14);
- *ve-niskeihem ke-mishpatam*, "as well as their libations, according to the relative law" (Exod. 29:6).

In all of these cases, the sense is "that which properly pertains to a thing," "that which is *jus* (a prerogative) of that thing."

God, too, has *mishpat*, that is, the things that He wishes us to do for His service, as in *mishpat Elohei ha-arets*, "the manner of the God of the land" (2 Kings 17:26). Similarly, in this section, after He concludes the *mishpatim* between man and his fellow, He records "the manner of the God of the land" as well, and this is, "Six days you shall do your labors, and on the seventh day you shall cease"; "Three times a year you shall celebrate to Me solemn festivals…" (Exod. 23:12-14).

The root *shafat* (which does not occur in Aramaic or Arabic) is derived, it seems to me, from *shevet* ("rod," "staff"), which was the title given to the head of a family, who served as the leader, law officer, and governor of his family members. Thus the [nation's] princes and leaders were called *shevatim*, as in, "Dan will defend his people, as an equal to one of the chiefs of [*shivtei*] Israel" (Gen. 49:16). One who was chosen by the people to perform the functions of a *shevet*—to decree a thing to be established [cf. Job 22:28], so that everyone heeded him as if he were the head of the family—was called (with the exchange of the *vet* for a *fe*) *shofet*.[1]

**that you shall present to them** *(asher tasim lifneihem)*. See above at 19:7.

**21:2. "When you make acquisition of a Hebrew servant, he will serve six years, and in the seventh he will go forth in freedom without paying anything.**

---

1. R. Samson Raphael Hirsch drew a similar connection between the roots *shavat* and *shafat*, understood by him to denote "control" and "create order and harmony," respectively. See Matityahu Clark, *Etymological Dictionary of Biblical Hebrew* (Jerusalem and New York: Feldheim, 1999), pp. 253-254, 268.

## *Mishpatim*

***When you make acquisition...*** The Torah, whose ways are ways of pleasantness and compassion, begins its laws with the law of the manservant and maidservant, who in ancient times were considered as animals, and a judge would not adjudicate their case or plead their cause against their masters.[2]

***a Hebrew servant*** *(eved ivri).* An Israelite; see Rashi and Ibn Ezra.[3]

***When you make acquisition of a Hebrew servant.*** In any manner, whether he sells himself or whether the court sells him; in either case, he goes free after six years. So seems to be the simple meaning of the verse, for the fact that it does not specify how this acquisition is made indicates that whatever the means of acquisition, he goes free after six years.

In the *baraita,* however (*Kiddushin* 14b), this matter is disputed: according to the first opinion, one who sells himself may be sold for six years or more, but one who is sold by the court may be sold for six years only; one who sells himself is not subject to piercing of the ear (below, v. 6), etc. Maimonides (*Avadim* 3:12) decided in accordance with this first opinion, but this is *contra* Rashi, for on Lev. 25:40 he wrote, "'He will serve with you until the year of the Jubilee'... if the jubilee befalls him before six years, the jubilee releases him," and that verse speaks of one who sells himself because of poverty (see my comment on v. 3 below) and, according to the first opinion, is not governed by the six-year rule, for he can sell himself for more than six years.

The words of R. Yohanan ben Zakkai, as they appear in *Kiddushin* 22b and in the Tosefta to *Bava Kamma* 7:2, indicate that even one who sells himself is subject to piercing of the ear, but as his words appear in the Mekhilta, they accord with the first opinion. Rashi (on v. 6, below), in citing R. Yohanan ben Zakkai, included both of his explanations.[4] However, Rashi's

---

2. Under the Jewish judicial system, judges were expected not only to decide cases but also to advance arguments on behalf of a disadvantaged party; see, for example, the comments of Rashi and Mahari (R. Joseph) Kara on Isa. 1:17, "Judge the fatherless, plead for the widow."
3. Rashi rejects the suggestion that the term refers to a non-Israelite servant who has belonged to an Israelite. Ibn Ezra rejects the suggestion that the term refers to a non-Israelite descendant of Abraham.
4. In *Kiddushin,* R. Yohanan says that if the servant refuses to go free at the end of six years, his ear is pierced because it is the ear that heard on Mount Sinai, "For it is to *Me* that the children of Israel are slaves" [Lev. 25:55], and yet he took himself another master (by selling himself). In the Mekhilta, however, R.Yohanan says that the servant's ear is pierced because it is the ear that heard, "Do not steal," and yet he stole and was sold into bondage.

comment on the present verse, "'When you make acquisition' from a court that sold him for his theft," was not intended to imply that one who sells himself is not covered by these laws; rather, his intention was to resolve the [apparent] superfluity of the verses, so as not to render redundant the passage, "And when a brother of yours becomes poor by you [and he is sold to you, you must not hold him in the servitude of a slave…]" (Lev. 25:39).

Here there is no mention at all of the jubilee, which was promulgated subsequently (Leviticus 25); there it states, "And he will serve with you until the year of the Jubilee. Then he will leave your house, together with his children…" (vv. 40-41). After the law of the jubilee was given, it cancelled to some degree the law that preceded it, and thus if the jubilee intervened within a six-year term, the servant went free in that year. Nevertheless, the law of six years was not canceled; the fact that it was written, "And he will serve by you until the year of the Jubilee" did not mean that the servant was obligated to serve beyond six years. We see that Jeremiah reproved his contemporaries with respect to this matter, saying, "Thus says the Lord, the God of Israel: 'I made a covenant with your fathers when I brought them forth… At the end of seven years you shall let go every man his brother that is a Hebrew, that has been sold to you and has served you six years, you shall let him go free from you…'" (Jer. 34:13-14).

Accordingly, the statement, "And he will serve with you until the year of the Jubilee" refers only to a servant whose ear has been pierced because he did not want to go free after six years, but it encompasses also a rule that if the jubilee intervened within [a regular servant's] six years, he would go free.

***in freedom*** *(la-ḥofshi).* The Heb. is a feminine noun, following an Aramaic form; cf. *nevali,* "dunghill" (Dan. 2:5). The Hebrew form would have ended in a *tav* (*ḥofshit*), on the model of *marbit* and *tarbit* ("usury").

**21:3. "If he will have come alone, alone will he go forth; if he is married, his wife will go forth with him.**

***If he will have come alone*** *(be-gappo).* The words *gaf, kaf,* and *ḥaf* all denote a "covering"; the addition of a *nun* yields *kenaf,* also meaning "covering" (Isa. 30:20 [*lo yikkanef,* "He will not hide himself"], and so also in Arabic). From this was derived *kenafayim,* "wings," in Aramaic *gappin,* so called because they cover a bird's body. *Be-gappo* denotes "in his covering," i.e., alone in his own garment (as per Rashi); cf. "With (only) my staff did I pass over this Jordan" (Gen. 32:11).

## Mishpatim

***if he is married.*** According to the plain meaning, his wife comes with him into the master's house and serves with him. This would be proper in the case of one who sells himself, for he can be sold with his wife. However, according to Rashi and some of the Rabbis, who understood this section to refer to one who was sold by the court, it would not have been proper for the wife to be sold for her husband's crime of theft, and for this reason they said, "Who brought her in that she should go forth? Rather, Scripture is indicating that one who acquires a Hebrew servant is obligated to support his wife and children" (Mekhilta; *Kiddushin* 22a). This rule was designed to increase the quality of mercy and compassion among Israel; even in the case of one who sold himself, the Rabbis did not allow the wife to enter into the master's house, but they obligated the master to provide for her and her children. She was to live in her own house, and she, not the master, was entitled to the proceeds of her work. So held Maimonides (*Avadim* 3:2) (although Nachmanides [in his comment on this verse] maintained that the master was entitled to the proceeds of the wife and children's work, except that she was under her own authority and did not enter his house to do his work).

Therefore, on the verse, "Then he will go forth from your house, together with his children" (Lev. 25:41), which undoubtedly refers to one who sells himself due to poverty, R. Simeon (*Kiddushin* 22a, cited by Rashi) says, "If he sold himself, who sold his children? [Rather, from here we learn that the master is obligated to support the servant's children]." However, it appears that just as the Torah permitted a father to sell his minor daughter, it also permitted him to sell himself along with his wife and minor children. It is well known that in ancient times, the father ruled over his household and held their lives in his hands (as is seen from Judah's statement, "Bring her [Tamar] forth and let her be burnt" [Gen. 34:28]). The Torah took this authority away from him and [for example] allowed a rebellious son to be put to death only by judicial decree. Similarly, a man's sale of his wife and children was permitted by the written Torah but forbidden by the Oral Torah. In addition, [the Sages] forbade a master to give a servant a Canaanite bondwoman [as a wife] unless the servant already had a wife and children (*Kiddushin* 20a), and the reason was (according to my student Moses Cohen Porto) that it was not fitting for a servant to beget servants for his master before fulfilling the commandment of *piryah ve-rivyah*, providing children in order to perpetuate his [own] name in Israel.

**21:4. "If his master gives him a woman and she bears him sons or daughters, the woman and her offspring will be her master's, and he will go forth alone.**

*a woman.* A Canaanite bondwoman; see Rashi [who, citing the Mekhilta, points out that a Hebrew bondwoman would go free after no more than six years].

**21:5. "If, however, the servant says, 'I love my master, my wife, and my children; I do not want to go forth in freedom' —**
**21:6. "His master will present him to the tribunal, and having caused him to approach the door, or the doorpost, the master will pierce his ear with an awl, and he will serve him forever.**

*to the tribunal (el ha-elohim,* lit., "to the gods"). To the judges; cf. below, 22:8. The reason is that he must go to the judges and perform the piercing before them, so that if the servant later changes his mind and abhors his servitude, he will not be able to deny that it was of his own free will that he stayed with his master, and he will not be able to go to the judges and complain that his master coerced him into servitude after six years.

*and he will serve him forever (le-olam).* Literally, but afterward the law of the jubilee was promulgated and partly canceled out what was said before; see above, v. 2.

The custom of piercing the ear has been found by world travelers to be practiced among the Persians and Indians, who pierce the ears of children to dedicate them to the service of their gods; in the language of India these children are called Dasa or Dasaia, meaning "slave" (Rosenmueller). Perhaps it was for this reason that God wanted ear piercing to be a symbol of servitude and shame, in order to distance Israel from this idolatrous practice.

According to the Korem (R. Herz Homberg), the piercing was to be a sign that the person was serving not out of obligation, but out of choice and free will.

**21:7. "And if a man sells his daughter for a maidservant, she will not go forth as servants go forth [but she will be married by her master or his son].**

*she will not go forth…* Not like a male Hebrew servant, who goes forth only after six years of servitude. Rather, if the girl is fit to be married before the fulfillment of six years, the master takes her to wife, as is specified below. This does not at all contradict was is said in Deut. 15:12, "When there is sold to you a Hebrew brother of yours, or a Hebrew woman, he [or she] will serve you six years," for there it does not speak of a minor girl who is sold by her father, but it refers to an adult woman who sells herself, and the law of *ye'ud* ("designation") does not apply to her (see next v.).

It is obvious that Scripture is not imposing a stringency on the girl, but is being lenient, for if six years are fulfilled before she shows signs [of puberty], she goes forth free after six.

**21:8. "If she does not please her master, so that he does not designate her to himself, he shall let her be redeemed [by some relative of hers]; but he shall not be master to resell her to a foreign people [to a person from another tribe, and who is not related to her], which would be to betray her.**

*so that he does not designate her to himself* (asher lo ye'adah). As he does not wish to designate her to himself for a wife (Rashbam). The principal meaning follows the word *lo* (לא) as written, but the phrase is abbreviated and its meaning is [as if it were written] *asher lo ye'adah lo* (אשר לא יעדה לו). Thus Aquila, Symmachus, and Theodotian all translated the phrase as "so that he does not (לא) designate her," and so also in the Syriac and Samaritan translations. Even Onkelos may have translated the phrase as די לא קיימינה ליה [similarly following the word לא as written], but [if so] the copyists deleted the word לא to conform to the *keri* [the Masoretic reading, which understands לא to be the homonymous לו, "to him"]. I have since found in a manuscript Targum [Onkelos] from the year 5171 (1411) or perhaps earlier the reading דלא קיימה ליה.

Rashi interpreted the phrase according to the *keri*: "who ought to have designated her to himself [לו]." Ibn Ezra and Nachmanides (also following the *keri*) interpreted this to mean that the master did not find her pleasing after acquiring her for the purpose of marrying her, for one who acquires and Israelite girl does so for that purpose, and as a rule she is designated to him.

*he shall let her be redeemed* (ve-hefdah). [The subject is] "her father"; he is forbidden to let her remain in her master's hands after the master declares that he does not wish to marry her, nor can the father resell her to foreign people, which would be to betray her, for it is betrayal for a man to sell his daughter to one who cannot marry her (Nachmanides), or to one who will not let her go after six years (my student R. Mordecai Mortara).

Because a foreigner would enslave her permanently, he would be able to offer a greater purchase price than an Israelite, who would keep her in servitude for no more than six years. Therefore the Torah had to admonish the father not to say, "I will sell her to a foreigner, who will pay more for her" (the late Jacob Hai Pardo).

Rashi explained the use of the *hif'il* conjugation [in *hefdah*] as indicating that the master was to give her the opportunity to be redeemed and go forth; this is in conformance with Hezekiah (*Kiddushin* 11b). Ibn Ezra was of the opinion that the master was to [actively] seek out her redemption and accept it.

**but he shall not be master to resell her to a foreign people** *(le-am nokhri).* This is an admonition to the court not to sell her to a non-Jew (Mekhilta); that is, the court was not to permit the father to sell her to a non-Jew. Perhaps, having seen that she did not please her master so that he did not designate her to himself, it might have occurred to the father to sell her to a foreigner (my student R. Shabbetai Ancona).

But today, 3 Adar 5599 (1839), it seems to me that the meaning of *ve-hefdah* ("he shall let her be redeemed") is that the master should make an effort to have one of her relatives redeem her; either an uncle, a cousin, any other family member, or any member of her tribe should redeem her. And the phrase "but he shall not be master to resell her to a foreign people [*le-am nokhri*]" means that the father may not sell her to a man from another tribe who is not her relative, for if such a person were to acquire her, he would keep her in servitude, unlike a man from her family, who would redeem and free her or else marry her.

We have seen that the word *am* [usually understood as "people" or "nation"] can denote "tribe," as in:

- "So that you [Jacob] give origin to an aggregate of peoples [*ammim*]" (Gen. 28:3);
- "And I will make you [Jacob] an aggregate of peoples [*ammim*]" (Gen. 48:4);
- "That one [Manasseh], too, will form a people [*am*]" (Gen. 48:19);
- "They [Zebulun and Issachar] invite their peoples [*ammim*] to the sacred mountain" (Deut. 33:19);
- "The princes of the peoples [*ammim*] are gathered together, the people of the God of Abraham" (Ps. 47:10).

We also find the word *nokhri*, meaning "foreigner," may be used to refer even to an Israelite, as in:

- "Yet God gives him not power to eat thereof, but a stranger [*nokhri*] eats it" (Eccl. 6:2);

- "Lest strangers be filled with your strength, and your labors be in the house of an alien [*nokhri*]" (Prov. 5:10);
- "Let another man praise you, and not your own mouth; a stranger [*nokhri*] and not your own lips" (Prov. 27:2);

and similarly, every instance of the word *nokhriyyah* ("foreign woman") in the book of Proverbs.

In ancient times, when people kept genealogical records, each member of a given tribe used to recognize his kinship with another, and it would have been likely that a tribal member would redeem a daughter of his tribe. However, members of two different tribes would not have been considered as relatives; rather, they would have been strangers to one another. Later, with the passage of generations, the sense of kinship between members of a given tribe was forgotten, and even such members were strangers and foreigners to each other, and no man would redeem anyone but his close relative. For this reason the Rabbis were constrained to interpret the phrase *le-am nokhri* as *li-gevar oḥoran* ("to another [Israelite] man") [as per Onkelos], for they knew that any Israelite, even one from the same tribe, would be a "stranger" to the girl and would not redeem her to set her free; rather, if he acquired her, he would keep her in bondage as a maidservant.

**which would be to betray her** *(be-vigdo vah,* lit. "in betraying her"). For if he were to sell her to a *nokhri* who was not of her family, this would constitute a betrayal of her.

**21:9. "If he, then, destines her to his son, the latter will treat her according to the right of girls [that is, as a wife and not as a maidservant].**

*according to the right of girls.* The son who takes her must treat her in the manner of daughters of Israel, that is, [he must provide her with] food, clothing, and cohabitation (Rashi, following the Mekhilta); she is not to be lightly esteemed or degraded by him as a maidservant would be.

**21:10. "If, then, (the master marries her, but) takes (also) another one, he must not diminish her [the first one's] food, clothing, and cohabitation.**

*If, then, (the master...) takes (also) another one.* If the master takes her, but also takes another wife besides her.

***her food*** *(she'erah)*. Her nourishment, as in, "He caused meat [*she'er*] also to rain upon them as the dust" (Ps. 78:27) (Mekhilta, followed by most of the [Jewish] commentators and Rosenmueller and Gesenius). Ibn Ezra explained that food is called *she'er* [lit., "flesh"] because it sustains one's flesh.

***and cohabitation*** *(ve-onatah)*. This is *derekh erets* (coitus), according to R. Josiah, followed by most of the commentators. R. Josiah, in the Mekhilta, interpreted the word *onatah* in the sense of *va-yishkav otah va-ye'anneha*, "and he lay with her, doing violence to her" (Gen. 34:2), but this is most unlikely.

Ibn Ezra wrote, "*Ve-onatah* is to be interpreted as referring to coitus, which is called *et dodim* ('the time of love'), for the word *et* is missing a *nun*, like *emet*."[5] Similarly, Kimhi wrote [in *Shorashim*], under the root עון, "*Ve-onatah* means a set time for coitus, as the Rabbis said, 'The *onah* for a scholar is from Sabbath eve to Sabbath eve...' (*Ketubbot* 62b)." However, it does not stand to reason that the Torah would designate a man's relations with his wife by the term "set time," besides the fact that nowhere in the Torah is there any timetable for this matter.

As I see it, Ibn Ezra was correct in deriving the word [*onatah*] from *et* and in saying that *et* is missing a *nun*; similarly we find in Aramaic the forms *ke-an* ("now") and *ke-enet* ("correspondingly") with a *nun*, and *ke-et* [an alternative form of *ke-enet*] without a *nun*. However, it seems to me that the word *et* does not primarily refer to time; rather, its primary meaning is that of the root from which it is derived. The root *anah* refers most basically to speech in response to another's speech, and it also denotes (1) the singing of two choruses of people who sing in response to each other, and (2) the fulfillment of another's request.

From this root is derived *ya'an* ("because"), which signifies the relationship between a result and its cause, and also *le-ma'an* ("so that," "in order that"), which signifies the relationship between an act and the result that is sought from it. Similarly, the word *ke-an* ("now") does not primarily refer to time, but rather links the consequence of a thing with what precedes it, in the sense of "if so" or "therefore," as in:

- "There is a man in your kingdom... Now [*ke-an*] let Daniel be called, and he will declare the interpretation" (Dan. 5:11-12);
- "But I have heard of you, that you can give your interpretations and loose knots; now [*ke-an*] if you can read the writing" (Dan. 5:16);

---

5. In other words, the original forms of these words were *ent* and *ement*, but in both cases the *nun* fell away.

- "All the presidents of the kingdom... have consulted together.... Now [*ke-an*] O king, establish the interdict" (Dan. 6:8-9);
- "Be it known now [*ke-an*] to the king that if this city is built" (Ezra 4:13);
- "Now [*ke-an*] because we eat the salt of the palace... therefore we have sent and announced to the king" (Ezra 4:14);
- "Make you now [*ke-an*] a decree" (Ezra 4:21).

So also the [Hebrew] work *attah*, as in, "May you now [*attah*] be blessed of the Lord" (Gen. 26:29); "Now, then [*attah*], may you be cursed" (Gen. 4:11); and many other such examples. Similarly, the word *ke-enet* or *ke-et* (Ezra 4:10, 11, 17, and 7:12) seems to me to be the equivalent of *ke-an* and *ve-attah*, and it was commonly used by Arameans at the beginning of their letters after the salutation.

Because time is one of the most abstract concepts, it did not receive a designation describing its actual essence; rather, they called it *enet*, *onah*, or *et*, signifying the proper conditions which, upon their fulfillment, bring about certain results, as in, "A time [*et*] to love and a time [*ve-et*] to hate," and all the other "times" listed in Ecclesiastes ch. 3. Similarly, "And your princes eat in due season [*ba-et*]" (Eccl. 10:17), i.e., under the proper conditions. So also, "And behold, your time [*ittekh*] was the time [*et*] of love" (Ezek. 16:8), i.e., you fulfilled the proper conditions ("your breasts were fashioned, and your hair was grown" [ibid., v. 7]) for the act of love. Also, "And a word in due season [*be-itto*], how good is it!" (Prov. 15:23).

In a similar vein, the word *onah* in Rabbinic Hebrew signifies the proper conditions that make a thing fit for another thing; for example, "one who donates his fruits to the Temple before they came into the time of tithing [*le-onat ma'aserot*]" (*Peah* 4:8, *Ḥallah* 3:4), interpreted by Bertinoro (in *Ḥallah*) to mean, "Each one according to the rule specified in the first chapter of *Ma'aserot*." In turn, *Ma'aserot* 1:2 specifies, "When do fruits come under the obligation of tithing? Figs, when they begin to ripen; grapes and wild grapes, when they are in an early stage of ripening...." Later the word *onah* was transferred to refer to "time" in general, just as the word *et* was transferred; see *Arukh*, s.v. ע"ן, sixth entry.

After all these considerations, I say that *onatah* ("her *onah*") is the condition befitting the woman inasmuch as she is married, and this condition is undoubtedly cohabitation. The Torah admonishes the master who has taken his maidservant as a wife that even if he takes another wife, he may not diminish what is due to the first one; just because her father was so poor that he was forced to sell her as a maidservant, she is not to be more lightly esteemed than the other wife whose father is rich. Rather, it is proper for the husband to remember always that when he married the first wife, he became obligated to her with all his wealth and powers, and that before he marries a second wife, he must see if his wealth and powers are sufficient for two wives; if not, he should not take a second wife. All of this the Torah said about one who marries his maidservant; *a fortiori* it applies to one who marries a free woman, that is, he is undoubtedly obligated to her with respect to food, clothing, and cohabitation according to the extent of his wealth and powers. The Torah, however, did not enter into the details of these matters, which are endless.

The Rabbis, doing what they always did with respect to all the other parts of the Torah, specified set amounts (*Ketubbot* 162a) such that if the husband were to diminish the amount established for him according to his individual circumstances, his wife would be entitled to bring a claim against him before the court, which would investigate whether he was a voluntary offender or was constrained to act as he did. If he was a voluntary offender, they would order him to give her what was due her, or else send her free from his house.

In their wisdom and righteousness, the Rabbis saw that a woman is not a vessel and was not created for a man's use or benefit alone; rather, a man and wife are two partners who have willingly joined together to help one another in love and affection. Not only were the Rabbis vigilant to prevent a man from diminishing his wife's due, but they were also vigilant with respect to the finer details, so that a man should not diminish his wife's pleasure, as for instance if he says that [he will have intercourse with her only if] he wears his clothes and she wears hers, [then he must send her free and pay her *ketubbah* (*Ketubbot* 48a)]. How honorable was their statement with regard to the reward due to men who contain themselves (*Niddah* 31a-b).[6]

In contrast to this, on the one hand, are the ways of churlish men who seek nothing but their own pleasure, always looking about to seek out lewdness while their wives, who are despised in their eyes, sit suffering in living widowhood. And in contrast, on the other hand, are the ways of sophisticates *(mit'ḥakkemim)* for whom a wife is like a maidservant and a medication for the preservation of their health ("One should not engage in intercourse unless he finds that his body is exceedingly healthy and strong..." ([Maimonides] *Hilkhot De'ot* 4:28).[7] However, one whose Torah is the Torah of Moses, the

---

6. "Because they [the men of Ulam, 1 Chron. 8:40] contained themselves during intercourse in order that their wives should emit their 'seed' first... Scripture attributes to them the same merit as if they themselves increased the number [not only] of their sons, [but also] of their sons' sons."

7. There Maimonides specifies the conditions under which intercourse is deemed medically beneficial for a man.

Mishnah, and the Talmud will love his wife as much as his own self and will honor her more than himself; of such a man it is said, "And you shall know that your tent is in peace" ([Job 5:24, as cited in] *Yevamot* 62b).

Rashbam and others interpreted *onatah* as derived from *ma'on*, meaning "dwelling place." Rosenmueller and Gesenius likewise derived it from *ma'on* and translated it as *cohabitatio* (lit., "living together"), which is a euphemism for intercourse.

R. Jonathan, in the Mekhilta, interpreted the words *she'erah kesutah* as "clothing that falls to her lot," i.e., if she is a young girl, the husband is not to give her clothing for an old woman, and if she is an old woman, he should not give her a young girl's clothing; likewise, he should not give her clothing for the sunny season during the rainy season or vice versa, but rather he should give her each one *be-onatah* [i.e., "in its proper season"]. Nachmanides had another opinion, which is quite far-fetched.[8]

**21:11. "If (any of) these three things [marrying her, giving her to his son, or letting her be redeemed] he does not do to her, she will go forth [once she has reached the age of marriage], without any payment.**

*If these three things* (*ve-im shelosh elleh*). Any of these three (cf. "If the contamination of a dead body touches all these [i.e., 'any of these']" – Haggai 2:13), that is, taking her for himself or for his son, or allowing her to be redeemed (so the Rabbis and most of the commentators). However, many have thought (as Ibn Ezra attests) that the reference is to "her food, clothing, and cohabitation" (v. 10 above); this was also Hizkuni's opinion, and Abravanel tended toward this interpretation as well. This does not seem likely to me, for if the master has already taken her, she is a lawfully married woman, and how could she go forth from him without a bill of divorcement freeing her to any other man? The expression "she will go forth, without any payment" is appropriate for a maidservant, not a married woman. And if you say that he is forced to give her a *get*, then the main [rule of law] is missing [from this verse].

If you say that in another place it is written, "When there is sold to you a Hebrew brother of yours, or a Hebrew woman, he will serve you six years," (Deut. 15:12) and that if so, even a young girl must serve for six years and does not go forth when she shows sign of puberty, know that according to the

---

8. According to Nachmanides, the entire phrase *she'erah kesutah ve-onatah* refers to conjugal rights: the husband is not to diminish the first wife's right to "flesh" (i.e., his proximity), her bedclothes, and her time of love.

plain meaning of that verse, it is speaking of one who sells herself and who is not a minor, i.e., she has already reached puberty; in that case she must serve six years. Here, however, the reference is to a minor who has been sold by her father and, when she is grown, the master does not wish to marry her, give her to his son, or let her be redeemed; in that case, she goes forth free without any payment of redemption.

**21:12. "One who strikes a man, and the latter dies of it, will be put to death.**

***One who strikes (makkeh) a man.*** With anything, even his hand, whether or not he causes him a wound. The term *hikkah* refers most basically to the beating of one body against another, and it was later transferred to denote "killing," as in, "The Lord struck [*hikkah*] every firstborn" (Exod. 12:29).

***and the latter dies of it*** *(va-met).* Whether immediately or after some time, for it does not say "dies under his hand" as in the case of a slave (below, v. 20), and as we learn below (vv. 18, 19), from the fact that it is written that even if the case of one who strikes another in a fight and the victim does not die but remains confined to bed, the one who causes the wound is not exempt unless the victim rises and walks outside his home. The reason that this is specified below [and not here] is because [of the need to distinguish that case from that] of the slave who survives [a striking] one day or two, in which case he is not avenged [by the master's death; see below, v. 21].

According to the plain meaning, even if the striker did not intend to cause death when he knowingly and intentionally struck, he is put to death if the victim dies of the beating and not of some additional cause that happens to occur. This matter may indeed be broken down into innumerable details, and the Torah leaves the judgment to the judges. The Rabbis tended to be lenient rather than strict in this matter; see *Sanhedrin* ch. 9.[9]

***will be put to death.*** By a court, but if the victim has a redeemer (*go'el*), the latter is permitted to avenge the victim's blood. This can be deduced from what immediately follows: "For one, however, who will not have acted with premeditation… I will designate a place where he will flee" (next v.), i.e., he is to flee from the redeemer (as is stated specifically in Num. 35:12, "for a refuge from a redeemer"), for if this were not so, why would he flee? Given

---

9. In *Sanhedrin* 9:2, it states that the striker is not subject to the death penalty unless he intended to cause death and used lethal force.

## Mishpatim

the fact that the judges would not put him to death without interrogating and investigating whether he killed unintentionally or with intent, it would have been enough to say, "However, one who does not act with premeditation, but God causes the matter to happen to him, will not be put to death."

Conversely, the Mekhilta states, "'He will be put to death': by a court, or perhaps not by a court? Scripture teaches, 'So that the manslayer is not put to death unless he stands before the congregation for judgment' (Num. 35:12)." But it seems clear to me that if the Torah's intention was to forbid blood-vengeance absolutely, what need would there have been for the cities of refuge? Now the Torah intended to discourage blood-vengeance, but it did not forbid it; if the redeemer killed the manslayer outside the cities of refuge, he was not culpable. However, not everyone has a redeemer, and not every redeemer would be willing to put himself in danger in order to kill a manslayer.

In several other contexts, this expression "he will be put to death [*mot yumat*]" is used, and there is no doubt that the meaning is "put to death by a court." It is unlikely that the judges would render [such a] judgment without testimony, and elsewhere it is specified that there must in fact be two witnesses. The Rabbis added the requirement of *hatra'ah* (the warning of the perpetrator by the witnesses) so as to distinguish between unintentional and intentional conduct; this, too, was for the sake of leniency.

***will be put to death.*** "By sword... or perhaps rather by strangulation?... But the text teaches us, 'He who sheds a man's blood will have his blood shed by a man' (Gen. 9:6). I might still say, let him be made to bleed from two limbs and then let him die. But the text teaches us, 'There, in that valley, they will slaughter the heifer... You will thus remove from your midst the innocent blood [of the victim of an unknown killer]' (Deut. 21:4, 9). The Torah thus makes an analogy between those who shed blood and the *eglah arufah* (beheaded heifer); just as the *eglah arufah* dies by beheading, so all shedders of blood die by beheading" (Mekhilta). This enactment, too, was a leniency, for the sake of speeding his death, in keeping with the Rabbis' teaching, "'Love for your neighbor that which you love for yourself' (Lev. 19:18)—he prefers an easy death" (*Ketubbot* 37b). See also below, v. 15.

**21:13. "For one, however, who will not have acted premeditatedly, but to whom God will have caused the case to happen [to be the cause of another's death], I will designate for you a place where he will flee.**

***who will not have acted premeditatedly*** *(va-asher lo tsadah).* The word *tsadah* is related to the root *tsud* and means to ambush and to seek to harm, as in:

- "Though you lay wait [*tsadeh*] for my soul to take it" (1 Sam. 24:12);
- "[Or if he threw upon him some object] intentionally [*bi-tsediyyah*]" (Num. 35:20);
- "[Or if he threw upon him some implement] inadvertently [*be-lo tsediyyah*]" (Num. 35:22).

Similarly, a hunter (*tsayyad*) lies in wait for animals and seeks to kill or trap them.

***but to whom God will have caused the case to happen.*** To whom God caused an unfortunate accident, so that he kills his neighbor unintentionally. Anything that a person does not do purposely and willingly is ascribed to God, the Prime Cause, for what we think of as an "accident" occurs by God's decree.

***I will designate for you a place.*** "I will establish for you cities of refuge when you arrive in the land" (so Rashbam) [*contra* Rashi, who maintains (following *Makkot* 12) that even in the desert, unintentional killers were to take refuge in the Levite camp].

***where he will flee.*** From the blood-avenger; see [the comment on] the previous verse.

**24:14. "But when one rises audaciously against his neighbor, killing him with forethought, from My very altar shall you tear him away, so that he may die.**

*from My very altar.* Holy places and altars were places of refuge among the ancients; therefore, after it says that "I will designate for you a place where he will flee," it adds that there is no refuge for an intentional killer, and that even if he takes hold of the prominences of the altar, they are to take him away from there and put him to death.

**21:15. "One who strikes his father or his mother [without their dying of it] will be put to death.**

***One who strikes his father...*** Even if he does not die of it. This, too, may be broken down into innumerable details, for it is unlikely that the person would be put to death for any blow whatsoever. The Rabbis interpreted this to refer to one who causes a wound.

***or his mother*** *(ve-immo*, lit., "and his mother"). Ibn Ezra and the Efodi [Profiat Duran], in his *Ma'aseh Efod*, interpreted this phrase [as if it said] "One who strikes his father, and one who strikes his mother"; this also seems to be the opinion of the accentuator [who placed a disjunctive *tevir* at the word *aviv*, "his father"].

***will be put to death.*** "By strangulation—or perhaps by one of the other [more severe] methods of execution mentioned in the Torah? Say then that this is the principle of the Torah: any death mentioned in the Torah without specification cannot be interpreted with severity, but must be interpreted leniently, according to R. Josiah" (Mekhilta).

**21:16. "One who steals a person and sells him, and he is found in his hands [in the act of sale], will be put to death.**

***One who steals... and sells him, and he is found in his hands.*** Formerly I explained this as per the Korem: "and sells him *or* he is found in his hands"; I gave a similar interpretation to the phrase *ve-hit'ammer bo u-mekharo* (Deut. 24:7)—"and treats him in the manner of a master, *or* sells him." But now (4 Sivan 5619 [1859]) it seems to me that it would be unjust for the thief to be put to death if he merely brought a free man into his house and enslaved him; however, if he sold him to others, then the evil deed would be complete, as that man's freedom would be lost permanently, for the person who bought him would have done so with money and thought that he was legally justified in enslaving him, because the man was his chattel.

The phrase "and is found in his hands" is to be understood to mean "at the time of the sale"; if there are witnesses who know that he is a free man and who saw him in the thief's hands as he was selling him to others, then the thief is sentenced to death. The Rabbis imposed a further restriction before the thief could be so sentenced, and they required witnesses to the theft itself; after all, even if the witnesses know that the victim is a free man, it is possible that others stole him and sold him to the suspect.

**21:17. "One who curses his father or his mother will be put to death.**

***One who curses his father,*** *etc.* In ancient times the father was the ruler of the household, with authority to punish and put to death, as is known from the annals of the nations. In the Torah, too, we find that Judah says, "Bring her forth, and let her be burnt" (Gen. 38:24). The Torah took this authority away from the father and transferred it to the court, and therefore the Torah imposed a severe rule on the children, who would have been used to such a rule. However, the judges would undoubtedly tend to leniency, in accord with what Moses transmitted to them orally; thus we find the Rabbis requiring the curse to have been uttered with the Name of God. Similarly, in the case of the "perverse and rebellious son" (Deut. 21:18), the Rabbis imposed many conditions, to the extent that his death was rendered virtually out of the question.

This, in fact, is a great general principle: many laws must be stated in a hyperbolic and threatening manner, but this does not mean that it would be just to carry them into effect without conditions that are unlikely to be fulfilled. These things must be transmitted to the judges in secret; for this reason we are commanded always to heed the judges of every generation.

With respect to the juxtaposition of the sections [above], it seems to me that Scripture progresses from the severe to the less severe, opening with homicide ("one who strikes a man, and the latter dies of it"); then setting forth its details (intentional and unintentional homicide); then mentioning one who strikes his parent without causing death; then one who steals a person without killing him but rather enslaving him; then one who curses his parent, which is an act of mere speech but is nevertheless punishable by death; then [next v.] one who strikes another in the course of a quarrel, which case is the least severe of all, since under some circumstances he is not deserving of death.

**21:18. "Whenever some men contend, and the one strikes the other with a stone, or with a fist, and the other does not die of it but remains confined to bed —**

***Whenever some men contend,*** *etc.* In a few books, the word *anashim* ("men") is accented with a [lesser disjunctive] *revia,* but there is no doubt that it is correctly accented with a [greater disjunctive] *zakef* [*katon*].

**21:19. "If he then rises and walks outside (the house) on his staff, the one who caused the wound will be immune; he will only indemnify him for the time that he will have had to remain idle, and he will assume the medical treatment thereof.**

## *Mishpatim*

***on his staff*** *(al mish'anto)*. The Heb. is the equivalent of *maklo* ("his stick"). [Once the wounded party rises and walks,] the wounding party immediately becomes immune, even if the wounded party subsequently dies, for it can be assumed that he brought it upon himself by failing to take proper care once he started to heal. R. Ishmael (in the Mekhilta) gave a kind of allegorical meaning to the phrase *al mish'anto*, interpreting it as *al buryo* ("in perfect health"); this is a stringency.

***he will only indemnify him...*** He will pay him the wages that he would have earned during his infirmity, when he was idled from work. The word *shivto* [lit., "his idleness," i.e., "the time that he will have had to remain idle"] is plausibly derived from the root *shavat* ("to cease work"), but is even more likely to have been derived from *yashav* ("to sit"), i.e., sitting in the house, which is the opposite of "walking outside" (Ibn Ezra).

***and he will assume the medical treatment thereof*** *(ve-rappo yerappei)*. The dressing of the wound, as well as other external treatments, whether done by the wounded party himself or by a physician. This verse does not speak of the case of one who cut off a person's hand or foot, but rather of one who caused an infirmity that was healed; therefore I have interpreted the payment of *shivto* as compensation for the victim's idleness from work during his infirmity, not his lifelong idleness caused by the wounding party's striking. However, the Rabbis did also speak of one who cut off a person's hand or foot, and they interpreted the payment of *shivto* as compensation for his idleness from work from then on, for the rest of his life; see below, v. 24.

Know that among the laws of the ancient Romans was also found the law of compensation for medical treatment, damages, and lost wages (*Digest* IX.3.7):

> When a freeman sustains bodily injury by something which is thrown down or poured out, the judge takes account of the cost of medical attendance and other expenses incurred in his recovery as well as the value of any employment which he lost or will have to lose because of his disability. However, no account is taken of scars or disfigurement because the body of a freeman is not susceptible of valuation.[10]

---

10. Alan Watson, ed., *The Digest of Justinian*, vol. 1 (University of Pennsylvania Press, 1998).

Here it is fitting to point out that the Rabbis required a person who injured his fellow to pay for pain and humiliation as well, but according to Roman law he was liable for medical costs, damages, and lost wages [alone], for (as it said), there was no compensation for a freeman's body. See how far from the way of truth were some modern scholars, who wrote that the Sages of the Mishnah learned their laws from the teachings of the Romans.

**21:20. "Whenever someone strikes his [non-Israelite] slave, or his bondwoman, with a staff, and the latter dies under his hand, he will be avenged [with the master's death].**

*his slave (avdo)...* A Canaanite slave;[11] see Rashi [who, citing the Mekhilta, observes that only such an *eved* can be referred to as his master's "money" (see next v.)] and Ibn Ezra [who gives the same reasoning and also observes that the case of an Israelite *eved* would, in this context, be no different from that of an Israelite freeman]. It is known that the master had the authority to put slaves to death, but the Torah took this authority away from him; if a slave died under his hand under circumstances suggesting that the master intended to kill him, the master was to be put to death. However, if the slave survived a day or two, under circumstances permitting an assumption that the master intended to discipline him but not to kill him, the slave was not to be avenged [see next v.].

Maimonides, in *Rotse'aḥ* 2:14, wrote: "It seems to me that one who strikes his slave with a knife or sword, or with a stone or fist or the like, reckoning that he would die—and he does die—is not covered by the law of 'a day or two'; rather, even if the slave dies a year later, the master is put to death for it. Therefore it says, '[Whenever someone strikes his slave] with a staff,' for the Torah did not give him permission to strike him other than with a staff, rod, strap, or the like, and not with a deadly blow."

*he will be avenged.* By means of execution by sword; see Rashi and Ibn Ezra [who support this view by citing the phrase "a sword that will avenge the (violated) pact," Lev. 26:25].

Among the Romans, the master had the authority to put his slaves to death by any cruel or unusual means, and for any reason at all; this continued

---

11. Shadal, in his text translation, distinguishes between the Israelite (Hebrew) *eved* and the Canaanite *eved*, rendering the former as *servo* ("servant" or "manservant") and the latter as *schiavo* ("slave"). Likewise, he translates the Israelite *amah* as *serva* ("maidservant") and the Canaanite *amah* as *schiava* ("slave," "bondwoman").

## Mishpatim

until the times of the emperors Hadrian and Antoninus, who had mercy on slaves and forbade their killing (Clericus).

Here it is fitting to mention the words of the Rabbis in the Mekhilta (cited by Rashi on this v. and also by the Yalkut [Shim'oni]: "Was (the Canaanite slave) not covered by the rule of 'one who strikes a man, and the latter dies of it [will be put to death]' (above, v. 12)? But Scripture removed him from this rule and subjected him to the rule of 'a day or two.'" Hence it is clear that according to the Tannaim, even Canaanite slaves were included in the rule of "one who strikes a man," and that an Israelite who killed them was subject to the death penalty. Nevertheless, the matter needs further study, for from the continuation of the words of the Mekhilta, it appears that the first Tanna, who said, "Was he not covered by the rule of 'one who strikes a man,'" would have interpreted the verse to refer to a Hebrew servant.

**21:21. "But if he survives a day or two, he will not be avenged, for he is his money.**

*But if he survives a day or two (yom o yomayim).* This terminology is used because *yom* ("day") sometimes includes both daytime and nighttime, but sometimes daytime only. Because it says *yom o yomayim*, one can infer that it is indicating a time that is close to both "a day" and "two days." If so, this is not merely a period of daytime, but at least a day and a night, that is, *me-et la-et* [i.e., time comprising part of two separate "days"], as our Rabbis said [in the Mekhilta].

*for he is his money.* And the master is thus permitted to discipline him; also, it is unlikely that the master would intend to kill him, for that way he would lose his money.

**21:22. "Whenever some men come to blows, and they push against a pregnant woman, and the latter miscarries, but the death (of the woman) does not occur, he (the guilty party) will be fined according to what the husband imposes upon him, and he will pay by the sentence of the judges.**

*Whenever some men come to blows (yinnatsu).* Hand-to-hand fighting, which is more serious than a *riv* ("quarrel"), as in, "He saw two Hebrew men who were coming to blows [*nitsim*]; and he said to the one who was in the wrong, 'Why are you beating your neighbor?'" (Exod. 2:13); "When he strove [*be-hatsoto*] with Aram-Naharaim" (Ps. 60:2). The term was transferred to denote a serious dispute even without hand-to-hand fighting, as in, "[Dathan and Abiram,] who contested [*hitsu*] with Moses and Aaron, in the congregation of Korah, contesting [*be-hatsitam*] with the Lord" (Num. 26:9).

**and they push against** *(ve-nagefu)*. They strike her belly by accident, as when she comes to separate them. [Although in the plural,] *ve-nagefu* refers to "one of them," on the model of, "[And when one takes a woman and her mother, it is turpitude;] he and they will be burned" (Lev. 20:14), i.e. one of the women (Ibn Ezra).

**but the death** *(ason)* **does not occur.** The word *ason* denotes an unusual death by means of an unfortunate accident, as in, "Some mishap [*ason*] could befall him" (Gen. 42:4). The meaning is that the woman does not die, for the fetus itself can be expected to die.

**he will be fined** *(anosh ye'anesh,* lit., "he will be punished"). A monetary punishment; cf. "And they will impose on him a penalty [*ve-aneshu oto*] of a hundred silver shekels" (Deut. 22:19).

**and he will pay by the sentence of the judges** *(ve-natan bi-felilim)*. The guilty party will pay his fine by the agreement of the judges, who will not allow the woman's husband to impose on him a fine that is excessive. Thus they said in the Mekhilta, "'According to what the husband imposes upon him' – I might understand this to mean all that he wants, but the text reads *ve-natan bi-felilim*, which tells us that he pays only what the judges decide." Nachmanides' opinion is similar, except that he explains that the husband is to fix the sum through the judges, so as not to impose on the guilty party an exorbitant amount.

**21:23. "If, however, the death (of the woman) occurs, you shall set life for life.**

*If, however, the death (ason) occurs.* The woman's death.

*you shall set life for life.* The one who struck will be put to death, even though he did not intend to strike the woman. The Rabbis were in dispute over the matter (*Sanhedrin* 79a-b); see Rashi [who notes that the dispute was whether to impose the death penalty or a monetary fine].

## Mishpatim

**21:24. "Eye for eye, tooth for tooth, hand for hand, foot for foot.**

***Eye for eye.*** This does not pertain in particular to one who strikes a pregnant woman, but since it says "life for life," it goes on to append "eye for eye," etc. This teaches that anyone who injures his fellow is to be given the same defect that he gave, regardless of whether he intended to injure the victim, as in the case of one who pushes against a pregnant woman. The Rabbis interpreted this to mean that he pays a monetary penalty (*Bava Kamma* 83b). From what is written, "And do not accept a ransom for the life of a homicide, who is guilty of death, but he must be put to death" (Num. 35:31), there is clear proof that the Torah permitted the taking of a monetary ransom in the case of other injuries that do not involve death. Similarly below, "But where it has been for some time a goring ox… also its owner will be put to death. If, however, a ransom is imposed on him, he will pay the ransom of his own life" (vv.29-30). the Torah permitted the taking of a ransom from one who did not directly cause a death but was negligent in guarding his ox.

This is one of the things that the Torah left to the judges, for if indeed there would be a rich person who did not mind losing his money and who took pleasure in injuring others, the judges would be able to impose the written penalty, "eye for eye." In the Roman laws (Twelve Tables) it is written, "If he has maimed a part of the body, unless he settles with him, there is to be retaliation [*talion*]."[12]

**21:25. "Burn for burn, wound for wound, bruise for bruise."**

***wound*** *(petsa).* A cutting. The root *patsa* is related to *batsa, baza* (Aramaic), *baka, puts, patsats, nafats,* all of which denote cutting, tearing, or breaking.

---

12. Michael Crawford, ed., *Roman Statutes,* London, Institute of Classical Studies, 1996. The law of *talion* (*lex talionis*) was the principle that criminals should receive as punishment precisely those injuries and damages they inflicted upon their victims. Modern scholarship echoes Shadal's view: "The central claim of the new research on talionic systems is that revenge coexisted with the option of compensation. Revenge was not phased out gradually, but was a central component of the whole idea of compensation" (Kaius Tuori, "Revenge and Retribution in the Twelve Tables: *Talio esto* Reconsidered," *Fundamina,* vol. 13, pp. 140-145 [2007]).

The normative halakhic view, as expressed in *Bava Kamma* 84a, is that the phrase "eye for eye" cannot be taken literally. According to Maimonides (*Ḥovel u-Mazzik* 1:3), the Torah's intention in using such terminology was not that the court should actually injure the guilty party in the same way that he injured his neighbor, but rather to express the thought that it would have been morally fitting to amputate his limb or injure him, just as he did to the injured party.

Rashi gave the Old French equivalent *navradure*, which is from the archaic root *navrer*, meaning *blesser* ("to injure, wound").

***bruise** (ḥabburah)*. A wound without a break in that which is "connected" (*ḥibbur*) [i.e., the skin]; rather the blood coagulates [under the skin], changing the skin's appearance; cf. "Or [can] the leopard [change] his spots [*ḥavarburotav*]?" (Jer. 13:23). Similarly in Arabic, the root חבר refers to that which is spotted in variegated hues. Rashi gave the Old French equivalent *tache*, which means "stain." R. Saadiah Gaon interpreted *petsa* as the breaking of a limb and *ḥabburah* as a blood wound.

**21:26. "Whenever someone strikes the eye of his [non-Israelite] slave, or the eye of his bondwoman, and destroys it, he will set him in freedom in compensation for his eye.**

***the eye of his slave** (avdo)*. A Canaanite slave.

***he shall set him in freedom.*** This will be a motivation for him to refrain from striking his slave with cruel blows, for if he destroys one of his body parts, even his tooth, the slave will go free and the master will lose his money (Ibn Ezra). The Rabbis said that for 24 other body parts the slave goes free: the 20 fingers and toes, the two ears, the nose, and the male organ. Apparently if the slave's hand or foot is destroyed, he would *a fortiori* go free; the Rabbis would not have had to mention them, since the destruction of a hand or foot would necessarily involve the destruction of the fingers or toes.

**21:27. "And if he causes a tooth of his slave, or of his bondwoman, to fall out, he will set him in freedom in compensation for his tooth.**
**21:28. "Whenever an ox gores a man or a woman, so that the person dies of it, the ox will be stoned, and the meat of it will not be eaten, and the owner of the ox will be immune.**

***Whenever an ox gores** (yiggaḥ)*. The act of *negiḥah* is specifically with a horn; cf. "And Zedekiah son of Kenaanah made him horns of iron, and said, 'Thus says the Lord: "With these you shall gore [*tenaggaḥ*] the Arameans"'" (1 Kings 22:11); "He is a majestic firstborn bull, provided with horns of a *re'em*, with which he gores [*yenaggaḥ*] simultaneously peoples and distant regions" (Deut. 33:17) (*Bava Kamma* 2b). The roots *nagaḥ, naga, nagaf, nakah, nakash,* and *yakash* are all related to each other in that they denote "striking," each one indicating a different means of striking.

***will be stoned*** *(sakol yissakel)*. By the throwing of stones upon it, as it says:

- "You shall stone him [*u-sekalto*] with stones" (Deut. 13:11);
- "And you shall stone them [*u-sekaltam*] with stones" (Deut. 17:5);
- "And you will stone them [*u-sekaltem otam*] with stones" (Deut. 22:24).

Similarly we find that Jezebel wrote, "Carry him [Naboth] out and stone him [*ve-sikluhu*]," and when this was done, it says, "And they stoned him [*va-yiskeluhu*] with stones" (ibid., v. 13). There is further proof from the statement above, "Let no hand touch him, but let him be stoned [*sakol yissakel*], or shot with an arrow" (Exod. 19:13; see my comment there). However, the Rabbis alleviated this method, with respect to the execution of a human being, in order to hasten the person's death (see *Sanhedrin* 6:4).[13]

The killing of the ox was not a punishment for the ox, but rather for the owner, so that he would properly guard his animals. It would have been possible for the ox to be taken from him without being stoned, but the stoning was for the purpose of making an impression on the entire people, that they should see, hear, and take fear. Furthermore, by this means an abhorrence of homicide would be reinforced in the people's hearts, for it would be impressed upon them that "he who sheds a man's blood"—whoever [or whatever] the shedder may be—"will have his blood shed by a man" (Gen. 9:6), as it says, "From every animal I demand account of it [i.e., 'your blood']; and from man, from man his brother, will I demand account of the life of man" (Gen. 9:5).

***and the meat of it will not be eaten.*** For the prohibition of eating a *nevelah* [an animal that died by means other than *shehitah*] had not yet been given. It is to be further understood (as per Rashbam) that the meat was not to be given over to a non-Israelite or a dog; that is, it was forbidden to derive benefit from it. The Rabbis said that even if the ox was slaughtered by means of *shehitah* before the stoning (after the sentence of stoning was pronounced), it was prohibited to derive benefit from it. This is a proper law (*din emet*), even though it does not reflect the plain meaning of the verse.

***and the owner of the ox will be immune.*** From death or any other penalty.

---

13. There, the halakhic procedure for stoning is described as: (1) pushing the guilty party off the roof of the "stoning chamber"; (2) throwing down a single stone upon the party's heart, if the fall did not kill him; and (3) throwing of stones by the general public, if the single stone did not kill him.

**21:29.** "But where it has been for some time a goring ox, and the owner has been warned of it and does not guard it, and then it causes a man or woman to die, the ox will be stoned, and also its owner will be put to death.

*a goring ox (naggah).* Accustomed to do so; the Heb. is on the model of *gannav* ("thief"), *dayyan* ("judge") [noun forms that denote a profession or a permanent character].

*for some time (mi-temol shilshom,* lit. "from yesterday and the day before"). An idiom meaning "beforehand," as in, "Not previously [*mi-temol shilshom*] having had animosity toward him" (Deut. 19:6); "For you have not passed this way heretofore [*mi-temol shilshom*]" (Josh. 3:4). Similarly, *ki-temol shilshom* means "as beforehand," as in, "The waters of the Jordan returned to their place, and went over all its banks, as aforetime [*khi-temol shilshom*]" (Josh. 4:18); and so also *temol shilshom,* as in, "And you have come to a people that you did not know heretofore [*temol shilshom*]" (Ruth 2:11).

The Torah did not specify how many times would establish a presumption that the ox was a "goring ox." The Rabbis said, "What is a *mu'ad* [i.e., an ox that has been "warned" about]? One that has been warned about three times" (*Bava Kamma* 23b) – that is, one that has gored three times previously.

*and the owner has been warned (ve-hu'ad) of it.* The Heb. denotes warning or admonition, as in, "That man declared [*ha'ed he'id*] to us" (Gen. 43:3);[14] "Go down, warn [*ha'ed*] the people" (Exod. 19:21).

*and does not guard it.* After being warned.

*and also its owner will be put to death.* The plain meaning is that the court would put him to death, but the Torah permitted the taking of a ransom [for his life], since he did not kill the victim with his own hands. The Torah left it up to the judges to judge, according to the nature of the person and the incident, whether he was worthy of death or worthy of being saved by a ransom, and what the amount of the ransom should be. However, the Rabbis said that he was [liable] to be put to death "by the hand of Heaven" [and not by a human court].

**21:30.** "If, however, a ransom is imposed upon him, he will pay the ransom of his own life, according to that which is imposed upon him.

---

14. Although Shadal's translation there reads "declared" (*protestato*), his comment on that verse interprets the words as meaning "warned."

## *Mishpatim*

***If, however, a ransom is imposed upon him.*** If the judges see that he is worthy of being saved from death, and they assess a ransom upon him. According to A.H. Mainster, this would happen if the relatives [of the victim] could be appeased with a ransom.

***the ransom of his own life*** *(pidyon nafsho)*. Money in return for his "soul" *(nefesh)*, according to what the judges assess based on his wealth, and on whether he was greatly or slightly negligent in guarding his ox. It does not appear likely that the phrase refers to the personal "valuation" of the guilty party or the victim [cf. Leviticus 27], for if so, it should have read *erekh nafsho*, and besides, the text would not have gone on to state "according to that which is imposed upon him [*yushat alav*]," but would have said "as they would evaluate him [*ya'arikhuhu*]."[15]

**21:31. "Equally, if it gores a boy or a girl, he will be treated according to the same law.**

***if it gores a boy or a girl*** *(o ven... o vat*, lit. "either a son or a daughter"). Minor children; even if their parent was negligent in failing to guard them, and even if they provoked the ox's anger upon themselves, nevertheless "he will be treated according to this same law."

**21:32. "If the ox gores a [non-Israelite] slave, or a bondwoman, he will give to his master the sum of thirty shekels, and the ox will be stoned.**

***a slave*** *(eved)*. A Canaanite slave.

***the sum of thirty shekels.*** This is not "the ransom of his own life," but rather a payment of damages that he caused to the master, and in addition he loses his ox.

***shekels.*** Modern scholars have weighed shekels that are still extant from the time of the Hasmoneans and have found them to weigh 215 to 229 "grains,"

---

15. The halakhic view, as reflected in Maimonides *(Nizkei Mamon* 10:4), is that the "ransom" is a compulsory penalty that atones for the guilty party's liability for death by the hand of Heaven. Rashi's comment on v. 30 maintains that the introductory word *im* (translated by Shadal as "if, however") is not conditional, but is the equivalent of *asher* ("when"); i.e., the payment of the ransom is not a matter of choice.

according to the weight system used by sellers of medications [apothecaries' weight], sixty to a dram (*drachma*). Undoubtedly their weight has diminished somewhat over the course of the two thousand years since they were made.[16]

**21:33. "When someone uncovers a cistern, or when someone is digging a cistern and does not cover it, and an ox or an ass falls into it —**

*When someone uncovers a cistern.* Which had been covered, and he opens it up (Rashi).

*or when someone is digging.* Or even if a person is digging a cistern and does not cover it over every day at evening when he leaves work, because he still needs to go back the next day and continue digging, and it is burdensome for him to cover it every day; nevertheless, the owner of the cistern is liable, whether he uncovers it or digs it (Rashbam).

The cistern at issue is made in a place of pasturing animals, which is public property, except that the cistern and the water contained therein belong to the person who dug it. This situation obtained in the days of Abraham and Moses, before the conquest of the land of Israel and its distribution; after the land was distributed to each tribe and family, the pasturing areas became private property as well. At that point, it would not have been possible for the cistern's owner to be liable for damages resulting from the cistern on his property, for who allowed his neighbor's ox to enter there? Therefore the Rabbis interpreted this case as involving a cistern on public property, and because it was a difficulty for them that Scripture should speak of "the owner of the cistern," they said that even though the cistern was not actually his, Scripture treated him as if he were its owner, in order to make him liable for the damages it causes.

**21:34. "The owner of the cistern will compensate, (that is) he will pay money to the owner (of the fallen animal), and the dead animal will be his.**

*and the dead animal will be his.* It will belong to the one who caused the harm, since he will have paid its entire value (Rashbam). The Rabbis, however, were lenient on him and said that he was not obligated to pay actual money, but that he could pay with anything, even bran (*Bava Kamma* 7a). Thus he would leave the dead animal with its owner, and he would pay him the amount by which the value of the live animal exceeded the value of the dead body. See below, v. 36.

---

16. A dram equals one eighth of an ounce.

## Mishpatim

**21:35. "When anyone's ox butts against the ox of another, so that it dies of it, they will sell the live ox, and they will divide its money, and they will also divide the dead one.**

*When anyone's ox butts against* (*yiggof*, lit., "strikes"). Whether with its horns or with its body, for *negifah* [as opposed to *negihah*; see on v. 28 above] is merely a synonym for *hakka'ah* ("striking").

*they will sell the live ox, etc.* This refers to oxen of the same value; see Rashi, [who points out that from here we derive the following rule]: he [the owner of a *tam*, i.e., an ox that has not been warned about three times] pays for half the damages.

**21:36. "Where, however, it is known that it was a goring ox beforehand, and the owner did not guard it, he will pay an ox in exchange for the ox, and the dead one will be his.**

*Where* (*o*, lit., "or")... *it is known.* However, if it is known.

*he will pay an ox in exchange for the ox.* This implies that the owner is to give another actual ox to replace the dead ox, in which case it would be clear that "the dead one will be his." However, the Rabbis were lenient and interpreted this case as above, v. 34 [i.e., they allowed a mere payment of full damages, with the dead ox counting toward the payment].

**21:37. "Whenever someone steals an ox, or a lamb, and slaughters it or sells it, he will pay five cattle in exchange for the ox, and four small cattle in exchange for the lamb."**

*Whenever someone steals an ox, or a lamb, etc.* Scripture was more stringent with respect to the penalty for one who steals an ox or lamb than it was with respect to other thieves, who pay only double, because animals grazing in a field are easy to steal, while it is hard to discover the theft after such an animal is slaughtered or sold. Thus the penalty is fittingly more severe in proportion to the shamefulness of the act and its ease of performance. As Maimonides wrote (*Guide for the Perplexed* 3:41):

> It is right that the more frequent transgressions and sins are, and the greater the probability of their being committed, the more severe

must their punishment be, in order to deter people from committing them; but sins which are of rare occurrence require a less severe punishment. For this reason one who stole a sheep had to pay twice as much as for other goods, i.e., four times the value of the stolen object; but this is only the case when he has disposed of it by sale or slaughter. As a rule, sheep remained always in the fields, and therefore could not be watched so carefully as things kept in town. The thief of a sheep used therefore to sell it quickly before the theft became known, or to slaughter it and thereby change its appearance. As such theft happened frequently, the punishment was severe. The compensation for a stolen ox is still greater by one-fourth, because the theft is easily carried out. The sheep keep together when they feed, and can be watched by the shepherd, so that theft when it is committed can only take place by night. But oxen when feeding are very widely scattered… and a shepherd cannot watch them properly; theft of oxen is therefore a more frequent occurrence.[17]

Similarly, the famous scholar Cesare Beccaria, in his fine book *Dei delitti e delle pene* ("Of Crimes and Punishments"), wrote: "Therefore the means made use of by the legislature to prevent crimes should be more powerful in proportion as they are destructive of the public safety and happiness, and as the inducements to commit them are stronger" [ch. 6].[18]

Rabbi Meir says [in *Bava Kamma* 79b] that the ox is compensated for fivefold because its owner was idled from work, that is, he was damaged for the day or two during which he did not have the ox with him to do his plowing; this was also R. Saadiah Gaon's view.

**22:1. "If the thief is found in the act of breaking the wall, and is stricken and dies of it, he has no blood [the thief who breaks the wall at night is not considered to be a living person, and one who kills him is not guilty].**

*If the thief is found, etc.* While he is digging under the house and breaks through the wall to enter; this occurs at night, for during the day he would not be digging. The next verse supports this (Ibn Ezra).

*he has no blood (ein lo damim).* For a long time I interpreted this as did Ibn Ezra, that ["he," i.e.,] the one who strikes the thief is not guilty of murder;

---

17. Trans. Friedländer, p. 571.
18. Trans. Edward D. Ingraham (1819).

## Mishpatim

this is what was printed in my commentary to the *parashah* of *Mishpatim* in the book *Ben Gorni* (Amsterdam, 5611 [1851]). But now (Shavuot eve 5619 [1859]) I see that the subject of the phrase in this verse and the one following is "the thief," not the owner of the house. The meaning of "he has no blood" is that he is not considered as a living person who has blood, but rather is viewed as if he were dead, and one who kills him has "killed a dead man." This is the opinion of Rashi, who wrote, "'He has no blood': this is not murder; he is considered to have been dead from the beginning." [On the other hand,] one who "has blood" is considered to be alive, and it is murder if the house owner kills him.

Ibn Ezra wrote, "One should be astonished at those who interpret *damim* ('blood') as 'life' [rather than 'bloodguilt'], for if so, what is meant by the expression *ish damim* (2 Sam. 16:8) and *damim bo* (Lev. 20:9)?" But his reasoning is void, for *damim* is certainly the equivalent of "life," since "the blood is the life" (Deut.12:23), but *ish damim* [lit., "a man of blood"] is an elliptical expression meaning "a shedder of blood," and likewise *damav bo* [lit., "his blood is in him"] is an elliptical expression meaning "the shedding of his blood, and his death, is no one's fault but his own." Similarly, the expression "otherwise [i.e., if you do not make a parapet for your roof] you would place *damim* in your house" (Deut. 22:8) refers to the shedding of blood. On the other hand, *ein lo damim* is not an elliptical phrase, but is meant in its plain sense ("he has no blood").

Support for this interpretation comes from the use of the formative letter *lamed* (in the phrases *ein lo damim*, *damim lo*), and similarly, "If, however, the homicide goes outside the border of the city of refuge... he has no blood [*ein lo dam*]," (Num. 35:26-27) meaning that he is considered as dead. In contrast, in the phrase *ve-hayah alekha damim* ("there would fall upon you a (crime of) homicide") [lit., "there would be blood upon you"] (Deut. 19:10), *damim* does mean "bloodguilt," and therefore the word is connected with [*ve-hayah*, "there would be"] by means of [a form of the preposition] *al*. I have said that this is "support," rather than complete proof, because we do find the phrase *ein la-na'arah het mavet*, "the young woman is not deserving of death" (Deut. 22:26), where the [subject and the] penalty are connected with the formative *lamed* [rather than a form of *al*].

The Rabbis of the Mishnah likewise understood the expression *ein lo damim* as referring back to "the thief," not to the owner of the house, for they said (*Sanhedrin* 72a), "If the thief is found in the act of breaking the wall... if he has blood, he is liable [for damages that he causes by breaking a barrel in the course of the act], but if he has no blood, he is exempt [from such damages, because he was subject to the death penalty, even though the owner did not kill him]."

The Torah exempted [from punishment one who shed] the blood of a thief who breaks in at night, because there are no witnesses present, and the owner who wants to save his property must rise against him; if the owner were not permitted to kill him, then the thief would kill the owner, or else the owner would have to look on and keep silent. Appropriately, the Rabbis taught, "If one comes to kill you, rise early to kill him"; similar is the statement of Rava (*Sanhedrin* 72a) [that the thief who breaks in "has no blood" because there is a presumption that the owner will not stand by his money without trying to defend it].

Given that the expression *ein lo damim* refers back to "the thief," who is considered as dead, it follows that not only the house owner but anyone else is permitted to kill him. So ruled Maimonides (*Geneivah* 9:7). Even though the Rabbis derived from this case the rule, "If one comes to kill you, rise early to kill him," he may be killed by anyone, because everyone is obligated to save a person who is being pursued [by a would-be killer], even at the cost of the pursuer's life.

It seems that even Ibn Ezra, in interpreting the expression to mean "the one who kills the thief has no bloodguilt," agreed that anyone was permitted to kill him; perhaps even he understood the word *lo* (lit., "to him") as referring back to "the thief," in which case the expression would mean "*for him* there is no bloodguilt," which is how Mendelssohn translated it. However, [it would seem that] both Ibn Ezra and Mendelssohn found this transferred and poetic Hebrew expression difficult—that a living person should be considered as dead and as if he had no blood—and felt constrained to interpret it to mean that there would be no bloodguilt for him. But Rashi had a discerning palate for Hebrew speech and understood the matter perfectly.

Jerome, Clericus, Gesenius, and others took the expression as referring to the killer, that he would have no bloodguilt. [Of these others,] only Gussetius understood that the [grammatical] subject of the phrase is "the thief," not his killer, but he did not understand that the thief was to be considered as dead, and so he, too, interpreted the expression in a transferred sense, albeit a greatly strained one. He said that the blood of a slain person would spurt upon the killer and bring upon him the guilt of murder, while in this case the Torah was saying that the blood of a thief who breaks the wall does not spurt upon his killer and does not bring guilt upon him. How far from reasonable this is! Blessed be He Who chose Rashi and bestowed upon His worshippers a seeing eye and a hearing ear.

## *Mishpatim*

Today, 5 Adar II 5624 (1864), my student Joseph Jarè showed me that Ibn Ezra, in his short commentary, expressed his view openly that *ein lo damim* refers to the thief: "the meaning is that there is no one who would seek to avenge his blood."

**22:2. "If, however, the sun has risen over him [that is, if it was day], he has blood. He would have paid; and if he could not have done so, he would have been sold for his theft.**

*If, however, the sun has risen over him* (im zareḥah ha-shemesh alav). If, while he is still digging (after having started at night), the sun rises, then it is forbidden to kill him or to seize the stolen goods from him by force, with a severe blow that would endanger his life, for in that case it would be possible to bring witnesses against him and take him to court; he would then pay, and if he could not, he would be sold for his theft.

For this reason, Onkelos translated [*im zareḥah ha-shemesh alav*] as, "If the eye of witnesses fell upon him." He interpreted correctly, for the house owner was permitted to kill the digger precisely because he could find no witnesses, but if this occurred at a time and place in which a human eye could perceive the thief, and the house owner could bring witnesses against him, an individual would not be allowed to execute judgment with his own hand unless there was an urgent need, for this is why courts were established.

Under this interpretation, even if this happens during the day, but with no one else present, the house owner is permitted to kill him; so states the Mekhilta, and so ruled Maimonides (*Geneivah* 9:7), but not Ra'avad or Rabbenu Hananel (who is cited by the author of the *Maggid Mishneh* commentary [Vidal of Tolosa] ad loc.). The Sages interpreted [the phrase *im zareḥah ha-shemesh alav*] to mean that if it is as clear to you as the sun that the thief does not come with murderous intentions [then do not kill him] (see Rashi [on this v.] and *Sanhedrin* 72a). This is a correct rule of law, only it is not the plain meaning of the verse, but merely an *asmakhta* [i.e., a scriptural support for a rabbinic enactment].

*He would have paid* (shallem yeshallem, lit., "he will pay"). If the thief escapes with the stolen good in his possession, and the house owner and witnesses see him, he must pay; therefore, it is forbidden to kill him, and one who does kill him is liable for it. Thus it is translated in the Jerusalem Targum attributed to Jonathan ben Uzziel, "And if he was saved from his [i.e., the owner's] hand, he will pay."

**22:3. "If the theft is found with him alive, whether ox, ass, or lamb, he will pay double.**

***If the theft is found,*** *etc.* This verse refers back to that which appears above (21:37): if a thief stole an animal and slaughtered or sold it, he must pay five cattle in exchange for an ox, etc.; however, if it is found in his possession (i.e., he has not sold it) and alive (i.e., he has not slaughtered it), he pays only double. This would be a means of discouraging him from hastening to slaughter and sell, and would also facilitate the discovery of the theft.

***alive.*** This refers back to "ox, ass, or lamb," as per Targum [Onkelos].[19]

***he will pay double.*** As is the rule for any thief (below, v. 6). This is measure for measure: he returns what he stole, and he loses from his own house another one like it.

**22:4. "Whenever someone causes the destruction of a field or a vineyard, that is to say that he lets his animal go to graze in the field of another, he will pay the best part of the field or of the vineyard.**

***Whenever someone causes the destruction*** *(ki yav'er ish)*. It seem to me that *yav'er* is used in the sense of *bi'ur*, "destruction." The statement that appears in Ibn Ezra's commentary, *ve-hu me-ha-binyan ha-dagush* (that *yav'er* is in the conjugation that is marked with a *dagesh*, i.e., *pi'el*) is merely a copyist's error and should be corrected to read (as is written in Ibn Ezra's short commentary) *me-ha-binyan ha-kaved ha-nosaf, u-vi'er me-ha-dagush* (that *yav'er* is in the "supplemented heavy" conjugation, i.e., *hif'il*, and the word *u-vi'er*, which appears later in the verse, in the the *pi'el*).

I have since inspected two Ibn Ezra manuscripts, and in one of them (written by R. Daniel, 5110 [1350]) it is written:

> And *yav'er* is used in the sense of *anaḥnu u-ve'irenu* ("we and our cattle" [Num. 20:4]), in the heavy conjugation, while [the word *bi'er* ("graze") in the subsequent phrase] *u-vi'er bi-sedeh aher* is similar, but is in the *dagush* conjugation; also similar is, "It is you who have eaten up [*bi'artem*] the vineyard" (Isa. 3:14).

---

19. *Contra* Rashi, who, following the Mekhilta, connects the word "alive" (*ḥayyim*) with "he will pay," i.e., he must repay for the theft with live animals or their value.

## *Mishpatim*

In the other manuscript, written in 5161 (1401), I found:

> And they say that *ki yava'er ish* is on the model of *anaḥnu u-ve'irenu*, and is in the heavy conjugation, while the meaning of *u-vi'er bi-sedeh aḥer* (here it is added in the margin *adam aḥer*, "another person") is similar, except that it is in the *dagush* conjugation; also similar is, "It is you who have eaten up [*bi'artem*] the vineyard."

**he lets his animal go.** This explains [what is meant by the preceding] general rule [and hence the words "that is to say" are supplied in the translation].

**his animal** *(be'iroh).* This Hebrew word [rather than some other, more common word for "animal" or "ox"] is used by way of a play on words with *ki yav'er* and *u-vi'er*. The laws [in this *parashah*] are set out in a somewhat poetic form, so that they should be impressed in the memory of the common people; similarly below (23:5), "You will refrain from abandoning the care to him alone [*me-azov lo*], but you will help him to unload [*azov ta'azov immo*]."

**the best part of the field,** *etc.* Of the injured party, according to R. Ishmael (*Bava Kamma* 6b), followed by Rashbam. Likewise, R. Idi bar Avin said, "As in a case where the animal ate one of several garden beds, but we do not know whether it ate a lean one or a productive one; he then pays a productive one" (*Bava Kamma* 6b). It seems to me that [the case is one where] the animal caused destruction, to a greater or lesser degree, to all the beds that it passed through, and the Torah placed the injuring party in the inferior position, making him liable to pay as if that which his animal destroyed were entirely the best.

Rava objected (ibid.) [that R. Idi's rule contradicted the principle] "one who seeks to recover from his fellow, upon him is the burden of proof." However, this principle justly applies when it has not been established that one person caused damage to another, but once the injuring party has been identified, it is not unlikely that the Torah would penalize him by making him pay as if the damaged property were the best. On the other hand, R. Akiva [ibid.] was of the opinion that Scripture merely intended to collect damages from [the *injuring* party's] best land; that is, if he offers to give the injured party land in compensation for the damages, he must give of his best land [but only so much of such land as is needed for compensation].

**22:5.** "Whenever a fire goes forth and finds some thorn bushes, and a heap of grain or the standing grain is consumed by it, or the field (is damaged), the one who has caused the fire will pay.

*Whenever a fire goes forth.* Even by itself (Rashi), or by means of an ordinary wind. In some places it is customary, before the arrival of the rainy season, to burn off the dry grass on the surface of the field (in Italian this is called *debbiare*, "to fertilize with ashes"), and the fire is likely to spread from one field to another and cause great damage. [Richard] Chandler, in his *Travels in Asia Minor* [1775], wrote that once a Turkish man came toward him emptying the ashes from his tobacco pipe, and a spark fell to the ground and set fire to the grass that had dried by the heat of the sun; the wind blew it, and as a result there was a great forest fire. Only after some hours and great effort and exertion were they able to extinguish the blaze.

*a heap of grain (gadish).* This is the term for grain after it is harvested, when it is heaped on the threshing floor (Kimhi). The word is derived from the root *gadash*, which is not [otherwise] found in the Bible but remained in Rabbinic Hebrew, in which the term *middah gedushah* refers to a "heaping" measure that exceeds the brim. Consequently, the dome that used to be built on top of a grave was called a *gadish* (Job 21:32) (Kimhi, citing R. Hai Gaon). The grave itself is so called in Arabic (Gesenius) after the dome; similarly in Latin, *tumulus* means both "heap" and "grave."

*the standing grain (ha-kamah).* Grain that is attached to the ground, so called because it stands (*kamah*) erect.

**22:6.** "When someone gives to his neighbor money or furnishings to guard, and (the object) is stolen from the house of that man, if the thief is found, he will pay double.

*When someone gives to his neighbor money or furnishings.* These are chattels, which the owner gives over to be guarded in the neighbor's house with his other possessions; therefore, if they are stolen from the neighbor's house, he is exempt, because he guarded them [merely] as he did his own possessions. However, in the subsequent section in which it is written, "When one gives to his neighbor as ass, an ox, a lamb, or any animal to guard" [below, v. 9], given that animals customarily graze in the field, it is certain that when the owner deposited them, he did so in order to have them guarded from thieves. Therefore, if they are stolen, the neighbor is liable (Rashbam).

## *Mishpatim*

The Rabbis interpreted this section as referring to a *shomer ḥinnam* ("gratuitous bailee") and the subsequent section as referring to a *shomer sakhar* ("paid bailee"). It is true that money or furnishings, which stay where they are put, are customarily guarded for free, while animals are difficult to guard, and so one customarily takes a fee for them. Yet this is not necessarily always the case, for it is conceivable that one might take it upon himself to guard his neighbor's animal with the rest of his own animals for free, and even though he would have had the right not to accept responsibility for the animal, once he has done so [it might be said that] he is liable for negligence if it is stolen, notwithstanding that he has taken no fee. [However,] the Rabbis were lenient, as was their custom, and said that he is not liable for negligence if he has not taken a fee.

***and (that object) is stolen from the house of that man.*** According to his own declaration (Rashi), for it is also possible that the object was not stolen from his house, but that he stole it for himself. In that case [i.e., if no thief is found], the judges are to investigate and decide according to what their eyes see, as is specified below: "And the one whom the judges condemn will pay double to the other" (v. 8).

**22:7. "If the thief is not found, the owner of the house [that is, the bailee] will present himself to the tribunal (so that it may be ascertained) if he has not put forth his hand on his neighbor's property.**

***if he has not put forth his hand*** *(im lo shalaḥ yado).* Rashi, Mendelssohn, and Rosenmueller interpreted this to mean that he is to swear that he did not put forth his hand; similarly below, "An oath (in the name) of the Lord will take place between the two, (to ascertain) if he has not put forth his hand on his neighbor's property" (v. 10). Mendelssohn and Rosenmueller maintained that the words *im lo* ("if not") introduce a [negative] oath, but this is a gross error, for every instance of the use of the words *im lo* in connection with an oath is meant in a positive and not negative sense, as in:

- "'If I am immortal,' says the Lord, 'just as you have expressed yourselves [*im lo ka-asher dibbartem*] before Me, so I will deal with you'" (Num. 14:28);
- "The Lord of hosts has sworn, saying, 'Surely as I have thought [*im lo ka-asher dimmiti*], so shall it come to pass'" (Isa. 14:24);
- "Yet surely I will make you [*im lo ashitkha*] a wilderness" (Jer. 22:6);

- "God do so to me, and more also, if you will not be captain of the host [*im lo sar tsava tihyeh*] before me continually instead of Joab" [i.e., "surely you will be captain of the host"] (2 Sam. 19:14).

So it must be, for anyone who says *im lo* means to say, "May such and such befall me *if* I have *not* done, or *if* I will *not* do, such and such." Surely such a person's intention is to say, "Truly I did or will do such and such." Conversely, when the meaning is negative, one says *im* without *lo,* as in, "I raise my hand [in an oath]… that not even a thread [*im mi-ḥut*], not even a shoelace, (in sum) I will not take anything that belongs to you" (Gen. 14:22-23); "Swear to me… that you will not be ungrateful [*im tishkor*] to me" (Gen. 21:23); there are many other such instances.

Here, where the bailee says *im lo shalaḥ yado,* if this statement were to be understood as introducing an oath, the meaning would be that he was swearing that he did indeed put forth his hand on his neighbor's property. Therefore I say that the phrase *im lo* as used here does not introduce an oath, but is to be understood literally; however, the verse is elliptical and should be taken to mean that the owner of the house will present himself to the tribunal *so that it may be ascertained* if he did not put forth his hand on his neighbor's property. This ascertainment was not to be by means of an oath, but rather by investigation of the judges according to what they would see. If they were to decide that he put forth his hand, i.e., that he was the thief, then he would pay double as stated in the next verse.

**put forth his hand** *(shalaḥ yado).* One who "puts forth his hand" (*shole'aḥ yad*) on something handles it with the power to do with it as he will, as in, "But on the spoil they laid not their hand [*lo shaleḥu et yadam*]" (Esth. 9:16). Here, likewise, if he "put forth his hand on his neighbor's property," this means that he stole it. According to the Rabbis, one who "puts forth his hand" on a deposited object to use it for his own benefit assumes responsibility for it (*Bava Kamma* 107b).

**22:8. "In any case of bad faith, whether it involves an ox, an ass, a lamb, a garment, (in sum) any lost thing that one says, 'It is this,' the dispute of the two will be brought to the tribunal, and the one whom the judges condemn will pay double to the other.**

***In any case of bad faith.*** After speaking of one who lies about a deposited object and says that it was stolen from him, the Torah speaks of one who lies

## *Mishpatim*

about a lost object or anything that has not been deposited with him; Reuben says to Simeon, "This thing in your possession is mine, and you stole it or found it," and then they both go before the court. The one whom the judges find to be in the wrong, whether the plaintiff or the defendant, pays double like a thief. Even if the plaintiff is in the wrong—in which case he is not a thief, but rather one who libels his neighbor—he still pays like a thief because of what he plotted against his fellow, that is, he sought to have him held liable as a thief.

***any lost thing.*** Any item that Reuben claims to have lost and says "it is this" which is found in Simeon's house; however, the Rabbis were lenient, as was their custom; see their interpretation in Rashi's comment.[20]

This verse does not deal with a bailee and thus is [strictly speaking] out of place. However, because it contains the phrase "the dispute of the two will be brought to the tribunal," similar to the phrase in the preceding verse, "the owner of the house will present himself to the tribunal," it therefore appears here (Judah Aryeh Osimo).

**22:9. "When one gives to his neighbor an ass, an ox, a lamb, or any animal to guard, and it dies, or is crippled, or is taken away without anyone seeing it —**

***When one gives to his neighbor,*** *etc.* See above at v. 6.

***or is taken away*** *(nishbah,* lit. "is taken captive"). The term *sheviyyah* ("capture") properly applies only to human beings, but here it is employed in order to provide a play on words with *nishbar* ("is crippled").

**22:10. "An oath (by the name) of the Lord will take place between the two, (to ascertain) if he has not put forth his hand on his neighbor's property, and the owner will receive [that which is found, that is, the dead or crippled animal], and the other will not pay.**

***An oath (by the name) of the Lord.*** In order to ascertain that he has not put forth his hand on his neighbor's property. Here, an oath will be helpful

---

20. Rashi, citing statements from the Mekhilta and *Bava Kamma* 107b, notes that the Rabbis took the phrase "it is this" (*ki hu zeh*) as a partial admission by the defendant, i.e., "it is this *only* that I owe you, but the rest was stolen from me." According to this view, only such a partial admission would obligate the defendant to take an oath.

to him, for the animal is present, whether dead or crippled, unlike the case above [v. 7], where the bailee claimed that a deposited object was stolen from his house. Even if the animal is not present and he claims that it was taken away, this is a more common occurrence than the theft of an object from a house, for animals graze in the field, and it was likely in those days that a troop [of robbers] would spread out and capture them by force.

***if he has not put forth his hand...*** To use the animal, for when the animal died or was crippled, it might be suspected that he put it to work for his own needs and by this means it died [or was crippled].

***and the owner will receive*** *(ve-lakah)*. The animal's owner will take it as it is, dead or crippled, and the bailee will not pay (Abravanel). The Rabbis took the work *ve-lakah* to mean that the owner was to "accept" the oath, but the meaning is the same, only that when the bailee claims that the animal was taken away, there is nothing [physical] for the owner to take, and thus the Rabbis said that he was to "take" [i.e., "accept"] the oath.

**22:11. "If, however, (the animal) has been stolen from him, he will pay for it to its owner.**

***If, however, (the animal) has been stolen from him.*** Even if he is not a paid bailee, given that he took it upon himself to guard an animal, which customarily wanders here and there, and is easy to steal, he is negligent and thus liable. However, the Rabbis were lenient [and applied this rule only to a paid bailee]; see above at v. 6.

**22:12. "If it has been torn to pieces [by some wild beast], he will bring him evidence of it [some piece]. He will not pay for the torn animal.**

***he will bring him evidence of it*** *(yevi'ehu ed)*. He will bring a few of the torn animal's limbs to serve for him as evidence and proof that the animal was torn to pieces, as it says, "As the shepherd rescues out of the mouth of the lion two legs, or a piece of an ear" (Amos 3:12) (Rashbam, Ibn Ezra). In the same vein, Jacob said [to Laban], "I did not bring you [for my justification] the (remains of the) animals seized [by the wild beasts]" (Gen. 31:39).

So it is translated in the Jerusalem Targum, in one of its versions, "He will bring him from among its limbs as evidence," while in another version (the one attributed to Jonathan ben Uzziel) there is a composite interpretation

## Mishpatim

derived from two readings, *ed* ("evidence") [which is the standard reading] and *ad* ("toward") [a reading based on a different vocalization of the same written word עד]: "He will bring him evidence, or he will bring him toward the body [*gufa*]." It seems to me that the latter word should read *guba* ("den"); i.e., he will bring the owner toward the preying beast's den. It goes without saying that the word *ha-terefah* ("the torn animal") [which word appears immediately after *yevi'ehu ed*] refers both forward and backward [so as to express two ideas]: *yevi'ehu ad ha-terefah* ("he will bring him to the torn animal") and *ha-terefah lo yeshallem* ("for the torn animal he will not pay"), in accordance with the Jerusalem Targum's interpretation [in the second version]. From here there is proof that the vocalization system (*nikkud*) was not yet fixed when the Targum was made; this is also the opinion of Zunz [*Die Gottesdienstlichen Vorträge*], p. 76 note C.

**he will bring him** *(yevi'ehu).* The Heb. means either "he will bring *him* [evidence]" or (as per Jacob Hai Pardo) "he will bring *it*," i.e., the torn animal, to serve for him as evidence, as in, "I did not bring you the animals seized" (Gen. 31:39). If no part of the torn animal remained, the preying beast having carried it off whole to its den, the law of the "captive" animal (above, v. 9) would apply, and the bailee would take an oath (A.H. Mainster).

**22:13. "When someone borrows from his neighbor (some animal), and (the latter) becomes crippled or dies, if the owner was not alongside him, he will pay for it.**

*if the owner was not alongside him (ba'alav ein immo).* The word *im* ("if") is missing in the Heb., as occurs in many instances. One who borrows an animal to work with will often take the owner along as well to stand over the animal in the course of the work. In such a case, it is the owner's responsibility to guard it against death or crippling. However, if the owner is not alongside him, the borrower is presumed to have overworked the animal or to have failed to watch over it properly, and thus he must pay.

**22:14. "If the owner was alongside him, he will not pay. If, however, he was a hired worker, he came for his wages [that is, if the animal's owner was there to work for hire, he could not watch over it, and then his presence does not exonerate the other from the obligation of paying him for it, if it dies or becomes crippled].**

## Shadal on Exodus

***If, however, he was a hired worker*** (*sakhir*), *etc.* But if the ox or ass is not borrowed but hired,[21] then the animal comes for its hire (*ba bi-sekharo*) into the hand of the hirer (*sokher*), not by way of borrowing, and the hirer does not get all the benefit, since it is by means of his payment that he makes use of the animal; thus the hirer is not governed by the law of the borrower to be held liable for accidental injury (Rashi). Consequently, he does not pay if the animal becomes crippled or dies [even if the owner is absent], for the animal does not come to him free of charge, but rather for its hire that he pays to the owner. It is under this condition that the ox's owner receives his hire, that if the ox dies or becomes crippled, the damages will be borne by him.

This is in accordance with Ibn Ezra's comment, "For this reason he received his hire." However, in his short commentary he wrote, "This misfortune come to him because of the hire that he received"; it seems that in his opinion, the verb *ba* ("comes" or "came") refers back to [the unstated subject] *ha-nezek* ("the injury"); this is the view taken by the Jerusalem Targum ascribed to Jonathan ben Uzziel, as well as Mendelssohn and the scholar Reggio. In my opinion, however, it would be more correct to follow Rashi's interpretation, "The ox comes for its hire," without having to make the verb *ba* refer back to an unstated subject, which would be *ha-ra* ("the misfortune") or *ha-nezek* ("the injury").

The hirer is exempt from accidental damages; that is, if the animal becomes crippled or dies, he does not pay. If, however, the animal is stolen or lost, he is liable to pay. This is the position of the anonymous Mishnah (*Shevuot* 8:1): "The paid bailee [*nosei sekhar*] and the hirer [*sokher*] take an oath with respect to that which was crippled or taken by force, and they pay for that which was lost or stolen." So ruled Maimonides (*Sekhirut* 1:3), and so logic suggests, for one who hires out his animal knows that the animal will not do its work without a person to supervise it, and when he delivers it to the hirer, he does so with that understanding, i.e., that the hirer is to supervise it and not leave it alone in such a way that it may be lost or stolen; therefore, if it is stolen or lost, the hirer must pay. However, in the *baraita* R. Meir and R. Judah dispute over this point (*Bava Metsia* 93, 95), and Rashi cites their dispute [in his comment on the present verse].

Mendelssohn was mistaken when he wrote that according to Rashi, Scripture does not specify what compensation the hirer must pay. Rather, according to Rashi, the phrase *ba bi-sekharo* teaches us that the hirer does not

---

21. The first part of this comment does not conform with Shadal's own translation. Note, however, that Shadal goes on to consider and ultimately adopt the interpretation given in the translation.

## Mishpatim

pay if the animal becomes crippled or dies, for he is not liable for accidental damages. Mendelssohn himself, at the end of his comment, contradicts what he states at the beginning, by saying that the phrase *ba bi-sekharo* refers to the coming of the ox to the hirer, in order to provide a reason why the law of the hirer is not like the law of the borrower. He is thus conceding that according to Rashi [who likewise holds that *ba bi-sekharo* refers back to the animal], *ba bi-sekharo* indicates that the law of the hirer is not like that of the borrower; that is, that the hirer does not pay if the animal becomes crippled or dies, as the borrower must do. How, then, can Mendelssohn say that according to Rashi, Scripture does not specify anything about the matter of payment?

Although Rashi did indeed write that Scripture "does not state explicitly what his law is," this means that even though the phrase *ba bi-sekharo* teaches that the hirer is not liable for accidental damages, Scripture does not specify what his law is with respect to theft or loss. Thus the Sages of Israel were in dispute on this issue.

Now according to this [explication above], the word *sakhir* ("hired") in this verse modifies "ox" or "ass." Similarly we find in Isaiah (7:20) the adjective *sakhir* transferred to modify that which is not human or even animal: "with a razor that is hired [*be-ta'ar ha-sekhirah*]." However, in the year 5596 (1836) it seemed to me that the reference was not to the animal but to the human, and this is how I interpreted the phrase: if the animal's owner was hired by the borrower to perform another labor alongside him, and not to stay by his animal, then the owner would not be able to supervise his animal, for "he came for his wages [*ba bi-sekharo*]" and he would have to do his work. Therefore the borrower would not be exempt from paying [accidental damages] on the ground that the owner was with him. Yet the Rabbis were lenient with the borrower and said that the rule of "if the owner was alongside him" applied whether the owner was there for the same work or for different work.

Subsequently, in the year 5604 (1844), it seemed to me that it could not be denied that *sakhir* modified "ox," for otherwise there would be no mention at all in the Torah of the law of the hirer. But now (Sivan 5619 (1859)) I have found that both R. Joseph Bekhor Shor and Hizkuni adopted the interpretation that I favored in 1836, and I hereby go back and affirm that interpretation. The point that I found difficult—that the Torah would then have made no mention of the law of the hirer—signifies nothing, for in Moses' time the people were not accustomed to hiring out animals; rather, everyone did his work with his own animals. If one sometimes needed more than he had, he would borrow it from his neighbor, and people would lend to each other for free: "Today you lend to me, and tomorrow I will lend to you." In all of Scripture we find no mention or hint of the hiring of animals. It is only at the time of the Babylonian exile (Zech. 8:10) that we find the expression *u-sekhar ha-behemah* ("any hire for an animal" or "profits from animals"), and even there, there is no proof that the reference is [specifically] to the hiring out of animals. Rather, the reference may be to any kind of benefit that a person may derive from his animals, i.e., their offspring, milk, fleece, or labor.

**22:15. "Whenever someone seduces a virgin who was not betrothed, and lies with her, he will endow her to himself for a wife [that is, he will marry her, first paying her father that sum that the husband customarily made a gift of to the wife's father].**

*Whenever someone seduces.* Generally, a man will not seduce a virgin who is worthy, according to his dignity, of marrying him; if it were so, then he would propose marriage to her. But those who consider themselves to be of a higher station, when they see common women who are attractive and they desire them, will seduce them by making them promises of marriage. The virgin will thus be willing, for the sake of marrying an upper-class man, but he will have no such thought or intention; he will think only of satisfying his desire with her and then leaving her. Therefore the Torah commands the seducer to endow her in the manner of a wife and marry her, even if she is not of his station.

If, however, the opposite occurs, and the girl is of a more honorable status than the seducer—and her father thus refuses to give her to him as a wife—then the man must weigh to her father as much money as is the bride-price of virgins (next v.), because he has disqualified her in the eyes of other young men (Abravanel).

*he will endow her to himself (mahor yimharennah lo) for a wife.* He will marry her, and he will give her father the amount of a virgin's bride-price (*mohar*), i.e., that which others would have given her father in order to take his daughter if she were a virgin. The bride-price (according to the Rabbis) was the fifty silver shekels specified in the case of rape (Deut. 22:29). Rashi interpreted this to mean that the man was to write her a *ketubbah* (marriage document), but the *ketubbah* was a [later] enactment of the Rabbis so that divorcing her should not seem easy to him.

## Mishpatim

**22:16. "If, however, the father refuses to give her to him, he must weigh [pay] as much silver as is the bride-price of virgins [that is, the seducer will pay the girl's father the above-mentioned amount].**

*he must weigh...* For he has disqualified her in the eyes of other young men, and it would be difficult for her father to find one who would be willing to take her and give him the bride-price; therefore, the seducer must give him what he has caused him to lose. Note that the Torah has consideration for the father, who may refuse to give his daughter to the seducer but does not thereby forfeit the bride-price, for otherwise a poor man could seduce a rich man's daughter and then marry her without paying the bride-price, to the father's ire.

**22:17. "A witch you shall not allow to live.**

*you shall not allow to live* (*lo tehayyeh*, lit., "do not cause to live"). Do not let her live but seek her out to kill her, for it is the way of witches to do their deeds in hidden places (Rashbam). Although a female witch (*mekhashefah*) is mentioned, the same law applies to a male, but Scripture spoke of the common case, since women were more usually involved in such practices (*Sanhedrin* 67a, Rashi, and Ibn Ezra). Thus we find:

- "So long as the harlotries of your mother Jezebel and her witchcrafts [*u-kheshafeha*] are so many" (2 Kings 9:22);
- "Because of the multitude of the harlotries of the well-favored harlot, the mistress of witchcrafts [*keshafim*], who sells nations through her harlotries and families through her witchcrafts" (Nahum 3:4);
- "Stand now with your enchantments, and with the multitude of your sorceries [*keshafayikh*, f. pl.]" (Isa. 47:12).

So attested Maimonides (*Guide for the Perplexed* 3:37), in accordance with that which he found in the books of the Sabeans, that most of the acts of witchcraft had to be performed by women.

The word *mekhashefah* is derived, in my opinion (as is the word *ashaf*, "enchanter"), from the root *shuf*, which denotes "covering" or "concealment," as in, "Surely the darkness shall envelop me [*yeshufeni*]" (Ps. 139:11). Similarly, *be-lateihem*, "with their arcane arts" (Exod. 7:22) denotes acts that are performed in secret and hiding (*artes occultae*). The reason that the witch was liable [to the death penalty] is that every witch is also an idolator (as per Maimonides in the *Guide, loc. cit.*) and furthermore brings the public toward belief in idolatry and its efficacy.

# Shadal on Exodus

**22:18. "Whoever lies with any beast will be put to death.**

***Whoever lies with any beast.*** It seems to me that this, too, was among the idolatrous customs, on the model of all other types of "commingled species" (*kil'ayim*), which were themselves standard practices in idolatry (as Maimonides attested [*Guide* 3:37]). This was also the opinion of Abravanel and the author of the *Akedah* [R. Isaac Arama], who cited as support a statement of the Rabbis about Balaam, that he used to cohabit with his donkey. For this reason was this law written between those concerning the witch and one who sacrifices to other gods. In addition, we know that in some locations in Egypt they worshipped goats, and that the women would engage in sodomy with them.

**22:19. "One who sacrifices to the gods will be destroyed, (one who sacrifices, that is, to any of them) except the Lord exclusively.**

***One who sacrifices… will be destroyed*** *(yoḥoram)*. We do not find the term *ḥerem* ("destruction," "ban") used in connection with [any other] persons who are put to death by a court. Nachmanides said that Scripture was likely including the sacrifice along with the sacrificer, i.e., that all would be destroyed. The Jerusalem Targum translates, "He will be put to death by sword and his possessions will be destroyed." This seems to me to be the plain meaning of the verse, i.e., "he and his property will be destroyed," as was to be done in the case of the city condemned for idolatry (*ir ha-niddaḥat*); there (Deut. 13:17) it says, "And nothing of the *ḥerem* will attach to your hands." This was likewise done with Achan (see Joshua 7).

***except the Lord exclusively.*** This is to be understood as, "Do not sacrifice except to the Lord exclusively."

***to the gods*** *(la-elohim)*. [The Heb. is to be understood] as in, "There is none like You among the gods [*ba-elohim*], O Lord" (Ps. 86:8); i.e., other gods; this is inferable from the context. The Samaritans emended the phrase to read *la-elohim aḥerim* ("to the other gods").

**22:20. "Do not oppress the foreigner, and do not molest him, for you (too) were foreigners in the land of Egypt.**

***Do not oppress the foreigner*** *(ve-ger lo toneh)*. [The term *hona'ah*] indicates the kind of exploitation that the strong impose upon the weak, who know that there is no one to champion their cause or strengthen their hand; such exploitation involves monetary matters, as it is written:

- "And when you make a sale [of some property] to your neighbor, or make a purchase from your neighbor, you must not abuse [*tonu*] one another" (Lev. 25:14);
- "And My princes shall no more wrong [*yonu*] My people" (Ezek. 45:8) [referring to land ownership];
- "The prince shall not take of the people's inheritance, to thrust them wrongfully [*lehonotam*] out of their possession" (Ezek. 46:18).

Similarly, the term *hona'ah* as used in Rabbinic Hebrew also refers to money, but in addition, *hona'at devarim* ("verbal *hona'ah*") is used in reference to any speech that causes pain to its hearer. The Rabbis explained (*Bava Metsia* 58b) that the prohibition given here, *lo toneh*, refers to verbal *hona'ah*, because we have already been commanded not to oppress our brothers monetarily in the verse, "And when you make a sale...." Nevertheless, this explanation provides no proof as to the [plain] interpretation of the present verse, for the warning against the oppression of foreigners is repeated several times. The correct interpretation is found in the statement in the Mishnah (ibid.), "Just as there is *hona'ah* in purchasing and selling, so there is *hona'ah* in words," i.e., the principal type of *hona'ah* is in purchasing and selling, but verbal *hona'ah* is also a contemptible thing that should be guarded against.

Scripture speaks here of the common case [i.e., the oppression of a foreigner], for the foreigner has no relatives to strengthen his hand; similarly it is stated afterward, "Do not mistreat any widow or orphan" (next v.).

**and do not molest him** *(ve-lo tilhatsennu)*. [This refers to] all other kinds of mistreatment besides exploitation and the theft of money, as above (3:9), "the oppression [*lahats*] that the Egyptians make them suffer." The root *lahats* is related to the roots *alats* ("to compel") and *its* ("to urge, press").

**for you (too) were foreigners in the land of Egypt.** So it is in the history of the human soul, that one's compassion is stirred when one sees a neighbor suffering a pain that he himself once felt (Mendelssohn). This is in the same sense as, "You indeed know the soul of the foreigner, for you were foreigners in the land of Egypt" (Exod. 23:9).

The Torah established two things as supports for its commandments, and they are Divine retribution (i.e., reward and punishment) and the sense of compassion, which is natural in humankind, but routine behavior may either increase or diminish its power.[22] The sense of compassion is truly the sturdiest and most permanent foundation for the Torah of humankind and the perfection of virtues; without it, a person would never do good to his fellow unless it were to his own advantage. On the one hand, the Torah bases its commandments on this sense of compassion, and on the other hand it provides supports for this sense in order to strengthen it and to safeguard it from diminution. This is accomplished by means of numerous commandments that are not intended for their own sake, but rather for this purpose, such as the prohibition against slaughtering a mother animal and its offspring on the same day (Lev. 22:28), and the like.

**22:21. "Do not mistreat any widow or orphan.**

*Do not mistreat (lo te'annun).* The Heb. is in the plural. The command is to the nation in general, that is, to the judges who will decide their cases; they are not to allow any individual to mistreat a widow or orphan without being punished. Therefore the penalty falls upon the nation at large: "And I will slay you [*etkhem*, pl.] with the sword" (below, v. 23).

**22:22. "If you mistreat him—for if he cries to Me, I will listen to his complaint—**

*If you mistreat him.* This phrase is attached to the verse below: "My wrath will be kindled," etc. The phrase "for if he cries to Me," etc., is parenthetical, and the meaning is, "Do not think that they have no one to save them, for indeed their Redeemer is powerful and will champion their cause against you; I am the Father of orphans and Judge of widows, and if they have no one to cry to or hear their complaints, I Myself will hear their cries."

**22:23. "My wrath will be kindled, and I will slay you with the sword, and your wives will remain widows, and your children orphans.**

---

22. This theme of the sense of compassion and the fear of Divine retribution as the two great foundations of the Torah is one that Shadal repeatedly returns to in his writings. See, for example, his *Yesodei ha-Torah,* translated by Noah H. Rosenbloom in *Luzzatto's Ethico-Psychological Interpretation of Judaism* (New York: Yeshiva University, 1965), in particular pp. 157-170, and see also his response to a friend's request for spiritual guidance, translated by Daniel A. Klein in "A Letter to Almeda: Shadal's Guide for the Perplexed," *Ḥakirah* vol. 10 (2010), in particular pp. 239-240.

## Mishpatim

***My wrath will be kindled,*** *etc.* I will take the actions of a redeemer, whose heart would be stirred to avenge the blood of his kin.

***and your wives will remain widows,*** *etc.* [This admonition is] in the same vein as, "For you (too) were foreigners" (above, v. 20), in that it is based on the heart's emotion, portraying the possibility of their wives becoming widows and their children orphans, and as a result, their compassion would be stirred toward the orphan and the widow.

**22:24. "If you lend money to My people, to some poor person near you, do not act toward him in the manner of a creditor; do not impose upon him (to pay any) interest.**

***If you lend money to My people.*** To an Israelite. A duty to lend free of interest is not imposed by the law of logic, and thus it is customary among all nations to take interest one from another as compensation for what the lender could have earned with his money if he had not loaned it. Yet the Torah commanded Israel to treat one another not according to law alone, but with compassion, mercy, and brotherhood.

***to some poor person near you.*** This elucidates the previous phrase: "I refer only to a poor person, who borrows out of necessity, not to a rich person who borrows in order to do business and amass wealth."

***near you*** *(immakh,* lit., "with you"). From among your brothers.

***do not act toward him in the manner of a creditor*** *(ke-nosheh).* "If he cannot pay at the specified time, and he asks you to extend the time for him, do not act as creditors do, extending the tine only with interest" (Rashbam similarly commented, "Do not impose interest upon him in order to extend his time"). The word נשא in Arabic means "to extend the time for a borrower" (Rosenmueller). [The Hebrew cognate *nosheh*] was later transferred to denote any lender, and still later the term *neshi* was applied to the loan itself, as in, "Pay your debt [*nishyekh*]" (2 Kings 4:7). The Torah goes on to specify, "Do not impose [*tesimun*] upon him interest," using the plural verb *tesimun* so as to address the nation at large, that is, the courts; they were not to allow the lender to demand interest from the borrower.

***interest*** *(neshekh).* So called because it "bites" *(noshekh).* Similarly, Lucan [in his book *Pharsalia*] (1.181) [refers to] *usura vorax* ("voracious usury") (Gesenius).

**22:25. "If you take as a pledge the garment of your neighbor, before the sun sets you will restore it to him.**

***the garment of*** *(salmat)* ***your neighbor.*** The *salmah* is a square or almost square garment without sleeves, customarily worn to this day by the Arabs who are called Bedouins; from them it came to us as well, and it is called *Beduine*. They wear it over their clothes when they go out, and they also cover themselves with it at night on their beds.

***restore it*** *(teshivennu).* This refers back to the [masculine] noun *ḥavol* ("pledge"), which [does not appear in the verse, but is understood] on the strength of the verb phrase *ḥavol taḥbol,* "take as a pledge" (Ibn Ezra).[23]

The verse does not say that the creditor may come back and take the garment in the morning. The plain meaning, it seems to me, is that since the debtor is so poor that he has nothing to give as a pledge but his garment, the Torah permits the creditor to take his garment from him for one day, so that the debtor will have to suffer the indignity of going out without a garment or else to be shut inside his home; but if he nevertheless does not pay, the Torah believes him that he cannot afford to do so, and it requires the creditor to return his garment to him and abandon the claim against him.

This would indeed be the law with respect to a *ḥovel*, i.e., a creditor who takes a pledge by duress, for the term *ḥavalah* ("indemnity") never refers to a pledge *(mashkon)* that is given willingly at the time of the loan, but rather denotes that which is taken from the debtor when the time for repayment arrives and he fails to pay (see Rashi). If, however, the debtor gives a pledge [of a garment] at the time of the loan, he is not covered by this law, for he has already made it clear (as per Gersonides) that he is able to do without this covering.

The Rabbis said (in the Mekhilta) that a creditor may take the pledge of a daytime covering by night and a nighttime covering by day, but he must return a daytime covering by day and a nighttime covering by night. They were thus lenient to the creditor, in order to avoid locking the door [of credit] in the face of borrowers. Still, how would the creditor benefit, given that he

---

23. The verb *teshivennu*, with the masculine suffix, cannot grammatically refer to *salmah*, a feminine noun.

## Mishpatim

would have to return the pledge daily? Saadiah Gaon responded that taking a pledge [even on such terms] would benefit the creditor in that the debtor would be deterred from going and borrowing money from another person and giving that person the pledge. My student R. Samuel Solomon Olper says that the fact that the debtor would be compelled to go every evening or every morning to take back his garment would ensure that he would make an effort to pay his debt.

**22:26. "For that is his only covering; it is his garment (needed) for his skin. In what will he lie [if the creditor does not give it back]? Now, when he cries out to Me, I will listen, for I am merciful.**

*For that is his only covering,* etc. All of this is stated in order to arouse compassion, so that [the creditor] will act beyond the line of strict justice.[24]

**22:27. "Do not curse the judges, nor shall you imprecate the prince of your people.**

*Do not curse the judges (elohim lo tekallel).* The term *kelalah* most basically refers to one who curses another to his face, for this causes shame (*kalon*) and degradation to the person who is cursed. On the other hand, the term *arirah* [as used here in the phrase "nor shall you imprecate [*ta'or*] the prince of your people"] refers to one who curses another outside of that person's presence and says, "Cursed [*arur*] be so-and-so"; when one says *arur attah* ("cursed be you"), then he is called a *mekallel* (my student R. Joseph Shabbetai Basevi). It was said of Abraham, "And he who curses you I will curse [*u-mekallelekha a'or*]" (Gen. 12:3), that is, if one would curse or slight [*yakleh*] Abraham to his face, God would subject that person to a curse (*arirah*) outside his presence, for God would not [deign to] reveal Himself to that wicked person to say to him *arur attah*.

Every instance [in Scripture] of the use of the verb *arar* refers to a curse outside of one's presence, e.g., "Curse ye [*oru*] Meroz... curse ye bitterly [*oru*

---

24. Shadal elaborates on this theme in *Meḥkerei ha-Yahadut* (Mosad ha-Rav Kook ed., p. 34), as cited by Nehama Leibowitz (*Studies in Exodus,* pp. 419-420): "The creditor quite rightly wishes to take a pledge when the debtor refuses to pay. If he has to turn it in every evening, there is no doubt that the borrower will never pay back his debt. Why should I return it? He has my money. How am I ever to get it back? What concern is it of mine in what he sleeps? So says the creditor. All the philosophers and honor-seekers will justify him. But the Torah, teaching us compassion and generosity, says to the creditor: 'In what else will he sleep!?'"

## Shadal on Exodus

*aror*] the inhabitants thereof, because they came not to the help of the Lord" (Judg. 5:23); and similarly, "Come, please, curse me [*arah li*] this people… and one whom you curse [*ta'or*] is cursed [*yu'ar*]" (Num. 22:6). Even though Balaam [the addressee in the latter verse] saw the Israelites when he stood to curse them, they did not see him and did not hear his words, and thus no shame or degradation would have come to them if he had [actually] cursed them.

Eventually, however, the use of the term *kelalah* was extended to include cursing outside of one's presence as well; thus it was said in connection with Balaam: "to curse you [*lekalelekka*]" (Deut. 23:5); "to curse you [*lekallel etkhem*]" (Josh. 24:9); "to curse him [*lekalelo*]" (Neh. 13:2). Similar examples are:

- "And they cursed [*va-yekalelu*] Abimelech" (Judg. 9:27);
- "And [Job] cursed [*va-yekallel*] his day" (Job 3:1);
- "But they curse [*yekalelu*] inwardly" (Ps. 62:5);
- "Curse not [*al tekallel*] the king, no, not even in your thought" (Eccl. 10:20).

With respect to the "prince" [in the present v.], it says *lo ta'or*, for it is unlikely that anyone would dare to curse him to his face, but with respect to "the judges," it says *lo tekallel*, using the general term for all types of cursing and reviling, whether within or outside one's presence.

**the prince of your people** *(ve-nasi ve-ammekha)*. Any kind of "prince," even the prince of a tribe, for a tribe itself may be called a "people" *(am)*. The Rabbis took the command *elohim lo tekallel* as an admonition against blaspheming God as well as cursing a judge. The case of blasphemy can undoubtedly be inferred *a fortiori* from the case of cursing judges, for the prestige of judges derives solely from the fact that they render God's justice, speaking words that are like God's own words, and thus they are referred to by the term *elohim* [lit., "God"]. Hence the admonition against cursing a judge encompasses blasphemy *a fortiori* (even though, according to the Rabbis, an admonition (*azharah*) that is logically derived, as from *a fortiori* reasoning, is not a true *azharah* [that would be the basis for punishment]).

Philo of Alexandria [*Life of Moses* 2:205] and Josephus Flavius [*Antiquities* 4:8] interpreted this verse to mean, "Do not curse the gods of other nations," but this was merely by way of ingratiating themselves with the nations.

**22:28. "Do not delay your solid and liquid produce [that is, the respective priestly privileges]. The firstborn of your sons you will give to Me.**

***your solid and liquid produce*** *(mele'atekha ve-dim'akha).* From the context it can be inferred that because it subsequently states, "The firstborn of your sons you will give to Me," and also, "The same will you do with your oxen and with your flocks" (next v.), which refers to the firstborn, here too the reference is to the tribute *(terumah)* of the first of the new grain, which is given to the priest, just as the firstborn son's redemption money goes to the priest and the firstborn of animals is eaten by the priest. R. Saadiah Gaon was likely correct in identifying the *mele'ah* as including the grain crop (as in, "Otherwise the product of the sowing [*ha-mele'ah ha-zera*] will become sacred," Deut. 22:9) as well as the wine crop (as in, "And juice [*ve-kha-mele'ah*] from the vat," Num. 18:27); the *dema* is the oil that come out [of the olive press] drop by drop, like a tear *(dim'ah).*

**22:29. "The same will you do with your oxen and with your flocks: seven days (the firstborn) will be with its mother, and on the eighth day you will give it to Me.**

***The same will you do with your oxen,*** *etc.* To sanctify the firstborn among them.

***and on the eighth day you will give it to Me.*** In the desert, they were able to present it on that same day, but when they came to the land of Israel, it was not always possible to bring it up to Jerusalem on the eighth day precisely. Therefore in the Mekhilta, the phrase is interpreted to mean "on the eighth day and afterward" (my student, the late R. David Hai Ashkenazi).

**22:30. "A holy people you will be to Me, and meat (found) on the field, (that is) an animal torn to pieces, do not eat; to the dog you will throw it."**

***and meat on the field, an animal torn to pieces*** *(u-vasar ba-sadeh terefah).* It seems to me that these words are to be taken to mean "meat that is found on the field, that is, torn to pieces," i.e., a wild beast has torn an animal to pieces, and its limbs remain on the field. The reason for the prohibition, according to R. Moses Ha-Cohen (cited by Ibn Ezra), Maimonides (*Guide for the Perplexed* 3:48), and Gersonides, is that this food is harmful. Abravanel said (following Nachmanides) that it produces a bad and corrupted temperament *(mezeg).*

It seems to me that the eating of inferior types of food, such as meat that remains from that which a beast has torn, as well as a carcass *(nevelah)* or creeping animals *(sheratsim),* cannot be separated from an inferior and lowly spiritual character. A person who eats such foods, other than by necessity, is an inferior and deficient person who has no sense of the exaltedness of humankind and who is likely to fall into all kinds of unworthy and evil conduct. In contrast, one who is aware of his superior nature is not so likely to defile himself with foul deeds. It is to this end, it seems to me, that the Torah commanded us to be a "holy people," that we should not contaminate our souls with inferior foods. For this reason it added, "To the dog you will throw it," that is, do not liken yourself to a dog, for *terefah* and *nevelah* are food for dogs, not food for people.

It was even more imperative for the Torah to elevate the soul of the children of Israel, for until that time they had been at an extreme point of degradation and enslavement, and there is no doubt that the level of their soul had sunk to the lowest depths. In addition, it was within the Torah's intention to separate Israel from the other nations, so that they would not learn from their practices, and thus the Torah had to impress upon their hearts their superiority over other peoples, so that they would not mix among them. The prohibition of inferior foods would help to further this goal, and so the Torah called the distancing from such foods *kedushah*, "holiness," making the achievement of the goal depend on our being holy individuals and a holy people, all for the sake of elevating the soul of Israel, thus distancing them from mixing with the nations and from stumbling into unworthiness.

**23:1. "Do not utter false reports; do not give a hand to the wicked, making yourself an iniquitous witness.**

*Do not utter false reports.* Do not let a false rumor escape your lips, so as to spread slander (Ibn Ezra); see above at 20:7.

*do not give a hand to the wicked (rasha).* To one who brings a false claim against his neighbor (Rashi). Because the matter of "uttering false reports" is included, in some respects, within the [previously stated] prohibition of "Do not give false testimony against your neighbor" [above, 20:13], the Rabbis made of it an admonition against listening to malicious gossip (*leshon ha-ra*), and against a judge's hearing a litigant's case when the opposing party has not yet appeared (*Sanhedrin* 7b).

**23:2. "Do not go after the many in evil matters; nor shall you give testimony in a cause, inclining after the many, in order to bend [twist] (justice).**

## Mishpatim

***Do not go after the many in evil matters.*** This seems to be referring to the giving of testimony, as is the subject of the previous verse and the latter part of the present verse, "nor shall you give testimony in a cause," etc., except that the end of this verse refers to a lawsuit, while the beginning of the verse refers to a context other than a lawsuit, as where one testifies [i.e., reports] about Reuben that he desecrated the Sabbath. Thus the verse says "... in evil matters [*le-ra'ot*]," for in a lawsuit, that which is "evil" for one party is good for the other, but where one reports that Reuben sinned when he did not in fact sin, there is no good involved, but only evil.

***nor shall you give testimony in a cause*** (*ve-lo ta'aneh al riv*). This is correctly explained according to Ibn Ezra: when there is a legal dispute, do not give testimony about something that you have not seen; do not rely on a multitude of other witnesses so as to testify about what you yourself have not seen, because a perversion of justice may result. If you say, "Since there are so many witnesses, the addition of one more will do neither good nor harm," it is nevertheless likely that the addition of a witness, if he is assumed to be valid, will cause the judges to be less thorough in their examinations than they would have been if none but the other witnesses had been present.

***inclining... in order to bend*** (*lintot... lehattot*). A play on words with two different meanings, on the model of, "Whenever someone causes the destruction [*yav'er*] of a field or a vineyard, that is to say that he lets his animal [*be'iroh*] go to graze" (Exod. 22:4). The Rabbis' homiletical interpretation of the phrase *aharei rabbim lehattot* [lit., "after the many in order to bend"], that it is obligatory to decide the law according to the majority (as per the Targum), is an *asmakhta* [a scriptural support for a rabbinic enactment]; undoubtedly there is no way to decide the law other than by majority, for it is unlikely that the opinion of each judge should be given equal weight. Rather, this verse does not speak [in its plain sense] in the context of judges, but refers to an individual who comes to testify.

Rashi departed from the Rabbis' interpretation and sought to resolve the verse according to its plain meaning, but he, too, interpreted it to refer to a judge and not a witness, and he was constrained to explain the words *lo ta'aneh* in an extremely forced manner.[25] It is quite astonishing that Rashi would have

---

25. Rashi explains as follows: If the defendant asks you about the judgment in his case, do not answer (*lo ta'aneh*) him with a statement that will incline after the corrupt majority, thereby twisting the judgment, but rather declare the judgment as it should be, and let the majority bear the responsibility if they outvote you.

thought that if the defendant were to ask a judge about his judgment, the judge should not answer him so as to incline after the differing majority, but should tell him the law as it is in his opinion. Such conduct would lead to many difficulties; it is a clearly stated law in the Mishnah (*Sanhedrin* 3:7), "How do we know that when one of the judges comes out [of the court chamber], he should not say [to one of the litigants], 'I found in your favor, and my colleagues found you liable, but what can I do? My colleagues have outvoted me'? Of such a one it says, 'He that goes about as a talebearer reveals secrets' (Prov. 11:13)." It is even more astonishing that the author of *Sefer Mitsvot ha-Gadol* [R. Moses of Coucy], in the Negative Commandments 195 and 196, quoted these words of Rashi without making any comment on them; similarly, Mizrahi and others [in their supercommentaries on Rashi] make no comment at all on this matter.

My student R. Mordecai Mortara says that the Mishnah is speaking about judges in general, that is, proper ones who do not intend to pervert justice, but who exonerate litigants or find them liable according to what is true and just on the basis of what their eyes see, while Rashi is speaking about wicked judges, as indicated by his introductory phrase, "If you see wicked people who are perverting judgment...." My student R. Moses ha-Levi Ehrenreich says that according to Rashi, the entire verse is not an admonition to one individual, but rather two individuals are targeted. "Do not go after the many in evil matters" admonishes a judge before whom litigants have appeared, and whose colleagues want him to pervert the judgment, while "nor shall you answer [*ta'aneh*] in a cause" admonishes a scholar who is not a judge, or who does not serve on the court in question but serves on another court. In the latter case, Rashi intends to say that if the litigant who has been found liable approaches another scholar and asks for his opinion as to the judgment to which the judges have subjected him, the scholar should not defer to them, but he should state the judgment as it should be.

**23:3. "To the poor one you will not render respect in (judging) his case.**

***you will not render respect*** *(tehedar)*. The root *hadar* in Aramaic denotes a drawing backward; similarly in Latin, *vereor* ("to respect," "to fear") is related to the root *vertor* ("to turn"). The meaning here is, "Do not tremble or draw back from finding him liable if he is liable." The Torah endeavors to strengthen the sense of compassion and mercy among individuals, while forbidding it among judges; the reason is that an individual gives of his own [funds], while a judge gives what belongs to others.

## Mishpatim

**23:4. "When you encounter the ox of an enemy of yours, or his ass, gone astray, you will restore it to him.**

*you will restore it to him.* "You will not turn aside and leave it on the road; even though the owners are your enemies, take the animal in and send it back to its owners." In the section above, the Torah mentions matters in which [misplaced] love may lead to an unjust result: "Do not give a hand to the wicked" (above, v. 1); "Do not go after the many in evil matters…" (v. 2); "To the poor one you will not render respect" (v. 3). Now the Torah adds matters in which hatred may lead to an unjust result: "When you encounter…" and "When you see…" (this v. and v. 5, below). Subsequently it adds, "Do not twist the judgment of your indigent one" (v. 6, below), because the disgrace that attaches to the indigent will likely result in an unjust outcome.[26]

**23:5. "When you see the ass of one who is ill-disposed to you, lying down under its load, you will refrain from abandoning the care to him alone, but you will help him to unload.**

*the ass of one who is ill-disposed to you* (sona'akha, lit. "one who hates you"). Here it speaks of one who is ill-disposed, while above it speaks of an "enemy," which is a more severe case. One might be afraid to come close to his enemy for fear of being killed; thus the Torah [in v. 4] obligated him only to return the lost animal without having to approach his enemy, as he would be able to send the animal back to him by means of others. With respect to one who is "ill-disposed," however, the Torah commands the person to come near him and cooperate with him in unloading his animal's burden; perhaps, as a result, the ill-disposed one will even make peace with him.

Today, 13 Elul 5620 (1860), my student Isaac Klineberger said that the Torah has consideration for the animal as well, and thus where an ass is lying down under its load and is suffering, the Torah commands anyone who sees it, even if from a distance, to approach it and help its owner unload the burden. If, however, the ass has [merely] gone astray, there is no element of suffering; therefore the Torah did not say that if one sees such an animal from a distance he should come near in order to return it to the owner. Rather, if he

---

26. Nehama Leibowitz (*Studies in Shemot*, p. 436, n. 2) finds Shadal's explanation of vv. 1-6 implausible because the first two verses in this section, in his own view, refer to the slanderer and the false witness. "Where then," she asks, "is the 'love which is the undoing of justice'?" However, Shadal's use of the word *ha-ahavah* ("love") is best understood here in the sense of "misplaced love" or "wrongful favoritism" toward fellow slanderers or false witnesses.

"encounters" the animal close by, [only] then is he obligated to watch over it so as to restore it to the owner.

***from abandoning the care to him alone** (me-azov lo),* ***but you will help him to unload*** *(azov ta'azov immo).* A play on similar-sounding words with different meanings, on the model of *yav'er* [and *be'iroh*], above, 22:4. *Me-azov lo* means allowing the owner to do the work himself without helping him; *azov ta'azov immo* means to release the burden from atop the animal so that the load falls to the ground, and the animal can have some rest from its exertion (Ibn Ezra, Mendelssohn).

**23:6. "Do not twist the judgment of your indigent one in (judging) his case.**

***Do not twist,*** *etc.* This admonition is the opposite of "to the poor one you will not render respect" (above, v. 3); the meaning is, "Take care not to find him liable [merely] because he is unimportant in your sight on account of his poverty."

**23:7. "Keep yourself far from (the risk of) giving an erroneous judgment, and the innocent and the just you will not kill, for (indeed) I will not absolve the guilty [that is, if you let a guilty party live, God will indeed know how to punish him, but do not let the innocent perish].**

***Keep yourself far,*** *etc.* An admonition to a judge that he should always fear to err in judgment, and that he should keep in mind that it is better to clear the guilty than to convict the innocent.

***for (indeed) I will not absolve the guilty.*** For God has many agents at His disposal to put the guilty to death (Rashi).

**23:8. "And do not accept bribes, for a bribe blinds the most sagacious, and it makes just men speak iniquitously.**

***And do not accept bribes.*** Even without any intent to pervert justice.

***and it makes just men speak iniquitously*** *(vi-y'sallef divrei tsaddikim).* It causes the words of just men to become distorted (*mesullafim*), that is, they will pervert the judgment.

## *Mishpatim*

**23:9. "Do not molest the foreigner; you indeed know the soul of the foreigner, for foreigners you were in the land of Egypt.**

*Do not molest the foreigner.* This [too] is addressed to the judge; after admonishing against injustice that results from [undue] familiarity, the Torah admonishes against injustice that results from unfamiliarity, for the heart of a native-born citizen (particularly in ancient times) was distant from a stranger who came from another land, especially because such a person was usually not wealthy and would not have been able to sway the citizen's mind by means of gifts. See the responsa *Ḥavvot Ya'ir* at the beginning of p. 126.[27]

**23:10. "And six years will you sow your land, and gather its products.**

*And six years.* After concluding the laws concerning judgment, the Torah states commandments that involve compassion and mercy, which go beyond the strict line of justice. With respect to the sabbatical year it says, "And you will abandon its produce, allowing the indigent of your people to eat of it" (next v.); with respect to the Sabbath day it says, "And the son of your maidservant and the foreigner may take respite" (below, v. 12). Kindness to animals, too, is commanded: "And that which remains of it let the wild beasts eat" (next v.); "So that your ox and your ass may rest" (v. 12).

**23:11. "And in the seventh you will leave it uncultivated, and you will abandon its produce, allowing the indigent of your people to eat of it, and that which remains of it let the wild beasts eat. The same you will do with your vine and your olive tree.**

*you will leave it uncultivated (tishmetennah).* Do not work the soil.

*and you will abandon its produce (u-netashtah).* That which grows of itself (Rashbam).

**23:12. "Six days will you do your work, and on the seventh day you will cease, so that your ox and your ass may rest, and the son of your maidservant and the foreigner may take respite.**

---

27. In the responsum in question, the author, R. Yair Hayyim Bacharach, ruled that there were circumstances under which a Jewish litigant would be permitted to offer a bribe to a non-Jewish judge, that is, if the litigant was convinced that he was in the right and that only a bribe could ensure against a wrongful ruling.

*the son of your maidservant.* One who is born in the [master's] house, that is, born into slavery. This is the lowest-ranking, most degraded of slaves, for he is a slave from birth and even *in utero*, but even he deserves to be treated by you with mercy.

**23:13. "You will observe exactly as I have already told you [the precepts of Chapter 20], and the name of other gods you will not invoke; let it not be heard upon your mouth.**

*You will observe exactly as I have already told you…* Having concluded the commandments between man and his fellow, the Torah returns to the commandments between man and God, and it finishes with that with which it began above, at the end of *Parashat Yitro* (20:20). There the Torah admonished against the making of images and commanded the building of an altar for His honor, and then it stated the laws between man and his fellow. Now, the Torah once again admonishes against idolatry and command that honor be given to God.

Thus, it says, "You will observe exactly as I have already told you," the reference being to, "Do not make (any god) beside Me: gods of silver and gods of gold do not make for yourselves…" (Exod. 20:20), and the subsequent commands until the end of the [above] *parashah*. Then God additionally commands the people not to invoke the name of other gods for praise or glory, in contrast to what is said above, "In every place that I will assign you to invoke My name, I will come to you, and I will bless you" (v. 21); see my comment there. God then adds, "Let it not be heard upon your mouth," which is to be understood literally: do not let the name of pagan gods be heard upon your mouth, that is, even on occasion or in passing. However, the matter is to be understood in context; the prohibition falls only on the mention of such a name for praise or glory, or by way of prayer or supplication. Utterance of the name of a pagan god is not absolutely forbidden, for Moses [himself] said, "For all those who followed Baal-Peor…" (Deut. 4:3).

**23:14. "Three times a year you will celebrate solemn festivals to Me."**

*times* (*regalim*, lit., "feet"). The Heb. is the equivalent of *pe'amim* ("times"), for the word *pa'am*, too, has the meaning of "foot," as in, "How beautiful are your steps [*fe'amayikh*] in sandals" (Songs 7:2) (Mendelssohn).

**23:15. "The feast of the unleavened breads you will observe: seven days will you eat unleavened breads, as I commanded you, at the established**

## Mishpatim

time of the month of the first ripening (of the barley), for in it you came forth from Egypt; nor shall My face be seen empty-handed.

*the month of the first ripening* (*ḥodesh ha-aviv*). See my comment on 13:4 above.

*nor shall My face be seen* (*ve-lo yera'u fanai*) *empty-handed.* My face shall not be seen—that is, do not come to see My face—if you come empty-handed. Coming to the House of God is referred to as "seeing God's face"; see my comment on Isa. 1:12.[28] The reason for this requirement is that the burnt offerings (*olot*) brought on the festivals increase the prestige of the festivities, and of the God Who is the object of such worship, in the eyes of the people, while the sacrifices of contentment (*shelamim*) that are brought then increase peace and love among the public.[29]

**23:16. "And also the feast of the harvest, of the first products of your labors, (of those, that is) that you will have sown in the field; and the feast of the gathering, at the going out of the year, when you draw in (the fruit of) your toils from the field.**

*when you draw in (the fruit of) your toils* (*ma'asekha*). The produce that results from a person's labor is called "his work" (*ma'asehu*), for the result of an action (*pe'ullah*) is [itself] called by the name of *pe'ullah*, and the recompense of a *pe'ullah* is also called *po'al* or *pe'ullah*, as in, "Who uses his neighbor's service without wages, and gives him not his hire [*u-fo'alo*]" (Jer. 22:13); "Behold, His reward is with Him, and His recompense [*u-fe'ullato*] before Him" (Isa. 40:10).

---

28. There, on the phrase *ki tavo'u lera'ot panai*, Shadal explains that in all such instances, the original idiom was "to see [*lir'ot*] God's face," but the Masoretic vocalizers—following a tradition passed down to them from the Sages of the Second Temple period—emended it to "to be seen [*lera'ot*] before God," in order to avoid anthropomorphic misunderstanding. In particular, Shadal refers to the present verse and says that *ve-lo yera'u fanai* is not to be interpreted as "the people will not be seen before Me [*yera'u le-fanai*]," since the Israelites are referred to in the second person and not the third person throughout the *parashah* of *Mishpatim*.

29. As Luzzatto comments on Lev. 1:2, such sacrifices had to be eaten "in companionship with others, for they were not permitted to leave any of it over till the next day or the day after.... One who fulfilled his vow to God for a kindness that He bestowed upon him would be obligated to have others rejoice with him, and as a result he would come to be bonded in affection with people that he had not known previously, or at least he would cause the poor and destitute to benefit from his festive meal."

## Shadal on Exodus

**23:17. "Three times a year every male of yours will appear before the Lord, the (supreme) Master."**

*Three times...* A general statement following particulars; it adds that the command pertains to males, and also that the command is patterned after a tenant farmer's going to see his master, the landlord. This is in order to impress upon the people's hearts that the earth is the Lord's, and from His hand it becomes theirs.

*before (el penei).* In some books it is written *et penei* [which would yield the translation "will see the face of the Lord"]. See my comment on Isa. 1:12 [and on v. 15 above].

**23:18. "Do not pour out over [that is, while possessing in the home] leavened bread the blood of My [paschal] sacrifice, nor shall the fat of the sacrificial animal remain until morning.**

*the blood of My sacrifice.* This is referring to the paschal sacrifice; below (34:25) [it states explicitly,] "Nor shall there remain until the morning the sacrifice of the feast of Passover." The first part of the verse is an admonition that the *hamets* should be removed before the paschal sacrifice is offered, in order that the people should perform the sacrifice when they are prepared and sanctified for the holiday, not in a haphazard manner; all this is for the purpose of augmenting the greatness of the holiday among the people.

*nor shall the fat... remain until morning.* So that the people should not tarry while burning the fat of the paschal sacrifices. Even though these sacrifices are numerous, none of the fat is to remain until morning; rather, that part of the sacrifice which is "food" for the One Above [i.e., the fat] is to be consumed that same night in which the meat is eaten by the common people. Otherwise, some of the Israelites would eat their paschal sacrifices before the fat was consumed on the altar, and this would be an act of disrespect toward God, similar to the actions of the sons of Eli.[30]

*Do not pour out (tizbah) the blood of My sacrifice.* It is difficult to understand how the term *zevihah* (lit., "slaughter") can refer to blood. However, it seems

---

30. In 1 Sam. 2:15, it is related that at the shrine in Shiloh, the high priest Eli's sons, Hofni and Phinehas, used to demand their share of the sacrificial meat "before the fat was made to smoke."

## Mishpatim

to me that the root *zavah* is derived from *zuv* ("to flow"), and the meaning of *zevihah* [here] is the spilling of blood. Similarly, the root *shahat* ("to slaughter ritually") is derived from *sahat*, meaning to squeeze and draw out the liquid that is absorbed within a body, as in, "and I took the grapes, squeezed [*va-eshat*] them into Pharaoh's goblet" (Gen. 40:11). Most of the laws of *shehitah* are designed to further the extraction of blood [from the meat].

**23:19. "The choicest first fruits of your soil you will bring to the House of the Lord your God. Do not cook a kid in the milk of its mother.**

*The choicest first fruits of (reshit bikkurei). Reshit* [lit., "first," "beginning"] signifies the choicest and most praiseworthy, as in, "Preeminent [*reshit*] among the peoples is Amalek" (Num. 24:20); "Sheep and oxen, the chief of [*reshit*] the devoted things" (1 Sam. 15:21).

*The choicest first fruits... Do not cook (tevashel) a kid...* By way of conjecture it seems to me that some nations, or some individuals even among the Israelites, had the custom of offering the firstborn of their flocks cooked in their mothers' milk, for just as the priest was presented with the first shearing, it seems likely that it would have been considered good and proper to offer the first of the milk. Thus they would have slaughtered the firstborn, cooked it in its mother's milk, and presented it as food for the priest (or else they would have given him the firstborn and the milk, and he would have cooked them together and eaten them; otherwise they might have cooked them and burned them whole upon the altar). In this manner they would have offered to Heaven the firstborn animals together with the first of the milk, and thus after mentioning the first fruits of the soil, the Torah also mentions cooking a kid in its mother's milk. It is understandable why the cooking and not the eating is mentioned, for the former and not the latter is the main thing—if there is no cooking, there is no eating.

The reason why this custom is forbidden, even though its intent was for the sake of Heaven, is (as per Rashbam, Ibn Ezra, and Johann David Michaelis) that there is an element of cruelty in cooking the offspring in the milk of the mother, along the lines of "Do not slaughter on the same day the mother [of a calf or lamb] and her offspring" [Lev. 22:28]. One might ask, given that slaughtering a kid is permissible, what does it matter to him or to his mother what liquid he is cooked in? But this act nevertheless fosters a negative character trait in the soul of the person who does or sees it. Imagine that a man were to make his father's bones into ladles and his skull into a bowl, and that he were to eat with them; there is no harm to his dead father, and yet this is an act of cruelty that damages the sense of compassion and mercy in him and in those who see him.[31]

Some of the Karaites interpreted this phrase to mean, "Do not let the firstborn kid 'mature' [*she-yitbashel*] and grow on its mother's milk, but give it to Me on the eighth day." However (as Ibn Ezra noted), even if we find the root *bashal* referring to the ripening of grains, since the heat of the sun "cooks" (*mavshil*) them as if it were fire, we do not find it referring to the growing of animals, since their growth is not by means of fire or external heat.

**23:20. "Here I send before you an emissary, so that he may guard you along the journey and conduct you to the place prepared by Me.**

*Here I send before you an emissary* (mal'akh). The early scholars interpreted this to mean an "angel." Herder and Rosenmueller understood it to refer to the pillar of fire and cloud, but according to this interpretation, the phrase "and pay him heed" [next v.] would be incomprehensible. It seems to me that Gersonides correctly explained that the *mal'akh* was a prophet, namely Moses, and that [it was only] because the people sinned and were detained in the desert [that] he did not bring them into the land [of Israel], and Joshua took his place.

**23:21. "Have regard for him and pay him heed; do not disobey him; for he cannot pardon your offenses, since My name is in him [that is, every command of his is inspired by Me].**

*for he cannot pardon your offenses.* Even though he is humble and patient, he lacks the power to pardon, and if you provoke him I will punish you, for you must pay him heed, since My name is in him and from Me come all his words.

---

31. Compare Cassuto's comment on this verse: "Although the first of the first fruits of your ground, that is, the best and choicest of the first fruits of your ground, you shall bring into the house of the Lord your God, just as the Canaanites bring the first-fruits to the house of their gods, yet you shall not boil a kid in its mother's milk according to the heartless custom that they practise on their festival of first-fruits. Maimonides (*Guide* 3:48) already conjectured that the prohibition of boiling a kid in its mother's milk was intended to keep the Israelites away from idolatrous customs, but he had no proof that the gentiles actually practised such things. Now we know from the Ugaritic texts that the Canaanites prepared such a dish particularly at festal ceremonies pertaining to the fertility of the soil" (A Commentary on the Book of Exodus, p. 305). Unfortunately, however, subsequent scholarship has cast doubt on this reading of the Ugaritic text in question (see, for example, Mark S. Smith, *The Rituals and Myths of the Feast of the Goodly Gods of KTU/CAT 1.23*, Leiden: Brill, 2006, pp. 52-53).

*My name.* My divinity, as in, "Behold, the name of the Lord comes from afar" (Isa. 30:27).

*since My name is in him.* This is connected to the beginning of the verse: "Have regard for him, since My name is in him" (Rashi). This explanation goes against the accents [which place the major disjunctive at the phrase "do not disobey him"], but in keeping with my interpretation [above], the verse can be understood in conformance with the accents as well.

**23:22.** "For if you pay him heed, and do as I speak, I will be an enemy of your enemies and an adversary of your adversaries.

*as I speak.* For all of his words are My words.

**23:23.** "Then My emissary will go before you and will lead you to the Amorites, to the Hittites, to the Perizzites, to the Canaanites, to the Hivites, and to the Jebusites; and I will exterminate them.

*My emissary.* The prophet mentioned above; it does not say that the emissary will destroy the nations, but rather, "I [God] will exterminate them."

**23:24.** "Do not prostrate yourself to their gods, and do not render them worship, nor shall you imitate their practices; but you must destroy them and break their statues in pieces.

*Do not prostrate yourself, etc.* Having mentioned their arrival among the idolatrous nations, the Torah warns the people not to learn from their practices.

**23:25.** "And you shall serve the Lord your God, and He will bless your bread and your water, and I will remove from your midst (every) infirmity.
**23:26.** "There will not be in your land any woman who loses her offspring, or any sterile woman; the number of your days I will make complete.
**23:27.** "I will make My terror precede you, and I will put into confusion every people into which you enter; and I will compel all your enemies to turn the back of their neck to you.

***and I will put into confusion*** *(ve-hammoti).* See my comment on Isa. 28:28.³² Rashi, after explaining most skillfully the grammar behind the word *ve-hammoti* [deriving it from the root *hamam* and identifying it as a variant of *ve-hamamti*], erred with respect to the word *ve-natatti* (ונתתי) by saying that it would properly have had three *tavs*: two as part of the root (*yesod*), as in the phrases *be-yom tet*, "on the day when [the Lord] delivered up" (Josh.10:12) and *mattat Elohim hi*, "it is the gift of God" (Eccl. 3:13), and the third as a suffix. However, the *dagesh* in the [second *tav* in the word] *ve-natatti* is in the place of [the missing root-letter] *nun*, not a *tav*, while in the word *tet*, the final *tav* is not part of the root but is a suffix, as in the word *ga'at* ("to touch"), which is from the root *naga*. In the phrase *mattat Elohim hi*, the word *mattat* takes the place of *matenat*.³³

**23:28.** "I will cause hornets to precede you, which will drive away from your presence the Hivites, the Canaanites, and the Hittites.
**23:29.** "I will not drive them away from your presence in one year, so that the country does not remain deserted and the wild beasts do not multiply against you.
**23:30.** "Little by little I will drive him away from your presence, until you, proliferating, can occupy the country.

***until you, proliferating, can occupy*** *(ve-naḥalta)* ***the country.*** The root *naḥal* signifies possession of a portion of an inheritance that goes to each one of a group of brothers. Thus it says that when you have children and grandchildren, each one of you will be able to take possession of his portion without the land becoming desolate. The root *naḥal* is derived from *ḥul* ("to fall upon"), as in, "Let it fall upon [*yaḥulu*] the head of Joab" (2 Sam. 3:29); "It should fall upon [*yaḥul*] the head of the wicked" (Jer. 23:19). It is used to describe one who is in possession of his inheritance and had taken hold of it (R. David Hananiah Viterbi). In *Bikkurei ha-Ittim* I said that the word was derived from the root *ḥalak* ("to allot"), but I hereby renounce that opinion.

**23:31.** "I will establish your territory from the Red Sea to the Sea of the Philistines, and from the desert to the river [Euphrates]; for I will give

---

32. There, on the phrase *ve-hamam gilgal* (which he translates as "he will scatter its chaff"), Shadal comments that *hamam* means "to scatter," "to make waste," and as an illustration he cross-refers to the present verse.
33. In other words, the root of the word meaning "to give" is *natan*. Rashi did not have access to the works of the grammarians who established the three-letter root system.

into your power all the inhabitants of the country, and you will drive them away from your presence.

*to the Sea of the Philistines.* This is part of the Mediterranean Sea. According to my son Ohev Ger [Filosseno], as far [north] as Akko it was called "the Sea of the Philistines," while from that point and beyond it was known as that of the Tyrians and Sidonians.

*and from the desert.* It has been said that this is the desert through which the Israelites traveled, but if so, it would be superfluous to mention it after the reference to the Red Sea. More likely is my son's view that this desert is to the east of the land of Israel, as it is in a straight line with the Euphrates River, just as the Red Sea and the Sea of the Philistines are in a straight line.

*and you will drive them away.* "I will give them into your power; then you, through your own efforts, will drive them away, and you must not establish any covenant with them." God gave them natural borders—the sea, the desert, and the river—so that they would be separated from all the idolatrous nations. If they had not kept foreigners among themselves, they would have stayed securely in their country forever, but they rebelled against His word. Yet in the end, all that happened was merely that which He intended, for as a result, the earth was filled with the knowledge of God.

**23:32. "You must not establish with them and their gods (any) covenant.**

*and their gods.* For if you establish a covenant with the people, you will perforce establish one with their gods, as you will have to let the people keep them; to force a person [with whom one has established a covenant] to abandon the faith with which he grew up is highly unlikely.

**23:33. "They must not remain in your country, for they would cause you to sin to Me, because you would serve their gods. Yes, (that people) would be to you a stumbling-block [a cause of ruin]."**

*Yes... would be to you a stumbling-block (ki yihyeh lekha le-mokesh).* The people to whom God referred (above, v. 30) in the singular, "I will drive *him* away from your presence," [is the unstated subject of this phrase]; that nation would be a stumbling-block to you if it lives in your country.

**24:1. To Moses then He said, "Go up to the Lord, you and Aaron, Nadab and Abihu, and seventy of the elders of Israel, and prostrate yourselves from afar.**

*To Moses then He said.* Up to this point, God had been telling Moses the laws that he was to say to all of Israel. Now, He told him what he was to do after he finished relating the laws to the people.

*and prostrate yourselves from afar.* To give praise and thanks before Him for the Torah that He gave to His people. Moses was to go up with them, like the faithful servant of a royal house who, when guests come to the King, goes before them and speaks on their behalf (Abravanel).

**24:2. "Moses alone will draw near to the Lord, and let them not draw near, and let the people not go up with him."**

*and let the people not go up with him.* Aaron and the others were to go up with him but not draw near with him, while the people were not to go up at all.

**24:3. Moses went, and he told the people all the words of the Lord, and all the laws; and all the people responded with one voice, and they said, "All that which the Lord has spoken, we will fulfill."**
**24:4. Moses wrote all the words of the Lord; then, having risen in the morning, he built an altar beneath the mountain, and (he erected) twelve tablets, according to (the number of) the twelve tribes of Israel.**

*all the words of the Lord.* This apparently refers to the Ten Commandments and that which follows, from "You have seen that from the heaven I spoke with you" (Exod. 20:19) until "Yes, (that people) would be to you a stumbling-block" (Exod. 23:33); this [segment] is called "the book of the covenant" (below, v. 7).

*and (he erected) twelve tablets (matsevah).* The word *hitsiv* ("he erected") [is missing but understood]; the verb comes on the strength of the noun [both of which are derived from the root *yatsav*, "to stand"].

**24:5. And he sent the young men of the children of Israel, who sacrificed burnt offerings, and slaughtered bulls as sacrifices of contentment, to the Lord.**

*the young men of the children of Israel.* The firstborns.

*who sacrificed burnt offerings…* In thanks to God for the Torah that He had given them, and in happiness for this. All this was a sign that the entire people was accepting this Torah and making a covenant concerning it.

*bulls.* It is not certain whether this word refers only to the "sacrifices of contentment" (as would be indicated by the accents [which place the major disjunctive at the word *olot*, "burnt offerings"]), or also to the "burnt offerings" (*Ḥagigah* 6a).[34]

**24:6. Moses took half of the blood, and he put it in the basins, and half of the blood he sprinkled on the altar.**
**24:7. And he took the book of the covenant, and he read it before the people; and they said, "All that the Lord spoke, we will fulfill obediently."**

*we will fulfill (na'aseh*, lit., "we will do"). The positive commandments.

*obediently (ve-nishma*, lit., "and we will obey"). The negative commandments, which do not involve an [affirmative] act, but rather require obedience to the voice of God (I have since found this explanation given by Kimhi [in *Shorashim*], under the root *sakat*).

**24:8. And Moses took the blood and sprinkled it on the people, and he said, "Here is the blood of the alliance that the Lord establishes with you, on the basis of all these commandments."**

*Here is the blood of the alliance, etc.* This blood would properly have been sprinkled in its entirety on the altar, it being the "food" of God; yet God commanded that half of it be sprinkled on the people, like one who receives a gift from His presence, by way of affection due to their acceptance of his Torah. It was as if they were eating at the table of God, at a festive covenantal meal marking the Lord's promise to be their God and to accept them as His people, as long as they did all that He commanded them, just as all parties to a pact of love dine together at a festive meal.

---

34. There, a controversy is recorded in which Beit Hillel maintains that the burnt offerings on this occasion were *olat tamid*, the continual offering which consisted of a lamb, while Beit Shammai held that these offerings were *olat re'iyyah*, the pilgrimage offering which consisted of a bull or various other animals.

***on the basis of all these commandments.*** Cf. below, "For on the basis of these commandments I establish an alliance with you and with Israel" (Exod. 34:27).

Onkelos made a change and translated [the phrase "and he sprinkled it on the people [*va-yizrok al ha-am*]" as] "and he sprinkled it on the altar [*u-zerak al madbeha*] to atone for the people" (such was the version of R. Bahya, which was also found by the author of the book *Ya'er* in a Spanish translation), but Rashi altered it and said, "The Targum renders it as *va-adi al madbeha*" [substituting an Aramaic synonym *va-adi* for *u-zerak*]; such is the reading in a manuscript Rashi in my possession. However, the printers failed to understand his intention [which apparently was to elucidate the Heb. *va-yizrok* by offering an Aramaic translation besides the cognate *u-zerak*], and they printed Rashi's comment as well [as Onkelos' translation itself] as "*u-zerak al madbeha* to atone for the people."

This same Aramaic translation appears also in the Targum ascribed to Jonathan. Apparently the Targum translators made the change for the sake of the common people and gentiles, so that they should not mock the Torah [by failing to understand the significance of sprinkling blood "on the people"] (27 Adar II 5624 [1864]) (my student, Shalom Simeon Modena).

**24:9. Then Moses and Aaron, Nadav and Avihu, and seventy of the elders of Israel went up.**
**24:10. And they saw the God of Israel [that is, the fire in which He appeared], and under His feet there was something similar in brightness to the whiteness [gleam] of the sapphire, and to the essence of the heaven [that is, to the pure and serene heaven].**

*And they saw...* This, too, was in order to glorify the people who has accepted His Torah; God wanted the most honorable among them to come close to Him, and He made Himself known to them in a vision.

***something similar*** *(ke-ma'aseh*, lit., "like a work"). It seems to me that the word *ma'aseh* is used to refer to any thing, whatever it may be. Here, too, the meaning is that they saw "something" that resembled (in appearance) the gleam of the sapphire.

***the whiteness of*** *(livnat)*. [The noun *livnat* means] "whiteness" (*loven*) and "brightness" (R. Jonah [Ibn Janah], Rashbam, Mendelssohn, Rosenmueller, and Gesenius). Mendelssohn thought that the same meaning was conveyed in the Jerusalem Targum, but this was an error, because there it is translated *ke-ovad lavan de-sapirinon*, and in Aramaic one does not say *lavan* but rather *ḥiver* to express the idea of "whiteness," while one says *livnin* to mean *levenim* ("bricks") [and thus the phrase in the Jerusalem Targum means "like sapphire brickwork"] (28 Adar II 5624 [1864]).

The thing that resembled the gleam of the sapphire also resembled "the essence of the heaven." All of this was a vision that the elect of the children of Israel saw, an honor that was created for that temporary occasion, but the people [as a whole] did not see any image at the time of the giving of the Torah. This was all in keeping with the adage, "The Kingdom of Heaven resembles an earthly kingdom" (*Berakhot* 58a); in ancient times, kings made themselves seen not to the entire nation, but only to a select group.

**24:11. Upon those elect among the children of Israel (God) did not thrust His hand [they did not undergo any punishment for having contemplated the Divine appearance]. They saw God, then they ate and drank.**

*Upon those elect.* Aaron and the others who went up with him.

*did not thrust His hand.* They were not harmed when they saw an image of God, for He wished to honor them.

*then they ate and drank.* After they saw what they saw, they went down and partook with their brothers of the meat of the sacrifices of contentment.

**24:12. Then the Lord said to Moses, "Ascend to Me to the mountain, and stay there, and I will give you the tablets of stone that I have written, and the laws and the precepts to teach them.**

*and I will give you the tablets of stone, etc.* The phrase "that I have written" [although appearing in the Heb. after "the laws and the precepts"] refers back to "the tablets," while the phrase "to teach them" refers to "the laws and the precepts." The import of the verse is, "I will give you the tablets of stone that I have written, and the laws and the precepts to teach them" [although a more literal rendering would have been, "I will give you the tablets of stone and the laws and the precepts that I have written to teach them"] This is in keeping with the statement in Deuteronomy (5:28), "And you stay here with Me, and I will communicate to you the precepts, the statutes, and the laws that I will teach them" (Nachmanides). The verb *ve-etnah* ("and I will give") principally refers to "the tablets," but by extension it refers also to "the laws and the precepts."

Mendelssohn translated, "And I will give you the tablets of stone, with the laws [*ha-torah*] and the precepts that I have written on them." However, it seems to me that it would not be correct to use the term *ha-torah* for the Ten Commandments, for they contain no conditional clauses, "If such happens, you shall do this, but if such happens, you shall do that." See my comment on Gen. 26:5 [where the term *torah* is defined as consisting of such provisions].

**24:13. Moses bestirred himself, with Joshua his servant; and Moses went up to the mountain of God.**
**24:14. And to the elders he said, "Wait here, until we return to you. Aaron and Hur remain with you; whoever has some lawsuit, let him present it to them."**

*Hur.* See above, 17:10.

**24:15. Moses went up to the mountain, and the cloud covered the mountain.**
**24:16. The majesty of the Lord lodged upon mount Sinai, and the cloud covered it for six days; then on the seventh day (God) called Moses from the midst of the cloud.**

*The majesty of the Lord.* This is the "devouring fire" mentioned in the next verse.

**24:17. The majesty of the Lord appeared to the eyes of the children of Israel as a devouring fire in the peak of the mountain.**
**24:18. Moses entered into the midst of the cloud, and went up to the mountain. Moses stayed on the mountain forty days and forty nights.**

# *Terumah*

*"They will make Me a Sanctuary"* • *Ark, cherubim, table, and candelabrum* • *"And you will make the tabernacle"* • *Curtains, covers, boards, and bases* • *The copper altar*

**25:1. The Lord spoke to Moses, saying:**

After the people accepted the laws and teachings, and God became King in Jeshurun, it was fitting that they should make Him a Sanctuary, as if their King were [physically] dwelling among them, for this would be a powerful cause for the preservation of the nation's unity and the continuity of their adherence to the Torah. Even though it had not yet been decreed that they should be detained in the desert, God did not want them to delay making Him a sanctuary until they conquered and allotted the land of Israel and they had a chosen place to serve as the center of the entire kingdom.

Rather, He commanded them to make a moveable sanctuary, so that even when they arrived in their land, they would be able to set it up in any place they wished, according to the need of the time. This Sanctuary served for 480 years until the Temple was built in Solomon's time (1 Kings 6:1).

**25:2. "Speak to the children of Israel, that they should collect for Me a tribute. From whoever will be inspired by his heart shall you receive My tribute.**

*that they should collect (ve-yikḫu*, lit., "that they should take") *for Me.* This was a command to the nation at large that they appoint officials to receive [contributions] from volunteers, as it says immediately afterwards, "From whoever will be inspired... shall you receive My tribute. And this is the tribute that you shall receive from them...." Similarly, Moses said to them, "Collect among yourselves a tribute to the Lord" (Exod. 35:5) (i.e., that persons appointed for this purpose were to take from others among the people and receive their voluntary contributions); "whoever is inspired by his heart will bring this tribute for the honor of the Lord" (i.e., to the appointees).

It seems to me, however, that the people did not appoint officials, but rather brought it [directly] to Moses themselves, as it is written, "And they [the craftsmen] took from before Moses all the tribute brought by the Israelites... and they brought him more offerings from morning to morning" (Exod. 36:3).

**25:3. "And this is the tribute that you shall receive from them: gold and silver and copper.**

*gold and silver.* According to Rashi, (see his comment below on 30:15), each person gave half a shekel, and they made a further donation of silver, each according to his will.

**25:4. "And blue wool, and purple, and scarlet, and linen, and goat hair.**
**25:5. "And sheepskins dyed red, and badger (?) skins, and acacia timbers.**

*and badger (?) skins (ve-orot teḥashim).* The word *taḥash* does not appear outside the account of the Sanctuary except for once, "And I shod you with *taḥash*" (Ezek. 16:10). According to the ancient translators, this was a type of leather dyed a particular color, and so held Bochart. The Sages of the Talmud said that it was the name of an animal (*Shabbat* 28a), and so held Gesenius, who said that it was *Phoca* [a genus of seals] or the like.

*acacia (shittim).* In Arabic, *shant*, and in Latin, *acacia* (see *Netivot ha-Shalom*).[1]

---

1. Mendelssohn's translation in *Netivot ha-Shalom* does not attempt to identify this tree, but renders *atsei shittim* simply as *Schitimholz* ("*shittim* wood"). The commentary presents arguments both for and against "acacia": On the one hand, *shittim* and the Arabic *shant* may well be related, as the *dagesh* in the letter *tet* in *shittim* could stand in place of the missing letter *nun*; acacia wood was well suited for construction; and travelers had reported seeing acacias in the Sinai

## Terumah

**25:6.** "Oil for illumination, spices for the oil of anointing [consecration] and for the aromatic incense.

**25:7.** "Onyx stones and stones for setting, for the dorsal and for the pectoral.

**25:8.** "And they will make Me a Sanctuary, and I will have residence in their midst.

**25:9.** "According to the model of the tabernacle that I will show you, and the model of all its furnishings, so in its entirety you will do.

**25:10.** "They will make an ark of acacia wood; two and a half cubits (will be) its length, one and a half cubits its width, and one and a half cubits its height.

**25:11.** "You will cover it with pure gold; within and without you will cover it; and you will make above it a cornice of gold round about.

*cornice (zer).* The Heb. is derived from *nezer* ("diadem," "tiara").

**25:12.** "And you will cast for it four rings of gold, and you will place them at its four corners; that is, two rings on its one side and two rings on its other side.

*its four corners (pa'amotav).* See 1 Kings 7:30, 34 ["And its four corners [*fa'amotav*] had undersetters.... And there were four undersetters at the four corners of [*pinnot*] each base"], from which there is proof that *pa'amotav* is the equivalent of *pinnotav*, "its corners." The prefix *vav* in [the first of the two phrases *u-sh'tei tabba'ot* (lit., "and two rings") denotes "that is"; cf. Gen. 24:41 [*ve-im lo yittenu lakh*, "If, that is, they will not give her to you"]; Exod. 14:19; Isa. 21:10; Jer. 2:9, 40:8, 46:26; Ezek. 23:37; 1 Sam. 28:3; and similarly, below v. 19.

**25:13.** "And you will make poles of acacia wood, and you will cover them with gold.

**25:14.** "And you will insert the poles into the rings along the (short) sides of the ark, to serve to carry the ark.

**25:15.** "In the rings of the ark will remain the poles; they must not be removed from them.

---

desert. On the other hand, a verse in Isaiah, "I will plant in the wilderness the cedar, the *shittah*..." (41:19), would seem to indicate that the tree in question was not customarily found in the desert, and this would lend support to the statement of the Sages (in Midrash Tanḥuma, followed by Rashi) that the Israelites brought the *shittim* timbers with them out of Egypt.

## Shadal on Exodus

**25:16.** "And you will place in the ark the Admonition [the Tablets of the Law] that I will give you."

***the Admonition*** *(ha-edut,* lit., "the testimony"). This means the Torah; [the word *edut* is used] in the sense of *ha'ed he'id banu ha-ish,* "That man declared to us" (Gen. 43:3).[2] Every *torah* [lit., "teaching"] is a warning and an admonition.[3]

**25:17.** "And you will make a cover of pure gold: two and a half cubits (will be) its length, and one and a half cubits its width.
**25:18.** "And you will make two cherubim of gold; you will make them one solid piece [not composed of separable parts], at the two ends of the cover.

***cherubim*** *(keruvim).* The Heb. *keruv* is like a reversed form of *rakhuv,* as per Gussetius and the scholar Reggio in *Bikkurei ha-Ittim* 5590 (1829), p. 7, although this is not because the *keruvim* were composites *(murkavim)* of various forms (as Reggio maintained), for the use of the term *harkavah* in this sense is a usage that was invented by moderns. Rather, the *keruvim* were so called because they were God's "vehicle" *(rekhev),* as in, "And He rode *[va-yirkav]* upon a cherub, and did fly" (2 Sam. 22:11); "And for the image of the [Divine] chariot *[ha-merkavah],* the golden cherubim" (1 Chron. 28:18).

***one solid piece*** *(mikshah).* The Heb. is derived from *kashah* ("to be hard, solid"), i.e., there were to be no hollow spaces; it is not derived from *nakash,* "to beat,"[4] because the *kof* has no *dagesh* [which would have indicated a missing letter *nun*]. Besides, the production of the cherubim and the candelabrum with its calyxes, buds, and flowers out of a single metal bar (below, v. 31) could not have been accomplished by beating with a hammer; rather, the main part of the work must have been done with a chisel and other cutting tools. Even Rashi [in his comment on v. 31 below, after stating that the candelabrum was made by beating,] wrote, "And [the craftsmen] cut it with a tool of the craft."

---

2. Although Shadal translated *ha'ed he'id banu* in Gen. 43:3 as "declared to us," his comment on this verse says that the phrase means "he warned us."
3. In *Bikkurei ha-Ittim* 5587 (1826), p. 194, cited in his commentary on Gen. 31:50, Shadal notes that *he'id* ("to testify") is the equivalent of "to remind," and that the term thus signifies "warning."
4. Some English versions translate *mikshah* as "beaten" or "hammered" work.

Gesenius argued against one who interpreted as I did, on the ground that we find in 1 Kings 6:23, 28, that the cherubim were made of olive wood overlaid with gold. I say, however, that one cannot bring proof from what Solomon did for what Moses did, for the cherubim made by Solomon were much larger and therefore were not made out of one solid piece of gold. Solomon's cherubim were ten cubits in height, but those of Moses could not have been so tall, for the entire Sanctuary was not taller than ten cubits, as it is said, "Ten cubits will be the length of the board" (Exod. 26:16), and the cherubim were placed on the cover, which in turn was placed on the ark, which was one and a half cubits in height.

It might have been possible to argue [that *mikshah* means "beaten work"] from the fact that we find the term *mikshah* used in connection with the silver trumpets (Num. 10:2), which were undoubtedly hollow. However, I say that it would still have been possible to have made them out of wood (or copper) overlaid with silver, and for that reason is said, "Solid [*mikshah*] [not silver-plated] will you make them" (Sivan 5619 [1859]). Compare the word *mikshah* in [the commentaries of] Maimonides and Bertinoro on *Middot* at the beginning of ch. 3.[5]

**25:19. "You will make, that is, one cherub on one end and one cherub on the other end; you will make the cherubim (as if) forming part of the cover at its [the ark's] two ends.**

*forming part of (min,* lit. "from") *the cover.* They were to be attached to and inseparable from the cover, as if they were a part of it; compare:

- "Its calyxes, its buds, and its flowers will be [inseparable parts] of it [*mimmennah*]" (below, v. 31);
- "[Inseparable parts] of it [*mimmennu*)] will be its prominences" (Exod. 27:2);
- "And it will have its prominences, [inseparable] from it [*mimmennu*]" (Exod. 30:2);

---

5. *Middot* 3:1 describes the dimensions and structure of the Temple's outer altar, which consisted of three layers. According to R. Ovadiah Bertinoro, the bottom layer was formed by building a frame of boards, 32 cubits squared in area and one cubit high. This frame was then filled in with stones, lime, pitch, and molten lead to create a *mikshah*. By a similar process, a second frame 30 cubits squared in area and five cubits high was filled in to create a *mikshah* forming the middle layer, and a third frame 28 cubits squared in area and three cubits high was filled in to form the top layer. Bertinoro's use of the term *mikshah* corresponds to Shadal's understanding of the term in the sense of "solid, not hollow."

- "And the band with which to bind it [the dorsal], which will be upon it [the pectoral], will be of the same work, forming part of it [*mimmennu*]" (Exod. 28:8);
- "[And the band,] forming part of it [*mimmennu*], is of the same work" (Exod. 39:5).

**25:20. "The cherubim will have their wings spread upward, sheltering with their wings over the cover, and they will have their faces one opposite the other; toward the cover will be the faces of the cherubim.**

***toward the cover will be the faces of the cherubim.*** Inclined slightly downward (Ibn Ezra). The cherubim had their wings spread upward as if they were taking flight, but they were not, Heaven forbid, a likeness of God. Rather, it was as Ezekiel saw (1:25-28): over the heads of the "living creatures" (*ḥayyot*) was a likeness of the layer of heaven (*rakia*), and over the *rakia* was the likeness of a throne, and over this was the Divine Presence.

**25:21. "You will place the cover on top of the ark, and within the ark you will place the Admonition [the Law] that I will give you.**

***and within the ark you will place the Admonition.*** Before stating that "there I will gather Myself to you, and I will speak with you from above the cover…" (next v.), the Torah mentions once more what was to be placed within the ark, in order to make it known that the ark's holiness was due to the tablets within it, not the cover and the cherubim (Iyyar 5624 [1864]).

**25:22. "And there I will gather Myself to you [I will be found with you], and I will speak with you from above the cover, from between the two cherubim situated on the ark of the Law, all that I will have charged you for the children of Israel.**

***And… I will gather Myself*** *(ve-no'adti).* There will be the place where I will come to speak with you. The root *ya'ad* may refer to either place or time, but here the meaning is the place [of meeting], not the time. Mendelssohn and Reggio translated [*ve-no'adti* as meeting] "at set times," but this is erroneous.

**25:23. "And you will make a table of acacia wood; two cubits (will be) its length, and once cubit its width, and one and a half cubits its height. 25:24. "And you will cover it with pure gold, and you will make for it a cornice of gold round about.**

## Terumah

**25:25. "And you will make for it an enclosure [a band], one handbreadth high, round about; and you will make a cornice of gold all around its enclosure.**

*an enclosure* (misgeret). On top, to close off (*lisgor*) that which is on the table so that nothing falls from it; this is why it was called a *misgeret*. If it had been underneath [the table top] to reinforce the table,[6] it seems to me that the term *misgeret* would not have been appropriate for it, as nothing would have been "enclosed" within it. My student Isaac Pardo adds that even so, it [i.e., the *misgeret*, understood as an "enclosure" above the table top] did serve to reinforce the table, for it was likely that the table did not rest on the tops of the legs, but that the legs entered into its thickness and that of the *misgeret*.

**25:26. "And you will make for it four rings of gold; and you will apply the rings upon the four corners, corresponding to its four legs.**
**25:27. "Beside the enclosure will be the rings through which to pass the poles, to carry the table.**

***Beside** (le-ummat) **the enclosure will be the rings.*** Inserted into the legs next to the enclosure.

**25:28. "And you will make the poles of acacia wood, and you will cover them with gold, and with these the table will be carried.**
**25:29. "And you will make its plates, and its bowls, and its goblets, and its libation vessels, with which the libations will be made; of pure gold you will make them.**

*its plates...* The explanations given by the Rabbis and Rashi for these vessels appear to conform with what existed in the Second Temple, but not with what existed in the desert.

*and its bowls (ve-khappotav).* The word *kaf* apparently signifies something that is bent [i.e., concave] (*kafuf*), like the palm (*kaf*) of the hand. Thus in *Tamid* 5:4: "And the *kaf* resembled a large *tarkav* [a measuring term] that held three *kabbim*." Similarly, "One bowl [*kaf*] of gold... full of incense" (Num. 7:14, 20, 26, etc.). If so, then the *ke'arah* ("plate") was flat, or less

---

6. As Rashi explains, some of the Rabbis were of the view that the *misgeret* was placed beneath the table top, running from leg to leg on all four sides, and that the table top rested on this ledge; see *Menaḥot* 96b and *Sukkah* 5a.

deep than the *kaf*; indeed, it is unlikely that it was absolutely flat, for the root *ka'ar* in Arabic signifies "depth" (and hence the term *ka'arurit*, "concavity"); nevertheless, the *kaf* was deeper and more concave than the *ke'arah*.[7]

**and its goblets** *(u-kesotav)*. The Mishnah [*Sanhedrin* 9:6] refers to "one who steals the *kasvah*," from which it may be inferred that [the *kasot*] were not the "attachments" [as described in *Menahot* 94a] or "canes" [i.e., half-pipes that supported and separated the loaves of bread, *Menahot* 96a], which were fixtures and difficult to steal. Rather, they [i.e., the *kasot*] were small vessels used for libation, as it says, *ve-et kesot ha-nasekh*, "and the libation vessels" (Num. 4:7). The word *menakkiyyotav* [translated in the present v. as "its libation vessels"] includes various other vessels used for libation.

The plates and the bowls served to dignify the table, so that it should not lack that which was customarily placed on tables, even though their functions were not for the use of the table, just as the goblets and the libation vessels were not for the table's use, but rather for the use of the altar.

**and its libation vessels** *(u-menakkiyyotav),* **with which the libations will be made** *(asher yussakh bahen)*. In the Syriac translation, *u-maikiyata de-metnake bahein*; similarly, the phrase *ve-nesekh lo tissekhu alav*, "nor will you make any libation over it" (Exod. 30:9) is translated in the Syriac as *ve-nukaya la tenakun aloha*. Thus it can be inferred that *menakkiyyot* is a term related to "libation" *(nesekh)*; likewise, *yussakh bahen* refers to *nesekh*, as Onkelos translates [*di-yitnassakh bahen*].

While it is true that the root *sakhakh* denotes "covering," the canes that Rashi mentions did not cover either the table or the bread.[8]

In addition, *menikta* is the Syriac translation of [the liquid measure] *log*, and Bar Bahlul explained that this was a measure that was called *kashat* in Arabic, containing two *cyathos*.[9] It may be deduced that the *kasot* and the *menakkiyyot* were "sisters," both of them liquid measures or small vessels that held drinks. Apparently, however, the *menakkiyyot* were larger than the

---

7. According to Rashi (following *Menahot* 97a), the *ke'arah* was a mold that fit the shape of the "bread of presentation" (next v.).
8. Rashi interprets the phrase *asher yussakh bahen* as "with which it will be covered" (understanding *yussakh* as derived from *sakhakh*) and as referring back to the *kasot*, which he takes to mean "canes."
9. *Cyathos*, lit., "gourd" or "ladle," was the smallest unit of Greek liquid measure, equal to 1/25 liter or 1/12 U.S. pint (see William Mole, *Gods, Men, and Wine* [Cleveland: World Publishing Co., 1966], p. 472). The *log* has been estimated to be 1/3 liter or 2/3 U.S. pint.

*kasot*, since the *menakkiyyah* was the size of a *log*, while the *kashat* was only the size of two *cyathos*, and Bar Bahlul erred in saying that the two measures were the same, for they were of different sizes.

**25:30. "And you will place upon the table bread of presentation, (which is to be) before Me continually.**
**25:31. "And you will make a candelabrum of pure gold; the candelabrum will be made one solid piece [not composed of detachable parts]; its calyxes, its buds, and its flowers will be (inseparable parts) of it.**

***its buds*** *(kaftoreha)*. The word *kaftor* is perhaps derived from *kaf tor*, i.e., *kaf shor* ("ox's foot"), "split hoof." An analogous expression is found in the Mishnah, *Kela'im: rosh tor* [a term for an angular plot of wheat whose point intersects with the side of a plot of barley; *Kela'im* 2:7; 3:3]. This term is not related to the expression *torei zahav* [generally translated as "circlets of gold," Songs 1:11, but understood by some as triangular ornaments] (as asserted by Bertinoro on *Kela'im* 2:7), and not every angle is called a *rosh tor*; rather, an angle that intersects a straight line (like this: V ) is so called, because it resembles the head of an ox (*rosh shor*) that has two horns.

**25:32. "And six branches will come forth from its sides, three candelabrum branches from its one side, and three candelabrum branches from its other side.**
**25:33. "Three calyxes (will be) incised in one branch, (that is) a bud and a flower, and three calyxes incised in the other branch, a bud and a flower, thus in all the six branches coming forth from the candelabrum.**

***Three calyxes*** *(gevi'im,* lit. "cups"). Each calyx consisted of a bud and a flower.

**25:34. "And in the candelabrum itself [that is, in the shaft] four calyxes; [there will be, that is] incised its buds and its flowers.**

***four calyxes.*** One below the place from which the branches came forth, and the three others consisted of a bud under each of the pairs of branches.

**25:35. "One bud (there will be) under two of its branches, one (other) bud under two of its branches, and one bud under (the other) two of its branches, for the six branches coming forth from the candelabrum.**

## Shadal on Exodus

**25:36.** "Their buds, and the corresponding branches, will be (parts inseparable) from it; it will be entirely a single solid body of pure gold.

***Their buds*** *(kaftoreihem).* Those of the branches. "And their corresponding branches" *(u-kenotam,* lit., "and their branches") means "those of the buds."

**25:37.** "And you will make its seven lamps; and (let them be made so that) when they are lit, (each one) may cast light toward that side which is facing (the candelabrum).

***and when they are lit*** *(ve-he'elah et neroteha,* more literally, "and when its lamps are raised"). [The lamps are said to be "raised"] because the flames rise upward. Similarly, "And a fire was kindled [*niskah*] against Jacob" (Ps. 78:21), and likewise the expression *massikin et ha-tannur* ("they light the oven"), for *nesak* [a synonym of] *seleik* in Aramaic means "to rise."

***toward that side which is facing (the candelabrum)*** *(al ever paneha).* All the lamps shed their light toward the side of the table, which was opposite the candelabrum, as it is said, "And the candelabrum facing [*nokhah*] the table" (Exod. 26:35). Similarly, "Make it so that all the seven lamps cast light toward the side that is facing the candelabrum" (Num. 8:2), i.e., toward the side of the table, which was opposite and facing it (Rashbam).

**25:38.** "And its snuffers and its tongs, of pure gold.
**25:39.** "Of one talent [three thousand shekels] of pure gold will the candelabrum be made, with all these furnishings.
**25:40.** "Contemplate, so as to then execute, their model that is shown to you in the mountain."

***Contemplate*** *(u-re'eh,* lit., "and see")... ***their model.*** The Heb. signifies close observation, as in, "And he [Moses] observed [*va-yar*] their burdens" (Exod. 2:11); "[For the king of Babylon... inquired of the teraphim] and looked into [*ra'ah*] the liver" (Ezek. 21:26).

**26:1.** "And you will make the tabernacle, (composed) of ten curtains, which you will make of twisted linen, of blue wool, of purple, and of scarlet, with figures of cherubim, the work of a tapestry weaver.

*of twisted linen, of blue wool, of purple, and of scarlet.* According to the plain meaning (*peshat*), each of these materials was used separately, since each one had its own color, and by such means [the weavers] would fashion designs of various hues. In the Rabbis' opinion, however, each thread was composed of the four materials.

*a tapestry weaver (ḥoshev,* lit., "a thinker"). One who makes multihued designs by weaving; see below at 28:39.

**26:2. "The length of one curtain (will be) twenty-eight cubits, and the width (will be) four cubits per curtain; one single measure all the curtains will have.**
**26:3. "Five curtains will be attached [sewn] one to the other, and (the other) five curtains attached one to the other.**
**26:4. "And you will make loops of blue wool on the edge of that curtain which is at the end of one series; and you will do the same on the edge of that curtain which is the last in the second series.**

*loops.* Each one was attached to the body of a curtain, fifty on one and fifty on the other, and a clasp was inserted in every two loops.

The length of the tabernacle, from east to west, was 30 cubits, and it width, from north to south, was 10 cubits; its height was 10 cubits, and its entrance was on the eastern side (see Kimhi on Ezek. 8:16). Upon its roof were four covers: (1) curtains of twisted linen, blue wool, purple, and scarlet; (2) curtains of goat hair; (3) a cover of sheepskins dyed red; and (4) a cover of badger (*taḥash*) skins.

The curtains of twisted linen, blue wool, etc., were 28 cubits long and 4 cubits wide. Because there were ten of them, it follows that their total width was 40 cubits, of which 30 were the length of the tabernacle, one corresponded to the thickness of the boards (below, v. 15) on the western side, and nine were behind the tabernacle (this is according to R. Nehemiah's view [*Shabbat* 98b], who held that the thickness of the boards was one cubit, while according to R. Judah, who held that the thickness of the boards was one cubit at the bottom but decreased to a finger's breadth at the top, there were ten cubits behind the tabernacle, and the bases [below, v. 19] were also covered). Of the 28 cubits of length, 10 covered the width of the tabernacle, one cubit on each side covered the thickness of the boards (as per R. Nehemiah), and 8 cubits on each side covered [8 out of 10 cubits of the height of] the boards, with the bottom 2 cubits exposed. According to R. Judah, only one cubit was exposed, and that was the cubit of the bases.

On top of these curtains were the goat hair curtains, which were 30 cubits long (2 cubits longer than the first curtains) and 4 cubits wide. There were 11 of them (one more than the first curtains) so that their total width was 44 cubits, and their length covered one more cubit on each side (down until the bases, according to R. Nehemiah, but including the bases in R. Judah's opinion; see Rashi on v. 8 below). Of their width, 30 cubits covered the length of the tabernacle, nine or ten were behind the tabernacle, and half of the remainder of the curtain (2 cubits) hung over the front of the tabernacle on the eastern side, while the other half hung over the back of the tabernacle (according to R. Nehemiah, one cubit was pulled over the ground, but according to R. Judah, both of them were).

On top of this covering were the covers of sheepskin dyed red and of badger skins; these were on top of the roof only, 30 cubits long and 10 cubits wide.

**26:5.** "**Fifty loops you will make on one curtain, and fifty loops you will make in the outermost curtain of the second series; the loops will be facing one another [that is, those of one curtain will correspond exactly to those of the adjoining curtain].**

**26:6.** "**And you will make fifty clasps of gold, and you will join the curtains one to another [by inserting them into the loops], and the tabernacle will be united.**

**26:7.** "**And you will make curtains of goat hair, to serve as a tent over the tabernacle; you will make eleven such curtains.**

**26:8.** "**The length of one curtain (will be) thirty cubits, and the width (will be) four cubits per curtain; one single measure (all) the eleven curtains will have.**

**26:9.** "**And you will attach five curtains on one side, and six curtains on one side; and you will fold back the sixth curtain in front of the tent.**

**26:10.** "**And you will make fifty loops on the edge of that curtain which is at the end of one series, and fifty loops on the edge of the curtain of the other series.**

**26:11.** "**And you will make fifty clasps of copper, and you will insert the clasps in the loops, thus joining the tent so that it will be united.**

**26:12.** "**The extra length that is in excess in the curtains of the tent, (that is) the half curtain that is left over [while the other half is folded in front], will trail behind the tabernacle.**

**26:13.** "**That cubit on one side, and that cubit on the other, left over in the length of the curtains of the tent, will hang at the (long) sides of the tabernacle, on one side and the other, to cover it [that is, to protect the underlying curtains of linen, etc, called those "of the tabernacle," while those of goat hair are called those "of the tent"].

**26:14.** "You will make for the tent a cover [a shelter] of rams' skins dyed red, and a cover of badgers' skins on top.

*You will make...* To accord with the view of R. Judah (*Shabbat* 28a) that there was only one cover (*mikhseh*) [made half of rams' skins and half of badgers' skins] (see Rashi), this verse would properly have been accented as follows:[10]

וְעָשִׂ֧יתָ מִכְסֶ֛ה לָאֹ֖הֶל עֹרֹ֣ת אֵילִ֣ם מְאָדָּמִ֑ים וּמִכְסֵ֥ה עֹרֹת־תְּחָשִׁ֖ים מִלְמָֽעְלָה׃

**26:15.** "And you will make the boards of the tabernacle, of acacia wood, standing erect [cut lengthwise].

**26:16.** "Ten cubits will be the length of the boards, and one and a half cubits the width of each board.

**26:17.** "Each board will have two pegs protruding, one facing the other; thus you will make all the boards of the tabernacle.

*protruding* (*meshullavot*). The *Arukh*, s.v. *shalav*, second entry, [cites a reference to] a pot of meat that has *shelivah* (*Shabbat* 112b), and explains, "This means like spigots of a basin that gush water." Thus, it is possible that *meshullavot* means "protruding"; similarly in Rabbinic Hebrew, the *shelivot* of a ladder are the wooden pieces that protrude from it and on which one steps. See Rashi on v. 25 below [where he says that *meshullavot* means "made like a rung [*shelivah*]"].

*one facing the other* (*ishah el ahotah*, more lit., "one to the other"). Onkelos translates *had le-koveil had* ("one corresponding to the other," "one opposite the other").

**26:18.** "You will make the boards of the tabernacle (distributed as follows): twenty boards on the side of the south, (otherwise called) the right side [in relation to an observer who is turned to the east; see 27:13].

*the side of the south... the right side* (*negbah teimanah*). The second term seems to be an amplification of the first, for the second is more common;

---

10. Shadal's proposed accenting would eliminate the major disjunctive [*etnahta*] that marks the word *me'addamim* ("dyed red").

# Shadal on Exodus

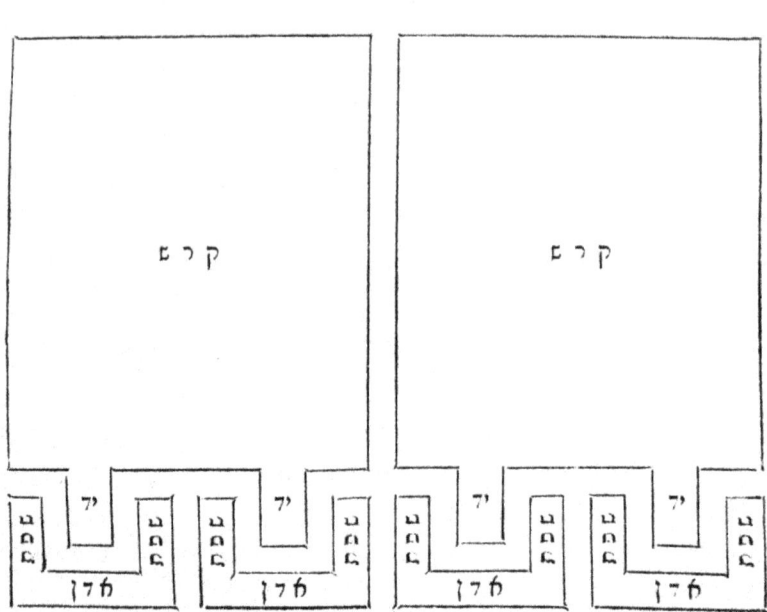

This illustration, which appears in the original 1872 edition of Shadal's *Pentateuco,* vol. II, p. 295, portrays Rashi's view of how the two pegs of each board were inserted into the bases.

cf. *kedmah mizrahah,* "eastward, toward the east" (Exod. 27:13), since the term *mizrah* was known to all. *Teiman* is derived from *yamin* ("right"), while "north" is called *semol* ("left"); when one faces east, one's right and is directed south and one's left hand is directed north.[11]

**26:19.** "And forty silver bases you will make under the twenty boards: two bases under one board, at its two pegs, and two bases under one board, at its two pegs.
**26:20.** "And on the other side of the tabernacle, (that is) on the northern side, twenty boards.
**26:21.** "And their forty silver bases, two bases under one board and two bases under one board.

---

11. To the ancient Israelites, east rather than north was the "orienting" direction; hence the term *kedem* ("forward") for "east" and *ha-yam ha-aharon* ("the rearward sea") for the "western" or Mediterranean Sea.

**26:22.** "And at the end of the tabernacle, (that is) at the west, you will make six boards.

**26:23.** "And two boards you will make at the corners of the tabernacle at the end.

**26:24.** "And they will be twins [they will fit closely together] at the bottom, and together they will finish at the top in one ring; such will be those two (boards): they will be at the two corners.

**twins** *(to'amim)*. As if they were twins *(te'omim)*. Similarly, [the subsequent phrase] *ve-yaḥdav yihyu tammim* is interpreted by Rashi to mean "they will be twins." However, I have translated the word [*tammim*] as vocalized (i.e., "they will finish"); the verse thus seizes upon a play on words, first *to'amim* (meaning "twins") and then *tammim*, as in the phrase *tam ve-nishlam* ("finished and complete").

**26:25.** "There will be (altogether) eight boards, with their silver bases, that is, sixteen bases, two bases under one board and two bases under one board.

**26:26.** "And you will make bars of acacia wood, five for the boards of one side of the tabernacle.

**26:27.** "And five bars for the boards of the other side of the tabernacle, and five bars for the boards of that side of the tabernacle which is on the end, (that is) to the west.

**26:28.** "The middle bar, then, (situated) at the half (of the height) of the boards, must run from one extremity to the other [while above and below it, each bar will be in two pieces].

**26:29.** "The boards you will cover with gold, and of gold you will make their rings, through which to pass the bars, and you will cover the bars with gold.

**and you will cover the bars with gold.** The word *pifiyyot* in Rashi's comment has a counterpart in the Italian language, *pippio* ("pipe"); see Rashi.[12] His

---

12. Rashi, following the *Baraita di-Melekhet ha-Mishkan* (ch. 1), expressed the view that the bars were not actually overlaid with gold, but rather on the boards there were fixed two gold *pifiyyot*, like two sections of a hollow cane, which made the bars appear to be covered with gold. The word *pifiyyot* (elsewhere usually understood as a plural of *peh* or *pifiyyah*, "mouth") appears in the text of the baraita itself, see Ish-Shalom's edition (Vienna, 1908), which notes a number of variants, such as *shefifiyyot* and *shefufiyyot* (apparently some sort of "bent" objects), but also *shefofarot* ("tubes" or "pipes"). It is possible that *pifiyyot* is derived from the Late Latin *\*pipa*, as are the English *pipe* and the Italian *pippio*.

phrase *sidkei kaneh ḥalul* means a hollow pipe split lengthwise (i.e., a half tube).

26:30. "Then you will erect the tabernacle in the proper manner that will be shown to you in the mountain.

26:31. "And you will make a door-curtain of blue wool, of purple, and of scarlet, and of twisted linen; it will be made with figures of cherubim in tapestry work

26:32. "And you will place it over four columns of acacia wood, covered with gold, with their hooks of gold, over four bases of silver.

26:33. "You will place, that is, the door-curtain under the clasps; and there, on the other side of the door-curtain, you will insert the ark of the Admonition; and the door-curtain will serve for you as a division between the holy place and the Holy of Holies [the most holy].

26:34. "And you will place the cover on the ark of the Admonition, in the Holy of Holies.

26:35. "And you will put the table outside the door-curtain, and the candelabrum facing the table, on the south side of the tabernacle, and the table you will place on the north side.

26:36. "And you will make a hanging at the entrance of the tent, of blue wool, and of purple, and of scarlet, and of twisted linen, the work of an embroiderer.

26:37. "And you will make for the hanging five columns of acacia wood, and you will cover them with gold, with their hooks of gold; and you will make for them, by casting, five bases of copper."

27:1. "And you will make the altar of acacia wood, five cubits in length and five cubits in width; square will be the altar, and three cubits (will be) it height.

27:2. "And you will make its prominences on its four corners; (inseparable parts) of it will be its prominences, and you will cover them with copper.

27:3. "And you will make its pots, in which to collect its ashes, and its shovels, and its basins, and its forks, and its paddles; all of its furnishings you will make with copper.

***its shovels.*** To gather the ashes [of the sacrifices].

***and its basins.*** To receive the blood.

*Terumah*

*its forks.* To turn the pieces of meat on the fire.

*its paddles.* To rake up the fire.

**27:4. "And you will make for it a grating of copper, a work (that is) in the form of a network; and you will makeover the network four copper rings, at is four extremities.**

*And you will make for it a grating, etc.* [The phrase is to be understood] as per Rashi and against the accents.[13] The grating surrounded the altar to catch falling pieces of meat and wood (Jerusalem Targum).

*and you will make over the network four copper rings.* With which to carry the altar; see below, 38:5-7 (Judah Aryeh Osimo). They were over the network, [that is] near the grating and above it, but they were not attached to the grating, but rather to the altar.

The grating was not a fixture, but was removable, for below (39:39) it is recorded that they brought to Moses "the copper altar, and its copper grating," and there is no mention there of its being fixed to an object, as were the loops, the enclosure, the cornice, the calyxes, the buds, and the flowers (A.H. Mainster).

**27:5. "And you will place it under the Karkov [?][14] of the altar, below; and the network will be (from the ground) up to half of the height of the altar.**
**27:6. "And you will make poles for the altar, poles (that is) of acacia wood, and you will cover them with copper.**
**27:7. "Its poles will be inserted in the rings; and the poles will be on the two sides of the altar, when it will need to be carried.**
**27:8. "Hollow, (formed) of boards, you will make it; as you have been shown in the mountain, so they will do.**
**27:9. "And you will make the courtyard of the tabernacle. On the southern side, (called) the right side, the courtyard will have curtains of twisted linen, a hundred cubits in length (that is) on one side.**

---

13. The Heb. word order and accents would make it appear that the meaning is, "And you will make for it a grating, in the form of a copper network." Rashi says that the word order is "transposed" (*mesoras*) and construes the phrase as Shadal does.
14. The word *Karkov*, left untranslated by Shadal due to uncertainty, has been understood by others as a "ledge" or "band."

27:10. "And (it will have) its columns, twenty, with their bases, twenty, of copper, and the hooks of the columns, and their ornamentations, of silver.

27:11. "And likewise on the northern side lengthwise (there will be) curtains (along the length of) a hundred cubits, with their respective twenty columns, and their twenty bases, of copper, and the hooks of the columns and their ornamentations, of silver.

27:12. "And the width of the courtyard, on the western side, (will have) fifty cubits of curtains, and their columns, ten, and their bases, ten.

27:13. "And the width of the courtyard on the forward side, (that is) on the east, (will be) fifty cubits.

27:14. "And fifteen cubits of curtains (there will be) on one side with their columns, three, and their bases, three.

*And fifteen cubits of curtains (there will be) on one side.* See Rashi on v. 13.[15]

27:15. "And on the other side fifteen (cubits of) curtains, with their columns, three, and their bases, three.

27:16. "And at the entrance of the courtyard (there will be) a hanging of twenty cubits, of blue wool, of purple, of scarlet, and of twisted linen, embroiderer's work, with their columns, four, and their bases, four.

27:17. "All the columns of the courtyard round about [that is, on its four sides] will have ornamentations of silver, and their hooks of silver, and their bases of copper.

27:18. "The length of the courtyard, one hundred cubits, and the width, fifty by fifty [that is, the courtyard proper was a square of fifty cubits, but with the inclusion of the tabernacle and twenty cubits of space on each side and behind it, the courtyard formed a rectangle of fifty by one hundred cubits], and the height, five cubits, (formed by curtains) of twisted linen, with their bases of copper.

*and the width, fifty by fifty.* See Rashi, and the diagram below.[16]

27:19. "All the furnishings of the tabernacle, for all that may be needed, and all of its pins, and all the pins of the courtyard (will be) of copper."

---

15. There, Rashi explains that the fifty-cubit eastern side of the courtyard had a twenty-cubit open entrance space in the middle, flanked on either side by fifteen curtained cubits.

16. Rashi's comment on this v. is the basis of the bracketed explanation in Shadal's translation.

*Terumah*

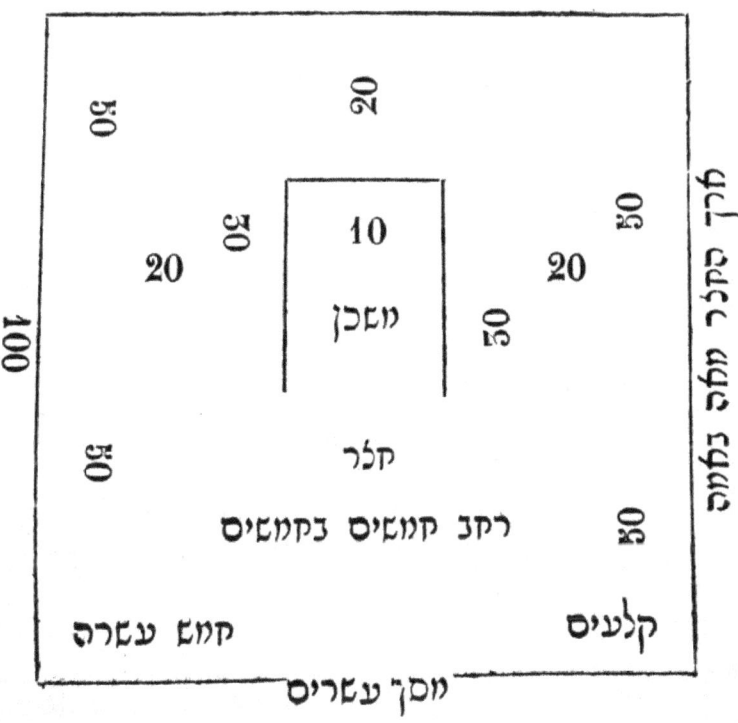

This illustration appears in the original 1872 edition of Shadal's *Pentateuco,* vol. II, p. 304.

# *Tetsavveh*

*Aaron's sacred garments • Installation of the priests
• The golden altar of incense*

**27:20. "And you will command the children of Israel that they bring you olive oil, clear, virgin [that is, extracted with one simple pressing of the olives], for illumination, to make a daily light burn.**

***that they bring you*** *(ve-yikḥu elekha*, lit., "that they take to you"). That they take and bring to you; cf. "Bring them here to me" (*kaḥem na elai*, lit., "take them to me") (Gen. 48:9).

***virgin*** *(katit)*. An adjective modifying *shemen* ("oil"), likewise, [the adjective] "clear" (*zakh*), and not *zayit* ("olive").[1]

***daily*** *(tamid*, lit. "everlasting"). Every evening, burning only from evening to morning, as is stated in the following verse.

**27:21. "In the tent of meeting, outside the door-curtain, situated before the (ark of) the Law, Aaron and his sons will arrange it (so that it burns) from evening to morning, before the Lord. A perpetual statute for the future age, charged to the children of Israel.**

---

1. In the Heb., "olive oil" is *shemen zayit*, so it might have seemed that the adjectives following these nouns modified the second noun *zayit*.

*charged to (me'et).* Cf. "For they received an allowance from [*me'et*] Pharaoh" (Gen. 47:22); "And this will be the right of the priests [to collect] from [*me'et*] the people, from [*me'et*] one who slaughters an animal" (Deut. 18:3).

**28:1. "You, now, bring near to you [declare close to you in rank] among the children of Israel Aaron your brother, and his sons with him, so that they may be priests to Me, Aaron (I say), and Nadab and Abihu, and Eleazar and Itamar, sons of Aaron.**

*You, now, bring near to you.* This does not mean that he was to call them to come to him; rather, this is similar to [Moses' statement to Korah], "And now that He has brought you near [to Him], and with you all of your brothers, the sons of Levi [will you also take the priesthood?]" (Num. 16:10), denoting a separation and setting aside for greatness and honor.

*so that they may be priests (lekhahano).* The *vav* suffix ("-*o*") is not a pronominal suffix [meaning "him"], but is in the manner of the Aramaic [verb forms] *lokatlah, lekatloteih*. Since the verb here is followed by the short word *li* ("to me"), it was made into a form with what resembles a pronominal suffix, and [Hebrew speakers] said *lekhahano li* in the same manner as [Aramaic speakers] would say *lekatloteih*. But to say that *lekhahano* is a transitive verb (i.e., "to make him a priest") is unlikely, for the verb *kihen* ("to serve as a priest") is found only as an intransitive, and besides, if it were transitive, it should have been *lekhahanam li*, "to make *them* priests to me."

The priesthood was distinguished by its clothing—thus the expression "as a bridegroom puts on a priestly diadem [*yekhahen pe'er*]" (Isa. 61:10)[2]— and therefore the Torah immediately proceeds to specify the garments that they were to make [for the priests].

**28:2. "And you will make sacred garments for Aaron your brother, for honor and for majesty.**
**28:3. "And you will speak to all the men of talent, to every man who has been endowed by Me with a talented spirit; and they will make Aaron's garments, with which he will be consecrated to be a priest to Me.**

*who has been endowed by Me (asher milletiv,* lit., "whom I have filled"). This refers to each one of "the men," although Ibn Ezra said that the pronominal

---

2. In his comment on that verse, Shadal suggests that the most basic meaning of the word *kohen* ("priest") was one who was distinguished from the rest of the people by his clothing, and he cross-refers to the verse here.

suffix [*-iv*, "him" or "it" (m.)] refers back to *lev* ["heart," in the phrase *ḥakhmei lev*, lit., "the wise of heart," translated as "men of talent"], but this is incorrect, for we find the following expressions:

- "And He has filled him [Bezalel] with the spirit of God" (Exod. 35:31);
- "He has filled them [Bezalel and Oholiab] with talent [*ḥokhmat lev*]" (Exod. 35:35);
- "And Joshua son of Nun was full of the spirit of wisdom [*ruaḥ ḥokhmah*]" (Deut. 34:9).

However, we do not find the expression "He filled *his heart* with the spirit of wisdom."

**28:4. "And these are the garments that they will make: pectoral, dorsal, mantle, embroidered tunic, mitre, and belt. They will make, that is, sacred garments for Aaron your brother and for his sons, with which they will be priests to Me.**
**28:5. "These [artisans] will receive the gold and the blue wool, and the purple, and the scarlet, and the linen.**
**28:6. "And they will make the dorsal of gold, of blue wool, of purple, of scarlet, and of twisted linen, the work of a tapestry weaver.**

*of gold...* The gold, blue wool, purple, and the other materials were each used individually.[3]

*the work of a tapestry weaver.* Who weaves threads of many colors, from which he produces various designs. As for that which is written, "They beat sheets of gold, and they cut them into threads, to be used amid [*be-tokh*] the blue wool, and amid the purple, and amid the scarlet, and amid the linen, the work of a tapestry weaver" (Exod. 39:3), this too, means that the gold threads were used in some places among the other threads that were used in the weaving.[4]

**28:7. "There will be two shoulder straps attached to its two ends, by means of which it will be connected (to the pectoral).**

---

3. *Contra* Rashi, who expressed the view (following *Yoma* 72a) that the five materials were intertwined in each strand; cf. above on 26:1.
4. Rashi, however, cites this verse in support of his view that the gold threads were intertwined with the threads of the other materials.

## Tetsavveh

28:8. "And the band with which to tie it, which will be on top of it, will be of the same work, forming part of it (the dorsal), of gold (that is), of blue wool, of purple, of scarlet, and of twisted linen.

*And the band with which to tie it* (ve-ḥeshev afuddato). The dorsal (efod) was worn only on the back, as Rashi commented on v. 6 above, but it had a band that circled the entire body, as it is written, "And he girded it [the dorsal] with the band of the dorsal, and with it he arranged [all these garments]" (Lev. 8:7), after which it says, "And he placed over it the pectoral [ha-ḥoshen]" (v. 8). It follows that before the pectoral was put on, the dorsal was girded on the body, and that which is "girded" must surround entirely. Thus the phrase "so that it [the pectoral] may be upon the band of the dorsal" (Exod. 28:28) can be well understood; i.e., the pectoral was literally placed upon the band of the dorsal, for the band circled the entire body.

28:9. "And you will take two onyx stones, and you will engrave upon them the names of the children of Israel.
28:10. "Six of their names upon one stone, and the names of the six remaining ones (you will engrave) on the other stone, according to their birth.
28:11. "An engraver's work in stone, the engraving of a seal, will you engrave in the two stones the names of the children of Israel; encircled by bezels of gold will you make them.

*An engraver's work in stone.* The Heb. would properly have been accented this way: מעשׂה חרש אֹבן; see Rashi.[5]

28:12. "And you will place the two stones upon the shoulder straps of the dorsal, stones of remembrance for the children of Israel; Aaron, that is, will bear their names before the Lord, on his two shoulders, as a remembrance.
28:13. "And you will make bezels of gold.
28:14. "And two chains of pure gold you will make of twisted thread, of cord work; and you will place those corded chains on the bezels.

---

5. The Masoretic accentuation is מַעֲשֵׂה חָרַשׁ אֶבֶן, with the disjunctive accent *zarka* setting off the word *ḥarash* ("engraver") from the following word *even* ("stone"). Rashi says that the words *ḥarash even* are closely connected, apparently understanding them to mean "an engraver of stone." Shadal's suggested re-accenting would facilitate this reading.

## Shadal on Exodus

**28:15.** "And you will make the pectoral of judgment [from which oracles were derived], the work of a tapestry weaver; similar to the work of the dorsal you will make it, of gold (that is), of blue wool, of purple, and of scarlet, and of twisted linen you will make it.

*the pectoral of judgment* (ḥoshen mishpat). So called because of the Urim and Tummim that were placed in it (below, v. 30).

**28:16.** "it will be a rectangle folded over [at the half of its length, to be able to contain the Urim]; it will have a span of length and a span of width.

*folded over.* In order to place the Urim inside it.

**28:17.** "And you will set in it, as (precious) stones are set, four rows of stone. One row: ruby, topaz, and emerald; (these will form) the first order.
**28:18.** "And the second order: carbuncle, sapphire, and diamond [?].[6]
**28:19.** "And the third order: jacinth, agate, and amethyst.
**28:20.** "And the fourth order: chrysolite, onyx, and jasper. Mounted in gold they will be in their settings.
**28:21.** "These stones will bear the names of the children of Israel, being twelve, according to their names; (engraved) with the engraving of a seal, they will represent the twelve tribes, each one with its name.

***These stones will bear the names, etc.*** *(tihyena al shemot benei Yisrael*, lit., "will be on the names of the children of Israel"). The meaning is that the names of the children of Israel will be upon them; cf. above (v. 11), "will you engrave in the two stones *al shemot benei Yisrael*," and similarly (Ezek. 48:31), "And the gates of the city shall be *al shemot shivtei Yisrael*… the gate of Reuben, one; the gate of Judah, one," etc., meaning that the gates will be named after the tribes of Israel, i.e., the names of the tribes will be called upon them. So here, the stones will be *al shemot benei Yisrael*, meaning that the names of Jacob's sons will be "called" and engraved upon them.

***being twelve, according to their names*** *(al shemotam)*. This is not a mere redundancy; rather, the meaning is that this is the reason that there were to be twelve stones, corresponding to the names of the tribes.

---

6. Heb. *yahalom*, "diamond" in Modern Hebrew, but understood here by some as "emerald" or "onyx."

## Tetsavveh

***with the engraving of a seal,*** *etc.* The stones were to be engraved with the engraving of a seal so that each tribe's name would be upon them; thus the stones were to represent the twelve tribes, serving as a sign and memorial for all the tribes.

**28:22.** "And you will make for the pectoral chains of twisted thread, of cord work, of pure gold.
**28:23.** "And you will make for the pectoral two rings of gold, and you will place the two rings on the two ends of the pectoral.
**28:24.** "And you will place the two cords on the two rings, at the ends of the pectoral.
**28:25.** "And the two ends of the two cords you will place on the two bezels, which you will place on the shoulder straps of the dorsal, on the front [that is, exterior] side.
**28:26.** "And you will make two (other) rings of gold, and you will place them on the two ends of the pectoral, on its edge that is against the dorsal on the inside.
**28:27.** "And you will make two (other) rings of gold, and you will place them on the shoulder straps of the dorsal, below, on the front [external] side, close to its juncture, above the band of the dorsal.
**28:28.** "And the pectoral will be laced from its rings to the rings of the dorsal with a string of blue wool, so that it may be upon the band of the dorsal, and the pectoral does not become detached from the dorsal.

***does not become detached*** *(yizzaḥ).* See Kimhi, *Shorashim.*[7]

**28:29.** "Aaron will thus bear the names of the children of Israel in the pectoral of judgment, upon his chest, when he enters into the Sanctuary, for remembrance before the Lord continuously.
**28:30.** "And you will place within the pectoral of judgment the Urim and the Tummim, and they will be upon Aaron's chest when he enters before the Lord; and Aaron will bear upon his chest always, (when he presents himself) before the Lord, the judgment [oracle] of the children of Israel.

***And you will place,*** *etc.* See below, Leviticus 8.[8]

---
7. There, the root of the Heb. is given as *zaḥah*, with a reference to the present verse.
8. There, on v. 8, Shadal comments that the Urim and the Tummim were not fixed inside the pectoral, but were sometimes removed and used as an oracle. He goes on to conjecture that they consisted of 22 pieces of wood or metal that the

**28:31.** "And you will make the mantle supporting the dorsal, all of blue wool.

*the mantle.* On which the dorsal was placed (Rashi); the term "dorsal" [here] includes the "pectoral" as well; cf. "[Abiatar] came down with a dorsal [*efod*] in his hand" (1 Sam. 23:6), where the meaning includes the dorsal and the pectoral together with the Urim and the Tummim.

**28:32.** "And it will have its upper opening (folded over) inside, its opening (that is) willhave a hem round about, of weaver's work; it will have an opening similar to that of a breast plate, so that it does not tear.
**28:33.** "And you will make at its edges pomegranates of blue wool, and purple, and scarlet, at its edges (I say) all around; and between these bells of gold all around.
**28:34.** "A bell of gold and a pomegranate, a bell of gold and a pomegranate (you will make) at the edges of the mantle all around.
**28:35.** "Aaron will put it on to officiate, and thus he will be heard when he enters into the Sanctuary, and when he exits, and he will not die [that is, otherwise he will die].
**28:36.** "And you will make a diadem of pure gold, and you will engrave upon it, in the manner of the engraving of a seal, 'Holy to the Lord.'
**28:37.** "And you will apply to it a string of blue wool, and it will be upon the mitre; it will be toward the front side of the mitre.
**28:38.** "It will be upon Aaron's forehead, and thus Aaron will bear [he will assume upon himself, and he will beseech from God the pardon for] the transgressions relating to the holy things that the children of Israel will consecrate, (relating, that is) to all the offerings consecrated by them. It will be on his forehead continually [every time he officiates], to obtain for them approval before the Lord.

*to obtain for them approval.* So that if they present and consecrate anything without purity of intent, their offering will nonetheless be approved, by means of the diadem upon which is written, "Holy to the Lord," in other words, through the merit of the high priest, who was holy and who was like an intermediary between the people and its God. In a manuscript of Rashi's commentary, it is written [not *she-memashmesh,* but] *she-yemashmesh.*[9]

---

*kohen* would remove one by one, spelling out a Divinely ordained response to his question, and that "the Urim and the Tummim" were so called because each letter was given a name, with the *alef* called "Urim" and the *tav* called "Tummim."
9. Rashi cites an opinion (based on *Yoma* 7b) that the high priest was supposed

# Tetsavveh

**28:39.** "You will make the tunic of linen, embroidered; and you will make a mitre of linen; and a belt you will make, the work of an embroiderer.

*the work of an embroiderer (rokem).* It seems to me that the work of *rikmah* was not originally done with a needle, but rather they would create an image in a garment itself and then attach it on another garment. From this was derived the expression "glistering stones and of divers colors [*avnei pukh ve-rikmah*]" (1 Chron. 29:2), i.e., stones that were attached to the wall for ornamentation; see my comment on Isa. 54:11.[10]

The root *rakam* is close to the root *karam*, which denotes stretching out skin that is attached to a body; also closely related is the root *raka*, which denotes stretching. In Aramaic, [*rekam*] means repairing a garment with a patch that is spread out and attached to it. Later people had the idea of creating *rikmah* by means of a needle without adding a cloth to a cloth, but the name *rikmah* continued to be used for such work as in previous times. Still later they had the idea of creating images within the weaving itself; such work was called *ma'aseh hoshev* ("the work of a tapestry weaver," lit., "the work of a thinker"), on account of the great talent and deliberation that it required.

**28:40.** "You will then make tunics for the sons of Aaron, and you will make them belts; you will also make them turbans, for honor and for majesty.
**28:41.** "You will have Aaron your brother, and his sons with him, don [the aforementioned vestments]; and you will anoint them, and you will install them, and you will declare them holy, and they will be priests to Me.

*You will have Aaron, etc.* See below, 29:9.

**28:42.** "Make them also trousers of linen, to cover their shameful parts; they will be from the loins down to the thighs.
**28:43.** "(These vestments) will be upon Aaron and on his sons, when they enter the tent of congregation, or when they approach the altar to perform

---

to touch (*memashmesh*) the diadem constantly so as to keep his attention upon it. The standard Rashi text has *she-memashmesh* ("that he touches"), while the manuscript cited by Shadal has the grammatically preferable reading *she-yemashmesh* ("that he should touch"). Chavel notes that this reading appears in the first printed edition of Rashi (Reggio di Calabria, 1475).
10. There, commenting on the phrase *marbits ba-pukh avanayikh*, Shadal identifies *pukh* with lapis lazuli, cross-refers to the phrase *avnei pukh ve-rikmah* in 1 Chron. 29:2, and says that this stone was encrusted upon other stones for ornamentation.

the sacred functions; otherwise they would incur transgression, and they would die. A perpetual statute for him, and for his progeny after him."

**29:1.** "And this is what you will do to them, to consecrate them, so that they may be priests to Me. Take a young bull and two immaculate rams. **29:2.** "And unleavened loaves, and unleavened cakes kneaded with oil, and unleavened cakes of soft dough anointed with oil; they (all) will be made of fine wheat flour.

***and unleavened cakes of soft dough*** *(u-r'kikei matsot).* Onkelos translated this as *espogin* ("spongy bread"), and I relied upon him in my translation.

**29:3.** "And you will put them in a basket, and you will present them [you will bring them to the courtyard of the tabernacle] in the basket. Likewise (you will bring there) the bull and the two rams.

***and you will present them.*** To the courtyard of the tabernacle (Rashi).

**29:4.** "And you will have Aaron and his sons present themselves at the entrance of the tent of congregation [that is, in the aforementioned courtyard], and have them bathe in the water.

***at the entrance of the tent of congregation.*** This is the courtyard of the tabernacle; see Rashi on vv. 3 and 11.

**29:5.** "And you will take the vestments, and you will have Aaron put on the tunic, and the mantle of the dorsal, and the dorsal and the pectoral, and you will arrange them for him with the band of the dorsal.
**29:6.** "And you will put the mitre on his head, and you will place upon the mitre the sacred diadem.
**29:7.** "And you will take the oil of anointing, and you will drip it on his head, and (thus) you will establish him as Anointed [that is, invested with his dignity].

***and (thus) you will establish him as Anointed*** *(u-mashaḥta oto,* lit., "and you will anoint him"). The meaning is that by means of this anointing, you will establish him as the anointed one *(mashiaḥ)*; that is, from that time on, he and all his descendants will be priests. The anointing was a sign of greatness and a sacred authority that would pass from father to son, and for this reason

Aaron's sons were not anointed, and neither were the sons of kings (except at a time of dispute, as in the case of Solomon on account of Adonijah's dispute).

Below in v. 29, where it says *lemoshḥah bahem* ("to become invested with their dignity through them") [referring to the sons of Aaron wearing Aaron's garments], the word denotes greatness without actual anointing. Similarly, where it says, "Because the Lord has anointed me [as a prophet]" (Isa. 61:1), and "Elisha the son of Shaphat shall you anoint to be a prophet in your stead" (1 Kings 19:16), these are transferred expressions by way of metaphor, for no actual anointing took place in those cases, nor would it have been likely for a prophet to be anointed, for his greatness was not passed on as an inheritance to his son.

**29:8. "Then you will have his sons approach, and you will have them put on their tunics,**
**29:9. "And you will gird them their belts, Aaron (that is) and his sons, and you will wrap them [the latter ones] their turbans; and they will acquire the priesthood as a perpetual right. Then you will install Aaron and his sons.**

***Then you will install*** (*u-milleta yad*, lit., "then you will fill the hand of") ***Aaron***. It seems that the root of this expression is that one who comes to serve as a priest approaches God's presence with his hands filled with an offering, as in the case of the wave offering (below, v. 24). Cf. "Who then offers willingly to consecrate himself [*lemallot yado*, lit., "to fill his hand"] this day to the Lord?" (1 Chron. 29:5), and similarly here, "And you will place it all on Aaron's palms" (below, v. 24). This matter requires further study.

**29:10. "That is, you will have the bull brought before the tent of congregation, and Aaron and his sons will lay their hands on the head of the bull.**
**29:11. "And you will slaughter the bull before the Lord, (that is) at the entrance of the tent of congregation.**
**29:12. "And you will take of the blood of the bull, and you will put it with your finger on the prominences of the altar, and all the (rest of the) blood you will pour out at the (site called the) foundation of the altar.**
**29:13. "And you will take all the tallow that covers the interior, and the network [omentum] that is on the liver, and the two kidneys, and the tallow that is on them; and you will burn (that is, all) on the altar.**

**29:14.** "And the flesh of the bull, and its skin, and its waste, you will burn outside of the encampment; it is a sacrifice of aspersion [that is, the blood of which must be sprinkled on the prominences of the altar].

*a sacrifice of aspersion (ḥattat).* See Leviticus 4.[11]

**29:15.** "And you will take one of the rams, and Aaron and his sons will lay their hands on the head of the ram.
**29:16.** "And you will slaughter the ram, and you will take its blood, and you will dash it on the altar, round about.
**29:17.** "And you will cut the ram into its quarters, and you will wash its inward parts and its legs, and you will put them near its quarters and its head.
**29:18.** "And you will burn all of the ram on the altar; it is a burnt offering in honor of the Lord, a propitiatory aroma, a sacrifice to be burnt to the Lord it is.
**29:19.** "And you will take the other ram, and Aaron and his sons will lay their hands on the head of the ram.
**29:20.** "And you will slaughter the ram, and you will take of its blood, and you will put it on the top of Aaron's right ear and on those of his sons, and on the thumb of their right hand, and on the big toe of their right foot; and you will dash the (remainder of the) blood on the altar, round about.
**29:21.** "And you will take of the blood that is on the altar, and of the oil of anointing, and you will sprinkle it upon Aaron and on his garments, and likewise on his sons and on their garments; and thus will be consecrated he and his garments, and with him his sons and his sons' garments.
**29:22.** "And you will take of the ram the tallow and the tail, and the tallow that covers the inward parts, and the network that is on the liver, and the two kidneys, and the tallow that is upon them, and the right leg, for it is the ram of installation.

*for it is the ram of installation.* And therefore the right leg was to be taken and burned with the *emurim* (portions of sacrifices offered on the altar), for we do not find the burning of the right leg with the *emurim* other than here; see Rashi.

---

11. There, in his comment on v. 3, Shadal states that the *ḥattat* is so called because there is a *ḥittui* ("aspersion," i.e., sprinkling) of the blood of the sacrifice, not because it is offered to atone for sin (*ḥet*).

# Tetsavveh

**29:23.** "And a round loaf, and a cake of bread with oil, and one of soft dough (you will take) from the basket of the unleavened loaves that is before the Lord [that is, in the courtyard].

**29:24.** "And you will place it all on Aaron's palms, and on the palms of his sons, and you will make of it a waving before the Lord [an act with which the priest received the consecrated object from the donor, and here Aaron and his sons were the donors, and Moses, who installed them, served as the priest].

*a waving (tenufah).* The *tenufah* consisted of lifting up and moving to and fro, for the priest would receive the offering from those who brought it and would lift it and move it about in order to symbolize the transfer of the offering from the domain of the owners to that of Heaven. Similarly, Aaron received the Levites, who had been "assigned" to God by the children of Israel, and he "waved" them (Num. 8:11, 21).[12] So also with regard to the sacrifices of contentment (*shelamim*), anyone who brings such sacrifices before God "with his hands will bring the parts to be burned to the Lord, he will bring (that is) the tallow upon the breast, with the breast to be made a waving [*tenufah*] before the Lord" (Lev. 7:30), meaning that he would bring the breast in order that the priest could wave the tallow upon it before the Lord. The breast served only as an object on which to spread the tallows that had to be waved, for they were to be burned upon the altar, and for this reason it was called *ḥazeh ha-tenufah*, "the breast of waving" (Lev. 7:34); it was left to the priest, like the basket in which the first fruits were placed.

In contrast, the [right] leg was a tribute (*terumah*) to God, Who in turn granted it to the priest, and thus it was called the *shok ha-terumah* ("leg of tribute"). On this occasion, which was the start of the sacrificial system and the consecration of Aaron and his sons, God wanted it to be known that the leg was Heaven's portion, and therefore it too was burned; Moses, who was serving as the priest, received only the breast, which he waved and which was then left to him.

The term *tenufah*, too, was used to denote a setting aside and donation to Heaven above, for anything that is so donated is designated in terms of "lifting" or "raising," e.g., "Every man who presented gold [*henif tenufot zahav*] in offering to the Lord" (Exod. 35:22); "All of the things that will be presented [*tenufot*] by the children of Israel [to the priests]" (Num. 18:11).

---

12. In Shadal's comment on Num. 8:11, he expresses the view that Aaron "waved" the Levites by having them walk around the altar.

See what I wrote at Deut. 16:10; there the words *millah yevanit* ("Greek word") were misprinted for *millah romit* ("Latin word").[13]

**29:25. "And you will take those things from their hand, and you will burn them on the altar with the burnt offerings, in a propitiatory aroma before the Lord, it is (that is, completely) a sacrifice to be burned to the Lord.**
**29:26. "And you will take the breast of the ram of installation, which belongs to Aaron, and you will make a waving of it before the Lord, and it will belong to you as (your) portion.**
**29:27. "And you will declare sacred the breast of which the waving was made and the leg of tribute [that is, of the priestly right, but on this occasion burned on the altar], which were waved and raised (in tribute) from the ram of installation of Aaron and of his sons.**

***And you will declare sacred*** *(ve-kiddashta).* For future generations; see Rashi. If the verse is so understood, then *ve-kiddashta* should not be connected with *me-eil ha-millu'im* ("from the ram of installation"), and the *etnaḥ* (major disjunctive accent) should have been placed at the word *ha-terumah* ("[the leg] of tribute") [instead of at the word *huram*, "raised"]. The words *asher hunaf va-asher huram* ("which were waved and raised") would thus be connected with *me-eil ha-millu'im*, i.e., the breast and leg that on this occasion were waved and raised in tribute from the ram of installation would in the future belong to Aaron and his sons (A.H. Mainster).

***which were waved and raised.*** Both [the breast and the leg] were waved before God, as is made clear here and in Lev. 8:27, 29. Both were offered as a tribute to God; the leg was burned, and the breast was allotted to Moses, who was serving as the priest during the days of installation and was eating from the table of Heaven.

**29:28. "And they will belong (in the future, the breast and the right leg) to Aaron and to his sons, as a perpetual right, (to be collected) from the**

---

13. There, commenting on the phrase *missat nidvat yadekha* ("those spontaneous sacrifices that you wish to offer"), Shadal derives the Hebrew word *mas* ("levy," "tribute") from *nasah* ("to raise"). He goes on to conjecture that the Aramaic word *missat* ("plenty," "enough") is actually a Latin word, derived from *satis* ("enough"), that entered the language during the Second Temple period. The misprint *millah yevanit*, which appears in the *Ha-Mishtadel* version of Luzzatto's commentary, was corrected to *millah romit* in the Deuteronomy volume of the *Pentateuco* (1876).

## Tetsavveh

children of Israel, for they are a (sacred) tribute. They will be a tribute of the children of Israel, (to be taken) from their sacrifices of contentment, the part (that is) that they will have to take for the Lord.

29:29. "The sacred garments of Aaron will belong to his sons after him, to become invested of their dignity with them, and with them to receive their installation.

29:30. "For seven days he will put them on, that one of his sons who will officiate in his place, who will enter into the tent of congregation to perform the sacred functions.

*he will put them on, that one of his sons who will officiate* (yilbeshem ha-kohen). Rashi's reading of the accents was ילבשם הכהן [with the disjunctive *tevir* separating the two words, though most texts have a conjunctive *darga* instead], and this is the proper reading, but in a manuscript in my possession and in two manuscripts belonging to Mendelssohn, [this comment of Rashi] does not appear. Indeed, it is not likely that the word *ha-kohen* ("the priest") is the equivalent of *ha-mekhahen* ("the one who serves as a priest").[14] Rather, the phrase *ha-kohen tahtav* is elliptical [and is the equivalent of] *ha-kohen asher yakum tahtav* ("the priest who will arise in his stead"), as it is rendered in the Jerusalem Targum.

29:31. "You will then take the ram of installation, and you will cook its flesh in a sacred place.

29:32. "And Aaron and his sons will eat the ram's flesh, and the bread that is in the basket, at the entrance of the tent of congregation.

29:33. "They will eat these things, with which expiation was made to install them, to consecrate them; and no stranger [that is, one who is not of the priestly family] will eat of it, for they are a sacred thing.

29:34. "And if there is left over some of the flesh (of the sacrifice) of installation, or of the bread, until the morning, you will burn that leftover, it will not be eaten, for it is a sacred thing.

29:35. "You will do thus to Aaron and to his sons, all that I commanded you; for seven days you will celebrate their installation.

29:36. "And a bull in a sacrifice of aspersion you will make each day, besides the (aforementioned) expiations, and you will sprinkle (the

---

14. The Rashi comment in question (which, as Chavel notes, does not appear in the first printed edition) expresses the view that *kohen* is actually not a noun but a participle, and implies that in the present verse, the words *ha-kohen tahtav* should be read together to mean "the one who serves as a priest in his place."

blood) on the altar, making expiation for it [that is, to purify it of every fault that might have been committed during its construction, or in the offering of its materials], and you will anoint it in order to consecrate it.
**29:37.** "For seven days you will make expiation for the altar, and (thus) you will consecrate it, and the altar will become a most holy thing; every thing that touches the altar will become holy.

***will become holy.*** See below, 30:29, comments of Rashi and Ibn Ezra. The Rabbis [followed by Rashi] distinguished between objects that were appropriate [for designation as holy] and those that were not appropriate: The altar, as well as all the sacred utensils, made holy any object that touched them if the object was appropriate for holiness, but not if it was inappropriate. However, it seems to me [in keeping with Ibn Ezra's approach] that even an object that was not appropriate for holiness, once it touched a sacred utensil, became one from which a stranger [not of the priestly family] was forbidden to derive benefit.

**29:38.** "And this is what you will do upon the altar: lambs born within the year, two a day every day.
**29:39.** "One lamb you will do in the morning, and the other lamb you will do toward evening.
**29:40.** "With a tenth (of an efah) of fine flour, mixed with virgin oil, a quarter of a hin, and the libation of a quarter of a hin of wine, for one lamb.
**29:41.** "And the second lamb you will do toward evening, accompanying it with the flour offering and the libation, like that of the morning, in a propitiatory aroma, a sacrifice to be burned before the Lord.

***ta'aseh lah*** *("you will do to it")* [these Heb. words, untranslated here, precede the phrase "in a propitiatory aroma"]. The word *lah* ("to it") refers to the *olah* (burnt offering) mentioned in the subsequent verse ("a daily burnt offering for all the ages to come").

**29:42.** "A daily burnt offering for all the ages to come, (to be done) at the entrance of the tent of congregation, before the Lord, where I will gather Myself to you, to speak to you there.
**29:43.** "I will gather Myself there to the children of Israel, and (that place) will acquire holiness through My glorious presence.
**29:44.** "I will sanctify the tent of congregation and the altar, and Aaron and his sons I will sanctify to be priests to Me.

## Tetsavveh

**29:45.** "And I will reside in the midst of the children of Israel, and I will be their [tutelary] God.

**29:46.** "And they will know that I, the Lord, am their God, Who brought them out of the land of Egypt, to reside among them. I am the Lord, your God."

**30:1.** "And you will make an altar on which to burn the incense; of acacia wood you will make it.

**30:2.** "One cubit (will be) its length and one cubit its width, it will be square, and two cubits its height; and it will have its prominences, (inseparable) from it.

**30:3.** "And you will cover it with pure gold, its upper surface, its walls all around, and its prominences; and you will make for it a cornice of gold round about.

**30:4.** "And two rings of gold you will make beneath its cornice, on its two sides, (two of them, that is) you will make on both of its sides, through which to pass the poles with which to carry it.

***on its two sides*** *(al shetei tsal'otav), etc.* Today, 25 Tammuz 5619 (1859), it seems to me that this means two that are [actually] four, i.e., two rings on both of its sides, not two in total but two on each side, just as there were on the ark, the table, and the altar for the burnt offerings, for with only one ring on one side and one on the other (as Rashi and R. Joseph Bekhor Shor maintained), it surely would not have been proper to carry it, as it would have tottered and shaken.

The reason why it is not plainly written "four rings" is merely for the sake of elegant variation, in keeping with the custom of the Hebrew language to express an idea twice using different words. It should be noted that in the case of all three of the [other] items where poles are mentioned, the wording always changes:

- Concerning the ark it is written, "And you will cast for it… two rings on its one side and two rings on its other side" (Exod. 25:12).
- Concerning the table it is written, "And you will make for it four rings of gold, and you will apply the rings upon the four corners" (Exod. 25:26).
- Concerning the altar of the burnt offerings it is written, "And you will make over the network four copper rings, at its four extremities" (Exod. 27:4). Then it is written, "The poles will be on the two sides of [*tsal'ot*] the altar" (v. 7)

Here, too, concerning the altar of the incense, the wording changes and it says "two rings," not "four rings," but it does specify that they are to be on both of its sides [*tsal'otav*], the same wording used with the altar of the burnt offerings, where there were four rings, not two. Then it specifically repeats "on both of its sides [*tsiddav*]," that is, two on each side.

I have since found that this is also the opinion of Abravanel, i.e., that there were four rings, except that he says that they were affixed to the corners, which is possible, but the word *tsal'otav* certainly does not mean "its corners." Perhaps Targum [Onkelos] chose [nevertheless] to translate the word as *zivyateih* ("its corners") because it was surprising and strange to mention the sides twice in close proximity, yet indeed the word *tsela* does not at all mean "corner."

**30:5.** "And you will make the poles of acacia wood, and you will cover them with gold.
**30:6.** "And you will place it in front of the door-curtain, which hangs over the ark of the Law, facing the cover that is upon the Law, where I will gather Myself to you.
**30:7.** "And Aaron will burn upon it the aromatic incense; from morning to morning, when he cleans the lamps, he will burn it.
**30:8.** "Likewise when Aaron lights the lamps toward night, he will burn it. A daily incense before the Lord, for all the ages to come.
**30:9.** "You shall not burn upon that (altar) any strange incense, nor burnt offering, nor flour offering, nor shall you make upon it any libation.
**30:10.** "And Aaron will make expiation upon its prominences once a year. Of the blood of the sacrifice of aspersion (of the day) of expiation, once a year, he will expiate upon it, in all the ages to come. A most holy thing to the Lord it is (that altar)."

# *Ki Tissa*

*The "evil eye" • Pride goeth before the fall • The half-shekel ransom • Anointing oil and incense • Betsalel and the men of talent • The Sabbath pact • A substitute for Moses • The calf of cast metal • The shattered tablets • "Let me, please, see Your majesty" • Thirteen Attributes • The new tablets*

**30:11. The Lord spoke to Moses, saying:**
**30:12. "When you make the review of the children of Israel, of those (that is) who are to be enumerated [excluding the minors and the women], each one will give to the Lord the ransom of his own person, when the enumeration is made of him; and thus no mortality will befall among them, when they are enumerated.**

*When you make the review, etc.* When a person counts his silver and gold, or when a king counts his troops, it is quite likely that he will trust in his wealth or in the multitude of his soldiers, and he will become proud and say, "My force and the vigor of my hand have procured or will procure me prosperity" (cf. Deut. 8:17). But then it will usually happen that the wheel of fortune will turn upon him and an unexpected disaster will befall him (for this is indeed one of the laws of Providence, that "pride goeth before the fall," and this has proven and continues to prove itself true in all generations with respect to individuals as well as nations and kings).

## Shadal on Exodus

From this resulted, among all the peoples, a belief in the "evil eye." Apparently this belief had already become widespread among Israel in the generations before the giving of the Torah. Now God did not wish to abolish this belief altogether, since it is based upon a belief in Providence and keeps a person far from trusting in his own might or wealth, and this is the main principle of the entire Torah. So then what did He do? He commanded that they be enumerated, just when they began to be a unified people, and that they give a ransom of half a shekel per head, and that this money be given over to the service of the tent of congregation as a remembrance before the Lord to ransom themselves. Thus from that day forward they could be counted without fearing the evil eye, for the Tabernacle that was made with the silver of ransom would effect expiation for them.

Now God said, "When you make the review of the children of Israel... each one will give to the Lord the ransom of his own person," etc., and the apparent meaning of these words is that this was to occur even in future generations; i.e., every time they would be counted without giving a ransom, a mortality would befall them. However, at the end of the matter it says, "You will receive from the children of Israel the silver of the ransom, and you will employ it for the use of the office to be done in the tent of congregation, and it will serve the children of Israel as a remembrance before the Lord, to ransom your persons" (v. 16). This indicates that the silver was to remain as a remembrance before the Lord for future generations, and that they would need no further ransom, for even though the enumerated persons needed to be ransomed, the tabernacle—which was constructed with the silver of the ransom—would effect expiation for them.

Accordingly, the command of *ki tissa* ("when you make the review...") was for that one time only, as per Abravanel. I disagree with him only insofar as he maintained that the main reason for this command was to collect the silver needed for the service of the tabernacle. I think that if it were not for this stratagem, they would have collected far more silver than the amount needed for the labor, as was collected from the gold, the precious stones, and all the other materials (see below, 36:5). Rather, the main intent of this command was that there should be one [amount of] tribute that would be the same for the rich and the poor, and that out of this tribute would be made the [silver] bases on which the tabernacle and the door-curtain would stand, so that the rich person could not say to the poor person, "My portion of the Sanctuary is greater than yours" (as the sages of the Tosafot wrote in *Da'at Zekenim* [on v. 14 below]).

## Ki Tissa

The second purpose of this command was to diminish the fear of the evil eye when the people were enumerated for a valid purpose, for the tabernacle, which stood on the silver that each person had given for his ransom, would effect expiation for them. So we find that several times after this, the children of Israel were counted and there is no mention of their giving a ransom, nor did any mortality befall them. All of this, however, obtained when the people were enumerated for a valid purpose. If they were enumerated for an invalid purpose, and only for the sake of the ruler's arrogance, then an evil occurrence would likely have stricken them as a punishment for pride and in accordance with Divine Providence. So it was said in Midrash Tanhuma: "Whenever Israel was counted for a valid purpose, they did not decrease; whenever for an invalid purpose, they decreased."

Thus it was that David, at the end of his life, was seized with a desire to know the number of the people, and this was for no valid purpose, for he was no longer waging war, but merely by way of pride and arrogance. For this reason Joab feared that this would provoke God's anger, and the king's order was abhorrent to him; indeed, God did send a plague upon the people (2 Samuel 24). It was at this time that David was stirred to build a House for God that would serve to expiate for Israel, and he donated and made great exertions to prepare gold, silver, copper, iron, wood, precious stones, and marble; he also requested of the public at large to make donations as well, and they immediately donated a large amount with a full heart. All of this was to expiate for Israel [even] in future generations.

Now I will come to the heart of the matter, that is, the "evil eye." I will note that some of the philosophizers (*mitpalsefim*), such as Gersonides, sought to explain it in a naturalistic way, expressing the view that the vapors that exude from the eyes of an observer toward the face of one who is seen can be toxic and may injure or kill that person, all according to the nature of the one receiving [such vapors]. Most of the scholars of our era, in contrast, mock the belief in the evil eye, just as they do many other things that cannot be understood in a naturalistic manner. In my view, both of these groups are mistaken. The world does not behave according to the laws of physical nature alone; rather, there are other laws that were framed by the Supreme Intelligence at the beginning of creation, according to which all events are caused, bringing upon nations and individuals alike both good and evil occurrences that attest to Providence. The [modern] philosophizer looks upon them and says that they are happenstance, while the common folk look upon them and say that they are miraculous. In fact, they are natural events that result inevitably from natural causes, but the events and their causes have all been arranged from the beginning of creation through the wisdom of the Supreme Regulator, blessed be His name.

It is this [wisdom] that decreed that the cold weather would be [unusually] harsh and early in the year 5573 (1812), in order to defeat a proud monarch and pacify the entire world.[1] It is this [same wisdom] that framed the decree that in the course of public and private events, "pride goeth before the fall" [Prov. 16:18, "Pride goeth before destruction, and a haughty spirit before a fall"]. From this it results that when a person (or likewise an entire nation) stands at the pinnacle of success and exults with pride, producing jealousy in the hearts of his observers, it will befall him that the wheel will turn and an unexpected disaster will come upon him. The common folk will attribute this to the evil eye, or sometimes to the curse of an enemy; but in truth, it is not the eye that does harm or curses that cause evil. Rather, justice is the Lord's, and it is He Who decreed the chain of causation of good and evil, and that "a man's pride shall bring him low, but he that is of a lowly spirit shall attain to honor" (Prov. 29:23). As a French poet said: *Du triomphe à la chute il n'est souvent qu'un pas* ("From triumph to fall there is often but one step") (Voltaire, *La Mort de César*).

The *Me'ammer* [R. Wolf Meir] wrote that the people of that generation had to give a ransom because they sinned with the Golden Calf and deserved destruction, but he did not keep in mind that this command preceded the incident of the Calf.

**30:13. "All those who will enter into the enumeration will give this: half a shekel, according to the weight of the Temple. The shekel is twenty gerah. The half shekel is the tribute (to be paid) to the Lord.**
**30:14. "Whoever enters into the enumeration, from the age of twenty years and upward, will pay this tribute to the Lord.**
**30:15. "The rich one will not give more, and the poor one will not give less, than the half shekel, to pay the tribute to the Lord, to ransom your persons.**

***to ransom your persons*** *(lekhapper al nafshoteikhem)*. A similar expression is *kesef ha-kippurim*, "the silver of the ransom" (next v.). The correct explanation is that of Mendelssohn, that [these derivations of the verb *kipper*] are used in the sense of *kofer nefesh* ("ransom of a soul"); so also, "For the blood, that can propitiate for the life [*ba-nefesh yekhapper*]" (Lev. 17:11),

---

1. A reference to Napoleon's disastrous retreat from Russia, October to December 1812.

*Ki Tissa*

i.e., it is the soul's ransom, "for the blood is the life" (Deut. 12:23), and one who brings a sacrifice is giving a life for a life.

30:16. "You will receive from the children of Israel the silver of the ransom, and you will employ it for the use of the office to be done in the tent of congregation, and it will serve the children of Israel as a remembrance before the Lord, to ransom your persons."

30:17. And the Lord spoke to Moses, saying:

30:18. "You will make besides a basin of copper, with its pedestal of copper, to be used for bathing; and you will place it between the tent of congregation and the altar, and you will put water in it.

30:19. "And Aaron and his sons will bathe their hands and feet in it.

30:20. "Entering into the tent of congregation, they will bathe themselves, otherwise they will die; likewise approaching the altar to officiate, to burn a sacrifice to be burned to the Lord.

30:21. "They will bathe their hands and their feet, and they will not die; and that will be for them a perpetual statute, for him (that is) and his progeny, for all the ages to come."

30:22. And the Lord spoke to Moses, saying:

30:23. "And you will take for yourself select spices: spontaneously flowing myrrh, five hundred (shekels in weight); aromatic cinnamon, half of the preceding, (that is) two hundred fifty; and aromatic [cinnamon] cane, two hundred fifty.

*And you will take,* etc. [This verse is to be understood] according to the accents, and as per the Jerusalem Talmud, *Shekalim*, beginning of ch. 6.[2]

30:24. "And cassia, five hundred, (all) with the weight of the Temple; and olive oil, one hin.

30:25. "And you will make of it an oil of sacred anointing, a fragrant compound, the work of a perfumer; oil of sacred anointing it will be.

---

2. The word *mahatsito* (translated by Shadal as "half of the preceding") is connected to the preceding words *ve-kinnemon besem* ("aromatic cinnamon") with the conjunctive accents *merkha-tipha*. Accordingly, the weight of the cinnamon would be 250 shekels, and the total weight of all the spices listed in vv. 23 and 24 would be 1,500 shekels. This total is confirmed in the Jerusalem Talmud, *Shekalim* 24b. However, Rashi (following the Babylonian Talmud, *Keritot* 5a) connects the word *mahatsito* with the subsequent words *hamishim u-matayim* ("two hundred fifty") and expresses the view that 250 was half the weight of the aromatic cinnamon.

30:26. "And you will anoint with it the tent of congregation, and the ark of the Law.
30:27. "And the table and all of its furnishings, and the altar of the incense.
30:28. "And the altar of the burnt offerings and all of its furnishings, and the basin and its pedestal.
30:29. "And you will declare them holy, and they will be a most holy thing; anything that touches them will become holy.
30:30. "And Aaron and his sons you will anoint, and you will consecrate them to be priests to Me.
30:31. "And to the children of Israel you will speak, saying, 'Oil of sacred anointing this will be to (the honor of) Me, for all the ages to come.
30:32. "'On the body of any person an ointment must not be made of it, and you shall not make of it anything similar with those same measurements. Holy it is, holy it must be for you.

**an ointment must not be made of it** *(lo yisakh).* [The Heb., a variant of *yusakh,* is] on the model of *va-yisem be-aron be-Mitsrayim* ("and he was placed in an ark in Egypt").[3]

30:33. "One who will compound something similar to it or will make use of it on a stranger will become extinct from the midst of his people."
30:34. And the Lord said to Moses, "Take for yourself spices: balsam, fragrant onycha, and galbanum, (and other) spices, and clear frankincense; let them be of equal measurements.

**and galbanum, (and other) spices** *(ve-ḥelbenah sammim,* lit., "and galbanum, spices"). Take the choicest balsam, onycha, and galbanum, such as are worthy of the term "spices," in keeping with that which is mentioned above [v. 23], *kinnemon besem* ("aromatic cinnamon") and *keneh vosem* ("aromatic [cinnamon] cane"). This is how it would appear to me according to the plain meaning, but the accents conform with the opinion of the Rabbis [i.e., the disjunctive *zakef katon* that marks the word *ve-ḥelbenah* separates it from the following word *sammim,* which was understood by the Rabbis the mean "other spices," as per Rashi and Shadal's own translation].

**let them be of equal measurements** *(bad be-vad).* Portion for portion, weight for weight; for each ounce of balsam, add one ounce of onycha. See above,

---

3. Gen. 50:26, where *va-yisem* is, according to Shadal, a variant of *va-yusam*; his comment there cross-refers to the present verse.

27:18 [where *hamishim ba-hamishim* means "fifty by fifty"]. When two things are combined or placed side by side, the preposition *be-* is used [as in *bad be-vad*], but when they remain separate, the preposition *ke-* is used, [as in] *helek ke-helek yokhelu*, "they will eat in equal portions" (Deut. 18:8) (A.H. Mainster).

**30:35. "And you will make of it an incense, a compound, the work of a perfumer, worked with purity and holiness.**

**worked** *(memullah)*. Ibn Ezra, Nachmanides, Rosenmueller, and Gesenius interpreted this word to mean that they were to add salt (*melah*) to it. It seems to me, however, that since we find the form *timlah* ("you will salt") in the *kal* conjugation [of the verb *malah* ("to salt"), the *pa'al* (participle) form ought to be *maluah* and not *memullah*. Onkelos translated the word as "mixed," and Rashi understood it as derived from the term *mallahei ha-yam* ("sailors of the sea"), who stir up the water with their oars, just as in the case of incense, various spices were well stirred and mixed together.

In my opinion, *mallahei ha-yam* is the equivalent of "[they that go down to the sea in ships,] that do business [*melakhah*] in great waters" (Ps. 107:23), and just as the verb *halakh* ("to go") was the source of *shalah* ("to send"), so *melakhah* was the source of *mallah* ("sailor," "sea worker").[4] Thus the meaning of the phrase [in this verse] *memullah tahor kodesh* is that the "work" [of the incense] was to be done in purity and holiness. The words *mumullah tahor* are masculine [adjectives], and thus they refer not to *ketoret* ("incense," f.) but to *rokah* ("compound," m.).

In a Rashi manuscript in my possession, [the text reads] *le'arevam helmon ve-helbon be-etsba'o be-vazakh*.[5]

**30:36. "And you will grind it into a fine powder, and you will make use of it before the (ark of the) Law, in the tent of congregation, where I will be found with you. It must be for you a most holy thing.**

---

4. More commonly, *mallah*/sailor has been derived from *melah*/salt. Thus, Strong's *Hebrew & Chaldee Dictionary of the Old Testament*, s.v. *mallah*, notes that a sailor follows "the salt," and Reuben Alcalay's *Complete Hebrew-English Dictionary*, s.v. *mallah*, includes the colloquial English word for sailor, "salt."

5. Translation: "to mix the yolk and white with his finger in a vessel." In standard editions, the text reads *le'arevam im ha-mayim, ve-khol davar she-adam rotseh le'arev yafeh yafeh mehappekho ve-etsba o ve-vazakh* ("to mix them [i.e., eggs] with water, and anything that a person wants to mix very well, he stirs them with his finger or in a vessel").

30:37. "This incense that you will make—you shall not make anything of an equal composition for your use—must be regarded by you as a thing holy to the Lord.
30:38. "One who makes anything similar to it, to enjoy its fragrance, will become extinct from the midst of his people."

31:1. The Lord spoke to Moses, saying:
31:2. "See, I call by name Bezalel, son of Uri, son of Hur, of the tribe of Judah.

*I call by name (karati be-shem).* This indicates a choosing; thus Onkelos translates it as *de-rabbeiti* ("that I have appointed"). Cf. "I have called you by your name; you are Mine" (Isa. 43:1).

31:3. "I have filled him with the spirit of God, with regard to wisdom, discernment, and knowledge, and every art.
31:4. "To think (new) ideas, to work in gold, and in silver, and in copper.
31:5. "And to work in gems to mount, and to work in wood, to work (in sum) in any art.
31:6. "I then assign to accompany him Oholiab son of Ahisamak, of the tribe of Dan, as well as all the (other) talented men, those (that is) who were furnished by Me with talent; and they will carry out all that I commanded you.

*as well as all the (other) talented men, etc.* (*u-v'-lev kol ḥakham lev natatti ḥokhmah*, lit., "and in the heart of every talented of heart I gave talent"). "I have also assigned to accompany him every talented man in whose heart I have given talent." This is analogous to *u-l'-khol bahen ḥayyei ruḥi* (Isa. 38:16) [lit., "and to all in which is the life of my spirit," translated by Shadal as, "And to my spirit, on which their life [i.e. that of my bones] entirely depends"].

31:7. "The tent of congregation and the ark for the Law, and the cover that is over it, and all of the furnishings of the tent.
31:8. "And the table, and its furnishings, and the pure [luminous] candelabrum and all of its furnishings; and the altar of the incense.
31:9. "And the altar of the burnt offerings and all of its furnishings, and the basin and its pedestal.
31:10. "And the netted cloths [that were spread over the sacred furnishings when the people and the tabernacle started a journey; see Num. ch. 4],

## Ki Tissa

and the sacred garments for Aaron the priest, and the garments of his sons for functioning.

*And the netted cloths* (*bigdei ha-serad*). [Various forms of the word *serad* serve as] the Targum [Aramaic translation] of *kela'im* ("hangings") and *mikhbar* ("grate") (Rashi, Rosenmueller, and Gesenius). These cloths were for covering the furnishings when the camp traveled; see Rashi at Exod. 39:1, where it is explained that they were made of blue wool, purple, and scarlet [but not linen, and thus unlike the priestly garments]. At the end of the *parashah* of *Bemidbar* [Num. 4:6-13] it is specified that they were of three kinds: cloth of blue wool, cloth of purple, and cloth of scarlet, and Scripture establishes which of these three kinds of netted cloths would cover each of the sacred furnishings.

In a manuscript of Rashi's commentary it is written *mefareshim* ("they interpret" or "all interpret"), not *yesh mefareshim* ("some interpret"), [and this is a preferable reading,] for everyone used to interpret *bigdei serad* as "garments of service," but Rashi, may his memory be blessed, came upon the correct interpretation on his own.

31:11. "And the oil of anointing, and the aromatic incense, for the Sanctuary. They will make it all as I commanded."

*And the oil of anointing, etc.* The oil served for anointing the sacred furnishings and the consecrated men.

31:12. And the Lord said to Moses as follows:
31:13. "And speak you to the children of Israel, saying, 'But My Sabbaths you shall observe, for it [the Sabbath] is a signal for all the ages to come [of the alliance, that is] between Me and you, so that it may be known that I, the Lord, have declared you holy.
31:14. "'You, then, shall observe the Sabbath, for it is [must be] holy for you; one who profanes it will be put to death; for whoever does work on it, that individual [if he is not punished] will become extinct from the midst of his people.
31:15. "'Six days will work be done, and the seventh is a day of great rest, holy to the Lord. Whoever does work on the Sabbath day will be put to death.

*a day of great rest (shabbat shabbaton).* The doubling is for emphasis; cf. *midaharot daharot abbirav*, "the prancings, the prancings of their mighty ones" (Judg. 5:22); *ra'at ra'atekhem*, "your great wickedness" (Hosea 10:15).

*Shabbaton* denotes cessation from labor and is used in connection with any festival (Exod. 16:23; Lev. 23:24, 39). Similarly, *shenat shabbaton* (Lev. 25:5) is a "Sabbatical year," i.e., a year of rest. *Shabbat shabbaton* indicates a "great rest" and is used only with respect to the Sabbath day and the Day of Atonement (Lev. 16:31, 23:32). Just as the Sabbath day is called *Shabbat* and also *Shabbat shabbaton,* so the Sabbatical year is called *shenat shabbaton* and also *Shabbat shabbaton* (Lev. 25:4, 5). The Sabbath day and the Day of Atonement are days of "great rest" because not even work for the preparation of food is permitted then, as per Rashi in some versions.

**31:16. "'The children of Israel will observe the Sabbath, celebrating the Sabbath in all the ages to come, as a perpetual pact.**
**31:17. "'Of the pact between Me and the children of Israel it will be a signal; for in six days the Lord made the heaven and the earth, and on the seventh day He ceased and rested.'"**
**31:18. Now, having finished speaking with Moses in the mountain of Sinai, He gave him the two tablets of the Law, tablets of stone, written with the finger of God.**

*Now, having finished, etc.* Rashi's words here are perplexing, and the gloss written here in later printings is correct, not the explanation of Mizrahi. See my comment on Jer. 7:22.[6]

---

6. Rashi's comment on this v. states that there is no chronological order in the Torah, and thus the episode of the Golden Calf (Exodus 32) occurred long before the command to work on the Sanctuary (Exodus 25ff.), for the tablets were broken (as punishment for the Calf incident) on 17 Tammuz, God became reconciled with the people on Yom Kippur (eighty days later), and the next day the people began contributing toward the Sanctuary. Mizrahi's supercommentary accepts this view and specifies that Moses *himself* must have received the command to build the Sanctuary only after Yom Kippur. However, some editions of Rashi contain an addition in parentheses, proposing an alternative view that would preserve the text's chronological order: God commanded Moses concerning the Sanctuary during the first forty days (at Sinai), before the Calf incident, but Moses did not communicate this command to the people until after Yom Kippur. This is Shadal's preferred chronology, as stated in his comment on 33:13 below and also in his comment on Jer. 7:22; in both of these places he expresses the view that the Calf incident caused a delay in the building of the Sanctuary; i.e., that if it had not been for the Calf incident and God's resulting anger with the people, the Sanctuary could have been built sooner.

## Ki Tissa

**32:1. But the people, seeing that Moses was slow to descend from the mountain, gathered near to Aaron, saying to him, "Arise, make us gods that may go before us [that is, images that, by means of heavenly influence, may serve us as a guide], for here, Moses, the man who led us out of the land of Egypt, we do not know what has become of him."**

*gathered near to Aaron.* The people gathered to him and forcibly demanded of him that he make them gods. He saw that if he did not do as they asked, they would kill him and then do as they wished, and then what good would his death do? On the other hand, by staying alive he would be able to distract them with dances so that there would not be war in the camp, as I explain at the verse, "Moses saw that the people were thoughtless" (below, v. 25).

**32:2. And Aaron said to them, "Take off the gold pendants that your wives, your sons, and your daughters have on their ears, and bring them to me."**
**32:3. And all the people took off the gold pendants that they had on their ears, and they brought them to Aaron.**

*took off the gold pendants* (*va-yitpareku et nizmei ha-zahav*, lit., "they stripped themselves the gold pendants"). They took the pendants off themselves; "pendants" is in the accusative, and the *hitpa'el* (reflexive) conjugation [i.e., *yitpareku*, the *hitpa'el* form of *parak*, "to take off"] includes an accusative: "they stripped themselves." Thus there are two actions included here, on the model of *va-yelammedehu da'at*, "who taught him wisdom" (i.e., "who taught him" and "who taught wisdom") (Isa. 40:14).

**32:4. He received (that gold) from their hands, he collected it in a bag, and he made of it a calf of cast metal; and they said, "This is [that is, represents] your God, O Israel, that brought you out of the land of Egypt."**

*a calf.* The calf was not an object of idolatry, nor did they accept it upon themselves as a god; rather, it was to be an instrument to receive Divine influence and to stand as a leader for them instead of Moses (Aaron would not have sufficed for them, for even he was merely human). This is the opinion of the *Kuzari* 1:96 and that of Ibn Ezra, Nachmanides, Hizkuni, and Gersonides. See *Bikkurei ha-Ittim* 5588 (1827), p. 89.[7]

---

7. There, Shadal posits that the Israelites could have (mis)construed the Second

***he collected*** *(va-yatsar).* The *kal* form of the root *tsor* ("tie," "bind"), as in *ve-tsarta ha-kesef,* "which money you will take with you" (lit., "and you will bind up the money," Deut. 14:25).

***in a bag*** *(ba-ḥeret).* Cf. *ha-ḥaritim,* "the purses," "the pockets" (Isa. 3:22) (Rashi, in one of the two explanations that he offers, and also the Jerusalem Targum, R. Joseph Bekhor Shor, Bochart, and Gesenius).

**32:5. Aaron, having seen this, built before himself an altar; then Aaron proclaimed and said, "A festival to the Lord tomorrow!"**
**32:6. Having risen in the morning, they immolated burnt offerings, and they presented sacrifices of contentment. The people sat down to eat and drink, then they arose to dance about.**

***to dance about*** *(letsaḥek,* Ital. *trescare).* The Heb. includes singing, playing instruments, and dancing; cf., "You will yet adorn yourself with tambourines, and go out in the dance of merrymakers [*mesaḥakim*]" (Jer. 31:3). David, who had been "leaping and dancing before the Lord" (2 Sam. 6:16), said, "Before the Lord will I make merry [*ve-siḥakti*]" (2 Sam. 6:21). So also, "Leviathan, whom You have formed to sport therein [*lesaḥek bo*]" (Ps. 104:26); the leviathan "sports" (*metsaḥek*) in the sea, that is, he moves about forcefully in it, stirring up the water as if he were dancing.

**32:7. And the Lord said to Moses, "Go, descend, for your people, that you led forth from the land of Egypt, committed a grave offense.**
**32:8. "They strayed quickly from the way that I have prescribed for them; they made themselves a calf of cast metal, and they prostrated themselves to it, and they made sacrifices to it, and they said, 'This is your God, O Israel, that brought you out of the land of Egypt.'"**

***from the way that I have prescribed for them.*** He did not say, "They strayed from Me," which indicates that they had not abandoned God to worship other gods.

---

Commandment as not forbidding a "likeness" (*pesel*) of a natural creature that would serve as a symbol of God, rather than an idol *per se*. That the calf was regarded as a mere symbol and receptacle of Divine influence, says Luzzatto, is indicated by the declaration, "This is your God, O Israel, that brought you out of the land of Egypt." "How could they have said of the calf that it had taken them out of Egypt," Shadal asks, "since at that time it had been nothing but gold ornaments in the ears of their wives?" He goes on to say that the people sought a leader that would never die, unlike Moses or Aaron.

## Ki Tissa

**32:9. And the Lord added to Moses, "I see that this people is a stiff-necked [stubborn] people.**

*stiff-necked* (*kesheh oref*). This implies that they had previously been attached to idolatry, as mentioned in Ezek. 20:7 [where God says to Israel, at the time of the exodus, "Do not defile yourself with the idols of Egypt"] (Mendelssohn). There is no need to say that they were attached to pagan worship per se; rather they would make images in honor of [the true] God.

Mendlessohn cited the words of Rashi and Ibn Ezra [commenting on the expression *kesheh oref*] without understanding that they express two opposite ideas: Rashi places the rebuker in front of the sinner, with the sinner turning his *oref* (the back of his neck) to him, while Ibn Ezra has the rebuker following after the sinner to make him turn from his path, with the sinner running ahead and not turning back. Ibn Ezra's statement itself is inexact, where he says [that the sinner] "does not turn his *oref* to the one who is calling him"; he should have said that he "does not turn his face" to the one who is calling. Undoubtedly the meaning of the expression is that the back of the person's neck is stiff and unmoving, and thus the person goes on his way without turning to face the one who is calling him from behind, that is, he does not heed the voice of his instructors.

**32:10. "Now let Me alone, and My wrath will burn in them, and I will exterminate them; then I will make you become a great nation.**

*Now let Me alone.* "And if you ask what I will do about My oath to the patriarchs, [My answer is that] I will make *you* become a great nation, for you are of their seed" (*Numbers Rabbah* 17:14; see Rashi on Num. 14:12).

**32:11. Moses then supplicated the Lord his God, and he said, "Why, O Lord, do You want Your wrath to burn in Your people, which You brought out of the land of Egypt, with great force and a powerful hand? 32:12. "Why do You want the Egyptians to say, 'With malice did He make them go forth (from here), to kill them among the mountains, and to exterminate them from upon the face of the earth'? Be calmed from the burning of Your wrath, and repent of the evil (threatened) to Your people. 32:13. "Remember Abraham, Isaac, and Israel, Your servants, to whom You swore by You [by Your immortality], and You promised, 'I will render your progeny as numerous as the stars of the heaven, and all of this land of which I spoke I will give to your progeny, and they will possess it in perpetuity.'"**

**32:14. And the Lord repented of the evil that He had said to do to His people.**
**32:15. And Moses, having turned, descended from the mountain, having in his hand the two tablets of the Law, tablets written on both faces, on the one side and on the other they were written.**

***on the one side and on the other*** *(mi-zeh u-mi-zeh).* As if to say, "front and back," except that with respect to a scroll it would be appropriate to speak of the front and back, since there is a difference in the parchment between one side and the other, but with stone there is no such difference, so it had to say *mi-zeh u-mi-zeh.*

**32:16. Those tablets were the work of God, and the writing was the writing of God, engraved on the tablets.**
**32:17. Joshua heard the people shouting, and he said to Moses, "I hear the sound of battle in the encampment."**
**32:18. And (Moses) said, "Those which are heard are not cries of victory, nor are they cries of defeat; sounds of songs I hear."**

***songs*** *(annot).* A response (*innui*) of everyone in unison (Mishnah, end of *Moed Katan* [3:8]).

**32:19. Then when he was near the camp, and he saw the calf and the dances, Moses became kindled with wrath, and he threw the tablets from his hands, and he shattered them at the foot of the mountain.**

***and he threw the tablets,*** *etc.* Not out of confusion or perplexity; rather, it seems that he did so to strike fear in the people and to show them that the pact between them and God had been broken.

**32:20. And he took the calf that they had made, and he burned [calcined] it in the fire, and he ground it until it turned to powder, which he then strewed upon the water and made the children of Israel drink it.**

***and he burned*** *(va-yisrof)* ***it in the fire.*** He mixed it with niter or some other substance that brought the gold to a state of calcination [i.e., the production of ash resulting from the thorough burning of a metal] and then he pulverized it; see Ibn Ezra, Mendelssohn, and Rosenmueller.[8]

---

8. Ibn Ezra commented on this v. that there was no need to understand "burned"

## Ki Tissa

**32:21.** And Moses said to Aaron, "What did this people do to you, for which you drew upon them a grave sin?"
**32:22.** And Aaron said, "Let not the wrath of my lord be kindled. You know the people, how it is inclined to evil.
**32:23.** "They said to me, 'Make us gods that will go before us, for here, Moses, the man who led us out of the land of Egypt, we do not know what has become of him.'
**32:24.** "I said to them, 'Who has gold?' (And at once) they took it off themselves and gave it to me. I cast it in the fire, and this calf came out of it."
**32:25.** Moses saw that the people were thoughtless [distracted by the amusements], for Aaron had rendered them so [by prescribing the festival], so that they would remain bewildered amidst those who would rise against them.

*for Aaron had rendered them so* (*ki fera'oh Aharon*, lit., "for Aaron had rendered them thoughtless"). See what I wrote in *Bikkurei ha-Ittim* 5589 (1828), p. 122.[9] An analogous incident is found in Tacitus, *Annals,* book I,

---

(*va-yisrof*) as "melted," because "there is a substance that, when placed in fire with gold, will instantly burn the gold and turn it black." Mendelssohn translated *va-yisrof* here as *kalzinirte*. Rosenmueller (*Scholia in Vetus Testamentum,* pt. 1, vol. 2, p. 490-491) noted that Moses could have learned the chemical arts of Egypt.

The chemist Georg Ernst Stahl (1660-1734) suggested in a 1715 work that Moses fused the Golden Calf with a mixture of potassium nitrate (niter) and sulfur, yielding a soluble compound (see Thomas Thomson, *A History of Chemistry* [London, 1830], p. 256). A modern scientist has found this to be a "plausible idea, since $KNO_3$ (niter) and sulfur were known in the biblical period, and they could certainly fuse metals in furnaces" (Susan V. Meschel, "Metallurgy in the Bible: Ironworking and the Disposal of the Golden Calf," *Jewish Bible Quarterly*, vol. 42:4, 2014, p. 266).

However, it has been observed that the "niter" of ancient Egypt (Heb. *neter*) was in fact not potassium nitrate ($KNO_3$), but rather "natron," which consisted essentially of sodium carbonate and sodium bicarbonate (A. Lucas and J. R. Harris, *Ancient Egyptian Materials and Industries,* New York: Dover Publications, 2012 [originally published 1926], p. 267). Natron, a cleaning and drying agent used in mummification, would not have lent itself to the calcination of gold.

Some alchemists were said to have calcined gold in a furnace with mercury and "sal ammoniac" (Ephraim Chambers, ed., *Cyclopaedia, or, An Universal Dictionary of Arts and Sciences* [London, 1728], s.v. "calcination"). Whether or not Moses would actually have had access to such materials or methods at Mount Sinai, he was regarded by alchemists well into the eighteenth century as a master of their craft (see, e.g. *Encyclopaedia Judaica,* s.v. "Alchemy").

9. There, Shadal explains that anyone who lets his hair grow long and unattended

where [the Roman general] Caecina caused the rebels to be killed through trickery.[10] My student R. Abraham Hai Mainster says that it was not Aaron's [actual] intention that the people should be too distracted to resist those who would rise against them, but when Moses saw that the people were thoughtless—for Aaron had rendered them so in such a way that they would be unable to resist—at once he said, "Whoever is for the Lord, come to me!" (next v.).

**32:26. And Moses stood at the entrance of the encampment, and he said, "Whoever is for the Lord (come) to me!" And all of the sons of Levi gathered near to him.**
**32:27. He said to them, "Thus says the Lord, God of Israel: 'Let everyone put his sword on his side, pass through the camp and back, from (its) one gate to the other, and kill [the worshippers of the calf] even if they be your brothers [close relatives], your friends, or your adherents.'"**

*Let everyone put his sword.* Even though the calf was not strictly speaking an idol, it constituted the beginning of idolatry, and God, at the start of the national experience, had to remove the sinners and leave the entire people with a terrible memory, so that they should not begin to resemble idol-worshippers.

**32:28. The sons of Levi fulfilled Moses' order, and on that day there fell (dead) of the people about three thousand men.**
**32:29. And Moses said [to the Levites], "You have today received your installation to the service of the Lord, yes, each one (has received it) with the (sacrifice of) his own son, and with the (sacrifice of) his own brother; and that will draw upon you today the (heavenly) blessing.**

---

(*parua*) out of laziness and carelessness will typically neglect his business and remain idle, and thus anyone who was lazy and neglectful was called *parua*, which Shadal translates as "thoughtless" or "careless." He goes on to interpret the present verse to mean that Aaron had purposely rendered the people thoughtless and distracted so they would not be aware of the righteous faction who would rise up against them; they would be too bewildered to offer any resistance, and thus they would be destroyed without open warfare.

10. This refers to an incident during a revolt of the Roman army's Rhine legions, ca. 14 C.E. Aulus Caecina Severus, ordered to punish the ringleaders, gathered loyal troops and "fixed a time for falling with the sword on all the vilest and foremost of the mutineers. Then, at a mutually given signal, they rushed into the tents, and butchered the unsuspecting men, none but those in the secret knowing what was the beginning or what was to be the end of the slaughter" (Tacitus, *Annals* I:48, trans. Church and Broadribb).

## Ki Tissa

***You have today received your installation*** *(mile'u yedkhem ha-yom*, lit., "they filled your hand today"). The word *mile'u* is a past tense verb in the *pi'el* conjugation, and it is an impersonal verb, similar to, "For they will no longer call you [*yikre'u lakh*] delicate and dainty" (Isa. 47:1), i.e., "those who call will not call." Here, too, *mile'u* means "those who filled, filled," except that this is said merely by way of figure of speech, as if there were actually people there who filled their hands. It is as if Moses said, "Your hand has been filled to God; you have received the filling of the hand [i.e., your installation] by means of your killing of your own sons and brothers."

***his own son.*** This means his daughter's son, who is not a Levite, and also his son-in-law, who is like a son to a father-in-law.

The word *mile'u* was properly understood by Rashbam as a past tense verb in the *pi'el* conjugation, as in *ki mile'u aharei YHVH*, "for they were fully faithful to the Lord" (Num. 32:12), and he properly interpreted it to mean *hinnekhu* ("they dedicated"). However, according to Rashi, Ibn Ezra, and Mendelssohn, the word is an imperative in the *kal* conjugation [i.e., "Fill your hand today"], but this is unlikely, for the expression *milui yad* is used only in the *pi'el*, and it is also unlikely that a person would fill his own hand and assume greatness for himself; rather, others must bestow the greatness upon him. Thus, in connection with the golden calves of Jeroboam, it is written in a deprecatory sense, "He would appoint [*yemallei et yado*] whomever he wished [as priest]" (1 Kings 13:33).

**32:30. On the next day Moses said to the people, "You have committed a grave sin. Now then, let me go up to the Lord [on mount Sinai], perhaps I will obtain pardon for your sin."**
**32:31. And Moses returned to the Lord, and he said, "Please, this people has committed a grave sin, and they made themselves a god of gold.**
**32:32. "Now then, either let You pardon their sin, or otherwise, please erase me from Your book of registry [that is, from the book of the living; in other words, it would be better for me to die]."**

***from Your book.*** The book of life; cf. "Everyone who is inscribed for life in Jerusalem" (Isa. 4:3); "May they be erased from the book of life, and let them not be inscribed with the righteous" (Ps. 69:29). This is the opinion of Rashbam and Mendelssohn; in the Talmud as well (*Berakhot* 32a), Samuel says that Moses surrendered himself to die for the people, for he said, "Otherwise, please erase me from Your book."

**32:33.** And the Lord said to Moses, "He who has sinned toward Me, him I will erase from My book.
**32:34.** "Now then, go, guide the people to the country that I have promised you. Indeed, an angel of Mine will go before you [that is, but I will not come with you, I will not reside among you; in other words, I will not permit you to build Me the Temple]. Then, whenever it may be, I will make them pay for their sin."

***Indeed, an angel (mal'akh) of Mine will go before you.*** Here the reference is to an actual angel [and not to Moses, who according to Shadal is the *mal'akh* referred to above, 23:20]; i.e., God's Presence itself would not go with them, or in other words, they were not to erect the Sanctuary, for the Sanctuary was to be a sign that God was in their midst.

***Then, whenever it may be, I will make them pay*** (*u-v'-yom pokdi u-fakadti*, lit., "and on the day of My accounting I will account"). [*Contra* Rashi,] this does not mean, "On another day of accounting, I will make them pay for this sin as well." Rather, this is a type of expression that is common in the [Hebrew] language; compare:

- *ve-shama ishah be-yom shome'o*, "And her husband becomes aware of it whenever it may be" (lit. "and her husband hears on the day of his hearing," Num. 30:8)—i.e., "he will hear when he will hear, whenever he hears";
- *ki yippol ha-nofel*, "when someone falls from it" (lit. "when the faller falls") – i.e. "when someone falls, whoever it may be" (Deut. 22:8);
- *ve-shama ha-shome'a*, "whoever hears," i.e., "the hearer will hear, whoever it may be" (2 Sam. 17:9); and so also,
- *ve-ḥannoti et asher aḥon*, "I will do favor to whom I wish to do it" (Exod. 33:19).

**32:35.** And the Lord sent a fatality upon the people, because they made [they wished to be made] the calf, which Aaron made.

***because they made the calf.*** For they said, "Arise, make us gods" [above, v. 1]. This was a delayed punishment, for this was not done immediately but only after some time had passed, as per Ibn Ezra. This is in keeping with God's statement, "Whenever it may be, I will make them pay," etc. (v. 34) (my student, Judah Luzzatto).

## Ki Tissa

33:1. The Lord said to Moses, "Go, depart from here, you and the people that you have led forth from the country of Egypt, toward the country that I have sworn to Abraham, to Isaac, and to Jacob, saying, 'To your progeny I will give it.'

33:2. "I send before you an angel, and I will drive out the Canaanites, the Amorites, and the Hittites, and the Perizzites, the Hivites, and the Jebusites.

33:3. "(Go, I say) to that country that flows with milk and honey, for I will not come in your midst, for you are a stiff-necked people, and I would not want to have to exterminate you along the journey."

*for I will not come in your midst.* I.e., "do not make a Sanctuary for Me."

33:4. The people heard this bad thing, and they grieved, and no one put on his ornaments.

*and no one put on his ornaments.* For the ornaments were a reminder of the calf, which had been made out of them. Otherwise, this was simply a sign of mourning, as per Ibn Ezra.

33:5. And the Lord said to Moses, "Say to the children of Israel, 'You are a stiff-necked people. If I were to journey in your midst [that is, if I were to permit you to erect the Temple], it could happen that in an instant I would exterminate you. Now then, you do well to strip yourselves of your ornaments, and I will decide how to deal with you.'"

*in an instant, etc.* He began speaking with them by way of affection, having seen their penitence in that they were grieving and had taken off their ornaments. Thus He said to them that the fact that He was not journeying with them was only for their own good, so that He would not exterminate them if they continued to sin, and that they would indeed do well if they were to keep refraining from wearing their ornaments. He then told them to trust in Him and let Him choose the way to manage them for their own benefit.

33:6. So the children of Israel stripped themselves of their ornaments, while they were near mount Horeb.

*while they were near mount Horeb* (me-har Ḥorev, lit., "from mount Horeb"). In other words, from then on.

**33:7. Moses then took his tent, and he pitched it outside of the encampment, far away from it, and he named it the tent of congregation. Now whoever wanted to consult the Lord would go out to the tent of congregation, situated outside the camp [that is to say, as the people were unworthy of having the temple of God within their midst, the revelations of God to Moses also could not take place within their quarters].**

*outside the camp.* Just as God did not want them to build a sanctuary and to have His Presence dwell among them, so it was not proper that His word should come to Moses within the camp.

**33:8. Now when Moses went out (to go to) the tent, the entire people arose, and everyone stood, each one at the entrance of his own tent, and watched after Moses until he entered the tent.**
**33:9. Now when Moses entered the tent, the pillar of cloud ascended, and it stayed at the entrance of the tent, and (God) spoke with Moses.**
**33:10. All of the people saw the pillar of cloud staying at the entrance of the tent, and all of the people, each one at the entrance of his own tent, rose and prostrated themselves.**
**33:11. The Lord spoke to Moses face to face, as a man speaks to his friend; then Moses returned to the camp, and the young man Joshua son of Nun, his servant, did not move from the tent.**

*face to face (panim el panim).* He sensed God's speech while he was awake; cf., "Face to face [*panim be-fanim*] the Lord spoke with you" (Deut. 5:4); a similar expression is *ayin be-ayin*, "eye to eye" (Isa. 52:8).

*then Moses returned to the camp...* Joshua had not been Moses' servant from his [earliest] youth (as Mendelssohn thought), for he had not been [with Moses] in Midian.[11]

*did not move from the tent.* The Divine Presence spoke with Moses at the entrance of the tent, but Joshua sat inside the tent (R. Judah Aryeh Osimo).

---

11. In Num. 11:28, Joshua is referred to as *mesharet Mosheh mi-beḥurav*, translated by Shadal as "servant of Moses, one of his most esteemed." In his comment on the word *mi-beḥurav*, Shadal says, "Ibn Ezra fittingly said that it is unlikely that *mi-beḥurav* should be understood as *mi-ne'urav* ("from his youth"), for this incident [i.e., the prophecy of Eldad and Medad] took place in the second year [after the exodus], and when would Joshua have served him previously, since he did not accompany him in Midian?"

## Ki Tissa

**33:12. And Moses said to the Lord, "See, you say to me, 'Have this people proceed,' but You have not let me know whom You will send with me. You Yourself said to me, 'I know you by name [I distinguish you, I prefer you], since you have found My favor.'**

***but You have not let me know...*** Whether it was to be a pillar of cloud or something else.

**33:13. "Now then, if I find Your favor, let me know Your intention, so that I may understand You, in order that I may merit Your favor; and consider that this nation is Your people."**

***Your intention*** *(derakhekha*, lit., "Your ways"). Written without a *yod* (דרכך), which would properly be read *darkekha* ("Your way"). In other words, "Let me know Your intentions, and how You conduct Yourself when leading this people, whether Your Presence will come with us or not." What he meant to ask was "whether You will give us permission to erect the Sanctuary or not." The *parashiyyot* of *Terumah* and *Tetsavveh*, which include [the instructions for] the making of the Sanctuary, were in fact told to Moses immediately after the giving of the Torah [i.e., the Ten Commandments and the laws of *Mishpatim*], during the first forty days, but the incident of the calf caused a delay in the construction of the Sanctuary, for the people were as if excommunicated by God, Who did not wish to cause His Presence to dwell among them. Moses did not communicate to the people the command of constructing the Sanctuary until God became reconciled with them; see Rashi's comment on v. 11 above [which says that Moses instructed the people as to the building of the Sanctuary only after he received the second set of tablets]. The word *letsavvoto* that appears there is an error; it should read *letsavvot* or *letsavvotan* [i.e., Rashi means to say that when Moses descended with the second tablets, he began to "command" or "command *them*" (the people) as to the building of the Sanctuary, not that God then began to "command *him*"].[12] See my comment on the *haftarah* to *Tsav*.[13]

When God was conciliated at Moses' request, He responded, *Panai yelekhu va-haniḥoti lakh*, (lit., "My face will go, and I will put you at rest"

---

[12]. Chavel's edition has *letsavvotam*, followed by *letsavvoto* in brackets; Rosenbaum and Silbermann have *letsavvotam*.

[13]. I.e., Jer. 7:21 ff. In his comment on v. 22, Shadal expresses the same views as he does here regarding the chronology of the command to build the Sanctuary and its actual construction.

(next v.), i.e., "I Myself will go with you, and I will bring you to the country of your rest and inheritance" (cf. Deut. 12:4); that is, "Make Me a sanctuary and I will walk among you." When Moses heard this, he made a further request: "If You Yourself do not come, do not make us depart from here" (v. 15), that is, "Since You have already been appeased to come with us, do not make us travel even one journey from here before the Sanctuary is built."

**33:14. And (the Lord) said, "I Myself will come, and I will put you at rest [that is, I will lead you to the promised land]."**

*I Myself will come* (*panai yelekhu*, lit., "My face will go"), *etc.* Rashi, Rashbam, and Ibn Ezra [all interpret *panai* as "I Myself"], and similarly Onkelos. The meaning is, in my opinion, "Make Me a sanctuary." Moses responded by asking that He not make them travel at all before they built the Sanctuary, so that they would not make even one journey without having God's Presence among them.

**33:15. And (Moses) said to Him, "If You Yourself do not come, do not make us depart from here.**
**33:16. "And in what way will it be known, then, that we have found Your favor, I and Your people, if it is not Your coming with us [that is, working miracles for us], so that I and Your people are distinguished from all the peoples that are on the face of the earth?"**
**33:17. And the Lord said to Moses, "This thing, too, of which you speak (to Me), I will fulfill, for you have found My favor, and I know you by name."**
**33:18. And (Moses) said, "Let me, please, see Your majesty" [as a sign of a solemn promise, as in Genesis ch. 15].**

*Let me, please, see Your majesty.* So as to make a covenant with him as He did with Abraham, [when the Divine Presence appeared to him in the form of fire and smoke:] "And behold, a smoking furnace" (Gen. 15:17) (Rashbam). This was in order to avoid the causation of sin, since the Israelites were a "stiff-necked people." [In contrast to the covenant with Abraham,] God did not say, "Provide Me [with various animals]" (cf. Gen. 15:9), for at the top of Mount Sinai there were no animals, nor was it permitted for them to go up there.

**33:19. And (the Lord) said, "I will cause to pass before you all of My goodness; I will proclaim, that is, before you the name [the attributes] of**

## Ki Tissa

the Lord; then (however) I will show favor to whom I will want to show it, and I will exercise mercy to whom I will want to exercise it [in other words, in promising to come with you, I do not promise indulgence to all the sinners]."

***I will cause to pass before you all of My goodness,*** *etc.* "All of My goodness [*tuvi*]" is analogous to "having with him his master's most precious articles [*tuv*]" (Gen. 24:10), and "the best [*tuv*] of all the country of Egypt" (Gen. 45:20), meaning anything good and precious. Here the meaning is, "I will cause to pass before you the most splendid vision possible, and yet do not think that I will make a covenant to cover up all sins, for even though I have said to you, 'This thing, too, of which you speak, I will fulfill,' know that I will show favor and exercise mercy only to those who are deserving of it. This I will make known to you by proclaiming the name of the Lord, setting forth My name and nature, and thus after the making of this covenant, I will show favor and exercise mercy as decreed by My attributes that I will announce to you."

***I will proclaim… the name (be-shem) of the Lord.*** "I will let you know My nature, the attribute of mercy and the attribute of justice; therefore I will not show favor to every sinner, but only to some of them, and I will punish some others."

The word *be-shem*, it seems to me, is in the *semikhut* (construct state) [i.e., the words *be-shem YHVH* are connected and mean "the name *of* the Lord"], and likewise below, 34:5 [where the same words appear], even though this is not the opinion of the accentuators [who marked *be-shem* with a disjunctive *tevir* in this verse and with a disjunctive *tipḥa* in 34:5].

The "proclaiming of the name of the Lord" referred to here is no different from any other "proclaiming of the name" (*keriyyah be-shem*) [mentioned elsewhere in the Torah]. Ibn Ezra thought that in the case of Abraham [*va-yikra be-shem YHVH*] (Gen. 12:8), the meaning is that he "called" people to the service of God, but this is incorrect, for if so, it would have said *le-shem* ("to the name"), not *be-shem* ("in the name"). The truth is that every instance of *keriyyah be-shem* means not "calling" ([German] *rufen*, "to call," "to summon"), but rather "raising the voice," so that *kara be-shem* means "he raised his voice in mention of the name of so-and-so," in order to give him honor and to tell his praises and virtues—as in, "Give thanks to the Lord, call on His name [*kir'u bi-shemo*]" (1 Chron. 16:8), and so here [God Himself was proclaiming His name] to tell of His attributes. Sometimes the expression is used to indicate that we are announcing our choice of someone, as in, "See, I call by name [*karati be-shem*] Bezalel" (Exod. 31:2); "I have called you [Israel] by your name [*karati be-shimekha*]; you are Mine" (Isa. 43:1).

**33:20. And He added, "You will not be able to see My face [that is, to see the front side of the apparition], for a man cannot see Me and remain alive."**

*You will not be able...* "As for the apparition that I have promised to pass before you, you will see it as it passes, but you will not be able to see its front, for by the nature of a human being this is impossible without his dying." All this was in order that people should not learn to make images.

**33:21. The Lord further said, "I have a place by Me [that is, on Sinai there is a cave], and you will wait upon the rock.**

*by Me.* "On Mount Sinai there is a place that is fitting for this purpose, for there is a cave in the rock there."

**33:22. "And when My Majesty passes, I will place you in the cave of the rock, and I will shelter you with My hand until I have passed."**

*and I will shelter you (ve-sakkoti) with My hand.* Cf. "And you will place as a partition [*ve-sakkota*] the door-curtain before the ark" (Exod. 40:3). Similarly here, "I will place My hand as a partition before you, so that you do not see My face."

The roots *sakhakh, sukh, shakhakh,* and *shukh* were all originally *sakh* or *shakh*; they denoted protection, whether from above or on the side. From this was derived *masakh* ("curtain"), a partition on the side; *sukkah*, a temporary abode that protects above as well as on the sides; and *mesukhah* ("hedge") and *seyag* ("fence"), which are partitions on the side. Originally the *sukkah* was made entirely of wood and vegetation, without any structure of stone, but later [the Rabbis] allowed it to be made within a house and to use the house's walls for the sides of the *sukkah*; from then on, the term *sekhakh* was used only for the covering, but in Biblical Hebrew, *sekhakh* refers to any protection, whether above or on the side. See Rashi on 35:12 below [where he says that anything that screens from above or in front is called *masakh* or *sekhakh*].

## Ki Tissa

**34:1.** And the Lord said to Moses, "Hew for yourself two tablets of stone like the previous ones, and I will write on those tablets the words that were on the first tablets that you broke.

**34:2.** "Be ready for tomorrow, and you will go up tomorrow to the summit of the mountain, and you will await Me there on the summit of the mountain.

**34:3.** "Let no one else go up with you, nor shall any person let himself be seen in all the mountain; and the flocks and herds shall not pasture toward that mountain."

**34:4.** And Moses hewed two tablets of stone like the first ones, and having risen in the morning, he went up to Mount Sinai, as the Lord commanded him, and he took with him the two tablets of stone.

**34:5.** And the Lord descended in the cloud, and He remained there by him, and He proclaimed the name of the Lord.

*and He remained there by him.* The cloud stayed by Moses, but the statement "The Lord, that is, passing before him" (next v.) refers not to the cloud, but to another vision, perhaps of fire.

*and He proclaimed the name of the Lord.* This is as He had promised him, "I will proclaim, that is, before you the name of the Lord" (Exod. 33:19). The statement "He proclaimed the name of the Lord" is a general statement, and the subsequent "the Lord, that is, passing before him" is a specific statement. Both above (33:19) and here, it seems to me that the word *be-shem* ("the name of") should have been marked with an auxiliary accent [see the comment on "I will proclaim," 33:19].

**34:6.** The Lord, that is, passing before him, proclaimed, "The Lord, (only) the Lord is a merciful and gracious God, forbearing and greatly benevolent and truthful.

*The Lord, the Lord.* The meaning is, "The Lord, the Lord alone, is a merciful and gracious God." The doubling signifies "exactly" and "no other"; cf., "I, I am (God), nor with Me [besides Me] is there any god" (Deut. 32:39); "I, only I [*anokhi anokhi*], am He Who comforts you" (Isa. 51:12).

These are the Thirteen Attributes according to the plain meaning: (1) a merciful God, (2) gracious, (3) forbearing, (4) greatly benevolent, (5) greatly truthful, (6) maintaining benevolence to the thousandth descendants, (7) tolerating sin without letting it go unpunished, (8) tolerating guilt without letting it go unpunished, (9) tolerating fault without letting it go unpunished, (10) demanding account of the sins of the fathers from the children, (11) demanding account of the sins of the fathers from the grandchildren, (12) demanding account of the sins of the fathers from the third generation, (13) demanding account of the sins of the fathers from the fourth generation.

When God began to enumerate His attributes, He first said that He was "God" (*El*), in which name is included the qualities of eternity, power, and wisdom, qualities that the gentiles also attributed to every god; but afterwards He specified the qualities that were unique to the God of Israel, starting with "merciful," denoting the feelings of compassion and love, combined with strength.

Then "gracious," meaning that He inclines to do good to one in need of it; then "forbearing," i.e., if He sees something contrary to His will, He is not easy to anger. Then "greatly benevolent," i.e., He has great love for those who do His will, and He treats them with benevolence. "Greatly truthful": once He loves someone, He remains faithful to that person, and His faithfulness is very great, for He maintains His benevolence even with the person's children to thousands of generations. If someone sins against Him, He tolerates sin and guilt and fault, yet He does not let it go unpunished, for He demands account of the sins of the fathers, etc.

The general principle that arises from these Attributes is that He is a God Who desires to do good and is slow to anger, but Who nevertheless punishes sinners as well. Even though there is no necessity, according to the plain meaning, for the Attributes to be [numbered as] thirteen,[14] this division that I have offered fits in well with the plain meaning. The following are various alternative opinions on this matter:

### The Thirteen Attributes

I. According to Rabbenu Nissim the Rosh Yeshiva, in *Megillat Setarim* (see Tosafot, *Rosh Hashanah* 17b):

(1) The Lord, (2) God, (3) merciful, (4) gracious, (5) forbearing, (6) greatly benevolent, (7) truthful, (8) maintaining benevolence, (9) to the thousandth descendants, (10) tolerating sin, (11) and guilt, (12) and fault, (13) and letting go unpunished.[15]

---

14. In *Rosh Hashanah* 17b, R. Judah refers to the covenant of the Thirteen Attributes (*middot*).
15. Heb. *ve-nakkeh*. Rabbenu Nissim and many of the other authorities listed here read this word separately from the subsequent two words *lo yenakkeh*, but

## Ki Tissa

II. According to Rabbenu Tam (ibid.), Ibn Ezra, Mendelssohn, and Reggio:

(1) The Lord, (2) the Lord, (3) God, (4) merciful, (5) gracious, (6) forbearing, (7) and greatly benevolent, (8) and truthful, (9) maintaining benevolence to the thousandth descendants, (10) tolerating sin, (11) and guilt, (12) and fault, (13) and letting go unpunished.

III. According to correction in Tosafot [ibid.]:

(1) The Lord, (2) God, (3) merciful, (4) gracious, (5) forbearing to the righteous, (6) forbearing to the wicked, (7) greatly benevolent, (8) and truthful, (9) maintaining benevolence to the thousandth descendants, (10) tolerating sin, (11) and guilt, (12) and fault, (13) and letting go unpunished.

IV. According to *Sefer ha-Ḥasidim*, sec. 250:

(1) Merciful, (2) gracious, (3) forbearing, (4) greatly benevolent, (5) and truthful, (6) maintaining benevolence to the thousandth descendants, (7) tolerating sin, (8) and guilt, (9) and fault, (10) letting go unpunished, (11) "and You can pardon our sins," (12) "and our faults," (13) "and treat us as Your patrimony."[16]

V. According to Abravanel:

(1) The Lord, (2) the Lord, (3) God, (4) merciful, (5) gracious, (6) forbearing, (7) and greatly benevolent, (8) and truthful, (9) maintaining benevolence to the thousandth descendants, (10) tolerating sin and guilt and fault, (11) and letting go unpunished, (12) not letting go unpunished, (13) demanding account of the sins of the fathers.

VI. According to R. Isaac Arama:

(1) The Lord, (2) the Lord, (3) God, (4) merciful, (5) gracious, (6) forbearing, (7) and greatly benevolent, (8) and truthful, (9) maintaining benevolence to the thousandth descendants, (10) tolerating sin, (11) and guilt, (12) and fault, (13) demanding account of the sins of the fathers.

---

according to the plain meaning, as stated by Shadal, the phrase *ve-nakkeh lo yenakkeh* forms a unit and means "and does not let go unpunished."

16. The last three elements are from v. 9 below.

# Shadal on Exodus

VII. Maimonides, in *Pe'er Ha-Dor*, sec. 90, says that the first "Name" [i.e., "The Lord"] is not counted among the Thirteen Attributes, which are:

(1) The Lord (or The Lord, the Lord), (2) God, (3) merciful, (4) and gracious, (5) forbearing, (6) greatly benevolent, (7) and truthful, (8) maintaining benevolence to the thousandth descendants, (9) tolerating sin, (10) and guilt, (11) and fault, (12) and letting go unpunished, (13) not letting go unpunished.

VIII. According to the Andalusians:

The phrase *ve-nakkeh lo yenakkeh* ("and not letting it go unpunished") is one single Attribute, and "demanding account of the sins of the fathers" is the thirteenth Attribute.

IX. According to A.H. Mainster:

(1) The Lord, (2) merciful God, (3) gracious, (4) forbearing, (5) greatly benevolent, (6) and truthful, (7) maintaining benevolence, (8) to the thousandth descendants, (9) tolerating sin, (10) and guilt, (11) and fault, (12) without letting it go unpunished, (13) demanding account of the sins of the fathers.

X. According to Judah Aryeh Osimo:

(1) Merciful God, (2) gracious, (3) forbearing, (4) greatly benevolent and truthful, (5) maintaining benevolence to the thousandth descendants, (6) tolerating sin, (7) tolerating guilt, (8) tolerating fault, (9) without letting it go unpunished, (10) – (13) demanding account of the sins of the fathers, etc.

XI. According to A.H. Mainster's interpretation of Abravanel:

(1) The Lord, (2) merciful God, (3) and gracious, (4) forbearing, (5) greatly benevolent, (6) greatly truthful, (7) maintaining benevolence to the thousandth descendants, (8) tolerating sin and guilt and fault, (9) without letting it go unpunished, (10) – (13) demanding account of the sins of the fathers, etc.

XII. According to A.H. Mainster's interpretation of Rabbenu Tam:

(1) The Lord, (2) the Lord, (3) merciful God, (4) and gracious, (5) forbearing, (6) greatly benevolent, (7) greatly truthful, (8) maintaining benevolence to the thousandth descendants, (9) tolerating sin, (10) and guilt, (11) and fault, (12) without letting it go unpunished, (13) demanding account, etc.

## Ki Tissa

**34:7.** "He maintains benevolence [demonstrated by Him to the good] even to the thousandth descendants; He tolerates sin, guilt, and fault, without, however, letting them go unpunished; demanding account, rather, of the sins of the fathers from the children and from the grandchildren, from the third and from the fourth descendants."
**34:8.** Moses then quickly bowed to the earth and prostrated himself.
**34:9.** And he said, "If I have indeed found Your favor, O Lord, let the Lord please come among us; for this is a stiff-necked people, and (only) You can pardon our sins and faults, and treat us as Your patrimony."

*let the Lord please come among us, etc.* Moses once again made his principal request, which was that the Presence of God be among Israel, that is, that He give them permission to erect the Sanctuary, and that the service [therein] atone for their sins and faults. Then God made him a promise; in so doing, He did not mention the matter of His Presence coming among them, for He had already assured him of this ("I Myself will come, and I will put you at rest" (Exod. 33:4). Rather, He mentioned the greatest merit that would result from His Presence being among them, which was that He would perform signs and wonders for them. This is the meaning of the statement, "Here I give (you) a solemn promise: in the presence of all the people I will make wonders..." (next v.).

**34:10.** And (the Lord) said, "Here I give (you) a solemn promise: in the presence of all the people I will make wonders that were never performed in all the earth, nor among any nation, so that all the people in whose midst you are, perceiving that which I will do for you, will see how awesome are the works of the Lord.

*so that all the people... perceiving, etc.* The verse is to be understood as follows: "The people will see that the works of the Lord are awesome [*ki nora hu*]," on the model of, "God saw that the light was a good thing [*ki tov*]," "that is, that which I will do for you."

**34:11.** "Pay heed to what I command you today. Here I am about to drive out from your presence the Amorites, and the Canaanites, and the Hivites and the Jebusites.
**34:12.** "Guard yourself that you do not make (any) covenant with the inhabitants of the country that you will occupy, so that, remaining in your midst, they do not become a stumbling block [a cause of ruin] for you.

*that you do not make (any) covenant.* The verse is to be understood as follows: "I am afraid that such and such will happen, that is, if you make a covenant with them, then they will engage in idolatry in your country, and you will gradually intermarry with them and worship their idols." This is why it says at the beginning [of this group of verses] in a general way, "So that… they do not become a stumbling block for you."

34:13. "But you will demolish their altars, and you will cut down their sacred groves.
34:14. "For you must not prostrate yourself to any other divinity, for the Lord is called jealous; a jealous God is He.
34:15. "Because if you make a covenant with the inhabitants of the country, they will fornicate after their gods [they will continue to worship them] and will make sacrifices to their gods, and they will invite you, and you will eat of their sacrifices.
34:16. "Then you will take from among their daughters (as wives) for your sons, and their daughters will fornicate after their gods, and they will cause your sons to fornicate after their gods.
34:17. "Gods of cast metal you shall not make.
34:18. "The festival of unleavened breads you shall observe: seven days you shall eat unleavened breads, (according to) that which I commanded you, at the established time of the month of the first ripening (of the barley); for in the month of the first ripening you came out of Egypt.

*The festival of unleavened breads.* After warning the people about idol worship, He concludes with that which they should do in honor of God.

34:19. "Every firstborn belongs to Me: of all your herds, that is, (you will sacrifice) the males, the firstborn of the oxen and of the sheep (and of the goats).

*Every firstborn belongs to Me.* Of men and animals; this is a general statement (*kelal*) that is followed by particulars (*perat*).

*of all your herds… the males* (ve-khol miknekha tizzakhar). The word *mikneh* ("herds") here is feminine [thus taking the feminine verb *tizzakhar*, which means], that is, "will be born male"; in other words, it is a command that when your herds are born male, you must separate out the males (so Ibn Ezra in his short commentary). Then it specifies that not all the males are meant, but only the firstborns. The letter *khaf* in the word *tizzakhar* is marked with a *kamats* (תִּזָּכָר) to indicate that the word is derived from the noun *zakhar* (זָכָר, "male").

## Ki Tissa

34:20. "And every firstborn of an ass you shall ransom with a lamb (or kid), and if you do not want to ransom it, you shall kill it; every firstborn of your sons you shall ransom; nor shall My face be seen empty-handed.
34:21. "Six days you shall work, and on the seventh day you shall rest; even in the season of the plowing and of the harvest you shall rest (on the Sabbath).

*in the season of the plowing and of the harvest* (*be-ḥarish u-va-katsir*). Even in those seasons you will rest on the Sabbath [the words "even" and "season" do not appear in the Heb. but are supplied in the translation]. So translated Mendelssohn, and this is correct, though some interpret the phrase to mean, "You will rest even from the labors of plowing and harvesting." If so, however, the text ought to have read *me-ḥarish u-mi-katsir*.

34:22. "You will celebrate likewise the feast of weeks, (feast of) the first fruits of the harvest of the wheat, and the feast of the reaping, the cycle of the year having ended.
34:23. "Three times in the year every male of yours will appear before the (supreme) master, the Lord, God of Israel.

*every male of yours will appear* (*yera'eh*). The Heb. is properly *yir'eh* ("will see"); see my comment on Isa. 1:12.[17]

34:24. "For I will drive out nations from your presence, and I will expand your territory; nor will anyone think to occupy your country when you go to appear before the Lord your God three times a year.
34:25. "You shall not pour out over [that is, while having in the house] leavened bread the blood of My sacrifice, nor shall there remain till the morning the sacrifice of the feast of Passover.

*the sacrifice of* (*zevaḥ*) *the feast of Passover.* That is, the *emurim* [the pieces of fat that had to be burned on the altar] (Rashi). Above it is written, "Nor shall the fat of [*ḥelev*] the sacrificial animal remain until morning" (Exod. 23:18), and here [too] Onkelos translates [*zevaḥ* as] "the fat [of the sacrifice]." Perhaps the word *zevaḥ* includes the fat and the blood, for both of them [may be described as] *zavim* ("oozing").

---

17. This comment is summarized in the footnote to 23:15, above.

34:26. "The most select first fruits of your land you shall bring to the House of the Lord your God. You shall not cook a kid in its mother's milk."

34:27. Then the Lord said to Moses, "Write for yourself these commandments, for on the basis of these commandments I establish an alliance with you and with Israel."

*for on the basis of these commandments.* Those stated in this section, starting from the words, "Here I am about to drive out" (above, v. 11) (Rashbam).

34:28. And Moses was there with the Lord forty days and forty nights; bread he did not eat and water he did not drink; and the Lord wrote upon the tablets the words of the pact, (that is) the ten commandments.

34:29. Now when Moses descended from mount Sinai—and the two tablets of the Law were in Moses' hands when he descended from the mountain—Moses did not know that the skin of his face had become radiant, while (the Lord) was speaking with him.

34:30. Aaron and all the children of Israel, seeing Moses, and perceiving that the skin of his face was radiant, were afraid to come near to him.

34:31. But Moses called them, and Aaron and all of the princes returned to him in the (place of) the assembly, and Moses spoke to them.

34:32. Afterward all the Israelites came near, and Moses commanded them all that the Lord had spoken to him on mount Sinai.

34:33. And when Moses had finished speaking with them, he placed a veil on his face.

34:34. When Moses then presented himself to the Lord, so that He might speak to him, he removed the veil until he left. He left and communicated to the Israelites that which had been enjoined upon him.

*so that He might speak to him* (ledabber itto, lit., "to speak with him"). So that God might speak with him; see the end of *Parashat Naso*.[18]

34:35. Then the Israelites saw Moses' face (that is, they saw) that the skin of Moses' face was radiant. Then Moses replaced the veil upon his face until he re-entered so that (the Lord) might speak to him.

---

18. There (Num. 7:89), where the same phrase *ledabber itto* appears, Shadal comments that nowhere else but there and here do we find a person "speaking with" God, and that the phrase should be understood in the sense of *she-yedabber itto*, "so that he might be spoken to with Him."

# Vayak'hel

*Contribution of materials • Construction of the Tabernacle • The totality of talented men • The women who came to work*

**35:1.** Moses had all the congregation of the Israelites assemble, and he said to them, "These are the things that the Lord has commanded to be done.
**35:2.** "Six days will work be done, and the seventh day will be holy for you, a great rest in honor of the Lord; whoever does work on it will be put to death.
**35:3.** "You shall not light a fire in any part of your residences [of your country] on the Sabbath day."

*You shall not light a fire.* Because it is mentioned above (12:16), with reference to the Feast of *Matsot*, that "only that which is wont to be eaten by every person, that alone may be made [prepared] by you," the Torah now says that on the Sabbath, "you shall not light a fire" [even] to bake bread or to cook meat, for fire is needed to prepare any food (Ibn Ezra).

**35:4.** Then Moses said to all the congregation of the Israelites as follows: "This is the thing that the Lord has commanded.
**35:5.** "Collect among you a tribute to the Lord—whoever is inspired of his own heart will bring it, this tribute, to the honor of the Lord—gold and silver and copper.
**35:6.** "And blue wool, and purple, and scarlet, and linen, and goat hair.

35:7. "And sheepskins dyed red, and badger (?) skins, and acacia wood.

35:8. "And oil for illumination, and spices for the oil of anointing [consecration] and for the aromatic incense.

35:9. "And onyx stones, and stones for setting, for the dorsal and for the pectoral.

35:10. "And whoever among you is a man of talent, come and (among them all) let them do all that the Lord has commanded.

35:11. "The tabernacle, its tent, and its cover; its clasps, its boards, its bars, its columns, and its bases.

35:12. "The ark, and its poles; the cover, and its dividing door-curtain.

35:13. "The table and its poles, and all of its furnishings; and the bread of presentation.

35:14. "And the candelabrum for illumination, and its furnishings, and its lamps, and the oil for illumination.

35:15. "And the altar of the incense, and its poles, and the oil of anointing, and the aromatic incense; and the entrance hanging, at the entrance of the tabernacle.

35:16. "The altar of the burnt offerings, and its copper grating, its poles, and all of its furnishings; and the basin and its pedestal.

35:17. "The curtains of the courtyard, and its bases; and the hanging at the entrance of the courtyard.

35:18. "The stakes of the tabernacle, and the stakes of the courtyard, and its cords.

35:19. "The netted cloths, for serving in the (transport of) the holy thing; the sacred garments for Aaron the priest, and the garments of his sons, with which to exercise the priestly functions."

35:20. All the congregation of the Israelites went forth from the presence of Moses.

35:21. And (at once) all those who felt raised by their hearts [moved to generosity], and stirred by their spirits, came and brought the tribute to the Lord for the work of the tent of congregation, and for every service thereof, and for the sacred garments.

35:22. Men and women came in multitudes; every generous heart brought brooches and earrings and rings and kumaz (?), every kind of gold furnishings, as well as every man who presented (unworked) gold in an offering to the Lord.

**brooches** *(ḥaḥ).* As in, "I shall place My hook [*ḥaḥi*] in your nose" (Isa. 37:29).

## Vayak'hel

*kumaz.* In Arabic, כמז is "a binding together and compression of a looser thing so that it is brought into a round form."[1] Similar to it is the root *kamas* ("to hide, store away"). It seems likely that the *kumaz* was placed beneath the breasts.

**35:23.** And all those who found themselves in possession of blue wool, or purple, or scarlet, or linen, or goat hair, or sheepskins dyed red, or badger skins, brought them.

**35:24.** Some brought in tribute to the Lord offerings of silver and of copper; and all those who found themselves in possession of acacia wood, (fitting) for various labors to be done, brought them.

**35:25.** And all the women of talent spun with their hands, and they brought yarn of blue wool, and of purple, and of scarlet, and of linen.

**35:26.** And all the women whose talent raised [distinguished] them for skill spun the goat hair.

**35:27.** And the princes brought the onyx stones, and the stones for mounting, for the dorsal and for the pectoral.

**35:28.** And the spices, and the oil, both for illumination and for anointing, and (the spices) for the aromatic incense.

**35:29.** Every man and woman inspired by their own heart to bring for all the work that the Lord, through Moses, prescribed to do—the Israelites (that is) brought offerings to the Lord.

**35:30.** And Moses said to the Israelites, "See, the Lord has called by name Bezalel, son of Uri, son of Hur, of the tribe of Judah.

**35:31.** "And He has filled him with the spirit of God, with regard to knowledge, discernment, and wisdom, and with regard to any art.

**35:32.** "And to think (new) ideas, to work in gold, and in silver, and in copper.

**35:33.** "And for labors in gems for mounting, and for labors in wood; for working (in sum) in any labor of talent.

**35:34.** "He also gave him the talent to teach others. (Such is) he, and (such is) Oholiab son of Ahisamak, of the tribe of Dan.

---

1. Shadal gives this definition in Latin, *rei laxioris collectio et compressio ut in formam rotundam redigatur*, without attribution. A search of this phrase indicates that his source was most likely Samuel Bochart (*Geographia sacra, seu Phaleg et Canaan*, first printed in Caen, 1646). Bochart's derivation of kumaz was echoed in later works by Matthew Poole (London, 1669) and Johann Braun (Leiden, 1680). These authorities seem to have viewed the kumaz as an ancient type of brassiere. In Braun's *Bigde kohanim, i.e., Vestitus Sacerdotum hebraeorum* (book 2, p. 459), the author follows his discussion of kumaz with the suggestion that the Latin word *camisia* ("shirt") might have been derived from Arabic and related to the root *kamas*, since a shirt covers and hides the body.

35:35. "He has filled them with talent for doing any work of a craftsman (smith, woodworker, and stoneworker), and of a tapestry weaver, embroiderer, and textile worker, in blue wool, in purple, in scarlet, and in linen. They are fit to execute every labor, and to make (new) inventions."

36:1. "And Bezalel and Oholiab, and all the men of talent, whom the Lord has endowed with knowledge and discernment to know how to work, will execute every labor of the sacred work, according to all that which the Lord has commanded."

*And Bezalel... will execute (ve-asah).* See *Ohev Ger*, p. 81.[2] Rashi, [commenting] in *Makkot* 12[a], understood that [the word *ve-asah* in this v.] is not in the past tense, but in his opinion it is in the imperative. If this were so, it should have read *ve-ya'aseh*, but *ve-asah* is in the future indicative [i.e., "he will execute"]; the meaning is, "I know that he will execute."

36:2. Then Moses called Bezalel and Oholiab, and every man of talent whom the Lord endowed with knowledge, everyone who felt himself animated to draw near to the work, to execute it [that is, to contribute to its execution].
36:3. And (the latter) took from before Moses all of the tribute brought by the Israelites for the labor of the sacred work, (they took it, that is) to execute it [the work]; and they brought him more offerings from morning to morning.
36:4. Then came all the artisans who executed all of the sacred works, each one from that work with which he was occupied.
36:5. And they said to Moses, "The people are bringing more than enough for the labor of the work that the Lord has commanded to do."
36:6. And Moses commanded, and a cry was made to go through the encampment, saying, "Let no one, man or woman, do any more work [that is, do not prepare more materials] for the sacred tribute." And the people refrained from bringing.
36:7. And the prepared material was such as to suffice for them [the artisans], for all of the work, to execute it, and to spare.

---

2. There (p. 87 in the 1895 ed.), Shadal says that to translate the word in the past tense, as did Mendelssohn and Jerome, is an "egregious error," for this verse is a continuation of Moses' speech to the people, which is followed by the statement (v. 2), "Then Moses called Bezalel." How, then, could it say that Bezalel "executed" the labor before he was called? Thus, says Shadal, the standard reading of Onkelos' translation of *ve-asah* should be emended from *va-avad* (past) to *ve-ya'avid* (future), which reading was in fact found by him in one version.

## Vayak'hel

36:8. The totality, then, of the talented men employed in the work made the tabernacle (composed) of ten curtains of twisted linen, of blue wool, of purple, and of scarlet, which it made with figures of cherubim, of tapestry work.

36:9. The length of the curtain (was) of twenty-eight cubits, and the width (was) of four cubits per curtain; one same measure had all the curtains.

36:10. And it attached[3] five curtains one to the other, and (the other) five curtains it attached one to the other.

36:11. And it made loops of blue wool on the edge of that curtain which is at the end of one series; and it made the same on the edge of that curtain which is the last in the second series.

36:12. Fifty loops it made in one curtain, and fifty loops it made on the last curtain of the second series; the loops were facing one another.

36:13. And it made fifty clasps of gold, and it joined the curtains one to another with the clasps, and the tabernacle was united.

36:14. And it made curtains of goat hair to serve as a tent over the tabernacle; eleven of such curtains it made.

36:15. The length of one curtains (was) of thirty cubits, and of four cubits the width of each curtain; one same measure had (all) the eleven curtains.

36:16. And it attached five curtains on one side and six curtains on one side.

36:17. And it made fifty loops on the edge of that curtain which is at the end of one series, and fifty loops it made on the edge of the curtain of the other series.

36:18. And it made fifty clasps of copper, to join the tent so that it would be united.

36:19. It made then for the tent a cover of rams' skins dyed red, and a cover of badgers' skins on top.

36:20. And it made the boards of the tabernacle, of acacia wood, standing erect [cut lengthwise].

36:21. Ten cubits (was) the length of the board, and one and a half cubits the width of every board.

36:22. Every board had two pegs, protruding one facing the other; thus it made for all the boards of the tabernacle.

36:23. It made the boards of the tabernacle (distributed as follows): twenty boards on the side of the south (otherwise called) the right side.

---

3. Heb. *Va-yehabber*, Ital. *Ed attaccò*. No subject for the verb is given in the Hebrew or Italian, but the unstated subject (given as "it" in the English translation) here and in many of the verses throughout ch. 36 refers back to "the totality... of the talented men" (Heb. *kol ḥakham lev*, Ital. *L'insieme... degli uomini ingegnosi*) mentioned in v. 8 above.

36:24. And forty silver bases it made under the twenty boards: two bases under one board, at its two pegs, and two bases under one board, at its two pegs.

36:25. And on the other side of the tabernacle, (that is) on the side of the north, it made twenty boards.

36:26. And its forty silver bases, two bases under one board, and two bases under one board.

36:27. And at the end of the tabernacle, (that is) at the west, it made six boards.

36:28. And two boards it made at the corners of the tabernacle at the end.

36:29. And they fit closely together at the bottom, and together they finished at the top in one ring; thus it made those two (boards), at the two corners.

36:30. There were (altogether) eight boards, with their silver bases, that is, sixteen bases; two bases under each board.

36:31. And it made bars of acacia wood, five for the boards of one side of the tabernacle.

36:32. And five bars for the boards of the other side of the tabernacle, and five bars for the boards of the tabernacle on the end, to the west.

36:33. It then made the middle bar, to run at the half (of the height) of the boards, from one extremity to the other.

36:34. And the boards it covered with gold, and with gold it made their rings, through which to pass the bars, and it covered the bars with gold.

36:35. And it made the door-curtain of blue wool, and of purple, and of scarlet, and of twisted linen; it made it with figures of cherubim, in tapestry work.

36:36. And it made for it four columns of acacia wood, which it covered with gold, with their hooks of gold; and it made for them by casting four silver bases.

36:37. And it made a hanging at the entrance of the tent, of blue wool, and of purple, and of scarlet, and of twisted linen, the work of an embroiderer.

36:38. Likewise its columns, five, and their hooks, and it gilded their tops, and of gold it made their friezes; and (it made) their five bases of copper.

37:1. And Bezalel made the Ark of acacia wood, of two cubits and a half cubit in length, one and a half cubits in width, and one and a half cubits in height.

37:2. And he covered it with pure gold within and without, and he made above it a cornice of gold round about.

## Vayak'hel

37:3. And he cast for it four rings of gold, at its four corners; that is, two rings on its one side, and two rings on its other side.

37:4. And he made poles of acacia wood, and he covered them with gold.

37:5. And he inserted the poles into the rings, along the (short) sides of the Ark, (to serve) to carry the Ark.

37:6. And he made a cover of pure gold, of two and a half cubits in length, and one and a half cubits in width.

37:7. And he made two cherubim of gold; he made them one solid piece, at the two ends of the cover.

37:8. One cherub on one end and one cherub on the other end; he made the cherubim (as if) forming part of the cover at its [the Ark's] two ends.

37:9. The cherubim had their wings spread upwards, sheltering with their wings over the cover, and they had their faces one opposite the other; toward the cover were the faces of the cherubim.

37:10. And he made the table of acacia wood, of two cubits in length, one cubit in width, and one and a half cubits in height.

37:11. And he covered it with pure gold, and he made for it a cornice of gold round about.

37:12. And he made for it an enclosure [a band], one handbreadth high, round about; and he made a cornice of gold all around its enclosure.

37:13. And he cast for it four rings of gold, and he applied the rings upon the four corners corresponding to its four legs.

37:14. Beside the enclosure were the rings through which to pass the poles, to carry the table.

37:15. And he made for it poles of acacia wood, and he covered them with gold, to carry the table.

37:16. And he made the furnishings to be placed on the table, its plates, and its bowls, and its libation vessels, and its goblets, with which the libations will be made; (all these furnishings he made) of pure gold.

37:17. And he made the candelabrum of pure gold; one solid piece he made the candelabrum, its shaft and each branch thereof; its calyxes, its buds, and its flowers were (inseparable parts) of it.

37:18. And six branches came forth from its sides, three candelabrum branches on one of its sides, and three candelabrum branches on its other side.

37:19. Three calyxes (were) incised in one branch, (that is) a bud and a flower; and three calyxes incised in the other branch, a bud and a flower; thus in all the six branches coming forth from the candelabrum.

37:20. And in the candelabrum itself [that is, in the shaft] four calyxes; (there were, that is) incised its buds and its flowers.

37:21. One bud (there was) under two of its branches, one (other) bud under two of its branches, and one bud under (the other) two of its branches, for the six branches coming forth from it (the candelabrum).

37:22. Their buds, and the corresponding branches, were (parts inseparable) from it; it was entirely a single solid body of pure gold.

37:23. And he made its seven lamps, and its snuffers and its tongs, of pure gold.

37:24. Of one talent of pure gold he made it, and all of its furnishings.

37:25. And he made the altar of the incense, of acacia wood, of one cubit of length and one cubit of width, square, and of two cubits of height, with its prominences, (inseparable) from it.

37:26. And he covered it with pure gold, its upper surface, its walls all around, and its prominences; and he made for it a cornice of gold round about.

37:27. And two rings of gold he made beneath its cornice, on its two sides, (two, that is) on both of its sides, through which to pass the poles with which to carry it.

37:28. And he made the poles of acacia wood, and he covered them with gold.

37:29. And he made the oil of anointing, sacred, and the aromatic incense, pure, the work of a perfumer.

38:1. And he made the altar of the burnt offerings, of acacia wood, of five cubits of length, and five cubits of width, square, and of three cubits of height.

38:2. And he made its prominences on its four corners; (inseparable parts) of it were its prominences; and he covered it with copper.

38:3. And he made all the furnishings of the altar, the pots, the shovels, the basins, the forks, the paddles; all of its furnishings he made of copper.

38:4. And he made for the altar a grating of copper, a work (that is) in the form of a network, (placed) under its Karkov [?], from below [that is, from the ground] up to its half [up to half of the height of the altar].

38:5. And he made by casting four rings at the four extremities of the copper grating, in which to insert the poles.

38:6. And he made the poles of acacia wood, and he covered them with copper.

38:7. And he inserted the poles in the rings, on the sides of the altar, to serve to carry it. Hollow, (formed) of boards, did he make it.

# Vayak'hel

**38:8. And he made the basin of copper, and its pedestal of copper, with the mirrors of the women who came to work at the entrance of the tent of congregation [who, besides their work, contributed their own mirrors, made of shining copper].**

***with the mirrors of the women who came to work.*** The copper of the mirrors was more burnished and polished than other copper, and therefore he chose to make the basin out of it (Abravanel).

***the women who came to work*** *(ha-tsove'ot asher tsave'u).* Perhaps the meaning is on the model of "all those who entered to take part in the ranks [*litsvo tsava*], to lend service in the tent of congregation" (Num. 4:23); and similarly, "Is there not a time of service [*tsava*] to man upon earth? And are not his days like the days of a hireling?" (Job 7:1), i.e., a fixed time for performing labor, whether one day or two, or whatever time it may be. Here, some of the women allotted themselves an assignment to go to the entrance of Moses' tent (which was called "the tent of congregation," above, 33:7) to perform service with the sacred tribute, such as weaving the goat hair or some other service, and it was they who donated their mirrors. So also the *tsove'ot* [mentioned in connection with] the sons of Eli (1 Sam. 2:22) would bring a sacrifice and remain there [at the Shiloh sanctuary] one day or two, "lingering before the Lord" (as was said of Doeg, 1 Sam. 21:8).

**38:9. And he made the courtyard. On the southern side, (called) the right side, (he made) the curtains of the courtyard, of twisted linen, a hundred cubits.**
**38:10. And its columns, twenty, and its bases, twenty, of copper; and the hooks of the columns, and their ornamentations, of silver.**
**38:11. And on the northern side, a hundred cubits (of curtains), with their respective twenty columns, and their twenty bases of copper; and the hooks of the columns, and their ornamentations, of silver.**
**38:12. And on the western side, fifty cubits of curtains, with their ten columns and ten bases; and the hooks of the columns, and their ornamentations, of silver.**
**38:13. And on the forward side, (that is) on the east, (the façade of the courtyard is of) fifty cubits.**
**38:14. Fifteen cubits of curtains (he made) on one side, with their columns, three, and their bases, three.**
**38:15. And on the other side, (that is) on either side of the entrance of the courtyard, fifteen cubits of curtains, with their three columns and three bases.**

38:16. The curtains of the courtyard all around are of twisted linen.

38:17. And the bases of the columns are of copper; and the hooks of the columns, and their ornamentations, of silver, and their tops are covered with silver. They are, in sum, ornamented with silver, all the columns of the courtyard.

38:18. And the hanging at the entrance of the courtyard is embroiderer's work, of blue wool, of purple, of scarlet, and of twisted linen; and it has twenty cubits of length, and of height (or in other words) of width five cubits, like the (other) curtains of the courtyard.

38:19. With their respective columns, four, and bases, four, of copper; and their hooks of silver, and their tops covered with silver, and their ornamentations of silver.

38:20. And the stakes of the tabernacle and of the courtyard all around are of copper.

# *Pekudei*

*The review • "Then was finished all the work" • "And the Majesty of the Lord filled the tabernacle"*

**38:21. This is the review that was made, by order of Moses, of the tabernacle, the lodging place of the Law, (entrusted to) the care of the Levites, under the direction of Itamar, son of Aaron the priest.**

***the lodging place of the Law*** *(mishkan ha-edut).* From the expression *aron ha-edut* ("the ark of the Admonition," i.e., "of the Law") (Exod. 30:26), meaning the Torah. The entire *Mishkan* (Tabernacle) was so named after the tablets of the Admonition and the ark of the Admonition, for they were the essence of [its] holiness. As is seen above (Exodus 25), [the commands that the people were to] "collect for Me a tribute" and "make Me a Sanctuary" are followed immediately by "They will make an ark."

**38:22. And Bezalel son of Uri, son of Hur, of the tribe of Judah, did all that the Lord commanded Moses.**
**38:23. And with him Oholiab son of Ahisamak, of the tribe of Dan, craftsman (smith, woodworker, and stoneworker), and tapestry weaver, and embroiderer in blue wool, in purple, in scarlet, and in linen.**
**38:24. All the gold used in the labor in all the sacred work, the gold (that is) of the offering was twenty-nine talents, and seven hundred thirty shekels, according to the weight of the temple.**

***talents*** *(kikkar).* The *kikkar* equaled three thousand shekels.

38:25. And the silver obtained from the enumeration of the community was one hundred talents, and one thousand seven hundred seventy-five shekels, according to the weight of the temple.

38:26. One beka per head, (that is) half a shekel, of the weight of the temple, for everyone entered in the enumeration, from the age of twenty years and upward, (that is) for six hundred and three thousand five hundred and fifty (individuals).

38:27. Now the hundred talents of silver served to make by casting the bases of the temple and the bases of the door-curtain; a hundred bases with a hundred talents, one talent per base.

38:28. And of the one thousand seven hundred and seventy-five (shekels) were made hooks for the columns, and their tops were covered with silver, and ornamentations were made for the same (columns).

38:29. The copper of the offering was seventy talents and two thousand four hundred shekels.

38:30. And of it were made the bases of the entrance of the tent of congregation, and the altar of copper, and its grating of copper, and all the furnishings of the altar.

38:31. And the bases of the courtyard round about, and the bases of the entrance of the courtyard, and all the pins of the tabernacle, and all the pins of the courtyard round about.

39:1. And of the blue wool, and of the purple, and of the scarlet, they made netted cloths, to serve in the (transport of) the holy things, and they made the sacred garments for Aaron, and the Lord commanded Moses.

39:2. And he made the dorsal, of gold, of blue wool, and purple, and scarlet, and twisted linen.

39:3. They beat sheets of gold, and they cut them into threads, to be used amid the blue wool, and amid the purple, and amid the scarlet, and amid the linen, the work of a tapestry weaver.

39:4. They made for it (two) attached shoulder straps; at is two ends it was connected (to the pectoral).

39:5. And the band with which to tie it, which is on top of it, forming part of it, is of the same work, of gold (that is), of blue wool, and of purple, and of scarlet, and of twisted linen, as the Lord commanded Moses.

39:6. And they worked the onyx stones, encircled by bezels of gold with the names of the children of Israel engraved in them with the engraving of a seal.

39:7. And he placed upon the shoulder straps of the dorsal stones of remembrance for the children of Israel, as the Lord commanded Moses.

## Pekudei

39:8. And he made the pectoral, the work of a tapestry weaver, similar to the work of the dorsal, of gold (that is), of blue wool, and of purple, and of scarlet, and of twisted linen.

39:9. A rectangle folded over they made the pectoral, of a span of length and a span of width, folded over.

39:10. And they set in it four rows of stones. One row: ruby, topaz, and emerald; (these form) the first order.

39:11. And the second order: carbuncle, sapphire, and diamond [?].

39:12. And the third order: jacinth, agate, and amethyst.

39:13. And the fourth order: chrysolite, onyx, and jasper. Encircled by bezels of gold they are in their settings.

39:14. These stones bear the names of the children of Israel, being twelve, according to their names; (engraved) with the engraving of a seal, they represent the twelve tribes, each one with its name.

39:15. And they made for the pectoral chains of twisted thread, cord work, of pure gold.

39:16. And they made two bezels of gold, and two rings of gold; and they placed the two rings on the two ends of the pectoral.

39:17. And they placed the two cords of gold on the two rings, on the ends of the pectoral.

39:18. And the two ends of the two cords they placed on the two bezels, which they placed on the shoulder straps of the dorsal, on the front [that is, exterior] side.

39:19. And they made two rings of gold, and they placed them on the two ends of the pectoral, on its edge that is against the dorsal on the inside.

39:20. And they made two (other) rings of gold, and they placed them on the shoulder straps of the dorsal, below, on the front [exterior] side, close to its juncture, above the band of the dorsal.

39:21. And they laced the pectoral from its rings to the rings of the dorsal with a string of blue wool, so that it may be upon the band of the dorsal, and the pectoral does not become detached from the dorsal, as the Lord commanded Moses.

39:22. And they made the mantle supporting the dorsal, of weaver's work, all of blue wool.

39:23. The mantle has its opening (folded over) inside, similar to that of a breast plate; its opening (that is) has a hem round about, so that it does not tear.

39.24. And they made at the edges of the mantle pomegranates of blue wool, and purple, and scarlet, twisted.

39:25. And they made bells of pure gold; and they placed the bells between the pomegranates, at the edges of the mantle, all around, alternating with the pomegranates.

39:26. A bell and a pomegranate,, a bell and a pomegranate, at the edges of the mantle all around, to officiate, as the Lord commanded Moses.

39:27. And they made the tunics of linen, of weaver's work, for Aaron and for his sons.

39:28. And the mitre of linen, and the ornaments (for the head, in other words) the turbans of linen, and the trousers of linen, of twisted linen.

39:29. And the belt of twisted linen, and blue wool, and purple and scarlet, the work of an embroiderer, as the Lord commanded Moses.

39:30. And they made the diadem, a sacred coronet, of pure gold; and they wrote upon it in characters (incised) with the engraving of a seal, "Holy to the Lord."

39:31. And they applied to it a string of blue wool, to place it on top of the mitre, as the Lord commanded Moses.

39:32. Then was finished all the work of the tabernacle of the tent of congregation, and the Israelites carried out completely all that the Lord commanded Moses.

39:33. And they brought the tabernacle to Moses, the tent and all of its furnishings, its clasps, its boards, its bars, its columns, and its bases.

39:34. And the cover of rams' skins dyed red, and the cover of badgers' skins, and the dividing door-curtain.

39:35. The ark of the Law, and its poles, and the cover.

39:36. The table, all of its furnishings, and the bread of presentation.

39:37. The pure candelabrum, its lamps, lamps of decoration [that is, for the purpose of ornamentation of the temple, not for actual use as lights, for the sacred place was not attended at night], and all of its furnishings, and the oil of illumination.

***lamps of decoration*** *(nerot ha-ma'arakhah).* Lamps that were not used for [actual] lighting, for there was no service at night, but were solely for display (by way of honoring the sanctuary). Mendelssohn did not understand this, and he left the word [*neroteha*, "its lamps"] untranslated.[1]

39:38. And the altar of gold, and the oil of anointing, and the aromatic incense, and the hanging at the entrance of the tent.

---

1. Mendelssohn's translation of this verse reads, *"Den Leuchter von reinem Golde, die daraufzusetzenden Lampe, alle Geräthe dazu, und das Oel"* ("The candelabrum of pure gold, the lamps placed upon it, all its utensils, and the oil").

## Pekudei

39:39. The altar of copper, and its grating of copper, its poles, and all its furnishings; the basin, and its pedestal.

39:40. The curtains of the courtyard, its columns, and its bases, and the hanging at the entrance of the courtyard, its cords, and its pins; and all the furnishings related to the service of the tabernacle of the tent of congregation.

39:41. The netted cloths to serve in the (transport of the) sacred things; the sacred garments for Aaron the priest, and the garments of his sons, for functioning.

39:42. In accordance with all that the Lord commanded Moses, so the children of Israel carried out all the labor.

39:43. And Moses saw all the work, and he found that they had carried it out entirely as the Lord had commanded; and Moses blessed them.

40:1. And the Lord spoke to Moses, saying:

40:2. "On the day of the first month [the new moon], (that is) on the first (day) of that month, you will erect the tabernacle of the tent of congregation.

40:3. "And you will place there the ark of the Law, and you will place as a divider before the ark the door-curtain.

*and you will place as a divider* (ve-sakkota). The Heb. is related to the word *masakh*; below in v. 21 it is clarified further: "And he put in place the dividing curtain [*parokhet ha-masakh*], screening [*va-yasekh*] the ark of the Law."

40:4. "You will bring in the table, and you will put in order its apparatus; and you will bring in the candelabrum, and you will light its lamps.

40:5. "And you will place the altar of gold, (that is, that) of the incense, before the ark of the Law; and you will put in place the hanging of the entrance to the tabernacle.

40:6. "And you will place the altar of the burnt offerings before the entrance of the tabernacle of the tent of congregation.

40:7. "And you will place the basin between the tent of congregation and the altar, and you will put water in it.

40:8. "And you will place the courtyard round about, and you will put in place the hanging of the entrance to the courtyard.

40:9. "And you will take the oil of anointing, and you will anoint the tabernacle and all that is in it, and (with that) you will consecrate it, with all its furnishings, and it will be a holy thing.

40:10. "And you will anoint the altar of the burnt offerings and all its furnishings; and you will consecrate the altar, and the altar will be a most holy thing.

40:11. "And you will anoint the basin and its pedestal, and you will consecrate it.

40:12. "And you will have Aaron and his sons present themselves at the entrance of the tent of congregation, and bathe themselves in the water.

40:13. "And you will have Aaron put on the sacred garments, and you will anoint him, and you will consecrate him, and he will be a priest to Me.

40:14. "And you will have his sons present themselves and put on the tunics.

40:15. "And you will anoint them, as you anointed their father, and they will be priests to Me; and that will result in their being invested with perpetual priesthood, for all their posterity."

40:16. And Moses complied, and he did fully as the Lord commanded him.

40:17. Now in the first month of the second year, on the first of the month, the tabernacle was erected.

40:18. Moses erected the tabernacle, and he placed its bases, and he put in place its boards, and he placed its bars, and he erected its columns.

40:19. And he spread the tent over the tabernacle, and he placed on top of it the cover of the tent, as the Lord commanded Moses.

40:20. He took (the tablets of) the Law, and he placed them in the ark, and he put the poles on the ark, and he placed the cover on top of the ark.

40:21. He brought the ark into the tabernacle, and he put in place the dividing curtain, screening (thus the view of) the ark of the Law, as the Lord commanded Moses.

40:22. He placed the table in the tent of congregation, on the northern side of the tabernacle, outside the door-curtain.

40:23. And he arranged upon it the apparatus of bread before the Lord, as the Lord commanded Moses.

40:24. And he put in place the candelabrum in the tent of congregation, facing the table, on the southern side of the tabernacle.

40:25. And he lit the lamps before the Lord, as the Lord commanded Moses.

40:26. And he placed the altar of gold in the tent of congregation, before the door-curtain.

40:27. And he burned upon it the aromatic incense, as the Lord commanded Moses.

## Pekudei

***And he burned upon it.*** In a Rashi manuscript in my possession it is written *Aharon shaḥarit ve-arvit* [i.e., it was Aaron who burned the incense in the morning and at night], and this was the reading that Nachmanides found as well; he said, "I do not know if this is a scribal error" (that is, whether the error was Rashi's own, for there is no doubt that the service [during the tabernacle's dedication] was done by Moses). See *Sefer ha-Zikkaron*.[2]

40:28. And he put in place the entrance hanging to the tabernacle.

40:29. And the altar of the burnt offerings he placed at the entrance of the tabernacle of the tent of congregation, and he burned upon it the burnt offerings and the flour offerings, as the Lord commanded Moses.

40:30. And he placed the basin between the tent of congregation and the altar, and he put there water for bathing.

40:31. And from that Moses, Aaron, and his sons bathed their hands and their feet.

40:32. At their entering into the tent of congregation, and approaching the altar, they bathed themselves, as the Lord commanded Moses.

40:33. And he erected the courtyard around the tabernacle and the altar, and he put in place the entrance hanging of the courtyard; and Moses finished the work.

40:34. Then the cloud covered the tent of congregation, and the Majesty of the Lord filled the tabernacle.

40:35. And Moses could not enter into the tent of congregation, for the cloud lodged above it, and the Majesty of the Lord filled the Tabernacle.

40:36. And when the cloud moved away from above the tabernacle, the Israelites advanced, in all of their journeys.

---

2. Chavel notes that the word *Aharon* does not appear in the first printed edition of Rashi, and properly so (for it was Moses who conducted the week's service), but that the Oxford manuscript (Bodley 2440) does have *Aharon*. Modern printed editions do not. The comment in *Sefer ha-Zikkaron* assumes that the reading with *Aharon* is the correct one and says that this reading explains Rashi's next comment (on the phrase "and he burned upon it the burnt offerings" in v. 29), that even on the eighth day, it was Moses who offered the public sacrifices—that is, v. 29 is once again referring to Moses, as in most of the rest of this section, and not to Aaron as in v. 27. *Sefer ha-Zikkaron* goes on to say that if the reading with *Aharon* is in fact a scribal error as Nachmanides claims, Rashi should be understood as saying, "Do not find it surprising that Moses burned the incense *and* offered sacrifices after the seventh day, for even on the eighth day, it was Moses who offered the public sacrifices, while Aaron offered only his private sacrifices."

**40:37. And if it did not move away, they did not advance, (and they waited) until the day that it moved away.**
**40:38. For the cloud of the Lord was upon the tabernacle during the day, and during the night there was fire within it (the cloud); (and thus it was) in the view of all of the house of Israel, in all of their journeys.**

*and during the night there was fire within it.* At night there was fire within the cloud; the cloud was always present day and night, but at night there was fire within it. See Num. 9:21 ["And sometimes the cloud remained from evening to morning… or (it remained) a day and a night"].

# Sources Cited by Shadal

## *Scholars and Commentators*

**Abravanel, (Don) Isaac** (1437-1508). Classic Torah commentator, philosopher, and statesman, born in Lisbon.

**Alexandrian translator.** The supposed author of the Greek Bible translation commonly known as the Septuagint (the translation of the "seventy elders"), written in Alexandria probably in the first half of the third century B.C.E. Shadal, expressing the view that this version had become so corrupt and unreliable as to be unworthy of the honorable title of "Septuagint," stated that "the soundest and most modern critics" referred to it instead as "that of the Alexandrian translator" (Luzzatto, *Introduction to the Pentateuch*, p. xxv).

**Ancona, Shabbetai** (Sabato). Student of Shadal, born in Venice, 1833; attended the Collegio Rabbinico 1854-1858. A newspaper article in 1899 reported that Professor Sabato Ancona was serving as rector of a community religious school in Venice.

**Apuleius, Lucius** (c. 123-c. 170 C.E.). Poet, philosopher, and rhetorician from North Africa. His *Apologia (De Magia)* was a defense speech in response to a charge of using magic to persuade his wife to marry him.

**Aquila** (second century C.E.). Jewish proselyte who translated the Bible into Greek, reputed to have been a native of Pontus, a relative of the Emperor Hadrian, and a student of R. Akiva. His translation, probably written in Palestine, was strictly literal.

# Shadal on Exodus

**Arama, Isaac** (1420-1494). Spanish Talmudist and exegete; author of philosophic Torah commentary *Akedat Yitshak*.

**Aristotle** (384-322 B.C.E.). Renowned Greek philosopher, student of Plato and tutor of Alexander the Great.

**Ashkenazi, David Hai** (David Vita Tedesco, 1820-1849). Student of Shadal, born in Venice; ordained in 1845. Wrote a translation of the prayers for five fast days (Leghorn, 1845).

**Ashkenazi, Hezekiah Matsliah** (Cesare Tedeschi). Student of Shadal, from Ferrara; admitted to the Collegio in 1862.

**Bahya ben Asher** (Rabbenu Bahya, thirteenth century). Bible commentator and kabbalist in Spain; his commentary was written in 1291 and first printed in Naples, 1492.

**Bar Bahlul, Hassan** (10th cent. C.E.). Scholar of the Assyrian Church of the East, in Baghdad; author of a Syriac lexicon.

**Basevi, Joseph Shabbetai** (Giuseppe Sabato, 1823-1884). Student of Shadal, born in Padua; ordained in 1847. Served as rabbi in Sabbioneta, Spalato, and Padua.

**Beccaria, Cesare** (Cesare Bonesana, Marchese Beccaria, 1738-1794). Italian philosopher and politician. His treatise *On Crimes and Punishments* (1764) was a founding work in the field of penology.

**Bekhor Shor, Joseph ben Isaac** (twelfth century). Exegete, Tosafist, and poet in northern France, pupil of Rabbenu Tam (see below). His Torah commentary was not published in its entirety until 1956-1960.

**Bertinoro, Ovadiah ben Abraham** (c. 1450-before 1516). Rabbi from northern Italy, author of the standard commentary on the Mishnah; spiritual leader of the Jerusalem Jewish community from 1488.

**Bochart, Samuel** (1599-1667). French Huguenot Bible scholar.

**Burckhardt, Johann Ludwig** (1784-1817). Swiss orientalist who explored Syria, Palestine, and the Sinai peninsula.

**Buxtorf, Johannes** (1564-1629). Swiss Hebraist; author of Hebrew and Aramaic vocabularies and lexicons, including *Lexicon Chaldaicum Talmudicum* (1640), completed by his son, Johannes II.

# Sources

**Cahen, Samuel** (1796-1862). French Jewish Hebraist and journalist, founder of *Archives Israélites*. Translated Bible into French, with critical notes and dissertations by himself and others (18 vols., Paris 1851).

**Caro, Isaac ben Joseph** (fl. 1492). Rabbi in Toledo and Constantinople; uncle of R. Joseph Caro, the author of the *Shulḥan Arukh*. Wrote the Torah commentary *Toledot Yitsḥak* (Constantinople, 1518).

**Celsus, Aulus Cornelius** (1st century C.E.). Roman medical writer.

**Chandler, Richard** (1738-1810). English antiquary and traveler. *Travels in Asia Minor* (1775).

**Clement of Alexandria** (150-?220 C.E.). Church Father whose writings were influenced by Philo. His *Stromata* is the third in a trilogy of works on Christian life.

**Clericus, Johannes** (Jean-Thomas Le Clerc, 1657-1736). French Huguenot encyclopedist and Bible scholar; commentary on Pentateuch, 1699.

**Coccejus (Koch), Johannes** (1603-1669). Dutch Calvinist Hebrew scholar.

**Cohen Porto, Moses** (Moisè Coen Porto, 1834-1918). Student of Shadal, born in Venice; ordained in 1859. Rabbi of Venice, 1876-1918.

**Crescas, Hasdai** (14th century, d. 1412?). Philosopher, theologian, and statesman in Spain. Author of *Or Adonai* (first ed. 1555), a philosophical work directed against the Jewish Aristotelianism of Maimonides.

**Curtius** (Quintus Curtius Rufus). Roman historian; wrote biography of Alexander the Great.

**De Dieu, Ludovico** (Louis, 1590-1642). Dutch Calvinist Hebraist.

**De Lira, Nicolaus** (Nicholas de Lyre, c. 1270-c. 1349). French theologian; his Bible commentary, written 1322-1330 and influenced by Rashi, was the first Christian commentary to be printed (Rome, 1471-1472).

**Della Valle, Pietro** (1586-1652). Italian traveler who, en route to Jerusalem in December 1615, climbed the two peaks traditionally identified as Horeb and Sinai.

**De' Rossi, Azariah** (Azariah min Ha-Adumim, Bonaiuto de' Rossi, c. 1511-c.1578). Renaissance Hebrew scholar in Italy, born in Mantua. Author of

# Shadal on Exodus

*Me'or Einayim* ("Light of the Eyes") (Mantua, 1573-1575), a revolutionary study of the development of the Bible and of Jewish history, chronology, poetry, and culture, drawing on a wide variety of Jewish and non-Jewish sources.

**De Wette, Wilhelm Martin Leberecht** (1780-1849). Rationalistic German Protestant theologian and exegete.

**Deyling (Dailing), Salomon** (1665 or 1677-1755). German Lutheran Hebraist.

**Diodati, Giovanni** (1576-1649). Swiss Calvinist theologian, author of Italian Bible translation (1607).

**Diodorus Siculus** (Diodorus of Sicily, first century C.E.). Greek author of a forty-book world history, containing some references to the Jews.

**Dioscorides Pedanius** (mid-first century C.E.). Greek pharmacologist of Anazarba, Cilicia.

**Dubno, Solomon** (*Maharshad*, 1738-1813). Author of the Genesis portion (except for ch. 1) of the commentary, or *Biur*, to Mendelssohn's *Netivot ha-Shalom* (see below). Also wrote *Tikkun Soferim* (Amsterdam, 1803), a commentary on the Masorah of the Pentateuch.

**Efodi** (Profiat Duran, Isaac ben Moses Ha-Levi, d. c. 1414). Anti-Christian polemicist in Spain, born in Perpignan, France; was forcibly converted to Christianity in 1391 but subsequently reverted to Judaism. His highly regarded grammar, *Ma'aseh Efod*, was first printed in Vienna, 1865.

**Ehrenberg, Christian Gottfried** (1795-1876). German naturalist; participated in scientific expedition to Middle East (1820-1825), including Sinai desert and northern coast of the Red Sea.

**Ehrenreich, Moses Ha-Levi** (1819-1899). Student of Shadal, son-in-law of Isaac Samuel Reggio (see below); born in Brody, Galicia; ordained in 1845. Rabbi in Modena, Casale, Padua, Trieste, and Turin; Chief Rabbi of Rome from 1890. Directed the Collegio Rabbinico Italiano when it was reconstituted in Rome, through his efforts, in 1887.

**Eichhorn, Johann Gottfried** (1752-1827). German historian and early Bible critic. *De Aegypti anno mirabili.*

**Euripides** (c. 480-406? B.C.E.). Greek dramatist.

# Sources

**Eusebius** (260-339 C.E.). Church Father, archbishop of Caesarea; his *Onomasticon* (c. 324) indentifies places mentioned in the Bible.

**Faber, Johann Ernst** (1746-1774). Professor at Kiel; his *Archäologie der Hebräer* was published in Halle, 1773.

**Foà, Hezekiah** (Cesare, 1833-1907). Student of Shadal, born in Sabbioneta; ordained in 1857. Rabbi in Sabbioneta and Soragna.

**Forskal, Peter** (Pehr Forskål or Forsskål) (1732-1763). Swedish physician and botanist, disciple of Linnaeus (see below). Died in Yemen, probably of malaria, during Danish-sponsored scientific expedition to Arabia. Was first to describe plant and animal life of Red Sea. Carsten Niebuhr (see below) published two of his works in 1775: *Flora Aegyptiaco Arabica* and *Descriptiones animalium, avium, amphibiorum, piscium, insectorum, vermium, quae in itinere orientali observavit Petrus Forskål*.

**Forster, Johann** (1496-1558). Swiss Lutheran Hebraist.

**Fullerus (Fuller), Nicholas** (1557(?)-1626). Anglican Hebraist.

**Gersonides** (*Ralbag*, R. Levi ben Gershom, 1288-1344). Bible commentator, mathematician, astronomer, and philosopher in France. His Torah commentary, written in 1329-1338, was one of the first Hebrew books to be printed (Ferrara, 1477).

**Gesenius, Heinrich Friedrich Wilhelm** (1786-1842). German Orientalist, lexicographer, and biblical scholar; professor of theology at University of Halle. Among his works are *Hebräisches und chaldäisches Handwörterbuch über das Alte Testament* (Leipzig, 1815), a later edition of which was translated as *A Hebrew and English Lexicon of the Old Testament*, ed. Brown, Driver, and Briggs (1907), and an Isaiah translation and commentary (Leipzig, 1820-1821, 1829).

**Gussetius (Gusset, Gousset), Jacques** (1635-1704). Protestant Hebraist of France and Holland.

**Hananel ben Hushiel** (Rabbenu Hananel) (d. 1055/56). Talmudic commentator and *posek* of Kairouan, North Africa.

**Hasselqulst, Fredrik** (1722-1752). Swedish botanist, student of Linnaeus (see below). Died during voyage to Egypt and Palestine to document biblical plants and animals. Author of *Iter Palaestinum* (Stockholm, 1757).

# Shadal on Exodus

**Hazak (Forti), David** (1832-1874). Student of Shadal, born in Verona; ordained in 1859. Rabbi in Pitigliano, Lugo, and Verona.

**Hefez (Gentili), Moses ben Gershom** (1663-1711). Author of *Melekhet Maḥashevet* (Venice, 1710), a philosophical-homiletical Torah commentary.

**Heidenheim, Wolf** (1757-1832). Hebrew scholar and exegete, born in Heidenheim, Germany. Published several editions of the Pentateuch, one of which was *Moda la-Binah*, including his supercommentary to Rashi, *Havanat ha-Mikra* (Roedelheim, 1818).

**Herder, Johann Gottfried** (1744-1803). German Protestant theologian; author of *Vom Geist der ebräischen Poesie* ("The Spirit of Hebrew Poetry," 1782-1783).

**Herodotus** (fifth century B.C.E.). Greek historian.

**Ibn Ezra, Abraham** (1089-1164). Classic Torah commentator, poet, grammarian, and philosopher, born in Tudela, Spain. Although Shadal often expresses criticism of Ibn Ezra's attitude and writing style, he frequently cites and often adopts Ibn Ezra's views in his Torah commentary.

**Ibn Janah, Jonah** (eleventh century C.E.). Influential Hebrew grammarian and lexicographer in Spain. His last work, translated from Arabic to Hebrew as *Sefer ha-Dikduk*, is the first complete book of Hebrew philology to be preserved in its entirety.

**Ibn Shem Tov, Shem Tov ben Joseph** (15th century). Spanish philosopher; author of commentary on Maimonides' *Guide for the Perplexed*.

**Igel, Eliezer Elijah** (Lazar Elias, 1825-1892). Student of Shadal, born in Lemberg (Lvov); ordained in 1847. In a letter to R. Samson Raphael Hirsch in Nikolsburg, dated August 8, 1849, Shadal said that Igel was seeking to serve the Jewish community of Teschen, Moravia, and he recommended him in the warmest terms (*Iggerot Shadal*, vol. 2, pp. 1063-1064). Although Igel apparently never went to Teschen, he became district rabbi of Czernowitz in 1854 and later chief rabbi of Bukovina, in which positions he succeeded in maintaining peace between the local Orthodox and Reform factions.

**Jablonski, Paul Ernst** (18th century). German Hebraist and Egyptologist; wrote *Opuscula quibus lingua et antiquitas Aegyptiorum* (1804-1813).

**Jacob ben Asher** (*Ba'al ha-Turim*, 1270?-1340). Torah commentator and author of classic halakhic work, *Arba'ah Turim*.

# Sources

**Jahn, Johann** (1750-1816). Austrian Hebraist.

**Jarè, Joseph** (Giuseppe, 1840-1915). Student of Shadal, born in Mantua; member of an old family that may have included R. Ovadiah Bertinoro (see above). Ordained in 1868; served as rabbi in Mantua and then in Ferrara from 1881 to 1915; published studies on Italian Jewish history.

**Jerome, St.** (Eusebius Sophronius Hieronymus, 342 C.E.-420 C.E.). Church Father, originally from Dalmatia; while living in Bethlehem, he learned Hebrew from Jewish teachers. Author of Latin translation of Bible (Vulgate), which became the official version of the Catholic Church, although he at first met with criticism for basing the "Old Testament" portion on the original Hebrew.

**Joseph of Orleans.** Tosafist who has been identified with Joseph ben Isaac Bekhor Shor (see above).

**Josephus Flavius** (c. 38 C.E.-c. 100 C.E.). Jerusalem-born historian in Rome; played a controversial part in the Jewish War of 66-70 C.E. Among his works is *Jewish Antiquities*, a history of the Jews from Bible times written in a Hellenistic style.

**Jost, Isaac Marcus** (1793-1860). Jewish educator and historian in Germany. Author of several multivolume, pioneering works of Jewish history, written from a political and social rather than religious viewpoint. *Allgemeine Geschichte des Israëlitischen Volkes* (1832). Corresponded with Shadal, who nevertheless criticized Jost's assimilationist tendencies.

**Judah ben Kuraish** (Ibn Quraysh) (second half of 9th century C.E.). Hebrew grammarian and lexicographer, regarded as one of the founders of comparative Semitic linguistics.

**Judah ha-Levi** (before 1075-1141). Hebrew poet and philosopher in Spain; author of the *Kuzari*, a defense of Judaism, translated from Arabic to Hebrew in the middle of the twelfth century and first printed in Fano, 1506. One of the authorities most admired by Shadal.

**Justi, Karl Wilhelm** (1767-1846). Professor of theology, University of Marburg; author of commentaries on Joel and Job.

**Juvenal** (Decimus Junius Juvenalis, 55-127 C.E.). Roman satirist.

**Kimhi, David** (*Radak*, c. 1160-c. 1236). Classic biblical commentator and grammarian, born and flourished in Narbonne, Provence. His book

## Shadal on Exodus

*Mikhlol* was a philological treatise consisting of a grammatical portion (Constantinople, 1532) and the *Sefer ha-Shorashim*, discussing Hebrew roots (before 1480).

**Klineberger, Isaac Judah.** Student of Shadal, ordained in 1863.

**Koppe, Johann Benjamin** (1750-1791). German biblical and classical scholar.

**Landau, Moses** (1788-1852). Head of the Prague Jewish community, grandson of R. Ezekiel Landau. Wrote a German translation and Hebrew commentary on several books of the Bible (1834-38).

**Levita (Bahur), Elijah** (c. 1458-1549). Hebrew philologist, grammarian, and lexicographer in Italy, born in Neustadt, Germany. Author of *Masoret ha-Masoret* (Venice, 1538) on Hebrew vocalization and accentuation. His *Tishbi* (1540-1541) was a lexicon of talmudic and medieval Hebrew.

**Linnaeus, Carolus** (Carl von Linné, 1707-1778). Swedish botanist who established the binomial system of scientific nomenclature.

**Lucan** (Marcus Annaeus Lucanus, 39-65 C.E.). Roman poet, born in Spain; author of *Pharsalia*.

**Ludolf, Hiob** (1624-1704). German scholar of Ethiopian history and culture. *Historia Aethiopica (New History of Ethiopia)*, 1682.

**Luzzatto, Hezekiah** (1761-1824). Shadal's father and teacher.

**Luzzatto, Judah** (Leon, 1841-1918). Student of Shadal, born in Venice; ordained in 1868. Served as Vice-Rabbi of Venice.

**Luzzatto, Ohev Ger** (Filosseno, 1829-1854). Shadal's firstborn, an Orientalist who wrote works on topics including Ethiopian (Falasha) Jews and Hebrew inscriptions. His death from cancer at the age of 24 was the crowning tragedy of his father's life.

**Lydius, Jacob** (1610-1679). Dutch clergyman and exegete.

**Maimonides, Moses** (*Rambam*, R. Moses ben Maimon, 1135-1204). Renowned halakhic authority, philosopher, and physician, born in Córdoba, Spain. Criticized by Shadal for adopting the world-view of Aristotelian philosophy, which valued the mind over the heart.

**Mainster, Abraham Hai** (1816-1882). Student of Shadal, born in Verona; ordained in 1841. Rabbi of Viadana, Rovigo, and Verona.

# Sources

**Meir, Wolf.** Author of Torah commentary *Ha-Me'ammer* (Prague, 1833-1837).

**Mendelssohn, Moses** *(Rambeman*, R. Moses ben Menahem, or Moses of Dessau, 1729-1786). German Jewish philosopher and Bible translator; his *Netivot ha-Shalom* (1780-1783), a German translation of the Torah printed in Hebrew characters, was accompanied by the *Biur*, a Hebrew commentary written in collaboration with Solomon Dubno (see above), Naphtali Herz Wessely (see below), Naphtali Herz Homberg (see below at *Korem*), and Aaron Jaroslaw.

**Michaelis, Johann David** (1717-1791). German Bible scholar, professor of Oriental languages in Goettingen. Translated Bible with notes (1769-1783).

**Mizrahi, Elijah** (*Re'em*, c. 1450-1526). Leading halakhic authority of Ottoman Empire, born in Constantinople. Wrote supercommentary to Rashi (Venice, 1527).

**Modena, Shalom Simeon** (Pacifico, 1830-1910). Student of Shadal, born in Modena. Director of the Talmud Torah of Alexandria, Egypt, 1884-1892.

**Mortara, Mordecai** (Marco, 1815-1894). Student of Shadal, born in Viadana; ordained in 1836. Rabbi of Mantua (1842-1894) and noted bibliographer.

**Nachmanides** *(Ramban*, R. Moses ben Nahman, 1194-1270). Classic Torah commentator, halakhic authority, and philosopher, born in Gerona, Spain.

**Nachtigal, Johann Konrad Christoph** (1753-1819). German Orientalist and Bible scholar.

**Niebuhr, Carsten** (1733-1815). German Orientalist. Surveyor-astronomer and lone survivor of a scholarly expedition to Syria, Palestine, Arabia, and Persia (1761-1767) initiated by Johann David Michaelis (see above) and financed by King Frederick of Denmark. Recorded data from the expedition in *Voyage en Arabie* (1774).

**Nissim ben Jacob ben Nissim ibn Shahin** (c. 990-1062). Talmudist and communal leader in North Africa, head of an academy in Kairouan. Author of *Megillat Setarim* (compiled by 1051), on a wide range of topics including *halakhah* and *aggadah*.

**Nissim ben Reuben Gerondi.** See *Ran*, below.

# Shadal on Exodus

**Olper, Samuel Solomon** (1811-1876). Student of Shadal, born in Rovigo; ordained in 1838. One of the few Italian rabbis to advocate Reform. Rabbi of Venice, 1838-1848; member of the revolutionary Assembly of Venice in 1848. Later served as rabbi in Florence, Casale, and Turin.

**Onkelos** (second century C.E.). Proselyte who translated the Pentateuch into Aramaic, reportedly under the guidance of R. Eliezer ben Hyrcanus and R. Joshua ben Hananiah. Some scholars maintain that the name is a corruption of Aquila (see above). His translation (Targum) is the subject of Shadal's *Ohev Ger*.

**Osimo, Judah Aryeh** (Leone, 1815-1869). Student of Shadal, born in Montagnana; ordained in 1841. Rabbi of Padua, 1867-1869.

**Ovid** (Publius Ovidius Naso, 43 B.C.E.-?17 C.E.). Roman poet.

**Pagninus, Xanthus** (Santes Pagnini, 1470-1536). Italian Hebraist whose Latin translation of the Hebrew Bible (Lyons, 1528) was the first since Jerome's to be based directly on the original text. His division of the text by chapter and verse has been retained to this day.

**Pappenheim, Solomon** (1740-1814). Hebrew linguist and poet in Germany; his three-part *Yeri'ot Shelomoh* (1784, 1811, 1831) was a study of synonyms.

**Pardo, Isaac** (1824-1892). Student of Shadal, born in Leghorn; ordained in 1847. Chief Rabbi of Verona.

**Pardo, Jacob Hai (Vita)** (1818-1839). Student of Shadal, brother of Isaac Pardo (see above); born in Ragusa (Dubrovnik). Wrote commentary on part of Micah at age 18, published by Shadal as a first supplement to his *Avnei Zikkaron* (Prague, 1841).

**Parhon, Salomon ben Abraham ibn** (twelfth century). Lexicographer in Spain and Italy, a student of Ibn Ezra and Judah ha-Levi. Wrote *Maḥberet he-Arukh* (Salerno, 1160), a popular biblical lexicon in Hebrew, incorporating elements of Ibn Janah's works.

**Paulus Jurisonsultus** (Julius Paulus, fl. c. 200 C.E.). Roman jurist.

**Petahiah of Regensburg** (12th century). Traveler in Erets Israel via Poland, Crimea, Armenia, and Babylonia. The account of his journeys (*Sibbuv* or "circuit"), written by others in third person, was first published in Prague, 1595, and was printed with an English translation by Abraham Benisch in 1856.

# Sources

**Philo Judaeus** (c. 20 B.C.E.-c. 50 C.E.). Alexandrian Jewish theologian and Hellenistic philosopher.

**Pitts, Joseph** (1663-1735?). English sailor who was captured by Algerian pirates and spent 15 years in captivity in the Middle East. After escaping, he wrote *A True and Faithful Account of the Religion and Manners of the Mohammetans* (1704), including a description of his visit to Mecca.

**Pliny** (the Elder, Gaius Plinius Secundus, 23-79 C.E.). Roman naturalist, author of *Natural History*.

**Plutarch** (c. 46-c. 120 C.E.). Greek biographer and moralist.

**Ra'avad** (R. Abraham ben David, c. 1125-1198). Talmudic authority in Provence; wrote critical notes on Maimonides' *Mishneh Torah*.

**Ran** (Rabbenu Nissim ben Reuben Gerondi, ?1310-?1375). Talmudist and halakhist in Spain. Among his main works is a commentary on the *Halakhot* of R. Isaac Alfasi to the Talmud.

**Rashbam** (R. Samuel ben Meir, 1080-1158). Classic Torah commentator and Tosafist, grandson of Rashi (see below). His commentary, to a greater extent that Rashi's, strictly adhered to the *peshat*, or plain meaning of the text.

**Rashi** (R. Solomon Yitshaki, 1040-1105). The preeminent classic Torah commentator, born in Troyes, France.

**Ravius (Rau), Christian** (1613-1677). Hebraist in Germany, England, and Sweden.

**Reggio, Isaac Samuel** (1784-1855). Italian rabbi of Gorizia; played a key role in formation and organization of the Istituto Convitto Rabbinico (Collegio Rabbinico) of Padua and helped to secure Shadal's professorship there. Wrote Torah commentary with Italian translation, *Torat Elohim* (Vienna, 1821).

**Ri** (R. Isaac ben Samuel, d. c. 1185). Leading Tosafist, of Dampierre, France; nephew and student of Rabbenu Tam (see below).

**Rosenmueller, Ernst Friedrich Karl** (1768-1835). German Orientalist, theologian, and exegete; included exegetical notes by Shadal, in French, on Isaiah as an introduction to his own Isaiah commentary (Leipzig, 1835). Rosenmueller's *Scholia in Pentateuchum* (Leipzig, 1828), was relied upon heavily by Shadal as a source of information and commentary.

# Shadal on Exodus

**Saadiah Gaon** (882-942). Leader of Babylonian Jewry, Talmudist, philosopher, and grammarian, born in Egypt; wrote commentary on and Arabic translation of Bible.

**Saphir, Jacob** (1822-1885). Jerusalem-based writer and traveler.

**Schultens, Albertus** (Albrecht, 1686-1756). Durch Orientalist and Hebraist at University of Leiden, pupil of Relandus (Hadrian Reland). Pioneer in the use of Arabic to illuminate Hebrew texts and vocabulary.

**Seneca, Lucius Annaeus** (c. 4 B.C.E.-65 C.E.). Roman philosopher.

**Servius** (Maurus Servius Honorius). Roman grammarian and commentator on Virgil, fl. late 4th century C.E.

**Sforno, Ovadiah** (c. 1475-c. 1550). Classic Torah commentator, Talmudist, and physician, born in Cesena, Italy.

**Shaw, Thomas** (1694-1751). English traveler in the Middle East; visited Egypt and Sinai (1721), Jerusalem, the Jordan, and Mt. Carmel (1722). Wrote *Travels or Observations relating to several parts of Barbary and the Levant* (Oxford, 1738).

**Simon, Richard** (1638-1712). French Hebraist.

**Symmachus** (after second century C.E.). Author of a non-literal Greek Bible translation; probably of Jewish origin or training, but said to have been either a Samaritan converted to Judaism or a Christian.

**Tacitus, Gaius Cornelius** (56?-117 C.E.). Roman writer, orator, and historian.

**Tam, Jacob ben Meir** (Rabbenu Tam, c. 1100-1171). Leading French Jewish scholar of the twelfth century, grandson of Rashi (see above) and brother of Rashbam (see above).

**Tanhum ben Joseph Ha-Yerushalmi** (c. 1220-1291). Philologist and rationalist exegete, known as the "Ibn Ezra of the East." Wrote biblical commentary, *Kitab al-Bayan*.

**Theocritus** (c. 310 B.C.E.-c. 245 B.C.E.). Greek poet, the creator of pastoral poetry (idylls).

**Theodotion** (second century C.E.). Diaspora Jew who revised the Septuagint, bringing it nearer to the standard Hebrew text.

# Sources

**Thévenot, Jean de** (1633-1667). Traveler in the Middle East and India.

**Toland, John** (1670-1722). Irish-born Deist in England; advocated naturalizing foreign-born Jews to attract them to England. His *Tetradymus* (1720) was a collection of essays in which, among other things, he interpreted various Old Testament miracles in a naturalistic manner.

**Vater, Johann Severin** (1771-1826). German exegete; wrote commentary on the Pentateuch (1802-1803).

**Viterbi, David Hananiah** (David Graziadio, 1815-1880). Student of Shadal, born in Mantua; ordained in 1839. Vice-Rabbi of Padua, 1842-1852, then Chief Rabbi till 1867. An early advocate (1842) of a *bat mitsvah* ceremony.

**Wessely, Naphtali Herz** (1725-1805). Poet, linguist, and exegete, born in Hamburg. Among his works are *Gan Na'ul*, a work on Hebrew synonyms and roots (Amsterdam, 1765-66); *Ruaḥ Ḥen*, a commentary on the Wisdom of Solomon (Berlin, 1780); *Shirei Tif'eret*, an epic poem on the life of Moses and the Exodus (1789-1802); and the commentary to Leviticus (edited by Mendelssohn) in the *Biur* (Berlin, 1782).

**Wolfsheimer (Wolffsheimer), Salomon Bernard.** Author of a medical dissertation on the fertility of the Hebrews, University of Halle, 1742.

**Yefet ben Ali ha-Levi** (second half of tenth century). Karaite scholar in Jerusalem; wrote biblical commentaries in Arabic, referred to by Ibn Ezra (see above).

**Zammatto, Elisha Hayyim** (Alessandro, 1844-1916). Student of Shadal, born in Padua; ordained in 1868. Rabbi of Padua, 1904-1916.

**Zunz, Leopold** (1794-1886). Founder of *Wissenschaft des Judentums* ("Science of Judaism"), the critical investigation of Jewish literature and ritual. *Die Gottesdienstlichen Vorträge der Juden, historisch entwickelt* (Berlin, 1832), a history of the Jewish sermon, establishes principles for the investigation of the Midrash and the *siddur*.

# Shadal on Exodus

## *Works Cited by Title Only*

***Anaf Ets Avot.*** Hebrew grammatical work by Reuben Grishaber (Fuerth, 1744).

***Arukh.*** Talmudic lexicon (completed in 1101, apparently first published in 1469-1472) by R. Nathan ben Yehiel of Rome (1035-c. 1110).

***Beḥinat ha-Dat.*** Book by R. Elijah Delmedigo (c. 1460-1497) on the relation between religion and philosophy (1497, first printed 1629, reprinted with Reggio's commentary, Vienna 1833).

***Ben Gorni.*** Collection of essays published (Amsterdam, 1851) by Gabriel Isaac Polak (1803-1869), Dutch Jewish educator.

***Bikkurei ha-Ittim.*** Literary-scientific periodical published in Vienna (12 volumes, 1821-1832, later volumes 1844 and 1845).

***Da'at Zekenim.*** Compendium of Torah commentary originating with the Tosafists of the 13th century, first printed in 1783 at Livorno.

***Der Orient.*** Weekly magazine (1840-1852) founded and edited by the Hebraist Julius Fuerst (1805-1873), with a scientific supplement, *Literaturblatt des Orients*.

***Encyclopédie.*** Full title, *L' Encyclopédie ou Dictionnaire raisonné des sciences, des arts et des métiers,* ed. Denis Diderot and Jean le Rond d'Alembert (1751-1772). Represented the thought of the Enlightenment; the editors' objective was to gather all the knowledge in the world.

***Halakhot Gedolot.*** A comprehensive code of all talmudic laws, compiled by an unknown author (identified by some as Simeon Kayyara) in the Geonic period.

***Ḥavvot Ya'ir.*** Monumental collection of responsa (Frankfurt, 1694) by R. Yair Hayyim Bacharach (1638-1702).

***Ḥizkuni (Ḥizzekuni, Ḥazzekuni).*** Torah commentary (mid-thirteenth century, first printed in Venice, 1524) by Hezekiah ben Manoah, of the school of Rashi.

***Ikkarim.*** Philosophical work on the principles of the Jewish faith, by R. Joseph Albo, completed in Soria, Castile in 1425.

# Sources

***Jerusalem Targum.*** Translation of the Pentateuch in Galilean Jewish Aramaic, written no later than the seventh or eighth century C.E., with a free aggadic handling of the text. Its mistaken ascription to Jonathan ben Uzziel, a pupil of Hillel, is believed to have originated with Menahem Recanati, a fourteenth-century commentator.

***Korem.*** Commentary on the Torah by Naphtali Herz Homberg (1749-1841), an extreme exponent of Haskalah; printed after *Ha-Mishtadel* and *Botser Olelot* in the 1846 edition of *Netivot ha-Shalom*.

***Ma'asei (Ma'aseh) Adonai.*** Rationalistic commentary on the Torah (first printed in Venice, 1583) by R. Eliezer ben Elijah Ashkenazi (1513-1586), rabbi and physician in Egypt, Italy, Poland, and other locations.

***Maggid Mishneh.*** Commentary on Maimonides' *Mishneh Torah* by Vidal of Tolosa, fourteenth-century Spanish scholar.

***Maḥzor Vitry.*** Halakhic-liturgical composition by Simhah ben Samuel of Vitry, France (d. 1105), a pupil of Rashi; contains responsa by Rashi and other authorities.

***Me'ammer.*** See Wolf Meir (above).

***Melitsat Yeshurun.*** A pioneering book on Hebrew poetics (1816) by Solomon Lewisohn (1789-1821).

***Netivot ha-Shalom.*** See Moses Mendelssohn (above).

***Otsar ha-Shorashim.*** Hebrew-German, German-Hebrew dictionary (Vienna, 1807-1808) by Judah Leib Ben Ze'ev (1764-1811).

***Pe'er ha-Dor.*** Compilation of responsa by Maimonides, translated from Arabic to Hebrew by Mordecai Tammah, published in Amsterdam, 1765.

***Sefer ha-Ḥasidim.*** Book of ethical teachings of the Ḥasidei Ashkenaz of medieval Germany, traditionally ascribed to R. Judah he-Ḥasid of Regensburg (d. 1217); printed in Bologna, 1538.

***Sefer ha-Zikkaron.*** Supercommentary to Rashi on the Torah (completed in Tunis, 1507; published in Leghorn, 1845, under the editorship of S.D. Luzzatto) by Abraham ben Solomon ha-Levi Bukarat (late fifteenth-early sixteenth century), exegete and poet in Malaga and Tunis.

# Shadal on Exodus

***Sefer Mitsvot ha-Gadol.*** Compilation of the positive and negative precepts, by Moses of Coucy (France, 13<sup>th</sup> century), first published some time before 1480.

***Shiltei ha-Gibborim.*** A detailed description of the Temple and its service (Mantua, 1612), by Abraham Portaleone (1542-1612), physician to the ducal house of Mantua.

***Siftei Ḥakhamim.*** Supercommentary on Rashi (1680) by Shabbetai Bass of Prague (1641-1718), publisher and bibliographer.

***Toledot Rambeman.*** A biography of Moses Mendelssohn, by Isaac Euchel (1758-1804), Vienna edition 1814.

***Zeitschrift für die Wissenschaft des Judentums.*** Periodical (1822-23) edited by Leopold Zunz. The first issue contained a lecture by Immanuel Wolf on Spinoza and the universal mission of the Jewish people.

## Early Manuscripts and Printed Works (Untitled)

***The Ya'er manuscript.*** Identified by Shadal, in most instances, only with the Hebrew letters *yod alef resh*. A manuscript of a commentary on Onkelos, discovered by Shadal in his youth in the genizah of the Trieste Talmud Torah, and purchased by him 33 years later, when it became the basis for his book *Ohev Ger* (see Margolies, Luzzatto, pp. 26-27). According to Meir Heilprin *(Ha-Notarikon ha-Simanim ve-ha-Kinnuyim*, Jerusalem: Darom, 5690 [1930]), the manuscript was so called by Shadal because the book as he found it had no title or author's name, but only the date *resh yod alef* (5211, or 1451). Apparently, Shadal rearranged the letters of the date in order to create his own nickname for the book, *Ya'er* or *Ya'or* ("it will shed light"). In his comment to Gen. 24:65, Shadal refers to the book by the alternate name *Sefer Patshegen*, which apparently was the real title; the book was published as *Patshegen* in Vilna, 1930.

***5171 Ḥumash.*** Identified by Shadal only with the Hebrew letters *kof ayin alef*, indicating the year 5171 (1411). Elsewhere *(Kerem Ḥemed* 4 [1839], pp. 178, 179), Shadal says that it had been in his possession since 1835, and he describes it as a manuscript on parchment containing the Pentateuch with Masorah and Targum, *haftarot, megillot,* and Job, signed by the scribe Isaac ben Simḥah. Referred to as "Codex 1411" by Isaac Hayyim Castiglioni in his introduction to Shadal's *Ohev Ger* (2nd ed., 1895), this manuscript has been identified as item 14 in the Loewe catalogue of Trinity College, Cambridge

# Sources

(F. 18.22-24), which tracks Shadal's description and notes that the work is in three volumes and in a German hand. C.D. Ginsburg *(Introduction to the Massoretico-Critical Edition of the Hebrew Bible*, pp. 753-759, under the heading "No. 55./ G. 4.") gives a more detailed description. The scribal date, given only as "Thursday, 16 Av," has been the subject of considerable conjecture. Shadal himself arrived at the year 5171 by calculating back from the owner's written date, "Tuesday, 3 Marheshvan 5174," but noted that the manuscript could have been much older. The Loewe catalogue gives the date as "c. 1400"; Ginsburg has 1400-1410.Malachi Bet-Arie dates the manuscript to 1230-1251.

## *Shadal's Own Works*

*Grammatica della lingua ebraica.* Hebrew grammar; Padua, 1853-1869.

*Il libro di Giobbe.* Translation of the Book of Job; Trieste, 1853.

*Ohev Ger.* A study of the methodology of Onkelos the proselye (*ger*) in his translation of the Torah; Vienna, 1830.

*Prolegomeni ad una grammatical ragionata della lingua ebraica.* An introduction to Hebrew grammar; Padua, 1836.

*Sefer Yeshayah Meturgam Italkit u-Meforash Ivrit.* Translation of and commentary on the Book of Isaiah; Padua, 1855-1867.

## Translator-Editor's References

Abrahams, Israel. "Samuel David Luzzatto as Exegete," *Jewish Quarterly Review* 57 (1966).

Adkins, Lesley, and Adkins, Roy. *The Keys of Egypt: The Obsession to Decipher Egyptian Hieroglyphs.* New York: HarperCollins, 2000.

Apuleius. *The Apologia and Florida of Apuleius of Madura,* trans. H.E. Butler. Oxford: Clarendon Press, 1909.

Aristotle. *The History of Animals* (350 B.C.E.), trans. D'Arcy Wentworth Thompson. Oxford: Clarendon Press, 1910.

Balsam, Yacov. "Who Was Re'uel? Finding a New Solution to an Age-Old Puzzle." *Ḥakirah,* vol. 8, pp. 157-179 (2009).

Beccaria, Cesare. *On Crimes and Punishments,* trans. Edward D. Ingraham, 2nd American ed. Philadelphia: Philip H. Micklin, 1819.

Benisch, Abraham, ed. and trans. *Travels of Rabbi Petachia of Ratisbon.* London, 1856.

Berger, Michael S. *Rabbinic Authority*. New York: Oxford University Press, 1998.

Blunt, Wilfred. *Pietro's Pilgrimage*. London: James Barrie, 1953.

Bochart, Samuel. *Geographia sacra, seu Phaleg et Canaan*. Caen, 1646.

Bonfil, Robert; Gottlieb, Isaac; and Kasher, Hannah; eds. *Samuel David Luzzatto: The Bi-Centennial of His Birth*. Jerusalem: Hebrew University Magnes Press, 2004.

Braun, Johann. *Bigde kohanim, i.e., Vestitus Sacerdotum hebraeorum*. Leiden, 1680.

Calimani, Riccardo. *The Ghetto of Venice*, trans. Katherine Silberblatt Wolfthal. New York: M. Evans and Company, Inc., 1987.

Cassuto, Umberto. *A Commentary on the Book of Exodus*, trans. Israel Abrahams. Jerusalem: Hebrew University Magnes Press, 1983.

Chambers, Ephraim, ed. *Cyclopaedia, or, An Universal Dictionary of Arts and Sciences*. London, 1728.

Chamiel, Ephraim. *Life in Two Worlds—The "Middle-Way" Religious Responses to Modernity in the Philosophy of Z.H. Chajes, S.R. Hirsch and S.D. Luzzatto* (Hebrew). Ph.D. dissertation, Hebrew University, 2006.

Chavel, Hayyim Dov (Charles), ed. *Perushei Rashi al ha-Torah*, 3rd ed. Jerusalem: Mosad ha-Rav Kook, 5743 (1983).

Chomsky, William. *Hebrew: The Eternal Language*. Philadelphia: Jewish Publication Society of America, 1964.

Clark, Matityahu. *Etymological Dictionary of Biblical Hebrew*. Jerusalem and New York: Feldheim, 1999.

David, Rosalie. *Handbook to Life in Ancient Egypt*. New York: Oxford University Press, 1999.

De'Rossi, Azariah. *The Light of the Eyes*, trans. Joanna Weinberg. New Haven and London: Yale University Press, 2001.

Deutscher, Guy. *The Unfolding of Language*. New York: Henry Holt and Co., 2006.

Elijah ben Solomon Zalman of Vilna. *Aderet Eliyahu*. Tel Aviv: Sinai (n.d.).

Euripides. *The Bacchantes*, in *The Plays of Euripides*, trans. Edward P. Coleridge. London: George Bell and Sons, 1907.

Ginsburg, C.D. *Introduction to the Massoretico-Critical Edition of the Hebrew Bible*. New York: Ktav, 1966.

Halivni, David Weiss. *Peshat and Derash: Plain and Applied Meaning in Rabbinic Exegesis*. New York: Oxford University Press, 1991.

Heilprin, Meir. *Ha-Notarikon ha-Simanim ve-ha-Kinnuyim*. Jerusalem: Darom, 5690 (1930).

# Sources

Herzog, Isaac. *The Main Institutions of Jewish Law.* London: Soncino, 1936.

Josephus. *The Works of Flavius Josephus: Volume 1: Antiquities of the Jews,* trans. William Whiston. Philadelphia: J. B. Smith (n.d.).

Judah ha-Levi. *Judah Hallevi's Kitab al Khazari,* trans. Hartwig Hirschfeld. London: George Routledge & Sons; New York: E. P. Dutton & Co., 1905.

Klein, Daniel A. "A Letter to Almeda: Shadal's Guide for the Perplexed." *Ḥakirah,* vol. 10, pp. 225-241 (2010).

Landa, Judah. "The Exodus: Convergence of Science, History and Jewish Tradition." *Ḥakirah,* vol. 14, pp. 187-235 (2012).

Leibowitz, Nehama. *Studies in Shemot (Exodus),* trans. Aryeh Newman, vols. 1 and 2. Jerusalem: Eliner Library, Joint Authority for Jewish Zionist Education, Department for Torah Education and Culture in the Diaspora, 1976.

Lockshin, Martin (Meir). "Some Approaches to the Tension between Peshat and Midrash Halakhah" (Hebrew). *Studies in Bible and Exegesis (Iyyunei Miqra u-Farshanut),* vol. 8, pp. 33-45 (2008).

Logue, Mark, and Conradi, Peter. *The King's Speech: How One Man Saved the British Monarchy.* New York: Sterling, 2010.

Lucas, A., and J.R. Harris. *Ancient Egyptian Materials and Industries.* New York: Dover Publications, 2012.

Luzzatto, Samuel David. *Beit ha-Otsar,* vol. 1. Lemberg: Evae Grossmann, 1847.

———. *Epistolario italiano francese latino.* Padua, 1890.

———. *Ha-Mishtadel.* Vienna, 1846-47.

———. *Iggerot Shadal.* Przemysl and Cracow, 1882-94.

———. *Il Pentateuco volgarizzato e commentato.* Padua: Francesco Sacchetto, 1871-1876.

———. *Index raisonné des livres de correspondance de feu Samuel David Luzzatto.* Padua, 1878.

———. *Meḥkerei ha-Yahadut.* Warsaw: Ha-Tsefirah, 1912/13; Jerusalem: Makor, 1970.

———. *Perush Shadal al Ḥamishah Ḥumshei Torah,* ed. Pinhas Schlesinger. Tel Aviv. Dvir, 1965.

———. *Perush Shadal al Sefer Yeshayah,* ed. Pinhas Schlesinger and Meir Hovev. Tel Avid: Dvir, 1970.

Maimonides, Moses. *The Guide for the Perplexed,* trans. M. Friedländer, 2nd ed. London: George Routledge & Sons, 1904. Reprinted, New York: Dover, 1956.

Margolies, Morris B. *Samuel David Luzzatto: Traditionalist Scholar.* New York: Ktav, 1979.

Meschel, Susan V. "Metallurgy in the Bible: Ironworking and the Disposal of the Golden Calf." *Jewish Bible Quarterly*, vol. 42:4 (2014).

Mole, William. *Gods, Men, and Wine.* Cleveland: World Publishing Co., 1966.

Ovid. *Metamorphoses*, trans. Garth, Dryden, et al. London, 1717.

Philip, Mosheh, ed. *Ḥumash ha-Re'em: Sefer Shemot.* Petaḥ Tikvah, 5753 (1993).

Pliny the Elder. *The Historie of the World, commonly called the Naturall Historie of C. Plinius Secundus*, trans. Philemon Holland. London: A. Islip, 1601.

Pliny the Elder. *The Natural History*, trans. John Bostock and H.T. Riley. London: Taylor and Francis, 1855.

Rosenbaum, M., and A.M. Silbermann. *Pentateuch with Rashi's Commentary.* New York: Hebrew Publishing Co., 1934.

Rosenbloom, Noah H. *Luzzatto's Ethico-Psychological Interpretation of Judaism.* New York: Yeshiva University, 1965.

Solieli, Menaḥem; and Mosheh Berkooz, eds. *Leksikon Mikra'i* (Lexicon Biblicum). Tel Aviv: Dvir, 1965.

Tacitus. *Annals I*, trans. A.J. Church and W.J. Brodribb. London: Macmillan and Co., 1869.

Thomson, Thomas. *A History of Chemistry.* London, 1830.

Touitou, Elazar. *Ha-Peshatot ha-Mitḥaddeshim be-Khol Yom: Iyyunim be-Feirusho shel Rashbam la-Torah.* Ramat Gan: Bar-Ilan University Press, 2003.

Tuori, Kaius. "Revenge and Retribution in the Twelve Tables: *Talio esto* Reconsidered." *Fundamina*, vol. 13, pp. 140-145 (2007).

Urbach, Ephraim. "The Derasha as a Basis of the Halakha and the Problem of the Soferim" (Hebrew). *Tarbiz* 27/2, pp. 166-182 (1958).

Vargon, Shmuel. "Samuel David Luzzatto's Critique of Rabbinic Exegesis Which Contradicts the Plain Meaning of Scripture" (Hebrew). *Jewish Studies, an Internet Journal*, vol. 2, pp. 97-122 (2003).

Watson, Alan, ed. *The Digest of Justinian*, vol. 1. University of Pennsylvania Press, 1998.

Wurzburger, Walter. "The Oral Law and the Conservative Dilemma." *Tradition*, vol. 3 no. 1, pp. 82-88 (Fall, 1960).

Yahuda, A.S. *The Language of the Pentateuch in its Relation to the Egyptian*, vol. I. London: Oxford University Press, 1933.

# Sources

## *Loeb Classical Library*

Juvenal. *Juvenal and Perseus*, trans. G. G. Ramsay.
Ovid. *Tristia/ Ex Ponto*, trans. Arthur Leslie Wheeler.
Pliny. *Natural History I*, Books I-II, trans. H. Rackham.
Seneca (vol. VII). *Naturales Quaestiones I*, Book II, trans. Thomas II. Corcoran.

# Primary Source Index

### Bible

### Genesis

| | |
|---|---|
| 1:11, | 246, 292 |
| 1:20, | 35 |
| 1:27, | 257 |
| 1:28, | 25 |
| 1:30, | 201 |
| 2:4, | 91 n. 1 |
| 2:7, | 257 |
| 2:21, | 257 |
| 2:22, | 257 |
| 2:23, | 125 |
| 3:12, | 225 |
| 3:15, | 90 |
| 3:19, | 206 |
| 3:23, | 134 |
| 3:24, | 201 |
| 4:4, | 85 |
| 4:11, | 325 |
| 4:23, | 57 |
| 8:22, | 168 |
| 9:5, | 339 |
| 9:6, | 329, 339 |
| 10:9, | 125 n. 26 |
| 11:3, | 41 |
| 11:8, | 85 |
| 11:12, | 45 |
| 11:28, | 286 |
| 12:3, | 365 |
| 12:8, | 445 |
| 14:14, | 208 |
| 14:18, | 226 |
| 14:22-23, | 352 |
| ch. 15, | 152, 444 |
| 15:7, | 92 |
| 15:17, | 444 |
| 15:19, | 444 |
| 16:7, | 230 |
| 17:12, | 155 |
| 17:14, | 143 |
| 18:6, | 152 |
| 18:8, | 271 |
| 18:25, | 294 |
| 19:1, | 206 |
| 20:1, | 230 |
| 20:15, | 269 |
| 21:23, | 352 |
| 22:2, | 247 |
| 22:4, | 247 |
| 22:14, | 92 |
| ch. 24, | 282 |
| 24:10, | 445 |
| 24:12, | 65 |
| 24:17, | 50 |
| 24:33, | 270 |
| 24:41, | 389 |
| 24:57, | 100 |
| 25:18, | 230, 286 |
| 25:21, | 126 |
| 25:22, | 48 |
| 26:5, | 386 |
| 26:29, | 325 |
| 27:40, | 159 |
| 28:3, | 322 |
| 28:9, | 228 |
| 28:14, | 40 |
| 29:32, | 55 |
| 30:30, | 41 |
| 30:37, | 236 |
| 30:38, | 56 |
| 30:43, | 41 |
| 31:7, | 116 |
| 31:27, | 228 |
| 31:39, | 354-355 |
| 31:50, | 390 n .3 |
| 31:51, | 201 |
| 32:11, | 318 |
| 32:22, | 287 |
| 32:26, | 208 |
| 33:2, | 73 |
| 33:20, | 252 |
| 34:2, | 324 |
| 34:5, | 181 |
| 34:10, | 269 |
| 34:28, | 319 |

35:16, 170
36:31, 219
36:40-43, 219
36:43, 219 n. 30

37:11, 153
37:36, 96

38:24, 332
38:29, 277

39:7, 135

40:11, 377
40:19, 276
40:20, 276

ch. 41, 282
41:43, 264

42:4, 336
42:7, 154
42:8, 154
42:17, 276
42:18, 276

43:3, 340, 390
43:34, 39, 43

45:20, 445
45:24, 218 n. 29
45:26, 16 n. 6

46:26, 35
46:29, 177

47:6, 269
47:11, 39, 40 n. 3
47:22, 407

48:4, 322
48:9, 406
48:19, 322

49:16, 316
49:19, 90
49:24, 188

50:26, 428 n. 3

**Exodus**

1:7, 43, 160
1:9, 125
1:11, 125
1:17, 42
1:18, 86
1:19, 150

2:3, 224
2:7, 51
2:11, 396
2:13, 335
2:17, 48

3:1, 259
3:9, 361
3:13, 200
3:14, 200
3:17, 67 n. 30
3:18, 82
3:21, 15, 67 n. 30, 135
3:22, 135

4:1, 115
4:9, 104
4:10, 93
4:11, 74
4:12, 73
4:13, 74
4:14, 75, 294
4:18, 78
4:19, 74
4:22, 79
4:23, 57, 79, 258
4:27, 76
4:30, 81

5:2, 64
5:6, 86
5:7, 85
5:10, 86
5:12, 83
5:14, 86
5:18, 84
5:21, 180

6:1, 67
6:9, 180
6:10-12, 97
6:13, 94
6:20, 17, 49, 152
6:26, 159, 160
6:29-30, 94

7:1, 227
7:3, 102
7:20, 17, 247
7:21, 105
7:22, 100, 108, 359
7:26, 103
7:27, 15-16, 130
7:28, 148

8:2, 111
8:3, 100
8:7, 116
8:10, 246
8:14, 100
8:17, 208
8:22, 71, 115 n. 19

9:3, 112
9:7, 113
9:10, 119
9:15-16, 98
9:15, 119
9:18, 120
9:23, 186
9:26, 43
9:27, 99
9:29, 89
9:31, 162

10:2, 112
10:4, 106
10:7, 123
10:8, 66
10:11, 66
10:13, 185
10:19, 131
10:23, 133, 243
10:24, 66

11:2, 69
11:3, 70

| | | |
|---|---|---|
| 11:4, | 117, 134 | |
| 11:15, | 292 | |
| 12:4, | 156 | |
| 12:6, | 26 | |
| 12:12, | 146 | |
| 12:13, | 150 | |
| 12:14, | 17, 161 | |
| 12:16, | 242, 455 | |
| 12:21, | 17, 142, 161 | |
| 12:22, | 80 | |
| 12:23, | 141 | |
| 12:28, | 159 | |
| 12:29, | 15, 17, 144, 328 | |
| 12:31, | 134 | |
| 12:33, | 89 | |
| 12:34, | 15, 17, 107, 145 | |
| 12:35, | 70 | |
| 12:36, | 70 | |
| 12:39, | 144-145 | |
| 12:40, | 17 | |
| 12:41, | 159 | |
| 12:43, | 26 | |
| 12:47, | 156 | |
| 12:48, | 151, 155 | |
| 12:51, | 96 | |
| ch. 13, | 144 | |
| 13:2-3, | 159 | |
| 13:3, | 167 | |
| 13:4, | 375 | |
| 13:5, | 60, 179 | |
| 13:9, | 28 n. 31, 170 | |
| 13:12, | 161 | |
| 13:13, | 161, 169 n. 25 | |
| 13:15, | 166 | |
| 13:16, | 165-166 | |
| 14:4, | 181 | |
| 14:6, | 178 | |
| 14:9, | 38 | |
| 14:11, | 232 | |
| 14:13, | 171 | |
| 14:18, | 187 | |
| 14:19, | 173, 175, 389 | |
| 14:20, | 174 | |
| 14:21, | 17 | |
| 14:24, | 174, 209 | |
| 14:25, | 177 | |
| 14:27, | 184, 201 | |
| 15:1, | 85, 197-198, 205, 229 | |
| 15:2, | 192 | |
| 15:3, | 15, 91 n. 1 | |
| 15:5, | 18, 209, 217 | |
| 15:6, | 203, 210-211, 222 | |
| 15:7, | 189, 191, 193 n. 15 | |
| 15:8, | 185, 209 | |
| 15:9, | 66 | |
| 15:10, | 66, 204, 207, 217 | |
| 15:11, | 222 | |
| 15:12, | 188 | |
| 15:13, | 164, 195 | |
| 15:15, | 211 | |
| 15:16, | 164, 207, 218-219 | |
| 15:17, | 49, 66, 193, 202, 219 | |
| 15:22, | 233 | |
| 15:23, | 227 | |
| 16:3, | 240 | |
| 16:4, | 231 | |
| 16:5, | 241 | |
| 16:6-8, | 233 | |
| 16:6, | 234 | |
| 16:10, | 234 | |
| 16:12. | 139, 208, 234 | |
| 16:13, | 233, 238 | |
| 16:19, | 240 | |
| 16:21, | 220 | |
| 16:22, | 233 | |
| 16:23, | 432 | |
| 16:25, | 241 | |
| 16:28, | 271 | |
| 16:29, | 133 | |
| 16:30, | 241 | |
| 16:31, | 237 | |
| 16:33, | 238 n. 35, 257 | |
| 16:35, | 257 | |
| 17:7, | 114 | |
| 17:10, | 386 | |
| 18:1, | 57 n. 22 | |
| 18:2, | 79 | |
| 18:5, | 267 | |
| 18:13, | 258 | |
| 18:16, | 260 | |
| 18:22, | 266 | |
| 18:27, | 253, 256-257 | |
| 18:31, | 256 | |
| 19:6, | 312 | |
| 19:7, | 281, 316 | |
| 19:8, | 270 | |
| 19:9, | 276 | |
| 19:10, | 212 | |
| 19:12, | 174 | |
| 19:13, | 339 | |
| 19:16, | 281 | |
| 19:19, | 274, 280 | |
| 19:21, | 276, 340 | |
| 19:24, | 206 | |
| 19:25, | 282 | |
| 20:1, | 15 | |
| 20:2, | 279 | |
| 20:3, | 18 | |
| 20:5, | 18, 288, 293-294 | |
| 20:6, | 295, 296, 298 | |
| 20:7, | 368 | |
| 20:10, | 15, 27, 242 | |
| 20:11, | 18, 215 | |
| 20:13, | 315, 368 | |
| 20:14, | 15, 279, 285 | |
| 20:15, | 280-281, 376 | |
| 20:16, | 278, 280 | |
| 20:18, | 278 | |
| 20:19-23, | 279 | |
| 20:19, | 382 | |
| 20:20, | 290, 374 | |
| 21:1, | 270 | |
| 21:2, | 320 | |
| 21:3, | 317 | |
| 21:6, | 20, 275, 317 | |
| 21:8, | 26 | |
| 21:9, | 315 | |

| | | |
|---|---|---|
| 21:12, 27, 335 | 24:4, 61 | 30:29, 420 |
| 21:13, 328 | 24:5, 61 | 30:32, 84 |
| 21:14, 213 | 24:7, 270, 382 | 30:34, 76 |
| 21:15, 197, 329 | 24:9, 275, 361 | 31:2, 446 |
| 21:16, 309 | 24:11. 275 | 31:13, 307 |
| 21:18, 328 | ch. 25, 465 | 31:15, 242 |
| 21:19, 328 | 25:12, 421 | ch. 32, 432 n. 6 |
| 21:20, 328 | 25:26, 421 | 32:1, 440 |
| 21:21, 328, 334, 361 | 25:30, 394 n. 7 | 32:19, 229 |
| 21:24, 333 | 25:31, 390-391 | 32:25, 433 |
| 21:28, 19, 343 | | 32:34, 298 |
| 21:29-30, 337 | 26:1, 408 n. 3 | |
| 21:34, 343 | 26:9, 350 | 33:4, 451 |
| 21:36, 342 | 26:15, 397 | 33:5, 58 |
| 21:37, 348 | 26:16, 391 | 33:7, 463 |
| | 26:19, 397 | 33:11, 174 |
| 22:1, 15 | 26:25, 399 | 33:13, 432 n. 6 |
| 22:2, 19 | 26:30, 316 | 33:19, 440, 447 |
| 22:4, 369, 372 | 26:35, 396 | |
| 22:6, 348, 353-354 | | 34:3, 262 |
| 22:7, 354 | 27:2, 391 | 34:5, 445 |
| 22:8, 320, 351 | 27:3, 188 | 34:6, 287 |
| 22:9, 350, 355 | 27:4, 421 | 34:7, 295 |
| 22:10, 351 | 27:7, 421 | 34:9, 449 n. 16 |
| 22:11, 27 | 27:13, 400 | 34:19-20, 161 |
| 22:13, 69 | 27:18, 429 | 34:11, 454 |
| 22:20, 363 | | 34:20, 169 n. 25 |
| 22:25, 310 | 28:8, 392 | 34:25, 142, 376 |
| | 28:11, 410 | 34:27, 384 |
| 23:1, 302, 371 | 28:21, 160 | 34:28, 285 |
| 23:2, 27, 371 | 28:28, 409 | |
| 23:3, 371-372 | 28:30, 410 | 35:2, 242 |
| 23:5, 349, 371 | 28:36, 167 | 35:5, 388 |
| 23:6, 371 | 28:39, 397 | 35:12, 446 |
| 23:9, 289 | | 35:22, 417 |
| 23:12-14, 316 | 29:9, 413 | 35:31, 408 |
| 23:12, 373 | 29:11, 414 | 35:35, 408 |
| 23:16, 138 | 29:24, 415 | |
| 23:18, 453 | 29:29, 415 | 36:3, 388 |
| 23:19, 389 | | 36:5, 424 |
| 23:20, 440 | 30:2, 391 | |
| 23:21, 374 | 30:9, 394 | 38:5-7, 403 |
| 23:24, 293 | 30:12, 18 | |
| 23:27, 187 | 30:15, 388 | 39:1, 431 |
| 23:30, 381 | 30:16, 424, 426 | 39:3, 408 |
| 23:33, 382 | 30:23, 428 | 39:5, 392 |
| | 30:26, 465 | 39:39, 403 |
| 24:1, 275, 278 | | |
| 24:3, 270 | | 40:3, 446 |
| | | 40:21, 469 |

## Shadal on Exodus

### Leviticus

| | |
|---|---|
| 1:2, | 375 n. 39 |
| 2:14, | 162 |
| 3:1, | 260 n. 6 |
| 4:3, | 416 |
| 7:18, | 24 |
| 7:23, | 226 |
| 7:30, | 417 |
| 7:34, | 417 |
| 8:7, | 409 |
| 8:8, | 409, 411 n. 8 |
| 8:27, | 418 |
| 8:29, | 418 |
| 10:3, | 286 |
| 10:18, | 121 |
| 11:34, | 203 |
| 13:42, | 119 |
| 13:49, | 151 |
| 13:57, | 119 |
| 13:58, | 109 |
| ch. 14, | 94 |
| 16:31, | 432 |
| 17:11, | 426 |
| 18:25, | 71 |
| 18:27, | 71 |
| 18:30, | 71 |
| 19:14, | 271 |
| 19:18, | 329 |
| 19:28, | 167 |
| 20:5, | 301 |
| 20:9, | 345 |
| 20:10, | 309 |
| 20:14, | 336 |
| 22:10, | 157 |
| 22:13, | 136 |
| 22:28, | 362, 377 |
| 23:24, | 432 |
| 23:32, | 432 |
| 23:39, | 432 |
| ch. 25, | 318 |
| 25:4, | 432 |
| 25:5, | 432 |
| 25:6, | 158 |
| 25:14, | 361 |
| 25:29, | 168 |
| 25:30, | 168 |
| 25:29, | 318 |
| 25:40-41, | 218 |
| 25:40, | 157, 317 |
| 25:42, | 222 |
| 25:43, | 41 |
| 25:45, | 157 |
| 25:46, | 41 |
| 25:55, | 317 |
| 25:53, | 41 |
| ch. 26, | 102 n. 9 |
| 26:25, | 334 |
| 26:40, | 299 |
| ch. 27, | 341 |

### Numbers

| | |
|---|---|
| 1:52, | 160 |
| 2:13, | 302 |
| 3:4, | 286 |
| 3:28, | 94 |
| 4:6-13, | 431 |
| 4:7, | 394 |
| 4:23, | 463 |
| 7:14, | 393 |
| 7:20, | 393 |
| 7:26, | 393 |
| 7:89, | 454 n. 18 |
| 8:2, | 396 |
| 8:11, | 417 |
| 8:21, | 417 |
| ch. 9, | 159 |
| 9:6-13, | 144 |
| 9:13, | 197 |
| 9:14, | 158, 316 |
| 9:18, | 234 |
| 9:21, | 472 |
| ch. 10, | 256 |
| 10:2, | 391 |
| 10:24-32, | 257 |
| 10:24, | 253 |
| 10:29, | 256 |
| 10:30, | 254, 256 |
| 10:31, | 256 |
| 10:33, | 173 |
| 10:35, | 85 |
| 11:4, | 151 |
| 11:5, | 232 |
| 11:8, | 244 |
| 11:9, | 236 |
| 11:16, | 215 n. 27 |
| 11:18, | 212, 214-215 |
| 11:21, | 215 |
| 11:28, | 442 n. 11 |
| 11:29, | 293 |
| 11:31, | 235 |
| 12:2, | 179 |
| 12:3, | 74 |
| 12:8, | 291 |
| 12:9, | 294 |
| ch. 13, | 160 |
| 14:12, | 208, 435 |
| 14:14, | 174 |
| 14:28, | 351 |
| 15:14-16, | 158 |
| 15:26, | 158 |
| 15:29, | 158 |
| 15:30, | 158, 178 |
| 15:33, | 83 |
| 15:39, | 142 |
| 16:10, | 407 |
| 17:5, | 58 |
| 18:11, | 417 |
| 18:15, | 169 |
| 18:27, | 367 |
| 19:10, | 158 |
| 20:8, | 118 |
| 20:4, | 348 |
| 20:14, | 219 |
| 21:14, | 226 |
| ch. 22-24, | 199 |
| 22:3, | 220 |
| 22:6, | 366 |
| 22:22, | 100 |
| 22:29, | 128 |
| 23:10, | 310 |
| 24:20, | 377 |
| 25:41, | 319 |
| 26:9, | 336 |
| 26:11, | 96 |
| 29:6, | 316 |
| 30:8, | 76, 440 |
| 31:28, | 139 |
| 32:12, | 439 |
| 33:12-14, | 246 |
| 35:12, | 328-329 |
| 35:15, | 158 |
| 35:20, | 330 |
| 35:22, | 330 |
| 35:26-27, | 345 |
| 35:31, | 337 |

# Shadal on Exodus

### Deuteronomy

ch. 1, 257
1:9-18, 257
1:9, 185
1:38, 269
2:4, 219
2:7, 185
2:15, 186
2:19, 262
2:25, 218, 286
3:11, 52
3:13, 293
3:25, 223
4:3, 374
4:8, 272
4:11, 202
4:12-13, 279
4:15, 291
4:16-18, 290
4.16, 290-291
4:23, 291
4:25, 291
4:36, 279
4:41, 213
4:44, 270
5:4, 442
5:5, 281-282
5:9, 293, 299
5:12, 304
5:14, 306
5:15, 306
5:19, 279
5:20, 279, 281
5:21, 279, 281
5:24, 281
5:28, 385
6:8-9, 166
6:8, 165 n. 23, 166
7:1, 60
7:9, 301
8:3, 238
8:17, 423
9:4, 71
10:16, 166
11:10, 142
11:26, 272
11:28, 81

11:32, 272
12:4, 44
12:11, 201
12:23, 345, 427
13:3, 293
13:11, 339
13:16, 295
13:17, 360
14:4, 139
14:21, 265
14:25, 434
15:12, 320, 327
15:13-14, 68
16:1, 153
16:3, 163
16:7, 163
16:8, 163
16:10, 418
17:3, 48
17:5, 339
17:11, 23 24, 29
17:16, 180
18:3, 315, 407
18:8, 429
19:6, 340
19:10, 161, 345
20:16, 45
21:4, 329
21:9, 329
21:16, 286
21:17, 315
21:18, 332
22:8, 345, 440
22:9, 211-212, 367
22:13-21, 67
22:19, 336
22:24, 339
22:26, 345
22:29, 358
23:5, 366
23:15, 213
23:18-19, 214
23:25, 208
24:7, 331
24:11-12, 306
24:16, 295
24:17 18, 306
25:18, 43
27:23, 254
28:4, 169

28:33, 41
28:65, 218
29:3, 98
29:21, 231
30:1, 272
30:19, 272-273
31:17, 114
31:21, 166
31:29, 88
ch. 32, 102 n. 9
32:1, 198
32:2, 198
32:4, 294
32:5, 151
32:7, 225
32:39, 447
32:40, 252
33:16, 194
33:17, 338
33:19, 322
34:8, 222
34:9, 408

### Joshua

2:1, 100
3:4, 340
3:5, 212
4:18, 340
5:2, 80, 245
5:4, 260
5:5, 48
ch. 7, 360
7:5, 220
7:13, 212
8:2, 69
8:20, 176
10:12, 380
14:10, 149
20:7, 213
24:9, 366
24:15, 271
24:16, 271

### Judges

1:16, 255
4:6, 144
4:10, 143

# Shadal on Exodus

| | | | | | |
|---|---|---|---|---|---|
| 4:11, | 253, 255 | 28:3, | 389 | 6:1, | 387 |
| 4:13, | 143 | 28:22, | 270 | 6:23, | 391 |
| 4:17, | 255 | 31:4, | 128 | 6:28, | 391 |
| 5:2, | 190 | | | 6:38, | 162 |
| 5:12, | 205 | | | 7:30, | 389 |

**2 Samuel**

| | | | | | |
|---|---|---|---|---|---|
| 5:22, | 432 | | | 7:34, | 389 |
| 5:23, | 366 | 3:17, | 87 | 8:13, | 223 |
| 5:26, | 37 | 3:25, | 202 | 8:39, | 223 |
| 5:27, | 207 | 3:29, | 380 | 8:43, | 223 |
| 6:15, | 219 | 5:14, | 48 | 8:49, | 223 |
| 7:20, | 264 | 6:16, | 434 | 9:6, | 272 |
| 9:27, | 366 | 6:19, | 196 | 10:29, | 177 |
| 10:8, | 41 | 6:21, | 434 | 12:12, | 84 |
| 11:34, | 228 | 7:11, | 47 | 12:14, | 145 |
| 11:40, | 168 | 7:13, | 224 | 13:3, | 99 |
| 14:19, | 164 | 7:14, | 302 | 13:4, | 143 |
| 19:25, | 128 | 7:16, | 302 | 13:33, | 439 |
| 20:15, | 122 | 8:4, | 176 | 16:31, | 49 |
| 21:21, | 229 | 10:8, | 176 | 19:3, | 52 |
| 21:23, | 229 | 11:10, | 170 | 19:16, | 415 |
| | | 11:14, | 213, 215 | 21:3, | 223 |

**1 Samuel**

| | | | | | |
|---|---|---|---|---|---|
| | | 12:14, | 48 | 22:3, | 181 |
| | | 13:3, | 36 | 22:11, | 338 |
| 2:3, | 84 | 13:8, | 85 | 22:13, | 339 |
| 2:15, | 376 n. 30 | 13:26, | 67 | | |
| 2:22, | 463 | 15:18, | 287 | | |

**2 Kings**

| | | | | | |
|---|---|---|---|---|---|
| 6:6, | 128 | 15:20, | 87 | | |
| 6:7, | 177 | 16:2, | 69 | 1:9, | 264 |
| 7:10, | 186 | 16:8, | 345 | 1:13, | 264 |
| 9:24, | 270 | 16:10, | 98 | 4:7, | 363 |
| 10:19, | 219 | 17:9, | 76, 440 | 4:43, | 271 |
| 12:3, | 41, 310 | 18:9, | 65 | 5:17, | 67 |
| 15:6, | 255 | 19:1, | 218 | 7:10, | 177 |
| 15:7, | 230 | 19:14, | 352 | 9:22, | 359 |
| 15:21, | 377 | 20:7, | 172 | 11:28, | 39 |
| 16:7, | 221 | 20:18, | 121 | 17:26, | 316 |
| 16:16, | 269 | 21:10, | 126 | 21:1, | 251 |
| 16:19, | 269 | ch. 22, | 190 | 23:7, | 214 |
| 17:30, | 262 | 22:11, | 390 | 24:15, | 220 |
| 17:35, | 45 | 22:17, | 54 | | |
| 17:49, | 201 | ch. 24, | 425 | | |

**Isaiah**

| | | | | | |
|---|---|---|---|---|---|
| 20:27, | 87 | 24:13, | 58 | | |
| 21:8, | 463 | 24:22, | 45 n. 8 | 1:2, | 198 |
| 21:12, | 229 | | | 1:11, | 179, 196 |
| 23:6, | 412 | | | 1:12, | 375-376, 453 |

**1 Kings**

| | | | | | |
|---|---|---|---|---|---|
| 23:23, | 219 | | | 1:13, | 143 |
| 24:12, | 330 | 2:28, | 213 | 1:14, | 103 |
| 25:23, | 206 | 5:27, | 39 | 1:17, | 191, 317 |
| 27:8, | 230 | 5:28, | 39 | 1:23, | 261 |

# Shadal on Exodus

| | | | | | |
|---|---|---|---|---|---|
| 1:25, | 136 | 34:10, | 252 | 2:7, | 223 |
| 1:26, | 63 | 35:8, | 70 | 2:9, | 389 |
| 2:9, | 121 | 37:18-19, | 264 | 2:10, | 71 |
| 2:19, | 205 | 37:29, | 456 | 2:30, | 303 |
| 3:14, | 348 | 38:11, | 200 | ch. 3, | 309 |
| 3:22, | 434 | 38:16, | 430 | 3:8, | 49 |
| 4:3, | 439 | 40:10, | 375 | 3:9, | 309 |
| 5:12, | 228 | 40:12, | 84 | 3:18, | 78 |
| ch. 6, | 77 | 40:14, | 433 | 4:1, | 89 |
| 6:3, | 178 | 40:19, | 290 | 4:30, | 303 |
| 6:10, | 77 n. 36 | 40:22, | 301 | 6:1, | 122 |
| 7:2, | 311 | 41:4, | 224 | 6:4, | 213 |
| 7:14, | 251 | 41:8, | 302 | 6:7, | 286 |
| 7:20, | 357 | 41:19, | 389 n. 1 | 7:21, | 443 n. 13 |
| 9:3, | 136 | 43:1, | 430, 446 | 7:22, | 432, 443 n. 13 |
| 9:5, | 252 | 43:21, | 164 | | |
| 10:3, | 298 | 44:10, | 290 | 8:4, | 90 |
| 10:31, | 122 | 44:13, | 293 | 8:5, | 88 |
| 11:23, | 202 | 45:5, | 204 | 9:9, | 58 |
| 13:1, | 302 | 45:13, | 196 | 9:11-12, | 272 |
| 13:3, | 213 | 47:1, | 439 | 10:14, | 290 |
| 14:3, | 207 | 47:7, | 304 | 12:5, | 205 |
| 14:11, | 239 | 47:12, | 359 | 12:16, | 47 |
| 14:21, | 300 | 49:15, | 165 | 13:23, | 338 |
| 14:24, | 351 | 50:10, | 185 | 14:5, | 264 |
| 17:11, | 207 | 51:9, | 136 | 14:20, | 299 |
| 18:4, | 224 | 51:12, | 447 | 15:10, | 54 |
| 19:6, | 50 | 52:8, | 442 | 16:3, | 48 |
| 21:10, | 389 | 53:7, | 129 | 16:19, | 193 |
| 21:12, | 241 | 54:11, | 413 | 17:8, | 174 |
| 23:13, | 122 | 54:16, | 290 | 18:3, | 44 |
| 24:20, | 311 | 57:6, | 90 | 18:17, | 183 |
| 25:6, | 223 | 57:13, | 303 | 18:19, | 73 |
| 25:7, | 223, 290 | 58:6, | 41 | 21:8-9, | 273 |
| 25:10, | 223 | 58:9, | 113 | 22:6, | 351 |
| 26:4, | 225 | 59:13, | 202, 308 | 22:13, | 375 |
| 26:13, | 313 | 61:1, | 415 | 22:15, | 224 |
| 26:19, | 300 | 61:10, | 407 | 23:6, | 251 |
| 27:8, | 183 | 62:4, | 251 | 23:10, | 58 |
| 28:4, | 37 | 63:11, | 54 | 23:19, | 380 |
| 28:13, | 308 | 63:12, | 53 n. 16 | 26:4, | 272 |
| 28:28, | 380 | 65:15, | 254 | 26:11, | 316 |
| 30:6, | 110 | 66:7, | 218 | 29:23, | 226 |
| 30:10, | 116 | | | 30:22, | 290 |
| 30:20, | 318 | **Jeremiah** | | 31:3, | 434 |
| 30:22, | 290 | | | 31:12, | 229 |
| 30:27, | 379 | 1:6, | 74 | 31:28, | 295 |
| 31:4, | 129, 143 | 1:12, | 170 | 31:29, | 42, 295 |
| 34:3, | 221 | 2:3, | 214 | 32:44, | 265 |

## Shadal on Exodus

| | | |
|---|---|---|
| 33:9, 218 | 38:23, 203 | **Habakkuk** |
| 33:17, 302 | 39:20, 176 | |
| 34:13-14, 318 | 43:11, 202, 291 | 3:2, 218, 304 |
| ch. 35, 255 | 45:8, 361 | 3:7, 218 |
| 35:3, 229 | 46:18, 361 | 3:8, 210 |
| 35:5, 271 | 47:5, 191 | |
| 38:6, 201 | 48:11, 410 | **Zephaniah** |
| 38:19, 129 | 48:35, 251 | |
| 38:22, 201 | | 1:7, 212, 214 |
| 40:8, 389 | **Hosea** | 3:6-7, 98 |
| 40:19, 290 | | 3:9, 78 |
| 44:1, 175 | 1:3, 48 | |
| 44:10, 272 | 4:9, 298 | **Haggai** |
| 46:4, 177 | 9:7, 298 | |
| 46:11, 303 | 9:9, 136 | 2:13, 327 |
| 46:14, 175 | 9:10, 162 | |
| 46:26, 389 | 10:12, 432 | **Zechariah** |
| 48:11, 208 | 12:10, 136 | |
| 49:23, 220 | 12:13, 42 | 1:14-15, 294 |
| 51:17, 290 | | 3:4, 265 |
| 51:29, 218 | **Joel** | 7:5, 265 |
| 51:34, 186 | | 7:14, 241 |
| | 1:14, 212 | 8:10, 358 |
| **Ezekiel** | 2:2, 131 | |
| | 2:19, 208 | **Malachi** |
| 1:4, 124 | 4:9, 213 | |
| 1:25-28, 392 | 4:18, 163 | 3:15, 47 |
| 2:9, 249 | | 3:20, 203 |
| 7:26, 117 | **Amos** | |
| 8:16, 397 | 3:12, 354 | **Psalms** |
| ch. 14, 102 | 4:1, 41 | |
| 16:7, 325 | 7:13, 213 | 2:8, 69 |
| 16:8, 325 | 9:11, 136 | 6:7, 221 |
| 16:10, 388 | 9:13, 220 | 9:20, 286 |
| 16:32, 309 | | 13:4, 310 |
| 17:13, 220 | **Micah** | 15:3, 302 |
| 18:2, 295 | 1:4, 221 | 16:4, 302 |
| 18:20, 295 | 2:1, 224 | 16:6, 195 |
| 18:25, 84 | 3:4, 359 | 17:15, 291 |
| 18:30-32, 297 | 3:5, 213 | 18:2, 190 |
| 20:7, 435 | 5:3, 205 | 18:15, 186-187 |
| 20:25, 121 | | 18:17, 54 |
| 21:26, 396 | **Nahum** | 18:8, 218 |
| 23:37, 389 | | 20:8, 313 |
| 27:26, 183 | 1:2, 294 | 22:8, 160 |
| 29:10, 175 | 2:7, 220 | 22:15, 220 |
| 30:6, 175 | 3:8, 185 | 28:1, 181 |
| 33:26, 159 | | 28:7, 193 |
| 34:4, 41 | | 29:1, 194, 211 |

| | | |
|---|---|---|
| 33:4, 223 | 92:10, 204 | 13:7, 37 |
| 33:7, 207 | 94:1, 204 | 15:22, 310 |
| 36:9, 59 | 94:3, 205 | 15:23, 325 |
| 46:2, 193 | 97:5, 220 | 16:2, 84 |
| 47:10, 322 | 100:4, 223 | 16:18, 426 |
| 48:8, 183 | 104:5, 224 | 17:14, 160 |
| 48:9, 224 | 104:8, 164 | 17:25, 139 |
| 50:16, 302 | 104:26, 434 | 21:2, 84 |
| 51:6, 308 | 104:27, 246 | 23:29, 293 |
| 52:11, 130 | 105:39, 174 | 26:20, 199 |
| 58:3, 224 | 107:23, 429 | 27:2, 323 |
| 58:6, 73 | 108:13, 81 | 29:23, 426 |
| 58:7, 206 | 109:1, 181 | 31:4, 205 |
| 60:13, 81, 195 | 109:14, 295, 300 | |
| 60:2, 335 | 109:16, 304 | **Job** |
| 65:5, 221, 366 | 116:10, 129 | |
| 65:7, 204 | 116:12, 193 | 1:10, 41 |
| 65:11, 220 | 118:5, 110 | 1:11, 286 |
| 65:13, 58 | 118:11, 162 | 2:7, 119 |
| 66:5, 216 | 119:62, 135 | 3:1, 366 |
| 68:3, 220 | 119:75, 250 | 3:21, 105 |
| 68:5, 121 | 119:117, 85 | 4:15, 287 |
| 68:7, 47 | 135:11, 188 | 4:16, 291 |
| 68:35, 194, 197 | 136:2, 190 | 5:2, 311 |
| 69:3, 201 | 136:6, 292 | 5:5, 244 |
| 69:15, 201 | 139:4, 193 | 5:18, 296, 301 |
| 69:29, 439 | 139:11, 359 | 5:24, 327 |
| 73:9, 124 | 141:4, 129 | 6:28, 286 |
| 74:2, 164 | 142:4, 164 | 7:1, 463 |
| 74:15, 188 | 144:6, 186 | 8:11, 191 |
| 77:17, 218 | 146:10, 225 | 8:12, 162 |
| 77:16-19, 186 | 147:18, 221 | 10:10, 207 |
| 78:9, 192 | 148:6, 225 | 12:6, 218 |
| 78:21, 396 | 149:3, 228 | 12:25, 132 |
| 78:26, 131 | 150:4, 228 | 13:9, 266 |
| 78:27, 324 | | 14:13, 50 |
| 78:45, 113 | **Proverbs** | 15:7, 142 |
| 79:1, 223 | | 16:14, 40 |
| 79:11, 221 | 3:3, 166 | 18:20, 162 |
| 80:13, 40 | 4:4, 61 | 19:19, 164 |
| 86:8, 360 | 4:8, 121 | 19:23, 250 |
| 88:7, 204 | 5:10, 323 | 20:4, 225 |
| 89:7, 210 | 5:23, 311 | 21:26, 239 |
| 89:10, 205 | 6:21, 166 | 21:31, 286 |
| 89:29-30, 296 | 7:3, 166 | 21:32, 350 |
| 89:31, 297, 302 | 7:20, 139 | 21:33, 144 |
| 89:33, 297, 302 | 10:1, 198 | 22:28, 316 |
| 89:52, 210 | 11:13, 370 | 27:21, 183 |
| 90:10, 149 | 11:22, 199 | 28:25, 84 |
| | | 29:3, 185 |

30:14,   136
34:25,   196
36:2,    193
38:6,    201
38:13,   188
38:11,   205
38:24,   85
41:13,   209
41:17,   211

## Ruth

1:21,    68
2:8,     266
2:11,    340
3:17,    68

## Song of Songs

1:2,     279
1:7,     193
1:11,    395
2:2,     198
3:7,     193
3:11,    202
4:8,     198, 205
4:9,     54
6:11,    162
7:2,     374
7:4,     221
7:7,     191
8:6,     165

## Ecclesiastes

3:13,    380
6:2,     322
7:16,    37
10:17,   325
10:20,   366
12:9,    84

## Lamentations

1:9,     304
1:10,    223
2:9,     201
3:15,    268
5:7,     295
5:10,    293

## Esther

1:4,     196
1:5,     137
1:20,    196
4:8,     196
9:16,    352
9:24,    186
10:3,    201

## Daniel

2:5,     318
2:36,    270
5:11-12, 324
5:16,    324
6:8-9,   325
9:19,    66
11:36,   210

## Ezra

4:10,    325
4:11,    325
4:13,    325
4:14,    325
4:17,    325
4:21,    325
5:17,    71
7:12,    325
7:17,    206
7:19,    174
7:23,    193

## Nehemiah

9:2,     299
9:12,    174
13:2,    366
13:3,    151
13:24,   193

## 1 Chronicles

2:55,    255
7:21,    150
7:27,    248
8:40,    326 n. 6
16:8,    445

21:23,   45
24:2,    286
25:1,    227
25:2,    228
25:3,    228
28:18,   390
29:2,    413
29:5,    415

## 2 Chronicles

7:13,    71
8:4,     39
8:6,     39
17:12,   39
20:7,    302
31:3,    196
32:28,   39

## APOCRYPHAL & CHRISTIAN SOURCES

### Wisdom of Solomon
19:7-8, 184 n. 8

### 2 Timothy
3:8,     100

## SHADAL'S WORKS

### Grammar
183,     241
258,     40 n. 3, 115
374,     60, 106
422,     60

### Ohev Ger
p. 13,   270
p. 19,   299
p. 48,   68
p. 81,   458
p. 95,   241
p. 112,  238
p. 116,  139

# Shadal on Exodus

## RABBINIC SOURCES

### Mishnah
Peah 4:8, 325

Kela'im
2:7, 395
3:3, 395

Ma'aserot 1:2, 325

Ḥallah 3:4, 325

Pesaḥim 5:3, 26, 14

Sukkah 9:6, 394

Mo'ed Katan
3:8, 436

Bava Kamma
6:4, 59

Sanhedrin
3:7, 370
6:4, 339
9:2, 328
9:5, 103

Shevuot 8:1, 356

Avot 5:8, 102 n. 9

Ḥullin 4:1, 170

Tamid 5:4, 393

Middot 3:1, 391 n. 5

Kinnim 3:5, 228

Parah 11:7, 126

### Tosefta
Bava Kamma
7:2, 317

### Talmud
Berakhot
3b, 185
7a, 295-296, 299
32a, 439
51b, 111
58a, 385

Shabbat
12a, 111
23b, 175
28a, 388, 399
36b, 83
86b-87a, 276
98b, 397
112b, 399

Eruvin
53a, 51

Pesaḥim
5a, 142
96b, 145 n. 15
116b, 144 n. 14

Shekalim
24b, 427 n. 2

Yoma
7b, 412
55b, 119
72a, 408 n. 3
75b, 236

Sukkah
5a, 393 n. 6

Rosh Hashanah
17b, 448

Megillah
9a, 153

Ḥagigah
6a, 383

Yevamot
62b, 327
70b, 155

Ketubbot
37b, 329
46a, 67 n. 30
48a, 326
62b, 324
162a, 326

Sotah
11a, 255
12b, 52 n. 15
30b, 189

Kiddushin
11b, 322
14b, 317
20a, 319
22a, 319
22b, 317
56b, 211

Bava Kamma
2b, 338
6b, 349
7a, 342
23b, 340
79b, 344
83b, 337
84a, 337
107b, 352, 353 n. 20

Bava Metsi'a
28b, 361
59b, 155
93, 356
95, 356

Sanhedrin
7b, 368
45a, 275
67a, 359
67b, 101, 111, 240
72a, 345-347
79a-b, 336
104a, 255

*Makkot*
12, 330
12a, 458
24a, 279

*Shevu'ot*
29a, 303

*Avodah Zarah*
22a, 21 n. 18

*Zevaḥim*
102a, 76
116a, 254

*Menaḥot*
85a, 100
94a, 394
96a, 394
97a, 394 n. 7
96b, 393 n. 6

*Bekhorot*
5b, 169 n. 25

*Arakhin*
15b, 235

*Keritot*
5a, 427

*Niddah*
31a-b, 326

**Midrash Rabbah**

*Exodus Rabbah*
1:7, 149
1:32, 55
9:12, 105
10:7, 105

*Numbers Rabbah*
17:14, 435

## MEDIEVAL JEWISH SOURCES

**R. Saadiah Gaon**
*Emunot ve-De'ot*
Intro, 245
4:4, 98

**Kuzari**
1:15-25, 284
1:96, 433
2:2, 92
3:37, 23 n. 20
3:65, 154
4:23, 288
5:9-10, 298

**Maimonides**

comm. to Mishnah
*Negaim* 14:6, 146

*Sefer ha-Mitzvot*
Pos. 1, 284

*Teshuvah*
6:5, 98

*De'ot*
4:28, 326

*Shevuot*
1:4, 303

*Nizkei Mamon*
10:4, 341 n. 15

*Geneivah*
9:7, 346-347

*Ḥovel u-Mazzik*
1:3, 337 n. 12

*Rotse'aḥ*
2:14, 334

*Avadim*
3:2, 319
3:12, 317

*Sekhirut*
1:3, 356

*Pe'er ha-Dor*
90, 450

*Guide*
1:36, 294
1:47, 280
1:54, 295
1:63, 63
2:33, 274
2:36, 280
3:37, 359, 360
3:41, 343
3:43, 307
3:48, 367, 378 n. 31

**R. Joseph Albo**
*Ikkarim*
4:25, 98

## GREEK & ROMAN SOURCES

**Apuleius**
90, 101

**Aristotle**
*History of Animals*
7.4, 149

**Clement of Alexandria**
*Stromata*
Bk. 1, 54

**Curtius**
*Life of Alexander*
5.2, 173
5.7,[1] 173

---

1. Shadal quotes this at 5.7, but standard editions list it at 3.3.

### Diodorus Siculus
*Bibliotheca Historica*
3.39, 184

### Herodotus
2:158, 39

### Josephus
*Antiquities*
2:9, 42, 54
2:14, 113
2:16, 1886 n. 11
3:2, 248

*Against Apion*
1:14, 36 n. 1

### Juvenal
*Satire*
15, 116

### Lucan
*Pharsalia*
1.181, 364
4.136, 50

### Ovid
*Ex Ponto*
I.2.57, 220

*Metamorphoses*
I.111, 163

### Philo
*Life of Moses*
1.130, 110, 113
2.205, 366

*Special Laws*
1.1-11, 150 n. 17
1.7, 150 n. 17

### Pliny
*Natural History*
2.49-56, 124 n. 25
2.50, 124 n. 25
2.49, 124
7.3, 149
13.13, 50
13.45, 50
30:1, 101
55.12, 80

### Seneca
*Naturales Quaestiones*
2.12, 124 n. 25
2.14, 124 n. 25
2.16, 124 n. 25
5.13, 124
5.23, 150

### Tacitus
*Annals*
I:48, 437, 438 n. 10

### Theocritus
*Idylls*
5, 163

### Virgil
*Aeneid*
2.200, 214 n. 26

# Subject & Author Index

Aaron, 49, 74, 75, 82, 88, 104, 105, 107-114, 117, 118, 125, 126, 129,130, 132, 137, 138, 146, 148, 153, 159, 160, 179, 227, 228, 232-235, 244, 259, 260, 275, 277, 278, 282, 382, 384-386, 454
   battle with Amalek, 248-250
   death of sons, 286
   garments, 407, 408-414, 419, 431, 456, 466, 468, 469, 470
   genealogy, 93-96
   Golden Calf, 433, 434, 437, 438, 440
   Korah rebellion, 336
   priesthood and priestly functions, 406-409, 411-420, 422, 427, 428, 431, 465, 470, 471
   speaking ill of Moses with Miriam, 294
   spokesman for Moses, 76, 81, 97, 99-103
Abihu, 96, 275, 286, 382, 384, 407
Abomination (*to'evah*), 71, 115, 214
Abraham, 58, 60, 64, 65, 71, 72, 91, 92, 95, 150, 152, 155, 200, 247, 289, 294, 297, 302, 342, 365, 435, 441, 444, 445
Abraham ben David (Ra'avad), 347
Abravanel, (Don) Isaac, 42, 54, 55, 107, 118, 120, 123, 135, 148, 152, 177, 179, 180, 185, 235, 238, 240, 245-247, 257, 259, 263, 278-280, 282, 284, 285, 327, 354, 358, 360, 367, 382, 422, 424, 449, 450, 463
Abstract and concrete terminology, 209n, 325
Acacia, 388, 389, 392, 393, 399, 401-403, 421, 422, 456, 457, 459-462

Accents and accentuation (*te'amim*), 42, 49, 51, 52, 86, 100, 105, 119, 124, 138, 140, 164, 194, 208, 210, 220, 222, 224, 226, 258, 276, 283, 286, 292, 331, 332, 379, 383, 399, 403, 409, 418, 419, 427, 428, 445, 447
Accidental death or injury, 329, 330, 336, 356, 357
Adultery (Seventh Commandment), 309, 311, 315
Albo, Joseph, 98, 284
Alexandrian translator (Septuagint, translation ascribed to seventy elders), 42, 54, 67, 110, 131, 145, 152, 163, 177, 244
Alfasi, Isaac, 144n
Alien multitude (*asafsuf*), 151
Alien people (*erev rav*), 150, 151
Altar, 61, 213, 251, 252, 313, 314, 330, 374, 376, 377, 382-384, 391n, 394, 413, 434, 452
   of burnt offerings (copper), 140, 402, 403, 415, 416, 417, 418, 420-422, 427, 428, 430, 453, 456, 462, 466, 469-471
   of earth, 313
   of incense (gold), 421, 422, 428, 430, 456, 462, 468, 469, 470
   of stone, 313
   prominences, 330, 391, 402, 415, 416, 421, 422, 462
Amalek, 43, 247-252, 254-256, 257n, 283, 377
Amram, 49, 94, 95
Ancona, Shabbetai, 322

# Shadal on Exodus

Angel, 59, 141, 173, 181, 182, 210, 378, 440, 441
  evil, 175
Anglo-Dutch War, 183n
Anointing, 389, 413-416, 420, 427, 428, 431, 456, 457, 462, 468-470
Apostate (*meshummad*), 153, 154
Apuleius, Lucius, 101
Aquila, 113, 321
Arabia, 35, 38, 106, 131, 235, 247
Arabic language, 133, 140, 154, 161, 170, 187, 196, 204, 215, 223, 228, 235, 237, 243, 291-293, 316, 318, 338, 350, 363, 388, 394, 457
Arama, Isaac, 47, 66, 257, 360, 449
Aramaic and Aramaisms, 41, 51, 53, 56n, 57, 58, 71, 84, 87, 100, 115, 162, 164, 169, 195, 196, 204, 206, 207, 215, 218, 222, 228, 237, 244, 256, 262, 268, 270, 285, 293, 299, 316, 318, 324, 337, 370, 384, 385, 396, 407, 413, 418n, 431
  in biblical poetry, 192, 193
Aristotle, 149
Ark
  of Noah, 52
  of the law (of the Admonition, of the pact of the Lord), 173, 244, 389-392, 402, 406, 421, 422, 428-430, 445, 456, 460, 461, 465, 468-470
"Arrows of God" (thunderbolts), 124, 186, 187, 209
*Asafsuf* (alien multitude), 151
Asher, 34, 35
Ashkenazi, David Hai (David Vita Tedesco), 214, 367
Ashkenazi, Eliezer, 280
Ashkenazi, Hezekiah Matsliah (Cesare Tedeschi), 152
*Asmakhta*, 255, 347, 369
Asses (donkeys), 77, 79, 117, 148, 149, 161, 169, 360
Avaris, 38
*Aviv*, 162, 375

*Ba'al ha-Turim* (Jacob ben Asher), 102, 103, 105, 144
Baal-zephon, 175, 176, 178
Bacharach, Yair Hayyim, 373n
Badger (*tahash*), 388, 397-399, 456, 457, 459, 468
Bahya ben Asher (Rabbenu Bahya), 79, 256, 312, 384
Bailments and bailees (*shomerim*), 350, 352-355
  borrower, 355-357
  gratuituous bailee (*shomer ḥinnam*), 351
  hired worker (*sakhir*), 355, 356
  hirer (*sokher*), 356, 357
  paid bailee (*shomer sakhar, nosei sekhar*), 351, 356
Bar Bahlul, Hassan, 394, 395
Barley, 126, 161, 162, 375, 395, 452
Basevi, Joseph Shabbetai, 137, 249, 365
Bass, Shabbetai, 226
Beccaria, Cesare, 344
Bekhor Shor, Joseph, 268, 277, 357, 421, 434
Benjamin, 34, 35
Ben Ze'ev, Judah Leib, 46n
Bertinoro, Ovadiah, 126, 325, 391, 395
Bezalel, 408, 430, 446, 457, 458, 460, 465
Birthing chair (*ovnayim*), 43, 44
Blessing, 150, 189, 272, 304, 310, 438
Blood, 214, 221, 329, 338, 339
  Nile (first plague), 73, 102-106, 108, 109, 111, 231
  of Moses' son, 79, 80, 81
  of sacrifices, 140, 142, 270, 376, 377, 383, 384, 402, 415, 416, 420, 422, 427, 453
  of thief, 344-347
  on doorposts of Israelites' houses, 140, 141, 145, 146, 159
Bloodguilt, 345, 346
Blood-vengeance, 329, 330, 347, 363

Blue wool, 388, 396, 397, 402, 408-412, 431, 455, 457-460, 464-468
Bochart, Samuel, 106, 131, 161, 388, 433, 457n
Boils (sixth plague), 102, 103, 118, 119
Borrowing and lending
　animals, 355-357
　money, 363-365
　upon leaving Egypt, 67n, 68-70
Bread, 142, 163, 232, 234, 235, 379, 453-455
　of presentation, 394, 395, 456, 468, 470
　from heaven (manna), 232, 234, 235, 238, 240, 243, 244
　unleavened (*matsah*), 142-145, 148, 151, 152, 161, 163, 164, 166, 374, 414, 417, 419, 452
Bribery, 372, 373n
Bricks and brickmaking, 41, 47, 83-88, 259, 385
Bride, 67n
Bride-price (*mohar*), 358, 359
Burckhardt, Johann Ludwig, 230
Burning bush, 59-61
Burnt offerings (*olot*), 61, 133, 313, 375, 382, 383, 416, 418, 420-422, 427, 428, 430, 434, 456, 469-471
Buxtorf, Johannes, 101

Caecina (Roman general), 438
Cahen, Samuel, 69, 70, 101, 146
Calcination, 436, 437n
Calf, Golden, 230, 290, 426, 432n, 433, 434, 436-438, 440, 441, 443
Canaan, 43, 71, 92, 150, 152, 172, 217, 218, 219, 245, 247, 251
Canaanites, 60, 65, 94, 163, 168, 174, 179, 219, 256, 378n, 379, 380, 441, 451
Canaanite slave, 154, 155-157, 319, 320, 328, 334, 335, 338, 341
Candelabrum (*menorah*), 390, 395, 396, 402, 430, 456, 461, 462, 468-470
Caro, Isaac ben Joseph, 152

Carriages, 176-178, 181, 185, 187, 188, 201, 227
Cassuto, Umberto, 44n, 293n, 378n
Cattle, 117, 118, 122, 123, 130, 133, 134, 150, 169, 232, 246, 343, 348
　small cattle (*tson*), 139
Celsus, Aulus Cornelius, 72
Chair, birthing (*ovnayim*), 43, 44
Champollion, Jean-François, 40n, 115n
Chandler, Richard, 350
Cherubim, 390-392, 396, 402, 459-461
Chiefs
　of Edom (*allufim*), 219
　of Israelites (*sarim*), 262-265
Children of Israel. *See* Israelites
Circumcision, 78-81, 150, 151, 154-159, 166, 289
Cistern, 342
Cities of refuge, 158, 213, 328-330, 345
Clement of Alexandria, 54
Clericus, Johannes
　comments cited approvingly or neutrally by Shadal, 39, 47, 67, 72, 80, 98, 101, 116, 119, 124, 131, 132, 144, 150, 182, 183, 185, 235, 257, 335
　comments at variance with Shadal's view, 42, 48, 119, 137, 143, 252, 346
Cloud at Sinai, 273, 274, 276, 278, 312, 386, 447
Cloud, pillar of, 159, 160, 173-175, 181, 182, 185-187, 209, 230, 233-235, 378, 442, 443, 471, 472
Coccejus, Johannes, 144, 160, 302n
Cohabitation (*onah*), 324-327
Cohen Porto, Moses, 79, 109, 174, 175, 249n, 319
Compound words or names, 54, 91n, 96, 199, 216
Concrete and abstract terminology, 209n, 325
Conjugal rights, 327

Copper, 388, 391, 398, 402-404, 421, 425, 427, 430, 455-457, 459, 460, 462-464, 466, 469
Coptic language, 115, 175n
Crescas, Hasdai, 280, 284
Curses and cursing, 254, 272, 273, 331, 332, 365, 366, 426
Curtius, 173
Cybele, priests of, 80

Damages, 333, 334, 337, 341-343, 345, 346, 349, 356, 357
Dan, 34, 35, 213, 316, 430, 457, 465
Dance, dancing, 228, 229, 433, 434, 436
Darkness
   at the Red Sea, 174, 181, 182
   ninth plague, 102, 103, 132, 133
David, 98, 189, 190, 296, 300, 302, 425, 434
Death penalty, 67n, 274, 275, 309, 319, 328, 329-332, 334-337, 339-341, 346, 359, 360, 431, 455
Deborah, 190
Deception
   of Pharaoh by Moses, 66, 67
   of Egyptians by Israelites, 69-71
De Dieu, Ludovico, 58, 238n
De Lira, Nicolaus, 257
Della Valle, Pietro, 59
De' Rossi, Azariah, 190
Desert, 65, 81, 82, 98n, 102, 114, 116, 172, 175, 176, 179, 180, 215, 233, 235, 236, 244, 258, 268, 330, 367, 378, 380, 381, 387, 393
   of Etham, 173
   of Shur, 230, 231
   of Sin, 232, 246, 304
   of Sinai (Horeb), 58, 59, 131, 237, 266, 267, 286n, 388n, 389n
Desire
   of Israel's pursuers, 207, 208
   tenth commandment, 285, 310, 311
De Wette, Wilhelm Martin Leberecht, 189
Deyling, Salomon, 78, 81

Diderot, Denis, 104
Diodati, Giovanni, 180
Diodorus Siculus, 184
Dioscorides Pedanius, 243
Donkeys (asses), 77, 79, 117, 148, 149, 161, 169, 360
Dorsal (*efod*), 389, 392, 408-412, 414, 456, 457, 466, 467
Dough, 107, 144, 145, 148, 151, 152, 243, 244, 414, 417
Dubno, Solomon, 53, 59, 87, 259

East wind, 131, 182, 183, 185, 206
Edom, 218, 219, 221
*Efod* (dorsal), 389, 392, 408-412, 414, 456, 457, 466, 467
Efodi (Profiat Duran), 331
Ehrenberg, Christian Gottfried, 232
Ehrenreich, Moses ha-Levi, 106, 120, 248, 370
Eichhorn, Johann Gottfried, 101, 103, 104, 106, 110, 111, 117, 119, 129, 133, 146
Elim, 232
Elders, 65, 66, 81-83, 144, 215n, 247, 260, 267, 269, 275, 278, 281, 382, 384, 386
Egypt and Egyptians, 34-38, 41, 48, 51, 53, 55, 56, 58, 60, 61, 80, 92, 99, 148, 179, 180, 231, 259, 268, 361, 435, 437n
   at the Red Sea, 181, 182, 185-189, 201, 202, 227
   attitude toward Israelites, 35-37, 68, 70, 135, 149
   attitude toward Moses, 135
   deception of, 67n, 69-71, 175
   enslavement of Israelites, 36-42
   fault of, 125
   fertility of, 149, 150
   gods of, 44n, 115, 116, 141, 146, 260, 312
   king of, 35-38, 42, 45, 56-58, 65-67, 77, 78, 82, 83, 93, 97, 176, 178 (see also Pharaoh)
   language of, 38, 40, 50, 54, 73, 96, 110, 115, 175

plagues. *See* Plagues of Egypt
pursuit of Israelites, 176-178
taskmasters, 83, 85-87
Eleazar, 96, 286n, 407
Eliezer
    servant of Abraham, 282
    son of Moses, 80, 258
Embroiderer and embroidery, 402, 404, 408, 413, 458, 460, 464, 465, 468
*Erev rav* (alien people), 150, 151
Esau, 95, 219, 247
Etham, desert of, 173
Ethiopians, 80
Euripides, 163
Eusebius, 101
"Evil eye," 424-426
Ezekiel, 295, 297

Faber, Johann Ernst, 173
False or vain oaths, 302-304
False reports, 368
False testimony or witness, 309, 310, 368, 369, 371n
Fatality
    as punishment for Golden Calf, 440
fifth plague (*dever*), 102, 103, 117, 118, 120
Father and mother, honor of (Fifth Commandment), 308, 309
Fathers, sins of, 292, 294-301, 448-451
Fertility of Egyptians and Israelites, 149, 150
Festivals
    Israelite, 31, 83, 138, 142, 151, 155, 306, 316, 374-376, 432, 452
    Golden Calf, 434, 436, 437
    pagan, 116, 378n
Fines, 335, 336
Fire
    burning bush, 59, 60
    destruction of Golden Calf, 436, 437
    during plague of hail, 124

during Revelation at Sinai, 273, 274, 276, 279, 281
in cloud over Tabernacle, 472
law of damage by, 350
pillar of, 159, 160, 173-175, 182, 185-187, 209, 230, 378
Sabbath prohibition, 455
symbol of God's presence, 384, 386, 444, 447
Firstborn
    as priests, 277, 383
    as sacred to God, 159-161, 366, 367, 452
    death of (tenth plague), 78, 102, 117, 120, 134-137, 141, 146, 147, 150n, 169
    Israel as God's, 78
    of animals, 160, 161, 166, 168, 169, 367, 377, 378, 452, 453
    of Moses, 78, 79
    ransom, 453
First fruits, 120n, 162, 377, 378n, 417, 453, 454
Flour, 414
offering, 420, 422, 471
Foà, Hezekiah, 249
Food and dietary restrictions, 367, 368
Foreigners
    *gerim*, 143, 156-158, 306, 360, 361, 373
    hirelings, 155, 156
    *nokhrim*, 153, 321-323
    resident foreigners (*toshavim*), 155-157, 256
Forskal, Peter, 40, 110, 132
Forster, Johann, 175
Freedom, 155, 156, 316, 318, 320, 331, 338
Frogs (second plague), 102, 103, 105-111, 113
Fullerus (Fuller), Nicholas, 170

Gad, 34, 35, 90
Gershom, 57, 79, 80, 258
Gersonides (Ralbag), 53, 67, 156, 159, 185, 238, 257, 263, 264, 279,

297, 298, 309, 364, 367, 378, 425, 433
Gesenius, Heinrich Friedrich Wilhelm
  comments cited approvingly or neutrally by Shadal, 39, 44, 50, 53, 54, 126, 137, 140, 146, 153, 170, 175, 177, 230, 232, 244, 300, 310, 323, 350, 364, 384, 431, 434
  comments at variance with Shadal's view, 47, 49, 96, 187, 188, 193, 204, 215, 228, 236, 244, 302n, 327, 346, 388, 391, 429
Goats, 139, 360, 452
  goat hair, 388, 397-399, 455, 457, 459, 463
  kids, 138, 139, 169, 377, 378, 453, 454
  rams, 220, 414, 416, 418, 419
God
  anger, 76, 287, 294, 298, 362, 363, 425, 432, 435, 448
  belief in, 81, 273, 283, 284, 287, 288
  burning bush, 59-61
  crying out to, 57, 58
  fear of, 36, 42, 43, 45-47
  "finger" of, 112, 113
  hardening Pharaoh's heart, 77, 97-99, 112, 128
  holiness, 210-212
  images of, 292, 313, 385, 392
  jealousy, 287, 292-294, 298, 305, 452
  mountain of, 58, 59
  names of, 62-65, 91, 92, 199, 200
  praying to, 108, 109, 116, 117, 125, 126, 132, 148, 181, 213, 225, 248, 300, 313
  proclaiming the name of, 444, 445, 447
  punishment of Egypt, 63, 69-71, 92, 99, 112, 141
  revelation, 59, 66, 274, 280, 289, 442
  summoning Moses, 60-79
  testing of, 246, 247
  Thirteen Attributes of, 295, 447-451
  unity (oneness) of, 147, 200, 285, 287-289, 308
  worship of, 61, 66, 102, 106, 113, 117, 120, 129-131, 133, 134, 148, 179, 217, 278, 284
Gods, pagan, 124n, 200, 210, 211, 213, 214, 259, 269, 284, 285-290, 292, 312, 313, 320, 360, 366, 374, 378n, 379, 381, 434, 452
  "Do not have other gods" (Second Commandment), 285-302
  of Egypt, 112, 115, 116, 141, 146, 260, 312
Gold, 68, 71, 135, 149, 165, 199, 221, 244, 290, 303, 312, 313, 374, 388-393, 395, 396, 398, 401, 402, 408-412, 417, 421-425, 430, 433, 434n, 436, 437, 455-457, 459-462, 465-470
Golden Calf, 230, 290, 426, 432n, 433, 434, 436-438, 440, 441, 443
  of Jeroboam, 213, 439
Goshen, 35, 38, 43, 106, 113, 117, 125, 133, 150
Gratuituous bailee *(shomer ḥinnam)*, 351
Gussetius, Jacques, 45, 47, 62, 78, 81, 145, 237, 346, 390

Hail (seventh plague), 43, 102, 103, 120-127, 130-132
Ḥamets, 142, 144, 145, 151, 152, 376
Ḥamsin, 133
Hananel ben Hushiel (Rabbenu Hananel), 79, 347
Hasselquist, Fredrik, 145
Hazak (Forti), David, 86, 180, 249, 311
Heber, 255
Hebrew language, 35, 43, 55, 76, 89, 192, 202, 203, 226, 421, 440
  Aramaic, relation to, 192, 193

compound words, 216
idioms, 72, 73, 87, 286, 302, 340, 375n
Rabbinic, 161, 206, 218, 226, 291, 292, 303, 325, 350, 361, 399
Hebrew maidservant, 320-328, 334n
Hebrews, 35, 42, 43, 46, 48, 51-53, 55, 56, 65, 82, 102, 103, 117, 120, 129, 149
Hebrew servant, 316-320, 334n, 335
Hefez (Gentili), Moses, 47
Heidenheim, Wolf, 285
Heliopolis, 39
Herder, Johann Gottfried, 378
Herodotus, 39, 80
Heroöpolis, 175
Hireling or hired worker *(sakhir)*, 155, 156, 355, 356
Hirer *(sokher)*, 356, 357
Hirsch, Samson Raphael, 316n
Hiwi al-Balkhi, 184, 238n
Hizkuni, 327, 357, 433
Hobab, 253-256
Holiness *(kodesh)*, 143, 210-216, 275, 368, 392, 420
Holland, 183
Homicide, 158, 328-330, 332, 337, 339
  manslaughter, manslayer, 213, 329
  murder and murderers, 213, 309, 315, 330, 344-346
Homberg, Herz (Korem), 37, 47, 55, 82, 88, 109, 154, 165, 166, 320, 331
Honor of father and mother (Fifth Commandment), 308, 309
Horeb, 58, 59, 247, 441
Horn *(shofar, yovel)*, 275, 276, 279-281, 311
Horsemen, 176, 178, 181, 185, 187, 188, 227
Horses, 117, 169n, 176-178, 185, 189, 191, 197, 227, 229, 230
Ḥoshen (pectoral), 389, 392, 408-412, 414, 456, 457, 466, 467

Hur, 248-250, 386, 430, 457
Hyksos, 36n
Hyssop, 145, 146

Ibn Ezra, Abraham
  comments cited approvingly or neutrally by Shadal, 42, 46, 53, 57, 59, 61, 83, 88, 96, 101, 102, 105, 109, 123, 131, 133, 134, 139, 140, 142, 148, 160, 165, 171, 177, 184, 195, 221, 226, 227, 231, 236-238, 240-244, 246, 248, 252, 258, 263, 266, 268, 275, 276, 279-282, 284, 309-311, 317, 324, 327, 331, 333, 334, 336, 338, 344, 348, 354, 359, 364, 367-369, 372, 377, 378, 392, 420, 433, 436, 440, 441, 442n, 444, 452, 455
  comments at variance with Shadal's view, 43, 49, 54, 56, 60, 68, 73, 74, 92, 105, 108, 112, 115, 126, 148, 149, 156, 159, 162, 164, 166, 185, 194-197, 202, 205, 208, 220, 224, 225, 230, 233, 239, 242, 248, 250, 251, 254, 256, 257n, 263n, 264, 266-268, 274, 275, 282, 283, 298, 309, 310, 321, 322, 324, 344-347, 356, 407, 429, 435, 439, 445, 449
Ibn Janah, Jonah, 44n, 126, 146, 154, 254, 384
Ibn Shem Tov, Shem Tov, 280
Idioms, Hebrew, 72, 73, 87, 286, 302, 340, 375n
Idols and idolatry, 115, 157, 287, 288, 290, 293n, 294, 295, 309, 313, 320, 359, 360, 374, 378n, 379, 433, 434n, 435, 438, 452
Igel, Eliezer Elijah, 83, 87, 92
Images, 289-291, 313, 314, 374, 433, 435, 446
  of God, 292, 312, 313, 385, 392
Incense, 389, 421, 422, 428-431, 456, 457, 462, 468-471

India, 231
Indian language, 320
Interest, 363, 364
Isaac, 58, 60, 64-66, 72, 91, 92, 95, 126, 152, 282, 435, 441
Isaac ben Samuel (Ri), 83
Israelites (children of Israel)
  acceptance of covenant and laws, 270-273, 382, 383
  battle with Amalek, 247-250
  camps and encampments, 172, 173, 175, 176, 178, 181, 182, 213, 232, 234, 235, 246, 267, 276, 416, 436, 438, 442, 458
  contributions to Sanctuary, 387, 388, 432n, 455-458, 463
  complaints and murmurings, 179, 180, 230-235, 246, 247
  elders, 65, 66, 81-83, 144, 215n, 247, 260, 267, 269, 275, 278, 281, 382, 384, 386
  enslavement, 36-42
  fertility, 149, 150
  genealogy, 34, 35, 93-96
  length of residence in Egypt, 95
  oppression in Egypt, 38-41, 60, 61, 64, 69, 259, 361
  population, 94, 149, 466
Israel, land of, 140, 150, 213, 223, 230, 250, 251, 255, 268, 342, 367, 381, 387
Issachar, 34, 35, 322
Italian language, 401
Ithamar, 96, 286n, 407, 465

Jablonski, Paul Ernst, 39, 40n, 54, 175
Jacob, 58, 60, 64, 65, 72, 91-93, 95, 152, 167, 189, 354, 441
  and family, 34, 35
Jacob ben Asher (*Ba'al ha-Turim*), 102, 103, 105, 144
Jacob ben Meir Tam (Rabbenu Tam), 111, 449, 450
Jahn, Johann, 153
Jarè, Joseph, 82, 107, 122, 138, 347

Jealousy of God, 287, 292-294, 298, 452
Jeremiah, 73, 273, 295, 297, 318
Jerome, 42, 67, 113, 145, 180, 346, 458n
Jerusalem, 145, 259, 367
Jerusalem Targum, 48, 132, 153, 174, 237, 354, 360, 385, 403, 419, 434
  version ascribed to Jonathan ben Uzziel, 100, 207, 285, 347, 354, 355, 356
Jethro, 57, 58, 77, 78, 253, 254, 256-261
Joseph of Orleans, 111
Josephus Flavius, 36n, 42, 54, 113, 186, 248, 366
Jochebed, 46n, 50, 94
  and infant Moses, 51, 53
Joseph, 34, 35, 36n, 73, 135, 154, 173, 177
Joshua, 80, 100n, 149, 212, 248, 250, 251, 271, 293, 378, 386, 436, 442
Jost, Isaac Marcus, 35, 38, 40, 95, 146, 175, 183, 187, 280, 281, 307
Jubilee, 138, 157, 317, 318, 320
Judah, 34, 47n, 96, 214, 255, 256, 319, 332, 410, 430, 457, 465
Judah ben Kuraish, 126
Judah ha-Levi, 92, 154, 284, 288
Judges and judging, 257, 260, 261, 264-266, 294, 295, 309, 315, 317, 320, 328, 329, 332, 333, 335-337, 340, 341, 351-353, 362, 365, 366, 368-370, 372, 373
Justi, Karl Wilhelm, 69
Juvenal, 116

Karaites, 139, 165, 166, 184n, 378
  Yefet ben Ali, 160
*Karet*, 103, 143, 197n
*Karkov*, 403, 462
Kenites, 255, 256
Kid, 138, 139, 169, 453
  cooking in mother's milk, 377, 378, 454
Kidnapping, 309

Kimhi, David, 39, 41, 58, 60, 82, 107, 121, 146, 162, 228, 229, 236, 254, 256, 290, 293, 310, 324, 350, 383, 397, 411

King
  George VI of Great Britain, 74n
  of Edom, 219
  of Egypt, 35-38, 42, 45, 56-58, 65-67, 77, 78, 82, 83, 93, 97, 176, 178
  (see also Pharaoh)

Klineberger, Isaac Judah, 50, 56, 371
Kneading, 145, 151, 152, 243, 414
kneading troughs, 107, 148
Koppe, Johann Benjamim, 95, 153
Korem (Herz Homberg), 37, 47, 55, 82, 88, 109, 154, 165, 166, 320, 331
*Kumaz*, 456, 457

Lambs, 148, 138-140, 161, 169, 228, 343, 348, 350, 352, 353, 377, 383n, 420, 453
Landau, Moses, 208
Latin, 115, 145, 161, 178, 192, 204, 208, 209n, 214, 225, 235, 291, 292, 302, 350, 370, 388, 401n, 418, 457n
Leaven and leavening, 142-145, 148, 151, 161, 376, 453
Leibowitz, Nehama, 67n, 365n, 371n
Leprosy, 72, 119
Levi, 34, 48, 62, 93, 94, 95, 407, 437, 438
Levita (Bahur), Elijah, 162, 202
Levites, 47n, 75, 76, 96, 147, 173, 306, 330, 417, 438, 439, 465
Levy (*mas*), 38, 39, 125, 418n
Lewisohn, Solomon, 192
*Lex talionis*, 337
Lice (third plague), 102, 103, 105, 110-113, 117
Lightning, 124, 185-187, 209, 245, 276
Linen, 388, 396, 397, 399, 402-404, 408-410, 413, 431, 455, 457-460, 463-468

Linnaeus, Carolus, 110
Locusts (eighth plague), 102, 103, 129-132
Lucan, 50, 364
Ludolf, Hiob, 80
Luzzatto, Hezekiah (father of Shadal), 34, 47, 49, 53
Luzzatto, Judah, 151, 440
Luzzatto, Ohev Ger (Filosseno, son of Shadal), 37, 39, 381
Lydius, Jacob, 178

Maidservant, 305-307, 310, 317
  Hebrew, 320-328, 334n
Maimonides, Moses, 62, 97, 98, 146, 274, 280, 284, 294, 295, 303, 307, 317, 319, 326, 334, 337n, 341n, 343, 346, 347, 356, 359, 360, 367, 378n, 391, 450
Mainster, Abraham Hai, 58, 59, 63, 64, 232, 237, 247, 251, 264, 341, 355, 403, 418, 429, 438, 450
Manetho, 36n
Manna, 172, 215, 220, 233, 234-245, 257, 282
  "bread" from heaven, 232, 234, 235, 238, 240, 243, 244
Manservant, 305-307, 310, 317
  Hebrew, 334n (see also Servant)
Manslaughter, manslayer, 213, 329
Marah, 230
Masoretes, Masoretic vocalizers, 45, 122, 224, 375n
Massah and Meribah, 247
*Matsah*, 144, 145, 148, 164, 166 (see also Unleavened bread)
*Me'ammer* (Wolf Meir), 196, 197, 226, 250, 257, 268, 301, 426
Measure, units of
  liquid, 394, 395
  solid, 245, 246
Meir, Wolf (*Me'ammer*), 196, 197, 226, 250, 257, 268, 301, 426
Memphis, 38, 50
Mendelssohn, Moses
  manuscripts in possession of, 258, 419

translations or comments cited approvingly or neutrally by Shadal, 34, 53, 55, 61, 69, 72, 76, 89, 96-98, 102, 111, 133, 141, 142, 148, 175, 181, 210, 227, 232, 233, 242, 246, 267, 282, 284, 301, 361, 372, 374, 384, 388, 426, 435, 436, 437n, 439, 453

translations or comments at variance with Shadal's view, 37, 39, 42, 47, 49, 52, 62, 65, 67, 88, 111, 114, 119, 137, 164, 228-230, 247, 250, 254, 261, 267, 299, 310, 346, 351, 356, 357, 384-386, 392, 439, 442, 449, 458n, 468

"Men of talent" (*ḥakhmei lev*, artisans), 407, 408, 430, 456, 458-460

Metaphor, 97, 119, 165, 166, 209n, 415

Michaelis, Johann David, 57, 101, 149, 150, 153, 157, 237, 377

Midwives, 42, 43, 45- 48, 125

Migdol, 175

Milk, cooking kid in mother's, 377, 378, 454

Milk and honey, land flowing with, 60, 65, 163, 441

Miracles, 70, 72, 73, 77, 81, 97, 98, 102, 112-114, 117, 118, 174, 212, 215, 221, 231, 444

battle with Amalek, 248, 249

manna, 237, 238, 239, 245

natural aspects of, 104, 173, 182-184, 237

quails, 235

splitting of Red Sea, 182-184, 218, 221

Miriam, 47n, 49, 74, 94, 95, 227-230, 248

and infant Moses, 51, 53

Mirrors, 463

Mixture (*arov*, fourth plague), 102, 103, 113, 114, 116-118, 208

Mizrahi, Elijah, 120, 370, 432

Moab and Moabites, 211, 218-221, 270

Modena, Shalom Simeon, 107, 384

Months

new moon, 266

numbering of, 138

Mortara, Mordecai, 54, 321, 370

Moses

Aaron as spokesman for, 76, 81, 97, 99-103

appearances before Pharaoh, 81-83, 108, 109, 114-117, 119, 125, 126, 129-137, 148

birth and infancy, 49-55

"bloodstained bridegroom" incident, 78-81

burning bush, 59-61

complaints to by Israelites, 179, 180, 230-235, 246, 247

construction of Tabernacle, 469-470

father, 48, 49, 94, 95

father-in-law, 57, 58, 77, 253, 254, 256-261

first ascent to Mount Sinai, 385, 386

receipt of first tablets, 432

flight from Egypt, 56

genealogy, 93-96

Golden Calf, actions in response to, 435-439

in Midian, 56, 57

judging, 260-262, 264-266

laws, announcement of, 144-146, 269-273, 382, 454-456

marriage, 57

mother, 46n, 50, 51, 53, 94

name, 53-55

second ascent to Mount Sinai, 447

descent with second tablets, 454

seeing God's Majesty, 444-451

sister, 47n, 49, 51, 53, 74, 94, 95, 227-230, 248

sons, 57, 79, 80, 258

staff, 72, 77, 99-104, 108, 110, 111, 117, 118, 123, 124, 134, 141, 181, 247-252

speaking difficulty, 73-75, 93
summoning by God, 60-79
wife, 57, 79, 80, 254, 258
Moses of Coucy, 284, 370
Mother and father, honor of (Fifth Commandment), 308, 309
Murder and murderers, 213, 309, 315, 330, 344-346
Sixth commandment, 309, 315
Music and musical instruments, 227-229, 434

Nachmanides
comments cited approvingly or neutrally by Shadal, 47, 48, 72, 88, 97, 103, 105, 111, 159, 164, 165, 181, 227, 231, 233, 236, 246, 273, 276, 286, 319, 321, 336, 360, 385, 433, 471
comments at variance with Shadal's view, 67, 109, 114, 122, 123, 145n, 152, 154, 160, 190, 191n, 217, 235, 251, 254, 256, 258, 294, 321, 327, 367, 429
Nachtigal, Johann Konrad Christoph, 189
Nadab, 96, 275, 286, 382, 384, 407
Naphtali, 34, 35
Napoleon, 426n
Nathan of Rome, 240
Netted cloths (*bigdei serad*), 430, 431, 456, 466, 469
Niebuhr, Carsten, 40, 183, 184, 231
Nile, 38n, 48-52, 73, 101-109, 121, 147, 149, 150, 175, 247, 259
Nissim ben Jacob ben Nissim ibn Shahin, 448
Nissim ben Reuben Gerondi (Ran), 144

Oaths, false or vain, 302-304
Oholiab, 408, 430, 457, 458, 465
Oil, 211, 212, 367, 414, 417, 420
of anointing, 389, 414, 416, 427, 428, 431, 456, 457, 462, 468, 469
of illumination, 389, 406, 456, 457, 468
Olper, Samuel Solomon, 102, 365
Onkelos
translations cited approvingly or neutrally by Shadal, 41, 48, 59, 80, 87, 121, 140, 145, 148, 151, 154, 244, 347, 348, 394, 399, 414, 430, 444, 453
translations at variance with Shadal's view, 42, 68, 111, 112, 143, 148, 178, 207, 214, 228, 236, 299, 304, 323, 384, 422, 429
variant readings, 68, 236, 321, 458
Onomatopoeia, 203
Oppression
of Israelites in Egypt, 38-41, 60, 61, 64, 69, 259, 361
monetary or verbal (*hona'ah*), 360, 361
Orphans, 191, 192, 306, 317n, 361-363
Osimo, Judah Aryeh, 46, 167, 353, 403, 442, 450
Overburdened animal, relief of, 371, 372
Ovid, 163, 220
Ox, 117, 161, 310, 337-341, 342-344, 348-350, 352, 353, 356, 357, 367, 370, 371, 373, 395, 452

Pagninus, Xanthus, 67
Paid bailee (*shomer sakhar*), 351, 356
Pappenheim, Solomon, 62
Papyrus, 49, 50, 53
Parallelism, 197-199
Pardo, Isaac, 67, 126, 167, 250, 393
Pardo, Jacob Hai, 43, 131, 322, 355
Parents
cursing, 331, 332
honoring (Fifth Commandment), 308, 309
striking, 197, 330, 331

Parhon, Salomon ben Abraham ibn, 80, 126
Paschal (Passover) sacrifice, 138-141, 144, 153-159, 163, 166, 197n, 316, 376, 453
Passover, 132, 140-148, 151, 155-157, 166, 179
Paulus Jurisonsultus, 150
Pectoral (*ḥoshen*), 389, 392, 408-412, 414, 456, 457, 466, 467
Pendants, 433
Persians and Persian language, 237, 320
Petahiah of Regensburg, 237
Pharaoh
  and midwives, 42, 43, 45- 48, 125
  enslavement of Israelites, 36-42
  exchanges with Moses and Aaron, 81-83, 108, 109, 114-117, 119, 125, 126, 129-137, 148
  hardening or strengthening of heart, 77, 97-99, 101, 104, 108, 110, 112, 113, 117, 118, 120, 127, 128, 132, 134, 137, 176, 178
  pursuit of Israelites, 176-178
  servants of, 89, 100-103, 107-109, 113, 114, 116, 117, 120, 123, 126-128, 130, 135, 137, 148, 176
Pharaoh's daughter, 52-55
Philistines, Philistia, 171, 217, 218, 219, 380, 381

Philo Judaeus, 110, 113, 150, 366
Phinehas
  son of Eleazar, 96, 302,
  son of Eli, 376n
Pi-ha-Hirot, 38, 175, 178, 182
Pillar of cloud, 159, 160, 173-175, 181, 182, 185-187, 209, 230, 233-235, 378, 442, 443, 471, 472
Pillar of fire, 159, 160, 173-175, 182, 185-187, 209, 230, 378
Pithom, 38, 39
Pitts, Joseph, 173

Plagues of Egypt
  blood, 73, 102-106, 108, 109, 111, 231
  boils, 102, 103, 118, 119
  classifications of, 102, 103
  darkness, 102, 103, 132, 133
  fatality (*dever*), 102, 103, 117, 118, 120
  firstborn, death of, 78, 102, 117, 120, 134-137, 141, 146, 147, 150n, 169
  frogs, 102, 103, 105-111, 113
  hail, 43, 102, 103, 120-127, 130-132
  lice, 102, 103, 105, 110-113, 117
  locusts, 102, 103, 129-132
  mixture (*arov*), 102, 103, 113, 114, 116-118, 208
Pledge, 66, 67, 306, 310, 364, 365
Pliny the Elder, 50, 80, 101, 124, 149
Plutarch, 116
Poetry and poetic devices
  Aramaisms, 192, 193
  archaic expressions and forms, 192, 206
  asyndeton, 207
  *mashal*, 165, 199, 302
  onomatopoeia, 203
  parallelism, 197-199
Polytheism, 285, 287-289
Portaleone, Abraham, 229
Prayer and praying, 108, 109, 116, 117, 125, 126, 132, 148, 181, 213, 225, 248, 300, 313, 374
Priestly garments, 407
  belt, 408, 413, 415, 468
  diadem (*tsits*), 167, 412, 413n, 414, 468
  dorsal (*efod*), 389, 392, 408-412, 414, 456, 457, 466, 467
  mantle, 408, 412, 414, 467, 468
  mitre, 408, 412-414, 468
  pectoral (*ḥoshen*), 389, 392, 408-412, 414, 456, 457, 466, 467
  trousers, 413, 468
  tunic, 408, 413-415, 468, 470
  turban, 413, 415, 468

Urim and Tummim, 410-412
Priests and priesthood
  Aaron, 406-409, 411-420, 422, 427, 428, 431, 465, 470, 471
  Egyptian, 36n
  firstborn as, 277, 278
  high priest, 167, 376n, 412
  Israelite (*kohanim*), 46, 47n, 76, 157, 160, 179, 212, 302, 315, 366, 367, 377, 407, 408, 413-415, 417-420, 428, 456, 470
  Midianite, 56, 58, 253
  of Cybele, 80
  "realm of priests and a holy nation," 269, 312
Proclaiming the name of the Lord, 444, 445, 447
Prophets and prophecy, 73, 97, 118, 165, 192, 193, 203, 211, 225, 227-229, 262, 273, 280, 291, 294, 297, 302, 378, 379, 415
Proselytes, 256
Puah, 42, 43, 47n
Purple (cloth), 388, 396, 397, 402, 408-412, 431, 455, 457-460, 464-468

Quails, 131, 140, 212, 233, 235, 283

Ra'amses, 38, 39, 40n
Ra'avad (R. Abraham ben David), 347
Rabbenu Tam (Jacob ben Meir Tam), 111, 449, 450
Rabbinic Hebrew, 161, 206, 218, 226, 291, 292, 303, 325, 350, 361, 399
Rameses, 35, 36n, 39, 40, 149
Rams, 220, 414, 416, 418, 419
Ran (Rabbenu Nissim ben Reuben Gerondi), 144
Ransom, 337, 340, 341, 423-427, 453
Rashbam (R. Samuel ben Meir)
  comments cited approvingly or neutrally by Shadal, 34, 41, 57, 61, 73, 76, 80, 89, 96, 102, 103, 105, 113, 114, 133, 134, 148, 156, 164, 178, 182, 217, 219, 227, 228, 231-233, 243, 244, 252, 259, 260, 275, 301, 313, 321, 330, 339, 342, 349, 350, 354, 359, 363, 373, 377, 384, 396, 439, 444, 454
  comments at variance with Shadal's view, 37, 42, 47, 49, 68, 69, 73, 80, 118, 159, 165, 202, 248, 251, 256, 298, 327,
Rashi
  comments cited approvingly or neutrally by Shadal, 39, 55, 59, 61, 65, 67, 68n, 72, 76, 78, 83, 84, 87-89, 92, 93, 97, 98, 108, 114, 119, 126, 134, 137, 140, 148, 150, 153, 155, 161, 168, 169, 174, 175, 194, 195, 208, 226, 227, 230, 233, 235, 242, 243-245, 247, 248, 258, 259, 261, 266, 277, 309, 311, 317, 318, 320, 323, 334-336, 338, 342, 343, 345, 346, 350, 351, 356, 357, 359, 364, 368, 372, 379, 380, 388, 389n, 390, 398-401, 403, 404, 409, 412, 414, 416, 418, 420, 431, 432, 434, 435, 443, 444, 446, 453
  comments at variance with Shadal's view, 46, 52, 92, 106, 107, 115, 132, 133n, 142, 143, 148, 156, 159, 164, 175, 182, 194, 196, 204, 214, 236, 238, 247, 250, 261, 268, 275n, 276, 278, 298, 299, 312n, 319, 321, 322, 330, 341n, 347, 348n, 353, 358, 369, 370, 380, 390, 393, 394, 399, 401, 408n, 419n, 421, 427n, 428, 429, 435, 439, 440, 458
  variant readings, 77, 120, 162, 195, 240, 303, 384, 412, 413n, 419, 429, 431-433, 471
Ravius (Rau), Christian, 153
Red Sea, 39, 132, 172, 175, 230, 235, 380, 381

splitting of, 102, 181-188, 227
song at. *See* Song of the Sea
Reeds, 49, 50-53
Refuge, cities of, 158, 213, 328-330, 345
Reggio, Isaac Samuel, 102, 119, 123, 168, 184, 257, 300, 306, 356, 390, 392, 449
Rekabites, 255
Rephidim, 267
Resident foreigners (*toshavim*), 155-157, 256
Retaliation penalty, 337
Reuben, 34, 93, 94
Reuel, 56, 57, 253, 254
Revelation, 59, 66, 274, 280, 289, 442
Ri (R. Isaac ben Samuel), 83
Roman law, 333, 334, 337
Romans, 116, 155, 438
Rosenmueller, Ernst Friedrich Karl
  comments cited approvingly or neutrally by Shadal, 39, 40, 47, 50, 53, 54, 58, 59, 72, 80, 88, 94-96, 98, 100, 101, 104, 110, 113, 119, 129, 131, 133, 140, 146, 153, 170, 175, 275, 310, 320, 324, 363, 384, 431, 436, 437n
  comments at variance with Shadal's view, 42, 43, 49, 52, 62, 66, 67, 82, 115, 119, 137, 160, 187, 193, 228, 237, 256, 302, 327, 351, 378, 429
  Shadal's comments included in work on Isaiah, 200

Saadiah Gaon, 59, 62, 92, 98, 146, 245, 258, 274-276, 338, 344, 365, 367
Sabbath, 143, 155, 211, 215, 233, 238-243, 324, 369, 373, 431, 432, 453, 455
  remembering the Sabbath day (Fourth Commandment), 304-308

Sabbatical year (*shemittah*), 157, 373, 432
Sacrifices, 65, 66, 82, 84, 88, 108, 114-116, 133, 134, 146, 148, 158, 211-214, 249, 260, 277, 305, 416, 427, 463
  burnt offerings (*olot*), 61, 133, 313, 375, 382, 383, 416, 418, 420-422, 427, 428, 430, 434, 456, 469-471
  flour offerings, 420, 422, 471
  of aspersion (*hattat*), 416, 419, 422
  of contentment (*shelamim*), 260, 313, 375, 382, 383, 385, 417, 419, 434
  of firstborns, 168, 169, 452
  of installation, 419
  paschal, 138-141, 144, 153-159, 163, 166, 197n, 316, 376, 453
  to other gods, 360, 452
Samuel ben Meir. *See* Rashbam
Sanctuary (*mikdash*)
  altar of burnt offerings (copper), 140, 402, 403, 415, 416, 417, 418, 420-422, 427, 428, 430, 453, 456, 462, 466, 469-471
  altar of incense (gold), 421, 422, 428, 430, 456, 462, 468, 469, 470
  ark of the law (of the Admonition, of the pact of the Lord), 173, 244, 389-392, 402, 406, 421, 422, 428-430, 445, 456, 460, 461, 465, 468-470
  basin, 427, 428, 430, 456, 462, 463, 469-471
  bread of presentation, 394, 395, 456, 468, 470
  candelabrum (*menorah*), 390, 395, 396, 402, 430, 456, 461, 462, 468-470
  cherubim, 390-392, 396, 402, 459-461
  cover of ark, 390-392, 402, 422, 430, 456, 461, 468, 470

furnishings, 389, 396, 402, 404, 428, 430, 431, 456, 461, 462, 466, 468-470
incense, 389, 421, 422, 428-431, 456, 457, 462, 468-471
netted cloths (*bigdei serad*), 430, 431, 456, 466, 469
table, 392-396, 402, 421, 428, 430, 456, 461, 468-470
Tabernacle (*mishkan*), 234, 244, 257, 275, 389, 396-404, 414, 424, 425, 430, 456, 459, 460, 464-466, 468-472
tribute (*terumah*), 39, 305, 367, 387, 388, 417-419, 424, 426, 455-458, 463, 465
Saphir, Jacob, 259
Sapphire, 384, 385, 410, 467
Saul, 189, 255
Scarlet (cloth), 388, 396, 397, 402, 408-412, 431, 455, 457-460, 464-468
Schultens, Albertus, 187
Seduction, 358, 359
Seneca, 124, 150
Septuagint (Alexandrian translator, translation ascribed to seventy elders), 42, 54, 67, 110, 131, 145, 152, 163, 177, 244
Serpents, 72, 99-102
Servant, Hebrew, 316-320, 334n, 335
Servants of Pharaoh, 89, 100-103, 107-109, 113, 114, 116, 117, 120, 123, 126-128, 130, 135, 137, 148, 176
Servius, 214
Seventy elders (Israelite leaders), 215n, 275
Seventy elders, translation ascribed to (Septuagint, Alexandrian translator), 42, 54, 67, 110, 131, 145, 152, 163, 177, 244
Sforno, Ovadiah, 43, 49, 51, 72, 78, 136, 151, 257, 259, 269,
Shaw, Thomas, 232
Sheep, 68, 139, 214, 232, 344, 452

lambs, 148, 138-140, 161, 169, 228, 343, 348, 350, 352, 353, 377, 383n, 420, 453
rams, 220, 414, 416, 418, 419
Sheepskins (rams' skins) dyed red, 388, 397, 456, 457, 459, 468
Shekels, 336, 341, 358, 396, 426, 427, 465, 466
half shekel, 388, 424, 426
"Shepherd kings," shepherd people, 35, 38
Shepherds and shepherding, 36, 37, 40n, 56, 57, 74, 117, 344, 354
Shiphrah, 42, 43, 46n
Shur, desert of, 230, 231
Silver, 68, 71, 135, 149, 173, 177, 221, 290, 312, 313, 336, 358, 359, 374, 388, 391, 400-402, 404, 423-427, 430, 455, 457, 460, 463, 464, 466
Simeon, 34, 94
Simon, Richard, 153
Sinai
desert or wilderness of, 131, 159, 232, 237, 266, 267, 388n
Mount, 58, 59, 61, 165n, 172, 184, 256n, 267, 268, 274-277, 280, 317n, 386, 432, 437n, 439, 444, 446, 447, 454
Singing, 49, 189, 190, 198, 199, 228, 229, 324, 434
Sins, 97, 98, 152, 158, 343, 344, 445, 449, 451
of the fathers, 292, 294-301, 448-451
Slander, 368, 371n
Slaves and slavery
bondwoman, 157, 319, 320, 334, 338, 341
Canaanite slaves, 154, 155-157, 319, 320, 328, 334, 335, 338, 341
Hebrew servants, 316-320, 334n, 335
Hebrew maidservants, 320-328, 334n
injury, 334, 335, 338, 341

Israelites in Egypt, 36-42, 57, 62, 66, 69, 70, 92, 161, 169, 171, 180, 282, 306, 307
jubilee, 157, 317, 318, 320
kidnapping and sale, 331
maidservants, 305-307, 310, 317
Sabbath rest, 307, 373, 374
under Roman law, 334, 335
Sodomy, 360
Song of Deborah, 190
Song of the Sea, 189-230
Sorcerers, 100, 101, 104, 105, 108, 111-113, 119, 120
Spices, 389, 427-429, 456, 457
Spinoza, Baruch, 200, 201
Stealing (Eighth Commandment), 309, 311, 315, 317n
"Stiff-necked people," 435, 441, 444, 451
Stoning, 115, 116, 275, 338, 339
Storehouses, 38, 39
Stranger (*ben nekhar, nokhri*), 153, 159, 322, 323
Straw for brickmaking, 66, 83, 85-88, 147, 259
Stray animals, restoration of, 371
Suez, 175, 182-184, 230
Superintendents of slaves, 83, 85-88
Supreme Court of United States, 308n
Swearing, 252, 351, 352
for falsehood (Third Commandment), 302-304
Symmachus, 321
Syriac, 51, 57, 111, 139n, 154, 161, 196, 204, 215, 238, 241, 293, 303, 321, 394

Tabernacle (*mishkan*), 234, 244, 257, 275, 389, 396, 402, 424, 425, 430, 455, 459, 464-466, 468-472
bases, 397, 398, 400-402, 404, 424, 456, 460, 463, 464, 466, 468-470
boards, 391, 397, 399-401, 403, 456, 459, 460, 462, 468, 470
construction, 469-470
courtyard, 403, 404, 414, 456, 471
covers, 397-399, 456, 459, 468, 470
curtains, 396-399, 403, 404, 456, 459, 463, 464, 469
door-curtain, 402, 406, 422, 424, 446, 456, 460, 466, 468-470
dimensions, 397, 398
materials for weaving (twisted linen, blue wool, purple, and scarlet), 396, 397, 402-404, 459, 460, 463, 464
pipes (*pifiyyot*), 401
Tablets of the Law, 244, 282, 284, 385, 386, 390, 392, 432, 436, 443, 447, 454, 465, 470
Tacitus, 437, 438n
*Tahash*, 388, 397
Tam, Jacob ben Meir (Rabbenu Tam), 111, 449, 450
Tangible and intangible concepts, 209, 214
Tanhum ben Joseph ha-Yerushalmi, 146
Taskmasters, 83, 85-87
*Tefillin*, 165-167, 170
Temple, 140, 155, 189, 190, 211-214, 223, 291, 325, 375n, 387, 391n, 393, 418n, 426, 427, 440-442, 465, 466, 468
Ten Commandments (*dibrot*)
First: "I am the Lord," 282-285
Second: "Do not have other gods," 285-302
Third: "Do not utter the name of the Lord your God (swearing) for falsehood," 302-304
Fourth: "Remember the Sabbath day," 304-308
Fifth: "Honor your father and your mother," 308, 309
Sixth: "Do not commit murder," 309, 315
Seventh: "Do not commit adultery," 309, 311, 315
Eighth: "Do not steal," 309, 311, 315, 317n

# Shadal on Exodus

Ninth: "Do not give false testimony," 309, 310, 368
Tenth: "Do not desire," 285, 310, 311
Ten Plagues. *See* Plagues of Egypt
Tent of congregation (*ohel mo'ed*), 413-415, 419, 420, 424, 427-430, 456, 466, 468-471
    Moses' tent outside the camp, 442, 463
    "women who came to work" (*tsove'ot*), 463
Tetragrammaton, 63, 199, 200
Thebais and Thebes, 38
Theft and thieves, 309, 318, 319, 331, 343, 344, 346-348, 354, 357, 361
Theocritus, 163
Theodotion, 321
Thévenot, Jean de, 44
Thirteen Divine Attributes, 447-451
Thunder, 124-127, 185-187, 209, 245, 276, 280, 281, 311, 312
Thunderbolts ("arrows of God"), 124, 186, 187, 209
Toland, John, 173
Tribute (*terumah*), 39, 305, 367, 387, 388, 417-419, 424, 426, 455-458, 463, 465
Typhon, 175

Ulcers, 118-120
United States Supreme Court, 308n
Unleavened bread (*matsah*), 142-145, 148, 151, 152, 161, 163, 164, 166, 374, 414, 417, 419, 452
Urim and Tummim, 410-412

Vain or false oaths, 302-304
Vater, Johann Severin, 153
Venetian dialect, 140
Venice, 122, 263n
Verb tenses, 61, 62n, 99, 106, 107, 110, 122, 125, 191n, 203, 217, 218, 225, 226, 264, 266, 439, 458
Vidal of Tolosa, 347
Viterbi, David Hananiah, 380
Voltaire, 426
Vowels and vocalization, 39, 44, 45, 49, 51, 57, 58n, 68, 81, 85n, 88, 124, 194-196, 202, 203, 207, 220, 222, 224-227, 239, 241, 266, 268, 292, 293, 313, 355, 375n, 401

Warriors, 177, 251
Water
    in the desert, 230-232, 246, 247
    of the Nile, 53-55, 73, 101-106, 108, 149, 150
    of the Red Sea, 182-185, 204, 206, 207
Waving (*tenufah*), 415, 417, 418
Weaving, 396, 397, 408, 410, 412, 413, 458, 463, 465-468
Wessely, Naphtali Herz, 37, 102, 123, 124, 168, 184, 247, 283
Widows, 191, 192, 306, 317n, 361-363
Wind
    east, 131, 182, 183, 185, 206
    north, 183
    *simoom* (*samum, samiel, ḥamsin*), 133
    south, 131
    west, 131, 132
Wisdom (*hokhmah*), 36, 37, 408, 426
Wisse, Y., 250
Witches and witchcraft, 359, 360
Witnesses, 310, 329, 331, 346, 347, 368, 369, 371n
Wolf, Immanuel, 200
Wolfsheimer (Wolffsheimer), Salomon Bernard, 150
"Women of talent" (artisans), 457
"Women who came to work" (*tsove'ot*), 463

Year, definition of, 168
Yefet ben Ali, 160

Zammatto, Elisha Hayyim, 59
Zebulun, 34, 35, 322
Zipporah, 57, 79, 80, 254, 258
Zunz, Leopold, 355

www.ingramcontent.com/pod-product-compliance
Lightning Source LLC
Chambersburg PA
CBHW031352160426

42811CB00092B/97